HANDBOOK OF THE INTERNATIONAL POLITICAL ECONOMY OF TRADE

HANDBOOKS OF RESEARCH ON INTERNATIONAL POLITICAL ECONOMY

Series Editors: Matthew Watson, *Department of Politics and International Studies, University of Warwick, Coventry, UK* and Benjamin J. Cohen, *Louis G. Lancaster Professor of International Political Economy, University of California, Santa Barbara, USA*

This highly original *Handbook* series offers a unique appraisal of the state-of-the-art of research in International Political Economy (IPE). Consisting of original contributions by leading authorities, *Handbooks* in the series provide comprehensive overviews of the very latest research within key areas of IPE. Taking a thematic approach, emphasis is placed on both expanding current debate and indicating the likely research agenda for the future. Each *Handbook* forms a prestigious and high quality work of lasting significance. The *Handbooks* will encompass arguments from both the British and American schools of IPE to give a comprehensive overview of the debates and research positions in each key area of interest, as well as offering a space for those who feel that their work fits neither designation easily. Taking a genuinely international approach these *Handbooks* are designed to inform as well as to contribute to current debates.

Titles in the series include:

Handbook of the International Political Economy of Governance
Edited by Anthony Payne and Nicola Phillips

Handbook of the International Political Economy of Monetary Relations
Edited by Thomas Oatley and W. Kindred Winecoff

Handbook of the International Political Economy of Trade
Edited by David A. Deese

Handbook of the International Political Economy of Trade

Edited by

David A. Deese

Professor of Political Science, Boston College, USA

HANDBOOKS OF RESEARCH ON INTERNATIONAL POLITICAL
ECONOMY

Edward Elgar
Cheltenham, UK • Northampton, MA, USA

Published by
Edward Elgar Publishing Limited
The Lypiatts
15 Lansdown Road
Cheltenham
Glos GL50 2JA
UK

Edward Elgar Publishing, Inc.
William Pratt House
9 Dewey Court
Northampton
Massachusetts 01060
USA

A catalogue record for this book
is available from the British Library

Library of Congress Control Number: 2014937777

This book is available electronically in the ElgarOnline.com
Social and Political Science Subject Collection, E-ISBN 978 1 78195 499 7

ISBN 978 1 78195 498 0 (cased)

Typeset by Servis Filmsetting Ltd, Stockport, Cheshire
Printed and bound in Great Britain by T.J. International Ltd, Padstow

Contents

Contributors

ABOUT THE EDITOR

David A. Deese is Professor of Political Science at Boston College in Chestnut Hill, Massachusetts. He is the author, editor, or co-editor of eight books, including *World Trade Politics: Power, Principles, and Leadership* (Routledge, 2008) and *Globalization: Causes and Effects* (Ashgate, 2012). He was the series editor for 11 volumes in the Library of Essays in International Relations, 2005–12, by Ashgate Publishing. He teaches and publishes on the politics and institutions of international economic relations, including specifically the leadership of international bargaining and negotiations, the comparative political economy of trade policy reform, the international drivers of political economic reform in developing states, the international politics of energy markets, and the interaction of economics and security in US foreign policy. Currently he leads a research project on the most feasible policies to address global climate change in the context of political deadlock in key countries. He is the founding director of the leading interdisciplinary degree program at Boston College, the International Studies Program, and a senior member of the Arts and Sciences Promotion and Tenure Committee. He is on the national roster of US Fulbright Specialist Scholars, and has served as adviser to major public international organizations, national foundations and governments, US federal and state agencies, US universities, and various energy firms.

CONTRIBUTORS

Susan Ariel Aaronson is Research Professor of International Affairs at the Institute for International Economic Policy, the George Washington University's Elliott School of International Affairs. She also was recently the Minerva Chair at the National War College. Her research focuses on the Internet, trade, and human rights, trade and conflict, and corruption, trade, and good governance. She has recently received grants from the MacArthur Foundation, the Ford Foundation, the Swiss National Science Foundation and the Ford Motor Company for her work on Internet freedom and trade, corruption, and business and human rights. She serves on the Advisory Board for Business and Human Rights and is a Senior External Advisor to the Business and Society Team of Oxford Analytica. She has advised the UN Special Representative on Transnational Corporations and Human Rights and the Congressional Human Rights Caucus. She has consulted for the International Labour Organization, the World Bank, Free the Slaves, the Ford Foundation, the Extractive Industries Transparency Initiative, the Stanley Foundation, several corporations, and the governments of Canada, Belgium, and the Netherlands, among others.

Mark Abdollahian focuses on designing and delivering advanced analytics for data-driven decision making. His global experience spans national policy, corporate strategy, economic development, finance, public–private partnerships, mergers and acquisitions, and business process reengineering. He creates, designs, and implements enterprise class data and strategy analytics used by the US government, the World Bank, and the United Nations, as well as private sector companies worldwide. He is currently Chief Executive Officer of ACERTAS and Clinical Professor at the School of Social Science, Policy and Evaluation at Claremont Graduate University. In addition to a bachelor degree from Case Western Reserve University, he holds an MA in foreign and defense policy and a PhD in political economy and mathematical modeling from Claremont Graduate University. He is author of dozens of articles and two books on data-driven strategy across business, politics, and economics.

Ari Afilalo is Professor of Law at Rutgers Law School, where he has taught since 2000. His areas of expertise include international trade, international investment, intellectual property, commercial and corporate law, international business transactions, European law, and public international law. He has published extensively on legal matters related to the GATT, NAFTA, and the European Union, including a co-authored book published by Cambridge University Press that explores the relationship between the structure of the international trading system and statecraft. He continues to work on the application of political theories of the state to international trade. He is a native of France and lived in Israel for several years before moving to the United States in 1986. He is fluent in French and Hebrew.

Greg Anderson is Assistant Professor in the Department of Political Science at the University of Alberta. He is also a Fellow of, and Research Director for, the Alberta Institute for American Studies at the University of Alberta. He holds a BA in history from Brigham Young University, an MA in history from the University of Alberta, and his PhD from the Paul H. Nitze School of Advanced International Studies of the Johns Hopkins

University (Johns Hopkins/SAIS) in Washington, DC. His research interests include Canadian–American relations, US foreign policy, and US foreign economic policy, with a particular emphasis on US trade policy and trade policy institutions. From 2000 to 2002, he also worked in the Office of the United States Trade Representative as a policy analyst in the NAFTA office.

Christopher Bliss is Emeritus Professor of Economics at the University of Oxford, UK, and a Fellow of Nuffield College, Oxford. Before his retirement he taught international economics and macroeconomics to Oxford graduate students. He has published on mathematical economics and development economics. His broad-ranging interests in development led him to intensive work in the 1970s with Nicholas Stern on the Palanpur village study in India, which remains highly influential. He has published five books and numerous journal papers, which are outlined on his homepage at the Nuffield College website.

Deborah Elms is Head, Temasek Foundation Centre for Trade and Negotiations (TFCTN), and Senior Fellow of International Political Economy at the S. Rajaratnam School of International Studies at Nanyang Technological University, Singapore. She is also a Senior Fellow in the Singapore Ministry of Trade and Industry's Trade Academy. Her research interests are negotiations and decision making, particularly in trade, with a current focus on the Trans-Pacific Partnership (TPP) negotiations. She conducts a range of teaching and training for Asian government officials, for members of parliament, for business leaders, and for graduate students. She has consulted for the governments of the United Arab Emirates, Sri Lanka, Cambodia, Taiwan, and Singapore. She holds a PhD in political science from the University of Washington, an MA in international relations from the University of Southern California, and a BA and BS from Boston University.

Marc D. Froese is Associate Professor of Political Science and the founding director of the International Studies Program at Canadian University College in Alberta, Canada. His research examines the politics of international economic law within the context of North American economic integration. He is the author or co-author of a number of books and articles examining the juridical and institutional aspects of the global political economy of trade, including *Canada at the WTO: Trade Litigation and the Future of Public Policy* (University of Toronto Press, 2010). His current work focuses on the uneven development of dispute settlement mechanisms in regional trade agreements, and the impact of non-compliance on the legitimacy of trade courts. Many of his articles have been uploaded to the Social Science Research Network and may be accessed at http://ssrn.com/author=887299.

Maria Garcia is a senior lecturer at the University of Bath in the UK. She was previously a senior Marie Curie Fellow at the School of Politics and International Relations at the University of Nottingham in the UK, and the National Centre for Research on Europe, University of Canterbury in New Zealand. Her research focuses on the dynamics of trade and free trade agreements in the Asia Pacific region and European–Asian relations. Her publications have appeared in numerous academic journals, including the *Journal of Common Market Studies* and the *Cambridge Review of International Affairs*.

Kathleen J. Hancock, PhD, University of California, San Diego, is Associate Professor at the Colorado School of Mines, where she teaches in, and was the previous Director of, the Master of International Political Economy of Resources (MIPER) program. In her book *Regional Integration: Choosing Plutocracy*, she develops a theory on how powers such as South Africa and Russia economically integrate neighboring states. She has published in journals such as *Foreign Policy Analysis, Asian Perspective*, and *China and Eurasia Forum Quarterly* and is the author of book chapters on energy security and Eurasian economic integration. She was previously a Senior Analyst in the National Security and International Affairs Division at the US Government Accountability Office. She has conducted research in countries from Central Asia to Europe and Africa. Her current research analyzes regionalism and natural resources.

Randal R. Hendrickson is Director of Faculty Development at the Jack Miller Center. He has written on themes ranging from republicanism to evolutionary psychology in such publications as the *Journal of Politics, Perspectives on Political Science*, and the *New Atlantis*. Before joining the Jack Miller Center, he was a Fellow in the Gerst Program for Economic and Humane Studies at Duke University, where he taught political theory for two years. Prior to that, he was a Fellow at the Symposium of Science, Reason, and Modern Democracy at Michigan State University and a Bradley Fellow in the Department of Government at Harvard University.

Bernard Hoekman is Professor and Program Director, Global Economics, at the Robert Schuman Centre for Advanced Studies, European University Institute in Florence, Italy. He has held various senior positions at the World Bank, including Director of the International Trade Department and Research Manager in the Development Research Group. Prior to joining the World Bank he worked as an economist in the GATT Secretariat. He has published widely on trade policy and development, the global trading system, and trade in services. He is a graduate of the Erasmus University Rotterdam, holds a PhD in economics from the University of Michigan, and is a Research Fellow of the London-based Centre for Economic Policy Research and a Senior Associate of the Economic Research Forum for the Arab countries, Turkey, and Iran.

Wei Liang is Associate Professor in the School of International Policy and Management at the Monterey Institute of International Studies, USA. Her research interests include the international political economy of East Asia, Asian regionalism, international trade negotiation, and global governance. She is the co-author of *China and East Asia's Post-Crises Community: A Region in Flux* (Lexington, 2012), co-editor of *China and Global Trade Governance* (Routledge, 2014), and author of several journal articles and book chapters. A graduate of Peking University, People's Republic of China, she received her PhD in international relations from the University of Southern California.

Mary Anne Madeira is Assistant Professor of Political Science at Queens College, City University of New York. Previously she was a Jean Monnet Fellow in the Global Economics research strand of the Global Governance Programme at the European University Institute. She received her PhD in political science from the University of Washington in 2013. She is the co-author, with James Caporaso, of *Globalization, Institutions and Governance* (Sage, 2011). Her research focuses on the domestic political and societal effects of global economic integration, particularly in the advanced industrialized economies. She also assesses the effects of regionalization on domestic social policies.

Rob Maxim is a Research Associate at the Council on Foreign Relations, where he focuses on competitiveness, immigration, and trade issues.. He holds a BA in international affairs and economics, and an MA in international trade and investment policy, both from George Washington University. His research interests include international trade, US economic policy, and Internet policy and governance.

Christian May is Research Associate in International Political Economy at Goethe University Frankfurt am Main, Germany. His research focuses on the domestic and international aspects of emerging economies and the role of language and culture in the political economy. Besides publishing on large emerging economies and comparative capitalism, he is co-editor of *Die großen Schwellenländer: Ursachen und Folgen ihres Aufstiegs in der Weltwirtschaft* (2013, with Andreas Nölke and Simone Claar) and *New Directions in Critical Comparative Capitalisms Research: Critical and*

Global Perspectives (Palgrave Macmillan, 2015, with Matthias Ebenau and Ian Bruff).

Erik Mitbrodt holds a JD from The Chinese University of Hong Kong as well as a BA from the University of Victoria. His interests combine anthropology and Latin American studies, and he researches the interaction between agricultural trade and economic development. He has broad-based experience of living and working in countries worldwide, including in many least developed countries.

Andreas Nölke is Professor of Political Science at Goethe University Frankfurt am Main, Germany. Within his field of international relations and international political economy he has published widely on topics such as financialization, transnational private self-regulation, the International Accounting Standards Board, and the nature of capitalism in emerging economies, in journals such as the *Review of International Political Economy, World Politics, Competition and Change*, the *Review of African Political Economy*, and the *Journal of Common Market Studies*. Currently, he is editing the volume *Multinational Corporations from Emerging Markets: State Capitalism 3.0* (Palgrave Macmillan, forthcoming), as well as special issues on "Brazilian Multinational Corporations and the State" (for *Critical Perspectives on International Business*) and "The Domestic Sources of China's Foreign Economic Policies" (for *International Politics*), both to be published in 2014.

Evgeny Postnikov is Lecturer in International Relations at the University of Glasgow. His research interests center on international political economy, particularly trade policy and its link with social issues, and European Union politics and external relations. He is especially interested in the rise of bilateralism in global trade and the role the EU and others play in it. He also researches the EU trade policy-making process through a comparative lens, contrasting it with that of the United States and other regional blocs. Prior to joining the University of Glasgow he completed his PhD in the Graduate School of Public and International Affairs, University of Pittsburgh, and was also educated in Germany and Russia.

John M. Rothgeb, Jr. is Professor of Political Science and Distinguished Scholar of the Graduate Faculty at Miami University in Oxford, Ohio. He is the author of numerous books and articles on international political economy, foreign policy, and the discipline of political science.

Elizabeth Smythe is a Professor of Political Science at Concordia University College in Edmonton, Alberta, Canada, where she teaches international and comparative politics. Her research interests include international trade and investment agreements and transnational social movements seeking to influence or resist these agreements. Her most recent research focuses on the global food system, international trade rules, especially standards around food labeling, and the influence of state and non-state actors on those rules.

Andrey Tomashevskiy is a PhD candidate at the University of California, Davis. His research interests focus on the impact of international trade and investment on domestic politics. More specifically, his current research examines the role of international investment for government stability in authoritarian regimes, the impact of financial flows on election outcomes in host countries, and the relationship between international investment and host nation corruption. He received his BA in political science from Kean University in 2006 and his MA from New York University in 2007.

Joel P. Trachtman is Professor of International Law at the Fletcher School of Law and Diplomacy. Recent books include *The Future of International Law: Global Government* (Cambridge University Press, 2013), *The International Law of Economic Migration: Toward the Fourth Freedom* (Upjohn Institute, 2009), *Ruling the World: Constitutionalism, International Law, and Global Governance* (Cambridge University Press, 2009), *Developing Countries in the WTO Legal System* (Oxford University Press, 2009), and *The Economic Structure of International Law* (Harvard University Press, 2008). He has consulted for the United Nations, the OECD, Asia-Pacific Economic Cooperation, the World Bank, the Organization of American States, and the US Agency for International Development. He has served as a member of the boards of the *American Journal of International Law*, the *European Journal of International Law*, the *Journal of International Economic Law*, the *Cambridge Review of International Affairs*, and the *Singapore Yearbook of International Law*. From 1998 to 2001, he was Academic Dean of the Fletcher School, and during 2000 and 2001 he served as Dean ad interim. He graduated in 1980 from Harvard Law School, where he served as editor in chief of the *Harvard International Law Journal*.

Silke Trommer is University Lecturer in Global Sustainable Development and World Politics at the University of Helsinki, Finland. She is associated with the Sir Walter Murdoch School of Public Policy and International Affairs in Perth, Australia, where she pursues a research project on the future of the World Trade Organization together with Ann Capling. She is author of *Transformations in Trade Politics: Participatory Trade Politics in West Africa* (Routledge, 2013). Her doctoral dissertation, on which the book is based, won the 2013 Best Dissertation Award from the International Political Economy Section of the International Studies Association. She has published articles on trade politics in *New Political Economy, Globalizations*, and the *Journal of Development Studies*, on trade law in the *Chinese Journal of International Law*, and on non-governmental organizations in *West European Politics*.

Gonzalo Villalta Puig is Professor of Law and Associate Dean (Development and External Affairs) of the Faculty of Law at The Chinese University of Hong Kong. He is a Barrister and Solicitor of the High Court of Australia and a Solicitor of the Senior Courts of England and Wales. A specialist in economic constitutional law, he researches the role of constitutional courts in the constitutionalization of free trade in federations and other non-unitary jurisdictions, mostly by a comparative approach. He has authored about 80 publications, mainly on matters of constitutional economics and legal issues of economic integration, including *Economic Relations between Australia and the European Union: Law and Policy* (Kluwer Law International, 2014), *The High Court of Australia and Section 92 of the Australian Constitution* (Lawbook Co., 2008), and *Boundaries of Commercial and Trade Law* (Sellier European Law Publishers, 2011, with Christian Twigg-Flesner). He is Convenor of the Research Group for Constitutional Studies of Free Trade and Political Economy of the International Association of Constitutional Law, a member of the Committee on International Trade Law of the International Law Association, and Associate Editor of the *Global Journal of Comparative Law*.

Zining Yang is a PhD candidate in political science in the School of Social Science, Policy and Evaluation at Claremont Graduate University. Her work focuses on the political economy of development, spanning environment and resource protection, diplomacy, and the political economy of Asian integration. She is also Research Associate at TransResearch Consortium, as well as a lecturer at La Sierra University and Claremont Graduate University. Her research interests include international political economy, conflict and integration, international relations in East Asia, computational economics, agent-based models, network analysis, and system dynamic models. She received her BA in international relations from Beijing International Studies University, and an MA in international studies from Claremont Graduate University in 2011.

Lyuba Zarsky is Associate Professor of International Environmental Policy and Business Administration at the Monterey Institute of International Studies in Monterey, California. She has written widely on the relationship between foreign investment and sustainability, including

"Can Extractive Industries Promote Sustainable Development? A Net Benefits Framework and a Case Study of the Marlin Mine" (*Journal of Environment and Development*, June 2013, with Leonardo Stanley) and *Enclave Economy: Foreign Investment and Sustainable Development in Mexico's Silicon Valley* (MIT Press, 2007, with Kevin Gallagher). She is a Senior Fellow at the Global Development and Environment Institute at Tufts University and holds a PhD in economics from the University of Massachusetts, Amherst.

1. Introduction: politics, trade, and the international political economy
David A. Deese

Trade is the area of international political economy (IPE) that is monitored the most directly by key actors, both public and private, from individuals to the global trade regime. It carries with it profound questions and issues about property rights and the role of the state, foreign direct investment and investment agreements, integration and regionalism, development strategy and inequality, international collaboration and governance, and transnational networks and coalitions. For research in international politics and IPE, trade is the preeminent domain for studying the interconnections of domestic and international politics. From understanding the evolution of labor and children's rights, to the horizontal and vertical shifts in authority levels under globalization, or the legalization of dispute settlement in both public and quasi-public domains and the establishment of a coherent body of international trade law, trade leads the way for other domains of IPE. Furthermore, trade is profoundly interconnected with the other main areas of IPE, from international production to investment, state-owned enterprises, energy markets, technologies and sustainability, money and exchange rates, and the Internet. In other words, trade is fundamentally political, as well as regional and inter-continental.

The Edward Elgar *Handbook of the International Political Economy of Trade* brings together the most important and promising research and policy questions regarding international trade. The authors are leading thinkers and writers from different countries representing a range of disciplines from political science and political economy to law and economics. Their work presented here begins with fundamental theory about trade as international communication, as well as its longer-term effects on growth and inequality. It then examines trends in the domestic politics of trade, and how government trade policies lead to optimal or suboptimal contributions to growth and development. In particular, the authors highlight how US and EU trade policy could be much more development-supportive, and how food and agriculture policies in particular call out for reform and opening.

The volume then covers in sequence the strong recent trend towards bilateral and regional trade (and investment) agreements and their implications, key issues of how trade is governed globally, and how trade continues to define and advance globalization. The conclusion highlights critical implications of the broader and deeper connections between societies worldwide caused by the flow of ideas over the Internet and of people through immigration.

In sum, this volume illustrates that over recent decades international political economy is the sub-field of international relations that has contributed the most in theoretical terms, and trade is very likely the most researched area of IPE. Thus it is no surprise to find frontier insights and debate in the IPE of trade about the basic politics of national economic policy as well as international economic exchanges, connections, and engagements.

THE FAILURE OF INTERNATIONAL POLITICAL LEADERSHIP IN ADVANCING GLOBAL TRADE NEGOTIATIONS

Perhaps the single most important dimension of trade policy and politics over the past decade is the crucial shortfall of international political leadership. Neither US, European, Brazilian, Indian, or other heads of state, nor the US Trade Representative, the EU Trade Minister, the World Trade Organization (WTO) Director-General, or other leading trade ministers have stepped forward alone, or especially in small groups, to provide the critical catalysts required to revitalize the global trade negotiation process. The July 2004 Geneva Package included significant aspects of what was not agreed in Cancun as of December 2003, but the progress stalled and then stopped after the July Package. Especially after the Hong Kong Ministerial in 2005 and its aftermath in 2006, scholars began to question whether the global process is even still relevant, and since then some have essentially declared it moribund.

This failure is sometimes attributed to the relatively low level, as compared to the Uruguay Round, for example, of business support and enthusiasm for the Round. This is certainly one contributing factor to the lack of leadership, and particularly by the largest market countries. At the same time, I believe that the deep political rift between US, European, and other leaders after the US invasion of Iraq in March 2003 is a more important explanatory factor in the lack of US and EU focus on, and initiative in, generating the critical small-N group consensus and leadership required to activate the Round. Additional key explanatory factors are the great recession of 2008–09 in the United States and the economic crises of several European states and the euro from 2010 to 2012. Certainly American foreign policy was consumed by the war on terror, the insurgency in Afghanistan by 2003, and the seriously escalating insurgency in Iraq by 2004–05. In addition, the overall reputation and public opinion of the US Bush administration by 2005–06 was not amenable to broad leadership, except for the war on terror, which was emphasized above all else. There were deep, enduring costs to US foreign policy of pursuing simultaneously the so-called "war on terror" and major counterinsurgencies in both Afghanistan and Iraq from 2004 onward. Other important foreign policy priorities were either no longer feasible, including intensive small group international trade policy leadership, or could not compete for the time and resources of top decision makers.

Furthermore, once profound economic crisis had gripped the US by late 2008, the highest-level US government efforts shifted to manage the crisis, and leaders were engulfed in crisis management for 2009–10 in response to the US great recession of 2008–09 and its international ramifications. Indeed, the new Obama administration was forced to focus its intensive efforts on damage control for the economy before it even formally began to govern in 2009. When the crisis reverberated internationally and European countries faced deep sovereign debt challenges by 2009 onward, all European leadership focus turned to managing the crisis in Europe. In light of the crisis gripping European economies from Ireland to Portugal, Spain, and Greece since then, it is no wonder that global negotiations have not been revitalized. Thus, it is important to acknowledge that crisis management dominated the years from 2008 to 2012. In addition, the processes engaged over the past few years to concoct multiple free trade agreements (FTAs) and regional trade agreements (RTAs) worldwide have taken up much of the political capital and time available for trade policy liberalization efforts in key countries. The US executive branch, for example, has made the European and Pacific deals, the Transatlantic Trade and Investment Partnership (TTIP), and the Trans-Pacific Partnership (TPP), respectively, its top international trade negotiation priorities. In addition, it has exerted considerable effort in reaching and implementing fully the bilateral agreements with South Korea, Singapore, and Australia, as well as expanded trade with the Association of Southeast Asian Nations (ASEAN) member states.

At the same time, however, leading public international organizations, economists, political economists, and trade policy experts generally agree that a substantial global trade deal would be one of the most helpful steps to longer-term economic growth and development of economies worldwide. There is little doubt that the most promising way to accelerate growth and broaden the base of its beneficiaries is to enact a substantive

Doha Round agreement that includes fundamental reforms to agricultural trade regarding export subsidies, tariffs, and domestic support programs. Yet political leaders are working on the most feasible instead of the clearly optimal. With the US wars in Iraq and Afghanistan over, the major economic and financial crisis in the EU apparently continuing to decline in intensity, and a second-term US president who will most likely be able to work with Republicans in the House on little else beyond trade policy reform, it is certainly the time to step up and advance a serious Doha Round agricultural and broader agenda.

US, EU, Indian, Brazilian, Japanese, and Chinese leaders might instead end up presenting the Bali Package agreed by all WTO trade ministers in December 2013 as their signature achievement. There is an argument for this agreement as not only substantive but also a breakthrough, as no new global deal had been agreed over the 18 years since the founding of the WTO in 1995 or the 12 years from the initiation of the Doha Round in late 2001. The customs clearance and transparency and efficiency elements of the trade facilitation, or primary focus of the deal, are both serious and substantive, and will contribute significantly to trade expansion and economic growth worldwide. In addition, to the extent that developing countries actually implement the specific reforms to reduce inefficiency and corruption inherent in trade flows across their borders rather than relying on opt-outs, a major fraction of the benefits of this agreement would flow to them. Furthermore, other narrow elements such as the reform, especially improved management and greater "filling," of tariff quotas for agricultural imports, as well as assuring the required financial and technology support for developing countries to implement the agreement, are also valuable contributions to productivity and efficiency in trade and its role in economic growth.

At the same time, with regard to the core issues of agricultural trade reform, phasing out export subsidies, sharply reducing tariffs, and further substantial reforms of domestic support programs, the agreement only specifies that members are committed to establishing a specific negotiating agenda and reaching a deal as soon as possible, and certainly before the next, tenth Ministerial meeting in 2015. This is hardly a breakthrough or any binding commitment that could trigger the necessary political compromises required of the key leaders, beginning in the several largest trading states. At best it provides some momentum towards a broader agreement, and it indicates that the prospect for major agricultural reform (still considerably narrower than the original Doha Development framework) is now more feasible.[1] Finally, however, I note that a recent WTO report on trade measures enacted by the largest, or G-20, states from mid- to late 2013 is not encouraging in that the number of new trade restrictions increased while the number of new trade-facilitating measures decreased, as compared to the prior period.

Leaders in many countries worldwide have shown their strong priority for a vast array of bilateral and regional trade, or trade and investment, agreements, and therein established a fundamental pattern of activity and arrangements. Trade policy processes do appear to be substitutable in that, when one level is stymied, others emerge in its place. In fact, some policy experts and scholars are musing whether the most likely route back to a broader, substantive global agreement is a major success with either the broad-based US–European framework or even a transpacific one. Indeed, it appears that the EU–Canada trade pact completed in 2013 (in principle) has helped to catalyze and accelerate EU–US negotiations, which might in turn help advance the transpacific process (or vice versa).

It is important to ask whether these RTAs could still be pursued in the larger US trade policy context of those in the 1980s and 1990s, or "competitive liberalization." If US leaders are willing to use progress with either of these large frameworks as a lever to help convince key countries to negotiate more positively in the Doha Round, then it is possible to see a wider range of options to energize small group international political leadership. However, it may be more that key countries this time around see the transpacific and transatlantic negotiations as stand-alone arrangements to substitute for still mainly "failed" negotiations at the global level. This view could be supported by the narrowness of the relatively modest agenda and outcomes of the December 2013 Bali Ministerial meeting within the Doha Round involving mainly trade facilitation and reform of tariff rate quotas in agriculture.

In this environment, it is important to ask whether any of these broad regional efforts promise the kind of economic stimulus and political platform required to once again connect trade policy liberalization with worldwide improvement in economic growth and poverty alleviation. After the conclusion of the Uruguay Round in 1994, the World Bank and most other estimates expected growth rates worldwide to be increased significantly over the following decade. It appeared that another noticeable boost to world growth could be generated as the Doha Round was launched in late 2001. Even the relatively modest negotiating modalities from the 2008 Ministerial have been estimated to provide very substantial increases in income for countries worldwide. Unfortunately, however, this vital opportunity for a major boost to growth has been forfeited, as the process, which had got bogged down by 2005, became relatively inactive by 2007–08. There is no better time than the second term of a US presidency, post-national elections in India in 2014, and very weak economic growth in Europe to have top US and EU foreign policy leaders reach out to form a G-5 consensus group for international political leadership on trade with India, Brazil, and China.

There is a serious difficulty with the exclusive focus on bilateral and regional agreements and commitments. Without global talks underlying all these new arrangements the overall effects are clearly suboptimal. First, large countries and markets as well as many intermediate-size ones are left out in part, if not entirely. Brazil, India, China, Russia, Argentina, and Indonesia are not included in either of the major US negotiating priorities. Thus, much of the world's trade is not included, and these countries will become ever more interwoven into their regional and inter-regional trade networks and likely less fully committed to making the global trade rules and procedures their highest priority. Second, crucial issue areas led by agriculture are likely to be substantially omitted and therefore continue as very closed, suboptimal market areas. (Note: The EU–Canada agreement does include some agriculture.) Indeed, the countries with the largest agricultural protection programs and barriers generally refuse to negotiate them in bilateral or multilateral deals in order not to lose leverage in global negotiations. This forfeits major potential boosts to growth, innovation, and market reform at the international as well as national level.

Next, it continues to bisect and trisect world markets into mainly more dynamic regions, and reinforces the most intensive bonds across OECD member states in intra-industry trade. Certainly, in more technical terms, each of the FTAs and RTAs becomes more efficient in its purposes and/or outcomes if there is a global agreement that reduces most favored nation (MFN) tariffs. Trade diversion is much less likely for members of new FTAs and RTAs if they also establish a new global reform framework. Finally, it leaves the new WTO Director-General, Roberto Azevedo, in particular and the more general global governance mechanisms without the international political leadership that is crucial to help stimulate deeper coordination in other issue areas such as foreign direct investment, environment and climate change, and labor and human rights.

International political leadership for the Doha Round will have to contend with the following:

1. It will have to turn around the weak support there has been from the US, EU, India, and Brazil since 2008. First and foremost, each of these countries or their top leaders would have to make this a high-level priority and commit to providing consistent pressure on the others. Indeed, it is particularly important to do so in 2014 instead of falling back on the excuse, rather than the "accomplishment," of the successful Bali Package of December 2013. Certainly the US president could, in principle, take up this leadership challenge in his second

term, despite the deep difficulties posed by a deadlocked congressional process. There is already some indication from US House Republicans that they might support a global trade reform agreement. The US and EU presidents will have to challenge the Chinese, Brazilian, and Indian heads of state to step up and re-establish common ground around foreign policies despite substantial differences in the domestic regulation of public procurement and foreign investment (see Chapter 19 in this volume). Furthermore, all of these states have significant overlapping (along with the conflicting) interests in related issue areas of food supply, energy markets, and climate change that might be linked informally.

2. With the concerted efforts mainly focused on RTAs at the moment, some new combination of emphasis would have to be constructed. Beginning with Indian, US, and EU leaders, they would have to exhibit their leadership by regularly announcing support for pursuing the agricultural reform efforts emphasized again in the Bali Package. One way to encourage this is once again to present significant early progress on the US–EU and Transpacific RTAs as a way to help engage India and Brazil, but there is no assurance that either of these large-scale regional negotiations will succeed before a global, WTO framework could be agreed.

3. Each key leader will have to break loose of, and offer targeted compensation in response to, serious domestic political constraints, including important labor groups in the US and EU. Top leaders have to build support for the global talks that is based on key advantages presented to the most powerful domestic constituencies, as well as gain the active support of the pro-liberalization groups such as green energy firms. Elections in India in 2014 may help increase its key leaders' willingness to negotiate a serious, substantive agreement on agricultural reform. This, in turn, could encourage US and EU negotiators to play a stronger international political leadership role.

THE THEMES, SCOPE, AND FINDINGS IN THIS VOLUME

Our definition and approach to trade are necessarily broad based. As Montesquieu argued, trade is as much about communication as it is strictly commercial activity. We understand today that it shapes, indeed defines, in part the nature of human, organizational, and national interactions. Some cultures are designed around trade; some economies are very heavily reliant on it; and what we call globalization today is substantially defined by intra-industry trade and the exchange of goods, services, and ideas within and across the regions of the globe. Indeed, as this volume will explain and document in detail, trade and related interconnections are advancing intra-regional integration even faster than global or inter-regional connectedness.

Ever more intense communication, exchange, and engagement challenge us, even our identities, and stimulate us at the same time to incorporate, contest, and reject elements of the "foreign." Individuals, firms, industries, regions, and states struggle to retain their advantages or establish new ones. The western countries, and many of their most "liberal" legislators, preach freedom and ever "freer" trade, while systematically supporting and protecting several key agricultural markets (as well as the flow of workers and immigration more generally) which could and should, in fact, be allowed to develop into truly international "markets." In any case, where trade is allowed, it tends to shape and re-shape production and even services within and across individual economies. This, in turn, shifts the interests of groups, firms, industries, and entire sectors and thus changes how they pressure and shape national and international institutions. Thus, just as politics is constantly shaping trade and its networks, politics is also modified, extended, and eventually even transformed by it.

Trade as an "Engine" of Integration, Growth, or Inequality? Development Strategy, Policies, Growth, and Inequality

Crucial to the international political economy research agenda are growth, integration, and inequality, as trade is often considered the most reliable or consistent source of national economic growth and development. Furthermore, we know that cultures are shaped by, and sometimes around, trade, for example the new silk road being mapped across the Middle East, India, and East Asia. As Randal R. Hendrickson presents in Chapter 2, trade represents much more than simple economic exchange. Indeed, Montesquieu argued that trade or commerce is much more natural to republics, and that the interactions involved in trading are much more extensive and important than only economics. Hendrickson explains for us Montesquieu's claim that "The history of commerce is that of the communication of peoples." Montesquieu's contribution was to transform the ancient concerns about acquisition and trade into a fuller understanding about human nature, its advancement, and how, in fact, a society and state encouraging acquisition and exchange will help develop and instill values of frugality, moderation, and an awareness of the needs of others. These are basic outcomes of commerce, competition, and interdependence pursued as it occurs naturally among people.

Pushing further to what we call today the "democratic peace" at the level of states, Montesquieu observed that commerce also induces peaceful relations, as dependence and interdependence create strong interests in avoiding the loss of trade during war among trading societies and therefore remaining at peace. In other words, almost three decades prior to the American Revolution and Adam Smith's *The Wealth of Nations*, Montesquieu explained what we still understand today to be the two core pillars of the "democratic peace" – the republican form of government and commerce among nations.

Trade is also closely related to some of the most important progress made across states worldwide over recent decades in terms of reforming economies and reducing poverty. What has trade contributed? In Chapter 3, Christopher Bliss emphasizes that manufactured exports have generated the revenues required for importing energy and other inputs to production, and world markets provide crucial demand for successful products. He also explains the quite dramatic decrease in the number of people in severe poverty as well as the profound transformation of the world economy. At the same time, Bliss cautions against overemphasizing the contributions of trade in the rapid growth paths of Brazil, China, India, and other, smaller countries. Certainly trade and globalization more generally have been important, but they have been enabled by the fundamental economic reforms and development of infrastructure executed at the national level.

In addition, Bliss documents very concerning, widespread increases in inequality within societies affecting not only the rich countries but also developing states such as India and China. As the supply of skilled or highly educated workers increases in the US and other well-off economies, the difference between the real wages of the skilled and unskilled increases, thus aggravating problems and consequences of inequality across essentially all income and wealth levels in these societies. Bliss believes that it may well be that technology advances and the demand for higher, as opposed to less, skilled manufacturing production are more important than trade to this growing gap. Still, it is likely that trade is especially favorable to high-productivity activities and firms and particularly challenging for low-productivity firms and low wage earners, including immigrants. Education, a minimum wage, and trade adjustment assistance can all help in this regard, but the changing structure of economies is more about technology advancement than it is about trade per se.

Despite these differential impacts of trade within societies, it also tends to cause gradual convergence in income and degrees of trade among all trading states. No matter what level of development and type of national economic structure, in Chapter 4 Zining Yang and Mark Abdollahian find that over the long run trade causes convergence in both growth rates and income level. This holds true despite other fundamental differences in the way that national economies are affected by the degree of trade connectedness and the nature of trade partners. More specifically, they find that the quality of trade connections can often matter the most for poor countries that, unlike the most developed ones, do not appear to benefit from any overall increase in the level of trade connectedness. In parallel with work by Hancock (Chapter 12) and Hoekman (Chapter 13), Yang and Abdollahian establish that RTAs provide benefits in both efficiency and productivity, but only for complementary (not competitive) market trade among relatively equal members. In sum, developing states should be careful and strategic in selecting trade partners. Importantly, they also show that for all countries close-in trade among neighbors is extremely important in advancing economic growth.

Domestic Politics, Development Strategy, and Democracy

Perhaps the richest of all research agendas in international politics is the interactions of international and domestic politics, and trade is the single most studied issue area in this fundamental set of questions and theories.

The ever increasing share of national and global economic growth based on trade is due in part to the opening up of economies to foreign direct investment (FDI), and the global search for efficiencies and competitiveness among key production sectors. Dramatically opened national markets for manufactures trade, and the EU expansion to 27 members in particular, have spawned extensive internationalization of production, probably the most distinctive aspect of contemporary globalization. In Chapter 5 Mary Anne Madeira explains why intra-industry trade, or that within corporate frameworks and networks, is the fastest-growing type of trade. Companies increasingly move similar goods from the same industry, whether semifinished or complete products, across borders as part of their global production chains. This is central to the politics of trade, as countries, such as most of the OECD members, with a high level of intra-industry trade tend to liberalize more readily between and among themselves, whereas those engaged in mainly inter-industry trade, such as many North–South interactions, experience more difficulties reaching trade agreements and benefiting from new trade.

Furthermore, Madeira shows that the most productive firms, including many large ones, are much more likely to export their goods, which helps the overall industry and economy by reallocating resources to higher-productivity activity. It also means a wider base of options for consumers and higher wages for exporting firms. Still, it creates increased competition within an industry, and, since most firms in an industry do not export, they incur losses or even failure as a result. With the distributional effects and pressures brought to bear on public actors, it is ever more difficult for class-based or sector- or industry-based coalitions to form as their interests diverge. Therefore, Madeira concludes, lobbying will be pursued more intensively by individual firms, where exporters prefer liberalization and domestically oriented firms do not.

For developing countries, FDI and supply chain participation offer potential social and environmental as well as economic and financial benefits. Indeed, FDI can be a pillar of a national sustainable development strategy, provided that host governments establish and implement coherent development and regulatory policies that capture the opportunities of FDI while managing its risks. In Chapter 6 Lyuba Zarsky warns, however, that good governance of FDI is often absent, most often in the extractives sector, which has been marked by intense conflict over human rights abuses and environmental degradation, especially in Latin America. Zarsky argues that, in three ways, current international investment rules impede host country governance for sustainable development. First, they constrict space for industry and investment policy. For example, investment agreements are restricted from including performance requirements that help developing countries selectively capture growth-enhancing technology spillovers from multinational corporations. Second, investor–state arbitration clauses, now virtually ubiquitous in investment agreements, have been used repeatedly to challenge environmental and social regulations. The prospect of costly lawsuits and settlements acts to "chill" domestic regulation. Finally, international investment agreements do not oblige foreign investors to uphold human rights and operate to high environmental standards. Zarsky suggests, however, that changing global business norms, as well as the urgency of a global response to climate change, are shaping international investment rules in ways that will promote sustainable development.[2]

As assessed by Christian May and Andreas Nölke in Chapter 19, development strategy and assistance are linked substantially to export-led growth, even if that may be changing to a more domestic orientation for some of the largest developing countries. Thus, the World Bank, among other organizations, dedicates extensive attention to trade policy and trade facilitation. Yet in Chapter 7 John M. Rothgeb, Jr. presents a reality check on the real world that developing countries confront as they seek to mobilize trade for development, or export-led growth. Exports can be crucial, as explained by Bliss in Chapter 3, but most producers in developed countries focus on domestic markets, and they are generally opposed to imported goods which compete with their products. This is especially pronounced in key agricultural markets, but, even for less expensive manufactured goods, developing countries' exports face a daunting array of "unfair" trade regulations, especially so-called antidumping and countervailing duties. Rothgeb advises these countries to seek out alliances with the firms importing their products in developed countries, as even their increasing use of dispute settlement at the WTO and the global trade negotiations are not proving to be adequate remedies.

In Chapter 8 Gonzalo Villalta Puig and Erik Mitbrodt stress the importance of expanding market access for developing countries' exports into developed economies in the always controversial area of agriculture. Many citizens are unlikely to recognize how extensively their countries' markets are in fact protected by a range of requirements imposed on less and least developed countries. Complex rules of origin and stringent "behind the border" barriers ranging from biosecurity to food safety measures are the culprit. Agriculture may provide only two percent of the GDP in developed economies, but it plays a vastly larger role, culturally and politically. Villalta Puig and Mitbrodt explain why protection for the rural aspects of culture and extensive political power and lobbying by large-scale agribusiness in both the EU and the US make it so difficult to open trade in agriculture, which is precisely where most people in developing economies are employed. Global trade talks and pacts such as the WTO's recent Bali Package, development assistance from the EU, US and elsewhere, and even the vast array of freer trade areas around the world are, ultimately, of only very limited value to the legion of farm-based less and least developed countries as long as the developed world shuts out agricultural trade with multibillion-dollar subsidies and support programs.

Important work has been done on not only economic and social but also political development, and the role of trade therein. International relations research has targeted very productively the questions surrounding how the conditions required for membership in the WTO and regional trade organizations may affect democratization, accountability of state institutions, and practices. Whitehead (1996) argued that the majority of transitions to democracy involved a substantial degree of pressure and coercion from external actors and forces. In Chapter 9 Andrey Tomashevskiy considers a more refined approach than prior scholars by assessing how states dependent on trade might make concessions in reforming domestic political processes and institutions in order to gain preferential access to important markets. If autocratic states are confronted with political conditions required in order to join a preferential trade area, a situation increasingly established by democratic states, then they may make incremental changes for that purpose. Tomashevskiy shows that, particularly when a state engages in a trade grouping with democratic members, democratization is more likely, because democratic trade partners press for political reform. Given the strong surge in RTAs and FTAs, as explained below, it is essential to understand both the increasing imposition of political conditionality on states seeking to enter organizations among democratic states and the use by autocratic states of their own regional organizations as alternatives to stand up against political reform.

Regions and Regionalism in the Lead

The coverage of regions and regionalism emphasizes the nature of, and variation in, regional trade arrangements and levels of integration, and the sharp contrasts from Africa to Asia, and the EU. It also maps out the rapidly changing and ever more complex connections between regions, and how the overall frenzy of regional activity affects global trade rules and negotiations.

As the WTO becomes ever more established as the locus for standing oversight and governance of the global trading regime, and less the site of dramatic global negotiations about major new treaties, bilateral and regional trade arrangements have become the main game in town. Indeed, as explained by Greg Anderson in Chapter 10, the world's largest traders from China to the US and the EU are intensively pursuing such negotiations. Once the Cold War ended, regions and regionalism blossomed, and in 1993 the EU finally forged the long-sought-after common market. This milestone was achieved in the same year that the Maastricht Treaty entered into force. The US had already declared the policy of "competitive liberalization" by 1985 as a way to use its bilateral and regional negotiations to pressure reluctant parties to agree to launch and close global trade negotiations. Indeed, with the US agreements of 1985 with Israel and 1987 with Canada, and the North American Free Trade Agreement (NAFTA) in 1993, it can be argued that the US triggered the entire process of pursuing deals at all levels, in part in order to press trade partners to act in accordance with its goals.

Anderson documents that by the late 1990s, even before the Doha Round was launched, regions and regionalism were ascendant, and liberal thinkers and several trade economists expressed concern that the complex, overlapping, and intermeshed regional arrangements created a "spaghetti bowl" of discriminatory preferences that threatened the open worldwide system. Furthermore, the Asian–global financial crisis of 1997–99 certainly stimulated intensive pursuit of regional deals in Asia.

In Chapter 11 Deborah Elms assesses the accelerating pace of regional negotiations and arrangements in east and southeast Asia which has taken on a life of its own. The region is alive with overlapping and crosscutting negotiations up to the level of, for example, the Trans-Pacific Partnership with 12 countries, including the US, Canada, Japan, Malaysia, and Mexico. At the same time, Asian countries, in ASEAN for example, do not include the breadth of issue area coverage, such as rigorous dispute settlement, and they tend to negotiate tariff reductions bilaterally even within regional organizations. Interestingly, Elms establishes that they are negotiating a series of agreements jointly with other key Asian countries, not unlike the EU's focus over the past several years. Over the past decade ASEAN has concluded agreements with countries from India to China, Japan, Australia, and New Zealand.

The EU, as by far the most advanced "region" in the world, and China, as the fastest-growing major state in the IPE, are ever more tightly bound by trade and investment flows and political engagement setting the context for their economic and financial interdependence. As Kathleen J. Hancock highlights in Chapter 12, the EU forged a new economic cooperation framework in 2000, the Cotonou Agreement, as a result of the perceived failure of prior arrangements to advance African development, trade, or market shares in the EU states. Unfortunately, the trade preferences granted to all African, Caribbean, and Pacific (ACP) countries were judged to be discriminatory by the WTO, and the EU has instead turned since 2002 to negotiating separate agreements with five different, and confusing, regional groupings. This process is not working, and in any case it runs counter to the larger goal of building broader markets across all of Africa. At the same time, Hancock concludes that the RTAs may be playing unexpected roles such as helping to support regional electricity grids and renewable energy development.

Sub-Saharan Africa is also an important focus of such work, as it is the region least integrated by, and benefiting from, trade agreements and interactions. Why is there less trade within Africa and its many RTAs than in other regions and groupings when the countries are strong exporters? Bernard Hoekman explains in Chapter 13 that this is due in part to their continued heavy reliance on producing and exporting natural resources, energy, and agriculture. He shows that, in addition to their large pool of unskilled labor and large endowments of energy resources, their trade costs are very high. For African states, trade policy liberalization is probably less important per se than administrative reform and restructuring. It is barriers along the transportation and border management or supply chain that are slowing and deterring much greater gains from trade. Thus, by effectively waiving the requirements of the current trade negotiations for African countries, it removes the pressure and incentives for them to work on vital service sector reform and trade facilitation. Hoekman analyzes the efforts of the WTO, World Bank, and other international development organizations to promote trade by African countries. Although he finds that much of value is being accomplished, he strongly recommends adding a "supply chain" approach that focuses on coherence and cooperation across the relevant government agencies and with business. He concludes that trade assistance and agreements will actually improve investment and employment if they are focused on opening the real, practical bottlenecks in moving goods and services through customs, handling, and processing.

At the opposite scale and level of the international trading system is the EU–China trading and investment relationship. This relationship starkly illustrates the politics of ever more tightly interwoven markets in relatively high technologies, and particularly where western market economies intersect state-managed and -directed ones. As these two very large players in trade advance their already extensive level of interdependence, we see what we would expect – an increasing number of bilateral issues that must be managed carefully along with increasing investigations, anti-dumping and related protectionist measures, and WTO dispute cases. In addition, this relationship points to the future of trade relationships and trade politics for countries worldwide as more economies move into trade based on supply chains, extensive foreign direct investment, and not only manufacturing but service sector industries which rely on imported equipment even more than domestic production. Furthermore, it highlights the serious challenges posed for the most advanced "region" in the world, the EU, in the issue area of trade that is supposed to be the most "common foreign policy," of actually executing a single policy when member states have divergent interests. Finally, it demonstrates the important role of the global trade regime in helping to guide regionalism in productive directions and backstopping it with worldwide dispute settlement and transparency norms.

Chapter 14 by Maria Garcia documents the bilateral, but also global, politics of trade, investment, and manufacturing in "green technologies." It traces a fascinating story of how the strategies and pathologies of the largest state-directed economy in the world, that of China, led to oversupply and (managed) bankruptcies in its own economy as well as the destruction of jobs and companies in the solar and wind industries in the countries that were the industry leaders. Her study maps out clearly the difficulties of forging a single trade policy among all the EU member states and their fundamentally different industrial, export, and investment interests in the context of an EU bureaucracy with its own agenda and strategies. It shows how China's industrial development plan must be meshed to some degree with the EU's strategy for economic and financial development. Garcia's study of how the EU–China solar panel dispute was resolved foreshadows the future of trade in general, but also of trade among the largest markets and particularly those governed by starkly different political regimes.

The Global Governance of Trade: Who Is Accountable and Who Governs?

The fundamental purposes, design, and legitimacy of public international organizations have been highlighted by the research and debate, as well as the opposition and protest politics, involving the WTO and broader global trade regime. Substantial research and some of the most interesting work on transnational networks and coalitions in interaction with states and public international organizations are vitally connected to trade. Groups seeking to block or enact reform in the global trade regime in general or the WTO in particular highlight questions about its legitimacy, credibility, and accountability. The relatively closed nature of the global trade regime to civil society, as defined very specifically by the WTO members, and the concern about privileging firms and their organizations and networks are the focus of serious and sustained study. Fundamental questions are raised about how and when civil society is allowed to intervene in a tightly member-driven organization, as opposed to, for example, the UN system. How should civil society be represented in the location of an international organization's headquarters, as opposed to only through national capitals?

At the same time, the trade issue area and WTO do not confront some of the fundamental international organizational adjustment difficulties experienced by the International Monetary Fund (IMF) and World Bank (WB), that is, adjusting quotas and decision-making power to accommodate the enhanced role in the global economy of emerging countries. Lacking the formal quota system and the intermediate level of governance by executive board of the IMF and WB, the WTO is able to adjust more incrementally and informally, and enable small and intermediate-size states, for example in the dispute settlement system, to gain experience and participate in bringing cases against the US and EU, and to have their leaders play major roles in standing and temporary committees. Indeed, the recently selected Director-General of the WTO comes from Brazil instead of the traditional path from Europe. Thus, on the dimension of inclusiveness the trade regime can be considered reasonably representative of its membership and thus more accountable than the IMF or WB.

In addition, the very success of trade agreements such as NAFTA, ASEAN, the WTO, and the EU have triggered extensive work on how trade agreements might help to advance (or retard) labor and human rights as well as environmental protection and sustainable development. In one way, the extraordinary degree of legally binding commitments represented by the WTO and its members have spurred efforts to see if this extraordinary capability can be linked or carried over to progress in other vital issue areas. This introduces the crucial question of how domestic and international levels interact and intersect.

As the WTO Dispute Settlement Body (DSB) gained traction and built de facto a relatively coherent body of international trade law, it intersects national environmental and social laws and regulations, and raises fundamental issues of when and how sovereignty over decision making is transferred or delegated to international bodies and authority. Both the WTO and NAFTA establish relatively authoritative dispute settlement mechanisms that can trump national law and regulations in ways that sometimes trigger protest and blowback.

In terms of international coordination and collaboration, for example the institutional designs of public international organizations, as well as "global governance," trade became the main focus of attention when the WTO was agreed and established in 1995. A rich and diverse set of research programs responded to the WTO dispute settlement system and the negotiations process (especially its failure to produce from 2001), but less so for the very important trade policy review (TPR) mechanism or the mechanism for advancing transparency and surveillance in trade, which is evaluated in Chapter 15 by Marc D. Froese. Despite all the research focused on the WTO DSB and process, the TPR process has been relatively neglected. This is unfortunate, as the TPR process works in parallel to dispute settlement and affects every member's trade environment from entry at ports to procedures at the highest levels of government. The detailed and fine-grained questions and information exchanged between the WTO Secretariat and national trade officials, and ultimately between the reviewed state and its trade partners serve both to open up actual and potential issues and to provide pressure on the state to resolve problems or deviations noted by trade partners.

Froese resolves a fundamental question, indeed perhaps an assumption by scholars, about how the TPR process likely triggers or otherwise encourages requests for dispute settlement. He finds that issues raised in the TPR process do not predict requests for dispute settlement, but that instead important problem areas raised by multiple members are indeed likely to end up in dispute settlement or to be already engaged in a case. Thus, in an important counterintuitive finding, Froese shows that an issue raised in a DSB case can well lead to its subsequent review in more detail in the TPR process.

This subtle and evolving relationship, then, between the transparency and the surveillance roles of the TPR is fundamental not only to the effective functioning of the WTO but much more generally to how public international organizations in all areas might provide more effective transparency functions linked closely to surveillance operations, even where the latter is not the primary or even an officially allowed role. For example, on a bilateral basis (outside the WTO DSB), the IMF and WB have greater degrees of direct surveillance roles and authority than the WTO with regard to member states borrowing from the WB and/or IMF. At the same time, the ability of the WB and IMF to produce high levels of transparency about these states is lower because members press hard for privacy and confidentiality of their national data and information. In addition, the IMF and WB do not have direct dispute settlement authority of the WTO. Thus, the IMF and WB help illustrate how strong surveillance and weak transparency work in combination, and the WTO demonstrates how strong dispute settlement interacts with weak surveillance and moderate levels of transparency provided by the TPR process. Perhaps most importantly, the WTO TPR highlights how multiple reviews, even if strung out over ten to 20 years for the smallest members, tend to raise and resolve issues from one review to the next until transparency is significantly improved and outstanding issues are gradually resolved.

Despite the relatively substantial WTO capabilities with regard to dispute settlement, transparency processes, and representation of smaller states in leadership roles, the overall relevance of the WTO and broader global trade regime is declining as newer issue areas emerge and grow in importance. As Chapter 16 by Wei Liang maps out, for the developed states, and their business interests in particular, the trade–investment–services nexus is their highest priority. Since bilateral and regional trade agreements more explicitly target this nexus, as required for example by growing emphasis on global supply chains, these negotiations have overtaken the global Doha Round as the most promising for the developed states. Liang explains that, while the main mechanism of WTO-based liberalization is the exchange of market access, FTAs and RTAs are better able to frame agreements on the domestic reforms necessary to investment and the wide range of service sector activity.

In addition to the relatively slow progress of the global trade regime in incorporating trade in services, at least for the majority of its members, and common regulations for foreign investment, progress in the global negotiations now requires greater inclusion of the large emerging market states and increased representation of the smaller states. For these reasons as well, Liang argues, we must expect the continuation of the worldwide focus on FTAs and their attractiveness to the US and EU in particular. Furthermore, to the extent that bilateral and regional deals incorporate these key new issue areas and the Doha Round and other Geneva-based negotiations do not, the WTO-based processes will become ever less relevant and urgent for most developed states. Unfortunately, as Liang highlights, since small and intermediate-size states have less leverage in bilateral and regional deals than at the global level, this means that they face a declining role in the governance of international trade.

In addition to the gradual evolution of governance at the global level, and rapid development at the bilateral and regional levels, very significant change is occurring worldwide at the level of individuals, groups, and firms. In Chapter 17 Ari Afilalo explains that it is not only that individuals can challenge states with regard to human rights across the EU but more that relations among individuals have come to challenge the very nature of traditional "sovereignty." He describes new forms of international economic arrangements and institutions that are transforming conventional forms of statecraft well beyond only trade and international finance. In place of, or at least alongside, the traditional vertical system is emerging a much more horizontal or integrated one that reflects the new realities of economic assets and regulatory systems that are no longer associated with any one state or set of national boundaries. As trade and capital are ever more intertwined, private actors establish access, for example through investment treaties, to legal processes that were available only to states in the past. In the new, horizontal system of international law, Afilalo argues, individuals will increasingly pursue legal claims and rights beyond any one state and be able to enforce them against even the most powerful states.

Trade as Globalization

The 1999 WTO Ministerial meeting in Seattle marked a key turning point because, among other reasons, civil society became a visible force in the politics of trade policy making. In the aftermath of this critical juncture in the role of civil society, scholars have focused on how interests and ideas intersect and frame foreign international economic policy outcomes. By this stage in the evolution of globalization, it was necessary to understand, as Silke Trommer explains in Chapter 18, that "the similarities between business and NGO 'campaigns' far outweigh their differences" and that therefore policy formation in the field "can be usefully viewed as a contest between two interest groups, without normatively privileging one group over another" (Sell and Prakash 2004: 144). Trommer shows that, as regional and global trade rules engage an ever broader spectrum of domestic regulatory and policy matters, we must expect civil society and corporate groups as well as state actors to press trade policy making in new and different directions as opposed to the conventional expectations, as mapped out for example in Chapter 5 by Madeira on intra-industry trade.

Perhaps the most fundamental question to be asked about the future of politics over trade and international political economy more generally is the nature of its underlying ideas and values. With the rise of the largest several newly emerging political economies to prominence, it is expected that the nature of their ideas, institutions, and foreign economic policies will play an ever greater role in IPE. Indeed, Christian May and Andreas Nölke argue persuasively in Chapter 19 that the large emerging political economies are much less based on liberal or redistributive principles and more on "reciprocity," or the interpersonal trust relationships between national capitalists and state agencies that essentially manage their economies. Contrary to the perceptions of key observers in the west, this study finds these long-standing, socially embedded reciprocal arrangements to be both efficient and productive.

In a fundamental argument, they show how external policies, for trade most specifically, replicate reciprocity in this sense, and lead to an IPE based on selective policies and preferential treatment instead of the most basic principles of non-discrimination and national treatment of the prevailing global trade regime. In other words, to the degree that these major new players insist that IPE reflects their own domestic reciprocal relations of loyalty and selectivity, the global trade order must be expected to favor bilateral over global institutions and to lead to a fundamentally different form of IPE in the future.

The evolution of conflicting ideas and interests in global markets and governance is starkly illustrated by the global food system. In Chapter 20 Elizabeth Smythe explains how globalization driven by national liberalization, new technologies, and international financial markets has carved out food markets distant from consumers, wherein a few large corporations play a central role and small farmers are less able to compete. In this core issue area of food and the wide range of differing food and agricultural markets, Smythe explains how the intense competition over the ideas and institutions forming the global food system has not only deadlocked the Doha Round and key international rule-making processes but also thrown into doubt both the viability and the legitimacy of the WTO.

Unlike other issue areas where governance is generally understood to require significant authority at the global level, the food system is being pressed hard by many civil society groups in countries worldwide, a range of broader publics, and food movements, for example for "food sovereignty" and security to support local markets and national (and EU) regulation and standards. In part the problem is driven by the failure of top-level political leaders in the US, the EU, Brazil, China, Canada, and Australia, the largest food exporters, to provide international leadership in the WTO-based negotiations, but it is also driven by strong domestic political pressure on major food-importing states such as India whose leaders have been less inclined to co-lead with the US and the EU than to work with like-minded states. Smythe shows that this issue area is also extremely difficult because the core issues have worsened substantially over the period since 2001, as the WTO-based negotiations failed to remove in the richest countries the hundreds of billions of dollars in annual export subsidies, the deeply embedded domestic payments systems, and the high levels of border protection. Consensus building is extremely difficult owing to the food price and access crisis of 2007–08, as well as the serious maldistribution of food across national markets, the dominance of key market segments by a few large firms, the inability to resolve serious disputes over genetically modified foods (despite final WTO rulings), and arguments that food is different because it is a basic right for all and unique from culture to culture.

For a significant number of developing countries, the most valuable asset they have to "trade" is their human resources. For many developing countries, human labor, whether shorter-term or long-term, but especially as workers, is a critical part of their need to exchange and engage in international transactions. And, as Joel P. Trachtman argues in Chapter 21, for the overall benefit of not only trade but also social welfare worldwide there is very clearly unprecedented value that can potentially be unlocked by greater opening of borders worldwide to a regulated and agreed movement of workers and migrants more generally. In light of the very wide range of wages paid worldwide, global welfare would be substantially advanced by allowing workers much greater freedom of movement.

Trachtman analyzes a set of scenarios for both exporting and importing states, and clarifies the possible trade-offs and bargains that might be struck. Indeed, the potential efficiencies and gains involved in this movement of people are so important that cross-issue or sector linkages seem appropriate, as well as necessary. He suggests that wealthy importing countries might accept more skilled and unskilled workers in exchange for poor-state reductions in tariffs, especially on manufactures, and barriers to investment and professional services.

The Future of Trade

The final part of this volume addresses the two most fundamental elements of international political economy, and of trade in particular, the global flow of people and of ideas and information. This part asks how the Internet accelerates trade and how trade might help to advance social standards.

Today's trade policy happens increasingly behind the border, and social standards are a crucial part of it. Labor and environmental provisions have become an important element of all EU and US FTAs. Furthermore, as the preference for "fair trade" grows stronger among both policy makers and their constituents in the developed world, Evgeny Postnikov shows in Chapter 22 that social standards will feature even more prominently on the trade policy agenda. He documents significant differences between the EU and US approaches towards the content and enforcement of these standards. Postnikov shows that the variation is due to the differing levels of the executive authority's insulation from the pressure of societal actors and control of legislators that characterize trade policy making in the EU and the United States. Indeed, the analysis of domestic political and institutional factors is central to understanding the design of FTAs more generally.

Labor and environmental standards in the trading system can be viewed as particularly valued commodities by some states, as they touch upon the deeply entrenched societal norms. Ironically, as Postnikov explains, social standards in FTAs could become the stumbling blocks in the negotiation process, undermining the whole function of bilateral agreements as an alternative to the complexities of the WTO system. The prolonged negotiation of the EU–Canada Free Trade Agreement, with the disagreements between the parties over the shape of social provisions, is a case in point. Finally, as the European Union and the United States negotiate the TTIP, the question of labor and environmental standards has become ever more important, testing our knowledge of international trade negotiations and providing the impetus to the richer analysis of new trade issues.

Because major countries worldwide have different priorities for privacy, security, the free flow of information, and trade policy openness, it is especially important for the US, the EU, Canada, and the other most democratic polities to provide leadership for coherent open trade and Internet policies. The US and the EU have made Internet freedom a priority. Yet Susan Ariel Aaronson and Rob Maxim argue in Chapter 23 that neither the US nor the EU has clearly defined Internet freedom or developed a compelling and consistent argument as to why Internet freedom and openness are important to both economic growth and political stability. Although the American, Canadian, and EU governments generally share a vision of Internet freedom, they have not collaborated to define the role of governments in supporting an open Internet, or to determine when it is appropriate to interfere in the affairs of other countries to protect netizens. Aaronson and Maxim find that policy makers do not make Internet-related trade policies by weighing the implications of their choices for Internet openness. As a result, US and EU policies to promote cross-border information flows seem disconnected from policies to sustain the open web.

NOTES

1. See, for example, the detailed proposal for a negotiation agenda post-Bali in Evenett and Jara (2013).
2. Rodrick (2000) would add that the crucial flaw in the development strategies of Latin American, Middle Eastern, and other states is the weakness of their domestic institutions of conflict management, which should form the front line in managing the challenges of globalization.

REFERENCES

Evenett, Simon J. and Alejandro Jara (eds.) (2013), *Building on Bali: A Work Programme for the WTO*, London: Centre for Economic Policy Research.
Rodrik, Dani (2000), "Institutions for High-Quality Growth: What They Are and How to Acquire Them," *Studies in Comparative International Development*, **35** (4), Fall, 3–31.
Sell, Susan and Aseem Prakash (2004), "Using Ideas Strategically: The Contest between Business and NGO Networks in Intellectual Property Rights," *International Studies Quarterly*, **48** (1), 143–75.
Whitehead, Laurence (ed.) (1996), *The International Dimensions of Democratization*, Oxford: Oxford University Press.

PART I

TRADE AS AN "ENGINE" OF INTEGRATION, GROWTH, OR INEQUALITY?

2.   Commerce as communication: Montesquieu's view[1]

Randal R. Hendrickson

> The history of commerce is that of the communication of peoples.
> (Charles-Louis de Secondat, Baron de La Brède et de Montesquieu, 1689–1755)

Here is Montesquieu, defining commerce not first as trade, but as communication. Others' manners and morals are *communicated* in the act of trade, and Montesquieu means to proclaim the good results. He means, along the way, to excuse and encourage the acquisitive drive natural to individuals, a drive traditionally repressed by the forces of politics, religion, and morality. And so it is against these forces that Montesquieu makes the case that commerce tends to improve morals and incline to peace. It morally shrinks the world, so to speak, averaging behavior across the globe and rendering nations not enemies but reciprocally dependent. Commerce is humanity's best hope for a "cure" of its "destructive prejudices." So much and more is for Montesquieu the work of commercial communication.

The Spirit of Laws (1748), Montesquieu's labor of 20 years, appears at a moment when commerce is hardly considered a theme of political science. It comes as something of a surprise, then, that a political philosopher should be so concerned with the subject.[2] It is remarkable, indeed, to find just how many matters reduce for Montesquieu to the commercial.

The instances abound. In his epistolary novel *Persian Letters*, a conqueror's inhumanity is likened to the wastefulness of a "madman" who acquires statues only to toss them into the sea (*Persian Letters* CXXI); in *The Spirit of Laws*, the war-mongering and tax-happy monarch recalls a reckless young spendthrift who forsakes the wise "order and economy" of a "good father" (*SL* XIII.12, 13).[3] Remarks on the alien nature of antique commerce open a work on Rome's grandeur and decline (*Considerations on the Greatness of the Romans and Reasons for Their Decline*, I). Related to it is a writing on the impossibility of contemporary expansion on the Roman scale that turns always on questions of commerce and trade (*Reflections on a Universal Monarchy in Europe*).[4] Commerce changes the law of nations and shapes individuals across classes (*SL* XIV.3, XIX.27, XX.1, 21). John Law, the financier, plays for Montesquieu a villain, Admiral Anson a hero – not so much for his military exploits as for his travelogue (*Persian Letters* CXLVI; *SL*

II.4, VIII.21). A shipwrecked Aristippus occasions reflection on the social meaning of money (*SL* XVIII.15). Montesquieu celebrates the exchange and the good political effects of invisible money, a civilizing currency less prone to Machiavellian "strokes of authority" and to be contrasted with a barbarous exchange of a pile of gold dust for a bigger pile of salt (*SL* XXI.20, XXII.1, XXII.10). The reader thrills to technological advances advancing trade, such as ship hull design, one of the two subjects that Montesquieu cannot leave behind, the other being Rome (*SL* XI.13, XXI.6). Odysseus is now a commercial man, who would have been a better one had he owned a compass, a marvel whose absence helped Homer to produce a work of poetry second only to the Bible (*SL* XXI.6, 7). And so it goes.

Commerce is treated poetically by Montesquieu not as a touch of honey to help the wormwood go down. Commerce (somewhat ironically) *is* poetic on his telling.[5] And so the books of *The Spirit of Laws* devoted to the theme are the work's most musical and open with a classical epigraph, an invocation to the muses, and a poem penned by Montesquieu himself. It is in this manner that *The Spirit of Laws* offers a tale moving from the "total privation of commerce" to its flourishing.

As might be gathered already, Montesquieu is no economist in any familiar sense, even if no less a figure than Keynes thought otherwise.[6] In place of the mathematical and theoretical sophistication, though, we get in *The Spirit of Laws* a transformative constitutionalism and the seeds of a politics of globalization, which Montesquieu champions rather before the fact. We get among the first and finest thinkers to contemplate the deep connection between a free constitution and what would come to be called the free market.

I will touch in this chapter on some of the highlights. I will consider Montesquieu's thoughts on the beneficence of commercial communication as he makes the case against its obstacles and celebrates its good effects. I will begin with the ancient republican repression of the acquisitive drive, with its problems and alternatives as Montesquieu presents them. I will then consider briefly the form of government that Montesquieu holds up as most amenable to the commercial spirit. From there I will consider some of the changes in behavior that commerce has brought (and ought to bring) in its wake.

FROM VIRTUOUS FRUGALITY TO "FRUGAL MORES"

The very international communication and mingling of manners that Montesquieu extols is a danger from the classical point of view.[7] *The*

Spirit of Laws drives a deliberate political and economic wedge between ancient and modern worlds. What emerges, among other things, is a contrast between two republics: one old and extinct, the other new and on the horizon.[8]

The old comes to light as rather repressive. Its motivating "principle," the passion that gives it life and keeps it together, is said to be virtue, defined at first in terms of a contrast. Virtue is neither Christian nor moral, says Montesquieu; it is "political"; it is "love of country" and "love of equality" (*SL* "Author's Foreword"). But, as Montesquieu goes on to develop the theme, he explodes the original contrast with a striking metaphor, as virtue is likened to a monkish love of repression, a sort of Stockholm syndrome whereby the monk loves the very order that "afflicts" him (*SL* V.2; *Pensées* no. 731). With that striking image established, and to come to the commercial point, virtue is now defined also as a "love of frugality" to be attained by a ceaseless effort to keep individual holdings equal and in check. This frugality is no ordinary thriftiness, then. It must be backed by the force of laws and the threat of punishment.

Laws meant to enforce frugality are meant to sustain the "love of equality," which might be expressed as a desire to see the great humbled, the very "genius" of republican government that pushes up against the stubborn fact of natural superiors (*SL* V.3, 8, VI.15). But the republican genius is not satisfied automatically. Natural inequality must be wrenched into an artificial equality, which plays upon the desire to keep our betters down, on the one hand, and, on the other hand, tells our betters that superior talents are but a further obligation their possessors owe to the good of the republic. And so the ancients recognized in human beings a desire for excess to be battled or in some way redirected: let the competition be not what you have but what you have done for the fatherland (*SL* V.3–4, 17, VII.1–3, VIII.4, 11). This is a never-ending race – not a Hobbesian pursuit for "power after power," but for sacrifice after sacrifice made on behalf of the *patrie* to which one will always owe something (*SL* V.3). To these ends, a self-renouncing frugality is instilled in a manner by which the human being "forgets himself" (*SL* I.1, V.2). And this, as Montesquieu tells the tale, is contrary to humanity's passionate and acquisitive nature. It is contrary to the "ordinary passions" that the monk's order represses.

It was in the name of their virtuous frugality that the ancients were uneasy with commerce, thought to be an activity too "vile" (*infâme*) for free men and to result in a material wealth that would be a distraction from the public good that demands a citizen's undivided attention, which is "always a very painful thing" (*SL* IV.8). So is there the moral dilemma born of the mingling with outsiders that commerce implies. For with foreign goods come foreign ways. While some have found Montesquieu to be sympathetic with the antique suspicion of commerce here and later in his masterwork, the rhetorical drift of *The Spirit of Laws* does not justify it, as the reflections of the early books are later repeated, and clearly not regretted, in the first chapter of the first book devoted to commerce.[9]

Commerce does corrupt virtue, Montesquieu there admits, but in the same breath he rejects the classical understanding of the requirements of a healthy polity: "One can say that the laws of commerce perfect mores for the same reason that these same laws ruin mores. Commerce corrupts pure mores: this was the subject of Plato's complaints; it polishes and softens barbarous mores, as we see every day" (*SL* XX.1). Here is a typically paradoxical formulation: moral progress has its source in moral decline.[10] It was in the name of what Montesquieu calls "pure mores" that ancient authors dreamed of self-sufficient orders unmixed with the manners of barbarous others.[11] But, for Montesquieu, this proves to be an aim too high. Pure morality is rooted in the "imaginary" needs of the state rather than the "real needs" of individuals (*SL* XIII.1). And so, finding international trade to be a movement reaching a crescendo, Montesquieu does not wrestle with the course of history as he sees it: "The history of commerce is that of the communication of peoples," he says approvingly (*SL* XXI.5). He looks to the effects of an international mingling of manners and concludes that "great things have resulted" from it, including this tendency to gentler morals (*SL* XIX.8, XX.1). Pure morality closes one off to the world and hardens one; it denies one the natural tendencies to acquisitiveness. In short, pure morality proves to be a goal that is "barbarous" in its consequences. Indeed, notice how Plato's "pure mores" are by the stroke of a pen themselves made to appear "barbarous."

Here is the flight to commercial mores. Its tale is anti-utopian and not a little Machiavellian. Machiavelli, who decided to turn away from the imaginary orders of Plato and others, did so in part for an awareness that "it is a very natural and ordinary thing to desire to acquire."[12] It is in a similar spirit that Montesquieu encourages readers to look elsewhere and notice exemplars less monkish and more in keeping with his own appreciation of things.[13] These are individuals who would rather flee than love the orders that afflict them, or "peoples who have engaged in economic commerce" (*SL* XX.5). Economic commerce, belonging to republics and to be distinguished from a monarchic commerce of luxury, is born of the "violence and vexation" of nature and governments alike.

Violent and vexing nature is beautifully exemplified by the republic of Marseilles, mentioned as Montesquieu offers something of a hymn to commerce: "Marseilles, a necessary retreat in the midst of a raging sea; Marseilles, that place where the winds, the shoals, the coastline order ships to put in, was frequented by seafaring peoples" (*SL* XX.5). He continues:

The sterility of its territory inclined its citizens to a commerce of economy. They had to be hard-working in order to supply what nature refused them; they had to be just in order to live among the barbarous nations which would come to make their prosperity; moderate in order for their government to be always tranquil; finally, of frugal mores, in order that they could live always by a commerce that they would more surely preserve when it would be less advantageous.

One has seen everywhere that violence and vexation have given birth to the commerce of economy . . . They had to subsist; they drew their subsistence from the entire universe. (*SL* XX.5)[14]

Here Montesquieu turns from the old civic stance, which had emphasized the *moral* difficulties besetting cities by the sea, and begins by making explicit the *natural* disadvantages of such a place, speaking as he does of "the sterility of its territory." He recalls without Locke's state of nature a Lockean view of nature as neglectful, as offering too little without human industry. Then he notes the qualities born of that natural condition. Call it necessity. By necessity, these people had to be "hard-working," "just," "moderate," and "of frugal mores." Forced by nature to acquire, they naturally acquire frugally.

Against the old education to frugality undertaken contrary to nature, then, Montesquieu suggests that a certain frugality ("frugal mores") compatible with commerce comes naturally.[15] Such people "had to subsist; they drew their subsistence from the entire universe." Necessity (in the form of scarcity and oppression) pushes up against these individuals, and those morals are born (see, for example, *SL* XVIII.1, 3–4, 6).[16] Notice the Machiavellian twist: the people of Montesquieu's peculiar island retreat were animated by those virtues, not with a view to higher ends, but because the situation called for it.[17] No education to virtue, no honorable notion of the self, and no religious restraint made them so. Natural necessity did it, and nature pays individuals for their efforts: "Nature is just toward men. It rewards them for their pains; it makes them hard-workers, because it attaches to greater work greater rewards" (*SL* XIII.3).

The promotion of states that practice a "commerce of economy" over others comes especially into view when the passage on Marseilles is compared to a later rumination on Athens. The passages are linked by a manner of style, as Montesquieu reserves for the two a rhythm and tone unique to them alone in all of *The Spirit of Laws* (*SL* XX.5, XXI.7). Note just their opening lines. Recalling the first: "Marseilles, a necessary retreat in the midst of a raging sea; Marseilles, that place where the winds, the shoals, the coastline order ships to put in, was frequented by seafaring peoples" (*SL* XX.5). Now the second: "Athens, filled with projects for glory, Athens, which increased its jealousy in lieu of increasing its influence; more attentive to expanding its maritime empire than making use of it" (*SL* XXI.7). The stylistic parallels abound, but it is the distinct thrust of each text that is decisive. Athens is motivated by glory; Marseilles is a hideout. Athens has all the right equipment for commercial greatness (good ships, silver mines, and a hefty slave population); Marseilles is the picture of barrenness. The one is full of advantages, the other of apparent drawbacks. But now the respective conclusions that tell the tale: with all of its potential, Athens's livelihood was limited to the Black Sea and its environs; Marseilles, with fortune's back turned, drew its sustenance from the "entire universe." And so now a Lockean twist: as the English philosopher had made a day laborer seem to surpass a native American king in his enjoyment of creature comforts, so with Montesquieu does Marseilles emerge superior in matters of sustenance to Athens itself.[18]

Aggrandizement is not for the author of *The Spirit of Laws* in the "true spirit" of republicanism, which, again, is "peace and moderation" (*SL* IX.2).[19] Athens could have lived off the universe, but (contrary to the republican spirit) it was too distracted by glory. Montesquieu presents the old pursuit of greatness as destructively prejudiced (e.g., *SL* X.4). And so he opposes it to commerce, which "cures destructive prejudices," such as those alive even in this most commercial of the imperial republics of antiquity (*SL* XX.1, XXIX.14).[20]

Commercial peoples will be more diffuse and less entangled in the bizarreries of honorific glory. Individuals and nations that trade together find each other better off alive than dead. You buy my beef and sell me your wheat, and so it is in my interest that no harm comes to you, indeed, that I do not offend you too grossly. Here, then, a space opens up for the pursuit of a less deadly form of aggrandizement. In place of the old pursuit of glory, then, Montesquieu now holds up a glory newly understood. He finds a certain "daring" (*hardiesse*) admirably at play in those moved by the entrepreneurial spirit (*SL* XX.4, XXI.11). All told, though, the morality and motivations born of the commercial spirit are rather more prosaic: "Commerce introduces into the same country different sorts of peoples, a great number of conventions, types of goods, and manners of acquiring" (*SL* XX.18).

What sort of political arrangement will best allow and manage the introduction of such diversity? What arrangement best gives rise to individuals who are "hard-working," "just," "moderate," "of frugal mores," and so on? Here we touch on the new commercial republic that Montesquieu imagines.

THE COMMERCIAL REPUBLIC OF SEPARATE POWERS

In the passages just preceding the description of a new order's institutional arrangement, Montesquieu exclaims: "Who would say it! Even virtue has need of limits" (*SL* XI.4). Virtue is abandoned in favor of a constitution that is a "disposition of things," whereby power – understood according to "sorts" relegated to distinct "bodies" – can check power (*SL* XI.6).[21] Montesquieu calls this government a republic.[22] But, unlike the ancient variety, this one is large and commercial, understood according to our "modern times," and the first to be true to the "true spirit of the republic," which, recall, is "peace and moderation" (*SL* IX.2, X.3). It is ordered by a constitution that has its basis not in political speech whereby diverse actors advance their claims to rule, *à la* Aristotle, but in a different sort of speech, in everyone's speech as it would unfold at the level of society, as it would reflect the universal concern for security. Not a will to virtue, then, but a more moderate thing, the will to security, informs Montesquieu's arrangement that begins from an abandonment of self-renouncing virtue. The will to security finds its fulfillment in the "political liberty" that the constitution supplies.

Political liberty is the "tranquility of mind [*esprit*] that comes from the opinion that each has of his security" (*SL* XI.6). Here is a liberty not rooted in the glory and aggrandizement of one's state, but in one's own sense of safety. It is political, as it is achieved politically, by an institutional arrangement. And it arises when "government is such that one citizen cannot fear another citizen." Political liberty is the "direct object" of Montesquieu's constitution of separate powers, and it is not defined until he announces what seems to be the essential separation, new with him, that of the power of judging from the executive. At the highest level, one citizen will not fear another when the executive may no longer execute individuals.[23] This "terrible power" must be removed from sight as far as it is possible. And it is in such an atmosphere that the "ordinary passions" now begin to fire quite freely, as Montesquieu makes clear in the rather more neglected complement to his much-studied formal description of the constitution devoted to liberty as the security of individuals.

By its constitution there is a citizenry made to feel secure and moderated – by institutional separation and by representation, respectively. Not being directly involved in governing, human beings will turn to a space now opened up, a social space enlivened by the "ordinary passions" traditionally squashed. This is the commercial sphere, contained by a constitutional republic that is a commercial republic. Montesquieu nods to this aspect of the new republic as he closes his discussion of its constitution, where what was until now a static description comes to hint at the arrangement's dynamic and informal effects. He draws on Herodotus to knock Harrington, who sought wrongly the limits of liberty in a constitution.[24] The English republican had "built Chalcedon with the shores of Byzantium before his eyes" (*SL* XI.6). Montesquieu, who opposes (among other things) the agrarian laws envisioned by Harrington and enacted by his ancient predecessors, turned his gaze across the Bosporus and saw the fruitful territory, the Golden Horn (a natural port), and thus the commercial potential, of Byzantium when he saw his constitution.

Such an order will put concerns of trade above others. Such an order has the potential to conquer the world in a way that benefits all who engage with it in commerce. This is the stuff of progress, a movement from civic, glorious, and otherworldly concerns to living off the universe. This, as Montesquieu understands it, is to overcome "barbarism."

THE TERMS OF ENGAGEMENT

Barbarism here is not meant to call to mind strange practices of others far from home.[25] Barbarism is systemic. It is barbarous to deny what is "naturally permitted," an act of repression against ordinary acquisitiveness that is synonymous with Plato's "pure mores" and all that that evokes. Now to the list of barbarous things are added the principles and practices of theologians and Machiavellian sovereigns, as one finds in a chapter titled "How Commerce Broke Through [*se fit jour*] Barbarism in Europe" (*SL* XXI.20). Whereas Montesquieu's remarks on Marseilles and other such states showed the commercial spirit flourishing in a state of natural "violence and vexation," here one finds some good effects of bad convention.

Montesquieu discusses here the moral and political obstacles to the spirit of commerce, highlighting its fugitive aspect at key moments in its movement through time and states. He presents a stylized history of commerce in Europe, where it was once indistinguishable from "the most atrocious usuries, monopolies, the levying of subsidies, and all dishonest means of acquiring money."[26] He speaks of European Jews becoming wealthy in those dark times by an "atrocious usury" that they carried on underground and of how they were "pillaged by princes" in turn. "In those times" – the times of barbarism, if one keeps the chapter title in mind – "men were regarded as lands" (cf. *SL* XXII.14). Like land, individuals were regarded as immobile and as matter from which an authority might derive profits and power. Jews in particular were "toyed with," says Montesquieu, having their goods confiscated when they agreed to convert to Christianity, or being burned at the stake when they did not. But, as it is the way of commerce to flourish on rocky shores, so does "one see commerce leave the bosom of vexation and despair." Jewish bankers, similarly treated across Europe, found a way to render their effects secure by inventing bills of exchange, "and in this way commerce was able to avoid violence and maintain itself everywhere; the richest trader had only invisible goods, which could be sent everywhere and leave a trace nowhere" (*SL* XXI.20).

In these circumstances, theologians were now "obliged to curb their principles." Montesquieu has economic principles in mind, and he finds in their retreat a good consequence born of "vexation and despair." It is a consequence that ought to be furthered, but Montesquieu prefers in these "matters of changing religion" to work by "invitations" rather than exhortations, which is to say he takes care (*SL* XXV.12). Indeed, often in *The Spirit of Laws* he is friendly to what he calls in a less friendly way the "religion of today" (*SL* X.3). When it is praised, Christianity is praised for its softening tendencies (e.g., *SL* XXIV.3), but, by that measure, commerce is more consistently held up as the most effective force.[27] It is no small matter that monks are the models of self-renunciation. Like conquerors, they are hardened, not gentle (*SL* VI.9),[28] whereas "it is almost a general rule that everywhere there are gentle morals [*moeurs douces*] there is commerce, and that everywhere there is commerce, there are gentle morals" (*SL* XX.1).[29] All told, the commercial spirit is fundamentally opposed to the Christian spirit insofar as the latter tends, in the words of Clifford Orwin, to "asceticism, hypocrisy, fanaticism, celibacy, and indifference to the exigencies of earthly prosperity."[30]

Montesquieu's approach is characteristically roundabout, as he turns to other objects and leaves it to the reader to notice what Japan (*SL* XX.9), Islam (*SL* XXII.19), ancient Rome (*SL* XXII.21-22), and medieval use of Aristotle (*SL* XXI.20) have to do with Christianity as an obstacle to the "great things" that commerce brings. He rethinks in these cases questions of competition, just price, the requirements of economic self-sufficiency, lending at interest, and the meaning of probity.

Competition makes the commercial world go round, and so nations must understand what establishes a just price in goods traded between them. Let nations not behave like Japan, this Eastern despotism at times cast as a double for the Church it would be imprudent to oppose in broad daylight.[31] Against the "true maxim," which is "to exclude no nation from one's commerce without great reasons," the Japanese trade with only two nations, which exploit the situation and earn artificially high profits to the detriment of those unjustly excluded (*SL* XX.9). Starting off in explicit opposition to the Japanese policy, Montesquieu arrives at a conclusion opposed to the Christian notion that there is a just price with its source in the nature of things, not a price that bends with the situation. Joining one

Thomas against the other, then, Montesquieu reiterates the Hobbesian view: "It is competition that puts a just price on goods and which establishes the true relation between them" (*SL* XX.9).[32] Competition, an activity subject to scarcity or surplus, to necessity, informs a standard of just price that replaces a standard rooted in a particular view of the nature of things that is informed by religious or natural laws.

States ought to know this and thus be open to trade with others, which ought not to be thought barbarous by virtue of their origins. It is on this point that Montesquieu provides a perfect close to the book that opened with a contrast between "Plato's complaints" and what "we see every day" (*SL* XX.1). The ancient position is again turned inside out, as self-sufficiency as a measure of a polity's health is rethought: "Let us say, then, that it is not the nations that need nothing that lose in engaging in commerce; it is those that need everything. It is not peoples sufficient to themselves, but those who have nothing at home who find an advantage in trafficking with no one" (*SL* XX.23).

To have "nothing at home" is to have none of the wider world's riches. Nations formerly mistook their isolation for "an advantage." Such nations understood the communication with others' ways implied by commerce, but they saw only a danger. They believed they were "sufficient to themselves," but by Montesquieu's lights they lacked everything. These lines thus amount to a turn from the old view of a state's self-sufficiency, once understood according to how little one needed others: the less, the better. But with Montesquieu it is a mark of a commercial people; it depends on international trade. Those who refuse trade with outsiders will "have nothing at home," while a people sufficient unto itself takes its livelihood from the "entire universe."

While international commerce depends on such reconsiderations of competition, just price, and self-sufficiency, particularly relevant to the domestic realm is the question of lending at interest, a practice traditionally condemned. Montesquieu begins his rehabilitation of it with remarks on Plato's student and the students of his student. True to form, he emphasizes the alien aspect of the ancients, speaking as he does of Aristotle having been "brought to the west" and reminding that the peripatetic came to us by strange hands from strange lands. Medieval scholastics were "infatuated" with Aristotle's thinking on lending at interest, which, Montesquieu notes in an aside, they just as well could have found in the Gospels. Led by pagan and sacred authorities, then, the scholastics wrongheadedly condemned lending at interest indiscriminately and always.[33] And so "commerce, which was only the profession of lowly [*vils*] people also became that of dishonest people: for every time that one prohibits a thing naturally permitted or necessary, one only renders dishonest the people

who do it" (*SL* XXI.20). So it is that Christianity piles righteous and otherworldly indignation on the old civic denunciation of the practice. It is
on this basis that Montesquieu considers the relation of natural necessity
to honesty, a virtue that takes on an economic aspect as he rescues it from
Christianity's hold. This he does by way of a critique of the ill effects of
Christian charity that he will employ here and again.

Now Rome is the analog. It serves to show how "extreme laws for good
give rise to extreme ill" (*SL* XXII.21). Montesquieu discusses a time of
political and economic instability: with the power of the people on the rise,
Roman magistrates scrambled to make laws pleasing to a pleb down on his
luck. Interest was lowered, and then forbidden. When a tribune wanted to
be loved, he began to speak of abolishing debts.[34] Montesquieu suggests
that tendencies of this sort, though certainly fine in themselves as private
preferences, have no place in the political sphere: "It is a very good action,
indeed, to lend one's money to another without interest, but one senses that
this can only be a counsel of religion and not a civil law" (*SL* XXII.19).[35]
When mixed up in the political realm, such Christian principles mirrored
by Roman policies stand opposed to "honest means of lending," because
they do not grasp, or will not entertain, the relation of natural necessity to
honesty. The effort proved disastrous in Rome, as usury was "naturalized"
by its very prohibition. It is thus through this brief reflection on a Roman
moment that Montesquieu suggests how Christian kindness and charity,
a wish to see things from the point of view of the debtor, might amount
politically to bad management and to laws ill conceived.

To run with the theologically inspired policy against lending at interest
is to go against nature's grain by opposing what is "naturally permitted
and necessary." Montesquieu suggests that the practice flourishes in spite
of a prohibition that is successful only in rendering dishonest those who
are not. Nature, in other words, has a way of reasserting itself. And so,
rather than fighting what cannot fruitfully be fought, Montesquieu seeks
to reconsider the effects of its prohibition. He suggests reconsidering what
constitutes "honest means of lending." There is a dishonest means, of
course, but the Christian religion fails to make the distinction, and here it
mirrors the "law of Mohammed," in so far as each "confuses usury with
lending at interest" (*SL* XXII.19). Montesquieu thus emphasizes the distinction between the two, the former being rightly understood as an unjust
and dishonest abuse of the latter.[36] And so he preserves a moral stance, but
he broadens its conception. Montesquieu wants to show that an orientation to economic commerce satisfies the human desire to acquire, which it
will manage, in turn, by its effects. He wants to show that the pursuit of
material satisfaction is "naturally permitted," "necessary," and properly
viewed as "honest."

He thus rethinks what constitutes "good faith" or "probity." Indeed, there is a noteworthy development in the meaning of this virtue that culminates here in the reflections on interest. At first, in *The Spirit of Laws, probité* is synonymous with the political virtue that animates the old republics (*SL* III.3, IV.6, V.15, VI.11). And so it is at first bound up with harsh and hardening self-renunciation. But, in the midst of such repression, lending at interest, "violently linked to bad faith, returned, so to speak, to the bosom of probity." To engage in what is "naturally permitted" is to engage in "good faith" (*SL* XIX.27). And so moral expectations are lowered to surer foundations, as good faith is reduced to good policy. Freed from its old republican and Christian definition, probity now takes on an economic aspect (*SL* XIX.27, XXI.2, 20).

All of this boils down to a self-interested morality. The same self-interest that is the engine of commercial activity informs the morality that will contain a commercial world.

COMMERCIAL MORALITY

Here, in a way, is the moral peak of *The Spirit of Laws*. "Happy it is for men to be in a situation where, though their passions inspire in them the thought of being wicked, they have an interest in not being so" (*SL* XXI.20). To the new situation belongs this morality rooted in one's interests, a morality that looks first to oneself but that makes for the good of the others who are not one's first concern. Though they do not require a repressive or extraordinary education, the interests do need training.[37] This is the popular enlightenment that Montesquieu in the very preface of his work says ought to be pursued. To enlighten the public is to "simplify the ideas," to make people able to see things from the point of view of reasonable self-interest. Interests will work somehow systematically, even predictably, moving according to the "laws of morality."[38] Ordinary individuals will not be attending seminars run by philosophers, of course; they will be shaped, rather, by legislators, who at best will listen to the legislators *par excellence* and learn the "spirit of moderation," a spirit that belongs with peace to republicanism newly understood (*SL* XXIX.1, 19).[39]

The workings of this morality are most visible in the commercial republic, which is a peaceful republic for its being a commercial one. But, "if the spirit of commerce unites nations, it does not in the same way unite individuals" (*SL* XX.2). Such places are peopled by "confederates rather than fellow-citizens," hardly moved by the old *we're all in this together* spirit (*SL* XIX.27). But commerce does produce in individuals certain virtues not called virtues. One, recall, is "exact justice," a certain mean between extremes born of the "total privation of commerce": banditry and a moral virtue that leads one to forget one's interests for others. So commerce doesn't make one simply good (*SL* XX.2, 5). Morality takes on some of the selfishness of banditry and some of the good effects of a virtue that in its pure form is too self-sacrificial. Commerce "cures" prejudice, says Montesquieu, and thus it reminds you of yourself. The new institutional arrangement and the commercial spirit harmonized in the new republic – all to the good of individuals.

The spirit of commerce reflects and satisfies the natural expansion of human desires. "One commerce leads to another: the small to the middling, the middling to the great; and he who had a desire to gain little finds himself in a situation where he wants no less to gain more" (*SL* XX.4). The desire to acquire is natural; the possibilities for acquiring are nearly endless; and the possibilities excite: Montesquieu likens engaging in commerce to playing the lottery, an enticement to which even the "wise" are susceptible, as is natural (*SL* XX.6). It is in everyone's interest to have (as it is in everyone's nature to want) more. If Montesquieu abandons the Hobbesian state of nature, he maintains something of the description of the human pursuit for "power after power" that the Malmesbury philosopher located in the prepolitical state and identified as an ingredient of its "war of all against all." But, here in the order that works best with the commercial spirit, self-interested behavior is restrained in the service of self-regard. Adam Smith later captured the spirit of it: "It is not from the benevolence of the butcher, the brewer, or the baker, that we expect our dinner, but from their regard to their own interest."[40]

While I have called this a moral peak in *The Spirit of Laws*, it will appear from another perspective to be rather low. Montesquieu recognizes as much and is clear that certain high things will be left behind. Indeed, there is a touch of regret as he speaks of French gallantry and *politesse*, whose natural place is monarchy. Citizens of commercial orders will have to let go of expectations of a society of high taste and courtly refinements of manner. They cannot expect acts of *noblesse oblige* or hospitality, a quality also found among those deprived of commerce: "Hospitality, so rare in commercial countries, is found admirably among bandit peoples" (*SL* XX.2). Montesquieu's morality, the substitute for repressive and self-forgetting virtue, also replaces the less extreme sort of self-forgetting at play in such *noblesse oblige*, where it is noble to deny one's lower interests. The aristocratic rejection of base self-interest is undermined in favor of the self-interested morality of commerce, its opposite. Self-interest is *ignoble*. It is so for its view to the basics and to the expansion of the basics. It is ignoble, too, for its unimpressive risks. The risks of self-interest can be calculated, and they are. It aims low, so it risks little. It is frugal when frugality is understood to be contrary to hospitality. Frugality, by a development I have touched upon in Montesquieu's work, comes to be compatible with acquisitiveness. In the old republic, frugality (identified with monkish virtue) told a citizen what he did not need; in the new republic it tells him that nothing is free, that he has to work. Hospitality runs against the grain, as it encourages one not to work for the expectation of getting something for free.[41]

Such things make little sense and cannot be sustained beneath the force of a commercial spirit that emancipates the steady pursuit of self-interest, which Montesquieu ultimately accepts and describes.[42] Such a pursuit belongs to the new republic "by its nature" (*SL* XX.4). Commercial activity comes naturally to the new republic, where the "ordinary passions" for the "comforts of life" are unleashed by an institutional arrangement and regulated by a morality that works when it has the opportunity. Its ways will be communicated to all who engage in trade, and that, for Montesquieu, is all to the good.

INTERNATIONAL POLITICAL ECONOMY: BACK TO MONTESQUIEU?

Montesquieu leaves us with the bracing image of individuals and states engaged in commerce, enjoying the goods that "the entire universe" has to offer. They are engaged in communication broadly understood – as various cultural norms are trucked along with goods in the act of trade. Here is commerce as so many instances of communicable values, tending peoples and nations toward peace. *The Spirit of Laws* shows what is politically and socially required for this happy state of affairs to come about.

There must be within states a shift in emphasis – from the enforcement of strict citizen virtue and isolation to constitutional liberty and an openness to the outside. Individuals must be left a social space to pursue their interests, a pursuit that will be contained by a morality that asks only that they follow their interests reasonably, which is to say peacefully. Much, then, is transformed as Montesquieu takes his reader from the "total privation of commerce" to its flourishing. Virtue, self-sufficiency, liberty, glory, barbarism, probity, poverty, work, and frugality are redefined according to a commercial spirit that is friendly to humanity's acquisitive nature and that finds its most ready venue in a particular arrangement, a commercial order that Montesquieu envisioned and that, in one shape or another, predominates today.

But it does not predominate simply. As foreign policy makers consider means to enrich and enliven recently war-torn and downtrodden regions, as with the United States' "New Silk Road" strategy, for instance, they might do well to return to Montesquieu's insights (which are at once profound and sensible) on what we might call the cultural-political prerequisites for a beneficent commerce. To take one example, it is difficult to imagine, say, Afghanistan as a great trade hub while it and its neighbors still have blasphemy laws on the books. We might say that what Sharia law demands is just the sort of strict citizen virtue that Montesquieu thought it necessary to abandon for the spirit of commerce to thrive. As with the lending at interest once forbidden by Christian authorities, the religious norms now enforced under threat of punishment in these parts of the world must be removed to the realm of private preferences. That is a tall order, indeed, a rush of realism's cold water.

The political is inseparable from the economic, and, for commerce to be more than merely trade, for it to have its good cultural effects, the political climate must be right. This would seem to be so uncontroversial as to go without saying. If the "history of commerce is that of the communication of peoples," then that historical march depends on an openness to communication. Montesquieu said it first and clearly, and his work is worth considering even now.

NOTES

1. Portions of this chapter are taken from Randal R. Hendrickson (2013), "Montesquieu's (Anti-)Machiavellianism: Ordinary Acquisitiveness in *The Spirit of Laws*," *Journal of Politics*, **75** (2), April, 385–96; and Randal R. Hendrickson (2014), "Ordinary Passions and Philosophic Morality: On the Uniqueness of Montesquieu's Commercial Republic," *Perspectives on Political Science*, **43** (1), 1–11.
2. Here is David Hume noticing as much: "Trade was never esteemed an affair of state till the last century; and there scarcely is any writer on politics, who has made mention of it. Even the Italians have kept a profound silence with regard to it, though it has now engaged the chief attention, as well of ministers of state, as of speculative reasoners" (Hume 1985: 88–9). On Montesquieu's influence on Hume's economic thinking, see Moore (2009) and references therein. On his possible debt to Hume on other matters, see Rahe (2009: 297–8 n. 46).
3. Citations of *The Spirit of Laws* (*SL*) refer to book and chapter, separated by a period. For all works but *Mes pensées* and *Le spicilège*, for which I have used Montesquieu (1991), I have used Montesquieu (1949). Translations are mine.
4. *Reflections* was originally meant to be published as a sort of final chapter of the *Considerations*, had Montesquieu not thought better of the pairing, based, it seems, on the *lettre de cachet* that the *Lettres philosophiques* earned Voltaire. On this, see Rahe (2009: 21).
5. Contrast Pangle (1973: 201–03).
6. Keynes: "Montesquieu was the real French equivalent of Adam Smith. The greatest of your economists, head and shoulders above the physiocrats in penetration, clearheadedness, and good sense" (quoted in Devletoglou 1963: 1). At the other pole is Schumpeter, who says that Montesquieu's economic thought is "insignificant – without

originality, force, or scholarship" (Schumpeter 1996: 135–6 n. 22). For an appraisal of Keynes's remarks, see Larrère (2001: 369–70).

7. See, for instance, Aristotle, *Politics* 1327a13–40; Cicero, *On the Republic* II.3–5; Juvenal, *Satires* VI.293; Plato, *Laws* 704b–705e, *Republic* 421d–423c.

8. That Montesquieu has republican leanings, classical or modern, is far from universally agreed upon. There is Montesquieu as monarchist (e.g., Shackleton 1961; Destutt de Tracy 1969; Althusser 1982; Carrithers 2001; Mosher 2001; Levy 2009), as a sort of relativist (e.g., Comte 1908; Condorcet 1962; Helvétius 1962; Durkheim 1965; Aron 1968; Shklar 1987; Berlin 2001; Rosen 2002), or as a proponent not of a particular form of government but of moderation in whatever form (e.g., Landi 1981; Cohler 1988; Goyard-Fabre 1993). The republican reading of Montesquieu, itself, is not uniform; on this see Rahe's (2009: 280–81 n. 40) excellent sampling and breakdown of varying views.

9. Larrère (2001: 337–40) thus errs when she suggests that "the general pattern remains that of classical republicanism" in commercial republics and that the books of *SL* devoted to the theme make it "very difficult to inscribe in Montesquieu an opposition between the ancients and the moderns" (Larrère 2009: 282–3). Nelson (2004: 155–64, 171–6) similarly finds in his treatment of wealth and property in Montesquieu the latter's "Greek scale of values" at work. See also Manin (2001: 573–602) and Spector (2004). Contrast with Pangle (1973, 2010) and Rahe (2009).

10. On Mandeville's moral influence, see *SL* VII.1, XIX.8; *Pensées* no. 1553; Rétat (1973); Larrère (2001: 340–41, 345–57); Spector (2002); Carrese (2005: 132–3); and Rahe (2009: 176–8).

11. Some nonetheless have identified Montesquieu's Platonism (for example, Kassem 1960; Nelson 2004).

12. See Machiavelli (1929), *The Prince*, chs. 3, 15.

13. I discuss the significance of Montesquieu's departures from Machiavelli at length in Hendrickson (2013).

14. Manent (1998: 39–42) has shined much light on this passage. On the good effects of harsh terrain, see Macfarlane (2000: 37–8). Pangle (2010: 113) emphasizes the example of Tyre (mentioned here in *SL*) for understanding the religious implications of the spirit of commerce.

15. Those who have considered frugality in Montesquieu have not accounted for his development of the theme and have thus thought him to be endorsing what he finds at work in the ancients. See, for instance, Nelson (2004) and Viroli (1995: 69–76).

16. In *SL* XVIII, Montesquieu suggests that nature's stinginess is good for human beings, as it forces them to labor and to create. The pursuit of needs against stingy nature leads to intellectual progress (*SL* XVIII.15), a point picked up now and again in the books on commerce (*SL* XXI.6).

17. See Machiavelli, *Discourses* I.1.12.

18. See Locke, *Two Treatises* II.41.

19. Montesquieu contrasts this with the "true spirit" of monarchy, which he defines as "war and aggrandizement" (*SL* IX.2), a spirit overtaken by that of commerce on his telling. Writing in the years after Louis XIV's expansionist efforts, the *philosophe* studies the king's failures in light of an increasingly commercial world and observes that the freest and wealthiest states at the moment are those that have favored trade over war; on this, see Macfarlane (2000: 4, 32–3, 39, 43, 51–2).

20. Montesquieu finds Athens strikingly similar to Rome, insofar as each is caught up in a politics of glory contrary to the spirit of commerce. Says the *philosophe*, "the Roman spirit was not commercial" (*SL* XXI.5); the Romans "rarely thought" about commerce (*SL* XXI.14); by its "political constitution," imperial "right of nations" (*droit des gens*) and "civil law," it was "inimical" (*accablant*) to commerce. Athens, he says, had "an abominable political law that followed from an abominable right of nations [*droit des gens*]" (*SL* XXIX.14).

21. A treatment of the functioning of the separation of powers is beyond the scope of this chapter. Scholarly views of the arrangement are numerous and varied. For suggestions

that Montesquieu here presents his ideal state, see Ilbert (1904: 32); Fletcher (1939: 107); Starobinski (1953: 67); Gay (1969: 470); Pangle (1973: 160, 163, 228); and Lynch (1977: 487–500). For readings that emphasize what is claimed to be Montesquieu's ambivalence toward the arrangement, see Merry (1970: 313, 339); Cohler (1988: 180ff.); Baker (1990: 173–9); Boesche (1990: 741–2); and Krause (2000). For those who note Montesquieu's historical inaccuracy, see Dedieu (1909: 228); Dodds (1929: 31); Merry (1970: 341–5); Plamenatz (1992: 285–94); Berlin (2001: 131); Courtney (2001: 279–80); and Claus (2005). And for the fewer who suggest or imply that historical accuracy is beside the point, see Pangle (1973); Mansfield (1989: 213–46); and Manent (1994).

22. Montesquieu calls this government a republic hiding behind a monarchy (V.19). Carrithers (1991: 252 n. 21) finds England (the actual state from which Montesquieu derives his government of separate powers) better described as a "mixed monarchy," taking his cue from Montesquieu's *Pensées* no. 238, where it is so called. But England is not, as far as I know, called a "mixed monarchy" in *The Spirit of Laws*, where it is later referred to as a republic (XII.19, first paragraph with chapter title, XXIX.19) and earlier left for the reader to determine whether it is a popular state or a despotism (II.4). As to the *Pensées*, Montesquieu says that one ought to be mindful of relying too much on his notebooks. Yet, should one consult them nonetheless, one would have to attend in this case to *Pensées* no. 1667, where Montesquieu refers to "the Republic of England."

23. See Mansfield (1989: 234–5).

24. See Herodotus, *Histories* 4.144.2.

25. See Schaub (1999), who has considered Montesquieu's rethinking of barbarism in a somewhat different light.

26. See Pangle (2010: 173 n. 25).

27. On the numerous points where Montesquieu raises doubts about Christian softness, see Pangle (2010: 103–08, 172 n. 18).

28. "Extremely happy men and extremely unhappy men are equally inclined to hardness [*dureté*]: witness monks and conquerors." Who is the happy one? Who the unhappy? In the confusion of the question, what is clear is that one shares the defect of hardness with the other. The notion that commerce softens manners comes to be known as the *doux commerce* thesis. On this, see Hirschman (1977: 60–63); Larrère (2001); and Force (2003: 164–5, 249–55).

29. In the *Dernier réponse* (the "Final Reply" to criticism of his first *Discourse*) Rousseau refers to this line and disputes it, referring to Montesquieu as that "celebrated philosopher." The editor of the Pléiade (Rousseau 1964: 72) mistakenly identifies Plutarch as "celebrated philosopher."

30. See Orwin (2009: 143).

31. Montesquieu says this of the Japanese emperor: "One punishes with death almost all crimes in Japan, for disobedience to such a great emperor as that of Japan is an enormous crime. It is not a question of correcting the guilty but of avenging the prince. These ideas are drawn from servitude and come above all from the fact that the emperor is the proprietor of all goods, such that almost all crimes are committed directly against his interests" (*SL* VI.13). In Montesquieu's notebooks, there is a nearly identical passage, with this notable addition: "The Japanese, then, reason with regard to their emperor in the same way we reason with regard to God: the fault is infinite that offends an infinite being" (*Le spicilège* no. 524, in Montesquieu 1991). See Pangle (2010: 109–10).

32. See Hobbes, *Leviathan*, ch. 15, § 14; contrast Aquinas, *Summa theologiae* II-II.78.1.

33. See Pangle (2010: 113–14).

34. Montesquieu here overturns what he says much earlier in apparent praise of Solon's cancellation of debt (*SL* IV.6). Nelson (2004: 173) notes Montesquieu's references to these legislators, particularly Montesquieu's praise and then blame of Solon – praising him for his cancellation of debts, blaming him for allowing one to leave one's property to others provided one had no children. Nelson fails to take into account the directly opposite position taken by Montesquieu later at *SL* XXII.22. And so I differ from Nelson

(2004: 173), who, not taking into account what unfolds in the present context, reads the earlier remarks on Solon as an endorsement.

35. Montesquieu distinguishes the "precepts of the gospel from its counsels" in one of his two direct confrontations with Bayle (*SL* XXIV.2, 6). In short, "precepts" are laws; "counsels" are recommendations. On the broader context, see Schaub (1999: 233–6) and Bartlett (2001: 13–44). As is glimpsed here in *SL* XXII.19, Montesquieu argues for something like a separation of church and state (cf. *SL* XXV.8). This is part of a larger project for religious tolerance to be accomplished especially by a plurality of religious sects in nations (cf. *SL* XIX.27, XXV.9–10). This is a sort of inversion of the practice of primitives, whom Montesquieu finds tolerant for their lack of religious dwellings: "Peoples who have no temples have little attachment to their religion: this is why the Tartars have always been so tolerant" (*SL* XXV.3). The civilized policy, in other words, is to multiply the temples, and the effects are the same: Montesquieu says of his English essentially what he says of the Tartars and others without temples (*SL* XIX.27).

36. See Pangle (2010: 114).

37. I have emphasized the repressive education of the old republicans, but the monarchic education has its drawbacks, too. Though this is not the place to dwell on the matter, the difficulty comes to sight in the monarchic education's preference for the "beautiful," "great," and "extraordinary" over the "good," "just," and "reasonable" (IV.2). In addition to excluding ordinary individuals, a society of individuals at the top trained according to the precepts of honor will not be open to the type of commerce that Montesquieu is describing.

38. Montesquieu seems to anticipate Adam Smith's "system of natural liberty," as we find in commerce an economic complement to the constitution that provides political liberty. See Adam Smith, *Wealth of Nations* II.iv.9; consider Sher (1994). I treat these oddly neglected "laws of morality" in Hendrickson (2014).

39. The chapter titled "On Legislators" is peopled entirely by philosophers (*SL* XXIX.19).

40. Smith, *Wealth of Nations* I.2.

41. See Mansfield (1995: 61).

42. Only accidentally and rarely does it find its way into monarchies, where it cannot long be maintained (XX.4). When monarchy is being itself, it is more taken with a commerce of luxury, less beneficial to the whole and given to all that inflames the arrogance of the sovereign. See Hulliung (1976: 32–6).

REFERENCES

Althusser, Louis (1982), *Politics and History: Montesquieu, Rousseau, Marx*, London: Verso.

Aron, Raymond (1968), *Main Currents in Sociological Thought*, New York: Anchor Books.

Baker, Keith Michael (1990), *Inventing the French Revolution*, Cambridge: Cambridge University Press.

Bartlett, Robert C. (2001), *The Idea of Enlightenment: A Post-Mortem Study*, Toronto: University of Toronto Press.

Berlin, Isaiah (2001), "Montesquieu," in Henry Hardy (ed.), *Against the Current: Essays in the History of Ideas*, Princeton, NJ: Princeton University Press.

Boesche, Robert (1990), "Fearing Monarchs and Merchants: Montesquieu's Two Theories of Despotism," *Western Political Science Quarterly*, **43**, December, 741–61.

Carrese, Paul (2005), "The Machiavellian Spirit of Montesquieu's Liberal Republic," in Paul A. Rahe (ed.), *Machiavelli's Liberal Republican Legacy*, Cambridge: Cambridge University Press, pp. 121–42.

Carrithers, David W. (1991), "Not So Virtuous Republics: Montesquieu, Venice, and the Theory of Aristocratic Republicanism," *Journal of the History of Ideas*, **52** (2), 245–68.

Carrithers, David W. (2001), "Democratic and Aristocratic Republics: Ancient and Modern," in Michael A. Mosher, David W. Carrithers and Paul A. Rahe (eds.), *Montesquieu's Science of Politics*, Lanham, MD: Rowman & Littlefield.

Claus, Laurence (2005), "Montesquieu's Mistakes and the True Meaning of Separation," *Oxford Journal of Legal Studies*, **25**, 419–51.

Cohler, Anne M. (1988), *Montesquieu's Comparative Politics and the Spirit of American Constitutionalism*, Lawrence: University Press of Kansas.

Comte, Auguste (1908), *Cours de philosophie positive*, Paris: Schleicher.

Condorcet, Marie Jean Antoine Nicolas de Caritat, marquis de (1962), "Observations on the Twenty-Ninth Book of *The Spirit of Laws*," in Antoine Louis Claude Destutt de Tracy, *A Commentary and Review of Montesquieu's Spirit of Laws*, New York: Burt Franklin.

Courtney, C.P. (2001), "Montesquieu and English Liberty," in Michael A. Mosher, David W. Carrithers and Paul A. Rahe (eds.), *Montesquieu's Science of Politics*, Lanham, MD: Rowman & Littlefield.

Dedieu, Joseph (1909), *Montesquieu et la tradition politique anglaise en France: Les sources anglaises de L'Esprit des lois*, Paris: Gabalda.

Destutt de Tracy, Antoine Louis Claude (1969), *A Commentary and Review of Montesquieu's Spirit of Laws*, New York: Burt Franklin.

Devletoglou, Nicos E. (1963), "Montesquieu and the Wealth of Nations," *Canadian Journal of Economics and Political Science*, **XXIX** (1), 1–25.

Dodds, Muriel (1929), *Les recits de voyages: Sources de L'Esprit des lois de Montesquieu*, Paris: Presses Modernes.

Durkheim, Emile (1965), *Montesquieu and Rousseau: Forerunners of Sociology*, Ann Arbor: University of Michigan Press.

Fletcher, F.T.H. (1939), *Montesquieu and English Politics*, London: Edward Arnold & Co.

Force, Pierre (2003), *Self-Interest before Adam Smith: A Genealogy of Economic Science*, New York: Cambridge University Press.

Gay, Peter (1969), *The Enlightenment: An Interpretation*, Vol. 2, New York: Knopf.

Goyard-Fabre, Simone (1993), *Montesquieu: La nature, les lois, la liberté*, Paris: Presses Universitaires de France.

Helvétius, Claude Adrien (1962), "Letters of Helvétius Addressed to President Montesquieu and M. Saurin, on Perusing the Manuscript of *The Spirit of Laws*," in Antoine Louis Claude Destutt de Tracy, *A Commentary and Review of Montesquieu's Spirit of Laws*, New York: Burt Franklin.

Hendrickson, Randal R. (2013), "Montesquieu's (Anti-)Machiavellianism: Ordinary Acquisitiveness in *The Spirit of Laws*," *Journal of Politics*, **75** (2), April, 385–96.

Hendrickson, Randal R. (2014), "Ordinary Passions and Philosophic Morality: On the Uniqueness of Montesquieu's Commercial Republic," *Perspectives on Political Science*, **43** (1), 1–11.

Hirschman, Albert O. (1977), *The Passions and the Interests: Political Arguments for Capitalism before Its Triumph*, Princeton, NJ: Princeton University Press.

Hulliung, Mark (1976), *Montesquieu and the Old Regime*, Berkeley: University of California Press.

Hume, David (1985), "Of Civil Liberty," in *Essays: Moral, Political, and Literary*, (ed.) Eugene Miller, Indianapolis, IN: Liberty Press.

Ilbert, Courtney (1904), *Montesquieu*, Oxford: Clarendon Press.

Kassem, Badreddine (1960), *Décadence et absolutisme dans l'oeuvre de Montesquieu*, Génève: Librairie Droz.

Krause, Sharon (2000), "The Spirit of Separate Powers in Montesquieu," *Review of Politics*, **62** (2), 231–65.

Landi, Lando (1981), *L'Inghilterra e il pensiero politico di Montesquieu*, Padua: CEDAM.

Larrère, Catherine (2001), "Montesquieu on Economics and Commerce," in Michael A. Mosher, David W. Carrithers and Paul A. Rahe (eds.), *Montesquieu's Science of Politics*, Lanham, MD: Rowman & Littlefield, pp. 315–73.

Larrère, Catherine (2009), "Montesquieu and Liberalism: The Question of Pluralism," in Rebecca E. Kingston (ed.), *Montesquieu and His Legacy*, Albany, NY: SUNY Press, pp. 279–303.

Levy, Jacob T. (2009), "Montesquieu's Constitutional Legacies," in Rebecca E. Kingston (ed.), *Montesquieu and His Legacy*, Albany, NY: SUNY Press.

Lynch, Andrew (1977), "Montesquieu and the Ecclesiastical Critics of *L'Esprit des Lois*," *Journal of the History of Ideas*, **38**, 487–500.

Macfarlane, Alan (2000), *The Riddle of the Modern World: Of Liberty, Wealth and Equality*, New York: Palgrave Macmillan.

Machiavelli, Niccolò (1929), *Tutte le opere: Storiche e letterarie di Niccolò Machiavelli*, Firenze: G. Barbèra.

Manent, Pierre (1994), *An Intellectual History of Liberalism*, Princeton, NJ: Princeton University Press.

Manent, Pierre (1998), *The City of Man*, Princeton, NJ: Princeton University Press.

Manin, Bernard (2001), "Montesquieu, la république et le commerce," *Archives européennes de sociologie*, **42** (3), 573–602.

Mansfield, Harvey C. (1989), *Taming the Prince: The Ambivalence of Modern Executive Power*, Baltimore, MD: Johns Hopkins University Press.

Mansfield, Harvey C. (1995), "Self-Interest Rightly Understood," *Political Theory*, **23** (1), 48–66.

Merry, Henry J. (1970), *Montesquieu's System of Natural Government*, West Lafayette, IN: Purdue University Studies.

Montesquieu (1949), *Oeuvres complètes de Montesquieu*, 2 vols., Paris: Bibliothèque de la Pléiade.

Montesquieu (1991), *Pensées, Le spicilège*, ed. Louis Desgraves, Paris: Bouquins.

Moore, James (2009), "Montesquieu and the Scottish Enlightenment," in Rebecca Kingston (ed.), *Montesquieu and His Legacy*, Albany, NY: SUNY Press.

Mosher, Michael (2001), "Monarchy's Paradox: Honor in the Face of Sovereign Power," in Michael A. Mosher, David W. Carrithers and Paul A. Rahe (eds.), *Montesquieu's Science of Politics*, Lanham, MD: Rowman & Littlefield.

Nelson, Eric (2004), *The Greek Tradition in Republican Thought*, Cambridge: Cambridge University Press.

Orwin, Clifford (2009), "Montesquieu's *Humanité* and Rousseau's *Pitié*," in Rebecca Kingston (ed.), *Montesquieu and His Legacy*, Albany, NY: SUNY Press, pp. 139–48.

Pangle, Thomas L. (1973), *Montesquieu's Philosophy of Liberalism: A Commentary on The Spirit of the Laws*, Chicago: University of Chicago Press.

Pangle, Thomas L. 2010. *The Theological Basis of Liberal Modernity in Montesquieu's Spirit of the Laws*, Chicago: University of Chicago Press.

Plamenatz, John (1992), *Man and Society: Political and Social Theories from Machiavelli to Marx*, London: Longman.

Rahe, Paul A. (2009), *Montesquieu and the Logic of Liberty*, New Haven, CT: Yale University Press.

Rétat, Pierre (1973), "De Mandeville à Montesquieu: Honneur, luxe et dépense noble dans L'Esprit des lois," *Studi francesi*, **50**, 238–49.

Rosen, Stanley (2002), *The Elusiveness of the Ordinary: Studies in the Possibility of Philosophy*, New Haven, CT: Yale University Press.

Rousseau, Jean-Jacques (1964), "Dernier réponse," in *Oeuvres complètes*, Vol. 3, (ed.) Jean Starobinski, Paris: Editions de la Pléiade.

Schaub, Diana (1999), "Of Believers and Barbarians: Montesquieu's Enlightened Toleration," in Alan Levine (ed.), *Early Modern Skepticism and the Origins of Toleration*, Lanham, MD: Lexington Books.

Schumpeter, Joseph A. (1996), *History of Economic Analysis*, Oxford: Oxford University Press.

Shackleton, Robert (1961), *Montesquieu: A Critical Biography*, Oxford: Oxford University Press.

Sher, Roger B. (1994), "From Troglodytes to Americans: Montesquieu and the Scottish

Enlightenment on Liberty, Virtue, and Commerce," in David Wooton (ed.), *Republican Liberty and Commercial Society*, Stanford, CA: Stanford University Press.

Shklar, Judith (1987), *Montesquieu*, Oxford: Oxford University Press.

Spector, Céline (2002), "Vices privés, vertus publiques: De *La Fable des abeilles* à *L'Esprit des lois*," in David W. Carrithers and Patrick Coleman (eds.), *Montesquieu and the Spirit of Modernity*, Oxford: Voltaire Foundation, pp. 127–57.

Spector, Céline (2004), *Montesquieu: Pouvoirs, richesses et sociétés*, Paris: Presses Universitaires de France.

Starobinski, Jean (1953), *Montesquieu*, Paris: Editions du Seuil.

Viroli, Maurizio (1995), *For Love of Country*, Oxford: Clarendon Press and Oxford University Press.

3.   Trade, development, and inequality[1]
Christopher Bliss

INEQUALITY AND INEQUALITIES

Inequality can be considered for any well-defined group for which data is available. One can feel unequal to a neighbour, or at an opposite extreme one may be concerned with inequality for the world population as a whole. Someone who claims to feel the pain of inequality in the second case as acutely as for the first may not be honest. Be that as it may be, all inequalities are proper concerns for economic analysis. The estimation of global inequality is an undertaking only embarked upon by the brave, or perhaps the foolhardy. Sala-i-Martin and Pinkovskiy (2009) tell us that the world Gini coefficient has declined from about 0.68 in the early 1970s to about 0.61 in 2006. These authors explain in detail how such an estimate is arrived at, with missing data being estimated by interpolation. While the exact numerical values proposed may not be worth much, the picture painted is surely correct. World inequality has been declining for the last several decades.[2] The extraordinary nature of this development should not pass without notice. Ever since the industrial revolution, rich countries have typically grown faster than poor countries. What has altered recently has been the rapid growth of incomes in populous and previously poor countries.

The rapid growth of incomes in poor countries that accounts for the declining world Gini coefficient is consistent with growing inequality within individual countries or regions, whether rich or poor. The point is well illustrated by the consideration of income inequality in the USA. Not only has this been increasing, but it has become the focus of academic debate and political argument. Yet the impact of even a substantial increase in inequality in the USA on the world Gini coefficient is small. A scholar of our world today can be embarrassed by how far the US is magnified in his field of vision, simply because of the richness of the data and literature from that country. Sometimes a focus on the trees rather than the wood is unavoidable.

Table 3.1 contains no entries for the European Union (EU). As the countries belonging to the EU or its predecessors have varied over time, an aggregate Gini coefficient would make no sense. Data for several European countries is given in Table 3.2. In five out of six cases the Gini coefficient

Table 3.1   Gini coefficients for various regions and times

	1980	1995	2010
Advanced	0.27	0.29	0.30
Asia and Pacific	0.36	0.38	0.37
Emerging Europe	0.35*	0.33	0.32
Latin America and Caribbean	0.46	0.51	0.48
Middle East and North Africa	0.30	0.37	0.36**
Sub-Saharan Africa	0.40	0.47	0.44**

Notes:
The numbers shown in the table are not true Gini coefficients, but rather averages of the coefficients for some of the countries that make up the regions concerned. The 36% for Asia and Pacific in 1980 is an average of 26.7% for Taiwan and 45.2% for Thailand!
* 1985; ** 2005.

Source: Bastagli et al. (2012).

Table 3.2   Gini coefficients for various countries and times

	1980	1995	2010
Brazil	0.55	0.58	0.52
China		0.33	0.42
France	0.29	0.29	0.30
Germany	0.24	0.27	0.32
India		0.32	0.37
UK	0.27	0.34	0.34
USA	0.30	0.36	0.39

Source: Bastagli et al. (2012).

in Table 3.1 is larger in 2010 than it was in 1980 (or 1985 for emerging Europe), although some of the differences are small. This justifies the claim made above that the decline in the world Gini coefficient is consistent with an increase in inequality in many regions.[3]

The Gini coefficient is not the only, or even the best, measure of inequality. In particular it is relatively insensitive to the tails of the income distribution. The right-hand tail notably, where the highest incomes are to be found, has been the theatre for spectacular increases in inequality in many countries. Over the last three decades the shares of the richest in pre-tax incomes have increased substantially in English-speaking advanced economies, as well as in China and India. The left-hand tail is also important, because it includes those living below an absolute poverty level. An example of an absolute poverty level would be the $1 a day test originally proposed by the UN, and subsequently adjusted for various reasons. The current level is $1.25 per day, or $2 per day at purchasing power parity. Some 1.4 billion people in developing countries are estimated to have been in poverty in 2005 (Chen et al. 2008). The proportion of a population living in absolute poverty can only be estimated,[4] but as with the world Gini coefficient the overall picture is clear. Over the last three decades there have been substantial declines in the numbers living in extreme poverty (Chen and Ravaillion 2004). This is the result chiefly of economic growth in previously poor countries, some of which has trickled down to the very poor. This observation should not blind us to the fact that the trickle-down effect is notoriously limited, and the substantial numbers living in poverty in China, India, and elsewhere remain an important and often neglected problem. The fact that trickle-down can make a significant and positive difference in poor countries is in contrast to the situation in rich countries, where it can be shown that trickle-down is largely ineffective (see OECD 2011).

The estimates of Gini coefficients shown in Tables 3.1 and 3.2 are for disposable income, that is after tax and transfers are taken into account. The importance of tax and transfers varies greatly between different regions, being more important for rich advanced countries than for poor developing countries. Typically tax and transfers reduce inequality, as do most public services, such as subsidized education and medical care. It is unfortunate for this reason that the regions shown in Table 3.1 with the greatest inequality are also those in which the redistribution affected by public policy is weakest. Bastagli et al. (2012) argue that fiscal policies have had positive redistributive effects in rich countries, although these effects have weakened since the 1990s. Arguably, point estimates of redistributive effects overestimate their power. If redistribution is viewed through its consequences for the lifetime welfare of different actors, the net burden of taxation on the rich will be seen to be lower than would otherwise appear. One reason is that the rich are more energetic in taking advantage of state benefits, such as subsidized transport and education. The rich also tend to live longer and hence to collect state pensions for more years than the poor. Only in the case of Brazil is the coefficient lower in 2010 than it was in 1980 (or 1995 in two cases).[5] Even for Brazil inequality first rose to 1995 before declining to 2010. In several cases the increase in inequality is large. That description applies to China, India, the UK, and the USA. It has been argued that the statistics for China have become increasingly unreliable over time, with massive unreported income and wealth for the high elite, some of whose scandals and corruption have been well publicized. The large increase in inequality for Germany took place between 2000 and 2010, so it was not affected by German re-unification.

EXPLAINING THE CHANGES

The changes that have taken place in our world during the last 30 years are enormous, and the same can be said of the majority of individual countries. To pick out from all those changes crucial and leading causes of economic development and alterations in inequality is a formidable undertaking. To consider just a short-list of possible influences, the following must be taken into account: demographic and health developments; democratization; urbanization; education; migration; technical change; and finally international trade and capital movements. These changes are not all independent of each other. For example, the great move towards urbanization has taken the world during the last decade to a point at which more than 50 per cent of the world's population live in cities. This has had large effects on inequality, notably by weighting more heavily the relatively higher incomes of the urbanized. Yet the move towards urban residence would have been far more difficult, if not impossible, had it not been accompanied by an increase in manufacturing employment. And that rise in manufacturing is often to be attributed to international trade, with the increased supply of manufactured goods going into exports, or import substitution.

A similar point applies in the case of technical change. In rich advanced economies the stagnation of unskilled wage levels has often been attributed to a bias in technical change that lowers the demand for unskilled labour. This is skill-biased technical change (SBTC) (see p. 62). That change is the result of two developments (see Autor and Katz 1999). First, technical change affects factor demands in specific activities. For example, the use of bar-code charging in supermarkets lowers the demand for unskilled sales staff in retailing. The employment of robots in motor vehicle assembly has had parallel consequences. Secondly, the mix of activities in rich countries has altered in favour of activities that are relatively skill-intensive in their employment. Again international trade has played a large role in these developments. The cheap prices of some manufactured goods on world markets have made domestic manufacture of these products in rich countries uncompetitive.

THE KUZNETS CURVE

In his famous paper Simon Kuznets (1955) argued that economic growth in poor countries would exhibit an inverse U-curve pattern for inequality, with inequality first increasing and then declining later as economic development reached a mature stage. This pattern could arise in more than one way. Kuznets saw the main driver as migration from the country to the city. As urban incomes are higher than rural incomes, the initial consequence of this migration is an increase in inequality. Later, as urbanization grows, and perhaps as the rural incomes for a minority remaining in the country converge to urban levels, inequality declines. A similar result could be observed with uneven regional development, if rapid economic growth takes off initially in the most favoured regions, such as coastal cities, but later embraces the whole country.

We have seen above that economic growth in China and India has been accompanied by an increase in inequality as measured by the Gini coefficient. So the rising section of the Kuznets curve looks plausible. Note however that increased inequality in China and India is accounted for both by variable growth between regions and by increased inequality within regions. Far more problematic is the right-hand section of the Kuznets curve, where inequality declines during the mature stage of economic development. Even if cities grow to account for a large share of the national population this does not necessarily imply great equality, as cities may include much inequality, and inequality in the city may rise over time for all kinds of reasons. If the right-hand section of the Kuznets curve reflects a decline in regional disparities, then where is the guarantee that this will be observed? Many regional inequalities persist for decades, even for centuries. In Italy, for example, the relative poverty of the South goes back at least as far as the Risorgimento, the unification of the regions of the Italian peninsula that created the nation that is now Italy. There is little indication so far that the South will catch up with the North, despite many policies designed to achieve that outcome.

The Kuznets hypothesis allows two interpretations, according to which variable is on the horizontal axis beneath the inverted U-curve. It may be time, as in the discussion above, or it may be per capita income, when we are looking at the relation between inequality and level of development. Both approaches have been tested empirically with generally negative findings for the Kuznets hypothesis (see Deininger and Squire 1998; and Fields 2001). A different approach again, adopted by Dobson and Ramlogan (2009), has the degree of trade liberalization on the horizontal axis, with the claim that some trade liberalization in largely closed economies causes increased inequality, while a movement to more complete openness reduces inequality. Here the Kuznets curve is connected directly to international trade. The hypothesis is tested using data from Latin American countries. The theoretical explanation for this finding is most unclear,[6] and it may be that one or more missing variables are playing an important role here.

INCREASING US INEQUALITY

The important example of the United States underlines the complexity of the issue of inequality and its connection to trade. Changes in general inequality are the result of numerous effects acting on different ranges of the income distribution. Take the top of the distribution, where incomes have diverged spectacularly from the average. Even this may be the consequence of more than one cause. The highest income earners come predominately from two groups. First there are the rentiers: people highly endowed with financial and real-estate assets, who live off the rents, dividends, and capital gains that these assets generate. This group have benefited from higher returns to their assets, notably in the form of capital gains on real estate. The second group of the rich are highly paid employees, notably those employed in the financial sector, plus chief executive officers (CEOs) of large companies. Also included are pop and sports stars. These people in turn have seen their incomes grow rapidly while other earned incomes have stagnated (see Gabaix and Landier 2008).

In the 1930s a fall in the incomes of capital owners had the effect of lowering inequality. In the later twentieth century most of the substantial increase in inequality is due to earned (wage) income (see Atkinson and Piketty 2007). It would be wrong to assume that earned and capital incomes are independent and separate categories. In fact, they are highly correlated across individuals (see Alvaredo et al. 2013). Alvaredo et al. (2013) also show how the explanation of the earnings of CEOs is a complex exercise, where several influences may be in play. The view that the rise in CEO earnings may indicate simply changes in supply and demand for these services, possibly influenced by globalization, is undermined by the observation that the trend towards increasing incomes for the top 1 per cent is largely a feature of English-speaking countries. An alternative explanation would look towards rent-seeking behaviour by top executives, who may use their power to control their own remuneration and to boost their incomes. But why would rent seeking increase over time, as it has done in recent decades? Here Alvaredo et al. (2013) propose the intriguing idea that the large variations in top tax rates, which have been seen particularly in English-speaking countries, may have played an important role. When top tax rates are as high as they have been in the past, the incentive to chase higher incomes, as against for example efforts to grow the firm, is greatly reduced.

Growing inequality is not explained solely by the divergence of the incomes of certain highly paid categories from the general average. There has also been increased inequality within many groups. The incomes of CEOs themselves, as well as the incomes of sports stars, lawyers, and authors, have all become more unequal during recent decades (see Katz 1992–93; and Autor and Katz 1999). This has been attributed to a 'winner takes all' tendency in employment searches, a trend that can be accentuated by the increasing influence of professional head-hunters. While these changes are fascinating to labour economists and to others, their connection to developments in international trade have not yet been analysed sufficiently.[7]

The question of how far increasing wage inequality in the US can be attributed to trade, specifically to imports from low-wage countries, has attracted the interest of several writers. Prominent among them is Paul Krugman. He has apparently changed his mind concerning this issue, from the view that trade is relatively unimportant (Krugman and Lawrence 1993) to the view that imports have played an important role (Krugman 2008). When Paul Krugman changes his mind the world should sit up and pay attention. However, a closer examination of the history shows that the seeming shift of Krugman's position is not a road-to-Damascus conversion. Rather, as Krugman explains, he has responded to a large change in the scale of low-wage imports into the US. He argues also that the Stolper–Samuelson result, which he discusses at length, is a long-term feature, requiring slow adjustment to a long-term equilibrium.

ECONOMIC THEORY: STOLPER–SAMUELSON

Many arguments about trade and inequality are constructed around the Heckscher–Ohlin trade model, which embraces factor price equalization, the Stolper–Samuelson theorem, and the Rybczynski effect (on the theory see Krugman and Obstfeld 2007). The Stolper–Samuelson theorem (Stolper and Samuelson 1941) is about the mapping from output (goods) prices to input (factor) prices. In the general case of many goods and factors, possibly unequal in number, this relation is complicated, and involves relations of complementarity and substitutability between inputs and outputs. Also, when output prices are arbitrary the theory predicts specialization if the number of goods exceeds the number of factors. In a world of general equilibrium, output prices will not be arbitrary but will take values consistent with the provision of all products demanded. In view of these facts, it is not surprising that theorists have concentrated on the two-factors and two-goods case, when inputs only can be substitutes.

That was the position adopted by Eli Heckscher, a precursor of the idea of factor price equalization, though he did not believe in that conclusion. For Heckscher the two factors are land and labour; the goods are food and manufactures; and the theatre is exchange across the Atlantic between the New and Old worlds. Ohlin also rejected the conclusion that trade would equalize factor prices because he considered a model with more than two factors (see Samuelson 1971). When the conditions for complete factor price equalization were established (Samuelson 1948), the two goods had become capital and labour, capital immobility being a reasonable assumption at that time. Today it makes sense to allow for capital mobility, although perfect capital mobility is hard to credit. That allows the two-factor case to focus on skilled and unskilled labour, a route adopted by Krugman (2008) (and see also Wood 1994).

When the two factors are taken to be skilled and unskilled labour the Stolper–Samuelson effect works as follows. The increased participation of poor countries, notably China, in international trade lowers the world price of goods produced with the intensive employment of unskilled labour, and hence lowers the prices of these goods in rich countries. These output price changes must translate to changes in input costs. With the cost of goods produced with the intensive employment of skilled labour unaffected, the only change possible is that one wage rate falls and the other rises. With this pattern it must be the wage rate of unskilled labour that falls and the wage rate of skilled labour that rises, because the opposite case would raise the price of the unskilled-labour-intensive good relative to the skilled-labour-intensive good, contrary to the world price movement assumed.

The implications of Stolper–Samuelson effects for inequality in both the rich North and the poor South are explored in Wood (1994) (see also Wood 1995). His two factors are again skilled and unskilled labour. His analysis reaches the conclusion that increased international trade will cause the convergence of goods prices between the rich North and the poor South. This will make unskilled-intensive goods relatively cheaper in the North, which will lower unskilled wages and lead to increased inequality there. In the South there will be an increase in the relative price of unskilled-intensive goods, and this will raise the relative wages of the unskilled, decreasing inequality. As was shown above, there has indeed been an increase in inequality in rich Northern countries. However, the same is true of the South. The data exhibited above concern general inequality of all sources of income, while Wood's model addresses only wage inequality. Uneven regional development also contributes importantly to global inequality and is clearly not covered by Wood's theory. Unfortunately for Wood's case, the wage differential between the skilled and unskilled in China, seemingly an ideal test bed of his model, has widened in favour of the skilled, the opposite of what his model predicts (see Yang et al. 2010, which covers the period 1978–2007). In defence of Wood it might be argued that his theory describes the long run, and that evidence taken from short periods, even nearly 30 years, cannot invalidate his theory. Retreating to the cover of the long run is a popular escape route for economists; the trouble is that this device often strips a theory of its relevance.

Following his earlier work, Wood's ideas have moved on. Wood (2002) considers a synthesis of three approaches: his own model with Anderson and Tang (Anderson et al. 2006); Feenstra and Hanson (1996); and Heckscher–Ohlin. Key to this modelling is the role of skilled labour in knitting together geographically separated activities in the North and in the South. When this is important, it is possible for the wage differential between skilled and unskilled labour to move in the same direction in all regions.

THE RYBCZYNSKI THEOREM

Of immediate relevance to recent changes in the world economy is the Rybczynski result (Rybczynski 1955), which will be described here in a rather general form. The basic idea behind the Rybczynski theorem is that an increase in the supply of a factor causes increased production of the good that employs that factor intensely, plus a substitution of that factor for the other factor in all production. To get a more general view it is helpful to adopt a technique first suggested by Dixit and Norman (1980). These authors propose that we first consider the integrated economy. This means that we unite both (or in general all) countries as a single economy, jointly endowed with the sum of their factor supplies. A production equilibrium is then derived. This of necessity has one set of factor prices. Now the question is whether the total productions in the integrated equilibrium can be devolved to the individual countries, using the production techniques of the integrated equilibrium, and consistent with these countries' factor supplies. If this can be done, we have factor price equalization; if not, we do not have factor price equalization.

Now perturb the integrated equilibrium by adding a small amount of one of the factors to one of the countries. Call it the additional factor. For the moment hold output prices constant. We then observe a pure Rybczynski effect. The extra factor endowment can be absorbed by expanding the production level of the process that uses the additional factor more intensely. This expansion requires more input of the other factor, and that is supplied by a contraction in the production level of the process that uses the additional factor less intensely. Rybczynski's doctoral thesis, which gave us his result, was concerned with migration of particularly labour into a small economy open to trade with the outside world. He showed that such in-migration need not depress the wage rate of the labour augmented by migration, at least not in the long run, as adjustments in production levels could absorb the additional labour at constant factor prices.

Notice that the simple Rybczynski result depends upon constant output prices, or equivalently on confining attention to one small country. Further examination of the integrated equilibrium for the two-country case permits an easy generalization to a world economy. So, again, we increase the supply of unskilled labour in one of the countries (call it China for convenience). This is the same as an increased supply of unskilled labour to the integrated economy. It does not even need to be a genuine addition to the labour supply. When China starts to participate in world trade, where before it failed to join in, the result is much the same. Once again we see a Rybczynski effect: the unskilled-labour-intensive sector expands. Now, with normal demand functions, the price of the unskilled-labour-intensive good will fall relative to the price of the other good, so that demand can absorb the additional supply. That price change triggers a Stolper–Samuelson effect on top of the Rybczynski effect. The wage rate of unskilled labour will fall in the integrated equilibrium. If the production levels in that integrated equilibrium can be devolved to individual countries, we will have factor price equalization, and the unskilled wage rate will fall in all countries.

INCREASED UNSKILLED LABOUR IN GENERAL EQUILIBRIUM

The Heckscher–Ohlin–Samuelson (HOS) model has dominated international trade theory for many years. Its success is not difficult to explain. It is simple and elegant, and it leads to powerful results. That said, it includes several features that are quite special, and one should never lose sight of that fact. Notable is the assumption that factors located in different countries are essentially identical, plus the similar assumption that technologies of production are the same in all countries. The evidence does not support these assumptions. Much ink has been spilt trying to explain the high productivity of US manufacturing in comparison with its international competitors.

The famous Leontief Paradox is revealed by contracting US foreign trade, replacing imports with domestic production, and computing the consequent change in demand for inputs. The paradox is that the exercise reveals an increased demand for capital, and a fall in the demand for labour. It appears then that US imports are relatively capital intensive, with that intensity measured by US techniques, contrary to what HOS theory predicts. Among the many solutions proposed to the Leontief Paradox, one of the most interesting came from Leontief himself. He suggested that US labour might be uniformly more productive than foreign labour. This is equivalent to a Harrod-neutral shift in favour of the US for both techniques of production. The idea is that the apparent capital abundance and labour scarcity of the US might be illusory. Taking the efficiency of US labour into account, could the US be a labour-abundant country after all?

This is not the place to pursue the Leontief Paradox and its solution in detail. Of more general interest is the point that Leontief's idea gives us a glimpse of a more general treatment of international trade equilibrium, in which countries are not assumed to have identical production possibilities and identical factors. Then the obvious question is: why not go all the way, and apply general equilibrium theory to the analysis of our leading problem? Recall that this leading problem is the analysis of the implications of China's wholehearted entry into the world economy, treated simply as an increased supply of unskilled labour in China. That trade theory modelling uses general equilibrium theory is not a new idea; it goes back to Jones (1965). However, the title of Jones's paper is revealing. It includes the term 'simple general equilibrium models', indicating the author's clear understanding that the HOS model is a notably special case of general equilibrium theory. So a more radical approach would be to go all the way and apply a more general version of general equilibrium theory, subject only to the restrictions that there should be only two tradable goods and two immobile factors.

General equilibrium theory is the pride and sorrow of economics. It is our pride because it represents perhaps one of the few mathematical frameworks that economists have produced that can sustain comparison with theoretical physics. The proof that at least one general equilibrium exists requires the application of a fixed-point theorem, which is an advanced piece of topology. The sorrow is that the resulting theory yields almost nothing of use beyond the existence theorem itself. In general, equilibrium need not be unique and may not be stable even if unique, and unambiguous comparative statics results, the working tools of economic theorists, may not be available. The only solution to these disappointing conclusions is that the theory has to be made more special and restrictive if it is to be usable. The restriction that has proved to be invaluable is the assumption that the excess demand functions for all goods and factor supplies satisfy the following property:

Definition 1: Goods, including factor supplies, in general equilibrium will be said to be gross substitutes if an increase in the price of any good lowers the excess demand for that good, and increases the excess demand for all other goods.

The definition corresponds to what may be called strong gross substitutes. A weaker version of the definition would allow excess demands not to change, provided that they do not move in the opposite direction to that required by the definition. The effect of the gross substitutes assumption is to make a general equilibrium system behave in accord with what partial equilibrium analysis would lead one to expect. The reference to a price change has to be made meaningful by specifying the numeraire in terms of which prices are expressed. The numeraire that will be used here is the general composite basket of goods, consisting of one unit of each of the goods in the model.

Now Chinese unskilled labour is a different good from labour elsewhere. If we assume gross substitutes, what can we conclude if the supply of Chinese unskilled labour increases? To absorb that additional supply the price (wage rate) of that labour must fall. Then Definition 1 says that the demand for all other goods will increase, when their prices must rise to curtail those higher demands. The implication is that Chinese unskilled workers will be worse off in terms of their real wages, although their employment will have increased. Unskilled workers in another country, taken to be a rich industrial country such as the US, will be better off. And, if the supply of this last factor is inelastic and its price flexible, it will not suffer a loss of employment. How large the gain to these last workers will be depends upon details of the model.

We have arrived at a conclusion in sharp contrast to the implications of the HOS model. There we saw that an increased supply of Chinese unskilled labour leads to an increased supply of the unskilled-labour-intensive good, a fall in its price, and a Stolper–Samuelson fall in the unskilled-labour wage rate in the rich country. There is only one explanation for the different conclusions from the two cases. The HOS simple general equilibrium model does not feature gross substitutability, and the reason is plain. An increase in the price of Chinese labour cannot increase the demand for rich-country unskilled labour, because these two types of labour are perfect substitutes in a Dixit–Norman integrated equilibrium.

It is interesting to imagine a totally integrated world economy, in the manner of Dixit and Norman, in the form of a world production function with inputs of labour, skilled and unskilled, plus capital. Then China's entry to this economy takes the form of a large influx of unskilled labour. This will lower the marginal product, which is the wage rate, of unskilled labour. It must increase the marginal product of at least one other factor, and possibly of both other factors. Complementarity means that a fall in the price of one input increases the marginal product of another input. If the two other inputs are substitutes for each other the demand for both will increase. This is what is assumed here.[8]

So which model is pointing us to the correct conclusion? Economic theory is never that simple. Each of our models gives us at best a partial view of reality; like the elephant of Jainist tradition that seemed very different to the blind men who examined it, depending upon whether they felt the tusks, the trunk, or a leg. The Stolper–Samuelson conclusion highlights a genuine and important effect produced by international competition among goods produced with similar technologies employing similar factors. The general equilibrium model allows for different technologies and factors, and more importantly permits non-tradable goods. So consider the consequence of increased Chinese production of simple goods. This is bad for the factor producing the same goods in competition with Chinese output. But there is also a positive income effect in the rich country, because a good previously purchased at a high price is now cheaper. This income effect will increase the demand for other goods, including non-tradables produced by unskilled labour (e.g. cleaning and waiting on restaurant tables). Therefore it is not amazing that rich-country unskilled labour might benefit. In the end we come back to empirics. Real hourly wages in rich countries, notably the US, have not been increasing. So it looks as though Stolper–Samuelson is the card that trumps gross substitutability. Unfortunately, reality is more complicated than either simple model, because other influences, such as technical change and unionization, will have made their contributions to the final outcome.

SPECIALIZATION AND MANY FACTORS

The simple two-country two-factor two-good model with identical technology in all countries does not invariably lead to factor price equalization and Rybczynski-style predictions. Where factor endowments are very different in the two countries, it is normal for one of the countries to specialize in the production of one of the outputs. When that happens a small increase in factor supply to the specializing country will increase the production level of its single product. However, unlike the standard Rybczynski case, factor prices will alter to accommodate the changed factor supplies. With only two outputs it is not easy to judge whether specialization is realistic. Yet interpreting the two goods as aggregates of good types, the possibility of specialization must be taken seriously. Below we will encounter the vexed question of whether China has specialized in the labour-intensive low-tech segment of information technology production.

Attempts to go beyond the two-factor case are rare. Bliss (2007) looks at a model in which there are two goods but three immobile factors. To avoid the horrible complications that might result from this specification it is assumed that one of the factors is only employed to a significant extent in the production of one of the goods. Call this the special factor. Then, provided that the special factor is a substitute for the other two inputs where it is employed, its return moves in the same direction as the relative price of the output it produces. The consequence is that the price of the special factor acts as a buffer which weakens the force of the Stolper–Samuelson effect on the other two factors. Regardless of the buffering effect, the direction of change is still as for Stolper–Samuelson. The model might be interpreted as applying to labour, skilled and unskilled, plus immobile capital. The two goods could be high-tech and low-tech. Then an audacious assumption would make skilled labour the special factor, only employed in the high-tech sector. The implication would then be that a fall in the relative price of the low-tech good, owing to increased exports from developing countries, will raise the skilled wage level, lower the unskilled wage level, and increase the return to capital. These conclusions seem to be attractive, as the model predicts both a fall in the unskilled wage rate and a rise in the return to capital. Both these changes are consistent with what has happened in advanced economies. However, caution is advisable here. The recent rise in the return to capital owes much to falling real wages, and these in turn are the result of economic recession. That is not part of the model.

Atkinson (2008b) is a further example of modelling that goes beyond the basic HOS 2×2×2 case. Atkinson (2008b) proposes a 3×3×3 framework in which the factors are labour, skilled and unskilled, plus capital. The goods are two tradables, intensive respectively in skilled and unskilled labour, plus a non-tradable service. The countries are one developing country, plus Europe and the US. The reason for distinguishing between Europe and the US is that the author is interested in the future of the welfare state in a globalized world. Europe is modelled as a high-welfare region, which means in this context a floor on the wage level, plus a high cost of welfare in the government budget. The US is the opposite to Europe, with no wage floor. Atkinson (2008b) reveals the differential impact of globalization on Europe and the US, with unsurprisingly unemployment playing a larger role in Europe than in the US. An important conclusion is that the non-tradable sector absorbs some of the shock provided by cheap imports from the developing country, moderating the effect on wages.

SKILL-BIASED TECHNICAL CHANGE (SBTC)

In the US notably, and to a lesser extent in other rich countries, the gap between the real wages earned by skilled workers, for example college-educated workers, and unskilled workers has widened during the last few decades. If skill is measured by years of education the observation is similar.[9] This is a striking outcome, and one that requires explanation. It is a challenge to economic theory, and it brings with it potentially disruptive political implications. The theoretical conundrum is seen to be great when it is noted that the supply of skilled workers has increased relative to the supply of the unskilled, as a larger proportion of the young population acquire college qualifications.

As a simple tractable model is required, it is no surprise that analysis based on an aggregate production function with inputs of two labour types, skilled and unskilled, is attractive. Card and DiNardo (2002) provide a thorough investigation of this model. The production function is CES with time-changing parameters. The CES function depends essentially upon two parameters. The elasticity of substitution itself is one of these. The other measures the relative weights on the two factor inputs. There is also the effect of technical change, which can influence the model parameters, and also a total factor productivity parameter, which measures Hicks-neutral technical change. When we are interested in the relative earnings of the skilled and unskilled, total factor productivity is irrelevant. We want to see whether this model can explain an increase in the wage rate (the marginal product) of skilled labour relative to the wage rate (the marginal product) of unskilled labour. With one trend in relative wages, and all those parameters and their trends, it is to be expected that the model parameters are under-identified.

The way around this difficulty taken by Card and DiNardo (2002) is to make use of an independent measure of skill-biased technical change. As the observation to be explained is the increase in the relative earnings of the skilled, despite the increase in their relative supply, they focus on a variable likely to be responsible for that observation: the use of micro-computers. As the rate of increase in this variable over about 40 years is not constant, this allows comparisons of the timing of micro-computer adoption, and the timing of changes in relative wages. More detailed analysis permits application of the same techniques to relative female/male and black/white earnings. The final conclusion might be well described as the statement that the model can be fitted to the data, rather than a claim that the data shows the model to be the truth. In view of the identification issue mentioned above, this is not surprising.

Just as the issue of timing is encountered with micro-computer adoption, so it arises with regard to policies, notably the level of the minimum wage. Card and DiNardo (2002) claim that the 1980s is an exceptional period, in particular because a rapid rise in the demand for skilled labour at that time met a sluggish supply, and also because the real value of the minimum wage was allowed to fall. Autor et al. (2008) argue that these views, which they dub 'Revisionist', are incorrect. They note, especially, that the secular rise in upper-tail inequality cannot owe much to the minimum wage or to unionization. Rather these authors argue that skill-demand shifts have played a central role in the trend towards more inequality, both in the 1980s and in later decades.

A proper understanding of what has happened to the inequality of earnings in rich countries requires a close examination of the detailed evidence, both across countries and over time. How a superficial look at the evidence can be misleading is demonstrated by a statistic often cited, the 90/10 ratio. This is the ratio of the earnings of the top-decile individual (the earner just in the top 10 per cent of earners) to the bottom-decile individual. This 90/10 ratio has increased since 1980 in the US and elsewhere. Yet it is wrong to use this number as evidence of how SBTC, or anything else, has worsened the position of low-skill earners. This is because the largest influence on the ratio has been changes at the top of the earnings distribution (Atkinson 2008a). And these developments in turn have been more marked in English-speaking countries than elsewhere.

While it is accurate to see the trend in earnings inequality as an upward climb from the 1970s, a longer time perspective is illuminating. The late 1960s and 1970s were a period of earnings compression in a number of European countries, including the UK. And declines in the bottom decile after 1980 can be seen as a part-reversal of 1970s compression. From 1950 to the mid-1960s there is already a rise in the top decile of the earnings distribution (with the exception of Germany), accompanied in some cases by drops in the bottom decile or lower quartile (Atkinson 2008a). Ideally theories of earnings should be able to explain most of what is observed over this long span of 60 years. However, there has been no attempt to do this.

What is the connection between the SBTC hypothesis and international trade? An aggregate national production function producing GNP seems to indicate that the nature of output is unaltered, while we focus on changes in inputs and their productivity. That is evidently not the case. When international trade alters national specialization, we are back to the Rybczynski effect. This means that one unit of GNP demands different inputs when input prices are constant. In the case of the US, that translates to an increased requirement for skilled labour, even when wages and technology are unaltered. That effect can presumably be subsumed into parameter changes in the Card and DiNardo model. The model does not seek to explain why the technical changes observed happened, so, if international trade is a driver, there is no problem. Even so, this argument indicates that the SBTC hypothesis and trade effects are not strictly alternative hypotheses.

RICH-COUNTRY LABOUR MARKETS

Even a cursory examination of the abundant literature concerned with rich-country labour markets will quickly convince the reader that the simple models of trade theory are inadequate when it comes to explaining the changes that have been observed in the last two or three decades. When the labour force is divided arbitrarily into two mutually exclusive categories, such as skilled and unskilled, it appears that a simple trade model might have some purchase. If the skilled are taken to be the educated, then what counts as education? Is it to be completing high school, university graduation, or a higher degree? The question is important because, for example, the wage premium for a basic undergraduate qualification has grown far less than the premium for higher-degree qualifications. In addition, it is important not to imagine that all the forces acting on wage levels are simple supply and demand effects. The institutions of wage setting may have important consequences, as may legal changes (ILO 2012). It is notable in this connection that, while skilled/unskilled wage differentials have widened in all industrial countries, these changes are far more marked in English-speaking countries than elsewhere. The differential influence of trade unions, and of minimum wages, may be part of the explanation for this difference. At the same time as this has happened, female/male differentials and black/white differentials have narrowed. In the UK the introduction of a national minimum wage has undoubtedly helped to improve the relative income position of employed women.

As with many theoretical questions, the issue of the effect of migration on wages and inequality is politically charged. For the USA, and probably for many other rich countries, the skill profile of arriving migrants is bi-modal (see Katz 1992–93). This means that migrants include high densities for very low skills, and also elevated densities for the well-qualified. The well-qualified include medical staff and information technology specialists, whose skills are easily recognized by and absorbed into the domestic economy. These individuals form part of the increased supply of highly educated workers, already noted above, whose wages have been rising notwithstanding the growing supply. At the lower end of the skill distribution, increased labour supply is adding to the pool of native-born workers with poor or no education. These individuals have been losing badly in rich-country labour markets ever since the 1970s (Autor and Katz 1999). A major reason for this outcome has been the contraction of manufacturing jobs for low-skilled workers. And the reasons for the decline in the demand for these low-skilled workers are twofold. First, there is less manufacturing. Secondly, what manufacturing remains has become more skilled-labour intensive. In the 1950s almost anyone could get some kind of job, if that only amounted to pushing a broom around a factory floor. Today such jobs have been mechanized out of existence. It is difficult to quantify the effect of migration on wages and inequality, but it looks likely that it has not made the problems in this area easier.

In a deep and rich study, Goldin and Katz (2008) examine the consequences of US education (both high school and college) for US economic dominance during the twentieth century. These authors see education chiefly as the accumulation of human capital, and argue that the efficiency and wide spread of US education, across classes and the genders, is what accounts for the high and growing per capita wealth of the US. This makes the twentieth century 'America's century', which leads directly to the question of whether the final decades of that century may not show the decline of US economic predominance, as other nations catch up with and surpass the US. Goldin and Katz provide their own version of a supply-and-demand account of wage growth and wage differentials similar to that demonstrated by Card and DiNardo (2002). Their vision is captured by their title, *The Race between Education and Technology*. In the first half of the century, it is argued, the increased supply of human capital was not offset by technical change that boosted the demand for that input. In the second half of the century the balance between these two forces was reversed in favour of the demand side. Hence there was a widening wage differential between the unskilled (low human capital) and skilled (high human capital).

We can see the major disconnect in the discussion of trends in wage differentials in that, on the one hand, writers such as Krugman and Wood place great emphasis on the effect of international trade, while Goldin and Katz do not even mention this effect. These last authors discuss migration only in terms of its consequences for education and human capital.

While most of the literature fails to make a connection between international trade and the details of rich-country markets, an important exception is Helpman et al. (2010), whose paper builds on the combination of variation in the productivity of firms, on the one hand, and search models of wage determination, on the other. Firms with high productivity find intensive search for workers to be more worthwhile, and end up with a better work force. Then a higher dispersion in firm productivity produces greater wage inequality among workers, who aside from quality variation are essentially one type. Add international trade to this recipe, and initially only high-productivity firms find it profitable to participate. This increases the dispersion of firm productivity, and consequently increases wage inequality. Later, if all firms participate in international trade, the export productivity premium disappears, and inequality declines.

POLITICAL ECONOMY AND OUTSOURCING

Economic theory can sometimes be a theatre for battles that have to do with politics and policy. Consider as an example the issue examined above: is growing wage inequality due to the character of technical change, or is it the result of trade and globalization? In either case one can imagine a policy intervention to offset some of the inequality. If the problem is technical change there is little, beyond the disastrous, that can be done about it. However, improvements in the educational system, and some redistributive taxation, might help a little. If on the other hand globalization is the source of our difficulties, there are tempting interventions to consider in the form of protection and trade restrictions. On policies to address wage inequality, see Freeman (1996–97).

Political pay-off attaches to trade protection when times are troubled. As an example, take President Obama's unfortunate attack on outsourcing during his 2012 campaign to be re-elected. The notion that outsourcing always costs jobs in the home economy is simplistic. It is true that, when a firm outsources some of its activities, less employment remains at home. However, outsourcing may save a firm that would otherwise fail, reducing the overall fall in employment. The total effect on employment depends upon the particular case. For better or worse, fragmentation of production is a growing trend in the world economy, and to resist this development would be foolish and counter-productive (see in this connection Arndt and Kierzkowski 2001).

With regard to outsourcing, it is useful to refer to the issue of the nature of Chinese exports. Krugman (2008) provides an excellent discussion. IMF trade statistics report that China exports a large volume of hi-tech goods, such as computers and mobile phones. This seems to run counter to what the HOS model would lead one to expect. To many people this puzzle will seem to admit of an obvious explanation. China is not really producing these products; it is rather providing a labour-intensive stage in the fragmentation of production that is more and more common in the world economy of today. Here is an issue which seems to allow for a straightforward empirical resolution. As Krugman demonstrates, it is not that simple. The trade statistics are far too coarse to distinguish between the value-added provided by a computer chip producer and the value-added provided by a Chinese assembly plant that mainly puts the parts together to yield a lap-top. So while anecdotes may support the view that the Chinese production is low-tech, and unskilled-labour intensive for that reason, there is no proof that such is the case.[10]

FINAL WORDS

The transformation in the world economy, and in worldwide inequality, has been dramatic. Essential to this development has been accelerated economic growth in Brazil, China, India, (the BRIC nations), and other, smaller countries. These changes have often been attributed to globalization and to increased international trade. This is partly true, but it misses an important aspect of economic development in the BRIC countries. This has been founded in fundamental economic reforms. These basically removed huge barriers to economic growth, in the form of protection, which is about trade, but also stifling bureaucracy, and public policies that confiscated the pay-offs from effort and innovation. China provides the most striking illustration of this point. People sometimes refer to the Chinese economic miracle, meaning the dazzling economic growth that followed the economic reforms of the 1980s. One might as well describe the history of China under Chairman Mao as an economic miracle. To reduce that great nation, with its long history of civilizations, and its outstandingly talented and adaptable people, to stagnation and starvation was surely miraculous.

It is clear that exports have been crucial to rapid economic growth in China. However, the country is not just a giant export machine. A large slice of Chinese national product is accounted for by the massive reconstruction and extension of the national infrastructure. If trade is not the fundamental explanation of increased economic growth in poor countries, it is nevertheless crucially permissive. While China and India could have experienced rapid economic growth based on their huge home markets, that route would have run into difficulties. First, these are countries lacking the resources in the form of energy and minerals necessary to provision their economic growth. So they had to import the commodities needed to fill that gap. Cheap manufactured exports provided the revenues that made the essential imports possible.

The second reason why trade has been crucially permissive with regard to economic growth is that it breaks the bounds of demand in the home market. Even though the home market is large in large countries such as the BRIC nations, it is small in comparison with the world market. When rapid economic growth takes off it soon finds that demand for its successful products in the home market is too sluggish to match the growing supply potential. This is what happened with cotton cloth production during Britain's industrial revolution, when home demand could not keep up with the rocketing productivity of the mills, and exports came to play an essential role. Then the argument proposed by among others Adam Smith and Myint (1958) comes into its own. Trade provides a vent-for-surplus. The space provided by exports has been far more marked in the case of China than that of India. From 1980 to 2010 India's share of world exports rose from 0.4 per cent to 1.4 per cent. China's share by contrast rose from 1.3 per cent to an astonishing 37.4 per cent (Joshi and Kapur 2013).

We have seen above that international trade is not always the explanation for growing inequality, particularly in rich countries. However, for the growing equality the world has depended crucially on international trade as a permissive factor.

NOTES

1. I acknowledge sympathetic and valuable comments from Anthony Atkinson, Vijay Joshi, and Adrian Wood. None of these, of course, are responsible for any shortcomings in this chapter.
2. The Gini coefficient is a single summary measure of the inequalities fully demonstrated by the Lorenz curve. Despite the increased equality evidenced by the Gini coefficient, there has been a rise in inequality at the bottom of the world income distribution, this chiefly reflecting the poor performance of many sub-Saharan African countries.
3. A change in inequality sometimes takes the form of an upward step rather than a trend. In the UK for example overall inequality has scarcely changed since 1990.
4. The estimation of poverty levels is always difficult and uncertain. It requires the local pricing of essentials and the conversion of these prices to the US dollar.
5. In Latin America in general, as shown in Table 3.1, a similar change in trend has attracted a lot of attention.
6. See, however, the discussion of Helpman et al. (2010) below.
7. Anthony Atkinson has pointed out to me that the "reach" of top performers has been extended by globalization. The fact that Manchester United has over 200 million supporters in China is related to the ability to sell Manchester United merchandise there.
8. This highly aggregated model hides an issue that has been debated. To what extent has rapid industrialization in China caused de-industrialization in other, particularly Asian, countries? (See Mayer and Wood 2011.)
9. The changes over time of earnings inequality do not follow a simple linear trend. In the UK the share of the bottom decile has remained the same percentage of the median since 1990. There has equally been little change in the US (it was in the 1980s that the bottom decile fell). So a simple high-school versus college account is inadequate.
10. Adrian Wood informs me that detailed breakdowns of the inputs to particular products such as iPads, and input–output analysis of Chinese firms and sectors, seem to give strong support to the view that China is contributing mainly labour-intensive assembly.

REFERENCES

Alvaredo, Facundo, Anthony B. Atkinson, Thomas Piketty and Emmanuel Saez (2013), 'The Top 1% in International and Historical Perspective: Causes and Consequences', *Journal of Economic Perspectives*, **27** (3), Summer.

Anderson, Edward, Paul J.G. Tang and Adrian Wood (2006), 'Globalization, Co-operation Costs, and Wage Inequalities', *Oxford Economic Papers*, **58**, 569–95.

Arndt, S.W. and H. Kierzkowski (2001), *Fragmentation: New Production Patterns in the World Economy*, Oxford: Oxford University Press.

Atkinson, Anthony B. (2008a), *The Changing Distribution of Earnings in OECD Countries*, Oxford: Oxford University Press.

Atkinson, Anthony B. (2008b), 'The Economics of the Welfare State in Today's World', *International Tax and Public Finance*, **15**, 5–17.

Atkinson, Anthony B. and Thomas Piketty (2007), *Top Incomes in the Twentieth Century: A Contrast between European and English-Speaking Countries*, Oxford: Oxford University Press.

Autor, David H. and Lawrence F. Katz (1999), 'Changes in the Wage Structure and Earnings Inequality', in O. Ashenfelter and D. Card (eds), *Handbook of Labor Economics*, Vol. 3A, Amsterdam: North-Holland.

Autor, David H., Lawrence F. Katz and Melissa S. Kearney (2008), 'Trends in US Wage Inequality: Revising the Revisionists', *Review of Economics and Statistics*, **90**, May, 300–323.

Bastagli, Francesca, David Coady and Sanjeev Gupta (2012), 'Income Inequality and Fiscal Policy', IMF Staff Discussion Note.

Bliss, Christopher (2007), *Trade, Growth, and Inequality*, Oxford: Oxford University Press.

Card, David and John E. DiNardo (2002), 'Skill Biased Technological Change and Rising Wage Inequality', *Journal of Labor Economics*, **20** (4), 733–83.

Chen, Shaohua and Martin Ravaillion (2004), *How Have the World's Poorest Fared Since the Early 1980s?*, World Bank Policy Research Working Paper 3341, Washington, DC: World Bank.

Chen, Shaohua, Martin Ravaillion and Prem Sangraula (2008), *Dollar a Day Revisited*, World Bank Policy Research Working Paper, May, Washington, DC: World Bank.

Deininger, Klaus and Lyn Squire (1998), 'New Ways of Looking at Old Issues: Inequality and Growth', *Journal of Development Economics*, **57** (2), 259–87.

Dixit, Avinash and Victor Norman (1980), *Theory of International Trade: A Dual Equilibrium Approach*, Cambridge: Cambridge University Press.

Dobson, Stephen and Carlyn Ramlogan (2009), 'Is There an Openness Kuznets Curve?', *Kyklos*, **62** (2), 226–38.

Feenstra, Robert C. and Gordon H. Hanson (1996), 'Foreign Investment, Outsourcing and Relative Wages', ch. 6 in Robert C. Feenstra, Gene M. Grossman and Douglas A. Irwin (eds), *The Political Economy of Trade Policy*, Cambridge, MA: MIT Press.

Fields, G. (2001), *Distribution and Development: A New Look at the Developing World*, New York: Russell Sage Foundation and Cambridge MA: MIT Press.

Freeman, Richard B. (1996–97), 'Solving the New Inequality', *Boston Review*, December/January.

Gabaix, X. and A. Landier (2008), 'Why Has CEO Pay Increased So Much?', *Quarterly Journal of Economics*, **123** (1), 49–100.

Goldin, C. and Lawrence F. Katz (2008), *The Race between Education and Technology*, Cambridge, MA: Harvard University Press.

Helpman, Elhanan, Oleg Itskhoki and Stephen Redding (2010), 'Inequality and Unemployment in a Global Economy', *Econometrica*, **78** (4), 1239–83.

ILO (International Labour Office) (2012), *Global Wage Report 2012/13*, Geneva: ILO.

Jones, Ronald (1965), 'The Structure of Simple General Equilibrium Models', *Journal of Political Economy*, **73**, December, 557–72.

Joshi, Vijay and Devesh Kapur (2013), 'India and the World Economy', in Delia Davin and

Barbara Harriss-White (eds), *China–India: Pathways of Economic and Social Development*, London: British Academy.

Katz, Lawrence F. (1992–93), 'Understanding Recent Changes in the Wage Structure', *NBER Reporter*, Winter.

Krugman, Paul (2008), 'Trade and Wages, Reconsidered', *Brookings Papers on Economic Activity*, Spring.

Krugman, Paul and Robert Lawrence (1993), *Trade, Jobs, and Wages*, NBER Working Paper No. 4478, September, Cambridge, MA: NBER.

Krugman, Paul and Maurice Obstfeld (2007), *International Economics: Theory and Policy*, Boston, MA: Addison-Wesley.

Kuznets, Simon (1955), 'Economic Growth and Income Inequality', *American Economic Review*, **45**, March, 1–28.

Mayer, Jörg and Adrian Wood (2011), 'Has China De-industrialized Other Developing Countries?', *Review of World Economics*, **147**, 325–59.

Myint, H. (1958), 'The "Classical Theory" of International Trade and Underdeveloped Countries', *Economic Journal*, **68**, 317–37.

OECD (2011), *Divided We Stand: Why Inequality Keeps Rising*, Paris: OECD Publications.

Rybczynski, T.M. (1955), 'Factor Endowment and Relative Commodity Prices', *Economica*, **22** (88), 336–41.

Sala-i-Martin, Xavier and Maxine Pinkovskiy (2009), *Parametric Estimations of the World Distribution of Income*, NBER Working Paper No. 15433, Cambridge, MA: NBER.

Samuelson, P.A. (1948), 'International Trade and the Equalization of Factor Prices', *Economic Journal*, June, 163–84.

Samuelson, P.A. (1971), 'Ohlin Was Right', *Swedish Journal of Economics*, **73** (4), December, 365–84.

Stolper, W. and P.A. Samuelson (1941), 'Protection and Real Wages', *Review of Economic Studies*, **9** (1) 58–73.

Wood, Adrian (1994), *North–South Trade, Employment, and Inequality: Changing Fortunes in a Skill-Driven World*, Oxford: Clarendon Press.

Wood, Adrian (1995), 'How Trade Hit Unskilled Workers', *Journal of Economic Perspectives*, **9** (3), Summer, 57–80.

Wood, Adrian (2002), 'Globalization and Wage Inequalities: A Synthesis of Three Theories', *Weltwirtschaftliches Archiv*, **138** (1), 54–82.

Yang, Dennis Tao, Vivian Chen and Ryan Monarch (2010), *Rising Wages: Has China Lost Its Global Labor Advantage?*, IZA Discussion Paper No. 5008, Bonn: IZA.

4. Trade networks, regional agreements and growth
Zining Yang and Mark Abdollahian

INTRODUCTION

Over the course of the last century, trade brought great changes to every corner of the globe, increasing the internationalization of production, distribution and marketing of goods and services as well as promoting economic integration. Like other economic transactions, trade enables parties to gain through exchange with more choices, better quality, lower prices and more competition. Over time, trade has become an increasingly important source of economic growth for many countries. Some argue that, as a nation expands its trading networks, more opportunities, better jobs and economic growth are created at home (Zoellick 2002). For instance, exports accounted for about 25 percent of US economic growth over the course of the 1990s and supported an estimated 12 million jobs (Drezner 2005). By lowering prices through imports and increasing incomes, regional trade agreements (RTAs), such as NAFTA, and multilateral trade frameworks, such as the Uruguay Round agreements, have benefited the average American family of four by $1300 to $2000 each year (Langerfels and Nieberling 2005).

In addition to local and individual effects, trade serves as a global economic health indicator. Many also define globalization simply as openness to foreign trade and long-term capital flows (Bardhan 2004). Thus, the prospects of increased trade opportunities strengthen foreign direct investment and confidence in financial markets, priming the global economy. Proponents of free trade posit that more open global markets enable regional and transnational businesses to realize gains from wider sourcing and sales networks, creating productive interconnections, top- and bottom-line value creation and increased market size (Zoellick 2002). Others view the development of global trade from a cultural perspective (Krugman 1991; Hummels 2007), emphasizing the importance of geographical distance, or how colonial histories and cultural traditions matter in differentiating trade patterns (Huntington 1996; Rauch 1999).

Most scholars identify three main causes that propelled globalization: first, post-World War II growth and industrialization, second, a long process of investment and trade liberalization in industrialized nations and regional economic integration agreements, and, finally, the impact of robust technological change with respect to transport and communications technologies creating a dramatic compression of economic space (Harris 1993). Between 1950 and 2000, international trade in manufactured goods increased more than 100 times, from $95 billion to $12 trillion annually (Schifferes 2007). New communication technologies made transactions among different cultures less and less problematic (Castells 2000; Friedman 2005), and innovation in transportation lessened geographical friction in global trade (Harvey 1989; Dicken 2003). Similarly, since the 1990s, RTA membership among the major trading nations of China, Japan, Russia, the US and Europe have increased over 400 percent (te Velde 2011), while difficulties still linger for a solidified, multilateral WTO framework.

With the above challenges in mind, we explore the evolution of the global trade system throughout the twentieth century through the lens of social network methods. First, we map dyadic trade flows for over 180 countries from 1960 to 2009. Second, we derive network measures for global connectivity using social network metrics to measure structure and change in global trade patterns. Third, we visually explore these patterns for major trading nations from 1920 to 2010, tracing their trading relationships with four social network metrics. Finally, we empirically test our networked trade effects with RTA membership and agriculture, manufacturing and service sector production shares across levels of development to illuminate the impact of trade equalization on both income level and growth rate convergence using fixed effects panel regressions.

Despite the frequent warnings about how globalization aggravates inequity, we find strong evidence for trade convergence and equalization that supports traditional income convergence dynamics across all levels of development and all stages of economic production. We find not only both sigma and beta income convergence, but more importantly trade convergence and equalization on all four social network metrics. Moreover, RTA membership has a positive effect on conditional convergence depending on income levels.

PAST WORK ON TRADE, GROWTH AND REGIONAL AGREEMENTS

Several political economy scholars explore the relationship among trade, growth and globalization with both confirmatory and contradictory outcomes. Soros (1998) argues that globalization brings countries together all over the world, with national economies becoming steadily more integrated as cross-border flows of trade, investment and financial capital increase. New trade theory focuses on the role of increasing returns to scale and network effects. Krugman (1986) argues that there are many economies-of-scale goods, resulting in increasing volumes, especially between similar countries. Shiozawa (2007) generalized Krugman's model and emphasized the importance of intermediate goods. He argues that volumes increased for intermediate goods when transportation costs decreased, altering the pattern of comparative advantage and enlarging the world production possibility set.

Unfortunately, globalization and trade have not benefited all equally, with significant differences in perceptions between developed countries and developing countries. In the Third World, there is a growing sense that globalization is proceeding too rapidly, increasing income disparities, producing unequal growth economies between urban and rural areas and leading to the infusion of domestic civil strife. As a result of the divergent perspectives, developing countries have kept high tariffs and non-tariff barriers, while industrializing countries remained closed to their exports, perpetuating a double standard in the international trading system. Conversely, under the auspices of the General Agreement on Tariffs and Trade (GATT), postwar trade barriers among major industrial countries declined significantly, while RTA initiatives proliferated, including the European Common Market, the North American Free Trade Agreement and the Association of Southeast Asian Nations Free Trade Area (AFTA). World trade grew by approximately 6 percent per year from 1950 in real terms, about 50 percent faster than world output growth over the same period (Hummels 2007).

Unfortunately, there is no clear consensus on how such RTAs affect growth through output and productivity effects, including domestic and global competition and scale. Viner (1950) originally suggested that the effects of regional integration on trade can be trade creating, when trade replaces or complements domestic production, or trade diverting, when trading partners' production replaces trade from the rest of the world. Others argue that the effects of RTAs are dynamic, as competition creates more efficient industry, growth and higher long-run productivity (Grossman and Helpman 1991; Neary 2001). Blomstrom and Kokko (1997) posit that regional integration leads to efficiency gains and higher growth owing to more efficient resource allocation. Specifically, Vamvakidis (1998) explores if and how RTAs affected growth from 1970 to 1990, but finds little substantive impact when controlling for other economic determinants such as openness. Sally (2006) argues that RTAs can actually have a negative impact on multilateral global trade, weakening regional economies by distracting attention from the WTO, unilateral liberalization and necessary, yet politically difficult, national structural reforms.

Besides geographical distance (Krugman 1991; Frankel 1997; Hummels 2007) and colonial histories and civilization traditions (Huntington 1996; Rauch 1999; Guiso et al. 2004), patterns of trade continue to define globalization's winners and losers. Neoclassical growth (Solow 1956; Swan 1956) and endogenous growth economists (Romer 1987; Rebelo 1991) seek to explain these differences by examining the fundamental drivers of economic development. Income convergence and conditional income convergence purport that less developed nations, if able to escape the poverty trap, will grow at faster rates than developed countries owing to larger potential labor pools, increasing marginal returns in mobilizing productivity gains and leapfrogging more advanced economies through technology transfer (Barro 1991; Levine and Renelt 1992).

Prior studies (Mankiw et al. 1992; Sala-i-Martin 1996; Ramajo et al. 2008; S. Sperlich and Sperlich 2011; Y. Sperlich and Sperlich 2012) identify two specific types of convergence: *sigma* and *beta*. Sigma convergence refers to income across economies reaching similar levels within a certain error bound σ, whereas beta convergence shows how less developed societies will grow at higher rates β until they reach similar income levels. Beta convergence explains how developed countries on average grow at a lower rate of 2.3 percent, while developing nations grow on average at 4.5 percent, and least developed countries average under 2 percent (Sachs and Warner 1997). Lau and Wan (1994) argue that trade is a necessary, but not sufficient, condition for developing countries to converge. Fischer and Serra (1996) suggest that trade accelerates growth and the rate of income convergence in poor countries and slows down growth and income convergence in rich countries. They also argue that in long-run equilibrium trade ensures that growth rates and incomes converge across countries.

Turning to the inter-relationship between trade, growth and RTAs, Williamson (1996) and O'Rourke and Williamson (1999) stress that reductions in postwar trade barriers and the resulting globalization propelled economic growth and were a key engine driving income convergence throughout the world. They find that convergence occurs under open economic policy preferences and divergence during spates of trade contraction. Epstein et al. (2003) discover that trading interactions do affect income convergence across the globe, albeit differently for countries according to level of development and time periods. Using standard growth models for nearly 100 developing countries over 1970–2004, te Velde (2011) does not find robust growth effects of regional integration. However, other regional integration measures yield positive effects through trade and investment. He concludes that trade and FDI promote growth and, since RTAs increase trade and FDI, regional integration can still have a positive impact on growth. It is upon this foundation that we formulate a new trade convergence approach below.

TOWARDS AN INTEGRATED APPROACH

While each of these scholars focuses mainly on import and export volumes, most ignore the interactive effects of trade networks, RTAs and stages of economic production and development. For example, what are the differential trade impacts if a country trades only with a few of its regional partners or has a relatively high or low global reach? What roles do trade and global connectivity have at different stages of agricultural, manufacturing and service sector production? How does RTA membership affect growth in the global trade network? Do RTAs benefit lesser-income or high-income countries? And, finally, how do trade networks impact economic development? To begin addressing these questions, we introduce several social network metrics of connectivity, enabling us to explore trade partnerships, development and change in connections over time.

This chapter extends previous work (Abdollahian and Yang 2013) exploring the evolution of the global trade system throughout the twentieth century via social network methods. First, we map dyadic trade flows for over 180 countries from 1960 to 2009, based on the International Monetary Fund (IMF) Direction of Trade Statistics and the Correlates of War data sets. Measuring structure and change, we derive metrics for global connectivity using degree, closeness, eigenvector and k-core network centrality measures. Degree, or trade, connectivity simply measures the total number of trading partners at a particular time. Closeness measures the distance of a nation to all others in the global network. This helps identify which nations are central to trade networks owing to their volume of trade. Eigenvector measures the influence of nations that bridge other highly active trading partners, identifying dominant nations that can easily expand trade and affect others' trade volume. K-core identifies regional clusters, or cliques, formed by trade networks. This measure classifies how well nations form local and regional subgroups within the global trade network.

We then visually explore these patterns for seven major nations – the UK, the US, France, Germany, Japan, Russia and China – from 1920 to 2010, tracing their trading relationships vis-à-vis each other with our four social network metrics. This allows us to interpret major historical political economy events through trade connectivity in order to explore globalization's impact and the implications for new trade theories. Finally, we present a generalized empirical test for our networked trade effects. Here we focus on the impact of RTA membership and agriculture, manufacturing and service sector production shares across levels of development to see the impact of trade equalization on both sigma levels and beta income convergence rates using fixed effects panel regressions. We argue that our trade network metrics reveal important implications for new economic theories of growth and development over the next century.

TRADE NETWORK METRICS AND PATTERNS

The social network perspective is an important empirical research tool as well as a paradigm for understanding connectivity. Breiger (1981) calls it "a natural wedding" between world-system dependency theory and a general strategy for the analysis of multiple networks. Many sociologists adopt a network analysis approach in examining the world as a system (Snyder and Kick 1979; Steiber 1979; Breiger 1981; Smith and White 1992; Kali and Reyes 2007), which in turn highlights relationships between economic development and position in the network.

Here we use social network metrics to examine the global trade system as a complex and interdependent web. First we adopt exploratory data analysis from a political economy and historical perspective, which suggests new hypotheses and inferences about global economic development and structure for the next century. This enables us later to derive patterns describing the structure and evolution of global trade in ways that traditional econometric approaches cannot, such as the two-way, interactive effects of individual states and their importance in global trade.

We begin by coding annual trade data from both the IMF's Direction of Trade Statistics and the Correlates of War for all politically relevant dyads from 1920 to 2009. Owing to World War II, we have missing observations between 1939 and 1947. Trade volume is reported in current US millions of dollars, calculated as the natural logarithm of the sum of dyadic imports and exports, then rescaled for comparability. We then convert the data into matrix form with columns and rows representing country names symmetrically. Finally, we use UCINET to assess network structure and calculate the network similarity attributes of degree, closeness, eigenvector and k-core measures. This network approach leads to a richer understanding of trade patterns and relationships, which we then combine with sigma level and beta rate income convergence models as well as trade equalization. We believe that studying dynamic trade network connectivity across societies over time has useful applications in academia and policy circles alike (De Benedictis and Tajoli 2011).

Below we explore various trade network attributes for major powers between 1920 and 2000. We focus on the US, the UK, Germany, France, Russia, China and Japan, in order to examine if, when and how trade disparities appear or disappear, as well as the effects on convergence.

DEGREE CONNECTIVITY

Our first measure of trade connectivity, degree, simply identifies the number of trading partners a nation engages with annually. Figure 4.1 shows the total number of trading partners among major powers from 1920 to 2000. With the development of faster, cheaper and more efficient transportation in addition to economies of scale within markets, the number of trading partners clearly increases in general throughout the twentieth century for all major powers. However, the differential pattern of connectivity between developed Europe and the rest of the world is very interesting. Here we see both the Europeans and the US move at very similar levels of trade connectivity in volumes over time. This indicates clear sigma convergence, not on income, but trade connectivity itself, among the developed economies as the number of their respective trading partners is within a tight band of less than plus or minus 10 percent. There is also early sigma trade convergence among Asian nations before World War II. Interestingly, since the 1950s, we see beta trade convergence by Japan and even more clearly with China, as their relative rate of increasing trading partner connectivity clearly outpaces that of the other major powers.

Although degree connectivity varies, trade convergence markedly happens by the end of the century for almost all major powers. We see a structural break induced by the Great Depression and hints of the effects of World War II for trade and globalization. After 1950, there was higher worldwide economic growth, and the rate of trade expansion begins to increase for all countries owing to the development of globalization and regionalization. The US, the UK, France, Germany and Japan increased at similar rates within a tight band, outpacing China and Russia for almost four decades, until China had caught up by 2000. Hence we see strong evidence of trade equalization among major economic producers by the end of the century. Below we explore degree connectivity variance coupled with each nation's economic history and specific policies. Not surprisingly, the UK, the US and France were the most open trading partners throughout most of the last century. They also illustrate homogeneity in both the number of and changes in trading partners. All three sought to protect domestic production by imposing new and higher tariffs and setting quotas on foreign imports during the time of the Great Depression. The

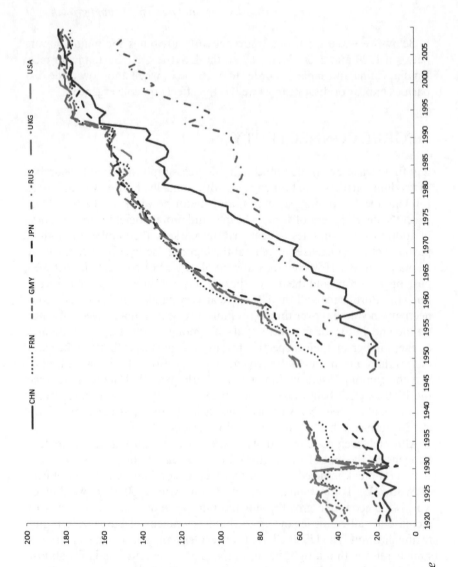

Figure 4.1   Trade degree

effect of these restrictive measures greatly reduced the volume of international trade, and by 1932 the total value of world trade had fallen by more than half, as country after country restricted the import of foreign goods (Hajdini 2010). During the postwar recovery era, all three countries continued to lead global trade in the number of trading partners. Between 1960 and 1990, as global and regional economies became more open (Keohane 1997), trade interdependence increased as most of the developed world experienced high rates of growth.

With regard to other key countries, China shows both beta and sigma trade convergence – increasing in three distinct stages in 1920–38, 1950–60 and 1970–2000. During the first stage, China's openness was limited after Japan's invasion in 1931 and subsequent economic slowdown, at one-seventh the number of trading partners compared to the US. With an estimated 20 million to 25 million citizens killed, China saw the previous decade's economic growth championed by Chiang all but vanish (Sun 2000). Industrial development was severely hampered and aggravated by the inflow of cheap substitutable American goods. By 1946, Chinese industry operated at only 20 percent capacity and a mere 25 percent of prewar output levels (Sun 2000).

During the second stage under a planned economy, it took China nearly three decades to recover. Mao's Great Leap Forward and Cultural Revolution caused a massive drop in living standards and low trade growth. During this period, China mainly exported minerals and agricultural and light industrial products, while it imported more sophisticated manufactured goods and the raw materials necessary for domestic production and consumption (MacDougall 1972). Deng's Reform and Opening Up Policy in 1978 led China to accept foreign investment and re-engage with global markets. Once again, trade assumed a dynamic of its own, as it accelerated economic growth and domestic political capital accumulation (Keohane 1997). By 2000, we see the China sigma converging with that of the rest of the major economic powers.

The trend for Russia is similar, albeit at lower levels and rates. After the devastation of World War II and the onset of the Cold War, Russia traded mainly within Communist bloc countries. Bereft of Marshall Plan assistance, foreign investment, technological assistance or GATT membership, it became increasingly economically isolated over time. These effects can be seen with the collapse of the USSR in 1991. The sharp decrease in central economic control that occurred just before and after the breakup of the Soviet Union decimated distribution channels across sectors, between suppliers and producers, and between producers and consumers throughout the region. Many non-Russian republics were dependent on Russian oil and natural gas, timber and other raw materials, while Russia bought food and other consumer goods in return. To ease transition effects, Russia forged multiple bilateral agreements with former client states to maintain the flow of goods. However, as in the case of the Central Europeans, such agreements proved impractical and, by the mid-1990s, accounted for only small amounts.

The cases of Germany and Japan are quite different from those of the other major powers. After World War I, Germany suffered hyperinflation owing to various Treaty of Versailles sanctions, while Japan began its ascension to major power status. With lower levels of economic performance, these two countries did not trade as much as the US, the UK or France. However, after the Dawes Plan in 1923, the German economy began to recover, bringing in more than 32 billion Deutschmarks in foreign investments and loans, softening war reparation burdens (Schuker 1988). This eventually stabilized the currency and opened up the economy to foreign markets (Schuker 1988) for Germany to perform similarly to its rivals. Japan also shared a similar pattern, but for very different reasons. Not satisfied with its post-World War I position, Japan began to develop its economy by exporting cheap goods to other Asian countries. By the end of the 1930s, Japan was seeing beta convergence with the Europeans and the US, and becoming more connected with foreign economies and integrated into the global market. Interestingly, some scholars argue that, in order to overcome the Great Depression and restrictions set in Versailles, both Germany and Japan initiated conflict (Grew 1944; Kitchen 2006). The implications surrounding the existence or nonexistence of either sigma or beta convergence and interstate conflict and cooperation we leave for other research (Tammen et al. 2000).

During World War II, both Germany and Japan's economies were devastated. Heavy bombing in World War II decimated German cities and left agricultural production at only 35 percent of prewar levels (Clodfelter 2002). About 40 percent of industrial plants and infrastructure were destroyed, and production reverted to levels from nearly 15 years earlier (Clodfelter 2002). Both Germany and Japan focused on developing their domestic economy through expanding international trade with the Marshall Plan in Europe and US assistance to Japan. As a result, trade and economic performance recovered as quickly for both the German and the Japanese economy. From the 1960s, the number of trading partners for Germany and Japan sigma converged with the US, UK and France, through to the end of the century. After reunification, German trade increased rapidly, while the export of Japan's high-tech industry flourished thousands of miles away. As these two countries became important global powers again, they began to trade globally, increasing market share with other developed countries. Thus we see both trade equalization and convergence on degree connectivity.

CLOSENESS CONNECTIVITY

Next we turn to the trade network measure of closeness, or how far a nation is from all other partners in the global trade network, measured by volume. This metric not only takes into account how many trading partners a nation has as degree connectivity, but indicates how close indirect trading partners can be reached through a country's trade network. High values for nations indicate ease of conducting trade with other partners. Figure 4.2 displays network closeness for all major countries, identifying countries in the most paths of other trading pairs of countries. Surprisingly, the UK, the US, Germany, Japan and France had the lowest levels of closeness throughout most of the twentieth century, owing in large part to their geographical distance from the majority of other nations. Compared with degree connectivity, we see similar variance, yet inverted levels. This documents the spurts of growth and trade disparities at different times. Despite inter-country differences and a narrow sigma trade band among major powers, we still see clear sigma convergence within 5 percent as well as beta trade convergence by China. What is fascinating is how being indirectly close to many other trading partners propels growth and the economic story for each one of our countries.

While the UK, the US, Germany, France and Japan's trade with both neighbors and former colonies easily gave them the highest degree connectivity for most of the last century, their indirect network partners remained low. The US did not take a leading role in global trade until after the Great Depression, when Congress passed the Reciprocal Trade Agreements Act of 1934 in order to stimulate employment, allowing the executive branch to negotiate bilateral trade agreements for a fixed period of time (Bolle et al. 2007). During the 1930s, the amount of bilateral negotiation under this act was limited but subsequently expanded the US's position globally. Trade in the UK, Germany and France tracked similarly, albeit at lower levels, but then precipitously declined right before World War II. Connecting Europe with America, closeness levels were low compared to the latter half of the century owing to limited trading partners and even less open economies in Asia and Africa. For every major economic power, both economic growth and trade closeness stagnated during the 1930s.

Almost immediately postwar, both the US and the UK developed two institutional innovations to expand and govern trade: the GATT and the International Trade Organization (ITO). Truman administration officials

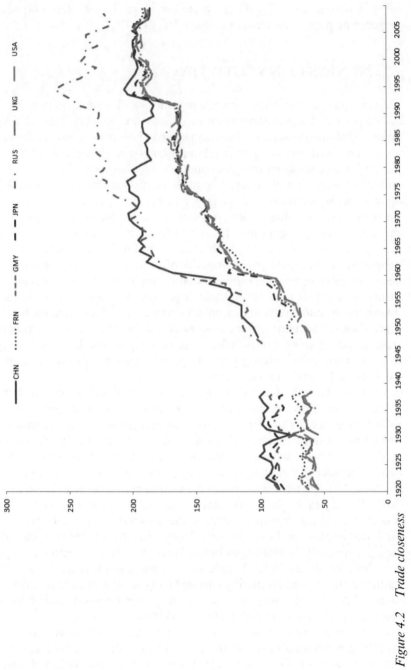

Figure 4.2 Trade closeness

believed that restoration of global economic prosperity would encourage peaceful relations among the world's powers. They recognized that a large and dynamic US economy could also benefit from open access to as many overseas markets and sources of supply as possible. Here we can see the large jump for the US, the UK and particularly France, all benefiting from a liberal trading regime at the birth of modern globalization. Concurrently, large-scale trade regionalization began in Europe, witnessed by the birth of RTAs. France and five other countries signed the Treaties of Rome in 1957, which extended the earlier cooperation within the European Coal and Steel Community (ECSC) and created the European Economic Community (EEC), establishing a customs union and the European Atomic Energy Community (Euratom) for cooperation in developing nuclear energy (European Commission 1960). The newly established European Community enhanced both European connectivity and the European role in the global trade system.

Not only did the number of trading partners rapidly increase during this period, but a distribution of new trade partners emerged, mostly in Asia, South America, North America and Africa, further magnifying trade closeness for the US, the UK and France. After a jump around 1960, all three countries tightly sigma-converge. However, their preeminence began to erode as global trade expanded and newly industrialized countries experienced strong economic growth. As Latin American business conglomerates became increasingly exposed to international competition, they countered by pressuring domestic governments to increase both export competitiveness and the protection of domestic products exposed to import competition (Kaufman and Segura-Ubiergo 2001). East Asia also played a more important role, as the four "Tigers" benefited directly from globalization through national export-oriented development policies (Dittmer 2002). Regionalization as well as globalization continued on two parallel tracks, stimulated by economic cooperation within and between developed and developing countries, resulting in both South–South and North–South cooperation movements (Jilberto and Mommen 1998; Urata 2002; Levy 2006).

Owing to geographic proximity and multiple bordering nations, China and Russia had high closeness scores throughout most of the twentieth century. Trade closeness also increased sharply after World War II with the rest of the world. In the case of China, while it had only three main trade partners at the beginning of the century, the UK, Russia and Japan, they were potentially much better connected through trade networks with other countries in the world. Russia and China had similar numbers of trading partners, but Russia's were all with better-connected European countries. As each of these economies began recovery, trade expanded, not only from Europe, but also from other continents. China developed significant trade partnerships with most African countries, including Kenya, Tanzania and Burundi. Conversely, Cold War polarization left few choices for Russian goods' market access. For China, we see clear beta trade convergence starting with its political opening and economic reforms in the 1970s and tight sigma convergence with all other major powers by 1995.

During the 1930s, Japan's closeness levels were similar to those of the US and the Europeans. In order to increase their economic strength and comparative political influence, Japan began to develop global trade partnerships after the war. Prime Minister Ikeda, former minister of the Ministry of International Trade and Industry (MITI), developed the "Double Income Plan" to open markets and push trade liberalization, eventually establishing trade and economic relationships to offset the loss of preferential colonial access. This, combined with massive US investment and government economic interventionism, was a critical step (World Bank 1993). Numerous allied foreign aid distribution agencies were set up to demonstrate Japan's willingness to participate in a new liberal international economic order and to promote exports. Japan's global economic integration was furthered by joining the GATT in 1963 and the IMF and the Organisation for Economic Co-operation and Development (OECD) in 1964 in an economic era associated with over 12 percent annual GDP growth rates. As a latecomer to modernization, Japan was able to avoid some of the trial-and-error lessons learned by Western predecessors in developing industrial processes. Specifically, Japan improved its industrial base through technology licensing, patent purchases and imitation with improvement of foreign inventions in the 1970s and 1980s. After the economic bubble burst in the 1990s, the government adopted policies to promote exports to countries all over the world, which led to sigma convergence by the end of the century.

Germany also tells a similar story in the postwar era. The Korean War led to an increased demand worldwide for goods. The resulting shortage helped overcome lingering resistance to the purchase of German products. At the time, Germany had a large pool of unemployed yet highly skilled and cheap labor, partly as a result of deportations and migrations that affected up to 16.5 million Germans. This helped Germany to more than double the value of postwar exports. Combined with the formation of the ECSC and EEC, Germany sigma levels tracked within the same tight band with other Europeans as they extended their global economic presence.

EIGENVECTOR CONNECTIVITY

Trade eigenvector measures which countries are most connected to other highly connected, trading countries measured by volume. It finds the most central trading nations with regard to the entire global trading system, identifying the nations that can trade easily with others. Eigenvector metrics help us place each of our seven major powers in the proper context relative to the global system. In Figure 4.3 our results show the strongest evidence for trade equalization and convergence in the twentieth century. Despite the Europeans and the US enjoying a 2:1 advantage over Asian economies in 1920, we see remarkable sigma trade convergence to less than 0.5 percent by 2000. Any real or perceived Western trade dominance over Asia continuously diminished, with both increased density of trade connectivity and the equality of trade access for all with the exception of Russia. The tight sigma eigenvector convergence demonstrates true global trade interdependence and equality at the start of the new century.

On eigenvector connectivity, it should also come as no surprise that the US, the UK and France have the highest scores, tracking within narrow sigma bands throughout most of the twentieth century. As the Second Industrial Revolution sprouted in the West, new manufacturing technologies widely proliferated, leading to one of the greatest increases in economic growth in a short time span. Living standards improved significantly as the prices of goods fell dramatically owing to the tremendous growth in productivity, transportation networks, industrial production and agricultural efficiency. With the US, the UK and France as the main recipients, trade relationships and networks also benefited from being closely degree-connected with other developed economies, as seen previously.

An important trend is that, despite large eigenvector disparities in 1920, a slow and steady march towards trade equalization and convergence emerges. One reason for this is the increased participation of developing nations in the global economy. Consistent with previous studies, on average every country traded with more countries in 1990 than in 1960 (Kim and Shin 2002). It has been repeatedly argued that national economies are steadily becoming more integrated as cross-border flows of trade, investment and financial capital have increased. As Soros (1998) argues, "the capitalist system can be compared to an empire that is more global in its coverage than any previous empire. It rules [an] entire civilization." With increasing numbers of newly industrializing countries also connected with trade hubs, naturally eigenvector values dropped for the three major trade centers. Another dramatic finding is tight sigma eigenvector convergence by 2000. Amongst the multitude of arguments concerning global trade inequities, our results strongly suggest otherwise.

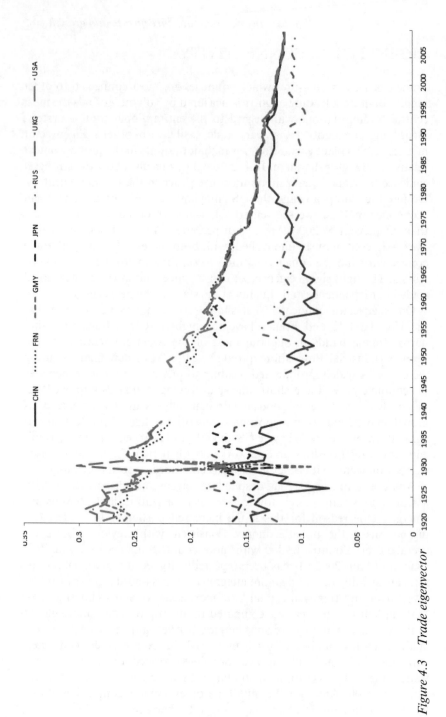

Figure 4.3   Trade eigenvector

Turning to China, we see an interesting path of beta and sigma eigenvector convergence. Once again, there are clearly three stages in Chinese trade development, 1920–38, 1950–60 and 1970–2000. At the beginning of the first stage, China developed a modern industrial sector, which stimulated modest but significant economic growth. Before the collapse of international trade and the onset of the Great Depression, China's share of world trade was 2.2 percent and its ratio of foreign trade to GDP achieved levels not regained for over 60 years (Brandt and Rawski 2008). While China established some key trading relationships, obviously the economy was heavily disrupted by the war against Japan and the civil war in the 1940s. Accordingly, its eigenvector connectivity dropped significantly, as seen by immediate pre- and postwar levels.

The second stage started in 1950, when the civil war ended and the Communists began economic reconstruction. The basic economic policy was the step-by-step organization of the farmers into agricultural collectives in order to promote efficiency and create the domestic savings necessary for the establishment of more beneficial heavy industry sectors. Private industry was gradually brought under joint state ownership. Economic output was realized through a series of programs involving state seizure of controlling interests (MacFarquhar 1987). The first five-year plan emphasized heavy industry development, with bilateral Soviet aid and technical advice contributing to early success. Combined with economic growth, China was able to increase trade by as much as 15 percent. However, its global trade relevance changed little, as trade openness was not a political priority. During the late 1950s, the domestic economy largely stagnated. The Great Leap Forward famine killed an estimated 30 million to 40 million citizens, while Cultural Revolution purges undermined individual incentive to improve (Brandt and Rawski 2008). Matters worsened with the withdrawal of Soviet economic assistance and technical advice during the Sino-Soviet split. Relatively low levels of economic growth during this period are strongly associated with hampered Chinese trade. Moreover, as the Cold War heated up, the relationship between China and most Western countries worsened, with declining trade volumes.

Deng's economic reforms signaled the third stage in the 1970s and marked the beginning of China's beta eigenvector convergence. Deng began with the de-collectivization of agriculture, opening up the country to foreign investment and granting permission for entrepreneurs to start up businesses. Progressing through the 1980s, privatization and some contracting out of state-owned industry occurred. The lifting of price controls, protectionist policies and regulations also liberalized the economy as the country opened up to foreign investment in 1994 for the first time since the Kuomintang era. Deng created a series of special economic zones for foreign investment that were relatively free of bureaucratic regulations and interventions. These regions subsequently became engines of national economic growth with significant trade centers. The success of China's economic reforms resulted in massive domestic structural changes, including economic infrastructure development, new labor migration patterns towards coastal manufacturing and urbanized trade centers, and poverty reduction. Enhanced Western relationships directly contributed to trade expansion growing faster than GDP for more than 20 years, resulting in the eigenvector sigma convergence.

The twentieth-century Russian story in trade is also interesting, with three associated stages, 1920–30, 1938–60 and 1970–2000. Immediately after the Communist revolution, the USSR remained generally an agrarian society, with an economy characterized by public industrial ownership, low investment and lack of access to foreign capital. Trade was intentionally kept to the minimum levels required for national prioritization of certain industrial development sectors, insuring national sovereignty to mitigate foreign threats. The second stage began with the New Economic Policy as Russia established more domestic organizations to deal directly with foreign partners in the buying and selling of goods. We see eigenvector trade levels decline sharply in the 1930s through the postwar and then remain almost constant for nearly three decades. The beginning of the Cold War imposed drastic trade changes, limiting foreign trade to only Eastern Europe and China, and leading to low eigenvector levels. The third stage started in 1970 with détente, as Russia exchanged energy and raw materials for Western capital goods. Growth in trade was substantial. The USSR relied heavily on various fuel and natural resource exports to earn hard currency, and Western partners regarded it as a dependable energy supplier. Heightened East–West political tensions slowed trade in the 1980s and also hampered domestic economic growth, as oil production costs increased and market prices declined. The 1991 collapse of the Soviet Union and the 1998 financial crisis further impacted both Russian trade and the economy, stunting eigenvector beta convergence. By 2000, Russia was the only major power that had not sigma-converged and equalized within a narrow range.

Patterns for Germany and Japan are also interesting given their respective industrialization paths. Before 1940, Japan's trading activities increased rapidly owing to economic development and colonialization. Simultaneously, the country progressively opened up to the West as the government focused on trade promotion. Germany also prioritized industrialization to recover after World War I, enjoying European geospatial proximity and bilateral links to other active trading countries such as the US, the UK and France. The Third Reich's trading policies were aimed at discouraging trade with countries outside the German sphere of influence, while making southern Europe largely dependent on German goods (Braun 1990). Both Germany and Japan were hit hard by the Great Depression. Some scholars argue that their economic interdependence with other Western countries triggered World War II (Grew 1944; Kitchen 2006). Successful reconstruction efforts in each country led to increasing trade openness and participation in a new liberal economic order under the Washington Consensus and resulted in their quick beta and sigma eigenvector trade convergence. German reunification in 1990 opened up the potential for further trade gains. The rapid appreciation of the yen in Japan during the 1980s made imports more attractive, causing greater trade openness policies in response to domestic pressures (Allen 1958; Huber 1994). These mechanisms propelled both Japan and Germany to eigenvector preeminence and equalization similar to most other major economic powers.

K-CORE CONNECTIVITY

Trade k-core measures which countries are most connected in subgroups, or cliques, given their trade volume and network patterns. K-core metrics help us place each of our seven major powers in the proper context relative to how well they are locally connected to other trading partners. In Figure 4.4, our results show strong evidence for trade equalization and convergence. All of our seven nations are tightly sigma-converged, with similar trade levels and variance. Sigma trade convergence throughout the twentieth century suggests that each of our seven powers had equal local partner trading access. This should be unsurprising given their major power status within their own respective regions throughout the century. With equal level and rate changes in k-core metrics, globalization had no differential local trading impact among our seven major powers. However, the same cannot be said for all other nations in the world, as we shall see later.

RTA MEMBERSHIP

Our final metric before testing trade networks and income convergence focuses on the distinct pattern of RTA membership detailed by many other scholars (Vamvakidis 1998; Dee 2004; Sally 2006; Bagoulla and Peridy 2011). For brevity, we will not repeat the well-documented economic history of RTA memberships, but briefly annotate how the number

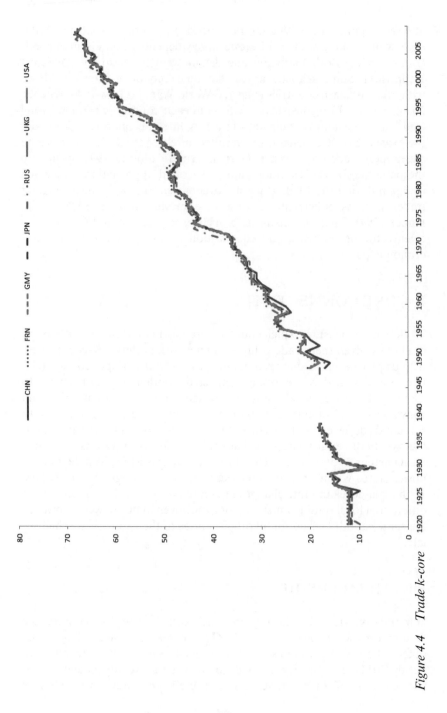

Figure 4.4   Trade k-core

90

of RTA memberships amongst our major powers varies and later explore RTA impact on growth for all countries.

Our three European countries, Germany, France and the UK, have similar patterns, joining only one RTA since the 1950s, albeit the largest and most economically powerful, the European Union (EU). Being members of the EU, they have close trade relationships with European countries, but also South American countries, African countries, Middle Eastern countries and Asian countries that signed reciprocal agreements with the EU. The US signed its first RTA with Israel in 1985, and then NAFTA in 1994 with Canada and Mexico. The US further increased indirect trade access from partners in the global trade network, including Singapore, Peru and Australia. China pursued RTAs after 2000, mainly to establish economic leadership in East Asia (Wang 2004; Sally 2006). It joined the Asia Pacific Trade Agreement (APTA) in 2002 and then enhanced economic cooperation within the Association of Southeast Asian Nations (ASEAN) by 2005. Besides Hong Kong and Macau, China also signed RTAs with Singapore and New Zealand. Currently, China has 14 FTA partners, including 31 economies, involving eight different agreements. However, many of China's trade agreements cover only specific sectors, which some see as a protectionist measure. Large industries and goods types are excluded from developing country partners with similar production structures and competing products. However, this minimizes mutual gains and increases the risk of trade diversion (Sally 2006). Japan also has a similar pattern of RTA membership. Anticipating the increasing amount of trade and investment in East Asia, it started signing RTAs with other Asian countries around the same time as China in order to benefit from market access and structural reforms. However, the level of Japanese RTA participation increased faster than that of China, owing to Japanese partnerships with countries spanning the globe, including Switzerland, Mexico and Brunei Darussalam. Russia quickly signed RTAs with former USSR members in 1993, and then joined the Commonwealth of Independent States (CIS), Eurasian Economic Community (EAEC) and Common Economic Zone (CEZ) a few years later.

AN EMPIRICAL TEST OF TRADE NETWORKS, REGIONAL AGREEMENTS AND CONVERGENCE

Based upon the economic history of major powers above, our network metrics are ripe for a compelling test of sigma level and beta rate income convergence models globally. Here we expand our sample to 180 nations from 1960 to 2009. In order to do so, we first build on te Velde's (2011) exploration of RTA effects on convergence models. Then we follow Lau and Wan (1994), Fischer and Serra (1996) and Kim and Shin (2002), exploring the differential impact of trade across levels of development and economic production with our detailed trade network metrics as additional, country specific determinants. We also control for stages of economic production, with interesting implications for development and globalization.

Machlup (1962), Bell (1974), Drucker (1993), Arthur (1996) and Pine and Gilmore (1999), among others, argue that types of production represent the current stage in a nation's economic development: from an agrarian economy extracting commodities, to an industrial economy manufacturing goods, to a service delivery economy, and finally a knowledge-based economy creating information. A country does not trade much in the first stage because its main function is to extract resources, which implies it can export only low-value-added commodities. In the manufacturing stage, developments in transportation technology allow for increases in the trade of goods, which happened after the Industrial Revolution in most of the West. Complex machines are traded for more efficient agricultural production, as well as inputs into more advanced and productive manufacturing processes. Subsequently, nations enter the third service stage of higher economic value production, benefiting from delivering services with larger economic multipliers. Finally, at least from the constraints of our current historical perspective, nations can enter a knowledge economy where advances in technology lead to even higher economic value multipliers.

The Europeans and Americans during the Second Industrial Revolution, as well as Japan and China more recently, all benefited from trade at different stages given their respective unique comparative advantages. Understanding which types of production goods and services are at which stages of development, prima facie, might be a key determinant for both income and trade convergence in the new century. Most Western nations including the US moved from manufacturing in the 1960s to higher-economic-value services by the 1990s, with a resulting increase in services in the trade portfolio. These countries went through each stage of economic development sooner than Japan or China owing to access to advanced technology, infrastructure, transportation and communication networks. The global reach of the internet, cheap international shipping and reduction of transaction costs can all propel trade more readily. For example, the large trade gap in 1920 between China, Russia and the West can be associated with communications technology. The number of telephone lines per 100 people was 34 in the US, 17 in the UK, 15 in Japan, 11 in Germany, eight in Japan, but nearly zero in China and Russia. However, this number changed dramatically in the last few decades. China increased from 0.2 in

1980 to 11 in 2000, while France and Germany doubled and the US and Japan increased by only 1.5 times. In the late twentieth century, about 73 percent of internet users in the world were in the US; Western Europe took another 15 percent, while China was left behind, which results in different trade performance. But, as China began to enter the third service stage with well-developed transportation and communication technology, the gap disappeared. In light of the 2008 global financial crisis, the lack of European capital and lower US consumer demand, some believe China is currently experiencing growing pains, transitioning from a manufacturing-centric to a service economy.

In order to understand the interactive effects of trade networks, growth and economic development, we follow the growth literature (Knight et al. 1993; Caselli et al. 1996), to build a simple growth model with the following specification:

$$\ln (Y_{i,t}) - \ln (Y_{i,t-\tau}) = \beta \ln (Y_{i,t-\tau}) + W_{i,t-\tau}\delta + \eta_i + \xi_i + \varepsilon_{i,t} \quad (4.1)$$

where $Y_{i,t}$ is per capita GDP for country i in time t, and $W_{i,t}$ is a vector of economic determinants, with η_i as country- and ξ_i as time-specific effects. We use economic growth, calculated as $\ln(Y_t) - \ln(Y_{t-1})$, as our dependent variable for sigma convergence. Our independent variables include percentage of agriculture, manufacturing and services as percentage of total GDP as the determinants of economic growth. For country-specific effects, we include four trade network attributes: degree, closeness, eigenvector and k-core centrality metrics as well as the number of RTA memberships for every country every year.

Table 4.1 shows data sources and descriptive statistics for our sample of over 180 countries from 1960 to 2009. Data is obtained from the World Bank's World Development Indicators, the World Trade Organization, the IMF's Direction of Trade Statistics and the Correlates of War Trade Data. Trade data is total volume of imports plus exports between any pair of countries in a particular year. Sigma is calculated as above showing income growth levels, while beta is calculated as $(\ln y_t - \ln y_{t-1})/y_{t-1}$ showing the speed of convergence. Agriculture, manufacturing and services are all measured as percentage of GDP. All variables have been logged and normalized for estimation purposes. Figure 4.5 displays the accompanying matrix plot of all variables, showing correlations and directionality of relationships as expected. It also suggests that we do not have any serious multi-collinearity issues.

Figures 4.6 and 4.7 visualize both sample distribution sigma level and beta rate income convergence by GDP per capita. As expected in both cases, we clearly see higher income level and growth rate variance at lower

Table 4.1   Descriptive statistics

Variable	Obs.	Mean	Std. dev.	Min.	Max.
Sigma	6867	0.0571268	0.1427864	−1.419804	1.181899
Beta	6867	0.0083028	0.0216993	−0.2367862	0.1852691
GDP per capita	7015	7.256475	1.637447	3.624781	11.79233
Agriculture	5763	3.862579	3.170818	0.008279	15.1995
Manufacture	5361	20.6869	2.749387	12.1007	28.2188
Services	5743	10.17501	2.822305	0.458988	17.6037
Degree	6863	6.418709	4.356766	0	18.2
Closeness	6863	2.617841	0.5479819	0	4.52
Eigenvector	6863	7.121536	3.740263	0	18.2
K-core	6863	40.42066	17.11662	0	68
RTA	7018	1.259618	1.703594	0	19

levels of development, with both convergence values tending towards zero as GDP rises.

Figures 4.8 and 4.9 depict the distribution of sigma level and beta rate income convergence by number of RTA memberships for our entire sample. Both figures show similar RTA effects of driving convergence, yet the impact might be nonlinear owing to the changing patterns as RTA membership increases. This suggests testing both linear and squared terms in our growth models to fully capture how RTAs impact income convergence.

Table 4.2 shows the result of our fixed effects OLS estimation approach for sigma income convergence. Model 1 establishes a baseline of our results for the full sample of all countries between 1960 and 2009. As the trade, income and growth literatures posit different effects from trade depending on levels of development, we subsequently run separate models 2 to 5 on subsamples given different stages of development as defined by the World Bank: low-income countries, low- to median-income countries, median- to high-income countries and high-income countries.

Model 1 focuses on the impact of economic growth and country-specific effects on convergence. As all variables are similarly scaled, we can interpret the relative magnitude of coefficients as importance of effects. GDP per capita has the highest negative impact ($\beta = -2.560$), consistent with neoclassical growth predictions. This supports most findings that argue countries relatively close to their steady-state output level will experience a slowdown in growth and conditional convergence. Agriculture has a much lower, but still significant, negative impact ($\beta = -0.378$), indicating higher proportions of agriculture production are associated with slower convergence. Manufacturing has the strongest positive impact ($\beta = 2.232$) on increasing convergence. The negative services coefficient ($\beta = -0.269$) has

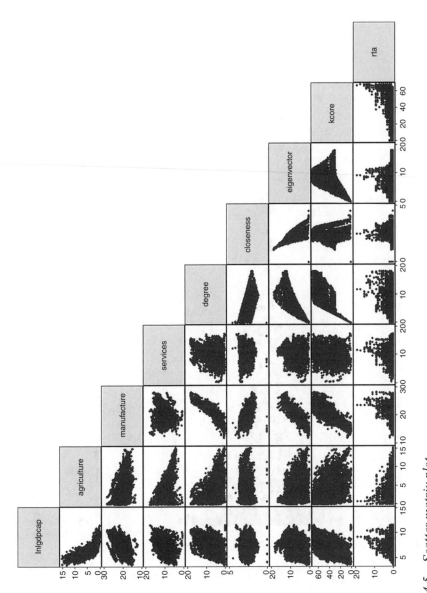

Figure 4.5   Scatter matrix plot

95

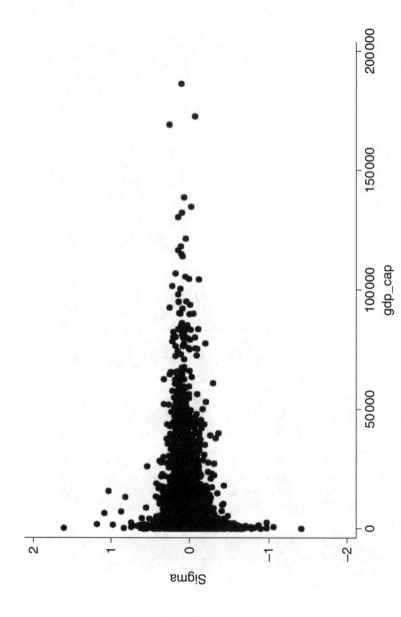

Figure 4.6 Sigma level vs. GDP per capita

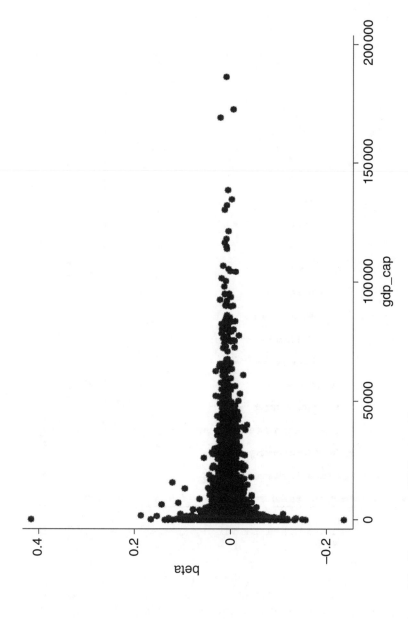

Figure 4.7 Beta rate vs. GDP per capita

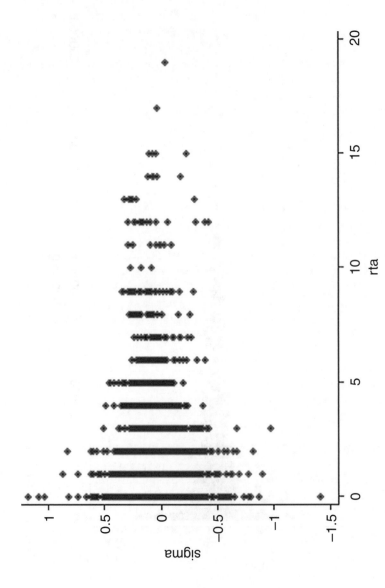

Figure 4.8 Sigma level vs. RTA membership

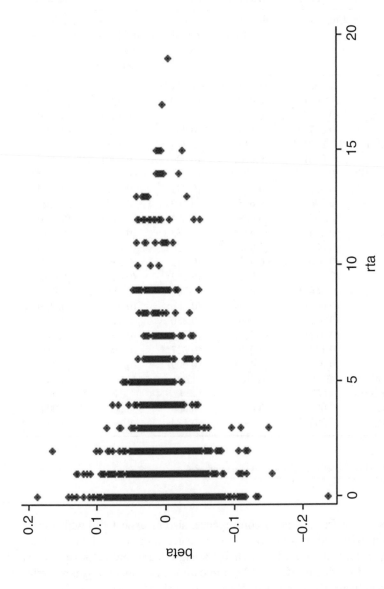

Figure 4.9 Beta rate vs. RTA membership

Table 4.2   Sigma convergence fixed effects OLS results

Sigma	Model 1	Model 2	Model 3	Model 4	Model 5
	Full sample	Low-income countries	Lower-middle-income countries	Upper-middle-income countries	High-income countries
lnlgdpcap	−2.560***	−1.258***	−1.564***	−1.901***	−1.620***
	(0.000)	(0.000)	(0.000)	(0.000)	(0.000)
agriculture	−0.378*	0.150	−0.141	−0.366*	−0.339**
	(0.017)	(0.588)	(0.450)	(0.022)	(0.005)
manufacture	2.232***	2.115***	2.368***	3.151***	1.123
	(0.000)	(0.000)	(0.000)	(0.000)	(0.071)
services	−0.269*	0.083	−0.105	−0.069	−0.639**
	(0.032)	(0.755)	(0.397)	(0.740)	(0.003)
degree	0.176	−0.655*	−0.163	−0.188	0.458
	(0.254)	(0.039)	(0.394)	(0.315)	(0.178)
closeness	−0.443***	−0.658***	−0.283*	−0.351	−0.406**
	(0.000)	(0.000)	(0.020)	(0.082)	(0.007)
eigenvector	−0.576***	−0.452**	−0.212	−0.375	−0.438*
	(0.000)	(0.002)	(0.252)	(0.050)	(0.010)
kcore	0.564***	1.023**	0.705**	0.688**	0.833***
	(0.000)	(0.007)	(0.006)	(0.005)	(0.000)
rta	−0.111	0.099	−0.180	−0.117	−0.206
	(0.078)	(0.563)	(0.284)	(0.293)	(0.070)
rta2	0.129*	0.079	0.327**	0.100	0.181*
	(0.010)	(0.493)	(0.009)	(0.148)	(0.049)
No. of obs.	4971	1018	1200	1469	1284
No. of groups	171	32	42	49	48
Prob. > F	0.000	0.000	0.000	0.000	0.000
Within R^2	0.203	0.291	0.234	0.247	0.254

Notes:
Standardized beta coefficients; p-values in parentheses.
* $p<0.05$; ** $p<0.01$; *** $p<0.001$.

a dampening effect on sigma convergence, also as expected; highly developed countries with a sophisticated service economy have already sigma-converged. RTA membership itself is not significant, but RTA squared is positive and significant ($\beta = 0.129$), indicating a nonlinear, U-shaped relationship between the number of RTAs and level of convergence. This suggests that RTAs can have a differential impact on growth with short-term, immediate impact that dissipates and then begins to accelerate later on.

Our network attributes demonstrate that closeness and eigenvector have nuanced but significantly negative impact (β = −0.443 and −0.576 respectively) for all nations. This suggests countries' convergence rates slow as they achieve prominence in the global trade network. K-core is positive and significant (β = 0.564), indicating that the more trading partners a country is tied with, the faster it moves towards convergence. Within R^2 indicates about 20 percent of the data is explained by our model.

Turning to our results across different levels of development, once again we find that GDP per capita has a strong negative impact on convergence consistent with neoclassical growth models. Agriculture coefficients are significant for more developed countries in Models 4 and 5, but insignificant in less developed countries in Models 2 and 3. This supports the increased drag of more expansive agricultural sectors in developed economies. Manufacturing has a consistent positive impact across all levels of development. Regardless of stages of development, manufacturing is a key driver for sigma convergence. Services are only negative and significant in high-income countries, showing the nonlinear relationship between the proportion of services in GDP and the level of convergence. RTA membership has a similar nonlinear pattern, as it is positive and significant for only lower-middle-income countries and high-income countries. This result suggests that RTA benefits accrue in asymmetric income partner relationships. This supports other scholars' findings that RTAs do provide efficiency gains and higher productivity, but only in partnerships where there is no direct market competition among equals.

Network attributes also prove differential impacts across levels of development. Degree has a negative impact for least developed countries only, suggesting globalization inequities based on connectivity only for those countries. Closeness is significant and negative for most except for upper-middle-income countries. This supports advantages for developing countries to strategically create trade partners within dense networks of trade volumes and partners. Eigenvector connectivity has a negative effect for low-income countries and high-income countries, but does not matter for middle-income countries. This indicates that, when a country is in the beginning or final stages of development, centrality of trade networks slows convergence. K-core is positive and significant across all stages of development and has a stronger impact than other network attributes. This indicates that local trading partnerships are critical to driving growth regardless of income level. R^2 shows that our approach fits best for low-income countries.

When testing beta convergence, we use $(\ln y_t - \ln y_{t-1})/\ln y_{t-1}$ as our dependent variable (Young et al. 2004). Similar to sigma convergence, we keep the same sets of determinants of economic growth and

Table 4.3   Beta convergence fixed effects OLS results

Beta	Model 6	Model 7	Model 8	Model 9	Model 10
	Full sample	Low-income countries	Lower-middle-income countries	Upper-middle-income countries	High-income countries
lnlgdpcap	−2.589***	−1.308***	−1.594***	−1.932***	−1.649***
	(0.000)	(0.000)	(0.000)	(0.000)	(0.000)
agriculture	−0.319*	0.165	−0.113	−0.370*	−0.350**
	(0.036)	(0.545)	(0.545)	(0.021)	(0.003)
manufacture	2.171***	2.128***	2.349***	3.008***	0.906
	(0.000)	(0.000)	(0.000)	(0.000)	(0.132)
services	−0.214	0.091	−0.091	−0.077	−0.653**
	(0.070)	(0.729)	(0.456)	(0.707)	(0.002)
degree	0.152	−0.572	−0.206	−0.190	0.408
	(0.332)	(0.055)	(0.298)	(0.303)	(0.241)
closeness	−0.463***	−0.631***	−0.296*	−0.354	−0.440**
	(0.000)	(0.000)	(0.011)	(0.072)	(0.003)
eigenvector	−0.629***	−0.422**	−0.259	−0.367	−0.523**
	(0.000)	(0.003)	(0.170)	(0.056)	(0.003)
kcore	0.597***	0.920*	0.740**	0.725**	0.901***
	(0.000)	(0.010)	(0.003)	(0.004)	(0.000)
rta	−0.124*	0.075	−0.177	−0.123	−0.201
	(0.047)	(0.642)	(0.283)	(0.264)	(0.064)
rta2	0.136**	0.075	0.319**	0.110	0.182*
	(0.005)	(0.494)	(0.009)	(0.114)	(0.040)
No. of obs.	4971	1018	1200	1469	1284
No. of groups	171	32	42	49	48
Prob. > F	0.000	0.000	0.000	0.000	0.000
Within R^2	0.203	0.299	0.240	0.258	0.283

Notes:
Standardized beta coefficients; p-values in parentheses.
* $p<0.05$; ** $p<0.01$; *** $p<0.001$.

country-specific effects. Table 4.3 shows the result of our five different models across levels of development: Model 6 for our all-country sample, Model 7 for low-income countries, Model 8 for lower-middle-income countries, Model 9 for upper-middle-income countries and Model 10 for high-income countries.

Looking at Model 6 results for all nations in our sample, once again we find a negative and significant GDP per capita coefficient ($\beta = -2.589$), supporting the literature's findings of lower growth rates for rich countries than for poor countries. In terms of beta convergence, agriculture has a negative impact ($\beta = -0.319$), slowing down growth at higher levels of development. Manufacturing ($\beta = 2.171$) has the largest positive impact on income convergence rates, supporting industrialization arguments for higher proportions of manufacturing to GDP to fuel economic growth. RTA is negative ($\beta = -0.124$), but more importantly RTA squared has a positive sign ($\beta = 0.136$), indicating increased RTA participation slows convergence. This result is stronger for countries with a very small number of RTAs or very large number of RTAs.

Clearly the results indicate that our trade network attributes impact beta convergence in different ways. Closeness and eigenvector both have significant negative impact ($\beta = -0.463$ and -0.629 respectively) for the full sample. This suggests that overall, if a country has strong trade relationships with other countries, especially hubs in the global trade network, it is likely to experience lower growth rates relative to countries that are not well connected with other trading countries. K-core is again positive and significant ($\beta = 0.597$), supporting faster convergence when involved with a large clique of other trading partners. Within R^2 explains about 20 percent of the variance.

Turning to Models 7 through 10 across different stages of development, once again we see high levels of GDP per capita as having a consistently negative impact of beta convergence as expected. Agriculture's negative drag on beta rates remains at higher levels of development, while manufacturing has a consistently strong and positive impact on economic growth regardless of development levels. The service sector has a negative impact on rate of growth for only high-income countries owing to diminishing returns. The number of RTAs is not significant, while RTA squared is positive and significant for lower-middle-income countries and high-income countries. This supports our early nonlinear findings of RTA membership benefiting low- and high-income countries.

Surprisingly, degree connectivity is not significant in any stage of development, which means the number of trading partners does not matter for rate of convergence. Closeness and eigenvector have very similar patterns: neither of them is significant in Model 9, and closeness is only weakly significant in Model 8, but they are both negative and significant for least developed countries and high-income countries. This indicates that these countries experience slower convergence if well connected with other active trading countries in the network. Once again, k-core is associated with a positive impact across all levels of development. Interestingly, this impact becomes more significant and powerful as income levels increase, suggesting the accretive regional effects. R^2 in our models controlling for levels of development are higher than the full sample, indicating that the relationship between trade and convergence does differ according to economic theory. This also helps to explain why many previous empirical assessments throughout the literature provide mixed results.

CONCLUSIONS AND FURTHER DIRECTIONS

Although in different proportions and significance at various income levels, we find strong evidence for trade equalization, supporting traditional income convergence dynamics. Our examination of the global trade system by volume shows increasing density and interconnectivity. This is not surprising given the emphasis on economic interdependence by economists since the late 1970s. Consistent with Epstein et al. (2003), trade interactions do affect income convergence for countries differently depending on development levels. First, despite Asian countries having started 200 percent behind Western nations in 1920, the number of trading partners a nation possesses has converged to within plus or minus 3 percent for all major powers with the exception of Russia. Second, both the UK and the US were preeminent trading hubs in the early part of the century at a 5100 percent advantage over Asian countries. This dramatically dropped to only a 28 percent gap by 2000, largely through strong manufacturing performance. Third, while the US and the Europeans enjoyed an 80 percent trading influence advantage over Asian nations in 1920, by 2000 that gap had narrowed to less than 1 percent. Each one of our measures shows clear trends towards trade convergence. Both sigma level convergence, where trade inequities disappeared, and beta rate convergence, where less developed economies' trade volumes grew faster than those of more developed economies, are present.

Our empirical results present some important implications and insights as well as directions for further enquiry. Consistent with many other scholars, we find strong empirical evidence for both income and trade convergence, with trade inexorably linked to growth and globalization. Lau and Wan (1994) argue that trade is a necessary but not sufficient condition for poor countries to income-converge, while we find via our eigenvector connectivity metric that the quality of trade connections can often matter most for poor countries. Fischer and Serra (1996) find trade accelerates economic growth and income convergence rates in poor countries, while slowing down growth and the rate of income convergence in rich countries. Here we discover a more detailed, granular pattern where sheer trade partner connectivity might help advanced countries converge and hinder less developed countries. However, targeted eigenvector connectivity can propel least developed societies' convergence faster than that of other nations. Consistent with many others (Williamson 1996; O'Rourke and Williamson 1999), we also see that in long-run equilibrium trade ensures countries grow at the same rate and income ratios tend to parity. Both our exploratory and empirical analysis across stages of economic production and levels of development supports these results.

RTA membership has a demonstrable, acceleratory effect on conditional convergence, yet is highly dependent on income levels. As both WTO globalization and regionalization developed rapidly in the postwar period, more and more countries became involved in the global marketplace. We also saw the trade system become more complex as decentralization and regionalization occurred simultaneously, benefiting low-middle-income and high-income countries the most. Regional organizations enhanced trade between members as these organizations emerged and proliferated. The rise of the European Free Trade Association (EFTA), AFTA, Mercosur and NAFTA, among others, not only stimulated growth but also propelled trade connectivity and convergence in the latter half of the century.

Our findings suggest that the addition of trade network metrics can play a significant and nuanced role for new economic theory formulation and empirical verification. Looking at global trade as a whole masks some very important network metrics and potential drivers of economic change missing from current explanations. Our approach of differentiating national economic development patterns through network measures, controlled for stages of economic production and development, can point towards generalizable trajectories. On conditional trade convergence, we find both beta rate convergence, where smaller and less integrated trading partners can grow faster than established trade leaders, and clear sigma level convergence among almost all major trading nations. We also find long-term trends of unilateral trade advantages disappearing and more global trade equalization. These new metrics and perspectives provide us with additional insights that cannot be derived from traditional trade volume, theories or growth models alone.

Here we do not evaluate convergence, whether caused by growth or trade, without further rigorous econometric testing using more sophisticated growth models and econometric techniques. However, our results dispel most claims of major power trade inequities based on volume and structural network connectivity alone. We have ventured only a first step towards further theoretical and empirical work linking trade, growth and globalization. Hopefully a network approach can lead to a better understanding of the global economic changes for this next century.

REFERENCES

Abdollahian, M. and Z. Yang (2013), "Towards Trade Equalisation: A Network Perspective on Trade and Income Convergence across the Twentieth Century," *New Political Economy*, **16** (3), 1–27.

Allen, G. (1958), *Japan's Economic Recovery*, Oxford: Oxford University Press.

Arthur, B. (1996), "Increasing Returns and the New World of Business," *Harvard Business Review*, **74** (4), 100–109.

Bagoulla, C. and N. Peridy (2011), "Market Access and the Other Determinants of North–South Manufacturing Location Choice: An Application to the Euro-Mediterranean Area," *Economic Systems*, **35** (4), 537–61.

Bardhan, P. (2004), "The Impact of Globalization on the Poor," *Brookings Trade Forum*, 271–84.

Barro, R. (1991), "Economic Growth in a Cross Section of Countries," *Quarterly Journal of Economics*, **106**, 407–44.

Bell, D. (1974), *The Coming of Post-Industrial Society*, New York: Basic Books.

Blomstrom, M. and A. Kokko (1997), *Regional Integration and Foreign Direct Investment*, Cambridge, MA: National Bureau of Economic Research.

Bolle, M. et al. (2007), *US Trade Statements: Expiration Dates and Mandated Periodic Reports to Congress*, available from: http://www.au.af.mil/au/awc/awcgate/crs/rl34196.pdf (accessed July 15, 2011).

Brandt, L. and T.G. Rawski (2008), *China's Great Economic Transformation*, Cambridge: Cambridge University Press.

Braun, H. (1990), *The German Economy in the Twentieth Century*, New York: Routledge.

Breiger, R. (1981), "Structure of Economic Interdependence among Nations," in P. Blau and R. Merton (eds.), *Continuities in Structural Inquiry*, London: Sage Publications.

Caselli, F., G. Esquivel and F. Lefort (1996), "Reopening the Convergence Debate: A New Look at Cross-Country Growth Empirics," *Journal of Economic Growth*, **1** (3), 353–80.

Castells, M. (2000), *The Rise of the Network Society*, Oxford: Blackwell.

Clodfelter, M. (2002), *Warfare and Armed Conflict: A Statistical Reference to Casualty and Other Figures 1500–2000*, Jefferson, NC: McFarland & Company.

De Benedictis, L. and L. Tajoli (2011), "The World Trade Network," *World Economy*, **34** (8), 1417–54.

Dee, P. (2004), *The Australia–US Free Trade Agreement: An Assessment*, Canberra: Australian National University.

Dicken, P. (2003), *Global Shift: Reshaping the Global Economic Map in the 21st Century*, London: Paul Chapman.

Dittmer, L. (2002), "East Asia in the 'New Era' in World Politics," *World Politics*, **55** (1), 38–65.

Drezner, D. (2005), "Trade Talk," *American Interest*, Winter.

Drucker, P. (1993), *Post-Capitalist Society*, Oxford: Butterworth-Heinemann.

Epstein, P., P. Howlett and M. Schulze (2003), "Distribution Dynamics: Stratification, Polarization and Convergence among OECD Economies, 1870–1992," *Explorations in Economic History*, **40** (1), 78–97.

European Commission (1960), *A Peaceful Europe – The Beginnings of Cooperation*, available from: http://europa.eu/about-eu/eu-history/1945-1959/index_en.htm (accessed August 16, 2011).

Fischer, R. and P. Serra (1996), "Income Convergence with and between Countries," *International Economic Review*, **37** (3), 531–51.

Frankel, J. (1997), *Regional Trading Blocs in the World Economic System*, Washington, DC: Institute for International Economics.

Friedman, T. (2005), *The World Is Flat: A Brief History of the Twenty-First Century*, New York: Farrar, Straus and Giroux.

Grew, J. (1944), *Ten Years in Japan*, New York: Simon & Schuster.

Grossman, G.M. and E. Helpman (1991), "Trade, Knowledge Spillovers and Growth," *European Economic Review*, **35** (2), 517–26.

Guiso, L., P. Sapienza and L. Zingales (2004), "Cultural Biases in Economic Exchange," Kellogg School of Management of Northwestern University Working Paper, available from: http://www.kellogg.northwestern.edu/faculty/sapienza/htm/cultural_biases.pdf (accessed April 3, 2011).

Hajdini, I. (2010), "The Role of the IMF in General and Its Role in Kosovo," unpublished bachelor's thesis, University for Business and Technology, Pristina.

Harris, R. (1993), "Globalization, Trade and Income," *Canadian Journal of Economics*, **26** (4), 755–76.

Harvey, D. (1989), *The Condition of Postmodernity*, Oxford: Blackwell.

Huber, T. (1994), *Strategic Economy in Japan*, Boulder, CO: Westview Press.

Hummels, D. (2007), "Transportation Costs and International Trade in the Second Era of Globalization," *Journal of Economic Perspectives*, **21** (3), 131–54.

Huntington, S. (1996), *The Clash of Civilizations and the Remaking of World Order*, New York: Simon & Schuster.

Jilberto, A. and A. Mommen (1998), *Regionalization and Globalization in the Modern World Economy*, New York: Routledge.

Kali, R. and J. Reyes (2007), "The Architecture of Globalization: A Network Approach to International Economic Integration," *Journal of International Business Studies*, **38** (4), 595–620.

Kaufman, R. and A. Segura-Ubiergo (2001), "Globalization, Domestic Politics and Social Spending in Latin America: A Time-Series Cross-Section Analysis, 1973–97," *World Politics*, **53** (4), 553–87.

Keohane, R. (1997), "Problematic Lucidity: Stephen Krasner's 'State Power and the Structure of International Trade,'" *World Politics*, **50** (1), 150–70.

Kim, S. and E. Shin (2002), "A Longitudinal Analysis of Globalization and Regionalization in International Trade: A Social Network Approach," *Social Forces*, **81** (2), 445–68.

Kitchen, M. (2006), *Europe between the Wars*, London: Longman.

Knight, M., N. Loayza and D. Villanueva (1993), "Testing the Neoclassical Theory of Economic Growth," *IMF Staff Papers*, **40** (3), September, 512–41.

Krugman, P. (1986), *Strategic Trade Policy and the New International Economics*, Cambridge, MA: MIT Press.

Krugman, P. (1991), *Geography and Trade*, Cambridge, MA: MIT Press.

Langerfels, J. and J. Nieberling (2005), "The Benefits of Free Trade to US Consumers: Quantitative Confirmation of Theoretical Expectation," *Business Economics*, July.

Lau, M. and H. Wan (1994), "On the Mechanism of Catching Up," *European Economic Review*, **38** (3), 952–63.

Levine, R. and D. Renelt (1992), "A Sensitivity Analysis of Cross-Country Growth Regressions," *American Economic Review*, **82**, 942–63.

Levy, B. (2006), "Emerging Countries, Regionalization and World Trade," *Global Economy Journal*, **61** (1), article 2.

MacDougall, C. (1972), "Chinese Trade since the Cultural Revolution," *World Today*, **28** (1), 23–9.

MacFarquhar, R. (1987), "The Succession to Mao and the End of Maoism," in R. MacFarquhar (ed.), *The Cambridge History of China*, Cambridge: Cambridge University Press.

Machlup, F. (1962), *The Production and Distribution of Knowledge in the United States*, Princeton, NJ: Princeton University Press.

Mankiw, N. Gregory, David Romer and David N. Weil (1992), "A Contribution to the Empirics of Economic Growth," *Quarterly Journal of Economics*, **107** (2), 407–37.

Neary, J.P. (2001), "Of Hype and Hyperbolas: Introducing the New Economic Geography," *Journal of Economic Literature*, **39** (2), 536–61.

O'Rourke, K. and J. Williamson (1999), *Globalization and History*, Cambridge, MA: MIT Press.

Pine, J. and J. Gilmore (1999), *The Experience Economy: Work Is Theater and Every Business a Stage*, Boston, MA: Harvard Business Press.

Ramajo, J., M.A. Márquez, G.J. Hewings and M.M. Salinas (2008), "Spatial Heterogeneity and Interregional Spillovers in the European Union: Do Cohesion Policies Encourage Convergence across Regions?," *European Economic Review*, **52** (3), 551–67.

Rauch, J. (1999), "Network versus Markets in International Trade," *Journal of International Economics*, **48** (1), 7–35.

Rebelo, S. (1991), "Long Run Policy Analysis and Long Run Growth," *Journal of Political Economy*, **99**, 500–521.

Romer, P. (1987), "Growth Based on Increasing Returns Due to Specialization," *American Economic Review*, **77** (2), 56–62.

Sachs, J. and A. Warner (1997), "Sources of Slow Growth in African Economies," *Journal of African Economies*, **6** (3), 335–76.

Sala-i-Martin, X.X. (1996), "Regional Cohesion: Evidence and Theories of Regional Growth and Convergence," *European Economic Review*, **40** (6), 1325–52.

Sally, R. (2006), "Free Trade Agreements and the Prospects for Regional Integration in East Asia," *Asian Economic Policy Review*, **1** (2), 306–21.

Schifferes, S. (2007), "Globalization Shakes the World," *BBC News*, January 21.

Schuker, Stephen A. (1988), *American "Reparations" to Germany 1919–33: Implications for the Third World Debt Crisis*, Princeton, NJ: Princeton University Press.

Shiozawa, Y. (2007), "A New Construction of Ricardian Trade Theory: A Many-Country, Many-Commodity Case with Intermediate Goods and Choice of Production Techniques," *Evolutionary and Institutional Economics Review*, **3** (2), 141–87.

Smith, D. and D. White (1992), "Structure and Dynamics of the Global Economy: Network Analysis of International Trade, 1965–1980," *Social Forces*, **70**, 857–93.

Snyder, D. and E. Kick (1979), "Structural Position in the World System and Economic Growth, 1955–1970: A Multiple Network Approach," *American Journal of Sociology*, **84**, 1096–1123.

Solow, R. (1956), "A Contribution to the Theory of Economic Growth," *Quarterly Journal of Economics*, **70** (1), 65–94.

Soros, G. (1998), *The Crisis of Global Capitalism: Open Society Endangered*, New York: Public Affairs.

Sperlich, S. and Y. Sperlich (2011), "Growth and Convergence in South–South Integration Areas: The Empirical Evidence," Université de Genève working paper, available from: http://www.unige.ch/ses/dsec/research/wps/12032_v2.pdf (accessed August 3, 2012).

Sperlich, Y. and S. Sperlich (2012), "Income Development and Sigma Convergence in South–South Agreement Areas," Université de Genève working paper, available from: http://www.unige.ch/ses/dsec/research/wps/12031.pdf (accessed August 3, 2012).

Steiber, S. (1979), "The World System and World Trade: An Empirical Explanation of Conceptual Conflicts," *Sociological Quarterly*, **20**, 23–36.

Sun, J. (2000), *Zhongguo Jingji Tongshi* [Economic history of China], Vol. 2: *1840–1949*, Beijing: China People's University Press.

Swan, T. (1956), "Economic Growth and Capital Accumulation," *Economic Record*, **32** (2), 334–61.

Tammen, R., J. Kugler, D. Lemke, A. Stam, C. Alsharabati, M. Abdollahian, B. Efird and A.F.K. Organski (2000), *Power Transitions: Strategies for the 21st Century*, New York: Chatham House.

Urata, S. (2002), "Globalization and the Growth in Free Trade Agreements," *Asia-Pacific Review*, **9** (1), 20–32.

Vamvakidis, A. (1998), "Regional Integration and Economic Growth," *World Bank Economic Review*, **12** (2), 251–70.

Velde, D.W. te (2011), "Regional Integration, Growth and Convergence," *Journal of Economic Integration*, **26** (1), 1–28.

Viner, J. (1950), *The Customs Union Issue*, New York: Carnegie Endowment for International Peace.

Wang, J. (2004), "China's Regional Trade Agreements: The Law, the Geopolitics and the Impact on the Multilateral Trading System," *2004 Singapore Year Book of International Law*, **8**, 119–47.

Williamson, J. (1996), "Globalization, Convergence and History," *Journal of Economic History*, **56** (2), 277–306.

World Bank (1993), *The East Asian Miracle: Economic Growth and Public Policy*, World Bank Policy Research Report, Washington, DC: World Bank.

Young, A.T., M.J. Higgins and D. Levy (2004), "Sigma Convergence versus Beta Convergence: Evidence from U.S. Country-Level Data," *Journal of Money*, **40** (5), 1083–93.

Zoellick, R. (2002), *Globalization, Trade and Economic Security*, available from: http://2001-2009.state.gov/e/eeb/rls/rm/2002/14014.htm (accessed May 4, 2011).

PART II

DOMESTIC POLITICS, DEVELOPMENT STRATEGY, AND DEMOCRACY

5. The new politics of the new trade: the political economy of intra-industry trade
Mary Anne Madeira

INTRODUCTION

International trade creates winners and losers. Though beneficial for society as a whole, trade makes some individuals within a society better off and it makes some individuals worse off. The categories of winners and losers shift along with one's analytical lens: men versus women, high-skilled workers versus low-skilled workers, employers versus employees, traded sectors versus non-traded sectors, capital-intensive industries versus labor-intensive industries, to slice it up just a handful of ways. As the advanced industrial democracies have grown ever more integrated into the global economy, societal groups have waged continual political battles over the direction of trade policy. The salience of these political battles varies dramatically, as do the players. Despite continued commitment to the liberal international trade regime, trade openness remains contentious in the advanced industrialized democracies. Analysts of trade policy have argued that, in the postwar era, lobbying has increased, protectionist lobbying specifically has increased and trade policy demands have become more heterogeneous.[1]

Before we can understand trade policy outcomes, we must understand why, when and how societal actors organize and mobilize themselves politically for the purpose of pressuring policymakers to adopt liberal or protectionist trade policies. In the United States, trade policy coalitions in the nineteenth century were well organized, highly active and broadly class-based or sector-based (Hiscox 2002). Over time, the nature of trade policy coalitions has changed dramatically. In the postwar period, coalitions both of industries and of labor have dissolved to a great extent, and lobbying today is primarily undertaken by industry-based rather than class-based groups, as well as by individual firms. Industry, labor, and political parties were all divided during debates over major pieces of trade legislation such as NAFTA and more recent bilateral trade deals with South Korea, Panama and Colombia, which stalled in Congress for years before being concluded. Likewise, in the European Union today, lobbying over trade is highly industry-based. Unions play a muted role in trade debates, and, while the vast majority of European manufacturing industry is free-trading, certain industries such as textiles and automobiles are deeply divided over their trade preferences.[2]

What explains the structure of trade coalitions? Why does this structure vary across time and place? Why are certain sectors and industries deeply divided over trade while others remain united in their positions? These questions, which bring us to the nexus of domestic and international political economy, motivate this chapter. To answer them I consider the growing importance of intra-industry trade for today's developed economies. I argue that the rise of intra-industry trade among these countries has undermined broad class and sector consensus over trade policies, as the costs of intra-industry trade fall primarily on individual firms rather than entire classes or industries. Intra-industry trade is trade by two countries in similar goods from the same industry, rather than different goods. It can include the exportation and importation of finished products. For example, the US exports automobiles to Germany and it also imports German automobiles. There is also intra-firm trade in semi-finished products (or intermediate goods) used in later stages of production. For example, Boeing imports many Chinese-made aircraft components that it uses in its final assembly of aircraft in the US. This importation of aircraft parts and exportation of finished aircraft is also intra-industry trade. The redistributive implications of this type of trade are profoundly different from those of the classic inter-industry, endowments-based trade, incentivizing individual firms to mobilize politically as the consensus underlying broader coalitions breaks down.

This chapter proceeds as follows. First, I review classic models of international trade and their political implications. Second, I discuss the nature of intra-industry trade and its economic foundations, as argued by economists working on the "new trade theory." Third, I discuss the distributional effects of intra-industry trade and the implications therein for societal preferences over trade, the politics of trade, and finally trade policy outcomes.

CLASSIC TRADE THEORY

Much of the seminal political science work on the politics of international trade is grounded in "classic" trade theory. According to the standard Ricardian model, comparative advantage drives international trade (Ricardo 1817). Each country will specialize in the production of the good it produces most efficiently (with the least labor) and it will trade for the rest. The Heckscher–Ohlin model builds on Ricardo's formulation by introducing factor endowments as the basis of comparative advantage.[3] Because countries differ in terms of factor endowments, they will each be relatively better at producing different types of goods, depending on what is the abundant factor in each economy. Firms specialize to produce goods exploiting abundant factors, and countries trade for goods that are produced more efficiently in other countries with different mixes of factor endowments. Trade is based on comparative advantage, and it occurs between countries with different factor endowments.

Rogowski's (1989) enduring contribution to the trade policy literature is his use of an extension of Heckscher–Ohlin, the Stolper–Samuelson theorem, to explain patterns in trade cleavages and coalitions between landowners, workers and owners of capital in a number of societies in different time periods. He argued that owners of the abundant factors in an economy will form a free trade coalition against owners of scarce factors, who will ally in favor of protection. For example, labor unions will hold different trade preferences than industrialists in countries where labor is scarce and capital is abundant. Much of the work that followed Rogowski's pioneering and parsimonious contribution sought to resolve a weakness of his study. As Rogowski himself noted (1989: 126–8), his expectations about the domestic effects of international trade struggled to explain postwar politics in the advanced industrial societies.[4] Numerous studies have attempted to improve upon Rogowski's model by developing more sophisticated measures of factor endowments or including additional productive factors (skilled labor versus unskilled labor, for example, as in Midford 1993). Others test his model using updated data (Jeong 2009) and/or survey data of individual attitudes (Scheve and Slaughter 2001; O'Rourke 2003), while others include additional political variables to better explain puzzling outcomes (Garst 1998, 1999).

Other scholars have argued that the Ricardo–Viner model better explains conflict over trade in the advanced industrial states where factor mobility is low. The implication of the Ricardo–Viner theorem is that sector-based cleavages composed of both workers and owners in a given industry or area will emerge as sectors that benefit from liberalized trade (those that use the abundant factor intensively) ally against sectors that lose out (those that use scarce factors intensively). Frieden (1992) argues that, when economic actors hold assets that are specific to a particular use or industry, sectoral conflict over liberalization is the likely result. Labor and capital are more likely to lobby together in support of policies beneficial to their industry, so cleavages and coalitions are likely to fall along industry lines. Frieden also argues that, in these cases, the government is likely to intervene on behalf of industry-based interest groups rather than more diffuse public interest or advocacy groups. Alt et al. (1999) support this theory with evidence that firms with greater asset specificity, measured as research and development investments and job immobility, are more likely to lobby for protective subsidies than other firms.

Still other studies have sought better measures of factor mobility. A central motivation behind many of these studies has been to put Stolper–Samuelson and Ricardo–Viner to the test, and the consensus is that, as the theorems themselves claim, Stolper–Samuelson effects tend to prevail when factor mobility is high and Ricardo–Viner when factor mobility is lower (Brawley 1997; Beaulieu 2002; Ladewig 2006). Hiscox (2002) developed one of the first measures of factor mobility in order to test the two models. He measured factor mobility over time in several advanced economies, and his findings confirm that, when factor mobility is high, political coalitions will form along broad class-based lines. When factor mobility is low, trade coalitions form along sectoral lines. Hiscox examines the policy preferences of political party, peak association and lobby groups to test these hypotheses.

These approaches certainly explain some of the variation we observe in trade politics and policy across time and across countries, although, as I argue here, they lose explanatory power as today's advanced economies move increasingly away from a Heckscher–Ohlin world of endowments-based, inter-industry trade and engage in an entirely different kind of trade: intra-industry trade.[5]

PUZZLING NEW TRADE PATTERNS IN THE SECOND WAVE OF GLOBALIZATION

Many analysts now question whether the classic Stolper–Samuelson and Ricardo–Viner models are the appropriate trade models to apply to today's developed countries (Alt et al. 1996; Gilligan 1997a; Ruffin 1999; Kono 2009; among others). The "new" trade theory, developed by economists such as Paul Krugman and Elhanan Helpman, seeks to explain the explosion of intra-industry trade among the developed economies in the postwar period. In all of the OECD economies, trade has become increasingly *intra*-industry rather than inter-industry (OECD 2002). Indeed, the developed economies are exceptional vis-à-vis the rest of the world for the high percentage of intra-industry trade in their trading profiles. Intra-industry trade is trade in similar goods, such as types of automobiles, mobile telephones or pharmaceuticals. As defined by Krugman, intra-industry trade (IIT) "consists of two-way international trade within an industry because firms in different countries will produce different differentiated products" (1990: 30). As discussed above, IIT can take the form of trade in finished products from the same industry as well as intra-firm trade in semi-finished products. In terms of the standard trade theories discussed above, the crucial distinction between intra-industry and inter-industry trade is that intra-industry trade occurs between countries with similar factor endowments.

Beginning with Adam Smith and David Ricardo, economists have explained international trade as a process by which countries specialize in the production of goods in which they have a comparative advantage and trade for the rest. As in the classic example, Portugal exports wine and imports British cloth. Indeed, from the mid-nineteenth century up until World War I, the time period often referred to as the "first wave of globalization," international trade patterns were primarily driven by comparative advantage. In the early twentieth century, even the manufacturing trade among the United States, Britain and the European Continent was inter-industry, with Britain exporting highly processed "old" manufactured goods such as textiles, clothing, ships and railroad materials, while the US and the Continent specialized in "new" industrial goods such as chemicals and steel. In 1910, 75 percent of Britain's exports were manufactures, and only 25 percent of its imports were manufactures. In the same year in land-rich and labor-scarce Canada, by contrast, manufactures accounted for 62 percent of imports and only 20 percent of exports (Baldwin and Martin 1999). Less industrialized nations (including many colonies) were important trading partners at this time, serving as sources of manufacturing inputs and receivers of manufacturing exports.

Trading patterns changed significantly after World War II with the onset of the "second wave" of globalization. In the postwar period, the United States and Western Europe embarked on a trade liberalization project embodied multilaterally in the General Agreement on Tariffs and Trade (GATT), and regionally within the European Community. At the same time, technological developments allowed transport costs to continue to fall. Also during this time, North–North trade and two-way manufacturing trade took on a greater importance than in the first wave of globalization (Krugman 2009). In the United Kingdom in 1993, manufactures accounted for 77 percent of imports (compared to 25 percent in 1910) and 97 percent of exports (compared to 75 percent in 1910). The advanced economies were exporting manufactures as well as importing them, and they were engaged in this two-way manufacturing trade with each other. In 1996, 83 percent of European exports were destined for Europe or North America, compared to 75 percent in 1910 (Baldwin and Martin 1999).

The growth in two-way trade for goods within the same industrial category, or intra-industry trade, became a significant feature of the global economy in the postwar period, but especially for the developed countries. It represents a major change in the structure of international trade. As shown in Figure 5.1, intra-industry trade in manufactured goods (defined at the 5-digit level according to the UN's Standard International Trade Classification) has increased between countries in all income groups, but it occurs at the highest levels among high-income countries. By 2006, intra-industry trade at this fine level of disaggregation accounted for approximately 40 percent of trade between developed countries, and this figure is even higher when trade is disaggregated to the 3- or 4-digit level, as it is in much of the literature.

Levels of intra-industry trade are the highest for manufactured goods, as these goods tend to be more differentiable than primary goods or raw materials. In 2006, only 11 percent of trade in primary goods was intra-industry, up from approximately 4 percent in 1962 (Brülhart 2009). Among manufactured goods, those with the highest intra-industry trade are the more sophisticated manufactured products such as transport equipment, chemicals and machinery, although this varies by country. More complex manufactured goods not only are more differentiable, but also may be the most subject to economies of scale in production (leading firms to specialize in fewer products, trading for the rest) as well as vertically disintegrated production across countries. This also contributes to the extensive intra-industry trade in intermediate goods, such as automobile parts. All these factors increase the likelihood of two-way trade within an industry. Across the high-income economies, food products tend to have the lowest levels of intra-industry trade, on average, typically around 40 percent or less in the 1990s (OECD 2002).

While high-income countries tend to have high IIT relative to lower-income countries, there is nevertheless considerable variation in IIT across the high-income countries, as shown in Table 5.1. In general, countries that are highly dependent on trade also tend to have very high levels of intra-industry trade. Krugman (1995) argues that highly open, "supertrading" economies such as Belgium, the Netherlands, the Czech Republic and Slovakia are heavily integrated into global production networks, exporting and importing a great deal of intermediate goods, and for this reason are likely to have high levels of IIT. Indeed, the OECD countries with the biggest increases in intra-industry trade in recent years are those that have received big increases in inward foreign direct investment, such as the Czech Republic, Slovakia and Hungary (OECD 2002). Volkswagen owns the largest exporting firms in these countries, firms that export not only automotive parts but also fully assembled automobiles. The countries with low and stable intra-industry trade tend to be those that are least reliant on manufacturing exports and most reliant on exporting agricultural and

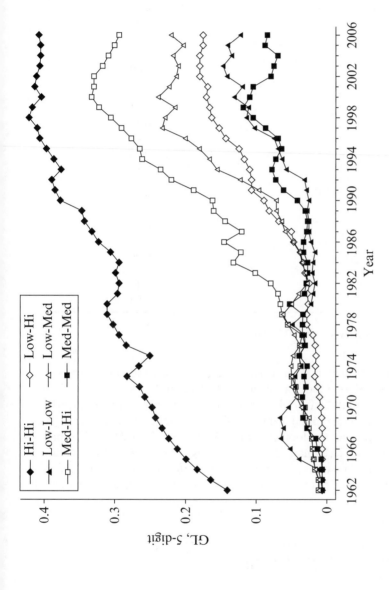

Notes:
Intra-industry trade is measured according to the Grubel–Lloyd index, as is standard in the literature.
Country groupings are defined by the World Bank.

Source: Brülhart (2009).

Figure 5.1 Evolution of global intra-industry trade by country income group, 1962–2006

Table 5.1   Intra-industry trade as a percentage of total trade, select high-income democracies, 2012

Belgium	0.73
Netherlands	0.70
Germany	0.64
France	0.62
Spain	0.60
Great Britain	0.57
Sweden	0.54
USA	0.54
Portugal	0.48
Slovenia	0.48
Switzerland	0.44
Canada	0.42
Finland	0.41
Japan	0.37
Greece	0.37
Ireland	0.36
Luxembourg	0.32
Australia	0.30
New Zealand	0.26
Iceland	0.11
Cyprus	0.08

Source: Comtrade data, 4-digit SITC sector level.

marine products, such as Australia, New Zealand, Iceland and Greece, as well as oil (Norway) and other raw materials (Iceland).

In sum, more than half of all global trade is now intra-industry (World Bank 2009). The World Bank calls intra-industry trade "perhaps the most important economic development since World War II" (2009: 171), but until the 1980s, as Krugman (2009) argues, existing trade theories could not explain this "new" trade. In the early 1980s economists set about developing new theories to understand the economic rationale for trade in similar goods.

"NEW TRADE THEORY" AND THE LOGIC OF INTRA-INDUSTRY TRADE

The economists who pioneered new trade theory, such as Dixit and Norman (1980), Helpman (1981) and Krugman (1981), all argue that the primary economic basis for trade between similar countries is increasing returns to scale and product differentiation.[6] These two factors are related, but different. Increasing returns to scale is a producer-driven cause of intra-industry trade, while demand for a variety of differentiated products is consumer-driven.

First, when products are similar but differentiated, firms have some control over pricing, and market structure becomes that of monopolistic competition. Under monopolistic competition with differentiated products, it is assumed that firms enjoy increasing returns to scale. When there are increasing returns to scale, producers have an incentive to specialize in their particular product variety and increase output of that product. Increasing returns to scale (IRS) is a property whereby an expansion of input use raises output more than proportionately. For example, a firm enjoys increasing returns to scale if it doubles the size of its factory and production more than doubles as a result. Increasing returns usually result from production that has high fixed costs. These are typically development costs, for example in industries such as pharmaceuticals and jet airliners, or the costs of setting up production lines. The high fixed costs associated with developing a new product line cause firms to specialize in a subset of products rather than to produce a full range of product varieties within an industry. Firms specialize and then seek increasing returns to scale as they ramp up production for an international market. Exports of differentiated, manufactured goods with IRS properties often go to countries whose firms produce similar goods, because, as firms specialize in a subset of products to capture increasing returns, each country is limited in the types of products available. There is likely to be a large market for additional product variety, as well as intermediate good inputs.

Consider an example from a classic IRS industry, motor vehicles. When trade in automobiles was liberalized between Canada and the US through the 1965 US–Canada Auto Pact, one of the first moves by Canadian producers was to rationalize plants and cut the number of automobile models they produced in half. By specializing in fewer automobile models, but maintaining output, Canadian manufacturers were able to capture increasing returns to scale and better compete with larger, more efficient US manufacturers.[7] Intra-industry trade between the US and Canada in this example is a result of firm-driven moves to specialize and enhance productivity. In this way, scale economies are a source of specialization, independent of factor endowments or comparative advantage, which induces countries to trade (Krugman 1990; Helpman 2011).

A second, though related, source of intra-industry trade is product differentiation. As discussed above, the variety of products available in one industry in a country will be limited by the gains firms can achieve by creating economies of scale in a smaller set of products. This country then has a consumer-driven incentive to trade for different goods in the same industry. For example, pharmaceutical companies invest heavily in the production of certain drugs and cannot produce a full range of drugs. Heavy investment in a subset of drugs leads to intra-industry trade with other countries whose pharmaceutical firms produce another subset of drugs. In order for consumers in one country to have access to a full range of pharmaceuticals, countries must engage in intra-industry trade with other pharmaceutical-producing countries. Thus, IIT is also driven by consumer preferences for a variety of products within the same industry (Helpman 2011). In a globalized economy, manufacturers seek to differentiate their products not only from those produced by other domestic manufacturers, but from goods produced by manufacturers around the world. As a result, in each country there is a limited product variety, but there is demand for all the different brands produced in the world economy. With greater product variety, prices fall as well, which is an added consumer benefit of trade in similar goods.[8]

In sum, increasing returns to scale, consumer love of variety and lower prices under expanded competition are all drivers of intra-industry trade among countries with similar technologies and factor endowments. Economies of scale create barriers to entry, which means a limited array of goods will be produced in each country. Thus, trade will increase the variety of differentiated but similar products. These products will come from countries with similar factor proportions. It is important to emphasize that models of intra-industry trade are complementary to classic trade models, rather than competing.[9] Comparative advantage explains *inter*-industry specialization and *inter*-industry trade: it explains why Germany specializes in high-tech manufactures while Argentina specializes in beef production, and it explains why these countries trade with each other for these goods. Increasing returns to scale, however, explain *intra*-industry specialization: they explain why German firms specialize in a subset of manufactures, such as luxury sedans, and seek to export these products. Consumers in countries whose firms make a similarly limited range of products will demand access to additional foreign varieties. In short, new trade theories explain trade between similar countries, while classic trade theories explain trade between different countries.

DISTRIBUTIONAL EFFECTS OF INTRA-INDUSTRY TRADE

The formation of new trade models to explain intra-industry trade was a major theoretical development in economics, but why does it matter to the political scientist? Krugman argues that theorizing about intra-industry trade is interesting to political economists because it is, in his words, "surprisingly non-disruptive" relative to endowments-based trade (2009: 339). As I will discuss in this section, intra-industry trade is politically important because it gives rise to different distributional, and hence political, implications than the standard trade models.

A primary argument from early contributions to new trade theory is that the economic adjustment costs of intra-industry trade are lower than for inter-industry, endowments-based trade. The argument is that IIT is generally welfare-enhancing and less redistributive within the economy, as it provides greater product variety and lower prices to consumers and allows firms market access both at home and abroad. The benefits to consumers are clear, but workers and industry face lower adjustment costs with intra-industry trade for one key reason: this trade most often takes place between countries with similar factor endowments and similar skills and technology profiles. Similarity between trading countries is key. If trade is not based on factor scarcity and abundance, it does not result in decreasing demand for scarce factors and heightened demand for abundant factors. When two trading countries are similar, scarce factors are scarce in both countries, and trade liberalization will not cause declining demand for this factor and the demise of industries that use scarce factors intensively.[10] Even if the scarce factor does incur losses via trade liberalization, Bernard et al. (2007) show that this decline will be less than in a Stolper–Samuelson setting. Part of the reason for this is that both scarce and abundant factors will be better off owing to the gains from a wider variety of goods (Krugman 1981).

The rise in intra-industry trade among OECD countries in recent decades has often been cited as a major factor in the smoothness of market liberalization among these countries in the postwar period (notably in Krugman 1981; Lipson 1982). It has also been cited as an explanation for why trade liberalization with Japan has been so much more controversial in the US than trade liberalization with other OECD states (Gawande and Hansen 1999). US trade with Japan is primarily inter-industry, while US trade with other wealthy countries, such as Canada, is much more intra-industry. For example, the US receives more automobile imports from Canada ($32 billion) than from Japan ($27 billion), but the US exports many more cars to Canada ($22 billion) than it does to Japan ($380 million).[11] Greater similarity between the US and Canada might also explain the relative ease of negotiating the US–Canada Free Trade Agreement, while the significant factor differences between the US and Mexico contributed to the highly contentious nature of the North American Free Trade Agreement. The political difficulties in liberalizing North–South trade, as evidenced not only by conflicts over NAFTA but also in World Trade Organization nego-tiations such as the ongoing Doha Round, are a key corollary to claims about IIT. Because North–South trade is predominately inter-industry and endowments-based, this trade should be more politically difficult to liberalize, and this appears to have been largely the case in the postwar era.

While the earlier wave of new trade theory emphasized the harmonious effects of intra-industry trade, the newest research on intra-industry trade finds that it actually has significant distributional effects, but these effects are *within* industries, rather than across industries. In a significant depar-ture from older "new trade" models, the newest trade models (sometimes referred to, clumsily, as the "new new trade theory") account for firm heterogeneity, rather than assuming that all firms within an industry have monolithic preferences and production behaviors. Melitz (2003) introduces firm-level productivity differences into trade models based on monopo-listic competition and increasing returns. He argues that firms within an industry vary in terms of their productivity levels, and exposure to trade causes only the most productive firms to self-select into export markets. At the same time, the least productive firms within the industry are forced to exit. Intra-industry trade, then, is a process that reallocates resources, and profits, away from less productive firms and to the most productive firms in an industry, the firms that are willing to undertake the significant entry costs into export markets. Melitz's model provides a theoretical basis for long-standing empirical observations about the gains that large firms reap from trade, while many other firms within the same industry, the "mom-and-pop stores," are forced to downsize or shut their doors entirely. Despite the significant losses incurred by less productive firms, the indus-try as a whole gains from trade owing to the reallocation of resources to the most productive firms. The economy as a whole receives net gains as well (Trefler 2004; Bernard et al. 2007).

Far from being harmonious, then, intra-industry trade has winners and losers. To find these winners and losers, we must look within industries at the individual firm level, something the older trade models did not do, and were unable to do without firm-level data, which has only become available in recent years. There are significant adjustment costs associ-ated with intra-industry trade, as less productive firms suffer losses of profit and market share, with important implications for trade politics. First, although exporters are often high-profile firms, the vast majority of firms do not export. Exporting is, in fact, a rare firm behavior even in net exporting industries (Melitz 2003; Kasahara and Lapham 2013). Intra-industry reallocations toward exporters mean significant short-term losses for the large number of workers in domestic-oriented firms. Second, intra-industry trade contributes to higher overall wages, but also higher wage inequality (Redding 2011). Larger firms tend to pay higher wages, as do exporting firms. Thus, trade-generated reallocation of resources to the most productive firms in an industry raises wages, but only in these leading firms. In the words of Amiti and Davis, "liberalization . . . raises wages for workers at firms which are most globalized and lowers wages at firms oriented to the domestic economy or which are marginal globalizers" (2011: 2). However, others argue that the reduced prices for consumer goods may be enough to raise the real wage of workers in less productive, non-exporting firms as well (Bernard et al. 2007).

This is the interesting aspect of intra-industry trade for political economists studying trade policy: it does not have the same distributional consequences that endowments-based trade does. As a whole, intra-industry trade enhances the welfare of the economy by increasing the size of the market, reallocating productive factors toward the most productive firms, raising wages in the most productive firms, and providing greater product variety for consumers. However, it increases competition among producers and can therefore drive less competitive firms to exit. Smaller firms that do not export, and their workers, are likely to be the primary losers of intra-industry trade.

INTRA-INDUSTRY TRADE AND TRADE PREFERENCES

Based on what we know about the economic basis of intra-industry trade, as well as its economic effects, we can deduce some expectations about preferences over trade openness in industries subject to intra-industry trade.

Consumers and Classes

First, we expect consumers to prefer open trade because of the gains they reap from enlarged markets, increased product varieties, and lower prices for consumer goods. Additionally, Krugman (1981) argues that, at least in the long term, any negative wage effects of trade will be offset by the gains from the larger market, and, as the market size grows and two-way trade grows, negative wage effects will decline.

In terms of broad factor-owning classes, it is difficult to form unified class-based preferences in countries with high levels of intra-industry trade. This is true for a few reasons. First, the formation of class-based preferences is based on factor scarcity and abundance. I have already established that intra-industry trade's factor-level effects are muted, because this trade is not rooted in comparative advantage and it occurs most frequently between countries with similar factor endowment profiles. Without income reallocation from scarce to abundant factors (Stolper–Samuelson effects), there is no basis for the formation of shared preferences across all workers or all industrialists. Second, in the economy as a whole, Ricardo–Viner effects are already more likely to hold than Stolper–Samuelson effects. As was theorized in the trade literature and demonstrated empirically by Hiscox (2002), when factor mobility is low, workers' fortunes are closely tied to the fortunes of the particular industries in which they work, and their preferences will align with those of their employers. With low factor mobility it is costly for workers to find employment in a different industry if their industry experiences trade losses and layoffs. In the developed economies, factor specificity and capital-intensive production have already made it unlikely that entire classes will hold unified trade preferences. High levels of economic development, as well as highly specific capital and skill investments, are key factors undermining unified class-based preferences in developed economies. This is true whether or not there are high levels of intra-industry trade, either at the country level or in particular sectors.

Industries

Industries will not hold unified preferences either, which is a departure from the expectations of the Ricardo–Viner model. Trade liberalization in IIT industries may benefit industries as a whole, but adjustment costs fall on individual firms. Depending on each firm's anticipated profits or losses from trade liberalization, firms within the same industry have different preferences over trade. Most generally, firms will prefer trade liberalization when they anticipate that their profits will be greater after liberalization than before, and they will prefer protection when they anticipate a loss of profits. Thus, in forming their preferences over trade, firms must weigh their expected gains from sales in foreign markets against the losses they will incur from increased import competition at home. This divides industry preferences across exporting firms and domestic-oriented firms that do not export and face losses from increased import competition.

With high factor specificity, workers are likely to have industry-specific skills that tie their preferences to those of their employers. Workers and firm owners will either jointly benefit from trade or suffer short-term and possibly significant losses. Because IIT leads to an intra-industry reallocation of resources away from small firms and toward the large exporting firms, trade liberalization creates winners and losers *within* industries. This means that trade preferences are formed at the firm level, not the industry level.

Exporting Firms

We can make assumptions about intra-industry trade's effects on preferences when we look at the heterogeneous nature of firms within industries. Specifically, exporting firms in IIT industries are likely to be winners from trade liberalization, while domestic-oriented firms are likely to be trade losers. Within manufacturing industries in developed countries, only a minority of firms are exporters, or expect to be exporters, after securing less costly foreign market access through a trade agreement. These firms will prefer liberalization when they expect the gains from expanding foreign market access will outweigh the increased import competition they will face in the domestic market. Exporters in IIT industries have an additional rationale for supporting domestic tariff cuts, and that is that these firms are likely to be importers as well. Domestic tariff cuts may help them reduce input costs.[12]

It is important to note that these expectations about exporter preferences for liberalization depend on a reciprocity-based trade liberalization regime, in which tariff rates are negotiated in the context of bilateral or multilateral trade agreements. In other words, a reduction of tariffs in country *a* is contingent upon a reduction of tariffs in country *b*. This is, in fact, the context in which tariff reductions are most often negotiated, whether in multilateral contexts such as WTO negotiation rounds, regional trade agreements such as NAFTA, or bilateral trade agreements.

When might exporters oppose trade openness? Simply, they will oppose openness when their gains from increased export opportunities are outweighed by the greater import competition in the domestic market. This might be the case in a few instances. First, exporters might oppose liberalization in industries where products are not sufficiently differentiated. In these industries, even small differences in factor prices across countries can lead to significant industry losses in the country in which factor prices are higher, even slightly so. For example, US and Canadian softwood lumber is not very differentiable. Trade liberalization in this industry between these two countries could lead to substantial losses in the country with relatively higher production costs, even when this difference is very small. This is supported empirically by the fact that US logging companies were one of the very few industries that opposed tariff cuts under the Canada–US Free Trade Agreement. Contrast this with trade in differentiated products. When products are sufficiently differentiated, some consumers will be willing to pay slightly higher prices for their preferred product variety; thus firms with higher production costs can remain competitive both in export markets and domestically. This is the case, for example, for luxury goods such as fine watches and luxury sedans.

Furthermore, with regard to intra-industry trade, for those industries producing sophisticated manufactures, exporters also tend to be importers. Even if an exporter does not expect that export gains will outweigh the costs of import competition, this exporter may still enjoy net profit gains after liberalization owing to cheaper imported inputs. In sum, although exporters may not always support trade liberalization, the economics of intra-industry trade suggests that exporters in IIT industries are likely to support liberalization, as these industries tend to enjoy increasing returns to scale, differentiated products, and trading partners that often have similar endowments and/or levels of development.

Domestic-Oriented Firms

While exporters generally stand to gain from trade liberalization in IIT industries, non-exporters expect trade losses. Even though in the long term the industry as a whole will gain from trade, as established by Melitz (2003), reduced protection will cause non-exporting firms to lose market share, or they may be forced to make costly adjustments to their product offerings, or even go out of business. It is likely that these domestic-oriented firms and their workers will have protectionist preferences. Since they do not export, they do not gain from reciprocal tariff cuts in foreign markets, and the increased import competition they face post-liberalization is not offset by higher export sales. These non-exporting firms are also less likely to import, as importing also involves considerable entry costs. Only the biggest, most productive firms are likely to import intermediate goods. Thus, in the short term, import competition will exert pressure on non-exporters to contract wages and/or employment, reduce their market share, and put downward pressure on prices. Many firms will exit the industry entirely. These short-term costs mean that both workers and owners in domestic-oriented firms are likely to have a strong preference for trade protection.[13]

POLITICAL COALITIONS, FIRM LOBBYING AND TRADE POLICY

Given these preferences about intra-industry trade, when will societal actors mobilize to influence trade policy, and what form will coalitions take? Although preferences over trade depend on a cost–benefit analysis of trade-related gains and losses, not all losing individuals or groups will undertake costly political action to demand protection. Because the distributional effects of intra-industry trade are located at the firm rather than the industry level, the rise of intra-industry trade has significant conse-quences for coalition formation and the degree to which industry-based coalitions will be politically active.

First, as discussed above, larger, more productive, exporting firms are likely to prefer trade liberalization, while smaller, less productive firms that do not export, or export very little, will be negatively affected by import competition. This heterogeneity in firm preferences will have the effect of weakening industry consensus over trade, and it will make it more difficult for industry-wide trade associations to secure broad support from firms. Firms may revoke membership or contributions if trade associations take an active lobbying stance for a trade position that is counter to their interests. The result of this in terms of trade policy lobbying is that trade associations may take weaker stances on policy to avoid losing members. They may also stop lobbying for particular trade positions altogether, or they may decrease the amount of resources they spend on lobbying over trade legislation. For example, this has been the response of the European Roundtable of Industrialists (ERT), a leading advocacy organization for EU manufacturing firms, to heterogeneous trade policy preferences among its members. While maintaining a general free trade policy stance, ERT does not lobby the EU over specific trade policy legislation. Similarly, lobbying over trade by EURATEX, the leading trade association for European textile and apparel manufacturers, has been limited because of heterogeneous demands from its members (Woll 2006).

As trade coalitions become less active in trade policymaking owing to competing trade preferences among their members, individual firms may become increasingly politically active. As discussed above, exporting and non-exporting firms will be split on their trade preferences, making collec-tive action difficult, at least at the industry level. However, both exporters and domestic-oriented firms have much at stake when trade policies are negotiated. The gains from trade are concentrated on exporters, while the costs are concentrated on domestic-oriented firms. The high stakes and the losses associated with an unfavorable policy outcome give both sides an incentive to participate in political activity. The constraints on coalitional political activity present an opportunity for individual firms to become more active in lobbying over trade policy.

Existing empirical analyses come to different conclusions about the relationship between intra-industry trade and political activity. In an early study on the effects of intra-industry trade on tariffs, Marvel and Ray (1987) argue that intra-industry trade significantly impedes the ability of domestic producers to secure protection of their products. They argue that producers seeking protection must compete politically not only with exporters, but with consumers of intermediate goods who have an interest in liberalization. These consumers are producers as well, and are better organized than consumers of final goods. Marvel and Ray expect that protectionist lobbying will be attenuated by these competing interests, and the result is less lobbying overall in intra-industry trade industries and lower levels of protection. Marvel and Ray test these arguments on US manufacturing industries in 1970 and find supportive evidence that higher intra-industry trade leads to lower protection.

Gilligan (1997a) puts forth a competing argument, arguing that intra-industry trade makes it easier for firms to lobby. Gilligan contends that lobbying becomes, in effect, a private good with excludable benefits. Individual firms are monopolists over their particular product variety, so they have more incentive to lobby for protection of that product. They do not, however, have an incentive to lobby for protection from imports of a different variety of the same product. In other words, firms will no longer form coalitions to lobby for industry-wide protections. As monopolists of their particular product varieties, they have an incentive to lobby only for protection of their own products. Since they face no collective action problems in doing this, protectionist lobbying will actually *increase* under IIT. Gilligan tests this counterintuitive argument with an analysis of firm complaints to the International Trade Commission (ITC), between 1988 and 1992. Gilligan finds that, as he theorized, firms in industries characterized by higher levels of IIT were more likely to lobby the ITC with complaints against foreign rivals.

Kono (2009) develops Gilligan's emphasis on collective action problems in trade policy, while focusing on policy outcomes rather than lobbying behavior. He introduces an important intervening variable by arguing that intra-industry trade is likely to lead to higher protection, but only when electoral institutions privilege small geographic constituencies. When electoral institutions give narrow interests disproportionate influence over politicians, IIT will increase firm incentives to lobby and lead to increased protection. When electoral institutions privilege broader coalitions of voters, intra-industry trade will not lead to increased protection, because firms will have less incentive to undertake costly political action. Kono tests these hypotheses in the US case over time and in a cross-section of OECD states (2005 data). His focus on the role of institutions in policy outcomes is a valuable one. His findings underscore the important and complicated relationship between economic and political variables on policy. As he puts it, "a given economic variable – including but not limited to the degree of intra-industry trade – may weaken a group's interest in a policy outcome but increase its capacity for collective action, or vice-versa" (2009: 886).

CONCLUSION

In conclusion, the distributional effects of intra-industry trade generate a new structure of trade preferences. When trade is endowments-based, classes or sectors are unified in their preferences about trade liberalization. When trade is intra-industry, class and industry consensus is undermined, as the costs of trade fall neither on entire classes, nor on entire industries, but on individual firms, depending on whether or not they export. The large firms that benefit from exports will prefer liberalization, while firms concerned with import competition will prefer protection. The question of which political coalitions and alignments will arise in place of traditional class and sector coalitions is important for contemporary students of trade politics. Thus far, political economists have reached neither theoretical nor empirical consensus about the implications of intra-industry trade for political coalition formation, or for the degree to which firms and coalitions will undertake costly political activity. The approach presented in this chapter suggests that intra-industry trade will make it more likely that firms will lobby individually over trade policy, rather than in the context of industry-based associations, and much of this lobbying will be in favor of liberalization. Nevertheless, the outcome of political contests among firms within the same industry remains an open question.

Finally, it must be said that no discussion of protection is complete without a consideration of some of the institutional factors involved in the provision of trade policy. It is for this reason that I have focused most of this analysis on the structure of political coalitions and trade policy lobbying – the demand side of trade policy – rather than policy output. One complication in bringing institutions into this analysis, and a fascinating one which is ripe for study, is that the new trade lobbying landscape in countries with high levels of intra-industry trade changes the societal "inputs" into the policymaking process. We cannot simply map existing institutional models of trade policy, which are likely to assume that policymakers are interacting with either broad class-based or sector-based coalitions, onto studies of protection in countries with high intra-industry trade. If coalitions are less likely to form and individual firms are to become more powerful lobbying actors, institutional models may need to be reworked to address the greater particularism in societal demands over trade policy.

NOTES

1. For example, see arguments by Gilligan (1997a, 1997b); Gibson (2000); Hiscox (2002); and De Bièvre and Dür (2005).

2. For in-depth analyses of the dynamics and composition of trade coalitions in the US and other developed economies, see Rogowski (1989); Hiscox (2002); and Chase (2009). For a discussion of trade politics in the EU, see Woll (2006); Dür (2008); and Greenwood (2011).
3. For Ricardo, the basis of comparative advantage lay in the amount of labor required to produce a good. His labor theory of value held that countries would specialize in the production of the goods that required the least amount of labor inputs relative to other goods.
4. His theory failed to explain why scarce US labor remained largely free-trading until the 1970s. He can't explain growing protectionism in the postwar period among trade unions and labor parties in labor-rich Europe. And finally his theory cannot make sense of what some see as growing protectionism among US capitalists since the mid-1970s (Midford 1993).
5. In the present analysis, I focus on the demand side of trade policymaking. I neglect the role of political and policymaking institutions almost entirely. This should not be taken as an indication that I think institutions do not matter. In fact I believe they are central to understanding trade policy outcomes and especially variation in trade policy across countries. However, I limit my task here to a consideration of the implications of intra-industry trade for societal trade preferences and trade policy demands.
6. Paul Krugman received the Nobel Prize in Economics in 2008 for his pioneering contributions to new trade theory.
7. See Trefler (2004) for an in-depth discussion. Another example is Boeing, which increasingly outsources the manufacture of aircraft parts to China, even though final assembly and additional part manufacture remain in the US. By specializing in the production of fewer intermediate parts and trading for the rest, Boeing captures increasing returns to scale.
8. As Helpman and Krugman (1985) argue, if all countries produced homogeneous products, then intra-industry trade would be zero and trade volumes would be better explained by differences in factor endowments. When there are differentiated products, however, intra-industry trade increases. As factor similarity across countries increases, intra-industry trade will increase at the expense of trade in homogeneous products. In the OECD countries, where the capital–labor ratio is similar relative to other countries, intra-industry trade of differentiated products should be higher, and the data confirm this. Helpman (1987) sampled 14 OECD countries and found that the share of intra-industry trade was larger in time periods when factor endowments were more similar. He argues: "differences in factor proportions are less important and intra-industry specialization is more important for trade between rich countries" (2011: 87).
9. This was formally modeled by Helpman and Krugman (1985).
10. Under inter-industry trade, resources are redistributed from scarce factors to abundant factors (or from industries using scarce factors to industries using abundant factors) as trade liberalization makes scarce factors less competitive.
11. 2010 trade data from the US Commerce Department.
12. Firms in IIT industries are more likely to import intermediate goods than firms in low-IIT industries. This is because the industries most subject to IIT are industries with highly differentiated products and increasing returns to scale. As products become less capital-intensive, firms tend to import fewer intermediate goods (Bernard et al. 2007).
13. While it would initially seem that exporters and non-exporters would hold competing preferences when trade is more endowments-based as well, this isn't the case. Though the Stolper–Samuelson and Ricardo–Viner models don't address firm heterogeneity, we would expect that in comparative advantage industries with homogeneous goods (such as agriculture, in land-abundant countries) exporters will strongly prefer liberalization and non-exporters will be indifferent. Because of comparative advantage, no firm within the industry will be significantly threatened by foreign imports, which would be higher-priced. Without product differentiation, consumers will have no reason to prefer high-priced foreign imports. In comparative disadvantage industries, on the other hand, industries as a whole will prefer protection.

REFERENCES

Alt, J.E., J. Frieden, M.J. Gilligan, D. Rodrik and R. Rogowski (1996), "The Political Economy of International Trade," *Comparative Political Studies*, **29** (6), 689.

Alt, James E., F. Carlsen, P. Heum and K. Johansen (1999), "Asset Specificity and the Political Behavior of Firms: Lobbying for Subsidies in Norway," *International Organization*, **53** (1), 99–116.

Amiti, M. and D.R. Davis (2011), "Trade, Firms and Wages: Theory and Evidence," *Review of Economic Studies*, **79** (1), 1–36.

Baldwin, R.E. and P. Martin (1999), *Two Waves of Globalisation: Superficial Similarities, Fundamental Differences*, NBER Working Paper Series No. 6904, Cambridge, MA: National Bureau of Economic Research.

Beaulieu, E. (2002), "Factor or Industry Cleavages in Trade Policy? An Empirical Analysis of the Stolper–Samuelson Theorem," *Economics and Politics*, **14** (2), 99–131.

Bernard, A.B., S.J. Redding and P.K. Schott (2007), "Comparative Advantage and Heterogeneous Firms," *Review of Economic Studies*, **74** (1), 31–66.

Brawley, M.R. (1997), "Factoral or Sectoral Conflict? Partially Mobile Factors and the Politics of Trade in Imperial Germany," *International Studies Quarterly*, **41** (4), 633–54.

Brülhart, M. (2009), "An Account of Global Intraindustry Trade, 1961–2006," *World Economy*, **32** (3), 401–59.

Chase, K.A. (2009), *Trading Blocs*, Ann Arbor: University of Michigan Press.

De Bièvre, D. and A. Dür (2005), "Constituency Interests and Delegation in European and American Trade Policy," *Comparative Political Studies*, **38** (10), 1271–96.

Dixit, A. and V. Norman (1980), *Theory of International Trade*, Cambridge: Cambridge University Press.

Dür, A. (2008), "Bringing Economic Interests Back into the Study of EU Trade Policy-Making," *British Journal of Politics and International Relations*, **10** (1), 27–45.

Frieden, J.A. (1992), *Debt, Development, and Democracy: Modern Political Economy and Latin America, 1965–1985*, Princeton, NJ: Princeton University Press.

Garst, W.D. (1998), "From Factor Endowments to Class Struggle," *Comparative Political Studies*, **31** (1), 22–44.

Garst, W.D. (1999), "From Sectoral Linkages to Class Conflict," *Comparative Political Studies*, **32** (7), 788–809.

Gawande, K. and W.L. Hansen (1999), "Retaliation, Bargaining, and the Pursuit of 'Free and Fair' Trade," *International Organization*, **53** (1), 117–59.

Gibson, M.L. (2000), *Conflict amid Consensus in American Trade Policy*, Washington, DC: Georgetown University Press.

Gilligan, M.J. (1997a), "Lobbying as a Private Good with Intra-Industry Trade," *International Studies Quarterly*, **41** (3), 455–74.

Gilligan, M.J. (1997b), *Empowering Exporters: Reciprocity, Delegation, and Collective Action in American Trade Policy*, Ann Arbor: University of Michigan Press.

Greenwood, J. (2011), *Interest Representation in the European Union*, Basingstoke, UK: Palgrave Macmillan.

Helpman, E. (1981), "International Trade in the Presence of Product Differentiation, Economies of Scale and Monopolistic Competition: A Chamberlin–Heckscher–Ohlin Approach," *Journal of International Economics*, **11** (3), 305–40.

Helpman, E. (1987), "Imperfect Competition and International Trade: Evidence from Fourteen Industrial Countries," *Journal of the Japanese and International Economies*, **1** (1), 62–81.

Helpman, E. (2011), *Understanding Global Trade*, Cambridge, MA: Harvard University Press.

Helpman, E. and P.R. Krugman (1985), *Market Structure and Foreign Trade: Increasing Returns, Imperfect Competition, and the International Economy*, Cambridge, MA: MIT Press.

Hiscox, M.J. (2002), *International Trade and Political Conflict: Commerce, Coalitions, and Mobility*, Princeton, NJ: Princeton University Press.

Jeong, G.-H. (2009), "Constituent Influence on International Trade Policy in the United States, 1987–2006," *International Studies Quarterly*, **53** (2), 519–40.

Kasahara, H. and B. Lapham (2013), "Productivity and the Decision to Import and Export: Theory and Evidence," *Journal of International Economics*, **89** (2), 297–316.

Kono, D.Y. (2009), "Market Structure, Electoral Institutions, and Trade Policy," *International Studies Quarterly*, **53** (4), 885–906.

Krugman, P.R. (1981), "Intraindustry Specialization and the Gains from Trade," *Journal of Political Economy*, **89** (5), 959–73.

Krugman, P.R. (1990), *Rethinking International Trade*, Cambridge, MA: MIT Press.

Krugman, P.R. (1995), "Growing World Trade: Causes and Consequences," *Brookings Papers on Economic Activity*, Spring, 327–77.

Krugman, P.R. (2009), "Prize Lecture: The Increasing Returns Revolution in Trade and Geography," in K. Grandin (ed.), *Les Prix Nobel*, Stockholm: Nobel Foundation, pp. 335–48.

Ladewig, J.W. (2006), "Domestic Influences on International Trade Policy: Factor Mobility in the United States, 1963 to 1992," *International Organization*, **60** (1), 69–103.

Lipson, C. (1982), "The Transformation of Trade: The Sources and Effects of Regime Change," *International Organization*, **36** (02), 417–55.

Marvel, H.P. and E.J. Ray (1987), "Intraindustry Trade: Sources and Effects on Protection," *Journal of Political Economy*, **95** (6), 1278–91.

Melitz, M.J. (2003), "The Impact of Trade on Intra-Industry Reallocations and Aggregate Industry Productivity," *Econometrica*, **71** (6), 1695–1725.

Midford, P. (1993), "International Trade and Domestic Politics: Improving on Rogowski's Model of Political Alignments," *International Organization*, **47** (04), 535–64.

O'Rourke, K.H. (2003), *Heckscher–Ohlin Theory and Individual Attitudes towards Globalization*, Cambridge, MA: National Bureau of Economic Research.

OECD (2002), *OECD Economic Outlook*, Vol. 71, Paris: OECD, pp. 159–70.

Redding, S.J. (2011), "Theories of Heterogeneous Firms and Trade," *Annual Review of Economics*, **3** (1), 77–105.

Ricardo, D. (1817), *The Principles of Political Economy and Taxation*, London: Everyman's Library.

Rogowski, R. (1989), *Commerce and Coalitions*, Princeton, NJ: Princeton University Press.

Ruffin, Roy J. (1999), "The Nature and Significance of Intra-Industry Trade," *Economic and Financial Policy Review*, 4th Quarter, 2–9.

Scheve, K.F. and M.J. Slaughter (2001), "What Determines Individual Trade-Policy Preferences?," *Journal of International Economics*, **54** (2), 267–92.

Trefler, D. (2004), The Long and Short of the Canada–U.S. Free Trade Agreement," *American Economic Review*, **94** (4), 870–95.

Woll, D.C. (2006), "Lobbying in the European Union: From Sui Generis to a Comparative Perspective," *Journal of European Public Policy*, **13** (3), 456–69.

World Bank (2009), *World Development Report*, Washington, DC: World Bank.

6. From "investor rights" to "sustainable development"? Challenges and innovations in international investment rules
Lyuba Zarsky

Since the 1992 Earth Summit, sustainable development has emerged as the guiding vision – at least rhetorically – for global economic governance. Stated as a central objective in the founding document of the World Trade Organization, sustainable development implies a trajectory that integrates improvements in human well-being and social equity with reductions in environmental risks and scarcities. In simple terms, it points toward a "green economy" that is "low carbon, resource efficient and socially inclusive" (UNEP 2011: 1).

Investment, both domestic and foreign, is crucial in moving from envisioning to implementing pathways to sustainable development. In the energy sector alone, the International Energy Agency estimates that an additional $750 billion to $1.6 trillion per year to 2030 and $1.6 trillion per year between 2030 and 2050 will be needed to halve global carbon emissions by 2050 (IEA 2010). UNEP estimates that $1.3 trillion per year is needed to halve carbon emissions as well as to achieve the Millennium Development Goals by 2050 (UNEP 2011).

Mobilizing private capital towards climate mitigation and, more generally, sustainable development requires domestic and international policies that enable investors to embed public purpose in the search for private return – that is, to "embed sustainability" in business strategy and management (Laszlo and Zhexambayeva 2011). Originating in the 1960s, current international investment rules have a much narrower aim, namely to protect the property rights of foreign investors in host countries. Missing in investment agreements are specified investor obligations to promote sustainable development through good environmental and social performance, as well as rights for host countries to regulate towards sustainable development.

In recent years, growing host country dissatisfaction with the current investment regime, as well as NGO activism in changing global business norms, has prompted innovation in investment agreements and calls for a new, more balanced international investment paradigm based on sustainable development.

This chapter analyzes the obstacles to sustainable development posed by current international investment rules. It first considers the potential role of foreign investment in promoting sustainable development, especially in developing countries, and describes the current international investment regime. It then analyzes three obstacles posed by investment rules to sustainable development: 1) lack of national policy space for development; 2) lack of specified investor environmental and social obligations; and 3) "regulatory chill" stemming from investor–state dispute resolution mechanisms. Next, the chapter examines innovations in global sustainability business norms that could go some way to overcoming these obstacles. The chapter concludes with models for "next-generation" investment governance based on the principle of sustainable development.

FDI AND SUSTAINABLE DEVELOPMENT

A sustainable development trajectory implies integrated progress along three axes:

1. *economic*: the deepening and broadening of productive capacities which generate economic growth and livelihoods, including technology, infrastructure, knowledge and skills;
2. *social*: improvement in social resilience and equity, including by increasing the income and quality of life of the poor;
3. *environmental*: reduction in environmental scarcities and risks.

Foreign direct investment (FDI) – investment by a foreign company, typically a large multinational, in a domestic company – offers potential benefits in each dimension. On the economic axis, greenfield FDI increases national income, including via capital inflow, employment, local procurement, royalties and taxes. More importantly, multinationals can transfer state-of-the-art technology and management systems which can generate productivity-enhancing knowledge and technology spillovers to domestic companies, including supplier firms. On the social axis, FDI can generate local employment, including for less skilled and unskilled workers, and companies can provide "social investment" in hospitals, schools, roads and so on in the communities in which they operate. On the environmental axis, foreign companies may disseminate newer, cleaner technology to local firms, as well as more stringent environmental management systems that reduce environmental risk.

The capture of potential sustainable development benefits from foreign investment by host states, however, is far from automatic. A large number of studies have found patterns of poor environmental and social practice by foreign companies, especially in mining, oil and gas, agriculture, forestry and other resource-intensive sectors. As a result, large-scale FDI projects in extractive industries have been found to increase environmental risk as well as violate human rights, while generating few lasting social or economic benefits to host states and local communities (Ajakaiye et al. 2011; Gauthier and Zeufack 2011; Blackmore et al. 2013; Zarsky and Stanley 2013). The empirical evidence that extractive industries fail to generate sustained economic growth is so pronounced that it has been dubbed a "resource curse" (Frankel 2010).

One of the most important potential benefits of FDI for developing countries is the capture of spillovers that can spur productivity growth and industrial transformation. Spillovers are positive externalities that "leak" from a multinational corporation (MNC) in a number of ways: the transfer of blueprints or other intellectual property to a domestic affiliate or joint venture partner; workers' acquisition of knowledge and skills that can be applied in a domestic company or their own start-ups; and local procurements, by which foreign firms can raise the quality standards and productivity of local supplier firms (Gallagher and Zarsky 2007). Spillovers for economic growth are also stimulated when foreign investment "crowds in" domestic investment by increasing demand for and raising the productivity of locally produced goods and services.

Evidence that foreign investment generates spillovers in developing countries is mixed. In a landmark study, Peter Evans (1995) compared the role of foreign investment in spurring growth in the electronics industries of three emerging economies – Brazil, Korea and India – and found three different outcomes. The primary difference stemmed from government requirements for accountability and performance by foreign investors. In a review of 11 empirical studies, Gallagher and Zarsky (2005) report that four studies found positive evidence for spillovers, two found none, and five studies found that "it depends" on exogenous variables, most notably the policy environment. Amsden and Chu (2003) found that proactive government policies were central in capturing benefits for industrial development from foreign investment in Taiwan. Moran (1998), however, found that spillovers occur when a liberal policy framework encourages the integration of local firms into MNC global sourcing and production networks. Agosin and Machado (2007), on the other hand, found that in the 1990s foreign investment "crowded out" domestic investment in Latin America, which had liberal investment policies, while it "crowded in" domestic investment in Asia, where investment policies were selective and performance-based.

Historically, OECD countries have accounted for the lion's share of FDI, in terms of both capital export and destination. In 2012, however, developing countries for the first time absorbed the majority (52 percent) of global FDI (UNCTAD 2013). Whether in extractive, manufacturing or services industries, however, the magnitude of FDI tells little about progress towards sustainable development. Rather than quantity, it is the quality of FDI that matters.

Whether or not foreign investment generates benefits for sustainable development largely depends on the institutions, norms and policies of host states: regulatory policies which reduce environmental risk and protect human rights; and investment and industry policies which promote productivity growth and innovation. In many developing countries, the institutions of environmental and social governance are weak and evolving. Moreover, international investment agreements condition and constrain both the regulatory and the industry policy space of host states.

THE INTERNATIONAL "INVESTOR RIGHTS" INVESTMENT REGIME

The legal framework governing international investment is a complex web of regional and bilateral investment agreements, free trade agreements with investment provisions, and economic partnership agreements (UNCTAD 2012b).

At the global level, efforts to negotiate investment rules at the WTO in the 1990s failed, largely owing to resistance by developing countries. However, investment provisions were incorporated in two WTO agreements, namely the Global Agreement on Trade in Services (GATS) and the Trade-Related Investment Measures agreement (TRIMS), both of which aimed to align investment with the WTO's "free trade" orientation. GATS requires states to list sectors for which they made liberalization commitments, while TRIMS restricts states from imposing development-oriented performance requirements, such as domestic content, local purchasing or joint venture (Mann 2013).

The WTO's failure to develop broad-based international rules in the context of burgeoning globalization led to an explosion of bilateral investment treaties (BITs). In 1990, there were some 450 signed investment treaties; by 2010, there were 3100 (UNCTAD 2012b). Investment rules are also contained in regional agreements, such as the North American Free Trade Agreement (NAFTA), as well as sectoral trade agreements such as the Energy Charter Treaty. With members primarily in Europe and Asia, as well as Australia, the Energy Charter covers all aspects of commercial energy activities including trade, transit, and energy efficiency, as well as investment.

Investment rules in all investment agreements aim to protect the property rights of foreign investors vis-à-vis host government actions and policies. Rights fall into two broad categories: pre-establishment, including the right to be treated the same as domestic and other foreign investors (national treatment and non-discrimination); and post-establishment, including protections from expropriation without compensation and broad guarantees of "fair and equitable" treatment. Moreover, bilateral and regional agreements generally follow TRIMS in prohibiting host countries from imposing performance requirements on foreign investors. In the event of a dispute, they give foreign investors the right to sue nation-states for compensation in an international court of arbitration – a right not available to domestic investors (Office of the US Trade Representative 2013).

The right to investor–state dispute settlement (ISDS) first emerged in 1994 in NAFTA's Chapter 11. Prior to NAFTA, dispute resolution was undertaken only on a state-to-state basis: foreign investors needed to engage their home country governments to take up their concerns with host country governments. With Chapter 11, investors in the three North American states were given the right to directly sue host country governments in international courts of arbitration for rights violations, most notably for actions that were "tantamount to expropriation" (Cosbey 2005).

The "tantamount to expropriation" provision triggered a torrent of suits charging that post-establishment changes in environmental and health regulations that had negative monetary impacts constituted expropriation. In one of the first cases, a US company, Metalclad Corporation, sued Mexico after it was denied the ability to establish a hazardous waste processing facility owing to a decree that created a nature reserve to protect a rare cactus species on the land sited for the facility. The tribunal ruled that Mexico's motivation or intent for the decree was irrelevant and found that Metalclad had been expropriated (Cosbey 2005).

The primary vehicle for international arbitration is the World Bank's International Center for the Settlement of Investment Disputes (ICSID). Some investment agreements specify ICSID as the court of arbitration, or one of several. NAFTA, for example, specifies that investors can bring cases in ICSID, the ICSID Additional Facility or the UN Center for International Trade Law (UNCITRAL). More commonly, however, BITs simply state that, in the event of a dispute, an arbitration panel will be established. These panels typically consist of three members, one appointed by each party and a third neutral member jointly appointed by both parties.

Since NAFTA, investor–state dispute resolution has become a standard feature of BITs. Not surprisingly, the number of investment arbitration cases has grown in tandem with the explosion of investor–state dispute resolution provisions in BITs. In 1996, 38 arbitration cases were registered at ICSID, increasing to 450 in 2011 (Eberhardt and Olivet 2012).

Unlike national courts, which are subject to rules of transparency and independence, international arbitration cases take place in shadowy spaces outside the parameters of international or national governance. Except for ICSID, which is required to make cases and rulings public, arbitration panels have no requirements for transparency or accountability. Moreover, they are not bound by precedent or subject to rules of fairness and independence. A small group of lawyers, many from only three legal firms, have acted as both arbitrators and counsel in the majority of known cases. According to a report by the Transnational Institute, only 15 arbitrators – some of whom have served on the boards of companies bringing suits – have decided 55 percent of all known investment-treaty disputes (Eberhardt and Olivet 2012).

OBSTACLES TO SUSTAINABLE DEVELOPMENT

Designed to protect the property rights of foreign investors, the current investment regime poses three obstacles to sustainable development.

First, strictures against "performance requirements" constrain the policy space needed by host countries to harness foreign investment to broad development goals, including economic growth, jobs, and enterprise growth. Proactive "first-generation" industry policies such as joint venture, export requirements, import controls, domestic content and targeted credit were central in the industrial emergence of the "four East Asian tigers" (Korea, Taiwan, Singapore, Hong Kong) in the 1980s and 1990s – before TRIMs – and in China since the 1990s (Studwell 2013; Szirmai et al. 2013). East Asian and other economies have also successfully utilized "second-generation" industry policies that aim broadly to overcome market failures, such as investment in industrial parks and research incubators and restrictions on speculative investment, both domestic and foreign (Stiglitz 2005).

With the exception of Brazil, Latin American countries have eschewed proactive industry policies in the embrace of investment liberalization – and experienced lower economic growth and greater dependence on primary resource extraction than East Asia (Chudnovsky and Lopez

2010). Lacking "linkage" policies, foreign investment in Costa Rica and Mexico failed to stimulate industrial deepening in high-tech sectors, instead creating "enclave economies" disconnected from the wider local economy (Gallagher and Zarsky 2007; Cordero and Paus 2010).

Proactive industry policies are also important in linking foreign investment to specific and increasingly urgent sustainability goals such as mitigating carbon emissions and increasing the climate resilience of the poor (Zarsky 2010). Climate-friendly industry policy aims to "shift production and consumption patterns towards the use of those primary commodities, means of production, and consumer goods that place a lower burden on the earth's atmosphere than the current GHG [greenhouse gas] intensive ones" (UNCTAD 2009: xiii). Linking climate change mitigation policies with traditional development goals, argues UNCTAD, "requires industrial policies that foster the creation of capabilities to produce or participate in the production of such goods and their subsequent upgrading" (UNCTAD 2009: xv).

There is ample evidence that proactive industry policies can be effective in promoting climate-friendly industrial growth. Rock and Angel (2005) show that proactive industry policies in East Asia are enabling a "sustainability transition." China's industry support policies propelled its emergence as a leader in solar photovoltaic and wind technology, as well as "clean coal" technologies such as direct coal liquefaction (UN-DESA 2009). Brazil's support for the development and deployment of a domestic sugar-based ethanol industry allowed it to capture a vibrant export market in the burgeoning global bio-fuels sector (UN-DESA 2009). In India, local government support enabled the emergence of a major domestic supplier of solar energy systems for households and industry (Wilson et al. 2008).

The second obstacle to sustainable development is that investment agreements fail to put obligations on investors to protect the public interest and create social value. Social and environmental protections are typically the purview of national governments. Developing countries, however, are still evolving in their institutional capacity to enact and enforce regulation, giving foreign companies the prerogative to determine their own social and environmental performance (Chidiak 2010).

In its *Guidelines for Multinational Enterprises*, the OECD makes recommendations for "responsible business conduct in a global context" in nine broad areas: disclosure (transparency); human rights; employment and industrial relations; the environment; bribery; consumer interests; science and technology; competition; and taxation (OECD 2011). All nine areas have implications for economic, social or environmental aspects of sustainable development. Despite the efforts of human rights and environmental groups to make them mandatory, including by attaching them to investment agreements, the Guidelines remain voluntary. The result is a lopsided emphasis in the investment regime on investor rights without responsibilities.

The third obstacle to sustainable development is the constraint on the "right to regulate" of host governments imposed by investor–state dispute settlement. The primary concern of arbitrators in investor–state compensation suits is whether foreign investors have been or will be financially harmed by environmental or health regulations, rather than whether such regulations are warranted in terms of public purpose. If the case goes against the host government, payouts can be very costly. In a high-profile case, the Canadian company Pac Rim sued the government of El Salvador for $77 million in ICSID for denying the company a mining permit in 2009. The denial was the result of intense opposition by local poor communities who claimed that the gold mine absorbed and polluted scarce water supplies (Kramer 2011).

Compensation claims in investor–state arbitration cases, in short, punish governments for regulating in the public interest. Even the threat of compensation could put a "chill" on developing new regulations that could negatively impact foreign investors. The risk is that regulatory measures would reduce the commercial value of investments and, therefore, could be considered expropriatory (UNCTAD 2012a, 2012b). Liability exposure creates incentives for host states to abstain from needed regulation.

The combination of the threat of investor–state arbitration and poor social performance by foreign companies can put developing country governments between a rock and a hard place. In Latin America, for example, FDI in extractive industries has skyrocketed in the past decade as a result of the commodities boom. Lacking adequate environmental oversight and human rights protections, mining projects have generated intense social conflict: as of mid-2013, over 200 communities were involved in conflicts over some 170 projects (OCMAL). Governments have responded by trying to increase regulation, but have confronted the reality or the threat of investor–state arbitration. Of 168 cases pending before ICSID in 2013, 49 involved oil, gas or mining ventures, 21 of them in Latin America (ICSID 2013).

GLOBAL SUSTAINABILITY BUSINESS NORMS

While investment agreements do not obligate good practice by foreign investors, global "sustainability" business norms are evolving rapidly. Generally, these norms articulate the environmental and social obligations of business to the communities and countries in which they operate.

In 1999, UN Secretary-General Kofi Annan triggered a spate of norm innovation with a call for a partnership between business and the UN that would give a "human face to the global market" (United Nations 1999). The Global Compact was launched as a voluntary initiative by which global corporations sign up to "embrace, support and enact" a set of "core values" in the areas of human rights, labor, the environment and anti-corruption. Derived from international law, including the Universal Declaration of Human Rights and the Rio Declaration on Environment and Development, the Global Compact's Ten Principles for business include respect for internationally proclaimed human rights, a precautionary approach to environmental management, and the development and diffusion of environmentally friendly technologies (Box 6.1). By 2013, over 10 000 companies and other stakeholders from over 130 countries were participants in the Global Compact, making it the largest voluntary corporate responsibility initiative in the world (UN Global Compact 2013).

The Global Compact complements the OECD Guidelines for Multinational Enterprises, differing primarily in implementation and monitoring mechanisms. In the Global Compact, individual businesses sign up to the Principles and produce public, annual "communications on progress" reports. The OECD Guidelines are embodied in a treaty between governments, which pledge to promote the Guidelines and to establish "national contact points" to act as citizen complaint and mediation mechanisms.

Another locus of global business norm setting is the UN Human Rights Council. In 2011, the Council endorsed the UN Guiding Principles for Business and Human Rights. Based on a "protect, respect and remedy" framework, the Principles for the first time established that business organizations have an independent duty – irrespective of the state law where they operate – to respect human rights. In operational terms, this means that businesses must uphold rights defined in international law, including rights to a clean environment and an adequate standard of living, both articulated in the International Covenant on Economic, Social and Cultural Rights (UNOHCHR 2011). While yet to make their way into investment agreements, human rights obligations are emerging in investment contract negotiations between developing countries and foreign investors (Cotula 2010).

Beyond voluntary guidelines, the de facto international standards for project finance are set by the International Finance Corporation's (IFC) Performance Standards on Environmental and Social Sustainability (Box 6.2). As the private sector arm of the World Bank, the IFC not only provides but leverages a substantial portion of global project finance, including in extractive industries. The IFC considers the Standards a

BOX 6.1   TEN PRINCIPLES OF THE UN GLOBAL COMPACT

Human rights

Businesses should:

1. support and respect the protection of internationally proclaimed human rights;
2. ensure that they are not complicit in human rights abuses.

Labor

Businesses should uphold:

3. freedom of association and the effective recognition of the
right to collective bargaining;
4. the elimination of all forms of forced and compulsory
labor;
5. the effective abolition of child labor;
6. the elimination of discrimination in respect of employment
and occupation.

Environment

Businesses should:

7. support a precautionary approach to environmental
challenges;
8. undertake initiatives to promote greater environmental
responsibility;
9. encourage the development and diffusion of environmentally friendly technologies.

Anti-corruption

Businesses should:

10. work against corruption in all its forms, including extortion
and bribery.

Source: UN Global Compact (2013).

BOX 6.2 IFC'S PERFORMANCE STANDARDS ON ENVIRONMENTAL AND SOCIAL SUSTAINABILITY

1. Social and environmental assessment and management systems.
2. Labor and working conditions.
3. Pollution prevention and abatement.
4. Community health, safety and security.
5. Land acquisition and involuntary resettlement.
6. Biodiversity conservation and sustainable natural resource management.
7. Indigenous peoples.
8. Cultural heritage.

Source: IFC (2012).

---

central part of its approach to risk management; demonstration that governments and companies are adhering to the eight Performance Standards is a requirement of project funding.

Global industry groups are another source of norm innovation. The International Council on Mining and Metals (ICMM), for example, a voluntary association of the world's largest mining companies, has developed a "Sustainable Development Framework" based on ten broad principles, including requirements to "uphold fundamental human rights" and "continually improve environmental performance." ICMM's 22 members are required to demonstrate that they are implementing the framework by producing annual public reports and undertaking independent, third-party assessment of company practice (ICMM 2013).

INNOVATIONS IN INVESTMENT RULES: TOWARDS SUSTAINABLE DEVELOPMENT?

In the past decade, host countries and NGO advocacy groups have begun to push back against international investment rules. In October 2013, the government of Ecuador announced the establishment of a commission to audit its bilateral investment treaties. Consisting of lawyers from throughout Latin America, the commission is charged with determining if the treaties are beneficial to Ecuador and whether they violate Ecuadorean sovereignty. In two high-profile cases, Ecuador is being sued in international arbitration by two multinational oil companies, Chevron and Occidental ("Ecuador Establishes" 2013).

Australia objected to investor–state dispute settlement in its 2004 free trade agreement with the US, and it was excluded from the treaty. After examination by an independent commission, Australia adopted a policy of excluding investor–state dispute from all future trade and investment agreements. Nonetheless, in 2011, under the terms of a Hong Kong–Australia BIT, Australia was taken to international arbitration by the tobacco company Philip Morris, on the grounds that new "plain packaging" regulation hurt the company's brand value (Sweet 2013).

The character and scope of investor–state dispute resolution could emerge as a controversial issue in the two biggest agreements currently being negotiated by the US: the Transatlantic and Trans-Pacific Partnerships on Trade and Investment (TTIP and TPP). A solution for Australia and by extension other countries might be an "opt-out" mechanism.

Changes that address the obstacles to sustainable development have begun to be incorporated in investment agreements (Bernasconi-Osterwalder and Johnson 2011). The 2012 US Model Investment Treaty, for example, a blueprint for future investment agreements, specifies environmental and labor obligations of both host and home countries. In both cases, parties agree to eschew a "race to the bottom" by agreeing that it is "inappropriate" to weaken standards or enforcement to attract, expand or retain investment. In the case of labor, they also agree that parties have obligations as ILO members to uphold core labor standards such as freedom of association and the right to collective bargaining (Office of the US Trade Representative 2013).

The US Model Treaty also seeks to better protect the "right to regulate" from investor–state arbitration challenges. The Treaty states that a party can take any measure it deems appropriate "to ensure that investment activity . . . is undertaken in a manner sensitive to environmental concerns" (Office of the US Trade Representative 2013: 18). However, the Treaty continues to grant investors the right to make arbitration claims when environmental regulation harms their financial interest. Given the ad hoc nature of arbitration tribunals and decisions, it is not clear what impact the Treaty will have on investor challenges to environmental regulation and, thus, the propensity of states to enact and enforce more stringent environmental oversight. Moreover, the Model Treaty does not address the lack of policy space for development.

A detailed approach to reform is previewed in the Model Agreement on Investment for Sustainable Development, created by a team from the International Institute for Sustainable Development (IISD) (Mann et al. 2005). The IISD Agreement starts from the premise that investor protections are necessary if not sufficient and specifies many of the currently articulated pre- and post-establishment rights, including national treatment and minimum international standards of treatment. However, it expressly addresses each of the three current obstacles to sustainable development.

First, it recognizes the right of states to set their own development objectives and allows them to impose performance requirements on investors. The Agreement lists seven such requirements, including domestic content, domestic procurement, export requirements and import controls. The expansion of "policy space" is controversial and runs contrary to TRIMS and the larger WTO liberalization agenda. However, developing country dissatisfaction with the restriction on performance requirements is a central reason that WTO talks have been stalled for over a decade.

Second, the IISD Model Agreement clearly identifies the social and environmental obligations of investors, as well as host and home states. The general obligation is to "contribute to the development objectives of host states and local levels of government" (Mann et al. 2005: 22). Reflecting evolving business norms, specific obligations include pre-establishment environmental and social impact assessment and post-establishment environmental management systems, as well as obligations to uphold international labor standards and human rights. Investors are also obliged to be transparent and accountable in their payments to host states, and to apply both OECD Guidelines for Multinational Enterprises and industry-specific codes of conduct.

Third, the Agreement protects the right of states to regulate in the public interest by not allowing investors access to international arbitration for disputes about existing or changing social and environmental obligations. For other disputes, it requires investors and states to engage in alternative dispute resolution, including a six-month "cooling-off period," and requires investors to exhaust domestic legal remedies before proceeding to international arbitration.

Another glimpse at "next-generation" investment governance is outlined in UNCTAD's 2012 *World Investment Report* (UNCTAD 2012b). UNCTAD's 11 Core Principles for Investment Policymaking for Sustainable Development address the same issues as the IISD Model Agreement – making sustainable development the goal, protecting the right of states to regulate, balancing rights and obligations – but also highlight the role of national policies and international cooperation in capturing sustainable development benefits from FDI (Box 6.3).

Investment agreements, including the TPP and TTIP, continue to be based lopsidedly on protecting investor rights rather than fostering

BOX 6.3   UNCTAD'S CORE PRINCIPLES FOR
INVESTMENT POLICYMAKING FOR
SUSTAINABLE DEVELOPMENT

1.   Investment for sustainable development: The overarching
     objective of investment policymaking is to promote invest-
     ment for inclusive growth and sustainable development.
2.   Policy coherence: Investment policies should be grounded
     in a country's overall development strategy. All policies
     that impact on investment should be coherent and syner-
     getic at both the national and international levels.
3.   Public governance and institutions: Investment policies
     should be developed involving all stakeholders, and
     embedded in an institutional framework based on the rule
     of law that adheres to high standards of public govern-
     ance and ensures predictable, efficient and transparent
     procedures for investors.
4.   Dynamic policymaking: Investment policies should be
     regularly reviewed for effectiveness and relevance and
     adapted to changing development dynamics.
5.   Balanced rights and obligations: Investment policies
     should be balanced in setting out rights and obligations of
     states and investors in the interest of development for all.
6.   Right to regulate: Each country has the sovereign right
     to establish entry and operational conditions for foreign
     investment, subject to international commitments, in the
     interest of the public good and to minimize potential nega-
     tive effects.
7.   Openness to investment: In line with each country's devel-
     opment strategy, investment policy should establish open,
     stable and predictable entry conditions for investment.
8.   Investment protection and treatment: Investment policies
     should provide adequate protection to established inves-
     tors. The treatment of established investors should be
     non-discriminatory.
9.   Investment promotion and facilitation: Investment policies
     should provide adequate protection to established inves-
     tors. The treatment of established investors should be
     non-discriminatory.

10. Corporate governance and responsibility: Investment policies should promote and facilitate the adoption of and compliance with best international practices of corporate social responsibility and good corporate governance.

11. International cooperation: The international community should cooperate to address shared investment-for-development policy challenges, particularly in least developed countries. Collective efforts should also be made to avoid investment protectionism.

Source: UNCTAD (2012b).

social value. The rapid evolution of global sustainability business norms, however, combined with the disillusion of many developing countries about the economic benefits of unfettered foreign investment, suggest that the balance is shifting. Given the urgency of global climate and other sustainability challenges, it is likely that the future of international investment governance will increasingly arc towards sustainable development.

REFERENCES

Agosin, Manuel R. and Roberto Machado (2007), "Openness and the International Allocation of Foreign Direct Investment," *Journal of Development Studies*, **43** (7), 1234–47.

Ajakaiye, Oyu, Paul Collier and Akpan H. Edpo (2011), "Management of Resource Revenue, Nigeria," in Paul Collier and Anthony J. Venables (eds.), *Plundered Nations? Successes and Failures in Natural Resource Extraction*, London: Palgrave Macmillan, pp. 231–61.

Amsden, Alice and William Chu (2003), *Beyond Late Development: Taiwan's Upgrading Policies*, Cambridge, MA: MIT Press.

Bernasconi-Osterwalder, Nathalie and Lise Johnson (2011), *Commentary to the Austrian Model Investment Treaty*, IISD Report, September, Winnipeg: International Institute for Sustainable Development, available from: www.iisd.org.

Blackmore, Emma, Danning Li and Sara Casallas (2013), *Sustainability Standards in China–Latin America Trade and Investment*, London: International Institute for Environment and Development.

Chidiak, Martina (2010), "Investment Rules and Sustainable Development: Preliminary Lessons from the Uruguayan Pulp Mills Case," in Kevin P. Gallagher and Daniel Chudnovsky (eds.), *Rethinking Foreign Investment for Sustainable Development: Lessons from Latin America*, London: Anthem Press, pp. 127–46.

Chudnovsky, Daniel and Andrei Lopez (2010), "A Missed Opportunity: Foreign Investment and Sustainable Development in Argentina," in Kevin P. Gallagher and Daniel Chudnovsky (eds.), *Rethinking Foreign Investment for Sustainable Development: Lessons from Latin America*, London: Anthem Press, pp. 77–98.

Cordero, Jose and Eva Paus (2010), "Foreign Investment and Economic Development in Costa Rica: The Unrealized Potential," in Kevin P. Gallagher and Daniel Chudnovsky (eds.), *Rethinking Foreign Investment for Sustainable Development: Lessons from Latin America*, London: Anthem Press.

Cosbey, Aaron (2005), "The Road to Hell? Investor Protections in NAFTA's Chapter 11," in Lyuba Zarsky (ed.), *International Investment for Sustainable Development*, London: Earthscan Press, pp. 150–71.

Cotula, Lorenzo (2010), *Investment Contracts and Sustainable Development*, London: International Institute for Environment and Development, available from: www.iied.org.

Eberhardt, Pia and Cecilia Olivet (2012), *Profiting from Injustice*, Brussels and Amsterdam: Corporate Europe Observatory and Transnational Institute.

"Ecuador Establishes Commission on Investment Treaties" (2013), *Dow Jones Business News*, October 8 (online).

Evans, Peter (1995), *Embedded Autonomy: States and Industrial Transformation*, Princeton, NJ: Princeton University Press.

Frankel, Jeffrey A. (2010), *The Natural Resource Curse: A Survey*, Working Paper No. 15836, Cambridge, MA: National Bureau of Economic Research.

Gallagher, Kevin P. and Lyuba Zarsky (2005), "No Miracle Drug: Foreign Investment and Sustainable Development," in Lyuba Zarsky (ed.), *International Investment for Sustainable Development: Balancing Rights and Rewards*, London: Earthscan Press, pp. 13–45.

Gallagher, Kevin P. and Lyuba Zarsky (2007), *Enclave Economy: Foreign Investment and Sustainable Development in Mexico's Silicon Valley*, Cambridge, MA: MIT Press.

Gauthier, Bernard and Albert Zeufack (2011), "Governance and Oil Revenues in Cameroon," in Paul Collier and Anthony J. Venables (eds.), *Plundered Nations? Successes and Failures in Natural Resource Extraction*, London: Palgrave Macmillan, pp. 79–113.

ICMM (International Council on Mining and Metals) (2013), available from: http://www.icmm.com/ (accessed August 11, 2013).

ICSID (International Center for the Settlement of Investment Disputes) (2013), Cases (website accessed October 10, 2013).

IEA (International Energy Agency) (2010), *Energy Technology Perspectives: Scenarios and Strategies to 2050*, Paris: IEA.

IFC (International Finance Corporation) (2012), *Performance Standards on Environmental and Social Sustainability*, Washington, DC: IFC.

Kramer, Anna (2011), "Giving Their Lives to Stop a Gold Mine in El Salvador," Oxfam (online), November 11.

Laszlo, Chris and Nadia Zhexambayeva (2011), *Embedded Sustainability: The Next Big Competitive Advantage*, Palo Alto, CA: Stanford University Press.

Mann, Howard (2013), "Reconceptualizing International Investment Law: Its Role in Sustainable Development," *Lewis & Clark Law Review*, **17** (2), 521–44.

Mann, Howard, Konrad von Moltke, Luke E. Peterson and Aaron Cosbey (2005), *IISD Model Agreement on Investment for Sustainable Development*, Winnipeg: International Institute for Sustainable Development.

Moran, Theodore H. (1998), *Foreign Direct Investment and Development: The New Policy Agenda for Developing Countries and Economies in Transition*, Washington, DC: Institute for International Economics.

OCMAL (Observatorio de conflictos mineros de America Latina), available from: http://www.olca.cl/ocmal/index.php (accessed August 10, 2013).

OECD (2011), *Guidelines for Multinational Enterprises*, Paris: OECD.

Office of the US Trade Representative (2013), "U.S. Model Bilateral Investment Treaty," available from: http://www.ustr.gov/about-us/press-office/press-releases/2012/april/united-states-concludes-review-model-bilateral-inves.

Rock, Michael and David Angel (2005), *Industrial Transformation in the Developing World*, Oxford: Oxford University Press.

Stiglitz, Joseph (2005), "Development Policies in a World of Globalization," in Kevin P. Gallagher (ed.), *Putting Development First: The Importance of Policy Space in the WTO and IFIs*, London: Zed Books.

Studwell, Joe (2013), *How Asia Works: Success and Failure in the World's Most Dynamic Region*, London: Profile Books.

Sweet, Melissa (2013), "The Philip Morris Case Illustrates Some Wider Dangers for Public Health from Trade Agreements," *Crikey Independent Media*, January 25.

Szirmai, Adam, Wim Naudé and Ludovico Alcorta (2013), *Pathways to Industrialization in the Twenty-First Century: New Challenges and Emerging Paradigms*, Oxford: Oxford University Press.

UN Global Compact (2013), (website accessed November 3, 2013).

UNCTAD (UN Conference on Trade and Development) (2009), *Trade and Development Report*, New York: United Nations.

UNCTAD (UN Conference on Trade and Development) (2012a), *Expropriation*, UNCTAD Series on International Investment Agreements II, New York: United Nations.

UNCTAD (UN Conference on Trade and Development) (2012b), *World Investment Report 2012*, available from: www.unctad.org/press.

UNCTAD (UN Conference on Trade and Development) (2013), *World Investment Report 2013*, available from: www.unctad.org/press.

UN-DESA (UN Department of Economic and Social Affairs) (2009), *Stronger Industrial Policies Needed to Face Climate and Development Challenges*, Policy Brief No. 23, August, New York: United Nations.

UNEP (2011), *Towards a Green Economy: Pathways to Sustainable Development and Poverty Eradication – A Synthesis for Policymakers*, available from: www.unep.org/greeneconomy.

United Nations (1999), "Secretary-General Proposes Global Compact on Human Rights, Labor, and the Environment in Address to World Economic Forum in Davos," Press Release SG/SG.6881, February 1.

UNOHCHR (UN Office of the High Commissioner on Human Rights) (2011), *Guiding Principles on Business and Human Rights*, New York: United Nations.

Wilson, Emma, Lyuba Zarsky, Ben Shaad and Ben Bundock (2008), "Lights On or Trade Off? Can 'Base of the Pyramid' Approaches Deliver Solutions to Energy Poverty?," in P. Khandachar and M. Halme (eds.), *Sustainability Challenges and Solutions at the Base of the Pyramid: Business, Technology and the Poor*, Sheffield: Greenleaf Publishing.

Zarsky, Lyuba (2010), "Climate-Resilient Industrial Development Paths: Design Principles and Alternative Models," in S.R. Khan and J. Christiansen (eds.), *Towards New Developmentalism: Market as Means rather than Master*, New York: Routledge, pp. 227–51.

Zarsky, Lyuba and Leonardo Stanley (2013), "Can Extractive Industries Promote Sustainable Development? A Net Benefits Framework and a Case Study of the Marlin Mine in Guatemala," *Journal of Environment and Development*, **22** (2), 131–54.

7. Developing countries and temporary trade barriers
John M. Rothgeb, Jr.

This chapter examines the trade barriers developing societies confront when they attempt to promote economic growth by exporting to advanced countries. The discussion focuses on the nature of the most frequently used protectionist barriers, some consequences of those barriers, and how effective developing countries have been when they turn to the World Trade Organization (WTO) to limit the effects of those barriers. American and WTO regulations are examined when appropriate to provide a reference point for the discussion.

TRADE AND DEVELOPMENT

Many developing countries seek to grow their economies by using exports to enlarge the customer base their corporations serve. Typically, local markets in less developed countries are limited by poverty and/or small populations, and local businesses need to export to acquire the capital to finance training for entrepreneurs and managers, and the construction of infrastructure, and to purchase industrial equipment and technology. With an exporting-for-growth development strategy, basic manufactured goods are sold in foreign markets, and the profits are used to move into more sophisticated industries in the hope that over time more and better jobs will become available for local workers and the standard of living for society as a whole will rise.

As developing countries have employed the export-based approach to growth over the past several decades, their share of world trade has increased substantially. For example, as Rothgeb and Chinapandhu (2007: 1) report, in 1970 countries classified by the World Bank as low and middle income accounted for 18 percent of world exports. By 1985, those same countries had approximately one-fourth of exports worldwide, and by the early twenty-first century their combined share stood at one-third. A similar pattern of growth occurred in the manufacturing sector, where by the early 2000s the developing country share of exports had more than tripled when compared to their 1970 total.[1]

These increases in export activity by developing countries have created mounting problems for producers in advanced societies which compete with less expensive goods from low and middle income nations and have brought demands for protectionist trade barriers to shield local firms and preserve jobs. This quest for protection, however, is affected by the trade deals that were negotiated from 1947 to the present under the auspices first of the General Agreement on Tariffs and Trade (GATT) and later the WTO. Under these agreements, participating countries pledged to lower their tariffs and other trade barriers and to establish standards and procedures that had to be followed before local producers could receive protection from imports. It is also understood that the failure to follow WTO rules might lead to trade penalties that could harm the economic performance of the offending country.

Given these WTO limitations on trade restrictions, one might presume that low and middle income country exporters would have little to fear from protectionism. This is not the case, however, for WTO regulations permit two types of temporary trade limitations (Bown 2010: 2). The first relates to fair trade, while the second pertains to unfair trade. These trade barriers are discussed briefly below.

FAIR TRADE PROTECTION

Fair trade is defined as commercial activity occurring within the context of a normally functioning market. Protectionist measures used within the context of fair trade are referred to as safeguards. As Jackson (1997: 176–7) notes, safeguards are meant to allow local producers that face competition from imports to have protection for a short time while they make adjustments to ensure that they will be competitive over the long run. Safeguards also can reduce the protectionist pressures political leaders often confront from those who feel swamped by imports (Lande and VanGrasstek 1986: 96; Destler 1995: 22; Bhala 2001: 1121). Under the WTO safeguards agreement, the protection provided cannot exceed four years, with the possibility of a four-year renewal. Once it expires, safeguard protection cannot be applied again to shield the same product until after a waiting period (WTO 1994b: 276).

In addition to being temporary, the protection afforded by safeguards must be nondiscriminatory and can sometimes lead to retaliation by the affected trading partners (WTO 1994b: 273, 276). Nondiscrimination means that the safeguard barriers cannot target selected exporters, but instead must be aimed at all foreign firms selling the product in the country enacting the safeguard measures. Retaliation is based on reciprocity, a central principle underpinning the WTO. According to this principle, members of the WTO open their markets to one another with the understanding that all members are making equivalent commitments. When a member sets up safeguard barriers it is in effect going back on its market opening commitments and as a result other members have the right to withdraw some of the market opening concessions they made to the member erecting the protectionist barrier (Jackson 1997: 193–4; Rothgeb 2001: 98). Hence, the attempt to help one industry can lead to lost export business for another.

According to WTO rules, safeguard protection can be enacted only after "an investigation by the [member's] competent authorities," which includes "public hearings . . . in which importers, exporters and other interested parties . . . present evidence" (WTO 1994b: 274). In the United States, the International Trade Commission (ITC), a quasi-independent agency, conducts the investigation and holds the hearings upon receipt of a petition from the president, a Congressional committee (the Ways and Means Committee from the House of Representatives or the Finance Committee from the Senate), or an affected party (a business, trade union, or industry association) (Lash 1998: 61).

Two questions are central to the ITC investigation: 1) has the producer in question been seriously injured, and 2) were imports a substantial cause of that injury? Serious injury is defined by the WTO and in U.S. trade law as the loss of market share, declining sales, plant closings, unemployment, and falling profits (WTO 1994b: 274; Lash 1998: 64). If the ITC establishes that a serious injury has occurred, it then considers the substantial cause issue. Under U.S. code, a substantial cause is one that is no less important than any other reason (for example, a recession or bad management) for an industry's woes. If another factor is regarded as more important than trade, then the petition for safeguard protection is denied, even if the industry has suffered a serious injury. An example of such a situation is an auto industry case in 1980 where the ITC found that the industry had experienced a serious injury but that trade was not a substantial cause because a recession was seen as a greater reason for the industry's problems (Lenway 1985: 148–50; Rhodes 1993: 159; Rothgeb 2001: 167). Hence, the petition was denied and the industry did not receive safeguard protection.

In the United States, if the ITC rules in favor of a safeguard petition (that is, the industry has experienced a serious injury and imports are a substantial cause of that injury), then the case is referred to the president. The president is charged by law with considering how the ITC recommendation for protection would affect the overall economy. The president may do any of three things: 1) accept the ITC recommendation and order that it be implemented; 2) overrule the ITC if it is determined that protection is not in the overall national interest; or 3) modify the ITC recommendation if another type of protection or course of action is regarded as more appropriate for the economy as a whole. Decisions to overrule or alter ITC recommendations usually are based on the costs protection might inflict on individual or corporate consumers of the product in question and/or on the probability that protection might lead to retaliation by other members of the WTO (Bhala 2001: 1144–5; Rothgeb 2001: 99).

Reflecting upon the way safeguards protection is handled, one can see that a producer seeking assistance confronts substantial hurdles relating to evidentiary standards, the degree to which the protection affects the overall national interest, and the need to abide by WTO rules. In light of this, one might expect those wishing to block imports to pursue other options. Unfair trade regulations provide an alternative.

UNFAIR TRADE PROTECTION

Unfair trade is the attempt to gain an advantage in international commerce by manipulating markets. Such manipulations most commonly involve either dumping or subsidies. Dumping is defined as selling exports at less than fair value, while subsidies are government payments to local businesses that allow them to export goods at lower prices. Since these activities are widely regarded as a form of cheating, they frequently evoke emotional responses from business and political leaders. This emotion means that politicians are often willing to rewrite the laws meant to combat dumping and subsidies whenever loopholes are detected in the already existing regulations (Lindsey 2000: 2; Rothgeb 2001: 95; Rothgeb and Chinapandhu 2007: 17–18). A summary of U.S. and WTO antisubsidy and antidumping rules is presented below.

Countervailing Regulations

Governments have provided local producers with monetary and other assistance for centuries. Usually this assistance is given either because the industry in question makes goods considered vital to national military or economic interests or because the business has political connections. When this aid is provided to corporations that export, it makes it possible to sell goods in foreign markets at prices that undercut the prices charged by local producers, which in turn complain to their government that they face an unacceptable form of competition. To prevent this, governments around the world have enacted antisubsidy, or countervailing, laws that are designed to counteract the benefits bestowed by subsidies.

In the United States, countervailing laws date from the late 1800s when Congress first sought to offset the bounties (an early type of subsidy) that some European governments paid exporters. One characteristic of these early laws that was carried over into later legislation was the absence of a role for the president when it came to making decisions about the imposition of countervailing duties (CVDs) to offset subsidies. In part, this reflected the Congressional belief that subsidies represented the cheating mentioned above and that in the face of such inappropriate behavior it would not be proper to allow the president to set aside or modify any investigative results that concluded that foreigners were engaged in illegitimate activities (CBO 1994: 22).

U.S. countervailing regulations were expanded in the early twentieth century when a federal appeals court ruled in 1901 that foreign tax breaks and refunds could be treated as subsidies. The Supreme Court affirmed this decision in 1903 (Viner [1925] 1966: 173–4). In addition, the Tariff Act of 1913 extended the initial definition of a subsidy to include payments by local governments. Further broadening the reach of American regulations, in 1930 the Smoot–Hawley Tariff permitted the Treasury Department, the cabinet agency that conducted subsidy investigations, to use estimates when determining countervailing duty rates (U.S. House of Representatives 2001: 84). Beyond this, U.S. laws did not require an injury investigation (as did later safeguards legislation) when deciding upon the application of countervailing penalties, since the act of providing a subsidy was regarded as automatically harming American firms. As Rothgeb and Chinapandhu (2007: 34) note, when combined with the lack of presidential discretion these features meant that before World War II foreigners wishing to export to the U.S. confronted substantial hurdles, because "American CVD rules [were] . . . the most stringent in the world."

Although the post-war period saw major reductions in trade barriers around the world, it also witnessed an expansion of unfair trade regulations, as can be seen by examining the U.S. experience. This increased reach of unfair trade rules in part reflected the political desire to provide producers beset by international competition with the means to shield themselves, especially when subsidies were involved. Accordingly, U.S. CVD rules were changed to make them tougher on imports.

Three major alterations came in the 1970s. In 1974, Congress stipulated that CVD investigations were to be completed within one year, and a 1979 law moved the authority for conducting those investigations from the Treasury Department to the Commerce Department. The 1979 legislation also permitted the use of the best information available (BIA) when foreigners were reluctant to provide data during investigations. Collectively, these moves favored U.S. complainants, in part because the bureaucratic culture in the Commerce Department was friendlier to domestic businesses than was the Treasury culture and in part because the combined effects of time limits and BIA meant that if foreigners attempted to stall American investigators by withholding information the Commerce Department was allowed to turn to alternative data sources (CBO 1994: 27; U.S. House of Representatives 2001: 91). Since the corporations filing the subsidy complaints sometimes were the source for the best information available, this change was especially troubling for foreigners (Nivola 1993: 94–5; Rothgeb and Chinapandhu 2007: 25).

In the 1980s, two additional changes to U.S. countervailing regulations expanded the definition of a subsidy. In 1984 Congress directed the Commerce Department to treat as a subsidy any circumstance in which a government provided financing to cover the production of a good that was used as a component for a product that was exported to the U.S. These were known as upstream subsidies (U.S. Congress 1984: 3035). An example would be payments to the manufacturers of the upholstery used to finish the interiors of cars exported to the U.S. The second definitional expansion came in 1988 when benefits provided by governments to producers without regard to export performance were classified as domestic subsidies. Special utility rates and infrastructure construction meant to serve a specific business are examples of such subsidies (U.S. Congress 1988: 1206–07; Horlick and Oliver 1989: 7–9).

Most of the above-mentioned conceptions of how a subsidy should be defined and treated found their way into the WTO Subsidies and Countervailing Measures Agreement (SCM) that emerged from the Uruguay Round of GATT negotiations. For instance, Article 1 defines subsidies as a "financial contribution by a government . . . or public body . . . [that] involves a direct transfer of funds . . . government revenue that is . . . foregone or not collected . . . [and the provision of] goods and services other than general infrastructure" (WTO 1994c: 229). Examples specifically mentioned include grants, loans, loan guarantees, and tax credits. As the reader might note, this definition includes the various conceptions of a subsidy that have been found in U.S. laws since 1890.

The WTO agreement also specifies time limits for investigations and allows for the use of BIA. Article 12.1.1 states that "Members [of the WTO] receiving questionnaires used in a countervailing duty investigation shall be given at least 30 days for reply," with the possibility of a 30-day extension (WTO 1994c: 243). And Article 12.7 permits the use of BIA, stating that "in cases in which any . . . Member . . . refuses access to, or otherwise does not provide, necessary information within a reasonable period or significantly impedes the investigation . . . determinations . . . may be made on the basis of the facts available" (WTO 1994c: 244).

The WTO SCM agreement additionally calls in Article 15 for a determination of material injury before duties can be applied. That is, simply finding that imports are subsidized is not a sufficient reason to apply a CVD. Instead, there must be a material injury as well, with material injury defined as "a significant increase in subsidized imports . . . significant price undercutting by the subsidized imports . . . or . . . depress[ed] prices to a significant degree" (WTO 1994c: 247). As will be discussed below, these injury standards differ greatly from those required in safeguards cases.

Almost all of the WTO SCM agreement standards and procedures were incorporated into U.S. trade law when the Uruguay Round Agreements Act was passed in 1994. Hence, current U.S. and WTO regulations regarding the handling of subsidies are closely aligned.

Antidumping Protection

As noted above, dumping is selling goods in a foreign market at a price that is less than fair value (sometimes also called normal value). The concern with dumping can be traced to the late nineteenth-century attempt to combat trusts and monopolies to ensure that single corporations would not dominate markets and use that control to harm consumers' interests. One tactic those seeking to dominate markets sometimes employed was "predatory pricing," a situation in which a large company would target smaller, more local competitors for destruction by setting prices at abnormally low levels in the areas serviced by the local competitor while maintaining higher prices elsewhere. Owing to its size, the larger firm would be able to make a profit across the full range of its activities even though it might lose money in the region where it dropped its prices. The smaller competitor, however, would find itself hard pressed and might eventually be forced to sell out or go bankrupt.[2]

By the early 1900s, many businesses, both in the U.S. and elsewhere, began complaining to their governments that foreign competitors were using predatory pricing to tilt the international commercial playing field in their favor. In the U.S., the complaints especially focused on British and German corporations that were allegedly selling goods at such low prices that American firms could not compete (CBO 1994: 18). As the local producers noted, such behavior was reminiscent of the tactics used to establish monopolies, except that in this case foreigners were the culprits, not such giant domestic companies as Standard Oil.

Two early attempts to counteract this foreign pricing behavior in the U.S. were the antidumping acts passed in 1916 and 1921. The 1916 law proved less than ideal, however, in part because it attempted to handle dumping as a criminal offense, which meant that it required evidentiary standards that prosecutors found difficult to meet (CBO 1994: 20; Lash 1998: 25). The 1921 law took a different approach. First, it specified that antidumping (AD) duties would be employed instead of fines and civil damages to combat inappropriate foreign pricing. Second, the determination of when antidumping duties should be imposed was made an administrative decision by the Treasury Department and was no longer handled by the courts (CBO 1994: 21; Mastel 1998: 19). Third, a new method was created to assess dumping. Previously, the determination of dumping involved a comparison of a good's price in its home market and in the U.S. If the U.S. price was lower, then the good was labeled as dumped. The 1921 law allowed the Treasury Department to employ a constructed value to assess dumping if the sales in the home market were negligible. According to this approach, the Treasury Department would estimate how much it should cost to make a good and market it in the U.S. If the U.S. price was lower than this constructed value, then the good was treated as dumped and an AD duty was imposed (CBO 1994: 21; U.S. House of Representatives 2001: 91–2).

The Antidumping Act of 1921 also replaced the need to establish predatory pricing intent, a feature of the 1916 legislation, with the far more easily established requirement that the Treasury Department demonstrate that foreign dumping was injuring or threatening to injure American producers. In 1930, Congress transferred the responsibility for injury investigations to the Tariff Commission (now the International Trade Commission) (U.S. Congress 1930: 217; Lande and VanGrasstek 1986: 108; Mastel 1998: 19–21).

As was the case with countervailing regulations, the more open trading system established after World War II was accompanied by a tightening of U.S. laws to make it easier to demonstrate that foreign firms were dumping. In 1954, Congress set a three-month time limit for antidumping investigations, and a 1958 law created a new means for assessing dumping, the third market comparison. This method was designed for circumstances in which it was suspected that a good was being dumped in the U.S., but sales in the home country market were negligible and the data for constructing a value were not readily available. U.S. investigators were now permitted to obtain information about how much the good cost in a third country and to compare that to the U.S. price; if the U.S. price was lower, the good would be regarded as dumped. This made it considerably easier for U.S. complainants to argue their case (Bryan 1980 8–9; U.S. House of Representatives 2001: 90).

The 1970s saw additional antidumping regulations. A 1974 law set a strict time limit on foreign firms for providing the pricing information needed in dumping cases and defined any sale in the U.S. that was below the cost of production as dumping. In 1979, the Commerce Department was put in charge of dumping investigations and was allowed to use the best information available. These moves had the same effects as described above during the discussion of subsidies. Additionally, Congress added the requirement that the Commerce Department conduct annual reviews of successful past dumping cases to ensure that previously imposed penalties were sufficient (CBO 1994: 24–7; Nivola 1993: 92–3; U.S. House of Representatives 2001: 90–91).

Congress approved more legislation in 1984 and 1988 in response to a growing chorus of complaints from American businesses about foreign dumping. A key feature of the 1984 law was a directive that the Commerce Department self-initiate AD investigations when there was "persistent injurious dumping" from multiple countries (Lande and VanGrasstek 1986: 119). Previously, the procedure followed in both dumping and subsidy cases called for investigations to begin only after an affected party filed a complaint with the Commerce Department.

The changes in 1988 included rules meant to combat circumvention and third country dumping. Circumvention is when a foreign firm facing AD duties seeks to avoid those duties by shipping goods to another country for a minimal degree of processing before exporting the goods to the U.S. Third country dumping involves selling goods in a foreign market at less than fair value, thereby displacing U.S. exports to that market. The new provisions in the 1988 law were meant to close these perceived loopholes in the U.S. AD code (U.S. Congress 1988: 5–6; Nivola 1993: 105; U.S. House of Representatives 2001: 102–03).

As was the case with subsidies and countervailing measures, the 1994 WTO antidumping agreement included many of the features found in U.S. laws. Article 2 defines dumping as sales at less than normal (or fair) value and sets three methods for determining when dumping is occurring: 1) a price comparison between the export market and the home market; 2) a price comparison with a third market; and 3) a comparison with a constructed value. Article 2.5 is meant to prevent circumvention, Article 14 sets procedures for investigations pertaining to third country dumping, Article 6.8 allows for the use of the best information available during investigations, and Article 6.1 fixes a 30-day time limit with a possible 30-day extension for providing data during an AD inquiry. Additionally, Article 3.7 specifies the use of a material injury standard based primarily on an increased flow of dumped goods and a significant depressing effect on domestic prices due to dumping (WTO 1994a: 145–63). The Uruguay Round Agreements Act of 1994 incorporated the provisions of the WTO antidumping agreement into U.S. law (Palmeter 1995).

Before turning to the effects the protectionist measures described above have had on developing countries, it is important to mention another U.S. unfair trade statute. This is the Continued Dumping and Subsidy Offset Act of 2000, better known as the Byrd Amendment (named after the late Senator Robert Byrd, a Democrat from West Virginia). Under this law, the money collected from AD and CVD duties goes not to the U.S. Treasury, but instead to the U.S. companies that filed the antidumping or countervailing complaint that led to the imposition of the duties (U.S. House of Representatives 2001: 104; Grimmett and Jones 2005: 2–3; Jones 2012: 19–20). This meant that U.S. firms might profit from filing cases, thereby providing those corporations with an additional incentive to take action against imports. As will be seen below, this law proved extremely controversial, led to WTO dispute settlement complaints, and eventually was rescinded as a result of those complaints.

TEMPORARY TRADE BARRIERS AND DEVELOPING COUNTRIES

Although some trade analysts argue that WTO safeguard regulations were designed to serve as the common form WTO members should use to address domestic calls for protection, over the past two decades the employment of antidumping and countervailing laws has far outstripped the use of safeguards (Lande and VanGrasstek 1986: 96; Jackson 1997: 177–9; Bhala 2001: 1126; Bown 2010, 2013).[3] Table 7.1 illustrates this by revealing the frequency with which safeguards and unfair trade cases have been initiated and duties have been imposed worldwide between the founding of the WTO in 1995 and 2012. As can be seen, 242 safeguard cases and 4416 antidumping and countervailing cases were initiated. That is, compared to safeguards initiations, there were 18 times more antidumping and countervailing filings. Looking at the measures imposed, one finds that there were 118 safeguards actions and 2819 antidumping and countervailing duties. This means that there were 24 times more antidumping and countervailing actions than there were safeguard measures. These figures starkly reveal just how great a role unfair trade barriers play in providing temporary protection.

Unfair trade measures have emerged as popular temporary protectionist devices for several reasons. One is the strict time limit associated with safeguard actions. As was noted earlier, a four-year time limit with the possibility of a four-year extension was built into the WTO safeguard agreement. The WTO antidumping and countervailing measures agreements, however, do not impose the same type of time restrictions, for, while the rules require a "sunset review" every five years after AD or CVD duties are

Table 7.1   Safeguards and countervailing and antidumping initiations and measures, 1995–2012

Safeguards initiations	242
Safeguards measures	118
Countervailing and antidumping initiations	4416
Countervailing and antidumping measures	2819

Source: WTO (2012a, 2012b, 2012c, 2012d, 2012e, 2012f).

imposed, one frequently finds that these reviews lead to a recertification of the need for the AD or CVD measures, and the penalty duties often remain in place for over a decade.

A second reason for the use of antidumping and countervailing protection is the much higher evidence standards required in safeguards cases. One may recall that before a safeguard measure can be imposed it must be demonstrated that local producers have suffered a serious injury and that imports are a substantial cause of that injury. The serious injury standard means that there must be declining sales, plant closings, unemployment, and/or reduced profits, and imports are regarded as a substantial cause only if they are no less important than any other reason for the industry's problems.[4] By comparison, antidumping and countervailing regulations have a less rigorous material injury standard requiring only that imports must be increasing in numbers and domestic prices must be depressed. One indication of just how great a difference these standards can make can be seen by noting that 48 percent of the safeguard cases initiated between 1995 and 2012 worldwide led to protection, while the proportion for dumping cases was 64 percent and for countervailing complaints it was 58 percent.[5]

Another evidentiary standard favoring the use of unfair trade protection has to do with de minimiz requirements. De minimiz refers to the level of subsidies and/or dumping that an investigation must find in order for a case to proceed. In the case of dumping, Article 5.8 of the WTO anti-dumping agreement calls for a 2 percent de minimiz. That is, if the difference between the price in the import market and the comparison market (or the constructed value) is not at least 2 percent, then the investigation is terminated (WTO 1994a: 152). For subsidies, Article 11.9 of the WTO Subsidies and Countervailing Measures Agreement sets a 1 percent de minimiz (WTO 1994c: 243). When these relatively low de minimiz levels are juxtaposed with the possible use of a constructed value based on the best information available, one has a recipe for findings favoring the firm filing the AD or CVD complaint, thus enhancing the attraction of unfair trade protection as compared to safeguards.

A third reason safeguards are less popular is the possibility of retaliatory measures by one's fellow WTO member countries if WTO safeguard procedures are not followed. As discussed previously, such retaliation is founded on the pledge WTO members make to one another to lower trade barriers in a reciprocal manner. Safeguard protections re-erect those barriers and violate the promise to maintain lower barriers in exchange for the reduced barriers of others. In this situation counteractions are considered warranted. Antidumping and countervailing measures, however, are a response to unfair trade. That is, they are a form of punishment for cheating. As long as the acting country conducts its investigations properly and can demonstrate that a subsidy or dumping as defined by the WTO has occurred, the targeted country has no right to retaliate. Hence, with safeguards there is a good chance that temporary protection will lead to damage to other parts of the actor's economy if trading partners retaliate, while if the temporary protection stems from the use of unfair trade measures there is a low probability that the action will lead to damaging retaliation.

Safeguards also are not employed as often as antidumping and countervailing regulations because the WTO requires that they be applied in a nondiscriminatory way. This makes safeguards protection a blunt instrument that cannot target especially troublesome foreign competitors. Since an important reason for creating protectionist barriers often includes the desire to strike at specific corporate opponents, nondiscrimination renders safeguards much less attractive than the alternatives available when unfair trade complaints are pursued, since those options can be aimed at selected foreign firms.[6]

The ability to target specific countries and corporations with antidumping and countervailing protectionist measures makes it possible to employ these laws to obstruct products from developing countries.[7] As can be seen in Table 7.2, worldwide more than 58 percent of the antidumping initiations and over 57 percent of the antidumping measures were aimed at products from low and middle income countries. The comparable figure for countervailing initiations was 64 percent, and for countervailing measures it was 66 percent. To place these numbers in perspective, it should be noted that between 1995 and 2012 low and middle income countries accounted for approximately 30 percent of world exports.[8] Hence, developing countries face unfair trade barriers at a rate that exceeds what should be expected, given their share of world exports.

Another way to examine how much low and middle income countries are affected is to look at which countries were targeted the most for AD and CVD investigations and duties. Table 7.3 reveals that seven of the top 11 targets worldwide for antidumping initiations are classified by the

Table 7.2   Antidumping and countervailing initiations and measures against low and middle income products, 1995–2012

	Antidumping	Countervailing
Total initiations	4125	291
Low and middle income initiations	2408	187
Percentage against low and middle income countries	58.4	64.3
Total measures	2649	170
Low and middle income measures	1503	112
Percentage against low and middle income countries	56.7	65.9

Source: WTO (2012a, 2012b, 2012c, 2012d).

Table 7.3   Most frequent country targets for antidumping initiations and measures, 1995–2012

Country	Initiations	Initiations per billion dollars 2012 exports	Country	Measures	Measures per billion dollars 2012 exports
China	884	.43	**China**	643	.31
Korea	299	.54	Korea	172	.31
U.S.	237	.15	Taipei China	142	.47
Taipei China	223	.74	U.S.	140	.09
Japan	170	.21	Japan	118	.15
Indonesia	168	.89	**Thailand**	109	.48
Thailand	168	.74	**Russia**	102	.19
India	160	.52	**Indonesia**	101	.54
Russia	127	.24	**India**	95	.31
Brazil	116	.48	**Brazil**	82	.34
Malaysia	105	.43	**Malaysia**	65	.26

Note: Developing countries are in bold.

Source: WTO (2012a, 2012b); CIA (2013).

World Bank as developing societies. The same proportion is found when AD measures are examined. Interestingly, an examination of antidumping initiations and measures per billion dollars of 2012 exports reveals that developing countries account for seven of the top nine targets both for initiations and for duties.[9]

Table 7.4   *Most frequent country targets for countervailing initiations and measures, 1995–2012*

Country	Initiations	Initiations per billion dollars 2012 exports	Country	Measures	Measures per billion dollars 2012 exports
China	57	.028	**China**	37	.018
India	54	.175	**India**	31	.100
Korea	19	.034	EU	11	.005
U.S.	14	.009	Italy	9	.019
Indonesia	14	.074	**Indonesia**	8	.042
Italy	13	.027	**Brazil**	8	.033
EU	12	.006	Korea	8	.014
Thailand	12	.053	U.S.	7	.004
Canada	8	.017	**Argentina**	4	.047
Argentina	7	.082	**South Africa**	4	.040
Brazil	7	.029			
Taipei China	7	.023			

Note: Developing countries are in bold.

Source: WTO (2012c, 2012d); CIA (2013).

Looking at comparable data for countervailing initiations and measures in Table 7.4 reveals a similar pattern. Six of the top 12 initiations targets worldwide were developing countries, and six of the top ten recipients of CVD measures also are classified as developing. When initiations and measures per billion dollars in exports are examined one finds that developing countries constitute six of the top seven targets both for initiations and for countervailing measures. Hence, one may conclude that products from developing societies are subject to antidumping and countervailing complaints and measures at a far higher rate than their export activity would indicate.

The disproportionate targeting of developing countries for antidumping and countervailing initiations and duties can lead to severe problems. For one thing, many of the affected products are important to the development strategies of the exporting nations (Nogues 1993: 41; Krueger 1999: 914). Another problem pertains to the sheer quantity of goods covered by the trade barriers. One illustration of this is provided by Bown's (2010: 5) estimate that 1.6 percent of China's exports to advanced countries are affected by antidumping orders.[10] In their case study of Thailand, Rothgeb and Chinapandhu (2007: 81–5) point out that the threat of AD duties inflicts substantial costs on Thai exporters because they must spend large amounts on foreign attorneys to monitor their compliance with AD regulations in other countries, and they must hire additional trade experts and administrative staff to ensure that they comply with WTO and other unfair trade regulations. Indeed, one scholar notes that sometimes developing country firms forgo exporting to certain markets because of "the attorney and other costs that would be required to defend against an [unfair trade] case" (Jackson 1997: 271). Vandenbussche and Zanardi (2010: 762) refer to this as a "chilling" effect, since the mere existence of AD actions can lead "to a lower level of exports [of other products] than would have otherwise been the case" (see also Krueger 1999: 914; Michalopoulos 1999: 136–7; Mukerji 2000: 69).

Examining the issue from a different angle, Bown (2010: 6) notes that between 1990 and 2007 the average proportion of the value of imports affected by antidumping duties in the U.S. was 13.37 percent, that the comparable figure for the EU was 9.62 percent, and that some countries have increased the value of the products they protect with unfair trade barriers by 1 percent per year. Beyond this, the shifting nature of the imported items covered by unfair trade barriers can "create substantial trade policy uncertainty for foreign exporters" (Bown 2010: 19), which can adversely impact the willingness of importers to do business with developing country exporters facing unfair trade actions.

MODIFYING PROTECTIONIST BARRIERS

As they grapple with the problems created by unfair trade barriers, many developing countries have turned to the World Trade Organization's dispute settlement understanding (DSU) and/or have used international negotiations to pursue more favorable WTO regulations. These efforts are described below.

WTO Dispute Settlement

The DSU allows WTO members to seek redress when a fellow member's trade policy does not conform to WTO regulations. The system allows an aggrieved party to request consultation with the alleged rule violator and, if the consultation does not yield an acceptable outcome, to request the formation of a panel of specialists to hear arguments from the complainant and the defendant. After the presentation of arguments, the panel members confer and reach a decision as to whether a violation has in fact occurred. If it is determined that a transgression has been committed, then the offender must cease and desist, offer acceptable compensation to the aggrieved party (or parties), or face the possibility of counteraction by the complainant that penalizes the violator's trade. Arbitration and appeals processes are included in the system (Jackson 1997: 124–7; Emens 2012: 18–48; Grimmett 2012: 2–3).

Developing countries have actively participated in the DSU system, filing 54 complaints (56.8 percent of all such complaints) alleging violations of the antidumping code and 25 protests (26 percent of the total) claiming infringements of the agreement on subsidies and countervailing measures.[11] While approximately 90 percent of these cases pertain to technical issues, a few address fundamental WTO regulations regarding unfair trade. Two issues relating to the U.S. stand out. One has to do with the Continued Dumping and Subsidy Offset Act of 2000 (the Byrd Amendment). The other relates to the use of zeroing in U.S. investigations. In each case, developing countries were joined by other WTO members in claiming that U.S. procedures did not conform to WTO rules.

As may be recalled, the Byrd Amendment called for distributing to the complainants the money collected when U.S. antidumping and countervailing duties were imposed. From the beginning, this law was controversial. Even President Clinton criticized the legislation as he signed it, stating that "this bill will provide select U.S. industries with a subsidy above and beyond the protection needed to counteract foreign subsidies" (Grimmett and Jones 2005: 3). In December 2000, Brazil, Chile, India, Indonesia, and Thailand joined Australia, the EU, Japan, and Korea in requesting consultation with the U.S. regarding whether the law violated WTO regulations. Mexico and Canada made the same request in May 2001. When these consultations failed to produce an acceptable outcome, a WTO panel was formed and the cases were merged (Grimmett 2012: 27).

The complainants presented three arguments: 1) the law gave American producers an unacceptable incentive to file unfair trade cases; 2) the legislation called for actions that exceeded WTO rules; and 3) the payments made under the law were themselves an unacceptable subsidy. The panel found the first two arguments valid, and the U.S. lost the case. The U.S. appealed and lost again. Following arbitration, authorization to impose countermeasures was granted in August 2004. The first such actions went into effect in May 2005 (Grimmett and Jones 2005: 10–12; Grimmett 2012: 27–8). Interestingly, several developing countries, including Thailand, opted to postpone penalties to avoid antagonizing the U.S. (Rothgeb and Chinapandhu 2007: 75).

Despite the loss of the WTO case and calls from the White House to rescind the law, Congress was unwilling to act. This was true even as the U.S. Court for International Trade ruled in April 2006 that the Byrd

Amendment violated provisions of the North American Free Trade Agreement (NAFTA), and therefore could not be applied to Mexico and Canada. Finally, Congress allowed the law to lapse in October 2007, but specified that such duties as were already imposed would still be paid to eligible firms until they expired (Chinapandhu and Rothgeb 2011: 24; Grimmett 2012: 26). Hence, even though the complainants secured a victory, over four years elapsed between the first consultation request and the initial imposition of countermeasures and nearly seven years passed before the offending regulations were eliminated. Even then, money was still distributed under the provisions of the Byrd Amendment for many additional months.

The zeroing cases followed a similar pattern. Zeroing is a technique employed by the U.S. when comparing prices in dumping cases. During such comparisons, average prices are often calculated both across time and across related products. When doing this, it is not uncommon to find that in some circumstances the U.S. selling price is higher than the comparison price (a foreign selling price or a constructed value), which is the opposite of dumping. Since there is no dumping, the Commerce Department assigns such transactions a value of zero (meaning no dumping) and then uses that zero to assess the average amount of dumping across time or across product lines. Doing this leads to higher dumping margins and increases the probability of a positive finding. Thus, foreigners facing U.S. dumping investigations resent zeroing. Interestingly, the Congressional Research Service notes that U.S. laws do not require the use of zeroing, and explains that zeroing is an administrative convenience adopted by the Commerce Department (Grimmett 2012: 20–22).

The EU filed the first WTO DSU consultation request regarding zeroing in June 2003.[12] Japan also made a request in November 2004. In October 2005, a DSU panel found that zeroing could not be used in initial investigations, and in April 2006 an appellate body said zeroing also could not be employed in administrative reviews. To comply with these decisions, in 2007 the Commerce Department promised to end zeroing in initial AD investigations (Jones 2006: 14–15; Grimmett 2012; WTO 2013a). The Commerce Department continued, however, to use zeroing in other phases of AD inquiries.

Developing countries joined the protest over zeroing when Mexico, Thailand, Ecuador, Brazil, China, and Vietnam filed DSU cases between 2006 and 2011. The U.S. received adverse panel rulings in the Thai and Ecuadoran cases and either recalculated the affected dumping margins without zeroing or revoked the dumping duties. In the other cases, the U.S. sought negotiated solutions for the complaints or requested arbitration (Jones 2006: 14, 2012: 20–22; Grimmett 2012: 17–18). The issue also became tied up in U.S. courts as several American corporations filed cases demanding that the Commerce Department employ zeroing in part because it favors U.S. firms when they file dumping complaints. Therefore, despite the unfavorable WTO rulings, zeroing is still used for several types of calculations when the Commerce Department handles dumping investigations. This illustrates once again that the WTO DSU provides only partial relief for those seeking redress for unfair trade rule violations.

International Negotiations

Developing countries have found the WTO Doha Development Agenda talks that began in November 2001 useful for conducting international negotiations regarding temporary trade barriers. For the most part, low and middle income countries have focused on the WTO antidumping agreement owing to the increasing frequency with which they have faced AD actions. To increase their bargaining power, several developing countries have joined with some more advanced nations to form the Friends of Antidumping (Friends). Members of this group include Brazil, Chile, China, Colombia, Costa Rica, India, Israel, Japan, Korea, Mexico, Norway, Singapore, Switzerland, Thailand, Turkey, and the EU (Jones 2006: 9; Rothgeb and Chinapandhu 2007: 79).

The antidumping issues at the top of the Friends' agenda include an outright ban on the use of zeroing in all phases of AD investigations, mandatory expiration dates for antidumping duties, the increased use of agreements whereby those accused of dumping can avoid penalty duties by raising prices (referred to as undertakings or suspension agreements), rules that would make it more difficult to demonstrate that dumping was injuring local producers, and an increase in the de minimiz that would require a much greater differential between a local selling price and the comparison price before antidumping duties could be imposed. While most of these issues have met opposition, there has been some willingness to bargain, in part because of the increasingly widespread use of AD regulations to hamper trade. This growing employment has even led many developing countries to adopt AD codes as a way to limit imports both from more advanced nations and from developing societies (Jones 2006: 10, 13–18; Vandenbussche and Zanardi 2009: 761; Bown 2010: 3).

To date, while the Doha negotiations have led to over one hundred suggestions for reforming the WTO antidumping agreement, little progress has been made (Jones 2006: 11). One reason is the emotion surrounding the issue of unfair trade, for negotiators often find that legislators and other politicians from their home countries demand tighter, not looser, rules. Another reason is that disagreements over other issues (for example agriculture, intellectual property, and trade in services) have stalled the Doha negotiations, making it difficult to address problems pertaining to unfair trade.

SUMMARY AND CONCLUSIONS

In recent decades, many low and middle income countries have employed an export-led growth strategy that has often met with resistance from competing producers in importing societies. At the heart of this resistance are the unfair trade regulations that many nations employ to deal with international commercial malfeasance. As has been demonstrated, developing countries are targeted for countervailing and antidumping actions at rates that exceed their share of world exports. These actions have resulted in lost business opportunities and substantial expense, as developing country exporters have been forced to defend themselves.

In an effort to reduce the problems associated with unfair trade barriers, many developing country governments have filed complaints with the World Trade Organization and/or have attempted to use the Doha Development Agenda multilateral trade talks to obtain modifications to the WTO antidumping and countervailing regulations that permit the most egregious protectionist actions by importing societies. Thus far, these approaches have brought only modest success. Regarding WTO dispute settlement complaints, low and middle income complainants have found that even when they win their cases, as was true in the Byrd Amendment and zeroing examples discussed above, the adjudication and negotiations associated with the cases stretched over long periods of time and that the losing side still found ways to postpone the full implementation of the changes required by the WTO panel ruling.

As for negotiations, some low and middle income countries have banded together in the Friends of Antidumping to form a coalition to enhance their bargaining position. However, at least two problems have emerged. The first is the widespread feeling in some nations that antidumping and countervailing rules should be strengthened, while the second is that the Doha negotiations have come to a standstill amid disagreements over a series of issues, many of which have nothing to do with unfair trade.

To make progress toward their unfair trade goals, developing countries might be advised to build alliances with partners within the nations receiving their exports. That is, they might seek out retailers and other corporate consumers of their exports and attempt to work with those businesses to put pressure on importing country political leaders to modify local regulations and their international unfair trade bargaining positions. Such an approach might work hand in hand with the Friends of Antidumping coalition to push importing governments toward an accommodation by confronting them with determined domestic and international bargaining. Additionally, low and middle income country leaders need to consider making trade-offs on other issues, such as concessions regarding intellectual property rights, to obtain changes in unfair trade regulations. After all, a key consideration in any negotiations must be what is most important in the near term, and, for many developing nations, lowering foreign temporary trade barriers to encourage economic growth through exports is a top priority.

NOTES

1. These data are from U.N., *Yearbook of International Trade Statistics* (various years), U.N. Conference on Trade and Development (UNCTAD), *Handbook of Statistics* (2005), and C.I.A., *World Factbook* (various years).
2. Yergin (1992: 35–55) describes how Standard Oil employed this tactic to dominate the American oil industry after the Civil War.
3. Bhala (2001: 1125) points out that one indication of the desire to promote safeguards as the preferred form of protection is that they can be used for three years without retaliation.
4. The substantial cause standard is employed in the U.S. Other countries sometimes use another approach.
5. These percentages were calculated from WTO data (2012a, 2012b, 2012c, 2012d, 2012e, 2012f). Please note that they are approximations, since the timing of initiations and measures can mean that some measures were based on initiations filed before 1995 and that some 2012 initiations have not yet received a final decision.
6. The ability to target particular foreign firms as a means for imposing burdens on troublesome competitors is especially true for dumping complaints. When combined with the specific WTO definition of a subsidy and the broader definition of dumping and with the relatively low de minimiz threshold, it should be no surprise that over 90 percent of unfair trade initiations and actions are for dumping (Chinapandhu and Rothgeb 2011: 27).
7. Bown (2010: 3–4) points out that in recent years several developing countries, including Argentina, Brazil, China, India, and Turkey, also have used unfair trade laws to hamper imports both from low and middle income countries and from advanced societies.
8. The figures for low and middle income country trade are from U.N., *Yearbook of International Trade Statistics* (various years) and UNCTAD, *Handbook of Statistics* (various years).
9. Dividing AD initiations and measures by total 2012 exports provides a convenient control for the size of the targeted economy.
10. Nogues (1993: 42) shows that even greater extremes can be found, noting that in the 1980s nearly 20 percent of Brazil's exports were covered by either antidumping duties or agreements to raise prices to avoid such duties.
11. These figures are based on WTO (2013a, 2013b) information relating to antidumping and countervailing complaints under the dispute settlement understanding.
12. The EU faced and lost its own zeroing complaint (WTO DSU case DS141) in 1998 (WTO 2013a).

REFERENCES

Bhala, Raj (2001), *International Trade Law: Theory and Practice*, New York: Lexis Publishing.

Bown, Chad P. (2010), *Taking Stock of Antidumping, Safeguards, and Countervailing Duties, 1990–2009*, Policy Research Working Paper 5436, Washington, DC: World Bank.

Bown, Chad P. (2013), *How Different Are Safeguards from Antidumping? Evidence from U.S. Trade Policies toward Steel*, Policy Research Working Paper 6378, Washington, DC: World Bank.

Bryan, Greyson (1980), *Taxing Unfair International Trade: A Study of U.S. Antidumping and Countervailing Duty Laws*, Lexington, MA: Lexington Books.

CBO (Congressional Budget Office) (1994), *How the GATT Affects U.S. Antidumping and Countervailing Duty Policy*, Washington, DC: CBO.

Chinapandhu, Benjamas and John M. Rothgeb, Jr. (2011), "The Problems U.S. Dumping and Subsidy Regulations Pose for Thailand: Evidence from the Steel and Pineapple Sectors," *Journal of Economics and Politics*, **19** (1), 19–34.

CIA (Central Intelligence Agency) (2013), *The World Factbook*, available from: www.cia.gov (accessed May 29, 2013).

Destler, I.M. (1995), *American Trade Politics*, Washington, DC: Institute for International Economics.

Emens, John D. (2012), *WTO Panel Dynamics: From Power-Based GATT Renderings to WTO Rule-Based Adjudication*, Saarbrucken, Germany: AV Akademiker Verlag.

Grimmett, Jeanne J. (2012), *WTO Dispute Settlement: Status of U.S. Compliance in Pending Cases*, CRS Report for Congress RL32014, Washington, DC: Congressional Research Service.

Grimmett, Jeanne J. and Vivian C. Jones (2005), *The Continued Dumping and Subsidy Offset Act ("Byrd Amendment")*, CRS Report for Congress RL33045, Washington, DC: Congressional Research Service.

Horlick, Gary N. and Geoffrey D. Oliver (1989), "Antidumping and Countervailing Duty Provisions of the Omnibus Trade and Competitiveness Act of 1988," *Journal of World Trade*, **23** (3), 5–49.

Jackson, John H. (1997), *The World Trading System: Law and Policy of International Economic Relations*, Cambridge, MA: MIT Press.

Jones, Vivian C. (2006), *WTO: Antidumping Issues in the Doha Development Agenda*, CRS Report for Congress RL32810, Washington, DC: Congressional Research Service.

Jones, Vivian C. (2012), *Trade Remedies: A Primer*, CRS Report for Congress RL32371, Washington, DC: Congressional Research Service.

Krueger, Anne (1999), "The Developing Countries and the Next Round of Multilateral Trade Negotiations," *World Economy*, **22** (7), 909–32.

Lande, Stephen L. and Craig VanGrasstek (1986), *The Trade and Tariff Act of 1984: Trade Policy in the Reagan Administration*, Lexington, MA: D.C. Heath and Co.

Lash, William H. (1998), *U.S. International Trade Regulation: A Primer*, Washington, DC: AEI Press.

Lenway, Stefanie Ann (1985), *The Politics of U.S. International Trade: Protection, Expansion, and Escape*, Boston, MA: Pitman Publishing.

Lindsey, Brink (2000), "The U.S. Antidumping Law: Rhetoric versus Reality," *Journal of World Trade*, **34** (1), 1–38.

Mastel, Greg (1998), *Antidumping Laws and the U.S. Economy*, Armonk, NY: M.E. Sharpe.

Michalopoulos, Constantine (1999), "The Developing Countries in the WTO," *World Economy*, **22** (1), 117–43.

Mukerji, Asoke (2000), "Developing Countries and the WTO: Issues of Implementation," *Journal of World Trade*, **34** (6), 33–74.

Nivola, Pietro S. (1993), *Regulating Unfair Trade*, Washington, DC: Brookings Institution.

Nogues, Julio (1993), "The Cost to Latin America of Adopting Unfair Trade Policies," in Mordechai E. Kreinin (ed.), *International Commercial Policy: Issues for the 1990s*, Washington, DC: Taylor & Francis.

Palmeter, David (1995), "United States Implementation of the Uruguay Round Antidumping Code," *Journal of World Trade*, **29** (3), 39–82.

Rhodes, Carolyn (1993), *U.S. Trade Policy and the GATT Regime*, Ithaca, NY: Cornell University Press.

Rothgeb, John M., Jr. (2001), *U.S. Trade Policy: Balancing Economic Dreams and Political Realities*, Washington, DC: CQ Press.

Rothgeb, John M., Jr. and Benjamas Chinapandhu (2007), *Trade and Development in a Globalized World: The Unfair Trade Problem in U.S.–Thai Trade Relations*, Lanham, MD: Lexington Books.

U.S. Congress (1930), *Tariff Act of 1930, Public Law 71-361*, Washington, DC: U.S. Government Printing Office.

U.S. Congress (1984), *Trade and Tariff Act of 1984, Public Law 96-573*, Washington, DC: U.S. Government Printing Office.

U.S. Congress (1988), *Omnibus Trade and Competitiveness Act of 1988, Public Law 100-418*, Washington, DC: U.S. Government Printing Office.

U.S. House of Representatives, Committee on Ways and Means (2001), *Overview and Compilation of U.S. Trade Statutes*, Washington, DC: U.S. Government Printing Office.

Vandenbussche, Hylke and Maurizio Zanardi (2010), "The Chilling Effects of Antidumping Proliferation," *European Economic Review*, **54** (6), 760–77.

Viner, Jacob ([1925] 1966), *Dumping: A Problem in International Trade*, New York: Sentry Press.

WTO (World Trade Organization) (1994a), "Agreement on Implementation of Article VI of the General Agreement on Tariffs and Trade (Antidumping Agreement)," available from: www.wto.org (accessed April 24, 2013).

WTO (World Trade Organization) (1994b), "Agreement on Safeguards," available from: www.wto.org (accessed April 24, 2013).

WTO (World Trade Organization) (1994c), "Agreement on Subsidies and Countervailing Measures," available from: www.wto.org (accessed April 24, 2013).

WTO (World Trade Organization) (2012a), "Antidumping Initiations by Exporting Country, 01/01/1995–30/06/2012," available from: www.wto.org (accessed May 20, 2013).

WTO (World Trade Organization) (2012b), "Antidumping Measures by Exporting Country, 01/01/1995–30/06/2012," available from: www.wto.org (accessed May 20, 2013).

WTO (World Trade Organization) (2012c), "Countervailing Initiations by Exporting Country, 01/01/1995–30/06/2012," available from: www.wto.org (accessed May 20, 2013).

WTO (World Trade Organization) (2012d), "Countervailing Measures by Exporting Country, 01/01/1995–30/06/2012," available from: www.wto.org (accessed May 20, 2013).

WTO (World Trade Organization) (2012e), "Safeguard Initiations by Reporting Member, 29/03/1995–30/04/2012," available from: www.wto.org (accessed May 20, 2013).

WTO (World Trade Organization) (2012f), "Safeguard Measures by Reporting Member, 29/03/1995–30/04/2012," available from: www.wto.org (accessed May 20, 2013).

WTO (World Trade Organization) (2013a), "Disputes by Agreement: Antidumping," available from: www.wto.org (accessed April 24, 2013).

WTO (World Trade Organization) (2013b), "Disputes by Agreement: Subsidies and Countervailing Measures," available from: www.wto.org (accessed April 24, 2013).

Yergin, Daniel (1992), *The Prize: The Epic Quest for Oil, Money, and Power*, New York: Simon & Schuster.

8. Agricultural trade and economic development: contradictions and incongruities between law and policy
Gonzalo Villalta Puig and Erik Mitbrodt

INTRODUCTION

This chapter critically assesses the problems that have emerged in the wake of the proliferation of developmental preferential trade agreements (PTAs) between the industrialized customs unions of the European Union (EU) and the United States of America (US) and those of less industrialized, agriculturally based economies. It argues that, without lessening the restrictions on trade in agricultural goods, developmental PTAs cannot benefit those underdeveloped economies that they seek to help.

The chapter first introduces the idea of development-through-trade as it reviews and comments on the exceptions to the most favoured nation (MFN) principle – the non-discrimination norm at the core of the multilateral trading system – in the various multilateral trade agreements of the World Trade Organization (WTO) that allow for the creation of developmental PTAs. Exceptions in favour of lesser-developed members are evident in the General Agreement on Tariffs and Trade 1994 (GATT), General Agreement on Trade in Services (GATS), and Agreement on Trade-Related Aspects of Intellectual Property Rights (TRIPS), as they are in various waivers specifically approved by the WTO. In contrast to the beginning of the chapter and in order to reveal the contradictions and incongruities between trade and development – law and policy – the chapter then reviews and comments on the exceptions to the MFN principle that the Agreement on Agriculture (AA) allows through its many qualifications to the obligations of the Agreement on Subsidies and Countervailing Measures (SCM), all in the name of self-sufficiency in the production of food and fibre. Here, the concern is with market access. The removal of tariffs and other border barriers does not always allow for more open markets, as subsidies, rules of origin, and biosecurity standards can take on a protectionist bent. Subsequently, the chapter examines the major developmental preferential trade schemes of the EU and the US, only to question whether these schemes can really help developing economies improve their welfare. Finally the chapter puts forward recommendations on how preferential trade access for the world's poorest countries can be improved.

DEVELOPMENT-THROUGH-TRADE AND THE WORLD TRADE ORGANIZATION

To examine the interplay between trade in agriculture and economic development, the chapter conveys the conflict between developed countries and developing countries as it translates to law and policy. Here, the concern is with developing countries everywhere and at every stage of development. Of course, in the interest of definitional certainty, the default reference must necessarily be to least-developed countries (LDCs), namely those countries classified by the United Nations (Economic and Social Council: Committee for Development Policy) as the poorest countries in the world. They are the worst off by almost every possible health and economic indicator. Currently, there are 49 LDCs, the majority of which are from Africa (UN-OHRLLS). Of these, 34 are members of the WTO and an additional nine are in negotiations to join the organization (WTO, *Understanding the WTO*). LDCs constitute 12 per cent of the world population (UN-OHRLLS) but account for only 2 per cent of world gross domestic product (GDP) and about 1 per cent of global trade in goods (UN-OHRLLS). The peoples of LDCs live below the poverty line – 'measured by the World Bank as less than $2.50 per day' – and have little or no access to basic services, including electricity, water, health care, and education (Thrasher and Gallagher 2008: 49). This classification is now a reference for many, a term which, as is evident from the SCM, the WTO adopts along with other agencies. LDCs are, therefore, the default reference of this chapter, but it is not an exclusive reference. The chapter is equally relevant to other developing countries. After all, agricultural trade is significant to the developmental expectations of almost 60 per cent of the world's population who, be they resident in LDCs or not, continue to live in poverty despite the efforts of the WTO (World Bank, *Global Poverty Indicators*).

Yes, the WTO primarily exists to supervise and liberalize international trade. Yet, like many other pillars of international economic law, it also has a mission to advance the welfare of the peoples of the world. International economic law runs parallel to international development law in that they both aim for a fairer, more equitable redistribution of world resources, which are often scarce and always arbitrary in their location (Qureshi and Ziegler 2011: ch. 17). That redistributive aspiration is, for Rawls, an obligation (Rawls 1971: 616). It is a duty born of justice that can only translate into a differential principle. The need for special treatment for the poorer motivates the United Nations Millennium Declaration, which through the Millennium Development Goals calls for new international development architecture to support the right to development (UN 2010): the right of states, that is, the need of peoples, in fact, to develop economically through fairer trade, socially through better governance, and sustainably through environmental protection. For the WTO, development is, most obviously, economic development. The WTO, thus, has a mandate to promote the economic development of the world's poorer countries through the removal of barriers to trade, through trade liberalization (Moon 2008: 38).

Despite an abundance of criticisms, controversy aplenty, and a legion of structural problems, over the years the WTO has taken positive steps to reduce the plight of the world's poorest countries, together with the World Bank and other organizations in the United Nations Development Group. Through the WTO, many of the world's developed countries have allowed for exceptions to MFN treatment in order to afford special, preferential treatment to poor economies. With the idea of development-through-trade at the base of the constitution of the WTO, exceptions in the GATT, GATS, and TRIPS allow developed countries to positively discriminate in favour of the poorest countries (Moon 2008: 31). Many of the exceptions set out to 'improve trading opportunities by allowing for longer time periods [to] implement agreements and commitments' (WTO, *Development*) and allow for developing countries to safeguard their trade interests by providing support to 'build infrastructure, implement technical standards, and provisions' (WTO, *Development*). The problem is that, in the main, these mechanisms are non-binding.

Agreement Establishing the World Trade Organization

As the Preamble of the Agreement Establishing the World Trade Organization suggests, when the WTO was established at the end of the Uruguay Round in 1995 the idea of alleviating world poverty and raising living standards was a central concern. The Preamble commits members to an open trading system that raises living standards, ensures full employment, and increases real income for poor countries:

> Recognizing that their relations in the field of trade and economic endeavour should be conducted with a view to raising standards of living, ensuring full employment and a large and steadily growing volume of real income and effective demand, and expanding the production of and trade in goods and services, while allowing for the optimal use of the world's resources in accordance with the objective of sustainable development, seeking both to protect and preserve

the environment and to enhance the means for doing so in a manner consistent with their respective needs and concerns at different levels of economic development.

Recognizing further that there is a need for positive efforts designed to ensure that developing countries, and especially the least developed among them, secure a share in the growth of international trade commensurate with the needs of their economic development.

General Agreement on Tariffs and Trade

As early as 1968, the United Nations Conference on Trade and Development (UNCTAD) recommended the creation of a 'generalized system of tariff preferences' that would permit industrialized countries to grant special concessions to developing countries. Three years later, the enactment of waivers to Article I GATT followed.

In 1979, the Enabling Clause further formalized the most significant exceptions to MFN treatment in favour of LDCs. These exceptions have become the legal basis for the Generalized System of Preferences (GSP), which allows developed countries to give differential and more favourable treatment to goods coming from developing countries. Another significant aspect of the Enabling Cause is that, under paragraph 2(c), it establishes the Global System of Trade Preferences (GSTP) in that it makes provision for '[r]egional or global arrangements entered into amongst less-developed contracting parties for the mutual reduction or elimination of tariffs and, in accordance with criteria or conditions which may be prescribed by the CONTRACTING PARTIES, for the mutual reduction or elimination of non-tariff measures, on products imported from one another' (Enabling Clause 1979).

Furthermore, Part IV GATT on trade and development contains an exception to the reciprocity normally applicable to PTAs. Article XXXVI:8 GATT permits an agreement to unilaterally favour a developing country by giving one-sided trade preferences: 'The developed contracting parties do not expect reciprocity for commitments made by them in trade negotiations to reduce or remove tariffs and other barriers to the trade of less-developed contracting parties.'

The obvious flaw of Part IV is that is does not create any binding obligations on developed countries to give preferential treatment. Preferential treatment is given largely on a unilateral, voluntary basis and can be easily withdrawn. Then again, such unilateral discretion is not necessarily exclusive to developed countries.

In that respect, Article XVIII GATT is notable. In conjunction with other WTO instruments, it allows a developing country to provide governmental assistance to economic development. The most significant implication of this provision is the unilateral discretion that it gives to developing countries, which can restrict trade temporarily either to safeguard the establishment or maintenance of infant and strategic industries from external competition or to safeguard their external financial position for reasons of economic hardship, specifically balance of payments difficulties (Decision on Differential and More Favourable Treatment, Reciprocity and Fuller Participation of Developing Countries 1979).

Despite these and other concerns, the WTO claims that exceptions for agriculture like that under Article XXXVI:4 GATT have helped poor countries increase the value of agricultural exports (WTO 2004: 16):

> Given the continued dependence of many less-developed contracting parties on the exportation of a limited range of primary products, there is need to provide in the largest possible measure more favourable and acceptable conditions of access to world markets for these products, and wherever appropriate to devise measures designed to stabilize and improve conditions of world markets in these products, including in particular measures designed to attain stable, equitable and remunerative prices, thus permitting an expansion of world trade and demand and a dynamic and steady growth of the real export earnings of these countries so as to provide them with expanding resources for their economic development.

Unfortunately, until the EU and US discontinue the payment of farm subsidies for their agricultural industries, access to their markets by developing countries will be of little benefit.

Article XXXVII:1(a) GATT commits the developed members of the WTO to give top priority to the removal of barriers to goods of export interest to developing countries:

> The developed contracting parties shall to the fullest extent possible . . . accord high priority to the reduction and elimination of barriers to products currently or potentially of particular export interest to less-developed contracting parties, including customs duties and other restrictions which differentiate unreasonably between such products in their primary and in their processed forms.

Regrettably, the language found in most WTO treaties is very ambiguous. The quotation from Article XXXVII:1(a) GATT above clearly demonstrates this problem, as the provision does not specify how full is 'the fullest extent possible' or how high is 'high priority'. Such ambiguity seriously brings into question the sincerity and the priorities of developed countries. It is still not clear that they are willing to put the developmental interests of the world's poorest economies over the interests of those that control their domestic agricultural industries.

General Agreement on Trade in Services

The GATS is comparable with the GATT in that it also provides exceptions to aid developing countries. A large proportion of the labour force in the developing world works in agriculture. Yet these countries often do not have the market access and the technologies that would otherwise allow them to be more productive.

Article IV:1 GATS, for example, promotes the increasing participation of developing countries:

> The increasing participation of developing country Members in world trade shall be facilitated through negotiated specific commitments, by different Members pursuant to Parts III and IV of this Agreement, relating to:
>
> (a) the strengthening of their domestic services capacity and its efficiency and competitiveness, inter alia through access to technology on a commercial basis;
> (b) the improvement of their access to distribution channels and information networks; and
> (c) the liberalization of market access in sectors and modes of supply of export interest to them.

The reality is that developing countries need much more than a mere provision. They need access to logistical technologies and services to strengthen their capabilities to trade with the world. Access to distribution channels is especially important in the agricultural sector, as most developing countries have poor infrastructures for efficient trade. Developed countries can and should provide aid to improve agricultural supply chains, distribution networks, and modes of export (WTO, *Technical Cooperation*).

Agreement on Trade-Related Aspects of Intellectual Property Rights

The TRIPS may well be the most controversial WTO agreement because of the obligations that it imposes on developing countries, obligations that did not previously exist. Intellectual property laws in developing countries prior to the introduction of the TRIPS served to promote local industry by providing easy access to foreign innovations and, thereby, facilitated technological development though imitation (Moon 2008: 29). Indeed, a minor concession in Article 66 TRIPS allows for developing countries to take a longer time-frame to implement the agreement and encourages the transferring of technology. In addition, Article 67 TRIPS makes several provisions for technical assistance.

Technology for agriculture is vital for a country that seeks to increase the productivity and efficiency of its agricultural sector. Intellectual property rights and the barriers that they create by preventing or limiting access to the necessary technologies can greatly hinder the agricultural capabilities of developing countries. For example, apart from the subsidies that the agricultural sector in the US receives, it has a further production advantage, namely access to high-yielding, genetically modified strains of crops, pesticides, and such other modern agricultural techniques.

Waivers

Lastly, in addition to the various provisions above, a system of waivers allows additional concessions to developing countries. These waivers need the approval of the Ministerial Conference and must comply with the procedures set out in Article IX:3 WTO Agreement. Instances of waivers include, for the US, the Caribbean Basin Economic Recovery Act (CBERC) (later the Caribbean Basin Trade Partnership Act, CBTPA) and the Andean Trade Preference Act (ATPA) (later the Andean Trade Promotion and Drug Eradication Act, ATPDEA) and, for the EU, the Cotonou Agreement and the gradual replacement of its unilateral preferences by economic partnership agreements (EPAs) with African, Caribbean, and Pacific (ACP) countries.

Binding Mechanisms?

A significant problem with the special and differential treatment provisions in aid of development is that there are currently no mechanisms to bind developed countries to the provisions sanctioning preferential treatment. Members have so far failed to agree to remedy this vital flaw, most recently during the Doha Development Agenda round of multilateral trade negotiations (Doha Round). In order for the above exceptions to be effective, they have to be binding (Wu 2008: 237).

Critics on both the right and the left of the political spectrum are all in agreement that more market access for less-developed economies to more-developed markets would be beneficial. Disagreement arises when developed countries do not honour their commitments and impose onerous requirements on developing countries. These requirements hide under substantial transformation rules of origin or, more often, take the form of apparently legitimate behind-the-border barriers. Biosecurity standards are, for many agricultural producers in developing countries, impossibly expensive to attain. Yet countries like the US and the EU insist on stringent food safety protocols even when the actual risk is relatively small or, at least, manageable. These hindrances to market access negate any gains from the removal of border barriers. Indeed, many are the commitments that the developed world has made in order to grant duty-free and quota-free treatment to agricultural products with, so far, limited success.

AGRICULTURAL SELF-SUFFICIENCY AND THE WORLD TRADE ORGANIZATION

Clothing and food are basic needs for the survival of human beings, yet they are also subject to the highest tariffs, subsidies, and protective measures imposed on external trade by developed countries. To make matters worse, the economies of underdeveloped countries are largely reliant on textiles and agriculture for domestic and export purposes.

As the collapse of the Doha Round suggests, the liberalization of trade in agricultural products has not followed the path of industrial products. In fact, the Doha Round has failed almost entirely because of the entrenched agricultural interests of the developed world.

Despite the difficulties in negotiating trade agreements on agriculture, this sector constitutes only 3 per cent of total world merchandise trade and so it accounts for an insignificant share of world GDP (World Bank, *2013 Economy*). Agriculture and, more specifically, food production are something of an abnormality in economic terms for the fact that their importance is highly overstated by developed countries. The attention given to agriculture is in complete disproportion to other more important areas of the economy. In the world's developed countries, agriculture accounts for only about 2 per cent of GDP (World Bank, *Employment in Agriculture*). In the Eurozone, for example, agriculture accounts for only 3 per cent of the GDP. Meanwhile, in low and middle income countries, agriculture accounts for a much larger 27 and 10 per cent of GDP respectively (World Bank, *2013 Economy*). The US and India are a case in point. In the US, agriculture accounts for about 1 per cent of its GDP and it employs only about 1 per cent of the population (World Bank, *Employment in Agriculture*), whereas in India agriculture accounts for about 18 per cent of the GDP and employs about 51 per cent of its people (World Bank, *Employment in Agriculture, Global Poverty Indicators*). For many poor Sub-Saharan African countries, such as the Democratic Republic of Congo, agriculture can account for up to 46 per cent of GDP and employ 60 per cent of the population (Bhala 2008; World Bank, *Global Poverty Indicators*).

Overall, a vast majority of the poor in developing countries live in rural areas where agriculture plays a large role in their daily livelihoods. In developed countries, agriculture has little economic impact, but it plays a disproportionately large cultural and political role. However, in the developing world, the success of agriculture is a matter of life and death.

The Multifunctionality of Agriculture

These revelations raise the question: if food production is not economically important for developed countries, why is it so special? There are many explanations to account for why food has been so controversial and difficult to negotiate in trade agreements bilaterally, regionally, and at the WTO level. The most compelling explanation appears to be the unique emotive value that humans give to food, given its centrality to survival and culture; it affects every person, every day (Bhala 2008: 69). Secondly, food security has historically been a critical component of a country's self-sufficiency, and this has been especially true for centrally planned economies after the Second World War. Electoral politics play a major role. Representative democracies like the US allow a disproportionate presence in the legislature to rural and farming concerns. Because of the strength of their agribusiness lobbies, these countries have a long history of agricultural protection, with supporting policies and payments that are almost impossible to remove without electoral harm. A third reason why compromise on agricultural policies has been so difficult is the technical difficulty inherent in the negotiation and conclusion of framework agreements for commodities (Bhala 2008: 69). Non-economic reasons have also been cited, such as stewardship of the countryside, environmental sustainability, and social advancement, though of course these reasons could also support a case for an end to agricultural protection, since payments for production can promote ecologically exploitative practices. The point is that, whatever the reasons, food production is a sensitive topic.

This sensitivity invariably points to an essential concern with self-sufficiency. Many are the countries that still measure the strength of their national sovereignty against their capacity for self-sufficiency in the production of food and fibre. Self-sufficiency in these two basic needs for human survival is still the main explanation for the protection that agriculture receives in world trade.

> The reason for such exceptional treatment lies in the sensitive nature of agricultural imports. Most governments share a concern for the security of their country's food supply and the level and stability of the income of their rural sector. This concern has translated itself in importing countries into caution about relying on imports for basic foodstuffs and a conviction that protection from overseas competition is necessary for the health of the rural economy. Those countries with export potential in the agriculture sector have long decried such sentiments, arguing that they can provide a regular supply of foodstuffs at

lower prices and that supporting inefficient domestic production is not a sound basis for development. But, as one might expect in a sector where governments still have considerable control over markets, negotiations to open up trade in farm products have tended to proceed at the pace of the most reluctant importers. (Josling 2009: 143)

Of course, that concern with self-sufficiency need not be without sophistication. The developed group of countries often justify such protectionist measures as production subsidies, high tariffs, or complex rules of origin with great nuance. The concern for the governments of the more industrialized economies is not with self-sufficiency perhaps but with the multifunctionality of agriculture itself: food safety, environmental protection, rural development, landscape preservation, or employment retention. Whatever the nature of the concern, be it a trade concern or a non-trade concern, the response to trade in agriculture is almost always the same: to bar it.

Barriers to Agricultural Trade

Despite the many provisions to facilitate development-through-trade in the various WTO agreements, the reality is that agricultural trade escapes them. It is very much the exception. The logic of wealth creation through free trade, it seems, is not compatible with the ideology of self-sufficiency that so heavily informs government policies to trade in agricultural products. Agriculture is still subject to special treatment. The GATT and, most specially, the AA permit a range of protectionist devices that insulate agricultural products from most liberalization efforts. Subsidies and tariffs are very much the norm.

The AA allows agricultural subsidies even if, in principle, they contravene the ban that the SCM imposes (Van den Bossche 2008: 600–603). Thus, Article 21 AA states: 'The provisions of GATT 1994 and of other Multilateral Trade Agreements in Annex 1A to the WTO Agreement shall apply subject to the provisions of this Agreement.' Agricultural subsidies come in two forms: agricultural export subsidies and domestic agricultural support measures. In relation to export subsidies, so long as these apply to agricultural goods itemized in Section II of Part IV of a member's GATT Schedule of Concessions and come under Article 9(1) AA, they are permitted. They are subject to reduction commitments and, thus, they cannot exceed the budgetary spending and quantitative obligation levels promised in the related Schedule. Nevertheless, the point is that export subsidies are allowed. Article 3(3) AA states:

a Member shall not provide export subsidies listed in paragraph 1 of Article 9 in respect of the agricultural products or groups of products specified in

> Section II of Part IV of its Schedule in excess of the budgetary outlay and quantity commitment levels specified therein and shall not provide such subsidies in respect of any agricultural product not specified in that Section of its Schedule.

Article 8 AA further confirms this provision: 'Each Member undertakes not to provide export subsidies otherwise than in conformity with this Agreement and with the commitments as specified in that Member's Schedule.'

An almost identical logic applies to domestic agricultural support measures. They too are subject to reduction commitments. Ultimately, however, members are permitted to provide domestic support so long as it does not exceed the reduction commitment levels pledged in the Schedule. Article 3(2) AA states: 'a Member shall not provide support in favour of domestic producers in excess of the commitment levels specified in Section I of Part IV of its Schedule'. Moreover, domestic agricultural support measures that do not provide price support to producers are actually exempt from the applicable reduction commitments. Such exempt measures are typically known as 'green box' and 'blue box' measures. These range from research and infrastructure projects to developmental subsidies. On 'green box' subsidies, Annex 2(1) AA states:

> Domestic support measures for which exemption from the reduction commitments is claimed shall meet the fundamental requirement that they have no, or at most minimal, trade-distorting effects or effects on production. Accordingly, all measures for which exemption is claimed shall conform to the following basic criteria:
>
> (a)   the support in question shall be provided through a publicly-funded government programme (including government revenue foregone) not involving transfers from consumers; and,
> (b)   the support in question shall not have the effect of providing price support to producers; plus policy-specific criteria and conditions as set out below.

On 'blue box subsidies', Article 6 AA makes several provisions. Of these, the provision under Article 6(2) AA is particularly notable: 'investment subsidies which are generally available to agriculture in developing country Members and agricultural input subsidies generally available to low-income or resource-poor producers in developing country Members shall be exempt from domestic support reduction commitments that would otherwise be applicable to such measures'.

In developed countries, agricultural barriers to free trade are paid by the consumers through higher prices and by the tax money that ultimately funds the subsidies given to the agricultural sector. More disturbingly, these policies have a detrimental effect on the world's poorest countries. All too often, agricultural tariffs and subsidies create perverse incentives and have the effect of lowering the prices of food commodities.

Aside from agricultural subsidies, countries often resort to customs duties – tariffs – in order to protect their capacity for self-sufficiency in food and fibre production. Despite the development-through-trade rhetoric, developed countries retain very high tariffs on what they perceive to be sensitive agricultural goods. They further protect themselves through a process of 'tariff escalation', which applies low tariffs to agricultural goods and such other non-processed goods and high tariffs to processed goods (Van den Bossche 2008: 409). Accordingly, less-developed countries have no tariff incentive to industrialize. These schemes are evident in the respective Schedule of Concessions, where Part I specifies the applicable tariffs and quotas to agricultural goods. Tariffs are indeed better than quantitative restrictions in that, at the very least, they do not close down trade altogether. In that respect, Article 4.2 AA places a laudable ban against quantitative restrictions on agricultural goods. However, in requiring the conversion of quantitative restrictions into tariffs, the AA encourages a 'tariffication process' that leads to higher customs duties (Van den Bossche 2008: 451). It also leads to a system of tariff quotas, which, if set low, as they are for many sensitive agricultural goods, attract prohibitively expensive customs duties for import quantities over the quota. Moreover, if tariffs and tariff quotas were not a significant enough trade barrier, the AA makes provision for the imposition of special safeguards subject to volume and price criteria. Article 5 AA states:

> any Member may take recourse to the provisions of paragraphs 4 and 5 below in connection with the importation of an agricultural product, in respect of which measures referred to in paragraph 2 of Article 4 of this Agreement have been converted into an ordinary customs duty and which is designated in its Schedule with the symbol 'SSG' as being the subject of a concession in respect of which the provisions of this Article may be invoked, if:
>
> (a) the volume of imports of that product entering the customs territory of the Member granting the concession during any year exceeds a trigger level which relates to the existing market access opportunity as set out in paragraph 4; or, but not concurrently:
> (b) the price at which imports of that product may enter the customs territory of the Member granting the concession, as determined on the basis of the c.i.f. import price of the shipment concerned expressed in terms of its domestic currency, falls below a trigger price equal to the average 1986 to 1988 reference price for the product concerned.

Tariffs, like subsidies and rules of origin, remain a substantial barrier to trade in agricultural goods.

Agricultural Subsidies

The production of agricultural goods is significantly subsidized in both the EU and the US (Moon 2008: 30). These subsidies make it practically impossible for developing countries to sell their products abroad owing to the artificially low prices that subsidies can and do create.

Developed countries use subsidies to protect their agricultural industries. The OECD economies as a whole are estimated to have spent about $366 billion in 2010 on agricultural subsidies, amounting to around 15 per cent of the total world agricultural output (World Bank 2012: 33). The largest agricultural subsidies come from the EU and the US, which together are responsible for about one-third of the world total (WTO 2006: xxxii). The EU, as a measure of its total agricultural output from 1995 to 2001, had the highest subsidy rates at an average of $96.1 billion (WTO 2006: xxxii). During this period, it subsidized, on average, the equivalent of between 83 per cent and 140 per cent of its overall agricultural production (Bhala 2008: 71). Meanwhile, the US equivalent was around 37 per cent (Bhala 2008: 71). In that same time period, US domestic support for agriculture totalled $66.2 billion (WTO 2006: xxxii). After the US and the EU, Japan is the largest payer of subsidies, accounting for $41.8 billion, about 15 per cent of the world total (WTO 2006: xxxii; Bhala 2008: 71).

Not surprisingly, many are the leaders of developing countries who have called on the EU and the US to end domestic farm subsidies as part of the Doha Round (Bhala 2008: 72). While developed countries continue to push developing countries to liberalize market access for foreign agricultural products by slashing tariffs, they do not seem to be willing to end their own domestic farm subsidies. On this basis, it is not surprising that negotiations have stalled. Thus far, domestic subsidies in industrialized countries have largely offset the benefits that would have been gained from drops in agricultural tariffs through, for example, developmental PTAs (Moon 2008: 30).

Agricultural Tariffs

Overall tariffs for agriculture are still high notwithstanding WTO commitments. This claim is especially true for raw goods, including vegetables, fruits, sugar, and dairy products. Furthermore, processed agricultural goods tend to have even higher tariffs than those applicable to raw goods. In 2013, for example, the EU average agricultural tariff was 14.8 per cent (WTO 2013: 45), and that of the US in 2012 was 8.5 per cent (WTO 2012: 103). Significant tariff peaks apply to agricultural products, which invariably attract (higher) non-*ad valorem* tariffs. Such tariff structures effectively exclude relatively unindustrialized nations from diversifying their exports into the far more lucrative processed foods industry (Moon 2008: 20). High tariffs, therefore, are counterproductive, since developing countries stand to benefit most from market liberalization in this sector (Bhala 2008: 69).

To make matters worse, developed countries have largely stymied efforts to allow substantial market access for agricultural imports by maintaining non-tariff, behind-the-border barriers. Technical standards, such as biosecurity measures, can be rather problematic for developing country producers (Bhala 2008: 69).

Rules of Origin for Agricultural Products

The protectionist role of rules of origin often determines whether or not products from developing countries can get preferential treatment in foreign markets (Laird 2012: 34). Rules of origin between countries vary widely from one tariff line to another, and they are far from consistent among WTO members (Laird 2012: 34). A key problem that agriculture poses for developing countries is that they often lack the ability to process their own agricultural goods. Because of a lack of technology and infrastructure, they often need to process their goods in a third country before the goods are ready for export to a developed country's market. Often, because of the substantial transformation requirements of many rules of origin, if the processing takes place in a third country, it is likely to become ineligible for preferential treatment (Laird 2012: 34).

And, even if the origin of the goods does qualify for preferential treatment under the rules, compliance with food safety standards and other biosecurity requirements may make market access impossibly expensive for many agricultural producers. Behind-the-border barriers are real. Subsidies, tariffs, and rules of origin are all instruments of trade policy that, with a protectionist configuration, can negate the use of agricultural trade by developing countries as a strategy for economic development. EU and US approaches to trade in agriculture respectively illustrate the difficult policy exercise that the development-through-trade model requires of developed countries.

EUROPEAN UNION APPROACHES TO TRADE IN AGRICULTURE

Historically, EU tariffs and export subsidies kept agricultural prices out of sync with those outside of the EU (WTO 2011: 104). In recent years, reforms to the Common Agricultural Policy (CAP) have worked to narrow the gap between EU and international prices for agricultural products. Since 1992, there has been a move in the EU towards a market reorientation of agricultural support, which has essentially decoupled payments to farmers from production. Moneys for agriculture in the EU now come from the European Agricultural Guarantee Fund (EAGF) and the European Agricultural Fund for Rural Development (EAFRD). The EAGF funds direct payments to farmers, while the EAFRD funds rural development programmes that range from assistance schemes for poorer regions to grants for environmental initiatives (WTO 2011: 104).

Despite many of the recent reforms to the CAP, MFN tariffs for agricultural products remain relatively high. EU average rates of tariffs for agricultural products are far higher than those for non-agricultural products. In 2013, the average agricultural tariff was 14.8 per cent, while the non-agricultural average was 4.4 per cent (WTO 2013: 45). Moreover, the EU tariff system for agricultural products is rather complex. The system allows compound and mixed duties as well as seasonal tariffs (WTO 2011: 109). In parallel, the EU also uses a system of tariff rate quotas on a 'first-come, first-served' basis (WTO 2011: 110). The EU further maintains the right to use export subsidies for agricultural products such as sugar, meat, eggs, and certain processed goods (WTO 2011: 110).

Third country access to the EU agricultural market is, therefore, very difficult. The combination of financial support for agricultural producers and high, complex tariffs makes agricultural trade with the EU unviable for most countries. Hence, developing countries, by necessity, require differential treatment.

The EU has long appreciated that trade can be one of the 'most effective tools to foster development' (European Commission 2004: 2). Its range of association agreements provides a most effective toolbox. They vary in scope, in some cases setting up free trade areas, while in other cases preparing a country for eventual membership. At the very least, agreements offer MFN treatment, but quite often they go much further (European Commission 2013c). In terms of developmental assistance, the reference for many years was the Cotonou Agreement between the EU and the ACP group of countries. The spirit of the Cotonou Agreement carries on in the series of EPAs that the EU plans to sign with regional configurations as diverse as CARIFORUM and the Southern African Development Community (WTO 2013: 35). One example is the interim EPA with Eastern and Southern African states such as Madagascar, Mauritius, Seychelles, and Zimbabwe. In fact, the EU has already given duty-free and quota-free market access to all ACP countries that have initialled an EPA, even if they have not yet ratified it or – what is more – signed it. These agreements are the EU's most recent initiative towards development-through-trade. EPAs are reciprocal in design, more akin to conventional PTAs except that they have a more obvious developmental application. In addition to fostering economic development, the EU has also been a pioneer, since 1995, in its approach to the use of PTAs as a tool to improve human rights and democratic principles in developing countries (European Commission 2013c). The provision that permits it to enter into association agreements with third countries is in Article 217 of the Treaty on the Functioning of the European Union: 'The Union may conclude with one or more third countries or international organizations agreements establishing an association involving reciprocal rights and obligations, common action and special procedure.'

The EU was the first customs union to implement the GSP in 1971 (European Commission 2004: 3). GSP schemes differ widely from country to country on the products that they cover and the rules of origin that they apply. The EU scheme came about to aid poor countries to industrialize by boosting infant industries through reduced tariff or tariff-free entry for manufactured products (Moon 2008: 31). The EU updates the GSP scheme on a regular basis and implements those changes on ten-yearly cycles (European Commission 2013c). A relatively recent development in this respect is the Special Incentive Arrangement for Sustainable Development and Good Governance (GSP+) (European Commission 2013b: 8). It is especially important for those countries that may be reluctant to enter into an EPA with the EU because their unique developmental needs require true differentiation without any commitment to reciprocate trade preferences.

Despite its apparent strengths, the GSP has many weaknesses. Ultimately, under the GATT, the EU unilaterally decides which products will have preferential entry into its market. Agricultural (processed) products, which are, in commercial terms, the most important exports for many developing countries, may not be included and, if they are, they may have onerous rules of origin requirements or other non-tariff barriers. Accordingly, the market advantage obtained by the move to lower tariffs has, overall, given little real advantage to developing countries (Moon 2008: 74).

Everything But Arms (EBA) is a special EU initiative that entered into force in 2001 in order to create special preferential treatment for UN-recognized LDCs (European Commission 2013a: 1). It is part of the GSP. It provides duty-free, quota-free access to the EU for all products from LDCs with the exception of arms and ammunition. Despite transitional arrangements for bananas, sugar, and rice, it now extends to agricultural produce. However, the problem is, once again, with the rules of origin requirements, which, because of the substantial transformation standard, can exclude many processed agricultural products (Bhala 2008: 74).

UNITED STATES APPROACHES TO TRADE IN AGRICULTURE

US agriculture policy currently comes under the Agricultural Act of 2014 (2014 Farm Bill), which replaces the Food, Conservation, and Energy Act of 2008 (2008 Farm Bill). The Farm Bill provides for agricultural subsidies and other support schemes. Agricultural support obviously has the reinforcement of tariffs. The average tariff for imports on agricultural products into the US was 8.5 per cent in 2012 (WTO 2012: 103). This rate is low when compared to the rates of most other members of the WTO.

Even though agricultural tariffs are comparatively low, market access is still difficult if not altogether impossible for most agricultural producers from developing countries. Thus, the US, like the EU, maintains a preferential trade scheme. US developmental PTAs come in the form of trade capacity building (TCB) programmes or 'aid for trade'. They ground the US claim to being the 'largest single-country provider of . . . TCB assistance in the world' (USAID 2012).

The US has varying political and economic motivations for negotiating PTAs for development. Historically, after the Second World War, the Marshall Plan was established to rebuild Western Europe and, thereby, prevent the spread of communism. Beginning in the 1990s, the US began to enter into PTAs both for political reasons, for example the Free Trade Agreement with Israel, and for economic reasons, for example that with Mexico and Canada under the North American Free Trade Agreement (Taylor 2009: 569). Since then, the US has been receptive to developmental agreements like those of the EU.

The most substantial of these agreements is the African Growth and Opportunity Act 2000 (AGOA). The official purpose of AGOA is to offer 'tangible incentives for African countries to continue their efforts to open their economies and build free markets'. However, this and other development agreements initiated by the US do not always come without conditions (Taylor 2009: 571). Market access for American companies and the protection of intellectual property rights are the kinds of concessions that the US expects, in return, from developing countries (Taylor 2009: 571).

DEVELOPMENT THROUGH AGRICULTURAL TRADE?

Preferential Trade versus Market Access

The problems that PTAs can pose for developing countries are substantial, so much so that PTAs can even be counterproductive. Despite these countries having large populations, their economies are small and fragile with few technical resources. Thus, during international negotiations, a developing country will usually but not always lack the diplomatic expertise necessary to negotiate and it will have little leverage to get the market access conditions that yield the greatest trade benefits (Taylor 2009: 601). This claim is certainly true of most developing countries, specifically LDCs, though, of course, not all such countries lack the diplomatic means. China's formidable Ministry of Commerce is a notable exception. Whatever the exception, multilateral trade negotiations are, objectively, difficult, more akin to contests of attrition where access to an ample reserve of resources does definitely help.

Indeed, so far, both the US and the EU have shown a certain reluctance to negotiate the kind of issues that would open up their agricultural markets substantially. Indeed, the PTAs that are actually in force often have restrictive rules that keep agriculture closed off to competition. Similarly, rules of origin requirements are so complex and costly to comply with that their administration alone can often negate any gains obtained. Moreover, record-keeping and legal costs are often brought about by the onerous enforcement rules stipulated in the agreements (Taylor 2009: 601). Another danger of PTAs for developing countries is eventual tariff phase-outs, which can leave an underdeveloped country open to competition from the US and EU agricultural sectors (Taylor 2009: 601).

Economic Development versus Human Development

WTO law and policy still remain firmly premised on the economic dimension of development (Bhala 2008: 78). A common criticism of the purely economic approach is its failure to provide a wider repertoire of development strategy options that may actually run counter to the standard model of trade liberalization (Bhala 2008: 64).

The emergence of alternative models of development has been encouraged by organizations such as the UN. The adoption of any new strategy for agricultural trade liberalization (UN 2002: 15) must necessarily come from the realization among stakeholders that a 'one-system-fits-all' approach is not always suitable for developing countries that need more than simple market access to improve their situations (Moon 2008: 23).

Amartya Sen (1999) proposed the concept of human development as an alternative to the traditional economic development models. He proposed that development be measured in terms of its capacity to free people from hunger, disease, and illiteracy (Moon 2008: 32). Since then, the UN has taken steps to realign the process of development with the need for human rights. In 2003, the UN Statement of Common Understanding on Human Rights-Based Approaches to Development Cooperation and Programming acknowledged the failure of globalization to resolve many of the fundamental problems that challenge human rights everywhere, from economic need to social exclusion. The World Bank has also moved in that direction. Its approach now is much more comprehensive. It is an approach that seeks to empower developing countries so that they can manage their own development strategies, ideally with the direct participation of civil society (Bhala 2008: 77; Moon 2008: 33).

The WTO, however, remains in a state of impasse, unable to progress the very necessary Doha Round. Because of the irreconcilable needs and wants that the different stages of development of its members bring to the negotiating table, the efficacy of the WTO as a forum for trade liberalization and, through it, economic development is very much in question (Rodrik 2001). The WTO has become little more than an international court of trade. The US, the EU, Japan, and the other developed country members do not show much concern for the eradication of poverty other than as an abstract neoliberal aspiration (Bhala 2008: 77). The WTO, as an organization, may remain true to that objective, but many of the members, it seems, do not. The failure of the WTO is its failure to discipline uncooperative members. Mechanisms like the bi-yearly Trade Policy Review exercise for the US and the EU are not enough (see Chapter 15 by Marc Froese). They are talkfests, inane gatherings where all members can voice their opinion of the policies and practices of the member under review to no avail whatsoever. The emergence of PTAs as a custom-made alternative to what, for the US and the EU, are unattractive multilateral trade negotiations is a case in point.

Multilateral Law versus Unilateral Policy

Indeed, a major problem with current PTAs, as with the GATT, the GATS, and the host of WTO agreements, is that they largely curtail the ability of developing countries to control their own policy. Once they are members of the WTO, they are obligated to liberalize their economies as specified in the agreements. The implication is that compliance can deprive them of the tools and policy control necessary for their long-term development.

In order to raise the standard of living of the world's poorest people, developing countries everywhere have to be given as many policy tools as possible. There is no doubt that the level playing field of the multilateral trading system does not give developing countries an even chance in the global economy (Roy et al. 2012: 15). They need the 'policy space' that countries like Japan, South Korea, Taiwan, or even China had to industrialize through a mix of liberalization, tariffs, and other tools (Thrasher and Gallagher 2008: 350). Neoliberal economics alone do little more than curtail the policy choices for developing economies. Then again, trade liberalization may potentially benefit developing countries at least in so far as trade among them is concerned (see Chapter 13 by Bernard Hoekman). Ironically, the very exceptions that the WTO allows for LDCs in the name of economic development may actually discourage trade creation between developing economies in the poorest of regions such as Africa (see Chapter 20 by Elizabeth Smythe).

In any case, developing countries, if given the right trade policy tools, could develop dynamic, comparative advantages and eventually use them to diversify into new industries outside of agriculture. Tools used by East Asian 'tiger' economies such as subsidies, tariff protection, local content requirements, or foreign ownership caps 'are no longer available' to developing countries (Abu-Ismail et al. 2011: 14). The levels of restrictions and tariffs imposed through the GATT, GATS, and TRIPS bind economic newcomers from underdeveloped economies and take away from them the ability to follow with ease the 'contemporary trajectory of development' (Abu-Ismail et al. 2011: 15). The developed world would not have much to lose if it were to grant more freedom of policy action to the poorest (Thrasher and Gallagher 2008: 348).

Challenges and Opportunities

Tariffs, generally, are already low for LDCs, which benefit from schemes such as the GSP. Improvements could be made for a greater range of coverage and stability: that is, more liberal rules of origin for LDCs. Having less restrictive rules of origin would also encourage investors who would otherwise be unwilling to invest in LDCs and other developing countries (Laird 2012: 3).

The US and the EU should implement the first batch of cuts on tariffs that were agreed in the agricultural and non-agricultural market access negotiations and unilaterally implement the more important developmental aspects of the Doha Round on a provisional basis (Schott 2011:

4). This would not be the first time that the US and the EU would have implemented an agreement on a provisional basis, for example the transparency mechanism for regional trade agreements of 2006 (Schott 2011: 4).

Of course, the most dramatic feat that the US and the EU could perform would be to eliminate agricultural export subsidies entirely. However, this option seems very improbable in the near future. Even in a time of harsh austerity, the EU's CAP spends somewhere around 40 per cent of the entire EU budget on agriculture (European Commission 2012). This is alarming given that the EU's entire agricultural industry generates less than 2 per cent of its GDP and employs under 5 per cent of its workers ('Milking the Budget' 2012). If agreement were ever reached, there would need to be measures to prevent the re-imposition of subsidies, even in the event that commodity prices fall (Schott 2011: 4).

Trade negotiations attract rent seekers (Woolcock 2007: 6), and for American and European political leaders it is unattractive to hurt the interests of those who benefit from the status quo. The European Commission is politically weak and unpopular. It needs the support of Europe's farmers, who are actually one of the few socio-economic groups with a strong reason to back it ('Milking the Budget' 2012). The American farm lobby is equally powerful.

CONCLUSION

The concept of 'development' is an eternally controversial topic yet a much-studied phenomenon. Both proponents and detractors of economic development often advocate conflicting policies, despite the fact that they are seeking to achieve the same ends: the end of poverty. Raj Bhala succinctly sums up the lack of agreement on development as follows:

> Doha Round negotiations . . . are mired in disagreement about development – its definition, its relationship to poverty and human capabilities as well as to economic growth, its links with trade (particularly when levels of development within a developing country vary greatly) and the most appropriate role for industrialized countries in supporting it globally. (Bhala 2008: 78)

Developed countries need to 'seriously work towards creating favourable market access conditions for all products originating in least developed countries' (UN 2011b: 25). All developing countries require quota-free, duty-free market access 'on a lasting basis', with 'simple, transparent and predictable' rules of origin (UN 2011b: 4).

Until the developed world eliminates the perverse agricultural subsidies that they provide to their farmers, developmental PTAs will have little effect in alleviating the poverty in the countries that they seek to help. Additionally, developed countries should take a leadership role and begin by unilaterally implementing the partial agreements struck in the Doha Round until further, multilateral accord can be reached. Future PTAs and WTO agreements should be drafted to allow developing countries to have a much wider policy space to enact strategic barriers when necessary. The combined economies of the world's poorest countries are so small that granting generous concessions to them would be of little comparative expense. In fact, the elimination of subsidies would actually be favourable for the consumers and taxpayers of developed countries. Wasteful spending on subsidies can perhaps be put to better use in these difficult economic times.

BIBLIOGRAPHY

Abu-Ismail, K., A. Moustafa and M. Arabaci (2011), *Is There Space for Development-Friendly Trade and Industrial Policies in Arab Countries?*, Arab Development Challenges Report, Background Paper 2011/04, New York: United Nations Development Programme.

Aggarwal, R. (2005), 'Dynamics of Agriculture Negotiations in the World Trade Organization', *Journal of World Trade*, **39** (4), 741–62.

Aksoy, Ataman M. and J. Beghin (2004), *Global Agricultural Trade and Developing Countries*, Washington, DC: World Bank.

Amin, Alavi M. (2009), *Legalization of Development in the WTO: Between Law and Politics*, Alphen aan den Rijn: Kluwer Law International.

Anderson, Kym (2013), *Trade, Development, and Agriculture: Essays in Economic Policy Analysis*, London: World Scientific.

Anderson, K. and J. Croser (2010), 'New Indicators of How Much Agricultural Policies Restrict Global Trade', *Journal of World Trade*, **44** (5), 1109–26.

Anderson, Kym and T.E. Josling (2005), *The WTO and Agriculture*, Cheltenham, UK and Northampton, MA, USA: Edward Elgar Publishing.

Anderson, Kym and W. Martin (2006), *Agricultural Trade Reform and the Doha Development Agenda*, Washington, DC: Palgrave Macmillan and World Bank.

Anderson, K., W. Martin and E. Valenzuela (2006), 'The Relative Importance of Global Agricultural Subsidies and Market Access', *World Trade Review*, **5** (03), 357–76.

Athukorala, P. (2004) 'Agricultural Trade Reforms in the Doha Round: A Developing Country Perspective', *Journal of World Trade*, **38** (5), 877–97.

Beierle, T.C. (2002), 'Agricultural Trade Liberalization: Uruguay, Doha, and Beyond', *Journal of World Trade*, **36** (6), 1089–1110.

Bhala, Raj (2008), *International Trade Law: Interdisciplinary Theory and Practice*, 3rd edn, Newark, NJ: LexisNexis.

Bureau, J., S. Jean and A. Matthews (2006), 'The Consequences of Agricultural Trade Liberalization for Developing Countries: Distinguishing between Genuine Benefits and False Hopes', *World Trade Review*, **5** (2), 225.

Croser, J. and K. Anderson (2011), 'Changing Contributions of Different Agricultural Policy Instruments to Global Reductions in Trade and Welfare', *World Trade Review*, **10** (3), 297.

Das, D.K. (2006), 'The Doha Round of Multilateral Trade Negotiations and Trade in Agriculture', *Journal of World Trade*, **40** (2), 259–90.

Delcros, F. (2002), 'The Legal Status of Agriculture in the World Trade Organization: State of Play at the Start of Negotiations', *Journal of World Trade*, **36** (2), 219–53.

European Commission (2004), *The European Union's Generalised System of Preferences*, Brussels: European Commission, Directorate-General for Trade.

European Commission (2012), *Budget 2012 in Figures*, 19 January, available from: http://www.ec.europa.eu/budget/figures/2012/2012_en.cfm.

European Commission (2013a), *Factsheet: Everything But Arms (EBA); Who Benefits?*, Brussels: European Commission.

European Commission (2013b), *Factsheet: The EU's New Generalised Scheme of Preferences (GSP)*, Brussels: European Commission.

European Commission (2013c), *Generalised Scheme of Preferences (GSP)*, 13 May, available from: http://ec.europa.eu/trade/policy/countries-and-regions/development/generalised-scheme-of-preferences/index_en.htm.

European Commission, *Association Agreements*, Brussels: European Union External Action, available from: http://www.eeas.europa.eu/association/index_en.htm.

Gylfason, T. (1998), 'Prospects for Liberalization of Trade in Agriculture', *Journal of World Trade*, **32** (1), 29–40.

Josling, Tim E. (2009), 'Agriculture', in Simon Lester and B. Mercurio (eds), *Bilateral and Regional Trade Agreements: Commentary and Analysis*, Cambridge: Cambridge University Press, pp. 143–83.

Khorana, S. (2007), 'Do Trade Preferences Enhance Market Access for Developing Countries' Agricultural Products? Evidence from Switzerland', *Journal of World Trade*, **41** (5), 1073–1109.

Laird, S. (2012), *A Review of Trade Preference Schemes for the World's Poorest Countries*, Issue Paper 25, Geneva: International Centre for Trade and Sustainable Development.

MacLaren, D. (2005), 'The Role of the WTO in Achieving Equity and Efficiency in International Markets for Agricultural Products', *World Trade Review*, **4** (2), 229–47.

'Milking the Budget: Charlemagne' (2012), *Economist* (online), 24 November, available from: http://www.economist.com.hk/news/europe/21567122-even-times-austerity-europe-spends-too-much-subsidising-rich-farmers-milking-budget.

Mohan, S. (2007), 'Reforming Agricultural Trade among Developing Countries', *World Trade Review*, **6** (3), 397.

Moon, G. (2008), 'The WTO-Minus Strategy: Development and Human Rights under WTO Law', *Human Rights and International Legal Discourse*, **2** (1), 37–71.

Orden, David, D. Blandford and T.E. Josling (2011), *WTO Disciplines on Agricultural Support: Seeking a Fair Basis for Trade*, Cambridge: Cambridge University Press.

Qureshi, Asif H. and A. Ziegler (2011), *International Economic Law*, 3rd edn, London: Sweet & Maxwell.

Rawls, John (1971), *A Theory of Justice*, Cambridge, MA: Harvard University Press.

Rodrik, D. (2001), *The Global Governance of Trade: As If Development Really Mattered*, Background Paper to the UNDP Project on Trade and Sustainable Human Development, New York: United Nations Development Programme.

Roy, R., K. Abu-Ismail and R. Almeida (2012), *Is There Fiscal Space for Financing an Arab Development Transformation?*, Working Paper No. 88, Brasilia: International Policy Centre for Inclusive Growth.

Schoenbaum, T.J. (2011), 'Fashioning a New Regime for Agricultural Trade: New Issues and the Global Food Crisis', *Journal of International Economic Law*, **14** (3), 593–611.

Schott, J.J. (2011), *Policy Brief: What Should the United States Do about Doha?*, PB11-8, Washington, DC: Peterson Institute for International Economics.

Sen, Amartya (1999), *Development as Freedom*, Oxford: Oxford University Press.

Smith, Fiona (2009), *Agriculture and the WTO: Towards A New Theory of International Agricultural Trade Regulation*, Cheltenham, UK and Northampton, MA, USA: Edward Elgar Publishing.

Taylor, C.O. (2009), 'Of Free Trade Agreements and Models', *Indiana International and Comparative Law Review*, **19** (3), 569–610.

Thrasher, R.D. and K.P. Gallagher (2008), '21st Century Trade Agreements: Implications for Long-Run Development Policy', *Pardee Papers*, **2**, 1–58.

UN (United Nations) (2002), *Economic, Social and Cultural Rights: Globalisation and Its Impact on the Full Enjoyment of Human Rights*, E/CN.4/2002/54, New York: UN Economic and Social Council.

UN (United Nations) (2010), *The Least Developed Countries Report 2010: Towards a New International Development Architecture for LDCs*, UNCTAD/LDC/2010, Geneva: United Nations Conference on Trade and Development.

UN (United Nations) (2011a), *The Least Developed Countries Report 2011: The Potential Role of South–South Cooperation for Inclusive and Sustainable Development*, UNCTAD/LDC/2011, Geneva: United Nations Conference on Trade and Development.

UN (United Nations) (2011b), *Outcome of the Fourth United Nations Conference on the Least Developed Countries 9–13 May 2011*, A/66/134, LDC-IV, Istanbul: Secretary-General of the UN.

UN (United Nations) (2011c), *Report of the Fourth United Nations Conference on the Least Developed Countries 9–13 May 2011*, A/CONF.219/7, Istanbul: Secretary-General of the UN.

UN-OHRLLS (United Nations Office of the High Representative for the Least Developed Countries, Landlocked Developing Countries and Small Island Developing States), *Least Developed Countries: About LDCs*, New York: UN-OHRLLS, available from: http://www.unohrlls.org/en/ldc/.

USAID (United States Agency for International Development), *Trade Capacity Building*, TC Boost, available from: http://www.tcboostproject.com/areas/trade_capacity_building.php.

Van den Bossche, Peter (2008), *The Law and Policy of the World Trade Organization: Text, Cases and Materials*, 2nd edn, Cambridge: Cambridge University Press.

Woolcock, S. (2007), *European Union Policy towards Free Trade Agreements*, Working Paper No. 3, Brussels: European Centre for International Political Economy, pp. 1–15.

World Bank (2007), *World Development Report 2008: Agriculture for Development*, Washington, DC: World Bank.

World Bank (2012), *World Development Indicators 2012*, Washington, DC: Development Data Group.

World Bank, *2013 Economy: 4.2 World Development Indicators: Structure of Output*, available from http://wdi.worldbank.org/table/4.2.

World Bank, *Employment in Agriculture (% of Total Employment)*, available from: http://www.data.worldbank.org/indicator/sl.agr.empl.zs.

World Bank, *Global Poverty Indicators: Poverty and Equity Data*, available from: http://povertydata.worldbank.org/poverty/home.

WTO (World Trade Organization) (2003), *World Trade Report 2003: Trade and Development*, Geneva: WTO Secretariat.

WTO (World Trade Organization) (2004), *Special and Differential Treatment for Least-Developed Countries*, WT/COMTD/W/135, Geneva: WTO Committee on Trade and Development.

WTO (World Trade Organization) (2006), *World Trade Report 2006: Exploring the Links between Subsidies, Trade and the WTO*, Geneva: WTO Secretariat.

WTO (World Trade Organization) (2011), *Trade Policy Review: European Union*, WT/TPR/S/248, Geneva: WTO Secretariat.

WTO (World Trade Organization) (2012), *Trade Policy Review: United States*, WT/TPR/S/275/Rev.2, Geneva: WTO Secretariat.

WTO (World Trade Organization) (2013), *Trade Policy Review: European Union*, WT/TPR/S/284, Geneva: WTO Secretariat.

WTO (World Trade Organization), *Development: Trade and Development Committee; Work on Special and Differential Provisions*, available from: http://www.wto.org/english/tratop_e/devel_e/dev_special_differential_provisions_e.htm.

WTO (World Trade Organization), *Technical Cooperation: Examples of Provisions for*

Differential and More Favourable Treatment of Developing Countries, available from: http://www.wto.org/english/tratop_e/devel_e/teccop_e/s_and_d_eg_e.htm.

WTO (World Trade Organization), *Understanding the WTO: The Organization; Least-Developed Countries*, available from: http://www.wto.org/english/thewto_e/whatis_e/tif_e/org7_e.htm.

Wu, M. (2008), 'Free Trade and the Protection of Public Morals: An Analysis of the Newly Emerging Public Morals Clause Doctrine', *Yale Journal of International Law*, **33** (1), 215–52.

9. Democracy and trade: which leads and how?
Andrey Tomashevskiy

INTRODUCTION

The spread of new democracies is one of the more important international phenomena characterizing the twentieth century. Despite the political importance of democratization, the role of international economic factors in producing democracy remains unexplained. A traditional approach to explaining democratization has focused on domestic factors such as internal economic development. Scholars such as Moore (1993), Boix and Stokes (2003) and Epstein et al. (2006) argue that democratization is produced through a process of internal development, typically captured in the growth of per capita GDP. This approach places significant weight on explaining democracy by reference to historical and developmental factors at the domestic state level. While domestic factors certainly play a critical role in producing movement toward democracy, states do not exist in a vacuum. Recent US experiences in Iraq and Afghanistan and the integration of East European countries into the European Union demonstrate that international factors matter for democratization. International trade is a particularly important component of democratization that has not been examined in sufficient detail.

Strong evidence exists that democratization is not solely driven by domestic development but also influenced by events outside of a country's borders. Scholars have examined the impact of factors such as diffusion (Wejnert 2005; Gleditsch and Ward 2006) and international institutions (Whitehead 1996b; Pevehouse 2002) and have found evidence to suggest that international factors do have an important role for democratization. International economic factors such as trade matter for democracy as well, as demonstrated by Li and Reuveny (2003), Eichengreen and Leblang (2008), Lopez-Cordova and Meissner (2008) and others. These studies have not produced a consensus on the effects of trade on democracy, however, with studies producing seemingly contradictory results. One possible explanation for these disparities relates to an inattention to the institutional and spatial context of trade; it is not simply trade in general that can produce democratization but trade conducted with democratic states through regional and global preferential trade agreements. The political regime of a trading partner matters, and all trade is not equal. Trade with authoritarian states may lead to different effects than trade with democratic states, and it is possible that trade with authoritarian states may actually dampen the development of democracy.

I argue that democratization is linked with trade not simply because of benefits for domestic development generated by trade but because of democratic conditionality imposed by democratic states. Democracies are unique in actively tying trade cooperation to particular political conditions. It is specifically trade agreements with democratic states due to the presence of conditionality, and not simply trade in general, that produces democracy. As I show in this chapter, democratization is driven by conditionality and is less likely to occur in the absence of democracy conditions. I demonstrate that trade alone may be insufficient to produce movement from autocracy to democracy. While I find that trade may indeed promote democracy, I show that this occurs only within the specific context of conditionality. I use data on democracy and trade and find evidence that trade with democracies is positively associated with democratization, while trade with autocracies is associated with movement away from democracy. This work refines the link between global economic integration and democracy by presenting an outline of the channels through which trade may lead to increased democracy. The context of trade matters: since only democracies impose democratic conditionality, democratic trade partners push for democratization but autocratic trade partners do not. In what follows, I review the literature on trade and democratization and discuss why conditionality may be a necessary component in the trade–democracy relationship. I test these arguments using empirical data while accounting for the potential effects of endogeneity. I then conclude with a discussion of the implications of this research for policy and strategies of democracy promotion.

INTERNATIONAL SOURCES OF DEMOCRACY

This work fits into the general tradition of international sources of domestic politics, a theoretical approach that has a significant history behind it. German and English historians at the start of the twentieth century, such as Otto Hintze, have hypothesized that a state's domestic regime is typically the outcome of international conditions. Hintze argued that democracies form in states that are insulated from external security threats and can afford to adopt a decentralized form of organization such as a democracy (Almond 1989). Gourevitch (1978), in reviewing the literature on the international sources of domestic politics, argues that the time at which states chose to industrialize played an important role in the selection of domestic regime; states that industrialized early, such as Britain, tended to be democratic, while states industrializing later in the nineteenth century, like Germany, tended to be non-democratic. World-system theorists such as Immanuel Wallerstein argue that a state's position within the international capitalist system affects its prospects for democracy. Periphery states that are economically dependent on core states are unlikely to democratize, especially if ruled by comprador-type ruling classes that derive support and legitimacy from external international sources.

If international factors have historically affected internal politics, what does this mean for democratization? Within the democratization literature, a number of international factors are identified as important for producing democratization. One of the more extreme forms of international influence involves forced regime imposition and occupation. This has been an important factor in the democratization of West Germany and Japan and was certainly the most important factor in Iraq. However, this form of imposition is rare and commonly involves the opposite process of authoritarian imposition. Examples of this type of imposition include Russian involvement in the suppression of the Hungarian revolutions of 1848 and 1956 and the 1968 invasion of Czechoslovakia.

There exist other, more subtle international mechanisms that are the focus of this chapter. One of the most basic mechanisms for the spread of democracy involves diffusion or "contagion" (Whitehead 1996a; Dobbin et al. 2007). The spatial and geographic environment of a state is important, as evidenced by waves of democratization occurring in spatially defined clusters. These clusters included the first wave of democratization in Western Europe, the democratizations in Latin America and the Caribbean basin and the waves of democratization in Eastern Europe and Africa in the 1990s. While some have suggested that transition to democracy is essentially a random and unpredictable event (Przeworski and Limongi 1997), the presence of geographically defined clusters is evidence that international factors are at play in affecting the occurrence of democratization. Thus, Gleditsch and Ward (2006) find that states are more likely to transition to democracy when bordered by other states that undergo the same transition, and Wejnert (2005) also finds evidence in favor of the diffusion hypothesis. This line of research suggests that the regional environment of a state plays an important role in predicting democratization; within regions, there appears to be a convergence process at play, producing homogeneity of regime types.

If the spatial and geographic context appears to play an important role in producing transition to democracy, what are the mechanisms that account for this diffusion? One argument regarding the causes of diffusion can be found in research that emphasizes the role of ideas and social processes and points out the emulative aspect of democratization (Finnemore 1996; Dobbin et al. 2007; Owen 2010). In this argument, democratization is conceptualized as a kind of fad where states democratize to emulate powerful and successful states in the international system. Thus, states in Eastern Europe democratized in an attempt to emulate the success of the United States and Western European nations, where this desire was an important cause of the revolutions in the region. This type of "follow-the-leader" process leads to norm cascades and tipping points, exponentially increasing the pace of democratization as more countries begin to emulate their regional neighbors. Using an apt metaphor, Huntington (1991) describes this process as "snowballing." Evidence shows that this type of diffusion takes place not only for democratization but for other policies, such as mass schooling (Finnemore 1996). The process of snowballing may be more effective in a regional context owing to existing historical and cultural ties among regional neighbors.

In addition to more general processes of diffusion, Pevehouse (2002) finds evidence that international organizations (IOs) have an important effect on democratization. States that are members of mostly democratic organizations are more likely to democratize through a similar process of diffusion. The impact of IOs on democracy is important for trade, since many organizations are specifically economic organizations dealing with matters of trade. Preferential trade agreements (PTAs) that lead to increased trade among states are a particular, economically oriented institution. Pevehouse argues that multilateral institutions produce democratization through mechanisms of socialization or through public social pressure applied by international organizations. In discussing the role of IOs, it is important to disaggregate IO types, such as security, trade and other regional institutions, since different institutional types may be associated with different internal mechanisms for democratization and diffusion.

There are several reasons why PTAs like NAFTA are different from other international institutions and should be considered separately. In particular, PTAs provide concrete economic rewards and should be associated with a more specific cost–benefit calculation. The channels through which a trade agreement influences democracy will be an economic channel, which may operate differently than a social mechanism. Kelley (2004) does not find social mechanisms of the type that Pevehouse discusses to be particularly effective in affecting domestic politics, and Kelley points to the effects of membership conditionality. This suggests that alternative mechanisms should be considered, including economic channels and the role of conditionality. Furthermore, the type of IOs that Pevehouse considers are multilateral, while PTAs are often bilateral. Bilateral institutions may be more effective at promoting democracy, since there is no collective action problem involved, as might be the case in a multilateral IO. In this sense, the mechanisms through which NAFTA produces democratization will be different compared to NATO or the Organization of American States (OAS), since membership in NAFTA will be associated with specific economic gains. Finally, Mansfield and Pevehouse (2008) find that democratizing states tend to be drawn to economic IOs compared to other regional organizations, which again suggests that analysis of institutional types should be disaggregated. Overall, there are reasons to believe trade institutions and conditionality may be more important for promoting democracy than simply IOs in general.

TRADE, CONDITIONALITY AND DEMOCRACY

Existing evidence suggests an important relationship between trade and democracy. The effect of trade on democracy has been examined within the context of globalization and increased international trade flows (Li and Reuveny 2003; Acemoglu and Robinson 2005; Rudra 2005; Eichengreen and Leblang 2008; Lopez-Cordova and Meissner 2008). There exist several arguments as to why integration into world markets is beneficial for democracy. Drawing on domestic development and modernization arguments, some scholars argue that globalization promotes democracy through development (Li and Reuveny 2003); democracy is more likely to take root in nations that achieve a high level of domestic economic development, where development is typically captured in GDP per capita (Boix and Stokes 2003; Epstein et al. 2006). Since globalization is assumed to increase development and provide economic benefits, globalization and increasing trade will indirectly lead to democracy by providing positive economic externalities. Evidence also suggests that economic development consolidates democracy and reduces the risk of authoritarian reversal (Svolik 2008). Globalization and trade may also decentralize power, strengthen institutions that promote democracy and increase the diffusion of democratizing ideas. Globalization can be detrimental for democracy as well. Globalization deepens government autonomy, produces domestic losers who may oppose a liberalizing economic regime and induces financial instability owing to the increased volatility of financial flows. Economic development may also enable authoritarian leaders to increase the legitimacy of authoritarian rule and reduces the likelihood of democratic transition.

The theoretical arguments for the trade–democracy link are therefore mixed. Empirical evidence is mixed as well. Li and Reuveny (2003) find that increased trade reduces democracy. Lopez-Cordova and Meissner (2008) find that trade openness increases democracy, and Eichengreen and Leblang (2008) also find a positive relationship between trade and democracy. Why is the empirical record so mixed? One reason is that the globalization literature fails to consider the institutional and spatial context of trade, where context accounts for the divergent empirical results. Trade is examined in a very general fashion; it is simply openness in general that matters, where openness is typically measured as imports and exports as a percentage of GDP (Li and Reuveny 2003; Eichengreen and Leblang 2008). Neither openness with respect to specific nations nor the specific nature of regional trade relations is taken into account. Not all trade flows are equal, and nations often place greater weight on trade relations with a specific nation or set of nations: for Mexico, maintaining good trade relations with the United States is more important than maintaining trade relations with Fiji. As the literature on diffusion and democratization suggests, the spatial and geographical context is important when considering the effects of globalization.

Why is the specific context of trade important? To answer this question, additional mechanisms of diffusion should be examined. Aside from simple unassisted diffusion of norms and ideals, coercion plays a very important role with respect to domestic policy diffusion. Coercion does not necessarily have to operate through direct invasion and imposition, but instead works by changing incentives and motivations. As Lawrence Whitehead argues:

> The essential point is that approaching two-thirds of the democracies existing in 1990 owed their origins, at least in part, to the deliberate acts of imposition or intervention from without . . . It is not contiguity alone but the policy of a third power that explains the spread of democracy from one country to the next. (Whitehead 1996b: 9)

The actions of third parties have been central to the spread of not only democracies but other policies as well, through a policy of external inducement.

In terms of trade and democratization, an important mechanism commonly used by powerful democratic states involves the use of political conditionality (Baylies 1995; Ethier 2003; Szymanski and Smith 2005; Finkel et al. 2007; Pridham 2008; Schimmelfennig and Scholtz 2008). The use of this mechanism is especially evident with regard to the EU/EC and international aid. There are a number of historical examples that demonstrate the explicit use of aid to achieve political goals. The EC froze aid to Greece after the colonels' coup in 1967 and halted negotiations on agricultural policy harmonization. This policy had a direct effect on the trajectory of Greek politics, since the EC "provided and absorbed roughly half of all Greek imports and exports respectively" (Tsingos 1996: 318). Furthermore, following a return to democracy, EC aid served to consolidate and stabilize further democratic development. As Basilios Tsingos argues, the EC worked to "establish a clear, causal connection between democracy, EC membership and prosperity for the now heavily subsidized countryside. This connection amounted to nothing less than recognition that personal and national prosperity were inextricably linked to Greece's new identity as a liberal democracy and EC member state" (Tsingos 1996: 341).

Since the end of the Cold War, the EU has been more explicit in using conditionality not only with respect to aid but also in terms of trade conditionality. Ethier (2003) and Schimmelfennig and Scholtz (2008) find that EU conditionality has been highly effective in promoting democracy when the reward involves EU accession. For non-member candidate states in the European Neighborhood Program (NEP) and the African Caribbean Pacific (ACP) states, the effects of trade conditionality are more ambiguous, and the impact of conditionality appears to be smaller. Despite this, Hafner-Burton (2005) finds that PTAs have a positive effect in promoting human rights, especially PTAs with "hard" standards that tie trade cooperation to human rights compliance. For example, the violation of democratic and human rights principles in Togo and Fiji caused the EU to suspend cooperation under the Lomé IV Convention, contributing to the reestablishment of democracy in those countries. The EU's strategy of conditionality is therefore evident not only in regional relationships but in a broad context as well. During negotiations with Mexico in 1997 to pass a Framework Agreement on bilateral trade liberalization, the EU included a democracy clause, which was also present in agreements concluded with other Latin American states, outlining a commitment to the "democratic foundations of cooperation" (Sanahuja 2000; Szymanski and Smith 2005). Finally, conditions on democracy and democratization were also in force during EU accession negotiations with Eastern European states, and here conditionality is considered to have achieved its most considerable success. Utilizing this type of conditionality mechanism, the EU was able to shift and alter the incentives towards democratization. While the effectiveness of conditionality declines when the prospect of EU membership is not on the table, conditionality still remains effective to some extent, as research by Hafner-Burton (2005) and others suggests.

These types of conditionality clauses need not be explicitly defined as in the EU case to be in operation; it is common for democratizing pressures to take place even in agreements that do not contain explicit democracy conditions, such as NAFTA or Mercosur. NAFTA is one example of ex ante, implicit conditionality. For Mexico, the prospect of NAFTA and the negotiation process served as a powerful impetus for the implementation of democratic reforms. Deliberations in the US Congress over the ratification of the treaty pushed Mexican leadership to enact a number of democratic reforms in order to ensure ratification of the treaty. Stephen Collins indicates that "NAFTA did not, in fact, include an explicit democracy codicil; rather, ex ante democratic conditionality was implicitly imposed by members of Congress at the ratification stage," further stimulating political reform in Mexico (Collins 2009: 377). Similarly, US government officials have often stated that further liberalization of trade with Belarus is conditional on the improvement of the political situation in that country.

How does conditionality interact with PTAs? Since states seek to join PTAs in order to secure market access, PTAs can be used as an incentive to promote domestic change. While states have a constant interest in securing preferential access to markets, they face an even greater incentive when multilateral trade negotiations such as WTO trade negotiations stall or fail (Mansfield and Reinhardt 2003). States thus have an interest in creating and joining PTAs in order to secure access to markets and to avoid being shut out of regional trading blocs. Conditionality may be ineffective if a given state does not have a need for a democratic PTA with conditionality attached: the targeted state may simply abstain from creating a PTA or seek out a PTA without political conditions. However, when a state is dependent on trade with democracies or stands to gain significant economic benefits from creating or joining a democratic PTA, democratization conditionality is more likely to prove successful. In such cases, democratic states may exert leverage over the domestic politics of potential trade partners by using conditionality (Levitsky and Way 2005). Such leverage will tend to be more effective if the potential trade partner stands to suffer higher costs by missing out on a PTA compared to the potential costs imposed by democratization.

If a state is not reliant on trade with democracies and can find other sources of aid or trade, democratizing pressure is less likely to succeed. In fact, it is possible that a reverse effect may occur in regional agreements composed mostly of autocracies. Autocratic regimes will not necessarily place "autocratization" clauses on entry but may instead provide support to certain factions that are viewed as reliable partners, regardless of whether such factions are committed to democracy. It is also possible that democratizing reforms may be more likely to stall, since elites that wish to consolidate their hold on power will have an easier time securing private goods abroad from other authoritarian states that have no explicit interests in promoting democratic norms. Ambrosio (2008) provides support for this idea and argues that the Shanghai Cooperation Organization has been used by its authoritarian member states to defend themselves against democratic trends and lock in authoritarian rule. In this way, ex ante democratic conditionality is the key channel through which democratization is produced.

To illustrate this logic, theories of internal leadership dynamics within authoritarian states provide a useful example. Although non-democratic states may desire a PTA for a number of reasons, one potential cause that may be unique to autocracies involves the prospect of domestic unrest. As Acemoglu and Robinson (2005) argue, although de jure political power in autocracies is monopolized by the autocrat or some group of elites, citizens continue to hold significant de facto power by virtue of their number. Acemoglu and Robinson (2005) define income of poor individuals in non-democracy by $y^p = \frac{(1 - \theta)\bar{y}}{1 - \delta}$ where θ is share of total income accruing to the elites and δ is proportion of elites where $\delta < 1/2$. Individual income y^i is a function of tax rate τ and θ; increases in θ represent increases in inequality, while increases in τ reduce θ and generate greater redistribution. Although elites prefer to set tax rates to zero and implement no redistribution, the threat of revolution from the general populace may induce elites to implement higher tax rates coupled with redistributive policies.

In Acemoglu and Robinson's (2005) model, as inequality increases and remains unaddressed by redistributive policies, the population threatens elites with revolution. In response to this threat, autocratic elites can respond with repression, with economic concessions and redistributive policies or with an expansion of political freedom. If repression is not feasible, autocrats may prefer to stave off revolution through concessions and limited redistributive policies. However, autocrats cannot credibly commit to provide such policies into the future; revolution may still occur owing to a time inconsistency problem, as the population does not trust the elites not to renege on their promises in future periods. Democratization takes place in the presence of a revolutionary threat because autocrats must credibly commit to redistributive policies. A change in domestic institutions from autocratic to democratic transfers de jure power to the population, thus locking in redistributive policies and eliminating the time inconsistency problem.

Since in this model elites prefer to keep tax rates at zero, democracy, and the resulting higher taxes, does not produce the optimal outcome for elites (Acemoglu and Robinson 2005: 176). However, the model does not account for possible external resources, such as PTAs and trade, that may be used to reduce inequality without changing tax rates. Economic gains from PTAs can be used to reduce inequality θ through Stolper–Samuelson effects and reduce the risk of revolution. Since the abundant factor of production tends to benefit from trade in the standard Heckscher–Ohlin/

Stolper–Samuelson model of trade and since many non-democratic countries are labor-abundant, the poor are likely to benefit more from increased trade compared to elites in an autocracy. Empirical evidence also suggests that trade can reduce wage inequality and improve welfare gains (Goldberg and Pavcnik 2004; Porto 2007). Similarly, growth has been shown to have effects on poverty reduction (Dollar and Kraay 2002). Joining an international trade agreement is a more credible mechanism than simple promises of reforms and concessions, since international agreements can work to lock in reforms and tie the hands of domestic leaders (Fernandez and Portes 1998). PTAs and subsequent gains from trade thus allow elites to reduce the revolutionary threat without giving way to democracy. PTAs and gains from trade reduce the risk of revolution by reducing inequality, θ, without increasing τ, the tax rate. PTAs may in fact produce a dampening effect on democratization by providing the autocrat with the resources to increase regime stability and reduce pressure for democracy.

Conditionality in democratic PTAs changes the logic of this interaction. The presence of democratic conditionality means that the autocrat cannot collect gains from trade without escaping democratization. All trade is not equal, and trading partners matter: democracies use conditionality to induce movement to democracy, while trade with autocracies helps lock in authoritarian rule. Depending on its regional location, the non-democratic state will have a limited choice of PTA partners. For non-democracies located in predominantly democratic regions where the "natural" trading bloc is composed of democracies (Frankel et al. 1995), the choice of PTA partner will be essentially limited to democracies. Autocrats can, of course, look for PTAs outside of their region, but these agreements will be less attractive because of increased transport costs and so may be less viable as a tool to buy off the population. Furthermore, since democratic states tend to be richer, democracies will be attractive PTA partners owing to the size of their markets. An autocrat in such a position is caught between a rock and a hard place: revolution on one side, conditionality on the other. In this case, democracies are better positioned to use the mechanisms of leverage to promote democratization (Levitsky and Way 2005).

Democratization induced by conditionality will not necessarily take the form of a direct democratic transition but may proceed more incrementally, as in countries like Brazil, Slovakia or Romania. Since PTAs provide benefits for the population and reduce inequality along with pressure for democratic transition, the elites implement a more limited set of reforms than in the absence of a PTA. Gains from trade can be thus used by elites to reduce the popular pressure for reform while still retaining some privileges via smaller steps to democracy.

In this sense, democratization generated by conditionality and democratic PTAs may actually be more limited compared to democratization that would have occurred from the threat of revolution alone. For the autocrat, this type of incremental democratization is the lesser of two evils, since positive economic externalities reduce the likelihood of revolution and allow the autocrat to hang on to some degree of power. Democracy conditions thus interact with the autocrat's need to maintain regime stability and avoid high redistribution to produce democratization. While the threat of revolution pushes autocrats to democratization, conditionality ensures that autocrats cannot use PTAs to escape this pressure by reducing inequality. A strategy of positive inducement thus reduces the costs of democratization so that the gains from compliance outweigh the costs. When conditionality is missing, the autocrats do not need to democratize to receive a PTA and can use economic gains from trade to reduce the threat of revolution.

DATA AND RESEARCH DESIGN

To test these arguments, it is necessary to model the conditionality process at work. Trade leads to democracy only if the trading partner is a democratic state. Separating the impact of the PTA on democracy from other, possibly endogenous, factors is more difficult, because past research shows that democratic states are more likely to form PTAs (Mansfield et al. 2002). Thus, if a PTA between state i and j is a function of i and j's domestic regime, as well as some other set of factors, an empirical model predicting the probability of PTA formation in a dyad would be written as:

$$PTA_{ijt} = \alpha + Democracy_{it}\nu + Democracy_{jt}\phi + X_{it}\beta + Z_{jt}\beta + \varepsilon$$

where X_i and Z_j are matrices of covariates specific to states i and j. Since I am interested in examining the impact of PTA formation on democracy, including an indicator for a PTA on the right-hand side in a model with democracy as a dependent variable would be equivalent to having democracy on both the right-hand and left-hand sides of the equation. To account for this endogeneity, I use a two-step approach which is consistent with similar approaches used by Lopez-Cordova and Meissner (2008) and Eichengreen and Leblang (2008). First, I replicate a model of PTA formation developed by Mansfield and Reinhardt (2003). This model is written as:

$$PTA_{ijt} = \alpha + X_{it}\beta + Z_{jt}\beta + \varepsilon$$

where X_{it} and Z_{jt} are matrices of covariates specific to states i and j at time t as above, and here I explicitly exclude regime types for i and j from the specification. This approach produces an estimate of a state's likelihood of PTA formation with a democratic state. To address the endogeneity problem, democracy is excluded from the model specification and the likelihood of PTA formation is expressed as a function of factors other than democracy. After estimating this model, I use the predicted probabilities from the PTA formation model as an independent variable in a model with democratization as the dependent variable:

$$Democracy_{it} = \kappa_i + W_{it}\delta + (\text{Pr } PTA_{it}) + \nu_{it}$$

where W_i is a matrix of covariates for state i. As the probability of PTA formation increases, states will have greater incentive to democratize and I therefore expect the coefficient for the PTA probability variable to be positive. A PTA may be more likely when the potential partner is attractive in terms of geographic distance, a shared alliance, high bilateral trade and other factors that have been found to increase the likelihood of PTA formation (Gowa and Mansfield 1993, 2004; Mansfield and Bronson 1997; Mansfield et al. 2002; Mansfield and Reinhardt 2003). These factors are accounted for by Mansfield and Reinhardt's (2003) model, which is among the more complete models of PTA formation, and so I use this model for the first stage estimation.

For their paper, Mansfield and Reinhardt (2003) estimate a logit model that includes a number of variables thought to influence the likelihood of PTA formation. This model uses directed dyad data for all states in the system in the years 1948–98. I make a modification to this model and I only include dyad observations up to the point where the members in the dyad concluded a PTA. Since observations after a PTA has been concluded do not provide information regarding the effect of conditionality, dyadic observations following the creation of a PTA are excluded from the model. I then generate predicted probabilities from this model as an estimate of PTA formation with a democracy. It is likely that not all PTAs will have an equal effect, since the prospect of a trade agreement with some states will be more important than with other states. To account for this fact, I weigh the generated predicted probabilities and multiply the predicted dyadic PTA probability by the ratio of dyadic trade between States 1 and 2 over State 1's total trade in a given year. If trade with State 2 accounts for a large proportion of State 1's total trade, State 1 will value a potential PTA with State 2 much more compared to other states that account for less trade. Since I am interested in the conditionality aspect of PTAs with democratic states, I also weigh the predicted probabilities by the Polity IV regime score of the second state in the directed dyad (Marshall and Jaggers 2002). I rescale the 21-point Polity scale to range from 0 to 21, with 0 corresponding to most autocratic states and 21 representing most democratic states, square the resulting value and weigh the predicted probabilities using this value. This ensures that dyads with more democratic trade partners contribute more than dyads with autocratic partners. I then keep the annual sum of predicted probabilities for State 1 in the original directed dyad. The resulting PTA variable for state *i* at time *t* can be formally expressed as:

$$\text{PTA}_{it} = \sum (Polity_{jt} + 10)^2 \times \left(\Pr(PTA_{ijt}) \times \frac{\text{Trade}_{ijt}}{\text{TotalTrade}_{it}} \right)$$

This procedure is done in order to facilitate analysis in the second stage. Since the first stage model uses directed dyad data and the second stage uses state–year data, transitioning between stages involves a transition between levels of analysis. I sum the annual state-level predicted probabilities to convert the information contributed by directed dyads into a state–year format and because conditionality is more likely to be effective when there is a prospect of PTA formation with multiple democratic states and so the effect will be cumulative.[1]

Using the PTA formation estimates, I regress a state's Polity score for all years 1948–98 at time *t* on PTA formation, log of GDP per capita, highest average IO score, mean regional regime score, mean regional number of conflicts, mean global number of conflicts and an indicator of military regime status. The dependent variable is the Polity IV regime score, which ranges from −10 to 10, with 10 indicating strong democracy and −10 indicating strong autocracy. The log of GDP per capita is included in order to control for domestic, endogenous sources of democratization and development. GDP per capita is the standard variable associated with modernization theory, and previous literature has found a link between development and democracy, indicating that there is reason to suspect that higher per capita income leads to an increased likelihood of democracy (Boix and Stokes 2003; Epstein et al. 2006). Using Polity IV data, I also calculate the average yearly democracy score for each region in the Correlates of War dataset. The regions include Europe, the Middle East, Africa, Asia, North America and South America, and this variable is designed to measure the effect of general diffusion and contagion processes.

As noted above, previous studies have found that states are more likely to democratize when located in a region with many other democratic states. Democratic norms and institutions are expected to spread across borders owing to increased contacts and interactions with other states, creating democratization through these contact-based mechanisms.

Similar pressure can be exerted through international organizations. Thus, Pevehouse (2002) finds that membership in international organizations with high democratic membership is predictive of democratic transition. To control for these effects I include a variable that corresponds to the highest average regime score for all international organizations that a state belongs to. The external security situation of a state can also play a role in producing democratization. As Hintze argues, states may be able to democratize more effectively when they do not face the threat of war or conflict (Almond 1989). Thus, unstable regional or international conditions will make it more difficult for states to democratize. To control for these effects, I calculate the total number of militarized interstate disputes taking place among states in the international system and on the regional level. Finally, I add a dummy variable to indicate if a state is under the control of a military regime in a given year. Military regimes are often more brittle and susceptible to regime change, and I include this variable to account for this higher likelihood of collapse, although it is unlikely that the collapse of a military regime will necessarily lead to democracy, and so I expect this variable to be negative (Geddes 1999).

Since state-level data are organized as repeated observations for states over time, I utilize a model for panel data. As a first cut, I use a fixed effects panel model with heteroskedasticity-corrected standard errors. Since it is likely that the effects of past democracy will persist into future periods, I also include a lagged dependent variable on the right-hand side.[2] The full model can be written as:

$$Democracy_{it} = \alpha_i + \beta\,Democracy_{it-1} + \beta\,PCGDP_{it} + \beta\,PTAProb_{it} +$$

$$\beta\,WorldMID_{it} + \beta\,RegionalMID_{it} + \beta\,RegionalDemocracy_{it} +$$

$$\beta\,MilitaryRegime_{it} + \beta\,IOscore_{it} + v_{it}$$

The results of the model are presented in the columns for Model 1 in Table 9.1.

These results provide some support for the hypotheses developed in this chapter. The coefficient on the PTA formation variable does not quite reach significance at the 0.05 level. The GDP variable is positive and significant, which is consistent with the endogenous democratization/modernization hypothesis. The IO variable is not significant in this model, which is somewhat puzzling given previous findings. These results also provide evidence for the diffusion hypothesis, since the regional democracy variable is positive and significant. The military regime variable is negative

Table 9.1 Fixed effects panel results

Variable	Model 1: full sample		Model 2: 1948–86		Model 3: 1986–98	
	Coefficient	(Std. err.)	Coefficient	(Std. err.)	Coefficient	(Std. err.)
Democracy, $t-1$	0.774**	(0.033)	0.745**	(0.041)	0.542**	(0.082)
ln PCGDP	0.184*	(0.085)	0.220*	(0.090)	−0.937	(0.894)
PTA probability	0.004	(0.004)	0.000	(0.003)	0.028**	(0.006)
International conflict	−0.014*	(0.006)	−0.024**	(0.008)	0.002	(0.009)
Regional conflict	0.046*	(0.015)	0.081**	(0.021)	−0.020	(0.032)
IO regime score	0.008	(0.020)	0.005	(0.022)	0.023	(0.075)
Military regime	−1.951*	(0.489)	−2.316**	(0.595)	−2.269**	(0.746)
Regional democracy	0.175*	(0.050)	0.206**	(0.061)	0.464**	(0.108)
Intercept	−0.642	(0.600)	−0.527	(0.597)	8.428	(7.173)
N	2746		2158		671	
R^2	0.742		0.739		0.49	

Notes: Significance levels: * 5%; ** 1%.

and significant and is consistent with Pevehouse's (2002) findings. The IO variable is not significant in this model, which might suggest that economic IOs may be responsible for most variation explained by the IO variable in other models. Finally, both of the international conflict variables are significant, although they seem to be pointing in opposite directions. This suggests that conflict has different effects on a regional level than on a global level. One explanation for this finding could involve the fact that new states were established out of former colonies following violent conflict and so new democracies were established following civil or interstate wars in the developing world.

To disaggregate the effects of PTA formation, I run the model for two separate historical periods, 1948–86 and 1986–98.[3] PTA formation has generally proceeded in two historical waves, a wave of PTAs during the 1960s and 1970s and a wave of PTA since 1989. We should expect to observe stronger effects in the post-1980 period, since conditionality became more widely used towards the end of the Cold War. More specifically, Baylies (1995) notes that World Bank conditionality became widespread in the mid-1980s and the EU officially began using conditionality in 1989. The results for these models are reported in the columns for Models 2 and 3 in Table 9.1.

The results of these models support the main hypotheses. The PTA formation variable is positive and significant in Model 3 but not in Model 2. This finding is consistent with the historical record, since use of conditionality became more widespread in the 1980s. The strong significance of the PTA coefficient in Model 3 indicates that the effect of conditionality is strongest in the post-1986 period, even though this effect was hidden by the full sample in Model 1. The coefficient for GDP is significant in the first period but not in the second. While the coefficient for diffusion remains positive and significant in both models, the effects of conflict appear to diverge. The lack of significance for both conflict variables in Model 3 could be related to the fact that democratizations taking place in the latter part of the twentieth century were mostly peaceful in nature and were not preceded by conflict. The decreased occurrence of violent regime change since 1980 could thus be pointing to alternative modes of democratic transition.

The fixed effects estimator may be problematic, since the regressor y_{it-1} is correlated with the error term, making the fixed effects estimator inconsistent. A more appropriate estimator for a dynamic model is the Arellano and Bond (1991) first difference estimator. First differencing eliminates unit-specific effects and uses short-run variation in the independent variables to explain short-run variation in the dependent variable. The full model can be written as:

$$\Delta Democracy_{it} = \beta \Delta Democracy_{it-1} + \beta \Delta PCGDP_{it} + \beta \Delta PTAProb_{it} +$$

$$\beta \Delta WorldMID_{it} + \beta \Delta RegionalMID_{it} + \beta \Delta RegionalDemocracy_{it} +$$

$$\beta \Delta MilitaryRegime_{it} + \beta \Delta IOscore_{it} + \Delta v_{it}$$

where Δ is the difference between year t and year $t-1$. A problem with this formulation is that the lagged dependent variable $\Delta Democracy_{it-1}$ is still correlated with the error term Δv_{it}. The Arellano–Bond estimator takes advantage of the fact that previous lags are not correlated with the error term and a matrix of lags can be constructed for use as instruments for the endogenous lagged dependent variable. For example, y_{it-2} is an instrument for y_{it-1} at $t = 3$, y_{it-2} and y_{it-3} are instruments at $t = 4$, $y_{it-2}, y_{it-3}, y_{it-4}$ are instruments at $t = 5$ and so on. When T is large, as it is in this case, many instruments are generated (969 for these data) and asymptotic performance becomes poor, with inconsistent standard errors. I restrict the use of available lags to 2, so that only y_{it-2} and y_{it-3} are used as instruments in period t.[4] With the GMM estimator it is also possible to relax the assumption of strict exogeneity, the assumption that $E[x_{is}v_{it}] = 0$ for all s and t. It is possible that a shock to democracy at time t will cause an increase of GDP at time $t+1$, meaning that $E[x_{is}v_{it}] \neq 0$ for $s > t$. This possibility is argued by Acemoglu et al. (2008), who suggest that democracy often has effects on

Table 9.2   Arellano–Bond GMM results

Variable	Model 4: full sample		Model 5: 1948–86		Model 6: 1986–98	
	Coefficient	(Std. err.)	Coefficient	(Std. err.)	Coefficient	(Std. err.)
Democracy, $t-1$	0.774**	(0.071)	0.702**	(0.088)	0.789*	(0.247)
ln PCGDP	0.460**	(0.177)	0.448*	(0.195)	−0.591	(0.934)
PTA probability	0.005†	(0.003)	0.002	(0.003)	0.018*	(0.008)
International conflict	−0.005	(0.009)	−0.019†	(0.010)	0.003	(0.009)
Regional conflict	0.011	(0.031)	0.084*	(0.035)	−0.025	(0.037)
IO regime score	−0.019	(0.028)	0.009	(0.022)	−0.286	(0.198)
Military regime	−4.402**	(0.955)	−5.068**	(1.062)	−1.251	(1.142)
Regional democracy	0.180*	(0.086)	0.184	(0.141)	0.317*	(0.127)
Intercept	−0.642	(0.600)	−1.996	(1.436)	9.228	(6.861)
N	2746		2158		671	
R^2	666.115		420.649		100.626	

Notes: Significance levels: † 10%; * 5%; ** 1%.

GDP just as GDP affects democracy. To account for this, it is possible to use instruments in levels in time periods that are unrelated to Δv_{it}, and I restrict available instruments for GDP to a single lag. This restriction, combined with the restriction for the dependent variable lags, generates 144 instruments at time t. This model is estimated using two-step GMM with heteroskedasticity-consistent robust standard errors. The results are presented in Table 9.2.

These results are consistent with the fixed effects results above. The PTA probability variable is now significant in the full sample at the 0.10 level. The other important difference involves the fact that the conflict variables are no longer significant, although regional conflict is significant at the 0.05 level in the pre-1986 period. Overall, these models show that the effect of PTA probability is robust across models.

The results so far seem to indicate that PTAs with democratic states have a significant impact on democratization. What kind of effects do PTAs formed with autocratic regimes have? Since autocracies do not use conditionality when creating PTAs, it is likely that autocratic PTAs will have no effect or a negative effect on PTA formation. To test this hypothesis, I modify the Polity weights on the PTA variable by subtracting 10 from the Polity score for state j. This gives greater weight to observations where PTAs were formed with autocracies. I re-estimate the fixed effects models and the first difference models using autocratic PTA formation

Table 9.3   Fixed effects autocratic PTA results

Variable	Model 7: full sample		Model 8: 1948–86		Model 9: 1986–98	
	Coefficient	(Std. err.)	Coefficient	(Std. err.)	Coefficient	(Std. err.)
Democracy, $t-1$	0.772**	(0.033)	0.743**	(0.041)	0.563**	(0.081)
ln PCGDP	0.163†	(0.086)	0.214*	(0.092)	−1.165	(0.869)
Autocratic PTA probability	−0.001**	(0.000)	−0.001**	(0.000)	0.104	(0.072)
International conflict	−0.014*	(0.006)	−0.024**	(0.008)	0.003	(0.009)
Regional conflict	0.047**	(0.015)	0.083**	(0.021)	−0.024	(0.031)
IO regime score	0.010	(0.020)	0.005**	(0.022)	0.024	(0.072)
Military regime	−1.977**	(0.488)	−2.334**	(0.596)	−2.186**	(0.727)
Regional democracy	0.183**	(0.051)	0.214**	(0.062)	0.475**	(0.108)
Intercept	−0.479	(0.605)	−0.608	(0.628)	10.247	(6.956)
N	2746		2158		671	
R^2	0.741		0.739		0.486	

Notes: Significance levels † 10%; * 5%; ** 1%.

Table 9.4   Arellano–Bond GMM autocratic PTA results

Variable	Model 10: full sample		Model 11: 1948–86		Model 12: 1986–98	
	Coefficient	(Std. err.)	Coefficient	(Std. err.)	Coefficient	(Std. err.)
Democracy, $t-1$	0.772**	(0.072)	0.697**	(0.087)	0.789 **	(0.228)
ln PCGDP	0.436**	(0.163)	0.415*	(0.183)	−0.800	(0.993)
Autocratic PTA probability	0.000	(0.000)	0.000	(0.000)	0.132	(0.081)
International conflict	−0.005	(0.009)	−0.020*	(0.010)	0.006	(0.010)
Regional conflict	0.015	(0.032)	0.090**	(0.031)	−0.035	(0.043)
IO regime score	−0.020	(0.030)	0.007	(0.021)	−0.312†	(0.165)
Military regime	−4.430**	(0.907)	−5.111**	(1.040)	−1.193	(1.205)
Regional democracy	0.187*	(0.092)	0.190	(0.134)	0.398*	(0.186)
Intercept	10.247	(6.956)	−1.714	(1.309)	11.150	(7.882)
N	2746		2158		671	
$\chi^2_{(8)}$	658.562		347.645		96.522	

Notes: Significance levels † 10%; * 5%; ** 1%.

as an independent variable. The results are presented in Tables 9.3 and 9.4.

As expected, these results provide additional evidence that it is PTAs with democracies that matter. In the fixed effects models, the autocratic PTA probability variable is significant and negative, indicating that trade with autocracies actually has a negative effect on democracy. For the GMM models, this variable is not negative but does not reach significance in any of the models. This finding provides further evidence for the fact that the positive effect on democracy is not produced by PTAs in general but only by PTAs formed with other democracies.

One possible explanation for the significance of the PTA probability variable could involve the role of the EU. Since the EU is unique in using explicit conditionality that is consistently applied, these results might be driven by the effects of EU conditionality. To explore this possibility, I create a dummy variable that is equal to 1 for all EU member states and 0 otherwise, and interact this variable with PTA probability. The GMM results are presented in Table 9.5. The overall pattern of results remains the same, and the interaction term does not reach significance in any of the models. However, the uninteracted PTA variable remains significant

Table 9.5   Arellano–Bond GMM interaction term

Variable	Model 13: full sample		Model 14: 1948–86		Model 15: 1986–98	
	Coefficient	(Std. err.)	Coefficient	(Std. err.)	Coefficient	(Std. err.)
Democracy, $t-1$	0.774**	(0.073)	0.703**	(0.091)	0.783**	(0.251)
ln PCGDP	0.455**	(0.169)	0.457*	(0.203)	−0.507	(0.920)
PTA probability	0.006†	(0.003)	0.004	(0.004)	0.004	(0.005)
International conflict	−0.005	(0.009)	−0.018†	(0.009)	0.003	(0.008)
Regional conflict	0.010	(0.032)	0.082*	(0.033)	−0.023	(0.035)
IO regime score	−0.019	(0.029)	0.008	(0.020)	−0.294	(0.182)
Military regime	−4.407**	(0.913)	−5.070**	(1.120)	−1.338	(1.161)
Regional democracy	0.178*	(0.091)	0.177†	(0.101)	0.307*	(0.130)
EU PTA probability	−0.003	(0.007)	−0.005	(0.005)	0.020	(0.012)
Intercept	10.247	(6.956)	−2.070	(1.499)	8.651	(6.843)
N	2746		2158		671	
$\chi^2_{(9)}$	732.097		507.302		136.33	

Notes: Significance levels † 10%; * 5%; ** 1%.

in the full sample, indicating that democratic PTA probability continues to have an effect when the EU dummy variable is equal to 0. It is likely that the EU by itself does not explain a sufficient amount of variance and that the inclusion of other regions is also important.

CONCLUSION

In this chapter, I have argued that external causes of democratization are often ignored in the literature. The international context plays an important role in affecting the likelihood of regime choice and democratization. The formation of preferential trade agreements and the conditions on entry imposed by democratic states are some of the important factors that are often overlooked. By estimating a panel data time series model, I have found evidence that PTAs with democracies play an important role in influencing the likelihood of democratization. Thus, when states were more likely to form PTAs with democratic states, they were also more likely to democratize. This is an important finding that challenges some previous work. While scholars have found that democracies are more likely to trade (Mansfield et al. 2002), it appears that democratization is first induced by the promise of PTA formation. This finding suggests that the international sources of domestic policy are important and the process of democratization is shaped to some extent by outside influence. This outside influence raises additional questions regarding the role of international power relations. Regional cooperation shifts the centers of power and is commonly associated with concerns of security and the international relations of power, not simply concerns about trade or democratic values. Lawrence Whitehead suggests that "it is inadequate to focus on the democracy-promoting potential of such regional groupings without also considering their power-political implications and the hegemonic tendencies they may also serve" (Whitehead 1996a: 406).

A more specific way to view this tendency is to think of conditionality as one item in a set of possible policy tools. States with large markets can use the prospect of market access as an incentive to achieve political goals in target countries. In this sense, the use of political conditionality represents the use of influence between unequal states. Conditionality is an important tool of influence, but it is important to determine why this particular tool is chosen. Why is conditionality used with respect to some countries and not for others? If PTA conditionality is a tool of influence, what are some other economic tools used by states and why do states choose one tool rather than another? A similar question relates to the goals of the democratic community in using conditionality. While the promotion of democracy is a central goal of US foreign policy, the promotion of democracy also relates to the strength of the democratic community and the incidence of war (Kadera et al. 2003). By strengthening the democratic community, democracies marginalize other regional groupings that feel threatened by the growing strength and cohesion of democratic groupings, creating the potential for increased conflict and major power competition. In this sense, organizations like the Shanghai Cooperation Organization are reactions that are designed to slow democratizing trends.

Finally, this line of research also raises additional implications regarding the question of positive inducement (Nincic 2006, 2011). This chapter suggests that the use of economic inducements has the potential to produce movement toward democracy and change the incentives of autocratic regimes. These are important questions, and answering them can provide additional insight regarding relations between powerful and weak states. Further research is necessary, along with additional controls to more fully explore the effect of PTAs on democratization.

NOTES

1. The results of the first stage model are presented in the Appendix to this chapter.
2. I performed the Wooldridge (2002) autocorrelation test, which returns a t-statistic of 142.718 and indicates that the null hypothesis of no panel autocorrelation can be rejected at the 0.000 level.
3. While conditionality became more widespread after the late 1990s and during the 2000s, trade conditionality was used by a number of democratic states in the time period captured by this sample. This sample also presents a more difficult test for my argument, since evidence in support of the conditionality argument when use of conditionality was less common suggests a stronger relationship when conditionality becomes more widespread.
4. To test if this is an appropriate specification, I perform the Sargan test of overidentifying restriction. This test finds that $prob > x^2 = 0.6319$ and indicates that the null hypothesis of valid overidentifying restrictions cannot be rejected.

REFERENCES

Acemoglu, Daron and James A. Robinson (2005), *Economic Origins of Dictatorship and Democracy*, Cambridge: Cambridge University Press.
Acemoglu, Daron, Simon Johnson, James A. Robinson and Pierre Yared (2008), "Income and Democracy," *American Economic Review*, **98**, 808–42.
Almond, Gabriel A. (1989), "The International–National Connection," *British Journal of Political Science*, **19** (2), 237–59.
Ambrosio, Thomas (2008), "Catching the 'Shanghai Spirit': How the Shanghai Cooperation Organization Promotes Authoritarian Norms in Central Asia," *Europe-Asia Studies*, **60** (8), 1321–44.

Arellano, Manuel and Stephen Bond (1991), "Some Tests of Specification for Panel Data: Monte Carlo Evidence and an Application to Employment Equations," *Review of Economic Studies*, **58** (2), 277–97.
Baylies, Carolyn (1995), "Political Conditionality and Democratisation," *Review of African Political Economy*, **22** (65), 321–37.
Boix, Carles and Susan C. Stokes (2003), "Endogenous Democratization," *World Politics*, **55** (4), 517–49.
Collins, Stephen D. (2009), "Can America Finance Freedom? Assessing U.S. Democracy Promotion via Economic Statecraft," *Foreign Policy Analysis*, **5** (4), 367–89.
Dobbin, Frank, Beth Simmons and Geoffrey Garrett (2007), "The Global Diffusion of Public Policies: Social Construction, Coercion, Competition, or Learning?," *Annual Review of Sociology*, **33** (1), 449–72.
Dollar, David and Aart Kraay (2002), "Growth Is Good for the Poor," *Journal of Economic Growth*, **7** (3), 195–225.
Eichengreen, Barry and David Leblang (2008), "Democracy and Globalization," *Economics and Politics*, **20** (3), 289–334.
Epstein, David L., Robert Bates, Jack Goldstone, Ida Kristensen and Sharyn O'Halloran (2006), "Democratic Transitions," *American Journal of Political Science*, **50** (3), 551–69.
Ethier, Diane (2003), "Is Democracy Promotion Elective? Comparing Conditionality and Incentives," *Democratization*, **10** (1), 99.
Fernandez, Raquel and Jonathan Portes (1998), "Returns to Regionalism: An Analysis of Nontraditional Gains from Regional Trade Agreements," *World Bank Economic Review*, **12** (2), 197–220.
Finkel, Steven E., Anibal S. Perez-Linan and Mitchell A. Seligson (2007), "The Effects of U.S. Foreign Assistance on Democracy Building, 1990–2003," *World Politics*, **59** (3), 404–39.
Finnemore, Martha (1996), "Review: Norms, Culture, and World Politics: Insights from Sociology's Institutionalism," *International Organization*, **50** (2), 325–47.
Frankel, Jeffrey, Ernesto Stein and Shang-jin Wei (1995), "Trading Blocs and the Americas: The Natural, the Unnatural, and the Super-Natural," *Journal of Development Economics*, **47** (1), 61–95.
Geddes, Barbara (1999), "What Do We Know about Democratization after Twenty Years?," *Annual Review of Political Science*, **2** (1), 115–44.
Gleditsch, Kristian Skrede and Michael D. Ward (2006), "Diffusion and the International Context of Democratization," *International Organization*, **60** (04), 911–33.
Goldberg, Pinelopi K. and Nina Pavcnik (2004), *Trade, Inequality, and Poverty: What Do We Know? Evidence from Recent Trade Liberalization Episodes in Developing Countries*, NBER Working Paper Series No. 10593, Cambridge, MA: National Bureau of Economic Research.
Gourevitch, Peter (1978), "The Second Image Reversed: The International Sources of Domestic Politics," *International Organization*, **32** (04), 881–912.
Gowa, Joanne and Edward D. Mansfield (1993), "Power Politics and International Trade," *American Political Science Review*, **87** (2), 408–20.
Gowa, Joanne and Edward D. Mansfield (2004), "Alliances, Imperfect Markets, and Major-Power Trade," *International Organization*, **58** (04), 775–805.
Hafner-Burton, Emilie M. (2005), "Trading Human Rights: How Preferential Trade Agreements Influence Government Repression," *International Organization*, **59** (03), 593–629.
Huntington, Samuel P. (1991), "Democracy's Third Wave," *Journal of Democracy*, **2** (2), 12–34.
Kadera, Kelly M., Mark J.C. Crescenzi and Megan L. Shannon (2003), "Democratic Survival, Peace, and War in the International System," *American Journal of Political Science*, **47** (2), 234–47.
Kelley, Judith (2004), "International Actors on the Domestic Scene: Membership

Conditionality and Socialization by International Institutions," *International Organization*, **58** (3), 425–57.

Levitsky, Steven and Lucan Way (2005), "International Linkage and Democratization," *Journal of Democracy*, **16** (3), 20–34.

Li, Quan and Rafael Reuveny (2003), "Economic Globalization and Democracy: An Empirical Analysis," *British Journal of Political Science*, **33** (01), 29–54.

Lopez-Cordova, Ernesto J. and Christopher M. Meissner (2008), "The Impact of International Trade on Democracy: A Long-Run Perspective," *World Politics*, **60** (4), 539–75.

Mansfield, Edward D. and Rachel Bronson (1997), "Alliances, Preferential Trading Arrangements, and International Trade," *American Political Science Review*, **91** (1), 94–107.

Mansfield, Edward D. and Jon C. Pevehouse (2008), "Democratization and the Varieties of International Organizations," *Journal of Conflict Resolution*, **52** (2), 269–94.

Mansfield, Edward D. and Eric Reinhardt (2003), "Multilateral Determinants of Regionalism: The Effects of GATT/WTO on the Formation of Preferential Trading Arrangements," *International Organization*, **57** (04), 829–62.

Mansfield, Edward D., Helen V. Milner and B. Peter Rosendorff (2002), "Why Democracies Cooperate More: Electoral Control and International Trade Agreements," *International Organization*, **56** (03), 477–513.

Marshall, Monty and Keith Jaggers (2002), Polity IV Project: Political Regime Characteristics and Transitions, 1800–2002.

Moore, Barrington (1993), *Social Origins of Dictatorship and Democracy: Lord and Peasant in the Making of the Modern World*, Boston, MA: Beacon Press.

Nincic, Miroslav (2006), "The Logic of Positive Engagement: Dealing with Renegade Regimes," *International Studies Perspectives*, **7** (4), 321–41.

Nincic, Miroslav (2011), "Getting What You Want: Positive Inducements in International Relations," *International Security*, **35** (1), 138–83.

Owen, John M., IV (2010), *The Clash of Ideas in World Politics: Transnational Networks, States, and Regime Change, 1510–2010*, Princeton, NJ: Princeton University Press.

Pevehouse, Jon C. (2002), "Democracy from the Outside-In? International Organizations and Democratization," *International Organization*, **56** (03), 515–49.

Porto, Guido G. (2007), "Globalisation and Poverty in Latin America: Some Channels and Some Evidence," *World Economy*, **30** (9), 1430–56.

Pridham, Geoffrey (2008), "The EU's Political Conditionality and Post-Accession Tendencies: Comparisons from Slovakia and Latvia," *Journal of Common Market Studies*, **46** (2), 365–87.

Przeworski, Adam and Fernando Limongi (1997), "Modernization: Theories and Facts," *World Politics*, **49** (2), 155–83.

Rudra, Nita (2005), "Globalization and the Strengthening of Democracy in the Developing World," *American Journal of Political Science*, **49** (4), 704–30.

Sanahuja, Jose Antonio (2000), "Trade, Politics, and Democratization: The 1997 Global Agreement between the European Union and Mexico," *Journal of Interamerican Studies and World Affairs*, **42** (2), 35–62.

Schimmelfennig, Frank and Hanno Scholtz (2008), "EU Democracy Promotion in the European Neighbourhood," *European Union Politics*, **9** (2), 187–215.

Svolik, Milan (2008), "Authoritarian Reversals and Democratic Consolidation," *American Political Science Review*, **102** (02), 153–68.

Szymanski, Marcela and Michael E. Smith (2005), "Coherence and Conditionality in European Foreign Policy: Negotiating the EU–Mexico Global Agreement," *Journal of Common Market Studies*, **43** (1), 171–92.

Tsingos, Basilios (1996), "Underwriting Democracy: The European Community and Greece," in Lawrence Whitehead (ed.), *The International Dimensions of Democratization*, New York: Oxford University Press.

Wejnert, Barbara (2005), "Diffusion, Development, and Democracy, 1800–1999," *American Sociological Review*, **70** (1), 53–81.

Whitehead, Lawrence (1996a), "Democratic Regions, Ostracism, and Pariahs," in Lawrence

Whitehead (ed.), *The International Dimensions of Democratization*, New York: Oxford University Press.

Whitehead, Lawrence (1996b), "Three International Dimensions of Democratization," in Lawrence Whitehead (ed.), *The International Dimensions of Democratization*, New York: Oxford University Press.

Wooldridge, Jeffrey M. (2002), *Econometric Analysis of Cross Section and Panel Data*, Cambridge, MA: MIT Press.

APPENDIX

Table 9A.1 PTA formation logit estimates

Variable	Coefficient	(Standard error)
Alliance, $t-1$	0.517**	(0.137)
Geographical distance	−0.484**	(0.041)
Bilateral trade, $t-1$	35.834**	(5.450)
GDP, State 1, $t-1$	−0.257[†]	(0.145)
GDP, State 2, $t-1$	−0.245[†]	(0.126)
Per capita GDP, State 1, $t-1$	−0.006	(0.006)
Per capita GDP, State 2, $t-1$	−0.005	(0.005)
GDP growth, State 1, $t-1$	−0.018[†]	(0.011)
GDP growth, State 2, $t-1$	0.008	(0.011)
PTA density, $t-1$	−33.310**	(4.566)
PTA density2, $t-1$	−194.617**	(72.321)
Trade partner PTA coverage State 1, $t-1$	3.636**	(0.223)
Trade partner PTA coverage State 2, $t-1$	3.463**	(0.210)
Year	−0.030	(0.023)
Detrended number of GATT members	0.234**	(0.035)
GATT round underway, t	1.259**	(0.189)
GATT dispute loss with third party, $t-3$	1.540**	(0.140)
New dispute between States 1 and 2, $t-1$	−0.383	(0.699)
New dispute with third party, $t-1$	0.505**	(0.155)
Former colonial relationship, t	1.223**	(0.331)
Postcommunist state, t	2.949**	(0.222)
Intercept	53.317	(46.270)
N	36421	
Log-likelihood	−901.848	
$\chi^2_{(28)}$	1150.189	

Notes:
Mansfield and Reinhardt (2003) logit model predicting PTA formation (six duration dependence splines omitted from the table, standard errors clustered by dyad, White heteroskedasticity-corrected standard errors used).
Significance levels: † 10%; ** 1%.

PART III

REGIONS AND REGIONALISM IN THE LEAD

10. Regionalism's past, present, and future
Greg Anderson

INTRODUCTION

Over the past two decades, regionalism in international trade has increasingly drawn the attention of policy makers and economists, quite often for very different reasons. Both economists and policy makers have long worried about the implications of regionalism for postwar multilateral order anchored by the General Agreement on Tariffs and Trade (GATT), renamed the World Trade Organization (WTO) in 1994. Yet economists and policy makers have slightly different sets of concerns where regionalism is concerned. Economists view regionalism with skepticism because of its corrosive effects on the efficiency and growth trade liberalization can bring. Policy makers are concerned with regionalism because of the many geopolitical ramifications attendant on the patchwork of economic preferences regionalism creates. Over the past two decades, both groups have worried about the ways in which regionalism has contributed to a series of phenomena that are increasingly difficult to reconcile with overall economic openness and liberal global trading.

All of this helps explain why trade, and regionalism specifically, is the quintessential international political economy (IPE) topic pitting the efficiency models of economists against the political imperatives of those implementing policy. Much of the contemporary debate about regionalism has treated it as though it was a recent and worrisome phenomenon, as well as an outlier in the history of international trade. Yet, in many ways, multilateralism is the historical outlier, and a postwar outlier on top of that. In fact, regionalism has been the default mode of governance in international trade for most of human history. As simple exchange gave way to long-distance trade, the logic of liberalization became more obvious, made vividly so by the eighteenth-century classical economists Adam Smith (absolute advantage) and David Ricardo (comparative advantage).

The end of World War II left most of the world's economies either smashed or exhausted, but presented a novel opportunity for postwar planners to recast the global trading system in the kind of efficiency and growth generating regime Smith and Ricardo had described two centuries before. The GATT put the global trading system on a path toward more efficiency and less discrimination in global trading patterns, but anachronistically left the door open to additional regionalism at the same time.

This chapter is about the anachronism of regionalism within the global trading system, its problems, its evolution, and its future. The plan of this chapter is as follows: first, it traces some of the thinking about regionalism from the interwar years and the run-up to the postwar multilateral system; it then outlines the concerns of politicians and economists concerning regionalism; it goes on to detail how regionalism and multilateralism continue to stand awkwardly beside each other in the same institutional structure; it then discusses the proliferation of regionalism over the past two decades; finally, it asks whether any of the "spaghetti bowl" can, or should, be reversed.

The broad conclusion of this chapter is that, despite its obvious drawbacks in terms of deviations from the efficiency and growth of global output, regionalism is here to stay. The proliferation of regional agreements, particularly after the end of the Cold War, concerns economists and policy makers both because of their efficiency implications and because of the challenges inherent in untangling them. Indeed, shortly after the conclusion of the Uruguay Round of the GATT and its transformation into the WTO in 1994, Jagdish Bhagwati warned that the penchant for regionalism risked undermining those hard-won multilateral gains by creating a complex "spaghetti bowl" of preferences (Bhagwati 1995). Yet regionalism's prominence today is also the result of geopolitics that favors the extension of preferential economic arrangements under rationales that have more to do with politics than economics, thereby making regionalism a quintessentially IPE topic.

PREWAR SPAGHETTI BOWL WITH NATIONALIST SAUCE

Contemporary academic treatments of the multilateral trading system almost universally begin with the postwar planning carried out at Bretton Woods, New Hampshire in 1944. There, the allied powers crafted the blueprints for a postwar economic order to be supported by two key institutions: the International Bank for Reconstruction and Development (World Bank) and the International Monetary Fund (IMF). As a key complementary body, postwar planners also conceived of a multilateral trading system anchored by the International Trade Organization (ITO), which some now consider a third pillar of Bretton Woods (Irwin et al. 2008: 98–9). The outlines of the ITO first emerged from the U.S. State Department in the fall of 1944, well after the July Bretton Woods Conference (Irwin et al.

2008: 49–50). As early as 1946, the United States and the United Kingdom were working on a parallel text designed as an offshoot of the larger ITO project, the General Agreement on Tariffs and Trade, which would govern tariff liberalization until the completion of the ITO (Irwin et al. 2008: 86, 98). After the failure of the ITO in the early 1950s, the GATT became the de facto set of rules governing multilateral trade, expanding to over 150 countries through its transformation into the World Trade Organization in 1994.

The GATT's modest beginnings – as well as its initial membership of just 23 countries – are part of the reason the GATT has not always been considered part of the Bretton Woods institutions. Yet the major principles undergirding membership in the GATT – most favored nation treatment, national treatment, and non-discrimination – have become cornerstones of a multilateral trading system designed to undo the patchwork of prewar trading arrangements some argued had contributed to the onset of war.

Years earlier, in the midst of the Great Depression, U.S. Secretary of State Cordell Hull became more fully convinced of the linkage between the economic nationalism implicit in protectionism and the rise of extremist political ideologies. In his memoirs, Hull wrote:

> Toward 1916 I embraced the philosophy I carried throughout my twelve years as Secretary of State, into the Trade Agreements, into numerous speeches and statements addressed to this country and to the world. From then on, to me unhampered trade dovetailed with peace; high tariffs, trade barriers, and unfair economic competition, with war. (Hull 1948: 211)

Indeed, one of the strongest reactions to the stock market crash of 1929 in the United States was the Tariff Act of 1930, more infamously known as the Smoot–Hawley Tariff Act. According to most accounts, re-election-minded legislators sought higher tariff rates on individual items of importance to constituents in their districts. The Smoot–Hawley Bill revised tariff schedules on more than 20000 items, most of which received increases, and, exacerbated by the price deflation of the 1930s, resulted in the highest American *ad valorem* equivalent tariff structure in the twentieth century at nearly 60 percent. While individual districts or sectors of the economy were the direct beneficiaries of protective tariff rates, consumers in particular suffered, as the Smoot–Hawley Bill raised the price of imports and contributed to a series of retaliatory tariff revisions by other nations that contributed to an exacerbation of the Great Depression (Schattschneider 1935; Pastor 1980: 77–84; Destler 1995: 11–13; Eckes 1995: 100–139; O'Halloran 1994: 32).

Convinced that economic nationalism in trade policy had contributed to economic decline and facilitated the rise of fascism in Europe and

Asia,[1] Hull persuaded President Roosevelt that competitive "beggar-thy-neighbor" policies were contrary to American interests and in 1934 received both presidential and congressional backing for the Reciprocal Trade Agreements Act, which initiated reciprocal tariff reductions of up to 50 percent (Anderson 2012a: 587–9). This basic approach to tariff reductions eventually formed the core of the GATT, with reciprocal reductions being multilateralized via their extension to all other members through the most favored nation principle.

Yet one of the most fascinating aspects of contemporary commentary and analysis of the multilateral trading system is the degree to which multilateralism is depicted as the default mode of governance of global trade (see Panagariya 1999; Crawford and Laird 2001; Majluf 2004; Baldwin 2006; Menon 2009). Indeed, Bhagwati's original conceptualization of regionalism as a "spaghetti bowl" of sorts depicts such arrangements as a relatively new corrosive phenomenon in global trade.

Yet, for much of human history, multilateralism – and the principles of most favored nation, national treatment, and non-discrimination – has been the exception rather than the rule. As Douglas Irwin's (1996) wonderful intellectual history of the evolution of free trade thought makes clear, the intellectual case in favor of openness in global trade was long in the making, its adoption as policy even more challenging, and continues to generate controversy. For centuries, trade has been viewed with suspicion. In contemporary debates, analysts have focused on forms of "protectionism" designed to shield domestic populations from the adjustment costs associated with openness and foreign competition. However, "protectionism" in the earliest patterns of human exchange frequently flowed from forms of xenophobia, including suspicions that the exotic goods borne by traders were the corrosive end of a wedge into society that would undermine domestic economic, political, or social stability (Irwin 1996: 10–25).

It is precisely this mixture of economic activity and politics that makes international trade the quintessential topic in IPE. As students of economics know well, the case in favor of trade liberalization was built over time, but finally coalesced in the writings of Adam Smith and David Ricardo in the late eighteenth and early nineteenth centuries. When we think about Smith's absolute advantage and Ricardo's comparative advantage, we rightly focus on the elegance of their thinking about the efficient allocation of scarce resources. That their ideas continue to act as a kind of "north star" guiding the global trading regime toward that efficiency in the twenty-first century is testament to their power. However, the power of those ideas has, over time, tended to obscure the fact that Smith and Ricardo, like many of their contemporaries, also thought deeply about the complications of politics in political economy (see Irwin 1996; Hoffman 2013).

Contemporary debates about economic policy have been dominated by the so-called rational market hypothesis: the idea that information flows easily and without cost in market economies and is rapidly reflected in asset prices such that few genuine opportunities for arbitrage exist. As Justin Fox so interestingly details in his book *The Myth of the Rational Market*, there are more caveats to this hypothesis than had been appreciated prior to the onset of the financial crisis in 2008 (Fox 2011). Doubts about the rational market hypothesis have re-kindled interest in behavioral economics, and a re-engagement with the work of psychologists on human rationality in decision making (Simon 1956, 1959; Tversky and Kahneman 1974, 1981).

The point is that regionalism in international trade is, in part, about the gap between the pure rationality of many economic models and the practice of politics. Hence, while economists worry about the inefficiency of regionalism, politicians often pursue it for reasons unrelated to economics.

WHO DOESN'T LIKE SPAGHETTI?

Economists fret about regionalism's impact on trade relations for a variety of reasons, almost all of which revolve around its role in undermining efficiency, and therefore the wealth-creating benefits of trade liberalization.

First and foremost, economists worry about trade diversion: the possibility that regionalism will foster the sourcing of imports from a less efficient regional partner over a more efficient supplier elsewhere (Panagariya 1999: 482–6). While a regional trading arrangement may in fact liberalize trade, it is the monetary difference between the benefits of liberalization between members and the trade diversion effect that troubles economists. If, for example, the United States and Mexico were to bilaterally liberalize their trade in agriculture, there might be a significant increase in agricultural trade between the two countries. However, if Mexico happened to have a relatively inefficient agricultural sector relative to Brazil, the United States might end up sourcing more of its agricultural imports from Mexico entirely owing to the preferences in their bilateral agreement rather than on the basis of growth-enhancing efficiency gains from liberalization (Panagariya 1999: 482–6). Preferences agreements can still yield enormous benefits for member countries (Panagariya 1999: 483). But economists worry about the rapid proliferation of these agreements, since they might incentivize the expansion of relatively inefficient production and trade among members (Estevadeordal et al. 2005; Menon 2009).

Moreover, economists have also knocked down a number of arguments proffered in support of regional preferences agreements, including the idea that "natural trading partners" exist or that preferences arrangements can accentuate the advantages of geography by reducing transport costs (Panagariya 1999: 486). Because preferences schemes do not entail the harmonization of trade policies, tariff schedules in particular, vis-à-vis non-members, complicated rules of origin are required to prevent the entry of non-member goods via the member country with the lowest tariffs. Yet rules of origin have in many instances become cumbersome and expensive administrative barriers to economic activity for all but the largest member country firms (Pastor 2011: 174–5).

Most critically, preferences schemes, such as free trade agreements, are inherently discriminatory, since they liberalize by extending privileges to members only. While not necessarily as worrisome as the economic nationalism of the interwar years that troubled Secretary of State Hull, the expansion of such preferences to new members has periodically prompted concerns that the global trading system was dividing itself into a small number of regional trading blocs (Thurow 1991). Yet controversy exists even where preferences have been extended for high-minded purposes like development in low-income countries. Specifically, evidence regarding the lasting benefits of preferential access to developed country markets for developing country exports is thin (Panagariya 1999: 489–91, 2002). Such schemes have too frequently been focused on a small number of commodities, too seldom incentivizing moves up the value chain or the kinds of governance reforms links such linkages are thought to provide (Panagariya 2002).

This then leads to the non-trade motivations for preferences schemes: geopolitics (Irwin et al. 2008: 188–200). International relations theorists familiar with the work of Immanuel Wallerstein will know the basic tenets of dependency theory (see Wallerstein 2004). In essence, global capitalism functions through a series of relationships in which rich and developed "core" countries engage in trading relationships with developing countries, or the "periphery," which are inherently exploitive. Developing countries export raw materials to developed nations, which are in turn processed into finished goods for export back to developing countries. This relationship repeats, preventing developing countries from moving up the value chain of production and keeping them economically "dependent" on core countries.

A variant of this line of thinking has emerged in the context of regional preferences schemes wherein large, developed countries, such as the United States, offer up market access to smaller partners as a way to draw them into the larger state's sphere of economic and political influence. Recent patterns of U.S. regionalism suggest support for this kind of hub-and-spoke dependence. Consider the 2005 agreement between the United States and five Central American countries (Costa Rica, El Salvador, Guatemala, Honduras, and Nicaragua) plus the Dominican Republic (CAFTA-DR). In economic terms, the impact of the agreement on America's $14 trillion economy was negligible, while the market access potential for CAFTA-DR countries was enormous.

Realist approaches look at the same patterns of trading relationship and posit that large countries dominate global trading relations through the maintenance of rules they themselves designed, in effect forcing smaller countries to play by them (Krasner 1976). More familiar to students of the political economy of postwar European integration is the perspective of liberal theorists wherein fostering economic linkages (interdependence) among states would render the price of political or military conflict unacceptably high, thereby securing peaceable relations (most famously Keohane and Nye 1977).

Regardless of the interpretation, the liberalization process required each of the CAFTA-DR countries to liberalize and reform a number of their economic policies as the price of membership. Here, another of the non-economic rationales for regionalism entails the "locking-in" of economic reforms by member (mainly developing) countries (Panagariya 1999: 489–90). Indeed, the "locking-in" of economic reforms in Mexico was a major argument undergirding U.S. support for the North American Free Trade Agreement (see Bush 1993; Krugman 1993; Panagariya 1999: 490; Lederman et al. 2005; Weyland 2009: 39; Pastor 2008: 85). These kinds of governance arguments in favor of regionalism are also not far removed from the promotion of democratic norms. For example, the proposed Free Trade Area of the Americas (FTAA) was launched with great fanfare at the Summit of the Americas in Miami in the fall of 1994. Its ambition and membership spanned the entire Western Hemisphere, included every country except Cuba, and attempted to both capitalize upon and consolidate the embryonic post-Cold War expansion of democracy in the region (Feinberg 1997; see also Dominguez 1998). Indeed, democracy was an explicit requirement for membership in the Summit of the Americas process and FTAA negotiations (see U.S. Department of State 1994).

Finally, one the most important non-traditional motivations for engaging in regionalism concerns overcoming the familiar collective action problems associated with large-N negotiations (Olson 1971; Yoshimatsu 2006). Although economists laud the potential global welfare gains from multilateral trade liberalization, political pragmatism suggests smaller groups of like-minded countries can more easily reach consensus on a greater range of issues. Relatedly, the United States, in particular, has used the collective action advantages of regionalism to push a policy of "competitive liberalization." Here, the lure of membership in an exclusive regional club anchored by the United States, coupled with the breadth and depth of the liberalization within the grouping, was thought to serve as a kind of leverage, spurring reluctant partners to the bargaining table (Evenett and Meier 2008).

Hence, there are many rationales for the pursuit of regionalism, nearly all of which depart from the efficiency arguments advanced by economists. And, while the postwar growth of the multilateral trading regime has evolved much more strongly in the direction of efficiency, supported as it is by the principles of most favored nation treatment, national treatment, and non-discrimination, the political rationales for engaging in regionalism continue to be the default mode of liberalization. In fact, while regionalism may be the bane of economists in pursuit of efficiency, the very design of the multilateral system has actually contributed to regionalism's growth.

HOW THE MULTILATERAL SYSTEM COOKED SPAGHETTI

In October 1947, 23 nations signed the General Agreement on Tariffs and Trade. It's easy to look at the GATT as having been a fantastically successful experiment in postwar multilateralism. Multiple rounds of successful negotiations reduced tariff barriers to the point that, once the Tokyo Round reductions were implemented, they were no longer serious impediments to global trade flows (Deardorff and Stern 1981; Koh 1992: 147). Moreover, the GATT slowly expanded its membership throughout most of the postwar period, expanded the range of issues considered for liberalization (post-Tokyo Round non-tariff barriers), and renamed itself the World Trade Organization in 1994.

However, all of these successes mask the fact that the GATT was in fact the byproduct of a series of collective action failures that beset the proposed International Trade Organization being negotiated in the late 1940s. Originally intended as an interim agreement, the original 23 members of the GATT were all that remained after the much larger, and more ambitious, ITO floundered and was effectively inoperable by 1950 (Pastor 1980: 97; Zeiler 1999: 2, 63, 134–6; Matsushita et al. 2006: 1–2).

Whereas the ITO fell apart because of the number of parties to the talks, the scale of the undertaking (over 100 countries), and the range of issues being tackled beyond tariff barriers, the GATT had just 23 members (many of them like-minded) and limited its focus to a relatively small range of issues – mainly numerical tariffs. Yet even the GATT contained provisions aimed at mollifying the original 23 signatories, including Article XXIV endorsing preferences arrangements within the multilateral structure (Matsushita et al. 2006: 548–56).

A major goal of American postwar planners with respect to the ITO and the GATT was not only the reconstruction of war-torn economies, but also the elimination (or at least reduction) of distortions to trade flows arising from existing preferences arrangements, notably the U.K.'s system of imperial preferences among its colonies and protectorates around the world (Dryden 1995: 9–32; Zeiler 1999: 27–36). There are many who argue that there is little inconsistency between multilateralism anchored in non-discrimination and most favored nation principles and the sanctioning of free trade areas in GATT Article XXIV (Matsushita et al. 2006: 554). Free trade areas conform to both the letter (Article XXIV) of the GATT and its spirit in that, unlike preferences systems, they are required to liberalize more trade between nations than they tend to divert or restrict.

In some respects, the apparent inconsistency is reduced even further when one considers that the multilateral process itself is a kind of complicated form of bilateralism wherein nations negotiate individually with each other on an item-by-item basis for the mutual reduction of tariffs. Tariff reductions by any two member countries are, in turn, offered to other GATT members on the basis of most favored nation treatment. However, the many concerns of economists noted above, coupled with fears about Article XXIV undermining efficiency by creating the "spaghetti bowl" effect, or lending itself to the "balkanization" of global trade into a small number of blocks, continue. Interestingly, the use of Article XXIV to engage in regional free trade has expanded dramatically since the end of the Cold War. As Panagariya notes, there were just 32 such agreements reported to the GATT as of 1990. As of 2002, that number had swelled to 172 such agreements (Panagariya 2002: 1415; see also Estevadeordal et al. 2005 for trends in the Western Hemisphere). Regional trade agreements have been proliferating at an especially fast pace in Asia, doubling in number between 2000 and 2004 (77 in total), with nearly 100 others in active negotiations or proposed (Menon 2009: 1383–7; see also Crawford and Laird 2001; Lee and Park 2005).

Scholars have traditionally tied the motivation for the Article XXIV regional exception within the GATT structure to the facilitation of Europe as a more unified postwar economic and political body (Chase 2006). Indeed, following the vision of Jean Monnet, and the logic of postwar planners who saw economic integration as dovetailing with peace, Europe has, by many measures, been a stunningly successful example of both the economic and the non-economic motivations for regionalism (Cooper 1968; Eichengreen 1996; Fransen 2001). The 1951 European

Coal and Steel Community created the initial foundation for the deep degree of European integration we see today. Postwar European regionalism has mostly been about the liberalization of economic barriers among members. However, starting with the Maastricht Treaty in 1992 paving the way for monetary union, the European Union moved heavily toward creating a true economic bloc, complete with supranational institutions and pooled sovereignty (see Anderson 2012b). Since 2008, some analysts have cast doubt on the stability of the European project. As an anchor for the peaceful rise of Europe as a unified and successful economic power, the regional exception to multilateralism allowing discrimination has been spectacularly successful. However, Chase (2006) points out that Article XXIV had a more immediate motivational source; the United States had secretly been negotiating a preferences arrangement with Canada to help it deal with postwar balance of payments problems (Chase 2006; see also Granatstein 1997).

Two additional caveats to the multilateral principles of most favored nation treatment – national treatment and non-discrimination – emerged in the 1960s and 1970s, both designed to aid developing countries. In 1965, GATT members added Part IV, designed to bring developing countries more fully into the multilateral system, and in 1979 then added the so-called "Enabling Clause," which granted waivers for developed countries to depart from GATT principles to engage developing countries in preferences schemes (Matsushita et al. 2006: 765–70; 772–9). Part IV was eventually responsible for the creation of the Generalized System of Preferences in 1971 granting preferential tariff treatment in developed countries for developing country textile exports (Panagariya 1999: 479; Matsushita et al. 2006: 773–6). However, as Panagariya (2002) has argued, many of these preferences schemes have not contributed the lasting benefits to the developing countries these exceptions were designed for. Instead of incentivizing developing country economic reforms, advances up the value-added production chains, and fuller integration into the multilateral regime, many of the schemes hatched under Part IV and the "Enabling Clause" have simply added more spaghetti to the bowl (Panagariya 2002).

Competitive Liberalization

While the regional genie had been out of the bottle since the inception of the GATT in 1947, such arrangements really began to proliferate in the late 1980s and early 1990s, driven in large part by the United States. In the early 1980s, the United States was promoting the launch of a new round of GATT negotiations with an ambitious agenda that would tackle a range of non-tariff issues. Yet, by 1982, much to the frustration of the United

States, GATT members were deeply divided about the agenda, or whether a new round ought to be launched (*New York Times*, November 28, 1982: A1, November 30, 1982: A1).

The Reagan administration was committed to the GATT process, but was increasingly prepared to work outside that process to achieve some of its goals if necessary. President Reagan announced in September 1985 that he was instructing American trade negotiators to try to accelerate the GATT process, "but if these negotiations are not initiated or if insignificant progress is made, I'm instructing our trade negotiators to explore regional and bilateral agreements with other nations" (U.S. President 1985: 2, 1129). The President's remarks appeared to be threats towards GATT members that the United States would pursue other options in lieu of a new GATT round. In October 1985, the 90-member GATT did finally agree to a new round of talks set to begin in 1986 (*New York Times*, October 3, 1985: D1). However, the President's remarks were more than just threats and might have been more accurate had they been uttered as facts instead. In February 1985, the United States concluded a free trade agreement with Israel, and in March formally launched similar talks with Canada. United States Trade Representative Clayton Yeutter advanced this argument again in May 1986 by arguing that:

> The United States will not be held hostage to the multilateral negotiating process . . . the administration is prepared to negotiate on a plurilateral or bilateral basis with like-minded nations. This path would become all the more important and urgent if the movement toward a new trade round is stalled. (U.S. Department of State 1986: 67–8)

In short, the United States was prepared to engage in Article XXIV liberalization as a way to put pressure on GATT members to complete a new, ambitious round of multilateral talks.

In the minds of some American policy makers, the strategy worked. After three years of talks, the Canada–U.S. Free Trade Agreement was completed in the fall of 1987. In 1990, Canada joined talks initiated between the U.S. and Mexico, and negotiations were completed on the North American Free Trade Agreement in late 1992. In December 1994, the Clinton administration spearheaded the launch of negotiations aimed at concluding the Free Trade Area of the Americas as part of the Summit of the Americas process. Coincidentally, in 1994, the Uruguay Round of the GATT was also completed at Marrakesh, Morocco, transforming the GATT into the World Trade Organization.

To the degree the U.S. strategy was successful, it was only a small number of Article XXIV agreements that seemed to do the trick. Each was ambitious in terms of the range of tariff and, most importantly, non-tariff measures the U.S. agreements dealt with. Many of these issues, such as investment, agriculture, services, or intellectual property, were also at the top of America's multilateral agenda.

As Menon argues, a major reason for the explosion of regional trade arrangements amounts to a "momentum effect" (2009: 1389) in which those left outside such arrangements feel pressure to bandwagon or be left behind. But was the multilateral system back on solid ground as a result of this early experimentation with competitive regionalism? Interestingly, the debacle flowing from the November 1999 WTO Ministerial Meeting in Seattle, Washington, the Battle in Seattle, suggested it was not. Moreover, those events, and the paralysis in the WTO that flowed from them, seemed to put competitive regionalism on everyone's agenda, as the spaghetti bowl thickened throughout the period with an explosion of regionalism, particularly in Asia after the financial crisis that spread through the region in the late 1990s (Lee and Park 2005; Menon 2009).

THE PRESENT: HOPE YOU LIKE SPAGHETTI

The Uruguay Round of the GATT negotiations, successful though it was, also left much to be done. Indeed, developing country members, many of whom had only recently joined the GATT/WTO, went along with the Uruguay Round text having been given assurances that major issues of importance to them (especially agriculture) would be addressed after the fact. Unfortunately, the process of trade liberalization was being subjected to increased public scrutiny throughout the 1990s, typified by the violence that seemed to accompany nearly every meeting of global leaders, not the least of which was the Battle in Seattle at the November 1999 WTO Ministerial Meetings. Those meetings fell apart over differences among the membership, many of which were now developing countries, on issues like agriculture, labor standards, and the growing importance of the environment. A new round of multilateral trade negotiations seemed unlikely in the near term.

Skepticism about the postwar orientation toward trade liberalization in the 1990s was also being felt in terms of regionalism, particularly in the United States. After ratification of the Uruguay Round Agreements, but particularly after the bruising political fight over the NAFTA between 1992 and 1994, the U.S. trade agenda stalled badly (Bergsten 2002, 2004). In the 1990s, U.S. policy makers twice failed to secure domestic negotiating authority to engage in either regional or multilateral talks (Destler 1997; Anderson 2012a). The United States was involved in negotiations in the period, notably bilateral talks with Chile and the larger FTAA. However, the lack of momentum was palpable. First steps on the Chile FTA were taken in 1992, but the final agreement implemented only in 2004. The FTAA talks, begun with such fanfare in 1994, were effectively dead in early 2002, primarily owing to differences between the U.S. and Brazil over the treatment of agriculture, but also because of the inability of the U.S. to commit to their completion.

However, the aftermath of the September 11, 2001 terrorist attacks on the United States brought an even greater sense of urgency to the Bush administration's renewed sense of enthusiasm for trade liberalization as they pushed for the launch of a new round of WTO talks, launched at Doha, Qatar in November 2001. The Doha Development Round (DDR), as it was dubbed, was designed to deal primarily with those agenda items "left over" from the Uruguay Round and of great importance to developing countries. Indeed, a consensus on launching the DDR depended on the support of developing countries, which by then accounted for a large majority of the WTO's membership.

Interestingly, the renewed sense of momentum also brought out a familiar set of rationales for liberalization, many of them unrelated to the efficiency arguments of classical economists. Similar to the rationales posited in the interwar years about the linkage between economic decline and the rise of extremism, the post-9/11 rationales for liberalization also included threads of rationales familiar to modernization and democratic peace theorists, linking interdependence, liberal capitalism, and liberal democracy, to peace and stability (see Fukuyama 1992; Zakaria 2003; Monten 2005; Inglehart and Welzel 2009).

Hence, the DDR was launched with the linkage between liberalization, economic interdependence, and political liberalization as part of the underlying rationale. It was a rationale that also played out in a renewed push into regionalism by the United States as the Bush administration engaged in a number of new bilateral and plurilateral preferences arrangements, most of them in the Western Hemisphere.[2] Perhaps buoyed by the experience of NAFTA's effects on Mexico's political opening, culminating in the election of Vicente Fox and the end of 70 years of rule of the Partido Revolucionario Institucional (PRI), the Bush administration saw democracy promotion as a major plank in the post-9/11 trade liberalization agenda (Dominguez 1998; Weyland 2009). As United States Trade Representative Robert Zoellick put it in his 2002 testimony to Congress:

> [Bilateral free trade agreements] can open up a new front for free trade. They can create models of success that help reformers break new ground for liberalization in changing or emerging sectors (e.g., biotech, high tech – including IPR [intellectual property rights]-related sectors – and services), build friendly coalitions to promote trade objectives in other contexts (e.g., biotech, SPS topics), add to

America's trade leverage globally, underpin links with other nations, and energize and expand the support for trade. Next, trade agreements also present fresh
opportunities to find common ground at home, and with our trading partners,
on the nexus among trade, growth and improved environmental and working
conditions. (Zoellick, quoted in Feinberg 2002: 140)

For many analysts, trade liberalization is over-hyped relative to the lasting
effects in terms of either greater efficiency and economic activity or the
non-economic motives swirling around governance (see Hufbauer and
Goodrich 2004; Aaronson and Zimmerman 2008).

Competitive Liberalization Revisited

The Clinton administration had a quirky relationship with trade liberalization, owing in large part to the heavy expenditure of political capital the
President expended early in his first term fighting the bruising battle over
the NAFTA. While Clinton launched the FTAA process with some fanfare,
his administration twice failed to secure "fast-track" trade-negotiating
authority from Congress in the 1990s, and, somewhat bizarrely, he seldom
mentioned the NAFTA again during his two terms in office (Destler 1997;
Pastor 2011: 55–6). Indeed, the Clinton trade agenda was rather quiet after
1994, picking up again only in his last year in office (2000) with his support
of both Permanent Normal Trade Relations (PNTR) for China (as part
of the process of ushering in Chinese WTO membership) and the African
Growth and Opportunity Act (AGOA). While both initiatives could be
interpreted as signals to the multilateral system after the Battle in Seattle
that the U.S. was looking to solidify links to emerging markets in lieu of a
new multilateral round, there is little evidence either initiative was part of
a broader strategy of competitive liberalization. Firstly, PNTR for China
was about bringing a large, rapidly developing country into the multilateral
system, not establishing a preferences scheme. And, while AGOA was a
preferences scheme of sorts, it essentially extended preferences in operation under the Generalized System of Preferences (GATT Part IV, 1965).

When the United States "re-discovered" its trade agenda after the election of President George W. Bush, competitive liberalization was revived
along with it, once again acting in parallel with an ongoing multilateral
negotiation. While the DDR was launched with much promise in 2001,
trouble emerged as early as 2003 when negotiations held at Cancun,
Mexico fell apart over developed and developing country differences on
agriculture and the so-called "Singapore Issues" important to developed
economies (see *Economist*, September 20, 2003; Bhagwati 2004).[3]

Much like the Uruguay Round before it, the DDR was generating
considerable frustration among U.S. policy makers, and has yet again pro-

vided the impetus for engaging in Article XXIV regionalism. U.S. Trade Representative Robert Zoellick writes of the DDR:

> To multiply the likelihood of success, the United States is also invigorating a drive for regional and bilateral free trade agreements (FTAs). These agreements can foster powerful links among commerce, economic reform, development, investment, security and free societies. The North American Free Trade Agreement (NAFTA) not only almost tripled American trade with Mexico and nearly doubled its trade with Canada, but also made all three members more competitive internationally. NAFTA proved definitively that both developed and developing countries gain from free trade partnerships. It enabled Mexico to bounce back quickly from its 1994 financial crisis, launched the country on the path of becoming a global economic competitor, and supported its transformation to an open democratic society. Ironically, a number of European publications that have criticised America's "competitive liberalisation" through regional and bilateral free trade negotiations were noticeably silent when the EU negotiated 30 such pacts; the United States only has three, but we are hard at work. (Zoellick 2002)

Has it worked? Has competitive liberalization generated momentum in the multilateral negotiations? While the Doha Round is not officially "dead," it has been on life-support for several years, with no prospects as of this writing for revival. Hence, the regionalism strategy pursued by the United States has yielded little on the multilateral agenda.

Has there been additional competition among potential U.S. trading partners to engage the United States to win market access? Evenett and Meier (2008) argued that there was little evidence that potential trading partners have pushed to engage the United States in preferences arrangements for market access advantages relative to rivals. As evidence, they point to the relative scarcity of these kinds of arguments in the public or press accounts of those countries' engagements with the U.S. (Evenett and Meier 2008: 55–6).

Yet America's latest bout with regionalism, the Trans-Pacific Partnership (TPP), suggests that competitive liberalization may have some strategic utility, in part, because of the paralysis in the DDR. What began in 2005 as a modest enterprise among an unlikely set of trading partners – Brunei, Chile, New Zealand, and Singapore – has since expanded to include a number of key Pacific Rim countries, including the United States.[4] With the addition of the United States to the TPP talks, several other countries soon thereafter expressed an interest in joining, notably Canada and Mexico. Yet the United States initially opposed having its NAFTA partners at the TPP table until the fall of 2012. Other countries, notably Colombia, with which the U.S. has an FTA, have asked to join and been denied access. One reason is very simple: the collective action problems of large negotiations are accentuated with each additional negotiating party. Indeed, the rationale for regionalism in the first place is that small-N negotiations can be quicker, cover more issues, and do so more "deeply" than large-N negotiations. Interestingly, the TPP currently excludes some of the Asia Pacific region's most important economies, notably China, Japan, and South Korea. The exclusion of China has raised hackles among some that the TPP is less about trade than it is about the "containment" of China as part of the Obama administration's "pivot to Asia" (Ross 2012). Moreover, the TPP has the potential to evolve into yet another hub-and-spoke trading bloc, as the only parties to the negotiation without a pre-existing preferences agreement with the United States are Brunei and Malaysia.

Finally, in early 2013, the United States and the European Union announced a new regional preferences negotiation, the Transatlantic Trade and Investment Partnership (TTIP), which would formally liberalize trade and investment between the globe's two largest trading blocs. For now, Canada and Mexico remain outside these negotiations, although both have large stakes in the outcome. Mexico already has a free trade arrangement with the EU (2000), and Canada is still in negotiations. There has long been talk among Atlanticists about some kind of transatlantic trade pact (Hart 1989), and, while much work remains to be done, the implications for the multilateral system of such an agreement could be profound in either jumpstarting the remnants of the Doha Round or killing it altogether. If the United States and Europe were able to come to agreement on new sets of protocols governing many of the so-called Singapore Issues, along with new disciplines on agricultural subsidies, the effect on the WTO structure, where developing countries now dominate, would be profound.

Unlike the Bush administration (2000–08), the Obama administration initially expressed considerable reticence with respect to engaging in more trade liberalization, candidate Obama opening questioning during the 2008 presidential campaign with whether the NAFTA should be re-opened and "fixed." The Obama administration has appeared less concerned with using trade policy as a competitive weapon in the same way as Obama's predecessor in the White House. Yet what we can say for certain is that the penchant for regional preferences agreements in the United States has been stronger than ever, and might even be characterized as "bandwagoning" in response to the expansion of regional preferences elsewhere and the apparent demise of the Doha Round.

Moreover, with more than a dozen recent preferences arrangements complete or in the midst of negotiations involving more than two dozen countries, the United States has contributed greatly to the proliferation of "spaghetti bowl" preferences in the global trading system. With the Doha Round in a state of effective hiatus, regional and bilateral liberalization is the only liberalization occurring anywhere. Hence, we return to the compatibility of GATT Article XXIV preferences within the multilateral trading system, and the main criterion to qualify under Article XXIV: do such agreements liberalize more than they restrict? As evidence on the growth of regionalism in East Asia suggests, the answer to that question is full of many "ifs" – as in "if" Asian regionalism evolves in certain directions (Lee and Park 2005).

THE FUTURE: IS LOW-CARB SPAGHETTI POSSIBLE?

The threat of the "spaghetti bowl" for global politics generates concerns among politicians that we could see a repeat of the interwar years in which economic and political nationalism created a toxic stew leading to conflict and violence. If such fears were going to be realized, the seriousness of the Great Recession (2008–10) in the United States and the European debt crisis (2009–present) should have given rise to much greater degrees of economic and political nationalism than we have seen. Protectionism in the face of the crises has crept upward, but has not become as serious a problem as first feared, and is nowhere approaching levels seen in the era of Smoot–Hawley (see *Economist*, June 30, 2012).

However, because the proliferation of Article XXIV agreements could collectively undermine the efficiency gains from multilateral liberalization, the "spaghetti bowl" represents a thicket of subtle protectionist measures in the form of discriminatory preferences serious enough to give economists cause to devise ways to undo some of it.

Consolidation

One way to deal with the "spaghetti bowl" would be for larger, more comprehensive agreements to supersede or nullify some of the patchwork of preferences arrangements that currently exist (Menon 2009: 1395). For instance, an agreement like the Trans-Pacific Partnership could ultimately supplant the North American Free Trade Agreement, since all three members of the NAFTA are currently at the TPP bargaining table. It would still require that the provisions of the TPP cover all or more content areas than the NAFTA, and at least meet or exceed the NAFTA's ambition in terms of the depth of integration. This particular scenario seems unlikely, since the NAFTA represents a kind of high-water mark for U.S. trade agreements generally, wherein dispute settlement mechanisms on trade remedy actions and investment were relatively robust and have not been extended to subsequent U.S. FTA partners

(Anderson 2013). Similarly, it is theoretically possible, although politically implausible, that the U.S.–EU Transatlantic Trade and Investment Partnership could ultimately replace the governance structures of both the NAFTA and the European Union. It would require a seismic shift in North America's political thinking about its tolerance for the levels of pooled sovereignty that currently exist in Europe, not the least of which would entail a decision as to whether the common currency would be the dollar or the euro.

Nevertheless, herein rests a possible silver lining in the growth of regionalism. As countries are increasingly tied together through networks of preferences anchored by large economic powers like the United States, a certain harmonization of practices and trading rules may ensue, eventually making the logic of consolidation or multilateralization stronger. However, it would require the acquiescence of those blocs (the United States, the European Union, China or Japan in East Asia, Brazil in South America) to a set of negotiations aimed at knitting the blocs together. Doing so assumes a willingness to forgo the non-traditional goals frequently undergirding regionalism in favor of efficiency, but small-N talks aimed at unwinding the blocs could be more fruitful than large-N efforts to unwind the "spaghetti bowls."

Multilateralization

Another means by which economists theorize about the rationalization of the "spaghetti bowl" is through a process Menon refers to as multilateralization. Here, the "hub" country in any "hub-and-spoke" system of preferences arrangements would simply extend to all of its preferences partners the most generous terms it had negotiated with any of its preferences partners (Menon 2009: 1397). In principle, this multilateralization would work in the same fashion as that in which the WTO currently extends negotiated reductions in trade barriers to all members through the principle of most favored nation treatment. In other words, the "hub" country would offer most favored preference treatment to all the "spokes" with which it had agreements. Hence, for the United States, the NAFTA's provisions regarding dispute settlement in trade remedy and investment, which are currently extended only to Canada and Mexico, could theoretically be extended to all other U.S. FTA and Trade Promotion Agreement partners. Given that the U.S. has stepped back from such robust provisions since the 1994 NAFTA, and given the current political climate in the United States, such an approach is a political bridge too far.

Dilution

Yet another means by which the patchwork of preferences could be dealt with would be to "water them down" by making some of their most discriminatory elements less onerous and incompatible with one another. Something as straightforward as harmonizing the various procedures under rules of origin (known as cumulation) to qualify for preferences treatment would go a long way toward reducing the degree of discrimination faced by the exports of non-member nationals. At present, different preferences agreements contain wildly different rules on how goods qualify for tariff-free treatment when crossing member country borders. If the process for the calculation of value-added production and inputs for duty-free treatment were harmonized, and broadened across different preferences areas, the effect would be the same as multilateralization of preferences (Menon 2009: 1400). The United States, for example, already looks for additional cumulation efficiencies with existing agreements as it enters negotiations with new partners.

Kickstarting the Multilateral Process

Finally, the most obvious and effective means by which to deal with the "spaghetti bowl" may actually be a renewed emphasis on the multilateral system itself. Such a kickstart seems hopelessly unrealistic given the paralysis of the DDR through 2013. However, the gains from completion of the Doha Round are widely thought to be enormous, particularly for trade between developing countries. Moreover, the multilateral system is the only institutional arrangement capable of dealing with the impulse to regional preferences agreements. Equally important, it may be the WTO alone that can and must deal with Article XXIV preferences, since it is the multilateral system's rules that sanctioned the creation of the "spaghetti bowl" in the first place.

CONCLUSIONS

Like it or not, the patchwork of regionalism we see evolving in the global trading system is here to stay. The irony is that a multilateral system that was designed to eliminate the sorts of preferences that lent themselves to the kind of economic nationalism witnessed in the interwar years sanctioned their longevity and proliferation in the postwar years by including Article XXIV in the GATT 1947. Having witnessed the demise of the International Trade Organization as it faded away in the early 1950s owing to over-ambition and the standard collective action problems of large-N bodies, the originators of the GATT may have believed that some trade liberalization, even that sanctioned by Article XXIV, was better than none. The GATT's originators also needed a pragmatic way to incorporate existing (imperial preferences) or contemplated (Europe, U.S.–Canada) discriminatory preferences that were motivated as much by geopolitics as they were by the gains from economic efficiency.

Moreover, with the GATT's earliest negotiating rounds focused on tariffs, the consolidation of postwar economic recovery, and the preservation of at least some trade liberalizing institution in light of the demise of the ITO, the GATT membership could not have been too concerned about any perverse incentives created by Article XXIV provisions. In short, there were larger postwar and emergent Cold War concerns to consider. Indeed, not until the late 1980s and early 1990s did the "spaghetti bowl" exist – until then, it was perhaps still a small side dish. Thereafter, the "spaghetti bowl" has grown larger and more complex with every concluded preference arrangement. Such arrangements are nominally about the efficiency gains that come from liberalization, but are often quickly overwhelmed in their purpose by numerous non-traditional and non-economic motivations that complicate efforts to untangle the "spaghetti bowl." Once hard-won preferences are established, nations are reluctant to permit them to dissipate.

This once again returns us to the nature of trade relations as part of a complex international political economy. While fiscal policy and monetary policy have far-reaching effects on economic performance that radiate out from the countries in which those policies are made, neither is as fraught with the mixture of economics and both domestic and foreign policy political imperatives as trade policy. Fiscal policy, particularly if poorly managed, can have significant foreign policy implications, but is nevertheless largely confined to the domestic sphere. Monetary policy is critically important internationally, but its abstract and arcane qualities make it a more narrowly prescribed preoccupation for bankers, corporations with overseas interests, or cross-border investors. The oft-poisonous mixture of economics and politics, both domestic and international, that infuses international trade makes it the quintessential subject matter of international political economy. As a component of the international political economy of trade relations, regionalism is often maligned as a counter-productive anachronism in a multilateral system designed to avoid the discrimination of preferences arrangements. Yet, as this chapter has argued, the characteristics of regionalism are as quintessentially a part of the politics of trade as trade is a part of international political economy.

NOTES

1. There is some debate about whether Japan was a fascist state in this period. See Willensky (2005).
2. U.S.–Chile FTA, completed 2004; CAFTA-DR (Costa Rica, El Salvador, Guatemala, Honduras, Nicaragua, and the Dominican Republic), completed 2005; U.S.–Panama Trade Promotion Agreement, completed 2007; U.S.–Peru Trade Promotion Agreement, completed 2009; U.S.–Colombia FTA, completed 2012.
3. Investment, competition policy, government procurement, and trade facilitation.
4. As of 2013, Australia, Brunei, Canada, Chile, Malaysia, Mexico, New Zealand, Singapore, the United States, and Vietnam.

REFERENCES

Aaronson, Susan A. and Jamie M. Zimmerman (2008), *Trade Imbalance: The Struggle to Weigh Human Rights Concerns in Trade Policymaking*, Cambridge: Cambridge University Press.
Anderson, Greg (2012a), "Did Canada Kill Fast Track?," *Diplomatic History*, **36** (3), June, 583–624.
Anderson, Greg (2012b), "Securitization and Sovereignty in Post-9/11 North America," *Review of International Political Economy*, **19** (5), December, 711–41.
Anderson, Greg (2013), "The Uncertain Politics of North American Integration," in Julian Castro-Rea (ed.), *Our North America*, London: Ashgate, pp. 45–66.
Baldwin, Richard (2006), "Multilateralising Regionalism: Spaghetti Bowls as Building Blocs on the Path to Global Free Trade," *World Economy*, **29** (11), November, 1451–1518.
Bergsten, C. Fred (2002), "A Renaissance for U.S. Trade Policy?," *Foreign Affairs*, **81** (6), November/December, 86–99.
Bergsten, C. Fred (2004), "Foreign Economic Policy for the Next President," *Foreign Affairs*, **83** (2), March/April, 88–101.
Bhagwati, Jagdish (1995), "U.S Trade Policy: Infatuation with FTAs," Discussion Paper Series No. 726, April, Department of Economics, Columbia University.
Bhagwati, Jagdish (2004), "Don't Cry for Cancun," *Foreign Affairs*, **83** (1), January/February, 52–63.
Bush, George H.W. (1993), "President Bush Address at Signing Ceremony of the North American Free Trade Agreement," Organization of American States, Washington, DC, *U.S. Department of State Dispatch*, **4** (1).
Chase, Kerry (2006), "Multilateralism Compromised: The Mysterious Origins of GATT Article XXIV," *World Trade Review*, **5** (1), 1–30.
Cooper, R. (1968), *The Economics of Interdependence: Economic Policy in the Atlantic Community*, New York: McGraw-Hill.
Crawford, Jo-Ann and Sam Laird (2001), "Regional Trade Agreements and the WTO," *North American Journal of Economics and Finance*, **12** (1), July, 193–211.
Deardorff, Alan and Robert Stern (1981), "A Disaggregated Model of World Production and Trade: An Estimate of the Impact of the Tokyo Round," *Journal of Policy Modeling*, **3** (2), 127–52.
Destler, I.M. (1995), *American Trade Politics*, Washington, DC: Institute for International Economics.
Destler, I.M. (1997), *Renewing Fast-Track Legislation*, Washington, DC: Institute for International Economics.
Dominguez, Jorge I. (1998), "Free Politics and Free Markets in Latin America," *Journal of Democracy*, **9** (4), 70–84.
Dryden, Steve (1995), *Trade Warriors: USTR and the American Crusade for Free Trade*, Oxford: Oxford University Press.

Eckes, Alfred E. (1995), *Opening America's Market*, Chapel Hill: University of North Carolina Press.
Eichengreen, B. (1996), "Toward a More Perfect Union: The Logic of Economic Integration," *Essays in International Finance*, **198**, 1–40.
Estevadeordal, Antoni, Kati Souminen, Pablo Sanguinetti and Alberto Trejos (2005), "Rules of Origin in Preferential Trading Arrangements: Is All Well with the Spaghetti Bowl in the Americas?," *Economia*, **5** (2), Spring, 63–103.
Evenett, Simon and Michael Meier (2008), "An Interim Assessment of the U.S Trade Policy of 'Competitive Liberalization,'" *World Economy*, **31** (1), 31–66.
Feinberg, Richard E. (1997), *Summitry in the Americas: A Progress Report*, Washington, DC: Institute for International Economics.
Feinberg, Richard E. (2002), *Latin American Politics and Society*, **44** (4), 127–51.
Fox, Justin (2011), *The Myth of the Rational Market*, New York: Harper.
Fransen, F.J. (2001), *The Supranational Politics of Jean Monnet: Ideas and Origins of the European Community*, Freeport, CT: Greenwood Press.
Fukuyama, Francis (1992), *The End of History and the Last Man*, New York: Free Press.
Granatstein, J.L. (1997), *Yankee Go Home? Canadians and Anti-Americanism*, Toronto: HarperCollins.
Hart, Michael (1989), "Almost but Not Quite: The 1947–48 Bilateral Canada–U.S. Negotiations," *American Review of Canadian Studies*, **19** (1), 25–58.
Hoffman, Tom (2013), "Where Art Thou, Adam Smith?," *Perspectives on Politics*, **11** (1), March, 193–203.
Hufbauer, Gary Clyde and Ben Goodrich (2004), "Lessons from NAFTA," in Jeffrey Schott (ed.), *Free Trade Agreements: U.S Strategies and Priorities*, Washington, DC: Institute for International Economics, pp. 37–50.
Hull, Cordell (1948), *The Memoirs of Cordell Hull*, 2 vols., New York: Macmillan.
Inglehart, Ronald and Christian Welzel (2009), "How Development Leads to Democracy," *Foreign Affairs*, **88** (2), March/April, 33–48.
Irwin, Douglas (1996), *Against the Tide: An Intellectual History of Free Trade*, Princeton, NJ: Princeton University Press.
Irwin, Douglas, Petros Mavroidis and Alan Sykes (2008), *The Genesis of the GATT*, Cambridge: Cambridge University Press.
Keohane, Robert and Joseph Nye, Jr. (1977), *Power and Interdependence: World Politics in Transition*, Boston, MA: Little, Brown.
Koh, Harold (1992), "The Fast Track and United States Trade Policy," *Brooklyn Journal of International Law*, **18** (1), 143–80.
Krasner, Stephen D. (1976), "State Power and the Structure of International Trade," *World Politics*, **28** (3), April, 317–47.
Krugman, Paul (1993), "The Uncomfortable Truth about NAFTA," *Foreign Affairs*, **72** (5), November/December, 13–19.
Lederman, Daniel, William F. Maloney and Luis Serven (2005), *Lessons from NAFTA for Latin America and the Caribbean*, Palo Alto, CA: Stanford University Press and World Bank.
Lee, Jong-Wha and Innwon Park (2005), "Free Trade Areas in East Asia: Discriminatory or Non-Discriminatory?," *World Economy*, **28** (1), January, 21–48.
Majluf, Luis Abugattas (2004), *Swimming in the Spaghetti Bowl: Challenges for Developing Countries under the "New Regionalism,"* Policy Issues in International Trade and Commodities Study Series No. 27, New York: United Nations.
Matsushita, Mitsuo, Thomas Schoenbaum and Petros Mavroidis (2006), *The World Trade Organization: Law, Practice, and Policy*, Oxford: Oxford University Press.
Menon, Jayant (2009), "Dealing with the Proliferation of Bilateral Trade Agreements," *World Economy*, **32** (10), October, 1381–1407.
Monten, Jonathan (2005), "The Roots of the Bush Doctrine: Power, Nationalism, and Democracy Promotion in U.S. Strategy," *International Security*, **29** (4), Spring, 112–56.

O'Halloran, Sharyn (1994), *Process, Politics, and American Trade Policy*, Ann Arbor: University of Michigan Press.

Olson, Mancur (1971), *The Logic of Collective Action: Public Goods and the Theory of Groups*, Cambridge, MA: Harvard University Press.

Panagariya, Arvind (1999), "The Regionalism Debate: An Overview," *World Economy*, **22** (4), June, 477–511.

Panagariya, Arvind (2002), "EU Preferential Trade Arrangements and Developing Countries," *World Economy*, **25** (10), November, 1415–32.

Pastor, Robert A. (1980), *Congress and the Politics of U.S. Foreign Economic Policy*, Berkeley: University of California Press.

Pastor, Robert (2008), "The Future of North America: Replacing Bad Neighbor Policy," *Foreign Affairs*, **87** (4), July/August, 84–98.

Pastor, Robert (2011), *The North American Idea*, New York: Oxford University Press.

Ross, Robert (2012), "The Problem with the Pivot," *Foreign Affairs*, **91** (6), November/December, 70–82.

Schattschneider, E.E. (1935), *Politics, Pressures, and the Tariff: A Study of Free Enterprise in Pressure Politics, as Shown in the 1929–30 Revision of the Tariff*, New York: Prentice Hall.

Simon, Herbert (1956), "Rational Choice and the Structure of the Environment," *Psychological Review*, **63**, 129–38.

Simon, Herbert A. (1959), "Theories of Decision-Making in Economics and Behavioral Science," *American Economic Review*, **49**, June, 253–83.

Thurow, Lester (1991), *Head to Head: The Coming Battle among Japan, Europe, and America*, New York: William & Morrow.

Tversky, Amos and Daniel Kahneman (1974), "Judgement under Uncertainty: Heuristics and Biases," *Science*, **185**, September, 1124–31.

Tversky, Amos and Daniel Kahneman (1981), "The Framing of Decisions and the Psychology of Choice," *Science*, **211**, January, 453–8.

U.S. Department of State, Office of Public Communication, Bureau of Public Affairs (1986), *Department of State Bulletin*, Vols. 83–88, Washington, DC: Government Printing Office.

U.S. Department of State (1994), *Declaration of Miami: First Summit of the Americas*, December, available from: http://www.state.gov/p/wha/rls/59673.htm (accessed April 14, 2014).

U.S. President (1985), *Public Papers of the Presidents of the United States*, Ronald Reagan, Washington, DC: Government Printing Office.

Wallerstein, Immanuel (2004), *World-Systems Analysis: An Introduction*, Durham, NC: Duke University Press.

Weyland, Kurt (2009), "Neoliberalism and Democracy in Latin America: A Mixed Record," in William C. Smith (ed.), *Latin American Democratic Transformations: Institutions, Actors, and Processes*, Chichester, West Sussex, U.K.: Wiley-Blackwell, pp. 35–52.

Willensky, Marcus (2005), "Japanese Fascism Revisited," *Stanford Journal of East Asian Affairs*, **5** (1), Winter, 58–77.

Yoshimatsu, Hidetaka (2006), "Collective Action Problems and Regional Integration," *Contemporary Southeast Asia*, **28** (1), April, 115–40.

Zakaria, Fareed (2003), *The Future of Freedom: Illiberal Democracy at Home and Abroad*, New York: W.W. Norton & Co.

Zeiler, Thomas W. (1999), *Free Trade, Free World: The Advent of the GATT*, Chapel Hill: University of North Carolina Press.

Zoellick, R. (2002), "Unleashing the Trade Winds," *Economist*, By Invitation, December 5.

11. Governing trade: regional leadership in the Asia Pacific
Deborah Elms

INTRODUCTION

There are many ways to organize the governance of international trade. It can be handled multilaterally, though organizations like the World Trade Organization (WTO). It can be handled unilaterally, as individual countries make decisions based on their own best interests. For example, a country might choose to lower barriers to trade in a particular sector or product entirely on its own to give producers and consumers cheaper access to that sector or product. Countries also create trade agreements at the bilateral level to lower barriers and streamline trade with one another. Finally, countries can elect to handle trade in a regional manner, coming together in groups larger than two, to lower trade barriers and draw up new rules to govern trade relations between the partners.

In Asia, countries have frequently chosen the path of governance at the regional level. What makes the Asia Pacific region so interesting for study from an international political economy perspective, however, is that the constellation of countries involved in trade governance vary from agreement to agreement.

CONTRAST WITH TRADE IN THE EUROPEAN UNION

Contrast this situation with that of Europe, which also practices trade governance at the regional level. In Europe, membership basically does not vary, except for the expansion over time of the number of countries included in the governance structures.

Nearly all the countries in Europe are now members of the European Union (EU). The EU grew out of the European Coal and Steel Community (ECSC), formed in 1951 to facilitate the movement of coal and steel between West Germany, France, Italy and the Benelux countries. A High Authority supervised the agreement, which also included provisions on free access to sources of production and rules about competition and price transparency. Thus the ECSC set down the first guidelines related to the common market in Europe.

By 1957, the Treaty of Rome had devoted an entire chapter to the liberalization of goods between members and also formed the members into a customs union. As a customs union, member states were obligated to maintain the same external levels of tariff protection.

To simplify the situation, tariffs can be thought of as a tax on imports and have been the primary means used by governments to provide protection for domestic producers of goods. To see how tariffs form barriers to trade, imagine two identical goods – one is an imported item subject to a high tariff of 100 percent, and the other is locally produced with no tariff at all. The local item can be priced significantly more cheaply. If the two items are the same, consumers will not buy the imported good because the tariff has made the price uncompetitive in the marketplace.

When ECSC members agreed to form a customs union, they also agreed to give up domestic control over the use of tariffs as a form of protection. From the very earliest days, then, trade policy was a core competence of Europe at a regional level. Agreements on tariff reductions in forums like the General Agreement on Tariffs and Trade (GATT), the predecessor to the WTO, had to be negotiated for a region by the members and not by individual member states.

With the implementation of the Lisbon Treaty in 2010, the EU moved to being fully regional in trade – the last exceptions that allowed individual member state actions on the trade front were eliminated and the 27 EU member states were required to operate as a regional group in all settings.[1] The EU Commission now negotiates all trade agreements (following directives issued by the European Council that have been adopted by a qualified majority). It also required that the European Parliament approve all future trade agreements. Hence, trade policy in Europe operates on regional lines for nearly all countries.

Those few countries in Europe that are not members of the EU also operate largely on a regional basis in trade.[2] Iceland, Liechtenstein, Norway and Switzerland have created the European Free Trade Association (EFTA), which handles their trade agreements with external parties. This includes an agreement between the EU and three EFTA members to create the Agreement on the European Economic Area (EEA).[3]

In short, for nearly all European countries, trade is conducted on a regional basis by a collective (either the EU or the EFTA) that operates on behalf of the individual member states. The membership in each grouping is largely fixed (other than expansion over time), and the scope for maneuver in policy space related to trade actions for countries has steadily decreased.

THE ASIAN EXPERIENCE

Asian countries do not operate in the same way. Trade is conducted along multilateral, unilateral, bilateral and – increasingly – regional tracks. The remainder of this chapter considers the most important regional structures governing trade in East and Southeast Asia, including: the (now) ten-member Association of Southeast Asian Nations (ASEAN); various agreements between ASEAN and other Asian countries; the Regional Comprehensive Economic Partnership (RCEP) between 16 parties; trilateral negotiations between China, Japan and Korea; the Trans-Pacific Partnership (TPP) agreement that has expanded through 2013 to include 12 member countries; and the Free Trade Area of the Asia Pacific (FTAAP) with 21 members of APEC. Each of these regional agreements contains a different set of member governments operating under different kinds of rules and objectives for trade.

ASEAN

The oldest regional trade governance structure for Asia is the Association of Southeast Asian Nations. ASEAN's pedigree is shorter than that of the EU. It was formed by Indonesia, Malaysia, the Philippines, Singapore and Thailand in 1967. Membership has since expanded to ten by including Brunei (1982), Vietnam (1995), Laos (1997), Myanmar (1997) and Cambodia (1999).

The regional trade integration efforts of ASEAN began in earnest in 1992 with the signing of the ASEAN Free Trade Area (AFTA). AFTA covered trade in goods among the (then) six member states and required members to successively lower tariff barriers to trade in goods with one another over a 15-year time period (subsequently the timeline was compressed to conclude in 2003).

By the early 1990s, the Japanese economy was booming. South Korea and Taiwan were rapidly catching up. Singapore and Hong Kong were part of the East Asian newly industrializing economies (NIEs), with breathless books written about their economic power and impressive growth (see Johnson 1982; Amsden 1989; Haggard 1990; Wade 1990; World Bank 1993). For much of the rest of ASEAN, it looked increasingly as if economic development and boom times might remain largely the province of Northeast Asia alone.

Instead, the countries decided to set themselves up in ASEAN as a single production base for companies. This, they thought, would help build up a comparative advantage for the region and overcome the challenges faced by the relatively small countries in the grouping. Because the six members had fairly high barriers to trade in goods with one another, this was the place to start liberalizing. In particular, most of the countries in ASEAN had high tariff barriers. High tariff walls make it difficult and expensive for businesses to move products back and forth across country borders.

AFTA was designed to lower internal tariff barriers among ASEAN countries. If tariffs were close to zero, officials believed that firms would increasingly find ASEAN an attractive location for investment and production, especially of more complex products like electronics and other high-tech manufactured products that were becoming too expensive to produce in Northeast Asia.

The method used by ASEAN members to cut tariffs and quantitative restrictions among themselves, however, was different from that of many other regional agreements. To simplify, for most free trade agreements (FTAs) elsewhere, the parties come together and cut tariffs to one another as a group. If Country A promises to lower barriers in canned tomatoes from 26 percent to 5 percent over a ten-year time frame, it extends this offer of tariff reductions to all the parties at the same time – every member gets the same tariff on canned tomatoes into Country A.[4]

However, ASEAN members have a number of particular challenges in creating a more common market. The members are an extremely diverse bunch in terms of per capita wealth, population and geographic size. Singapore's per capita GDP is significantly larger than the GDP of the rest (even of the original six members in 1992), even if its population size has always been much smaller. In 1992 when AFTA was negotiated, Brunei and Singapore's per capita GDP was already over US$15 000, while the Philippines' was $819 and Indonesia's was just $730.[5]

Indonesia, however, dwarfs the rest in population and geographic size. In 1992, Indonesia's population was 184 million, while Singapore had 3.2 million people, and tiny Brunei had only 269 000.[6] The extent of economic competitiveness varies quite a bit between them as well.

In part because of this diversity and also because the "glue" that holds ASEAN together is considerably less "sticky" than that in organizations like the European Union, ASEAN members have been much less eager to hand over sovereignty to the collective. They have been cautious about offering the same tariff liberalization, for example, to all parties simultaneously. Therefore, ASEAN trade opening for goods proceeded in a different manner.

Members split goods into four different categories. The first category (Inclusion List) had to be liberalized starting immediately.[7] Products in the second category could be protected from liberalization for an additional two to four years before being merged into the Inclusion List.[8] Items in the third category, the Sensitive List, could be protected for a longer period and were allowed higher tariffs in the interim.[9] Finally, a small list of goods could be placed on the General Exception List and excluded entirely from the FTA for reasons such as national security, public morals or the protection of human life and health.

What makes ASEAN negotiations different, however, is that, rather than cutting down tariffs on items like canned tomatoes to all ASEAN members simultaneously, ASEAN created a complex system of negotiating that appears to be closer to six bilateral deals than one regional agreement. This is because canned tomatoes were only opened under the agreement if and when more than one state agreed to open up canned tomatoes. If all countries placed canned tomatoes in the Inclusion List, then canned tomatoes would be subject to tariff reductions across the board in all ASEAN members. But, if Country B placed canned tomatoes in the Sensitive List instead, then Country A was not required to offer up tariff liberalization in canned tomatoes to Country B until such time as *both* Country A and Country B had placed canned tomatoes on the Inclusion List for liberalization. As a result, although AFTA was announced in 1992, tariff reductions to one another proceeded slowly.

A SIDE TRIP THROUGH TARIFF LIBERALIZATION

To liberalize trade in goods, officials use tariff schedules to determine product categories. Goods are arranged into different categories using a Harmonized System (HS) code.[10] HS codes can be thought of as a sorting system, with the greatest number of products bundled together at the two-digit level and more finely detailed information on products given as more digits are included. As an example, preparations of vegetables, fruits, nuts, etc. are found at the two-digit level in Chapter 20. Tomatoes prepared or preserved otherwise than by vinegar or by acetic acid are given the code 2002 at the four-digit level. Digging down further, 200210 is greater detail on the product: tomatoes, whole or in pieces (prepared or preserved; excluding by vinegar or acetic acid).

At this level of detail, goods are divided into over 5000 groups using six-digit HS codes. HS codes actually range from as few as two digits (where they aggregate into 99 product categories) to as many as ten digits. All countries use six digits, but not all countries use the eight- or ten-digit level of specificity.[11] In tariff negotiations, these are called domestic level headings. Some FTA negotiations are conducted at the level of domestic headings, which result in considerably more than 5000 tariff lines.

In countries with eight or ten digits, canned tomatoes are likely given a separate tariff line from other types of whole or pieces of tomatoes (for example, those mixed with herbs). Because individual countries set the criteria for these lines themselves, there is no international standard that applies across all products at the eight- or ten-digit level (unlike the two-, four- and six-digit categories determined by the World Customs Organization).

Agreements that liberalize trade at broader levels can actually open up the market more than those that use domestic-level tariff headings. Take the example of tomatoes again. A country that agrees to drop tariffs to zero (i.e., duty-free access for tomatoes) at the two-digit level for Chapter 20 will actually be dropping the tariff to zero on *all* preparations of vegetables, fruits, nuts, etc. This is likely to include a wide range of goods such as tomatoes, but also mushrooms, jams and jellies, nuts and fruit juices. But a country that agrees to open markets at the eight-digit level may be opening the market only for tomato paste.

When determining the level of market liberalization for any given agreement it is therefore critically important to determine how tariff liberalization was conducted. Although it seems counterintuitive, if liberalization was done along tariff lines at the domestic heading level, then an agreement that included 98 percent of all lines may be quite comprehensive. This means that a country agreed to open up nearly all the market to its partner at the level of tomato paste or frozen orange juice. But, if a country opened up 98 percent of the market on broader tariff lines, this may result in *less* market opening. This is because the country may have opted to keep the whole of Chapter 20, for example, closed or carved out the agreement as highly sensitive. No additional market access would be possible in any of the items in the chapter, including tomatoes, mushrooms, jams or fruit juices.

Chapter 20 may not seem particularly critical. However, given the relatively limited trade between some parties in FTAs, the bulk of trade between partners can often be localized to a very few tariff lines alone. If these items, such as canned tomatoes, frozen orange juice or non-agricultural products like automobiles with engine sizes of 1000 cc and below, are excluded from market liberalization efforts, the final assessment of the impact of the FTA may be significantly less than it first appears.

Officials will often argue that their coverage should reach a certain target of, for example, 90 percent of trade in goods.[12] This generally means that 90 percent of tariff lines ought to be included with tariff reductions (and 10 percent of tariff lines can be excluded from cuts) at the end of the implementation period. Better agreements include commitments at or near 100 percent of lines.

In short, determining the potential for market access requires a careful analysis of the terms of any trade agreement. In the case of ASEAN, the complex mechanisms used to open markets to one another meant that the promises made in AFTA for trade in goods took until the full implementation of the agreement to bear fruit. It was not until the complete agreement was phased in and all tariff lines (except for the relatively modest number of items placed in the General Exception List[13]) were opened to one another that firms were finally able to take full advantage of market access across the partner countries.

BACK TO ASEAN MARKET OPENING

The creation of a common market for goods was supposed to include more than just tariff reductions. It was also intended to tackle various types of non-tariff barriers that prevented or slowed the movement of goods across ASEAN member borders. This included the harmonization of standards, recognition of testing and certifications, removal of barriers to investment, and rules for fair competition. These other elements of the agenda moved forward at a crawl.[14]

Countries trade more than just goods with one another, however. Starting in 1995, ASEAN began discussions to open its markets for services among members, with initial opening at the end of 1997. Over time, the number of sectors covered by the agreement expanded as members gradually allowed greater competition within ASEAN in more service areas.[15] Barriers to investment also began to fall, starting with a limited agreement in 1998.

By 2007, most ASEAN countries had experienced strong economic growth. The per capita GDP had more than doubled for most.[16] The figures stood at US$36707 for Singapore, $32443 for Brunei, $1685 for the Philippines and $1859 for Indonesia. The newest members of ASEAN had much lower figures (Cambodia $632 and Myanmar $587, for example).

Population sizes had also increased since the creation of AFTA, so the increase in per capita GDP for the original ASEAN 6 countries was even more impressive than it first appeared. Indonesia now had 231 million people (up 47 million). Singapore had 5.16 million people, and even Brunei had increased to 402000.[17]

Most of the tariffs in ASEAN had fallen significantly. Yet, despite the decline in formal barriers to trade, intra-ASEAN trade levels remained quite low. In 2006, the total figure for exports was US$193 billion, although Singapore alone accounted for almost 44 percent of the total.[18] By comparison, the WTO calculated global trade figures for the same year of nearly $11.8 trillion.[19] This meant that barely 1.6 percent of global trade was taking place between ASEAN countries.

The regional trade grouping had not met its original intention of being a single production base, nor was it attracting the levels of inward foreign investment that members thought possible. In 2007, it reached US$69 billion.[20] In 2008, the intra-ASEAN FDI figure was US$10.7 billion.[21] Both figures, again, were relatively small given the overall pool of global FDI.

As a result, in 2007, ASEAN members took another important step forward by agreeing to create an ASEAN Economic Community (AEC).[22] The AEC is due to come into force in 2015, although this deadline is highly likely to slip. Under the AEC, the members have promised to have a free movement of goods, services, investment and skilled labor and a freer movement of capital. Once implementation is complete, the trade and investment figures for ASEAN are expected to soar.

But implementation of the AEC will be very challenging for ASEAN. For example, the ASEAN Secretariat is quite small and underfunded. In 2013, it had a staff of just 200 (compared to a staff strength of more than 30000 in the European Union responsible for crafting and implementing integration policies) (Economist Corporate Network 2013: 11). Nevertheless, to the extent that ASEAN achieves the AEC goals, it will involve a dramatic transformation of the marketplace in Southeast Asia.

ASEAN+ONE AGREEMENTS

Another way that trade is structured along regional lines in Asia is through a series of what are known as ASEAN+One agreements. These five FTAs link the ten ASEAN countries together with a partner country.[23] The other countries, called dialogue partners, include Australia, China, India, Japan, New Zealand and South Korea.

All ASEAN+One agreements have begun with negotiations over opening markets to one another in goods. Goods discussions have two key elements: rules governing trade in goods and mutual tariff reductions. The former are conducted between the ten members of ASEAN acting as a block and the dialogue partner. Tariff cuts, however, are largely negotiated by individual ASEAN countries (along similar terms to how ASEAN negotiated internally in AFTA). In technical terms, each ASEAN country maintains its own tariff "schedule" that spells out its own commitments for each good. The amount of goods covered in each of the ASEAN+ agreements varies, as noted below. Individual member countries offer different levels of liberalization to their partners.[24] In general, in the ASEAN+One agreements, ASEAN members have agreed to open 73.3 percent of tariff lines to all the dialogue parties, while refusing to open 0.9 percent. But nearly a quarter of all tariff lines may or may not be opened in any specific agreement.[25]

Of course, as noted above, the majority of trade (and often the majority of highly sensitive trade) may take place in a tiny handful of lines alone. So a pledge to open all but ten tariff lines may be considerably less impressive than it first appears if nearly all the trade of interest actually takes place in those ten lines. For some of the parties in the ASEAN+One agreements, this situation of highly concentrated trade in a small number of lines holds true. In most of the agreements, excluded tariff lines or lines subject to the longest implementation periods frequently coincide with the sectors with significant actual or potential for trade between parties.

The first agreement to be negotiated was ASEAN–China (ACFTA). Talks began in 2002, and the first elements of the agreement, tariff reductions on goods, were implemented starting in July 2005.[26] Over time, the agreement expanded to include modest commitments to open up markets to one another in services (July 2007) and rules governing investment (2010).

But ACFTA implementation did not go smoothly in all countries. Many farmers and manufacturers complained loudly when the tariff cuts came into force. For instance, in Thailand, officials faced protests from fruit farmers when imports of Chinese goods like apples rose by 117 percent or grapes soared by 4300 percent after signing a bilateral agreement.[27] Air conditioning manufacturers begged the Thai government for relief, and the silk industry warned strongly of serious damage to traditional producers.[28]

Indonesia delayed opening its market to China under ASEAN–China until 2010. Once tariff cuts began to take effect, protests also sprang up in a range of areas. Thousands of workers rallied in West Java to urge the government to delay the implementation of the agreement.[29] The protests in West Java and elsewhere led the government of Indonesia to try to renegotiate the deal with China in 228 categories of tariffs. China, however, declined to participate.[30]

In the meantime, ASEAN continued signing agreements with other dialogue partners. The other agreements have been much less contentious. In 2003, ASEAN launched talks with Korea, although negotiations did not get under way in earnest for two years. An agreement covering trade in goods entered into force in June 2007. The original tariff reductions covered 90 percent of trade in goods by 2010 among the ASEAN 6 countries, negotiated in a similar manner to the ASEAN–China FTA. An agreement on trade in services was added later in 2007, and both services and investment commitments began coming into force in 2009 as individual member countries ratified the agreement.

An agreement between ASEAN and Japan was signed in 2008 covering trade in goods. Japan's own commitments are lower (91.9 percent) than all but Cambodia (85.7 percent), Indonesia (91.2 percent), Laos (86.0 percent) and Myanmar (85.2 percent).[31]

The most comprehensive agreement of all was signed in February 2009 between ASEAN and Australia and New Zealand. Following Indonesia's ratification of AANZFTA, by early 2012 the agreement covered all 12 parties, with commitments to one another in goods (coverage of nearly 96 percent),[32] services (across 11 out of 12 sectors), investment, some movement of labor, electronic commerce, competition policy, intellectual property rights, and more. The agreement also included the most robust dispute settlement mechanism in all of the ASEAN agreements.[33]

The last agreement under negotiation has been the ASEAN agreement with India. The goods agreement was completed in 2009, but, three years later, Cambodia and the Lao PDR had not yet begun implementation. Coverage of goods, however, has been quite poor. India agreed to open 78.8 percent of its market, Indonesia committed to only 48.7 percent, and no country (but Singapore) pledged more than 88 percent.[34] Negotiations in services and investment were concluded in late 2012.

INTEGRATING ASIA

ASEAN began moving towards regional trade integration in 1992 in Southeast Asia. The rest of Asia, however, did not move as quickly or as early in pursuing regional integration. Instead, countries in Northeast Asia and Australia and New Zealand were busy pursuing multilateral trade and signing bilateral agreements. The ASEAN+One agreements linked up the various dialogue partners to ASEAN. The dialogue partners themselves were not well connected. However, in a few short years, the momentum in favor of regional agreements in Asia has changed dramatically. By 2013, Asia was involved in two mega-regional agreements, with 12 and 16 members, as well as a new set of smaller agreements.

REGIONAL COMPREHENSIVE ECONOMIC PARTNERSHIP (RCEP) OR ASEAN+SIX

Over the years that ASEAN was busily negotiating various agreements with its dialogue partners, different ideas also came and went about consolidating these agreements into a larger commitment. Everyone recognized the economic potential from hooking the 16 countries together in an integrated agreement with greater market liberalization.

Finally, in May 2013, the 16 countries involved in existing ASEAN agreements sat down in Brunei to launch the first round of negotiations on a new agreement, the Regional Comprehensive Economic Partnership. The 16 countries had a total population of over 3 billion people, and a trade share estimated at around 27 percent of global trade (based on 2010 WTO figures), covering GDP of around US$20 trillion (2011 IMF figures).[35]

RCEP is designed to be a comprehensive trade agreement. The Leaders' Statement, which provides the roadmap for officials, clearly indicates that RCEP is intended to provide significant improvements over the existing ASEAN+One agreements, subject to specific circumstances in individual countries.[36] The statement also pledges that RCEP will cover "trade in goods, trade in services, investment, economic and technical cooperation, intellectual property, competition, dispute settlement and other issues to be identified during the course of negotiations."

Early indications suggest that RCEP's quest for breadth and ambition may not be met right away by all 16 parties. From the earliest moments, officials were including calls for special and differential treatment, as well as additional flexibility for least developed country members.[37] This suggests that whatever provisions will be forthcoming in the RCEP will not apply to all members evenly, at least for some provisional period. Furthermore, the agreement includes the possibility that a member could join the agreement at a later date.

The roadmap called for talks to begin in 2013 and be concluded by 2015. However, given ASEAN's history of negotiations thus far, such a timeline for a comprehensive agreement is likely to be too ambitious.

TRILATERAL AGREEMENT: CHINA, JAPAN AND KOREA

At the same time as the RCEP negotiations were officially launched in November 2012, the leaders of China, Japan and Korea announced the start of formal negotiations in what have become known as the trilateral CJK talks.[38] These talks are to follow in the wake of bilateral negotiations already under way between Korea and China.

If the CJK were to get momentum, it might complicate negotiations in the RCEP, as the current plan for RCEP is to leave ASEAN "in the driver's seat." But given the economic weight of Northeast Asia relative to the rest of the countries in RCEP, if CJK were to create a true integrated market between the three countries, the center of gravity in the negotiations would shift northward and away from ASEAN. However, given the political and security difficulties between China, Japan and Korea, it is likely that CJK may be significantly delayed.

TRANS-PACIFIC PARTNERSHIP (TPP)

Another regional governance structure for trade in Asia includes several Asian countries – the Trans-Pacific Partnership (TPP). With the addition of Japan in mid-2013, the TPP includes 12 countries: Australia, Brunei, Canada, Chile, Japan, Malaysia, Mexico, New Zealand, Peru, Singapore, the United States and Vietnam. Negotiations began in earnest in 2010.

The TPP is significantly more comprehensive than the ASEAN-based agreements. The TPP opens the entire goods market to members – at or near 100 percent coverage at nearly zero tariffs once the agreement is fully implemented. It also includes extensive commitments to liberalize the market in services, using a different method of market opening from ASEAN+ agreements and RCEP.[39] Overall the TPP has nearly 30 chapters, which include promises on issues as diverse as intellectual property, environment, labor, competition, and regulatory coherence.

Coverage in the TPP is the same for all members. Even the developing country participants are required to follow the same levels and extent of commitments as the most advanced countries in the agreement (subject to slightly longer timelines and some technical assistance). This is because the TPP comes with a strong normative commitment to opening markets as a mechanism for spurring economic growth and development for all member participants.

Another key difference between the TPP and ASEAN+ agreements is the dispute settlement mechanism. Although ASEAN has a dispute mechanism, as well as the ASEAN+ agreements, in practice, these mechanisms have never been tested. The "ASEAN way" is one of consensus, which means that ASEAN members are extremely reluctant to confront one another. To the extent that the parties have an issue with one another, these issues are generally taken up in the dispute settlement system within the WTO. Such a stance is possible in the ASEAN agreements, because ASEAN commitments rarely go much beyond WTO promises. This makes it possible to adjudicate disputes in the WTO.

However, the TPP routinely ventures into territory that is not covered at all in the WTO. For example, the TPP has rules on electronic commerce. There are no rules yet at the global level on e-commerce. It is not possible to have a dispute at the WTO on e-commerce violations, as no WTO rules can have been broken. Therefore, the TPP members decided to include a robust dispute settlement mechanism in the agreement, which is intended to be used by participants.

The TPP has an accession clause that has already been used multiple times to admit new members. The process for membership requires countries to indicate their interest in joining and their willingness to undertake the commitments of the agreement. Then they must engage in bilateral consultations with each current TPP member. If all current members approve on a bilateral basis, the candidate country is considered by the collective membership. The TPP operates on consensus, so the new member must be approved by the whole group.

FREE TRADE AREA OF THE ASIA PACIFIC (FTAAP) AND APEC

Another institutional structure for trade in Asia is the Asia Pacific Economic Cooperation (APEC). APEC was launched in 1989 as a non-binding, advisory trade body, which includes 21 member economies: Australia, Brunei, Canada, Chile, China, Hong Kong, Indonesia, Japan, Malaysia, Mexico, New Zealand, Papua New Guinea, Peru, the Philippines, Russia, Singapore, South Korea, Chinese Taipei, Thailand, the United States and Vietnam. It is perhaps most famous for the photographs of the leaders taken every year in the costumes of the host country – ponchos in Peru, batik in Indonesia, or outback drover jackets in Australia.

The purpose of APEC is to develop economic growth and development in the region. Because the organization is advisory, it does not really have a mechanism for compelling members to follow through with economic liberalization plans. In particular, APEC itself has no mechanism for negotiating. So, starting in 2006, APEC members began discussing plans to create a true Free Trade Area of the Asia Pacific. By 2010, the leaders agreed that the plans to get to an FTAAP could take different formats. The Leaders' Statement endorsed three pathways – ASEAN+Three (ASEAN+CJK), ASEAN+Six (RCEP) and the TPP – among others. APEC itself pledged to provide "leadership and intellectual input into the process of its development, and [to play] a critical role in defining, shaping and addressing the 'next generation' trade and investment issues that an FTAAP should contain."[40]

Left unaddressed is how any of these three processes will convert or converge into an FTAAP at the end of the day. As one simple example of the problems to be faced, RCEP currently includes India, which is not an

APEC member (although it has been lobbying for APEC membership for years). Not all ASEAN countries are APEC members (Cambodia, Laos and Myanmar are missing). The TPP, likewise, has several non-APEC economies lining up to join the agreement.

The TPP and RCEP are likely to have different provisions, and merging the two might prove so problematic that it could be easier in the end simply to start over with a new FTAAP.

The level of commitments in the TPP, in particular, are likely to be a significant stretch for many APEC economies. If the FTAAP required similar levels of liberalization, many APEC members would likely not want to participate. Even some current TPP members might be reluctant to extent their current commitments to the wider, 21-member group.

AGREEMENTS WITH THE EUROPEAN UNION

To come back full circle in this chapter, the European Union decided, in 2007, to start negotiations with ASEAN on the creation of a new FTA. The EU thought that it could have two regional agreements connected together as a mechanism for spreading liberalization and economic cooperation between Europe and Asia. However, by 2010, the EU had decided to abandon the effort temporarily. The basic problem was that the EU had expected ASEAN to negotiate as a block, similar to the way the EU operates. However, as noted above, ASEAN does not negotiate as a collective. Instead, bargaining in goods becomes something closer to ten separate deals. From the European perspective, this approach was not attractive.

Thereafter, the EU switched away from this regional approach to trade. Instead, it launched negotiations on a bilateral basis with individual ASEAN countries, starting with Singapore in March 2010. The Singapore agreement was concluded in December 2012. In the meantime, the EU also started talks with Malaysia (2010), Vietnam (2012) and Thailand (2013). At some point, the EU still has aspirations to sign a region-to-region agreement.

NEW TRADE PATTERNS

Asia highlights changes in trade governance perhaps better than any other area. Trade is increasingly organized around a set of regional agreements that include differing groups of participating countries. Over time, these regional arrangements have themselves grown bigger with more members and more complex with more trade areas covered by the agreements. As a result, most Asian countries are involved in bilateral, regional and global trade commitments.

This shift is most pronounced in Asia, but other regions are following a similar path. This represents a rather profound shift in trade governance in a relatively short amount of time. Although ASEAN began trade integration in 1992 (and, of course, the EU started much earlier), the explosion in bilateral and smaller regional agreements took off in the late 1990s and early 2000s. Prior to this time, governments were largely content to rely on global trade initiatives in the GATT/WTO.

It is not clear where this stampede into bilateral and regional agreements will leave the multilateral trade system. It could be argued that liberalization of trade in any format is simply an extension of the original objectives of the GATT from the 1940s and therefore not a concern. However, the benefits of any free trade agreement are granted only to partners and not extended to others, so the reduction in tariffs or changes in regulations to allow foreign service operators into markets as a part of FTA commitments are not as market opening as similar commitments made in global agreements.[41] Some changes, though, cannot be confined only to partners. For example, new rules for speeding up customs or changes in procedures for handling investment may spill over to non-parties as well.

Of greater concern may be the spread of FTAs into new areas entirely. Agreements like the TPP are attempting to harmonize regulations and set standards across an ever-wider set of member countries. As these new standard-setting agreements spread, the potential grows for conflict between sets of countries in different agreements. It could become more difficult for exporters to navigate different sets of standards required by different FTA agreements.

Some of these new commitments, rules and regulations might eventually be brought back full circle into the global system. As countries find themselves taking on greater liberalization promises with bilateral and regional partners, they may discover that implementing new market access commitments is less threatening than originally envisioned. Dealing with multiple, overlapping FTAs may become so cumbersome that firms will start to lobby once more for sorting it all out at the system level. In the long run, the multilateral trade regime could become stronger as a result.

But, in the meantime, the shift in trade governance from the global level to new bilateral and regional levels looks set to continue and spread to other parts of the world. It therefore bears watching carefully, as it changes the nature of the global trading regime.

NOTES

1. The 27 EU members committed in the 2010 Lisbon Treaty included: Austria, Belgium, Bulgaria, Cyprus, the Czech Republic, Denmark, Estonia, Finland, France, Germany, Greece, Hungary, Ireland, Italy, Latvia, Lithuania, Luxembourg, Malta, the Netherlands, Poland, Portugal, Romania, Slovakia, Slovenia, Spain, Sweden and the United Kingdom.
2. One difference between EFTA and the EU, however, is that EFTA members do not negotiate as a block in the multilateral setting of the GATT/WTO.
3. Switzerland is not a member of the EEA, but has a separate bilateral agreement with the EU. The EEA includes the free movement of goods, services, persons and capital, but it does not mean that the EFTA countries are also members of the customs union. Nor do the EFTA members have the same EU commitments in all areas including the Common Agricultural and Fisheries Policies (CAP), the Common Foreign and Security Policy, Justice and Home Affairs, or Monetary Union (EMU).
4. Of course, only members get this benefit. Non-members of the group still must pay the 26 percent tariff. This is why many people refer to free trade agreements as preferential trade agreements (PTAs), since they guarantee preferences or benefits to members that are not granted to non-members. To ensure that non-member country firms do not have access to these tariff benefits, negotiators must also create what are known as "rules of origin" (ROO) to ensure that only products "from" member countries qualify for the preferential rates on offer. It is only by examining both the tariff reductions and the rules of origin criteria that it is possible to determine how open or closed a particular market actually is to other members, as a country could lower tariffs but create such difficult ROO criteria that hardly any products actually qualify for use of the lower tariff rates.
5. "GDP per Capita (Current US$)," World Bank Group, 2013, available from: http://data.worldbank.org/indicator/NY.GDP.PCAP.CD (accessed April 9, 2013).
6. "Growth of the Population per Country in a Historical Perspective, Including Their Administrative Divisions and Principal Towns," *Population Statistics*, available from: http://www.populstat.info/ (accessed April 9, 2013).
7. Products with tariffs of less than 20 percent had to be cut down to 0–5 percent faster than those with tariffs above 20 percent. When the four new members of ASEAN joined, they were given different deadlines to reduce tariffs to between 0 and 5 percent: Vietnam had until 2006, Laos and Myanmar had until 2008, and Cambodia had until 2010. The ASEAN Secretariat notes that average tariffs on products on the original Inclusion List for the ASEAN 6 in 1993 was 12.76 percent. See www.asean.org/communities/asean-economic-community/category/asean-free-trade-area-afta-council (accessed April 5, 2013).
8. Products on the Temporary Sensitive List (TSL) were moved starting on January 1, 1996, in five equal installments, concluding on January 1, 2000.
9. Sensitive products were unprocessed agricultural products. They were eventually split into two categories. Most were moved to the Inclusion List, starting between January 1, 2001 and January 1, 2003, with final tariffs of between 0 and 5 percent by 2010. Vietnam had to start the transition on January 1, 2006 and complete the transition to 0–5 percent by January 1, 2013. For Laos and Myanmar, the start date was 2008, with implementation by 2015. Cambodia had the same start date, but until 2017 for implementation of the Sensitive List tariff reductions. The exception (Highly Sensitive List) was rice from Indonesia, Malaysia and the Philippines.
10. The World Customs Organization manages the system and revises it periodically.
11. GATT/WTO commitments are therefore made at least at the six-digit level for all members.
12. Countries are not supposed to sign an FTA with very poor coverage of goods, because it would violate their commitments under the GATT/WTO. Under Article 24 of the GATT, countries must include "substantially all trade" in their free trade agreements.

This benchmark has not been defined by the members, but has been generally held to require something closer to 90 percent or more of lines for developed countries and slightly less for developing countries.

13. Mostly alcohol, tobacco and firearms products that are prohibited for moral or security reasons.
14. AFTA was replaced by the ASEAN Trade in Goods Agreement (ATIGA) on May 17, 2010. ATIGA consolidated various commitments on goods into one, more comprehensive legal instrument.
15. The eighth package under the ASEAN Framework Agreement on Services (AFAS) was signed in 2010. Mutual recognition agreements (MRAs) were signed to recognize qualifications between ASEAN members in surveying, architecture, nursing, engineering, dentistry, medicine and accountancy, starting in 2005.
16. "GDP per Capita (Current US$)," World Bank Group, 2013, available from: http://data. worldbank.org/indicator/NY.GDP.PCAP.CD (accessed April 9, 2013).
17. "Growth of the Population per Country in a Historical Perspective, Including Their Administrative Divisions and Principal Towns," *Population Statistics*, available from: http://www.populstat.info/ (accessed April 9, 2013).
18. See WTO (2006: Table I.22).
19. See WTO (2006: Table I.4).
20. ASEAN Secretariat, http://www.asean.org/communities/asean-economic-community/category/overview-14 (accessed April 10, 2013).
21. ASEAN Secretariat, http://www.asean.org/communities/asean-economic-community/category/overview-14 (accessed April 10, 2013).
22. The AEC is part of a larger package of reforms by ASEAN. Other changes included the introduction of an ASEAN Charter that included political and security elements.
23. Australia and New Zealand are linked with ASEAN in what might more properly be known as an ASEAN+Two agreement, AANZFTA.
24. Except for Singapore, which offers the same 100 percent coverage to all countries, since it has zero tariffs for all goods (except for six lines – tobacco and some alcohol products).
25. Fukunaga and Kuno (2012: 4, Table 2).
26. Not all goods are included in ACFTA – total coverage is just under 95 percent of goods at the end of the implementation period, which stretches as long as 2018, depending on the country and item. See Fukunaga and Kuno (2012: 2, Table 1). Note that Vietnam's data is not included in the calculation.
27. See Pongvutitham (2004).
28. "Thai Air-Con Manufacturers Feel the Heat of China FTA" (2009), *The Nation* (Thailand), August 29; and "Chinese Textiles to Flood Thailand" (2009), *The Nation* (Thailand), November 12.
29. "Indonesian Workers Rally to Urge Delay of Implementation of ASEAN–China FTA" (2010), *Jakarta Post*, January 7.
30. Killian (2010).
31. Fukunaga and Kuno (2012: 2, Table 1). Fukunaga and Isono (2013: 4) note that Indonesia had still not enjoyed the benefits of the ASEAN–Japan Comprehensive Economic Partnership (AJCEP) by the end of 2012 because it had not yet dealt with some technical issues in its tariff schedules.
32. This includes 100 percent coverage by Australia, New Zealand and Singapore. Even the new ASEAN countries of Cambodia (89.1%), Laos (91.9%), Myanmar (88.1%) and Vietnam (94.8%) took on relatively high commitments. See Fukunaga and Kuno (2012: 2, Table 1).
33. Disputes to be settled by consultation followed by an arbitration tribunal, although not all provisions of the agreement were included under dispute settlement (some sanitary and phytosanitary commitments, electronic commerce, competition and economic cooperation were excluded).
34. Fukunaga and Kuno (2012: 2, Table 1).

35. Data taken from New Zealand Ministry of Foreign Affairs and Trade, http://www. mfat.govt.nz/Trade-and-Economic-Relations/2-Trade-Relationships-and-Agreements/ RCEP/ (accessed April 24, 2013).
36. For a copy of the roadmap, see http://www.asean.org/images/2012/documents/ Guiding%20Principles%20and%20Objectives%20for%20Negotiating%20the%20Regio nal%20Comprehensive%20Economic%20Partnership.pdf.
37. "Special and differential (S&D) treatment" is a term used in the WTO to describe a situation where developing countries are given more favorable treatment than developed country members. In practice, members have requested S&D treatment such as additional time to implement commitments.
38. Starting in December 2008, the three countries launched a (nearly) annual Trilateral Summit to take place in rotation among the three countries. The Summit even set up a permanent Secretariat in Seoul in September 2011. However, the agenda of the meeting (which may last for as little as two hours) is largely non-economic in nature.
39. In formal terms, ASEAN and RCEP use a positive list, which means that countries open *only* sectors that are listed. In the TPP, countries agree to open every sector *except* for those that are listed, using a negative list. This also means that any new service industries are automatically opened for foreign providers unless they are explicitly added to the list during the annual review process.
40. APEC, Leaders' Statement, November 14, 2010, Yokohama, http://www.apec.org/ Meeting-Papers/Leaders-Declarations/2010/2010_aelm/pathways-to-ftaap.aspx.
41. Even if governments frequently offer more generous terms at the FTA level than at the multilateral level, knowing that fewer parties will take advantage of the benefits of the agreement.

REFERENCES

Amsden, A. (1989), *Asia's Next Giant: South Korea and Late Industrialization*, New York: Oxford University Press.
Economist Corporate Network (2013), *Riding the ASEAN Elephant: How Business Is Responding to an Unusual Animal*, Beijing: Economist Corporate Network.
Fukunaga, Yoshifumi and Ikumo Isono (2013), *Taking ASEAN+1 FTAs towards the RCEP: A Mapping Study*, ERIA Discussion Paper Series, No. ERIA-DP-2013-02, January, Jakarta: Economic Research Institute for ASEAN and East Asia.
Fukunaga, Yoshifumi and Arata Kuno (2012), *Toward a Consolidated Preferential Tariff Structure in East Asia: Going Beyond ASEAN+1 FTAs*, ERIA Policy Brief, No. 2012-03, May, Jakarta: Economic Research Institute for ASEAN and East Asia.
Haggard, S. (1990), *Pathways from the Periphery: The Politics of Growth in Newly Industrialized Economies*, Ithaca, NY: Cornell University Press.
Johnson, C. (1982), *MITI and the Rise of the Japanese Miracle: The Growth of Industrial Policy, 1925–1975*, Stanford, CA: Stanford University Press.
Killian, P.M. Erza (2010), "Rethinking the Current Free Trade Debate in Indonesia," *Jakarta Post*, April 13.
Pongvutitham, Achara (2004), "China FTAs Need Careful Thought," *The Nation* (Thailand), November 9.
Wade, R. (1990), *Governing the Market: Economic Theory and the Role of Government in East Asian Industrialization*, Princeton, NJ: Princeton University Press.
World Bank (1993), *The East Asian Miracle*, Oxford: Oxford University Press.
WTO (World Trade Organization) (2006), *World Trade Developments 2006*, Geneva: WTO.

12. African regionalism: the complex role of regional trade[1]
Kathleen J. Hancock

In May 1963, President Kwame Nkrumah of Ghana stood before the leaders of 32 newly independent African states and proclaimed:

> We must unite now or perish. I am confident that by our concerted effort and determination, we shall lay here the foundations for a continental Union of African States . . . Independence is only the prelude to a new and more involved struggle for the right to conduct our own economic and social affairs; to construct our society according to our aspirations, unhampered by crushing and humiliating neo-colonialist controls and interference. (Nkrumah 2013)

He called for a common currency and market, common development policies, and a central bank, as well as a common foreign policy and military. The next day, the leaders founded the Organization of African Unity (OAU), a weaker union than the United States of Africa that Nkrumah had dreamed of, but still an expression of their aspirations for true independence from colonial influence. Fifty years later, the African Union (the successor to the OAU) declared 2013 the Year of Pan-Africanism and African Renaissance. Nkrumah and his fellow leaders' vision from 50 years ago helps explain the regional trade agreements we see throughout Africa today as well as the enduring idea for a continental economic union. Yet, as this chapter shows, the African regional trade agreements which are meant as building blocks to the continent-wide union have a long way to go before accomplishing even this part of the pan-African dream.

Many US and European publications on trade largely ignore economic regionalism in Africa. This is a significant oversight, since the continent is home to the oldest customs union, the over 100-year-old Southern African Customs Union (SACU), and has more customs and monetary unions that any other world region. Geographically larger than Europe, the US, and China combined, sub-Saharan Africa (hereafter called "Africa") is home to 11 regional trade agreements, implemented to varying degrees and with an assortment of integration goals. In addition, three states (Cameroon, Côte d'Ivoire, and South Africa) have free trade agreements with the European Union (EU), and SACU has a free trade agreement (FTA) with the European Free Trade Association. Finally, four eastern and southern African states (Madagascar, Mauritius, Seychelles, and Zimbabwe) formed a new trade agreement, which they began implementing in spring 2012 (European Commission 2013a). As shown in Table 12.1, many states belong to more than one regional agreement, raising questions about overlapping commitments, particularly as the states move toward deeper integration, such as customs unions.

In this chapter, I analyze the types of regional economic integration agreements, why states in general and African states in particular might favor regional accords, and whether regionalism is working in Africa. I then summarize the major trade agreements between the EU and Africa and argue that Europe's recent focus on economic partnership agreements could be undermining the very regionalism Europe advocates for African states as well as other world regions. I suggest a new focus of research, *resource regionalism*, with a focus on two issues important to Africa: regional electricity grids (known as *power pools*) that link together members of the trade agreements, and regional water governance. My focus throughout is on regional agreements, as opposed to so-called multilateral or global trade covered by the General Agreement on Tariffs and Trade (GATT) and the World Trade Organization (WTO); for a focus on the global accords, see Chapter 13 by Hoekman.

TYPES OF REGIONAL ECONOMIC AGREEMENTS

Since the end of the Cold War, economic integration accords have proliferated. Virtually every world region, regardless of economic development, government type, or culture, boasts at least a few loosely specified accords. However, for analytical purposes, these accords should not be lumped into a single category of "integration," as some IPE scholars have done. Instead scholars should categorize agreements by depth (shallow to deep), as well as type (monetary and trade) and governance structure (plutocratic, supranational, and intergovernmental) (Hancock 2009). Looking only at trade, shallow integration accords include preferential and free trade agreements, customs unions are moderately deep agreements, and economic unions are deep agreements. At the maximum level of integration, states unite into a single political unit. Dividing agreements by depth immediately reveals an important difference in how often certain types of accords are signed: of the 354 regional integration accords registered with the World Trade Organization, only 14 are customs unions or deeper-level (such as monetary unions or common markets).[2]

Bela Balassa's seminal work on trade concisely defines integration as "the abolition of discrimination within an area" (Balassa 1961). He goes

Table 12.1 African regional trade agreements

	AU+	CEMAC*†	CEN-SAD¹+	COMESA*+†	EAC*+†	ECCAS+	ECOWAS*+†	SACU*†	SADC*+	WAEMU*†
Angola	X					X			X	
Benin	X		X				X			X
Botswana	X							X	X	
Burkina Faso	X		X				X			X
Burundi	X			X	X	X				
Cameroon	X	X				X				
Cape Verde	X		X				X			
Central African Republic	X	X	X			X				
Chad	X	X	X			X				
Comoros	X	X	X	X						
Congo, Rep. of	X	X				X				
Côte d'Ivoire	X		X				X			X
Dem. Rep. of Congo	X			X		X			X	
Djibouti	X		X	X						
Equatorial Guinea	X	X				X				
Eritrea	X		X	X						
Ethiopia	X		X	X						
Gabon	X	X				X				
Gambia	X		X				X			
Ghana	X		X				X			
Guinea	X		X				X			
Guinea-Bissau	X		X				X			X
Kenya	X		X	X	X					
Lesotho	X		X					X	X	
Liberia	X		X				X			
Madagascar	X			X					X	

270

Country											
Malawi	X			X							
Mali	X		X								X
Mauritius	X			X							
Mozambique	X			X							
Namibia	X			X		X					X
Niger	X		X	X		X					
Nigeria	X		X	X		X					X
Rwanda	X				X			X			
São Tomé & Príncipe	X		X	X		X					X
Senegal	X		X	X		X					X
Seychelles	X									X	
Sierra Leone	X		X			X					
Somalia	X		X								
South Africa	X			X			X			X	
South Sudan	X			X						X	
Sudan	X			X							
Swaziland	X						X			X	
Tanzania	X			X	X					X	
Togo	X			X	X	X					X
Uganda	X		X	X	X					X	
Zambia	X		X	X						X	
Zimbabwe	X		X								
TOTAL in SSA (inc. north Africa)	48 (54)	6	20 (24)	18 (20)	5	10	5	15	5	15	8

Table 12.1 (continued)

Notes:
Agreements are Community of Sahel-Saharan States (CEN-SAD), Economic and Monetary Community of Central Africa (CEMAC), Central African Economic and Monetary Community (COMESA), East African Community (EAC), Economic Community of Central African States (ECCAS), Economic Community of West African States (ECOWAS), SACU, Southern African Development Community (SADC), and the West African Economic and Monetary Union (WAEMU).

¹ CEN-SAD also includes the north African states of Egypt, Libya, Mauritania, and Morocco; COMESA includes Egypt and Libya.

† = customs union

* = agreement notified to the World Trade Organization

+ = agreement recognized by the African Union. The AU also recognizes as African "regional economic communities" the Inter-Governmental Authority on Development (IGAD), which focuses on drought, ecological degradation and economic hardship, and whose members include Djibouti, Ethiopia, Kenya, Somalia, Sudan, and Uganda; and the Arab Maghreb Union (UMA), which includes Algeria, Libya, Mauritania, Morocco, and Tunisia, all north African states.

Sources: World Trade Organization, Regional Trade Agreements database: http://wto.org/english/tratop e/region e/region e.htm, May 2013; Economic Commission for Africa, African Union, and African Development Bank Group. *Assessing Regional Integration in Africa, V,* 2012; and Intergovernmental Authority on Development: http://igad.int.

on to suggest varying forms, moving from shallow to deep integration, a schematic many scholars use today. These are ideal types in the sense that Max Weber used the term; they are used for analytical purposes and generally do not exist in their perfect or true form (Weber [1922] 1978: 19–22). For example, although the EU is generally held up as the best example of a common market, the deepest form of economic integration short of a political union, a number of barriers to trade still exist within its borders.

Shallow trade accords include preferential trade agreements, free trade agreements, and customs unions. Preferential trade agreements grant lower tariffs or duty-free access to signatory states. These can be broad-based, covering a significant percentage of traded goods, or highly selective, offering reduced tariffs on only a handful of products. Members retain some tariff and non-tariff barriers with each other. The members do not align their external trade policies; these are left as decisions for each individual state. For example, one state might have high tariffs on oranges for non-members, while another eliminates these tariffs.

Free trade areas (FTAs) are defined as those that deepen economic integration by eliminating all barriers to trade between the members, including differences in product standards, and harmonizing trade-related laws and customs administration. Members may impose import tariffs on nonmember states at their individual discretion. The distinction between a preferential and a free trade area is thus a matter of degree rather than of kind. The most sophisticated accords include regional rules on investment, competition, the environment, and labor. The EFTA, the North American Free Trade Agreement (NAFTA), the Southern African Development Community (SADC), and the ASEAN Free Trade Area are examples of FTAs. Most states sign preferential and free trade accords with numerous states. While leaders intend that the accords increase trade among signatories, the integration is relatively shallow and can be broken without significant economic and political costs compared to deeper forms of integration. As a result, free trade agreements dominate the number of formal integration arrangements; about 90 percent of all accords reported to the WTO are preferential or free trade accords (World Trade Organization 2013b).

Customs unions are moderately deep forms of integration. By definition, they require member states to remove barriers to trade among members, like free trade accords, and also to harmonize the members' tariffs and other trade policies that apply to nonmembers. Member states decide on a tariff, quota, or other restriction to impose on nonmembers and jointly impose this policy. Harmonizing external policies prevents nonmembers from diverting trade through the state with the lowest tariffs or other trade barriers and then transporting goods into member states with higher barriers. The oldest customs union is Africa's SACU, founded in 1910. Other current customs unions include the Southern Common Market (Mercosur), the East African Community (EAC), the Russia–Belarus–Kazakhstan Customs Union, and the Andean Community (World Trade Organization 2013b).

Customs unions differ from preferential and free trade accords in several other ways. First, states sign only one customs union agreement as opposed to a variety of preferential and free trade accords. This accounts for the much smaller number of customs unions compared to free trade accords. Second, the exclusivity of these accords means that states are signaling a significant, generally long-term, relationship with other members. Third, members of customs unions are contiguous with each other, whereas shallow accords often include partners in distant regions. Finally, because of the necessity of cooperating on a greater number of decisions, customs union members commit to greater levels of institutionalization. Intergovernmental accords can become cumbersome given that negotiators must remain loyal to their home states. This can lead to long bargaining sessions with few results, hampering the integration effort.

Common markets and economic unions are significantly more extensive than customs unions and are thus considered forms of deep integration. In the ideal-type common market, goods, services, investments, labor, and capital move freely among the member states. At the ultimate level of integration, short of giving up political autonomy, is an economic union in which states share a common currency and integrate other policies such as industrial and agricultural policy, taxation rates and collection, and community and regional development plans and financing. Such integration agreements may even move beyond economics, harmonizing domestic policing, armies, and other foreign policies, as the EU has done in some areas. These deeper forms of integration may signal that states intend to integrate politically, thus becoming a single state.

The name of agreements can be misleading, in that some are mostly aspirational rather than fully in force. For example, the members of the Eurasian Economic Community plan to integrate along the lines of the EU, with a common currency, trade policies, bargaining positions, and external tariffs, along with free movement of labor and capital, but in terms of implementation the members are closer to having a customs union than a common market or economic union. Furthermore, recall that these concepts are ideal types, which do not exist in their perfect form.

The African Union heads of state and government envision an African Economic Community, modeled after the EU and developed in six stages, moving from shallow to deep integration: first, strengthen sectoral cooperation; then establish regional FTAs, a continent-wide customs union, a common market, a monetary union and, finally, a full economic union (Bøås and Dokken 2002; Bach 2003; Economic Commission for Africa et al. 2012). They argue that progress can be accelerated by bringing together a subset of the regional groups, such as the Tripartite FTA, which includes the Central African Economic and Monetary Community (COMESA), the EAC, and SADC. The Tripartite effort brings together 26 states, with a combined population of 530 million and a GPD of $630 billion, or about half the continent's economic output (Economic Commission for Africa et al. 2012: xv). The staged approach is mostly behind schedule, with the exception of those agreements that have long been in force, some of which the AU does not recognize, such as the SACU.

WHY REGIONALISM?

Neoliberalism has become the dominant discourse in Africa. According to this model, states must look outward, beyond their national borders and toward the global market. State leaders must reduce barriers to trade, opening up their states to regional and then global competition (Söderbaum 2004; Söderbaum and Taylor 2008: 25). The regional agreements are thus meant as a pathway to increased trade, which in turn will lead to improved economic development (Frankel and Romer 1999).

In *Assessing Regional Integration in Africa, IV*, the UN's Economic Commission for Africa, the African Union, and the African Development Bank (2010) cite a plethora of studies indicating that, in the last few decades, increased trade and economic growth are significantly correlated (Vamvakidis 2002; Clemens and Williamson 2004). Teasing out causality is less straightforward. Some scholars have found that countries with high incomes, for reasons other than trade, may trade more than those with less income (Helpman 1988; Bradford and Chakwin 1993; Rodrik 1995; Singh 2010). Those focusing on low-income states have found that increased trade liberalization in the form of reduced tariffs leads to few adjustment costs compared to the benefits of trade and may increase employment (Matusz and Tarr 1999). Thomas, Nash, and their associates review a number of studies and conclude that greater liberalization can result in gains from 1 or 2 up to 10 percent of annual GDP. Because the removal of tariffs eliminates incentives to smuggle, lobby, and evade taxes, trade reform can lead to further economic benefits. Over the long run, increased investment and savings and exposure to advanced technology may further spur the economy (Thomas et al. 1991; Sachs and Warner 1995; Dollar and Kraay 2002; Greenaway et al. 2002; Berg and Krueger 2003; Kraay 2004). Other scholars have raised issues with some of these findings, based on methodological critiques, particularly of the earlier studies (Rodríguez and Rodrik 1999).

A related goal of increased trade is poverty reduction. The world has witnessed an astounding decline in global poverty: between 1990 and 2010, the percentage of people living in extreme poverty in developing states declined by half. If progress were to continue at this pace, extreme poverty, measured as living on less than $1.25 per day (in 1995 dollars), would be eradicated by 2030 (Chandy et al. 2013). However, while China and India have made significant strides in reducing poverty, Africa has stagnated at high levels: in sub-Saharan Africa, 70 percent of the population live on $2.00 or less a day (World Bank 2013c). Africa is expected to be the most difficult place to get poverty reductions, in part because so many of the region's extreme poor live in fragile states, where the government is ill equipped to reduce poverty (Chandy et al. 2013: 14).

Many of the studies linking trade to development are not focused on regional trade agreements, but rather on global trade. China's rise as a global economic powerhouse is a stark example of the benefits of liberalizing trade, but China gained not through regional economic agreements but through global trade, primarily with the US and Europe.

Given that the most significant studies on the role of trade in reducing poverty and growing the state's overall economy come from studies looking at global trade rather than regional accords, why are African leaders so focused on regionalism? There are four primary explanations: First, economists offer a number of explanations related to economic gains under RTAs. Second, there have been a plethora of regional agreements, pushing many states to sign their own, lest they be left out of their own accord and face barriers from others. Third, the EU has both actively advocated for regionalism, urging the Africans (and others) to follow in their footsteps, and passively been a model of success in raising GDP (and reducing security threats) for its members, suggesting that economic regionalism is a viable option for African security and economic growth. Finally, as with other formerly colonized regions, many African leaders want to eschew economic and other ties to the former colonial powers. Regional agreements offer the promise of growth by trading within the region rather than with Europe. This sentiment is consistent with the pan-African vision discussed earlier. The following sections elaborate on these reasons.

First, in deciding whether to integrate regionally, a state considers several benefits derived from economic theories (Chipman 1965). Many of the benefits suggested by economists are assumed to accrue to all members, regardless of their economic size relative to the other members, and from both global trade accords (GATT/WTO) and regional trade accords. Major economic benefits include: reduced transaction costs leading to greater economic efficiencies; a larger customer base that allows companies to specialize within a sector, leading to increased efficiencies, higher profits, and expanded employment; broadened competition that weeds out poor performers; tariffs collected from nonmembers that can be redistributed among members; lower administrative costs for internal customs houses, border guards, and other officials who regulate the borders; higher levels of foreign direct investment from nonmembers seeking to avoid tariffs and to take advantage of the larger market; and greater bargaining power due to the increased market size of the integrated states (Mattli 1999). Other benefits are associated specifically with regional accords, from the shallowest preferential trade agreements to deep economic unions. These accords with their smaller memberships allow states to focus on economic benefits specific to the members. For example, in free trade negotiations with Chile and Singapore, the US pushed for concessions on intellectual property rights and allowing the US to bid on government procurement contracts, two issues of particular importance to the US (Weintraub 2004). Usually, states integrate at deeper regional levels (customs unions and common markets) only when they are in economic crisis, when the loss of sovereignty is outweighed by the promised economic benefits of integration (Mattli 1999; Hancock 2009).

While some scholars consider general benefits, others argue that the benefits of integration vary according to the economic size of the state. States with the largest GDPs can use power asymmetries to extract more favorable provisions from other members (Antkiewicz and Whalley 2005). For small and newly independent states, regional accords provide a transitional space: domestic companies become more competitive in a smaller universe, in preparation for stiffer competition from the global trading partners they will confront under an increasingly open trading system (Schott 2004). Similarly, a smaller negotiating table with regional allies provides a comfortable classroom in which to learn skills needed for the global accords (Schott 2004). Fewer players may simplify the path to reaching agreements: collective action theory suggests that larger groups have greater difficulty resolving their differences. "When the numbers of parties to an agreement increase, there is an increased probability that members' preferences will diverge, the core will shrink, and the probability of a bargain will fall" (Haggard 1997: 25). Furthermore, in some cases, such as the SACU, tariff revenues collected from nonmembers may provide government revenue needed by developing or newly independent states (Leith and Whalley 2004: 335–6; Gibb and Treasure 2011).

Not all customs unions bring the same benefits. Economists generally concur that a customs union will be more welfare-enhancing the closer it comes to meeting the following six conditions:

1. Geographically proximate members. States that share borders will benefit more from removing trade barriers than those that are distant. The African regional agreements mostly meet this provision.
2. High levels of pre-union trade among members. When states have historically engaged in extensive trade, their consumers are familiar with the other states' products and will quickly increase purchases when prices fall under free trade conditions. As discussed in the section "Is regionalism working?" below, African states have generally not had significant trade within the regional accords.
3. High pre-union trade barriers. When trade barriers are already very low, removing them will have less effect than when barriers have been historically high.
4. Low customs union barriers on trade with the rest of the world. Trade is less likely to be diverted from nonmembers when external barriers are low.
5. A large number of members with sizable economies. Even aggregated small markets still add up to a small economy and thus insignificant scale benefits (McCarthy 2003: 608). In Africa, this is a significant challenge, as many of the states are low- or lower-middle-income states. For example, as noted above, the Tripartite FTA includes 26 states, but the members' combined GDP is only $630 billion, about the same as Switzerland's (World Bank 2013b).
6. Competitive (at equal levels of development) rather than complementary (some developed, some undeveloped) economies within the membership (Salvatore 2004: 327–8). For example, a regional organization with South Africa and Botswana, both upper-middle-income states, should perform better than a regional accord with South Africa and Mozambique, a low-income state. When some members are substantially more advanced than others, "backwash and polarization" can occur: advanced states attract more investments than their partners (*backwash*) and thus develop exponentially faster than the other members (*polarization*). This leads to lopsided development, exacerbating already unequal relations.

Even in a trade-diverting customs union, however, the collective terms of trade may well improve for members. Particularly for developing states, even when the customs union increases import costs, the gain of a somewhat larger market, and thus greater production, may be preferable to no gain at all. Consumers may benefit more from the growth in income and jobs than they lose in higher prices owing to trade diversion (McCarthy 2003: 607–08). Whether an individual member's terms of trade improve, decline, or remain the same depends on the details of the accord and the circumstances of the state, specifically in what sectors it has strength and how the newly unified tariffs affect those sectors (Viner 1950).

African pro-integrationists tend to focus on the argument that integrated economies will dramatically increase market size, leading to greater economic growth. For example, they argue, most African economies cannot support a steel industry, a potentially pivotal sector for industrialization. However, if states can provide the right investment conditions, such as stable policy, improved transportation and communication infrastructure, and coordinated and sound economic policy, they might be able to attract regional projects that would benefit from economies of scale (Economic Commission for Africa et al. 2012: 3).

A second factor behind interest in RTAs is a type of twenty-first-century integration race. It was not until after the Cold War ended that formal economic alliances proliferated the world over. Between 1990 and 1994, states notified the WTO of 33 new accords, more than twice the number that had previously been reported (Duina 2006: 3). This number has since skyrocketed. As of January 2013, WTO members have notified the organization of 546 regional trade agreements, counting goods, services, and accessions separately; of these, 354 are in force (World Trade Organization 2013b). Fear of being left out in the cold, while their neighbors form cozy, warm circles surrounded by high tariffs and other barriers to entry, drives state leaders to seek regional accords for their own states.

In a typical arms-race fashion, the European Union responded to the 1992 North American Free Trade Agreement by negotiating its own free trade accord with Mexico, which came into force in 2000 (Reiter 2003; Deardorff and Stern 2009). South American states responded to the race with a customs union of their own, Mercosur, noting in the preamble that a primary reason for the accord was "international trends, particularly the integration of large economic areas." On the other side of the world, China caught the wave of integration. At the dawn of 2013, it had completed accords with the ten-member ASEAN, the five-member Asia Pacific Trade Agreement, Chile, and Pakistan and was negotiating with Australia, Norway, and Switzerland, and with Taiwan, Penghu, Kinmen, and Matsu (World Trade Organization 2013b). Some have argued that the increase in regional accords is due to the WTO Doha Round stalling. While this may be a contributing factor, RTAs started significantly increasing in 1994, well before the Doha Round began in 2001 (World Trade Organization 2013a).

The integration race and stalled WTO negotiations do not explain the long-term interest in African regionalism, as many agreements predate the dramatic rise in regional accords. However, proliferating RTAs in all the world regions may legitimize Africa's interest in regionalism and spur on the continent's interest in these accords.

The third major reason for African interest in RTAs is the EU, both as a model of success and as an advocate of regionalism. The EU is widely viewed as the single most important economic integration agreement today. Although one cannot yet predict the outcome of the current euro crisis, which may significantly change the way other regions view the EU model, the EU has undoubtedly served for decades as the "gold standard" by which other integration agreements are measured (Grugel 2004; Bicchi 2006; Börzel and Risse 2009). Members have gone deeper and wider in terms of delegating to a central authority and issues areas covered than any other regional grouping. Whatever challenges the EU has faced along the way, its integration accords are viewed as having brought peace and prosperity to Europe, a continent once fraught with seemingly never-ending, and often catastrophic, warfare. Not only do other states view EU institutions as paradigms to be emulated to varying degrees, but the EU sees itself as a model for other world regions and thus has been actively promoting regional economic and political agreements around the globe.

The EU is not just a collection of agreements, institutions, and policies. It is an idea: the idea that states integrating their economies can cure the ills of persistent interstate conflict and low economic growth. There are five mechanisms for diffusing ideas, according to Börzel and Risse, four of which relate to the EU: coercion, which the EU does not employ; manipulation of utility calculations through positive and negative incentives; socialization by providing an authoritative model; persuasion through reason giving; and emulation through lesson drawing and/or mimicry (Börzel and Risse 2009). The EU allocated €116 million for 2008–13 to encourage regionalism in Africa, with 80 percent of that going toward economic regionalism. In addition, African leaders appear to be emulating the EU by using similar governance structures (though not supranational ones) and creating a timeline for increasing economic integration from preferential trade agreement to customs union, monetary union, and finally common market, along the lines of the EU. While it is impossible to untangle which of Börzel and Risse's four mechanisms has the greatest effect, it is clear that the EU sees itself as a role model for the region, that it has continued to play a vital role in encouraging regionalism, and that at least some of the regional agreements have benefited from the EU's backing.[3]

The final explanation for the African focus on RTAs relates to pan-Africanism, discussed at the beginning of this chapter. The desire to be free of the (former) colonial powers dates back to independence. The RTAs are thus seen as a means of escaping the European powers. Given the previous reason for RTAs, there is irony in this position. Nevertheless, the view holds sway with many Africans.

IS REGIONALISM WORKING?

At first glance, RTAs might seem to be working for Africa. Despite the global downturn since the 2008 economic crisis, African states' GDPs have grown well above 5 percent annually over the last decade. However, this growth has not translated into widespread economic advancements: 49 percent of sub-Saharan Africans survive on less than $1.25 per day, average life expectancy is 55 years, and average GDP per capita is $1447 (World Bank 2013d, 2013e). In addition, neither inter- nor intra-continental trade has increased substantially in the last 25 years. Africa's share of global trade has declined: having accounted for about 6 percent around 25 years ago, it now constitutes only 2 percent of global trade, and is even lower (1 percent) if South Africa is excluded (Economic Commission for Africa et al. 2010: 3). Furthermore, most of the trade is with states outside the continent, usually based on historical ties, particularly with former colonial powers. In the 1990–99 and 2000–10 decades, only 12 percent of trade in sub-Saharan Africa was with other sub-Saharan African states. While quite low, there has at least been a modest upward trend since 1970, as shown in Figure 12.1.

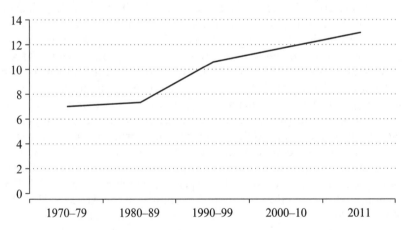

Note: Percentage of total exports.

Source: (Qureshi and Tsangarides 2011; World Trade Organization 2013b).

Figure 12.1 Intra-African trade

However, as shown in Table 12.2, trade within the RTAs has been averaging around 8–9 percent of overall trade; in other words, in the years
1995–2012, the members of an African RTA exported on average less than
10 percent of their overall exports to other members of the same RTA.
While more exports are going to Africa overall, compared to the rest of
the world, than in the past, the vast majority of exports still go to the rest
of the world, as Figure 12.1 shows. In addition, when comparing 2012
to 1995, intra-RTA trade has on average *decreased* 13 percent. Only two
RTAs – COMESA and EAC – show an increase since 1995. The decade
2000–10 shows a much smaller decline (0.94 percent), but still a decline.

This data only reports formal trade. Yet there is evidence that Africans
are trading a great deal through informal cross-border trade, defined as
trade transactions between residents and non-residents across the economic boundaries of two or more countries that are not recorded by
customs authorities (Guvele and Lautze 2000; Teka and Azeze 2002;
Lawrence and Mohiddin 2004; Muchomba and Sharp 2006; Umar and
Baluch 2007; Economic Commission for Africa et al. 2010: 161; Afrika and
Ajumbo 2012; Uganda Bureau of Statistics and Bank of Uganda 2012).
Uganda estimates that it alone exports informally as much as $200 million
more than its official numbers reflect (Uganda Bureau of Statistics and
Bank of Uganda 2012). However, the relationship between informal trade
and RTAs is unclear. If Uganda's informal trade was included in current
numbers, it would only further lower trade percentages within the RTA,
since the majority of its informal trade is with the Democratic Republic of
Congo, which is not a member of the same RTA as Uganda.

Why, despite the plethora of RTAs, have African states failed to increase
intra-African trade, either within the continent as a whole or within RTAs?
Unfortunately, there appear to be so many factors working against African
regional as well as global trade that low levels of trade are highly over-
determined. A variety of explanations point to issues that impede not only
trade but economic growth in general. These include: poor development,
maintenance, and connectivity of critical infrastructure, such as roads,
railways, ports, and communications; lack of reliable electricity; international and intra-state violence and armed conflicts; and poor health among
the population, including short life expectancy, high rates of HIV/AIDS,
malaria, and malnutrition (Economic Commission for Africa et al. 2010;
Mbekeani 2010; Sebitosi and Okou 2010; World Bank 2013e).

Other explanations focus on the RTAs and trade more generally.
The RTA member states have not fully implemented the agreements,
leaving in place tariffs and other barriers to trade, and local officials have
impeded trade through harassment, road blocks, and other illegal barriers (Economic Commission for Africa et al. 2010). Some have argued

Table 12.2 Intra-Trade of RTAs (per cent of total trade)

RTA	1995	2000	2005	2010	2011	2012	% change: 1995-2012	% change: 2000-2010
CEMAC	1.7	1.2	1.1	2.3	1.7	1.6	-1.58%	34.77%
CEN-SAD	7.9	6.6	6.5	6.8	6.3	6.7	-14.29%	1.30%
COMESA	5.6	4.7	5.2	7.4	9.3	7.1	28.08%	50.87%
EAC	17.2	17.9	18.6	19.8	19.2	20.9	21.46%	16.89%
ECCAS	1.2	0.9	0.7	1.5	0.9	0.9	-27.32%	-4.03%
ECOWAS	10.3	9.0	9.7	8.3	6.4	7.1	-30.73%	-20.67%
SACU	7.5	7.4	6.4	5.4	5.1	2.9	-61.49%	-60.99%
SADC	14.9	14.3	11.9	13.0	12.4	13.0	-12.79%	-8.73%
WAEMU	16.1	15.2	14.2	12.2	10.8	12.5	-22.26%	-17.85%
Average	9.1	8.6	8.3	8.5	8.0	8.1	-13.44%	-0.94%

Notes:
Regional Trade Agreements include Economic and Monetary Community of Central Africa (CEMAC), Community of Sahel-Saharan States (CEN-SAD), Central African Economic and Monetary Community (COMESA), East African Community (EAC), Economic Community of Central African States (ECCAS), Economic Community of West African States (ECOWAS), SACU, Southern African Development Community (SADC), and the West African Economic and Monetary Union (WAEMU).

Source: UNCTAD Statistical Database, June 2013.

that export-processing zones (EPZs) could be the missing link for Africa. Mauritius has had some success with EPZs, as have Bangladesh, Mexico, and the Dominican Republic (Economic Commission for Africa et al. 2012: 49). Taylor argues that the regionalist enterprise in Africa is undermined by a lack of common political culture among member states (Taylor 2011). Others point to problems with who is driving the agenda. Whereas Mattli (1999) finds that regionalism generally comes about owing to pressure from below, primarily businesses demanding more supportive trading regimes, in much of Africa the political elite have been the drivers (Bischoff 2012). Without interest from those who do the trading, there is unlikely to be much progress in the trade statistics. For many regional accords, a regional plutocrat (dominant economic power) designed and enforced the regional project, a role South Africa played in the SACU (Hancock 2009) but that is missing from many of the other African RTAs. The colonial powers formed some of the most effective unions, also playing the plutocratic role. For newer agreements, however, this key player is missing, and in the older ones it is often no longer active. Others have argued that the preconditions for Europe's success – developed economies, high trading rates and high tariffs, and a long-term security threat with a history of going global (Germany and France), *inter alia* – are mostly missing in Africa (Hancock 2011; Draper 2012), undermining the chances of success despite the integration push. Finally, African states perform poorly on a number of additional factors that encourage trade: they have the highest transport costs of any region (Economic Commission for Africa 2010), with the landlocked countries' transport prices accounting for 15 to 20 percent of import costs, or three to four times higher than most OECD states (Raballand and Macchi 2008); total trading costs are twice as high as in OECD countries (Portugal-Perez and Wilson 2008); the region has the lowest "ease of doing business" scores (World Bank 2013a); and Africa has notably high uncertainty of trading costs and time delays (Christ and Ferrantino 2011).

In sum, a substantial number of economic and political factors are working against African regionalism, overall trade, and economic growth. Ironically, the EU may be adding to the problems.

EUROPE INADVERTENTLY UNDERMINING RTAS

The EU's new approach to trade in Africa may further undermine Africa's RTAs. In the 1990s, the GATT and later the WTO ruled that the EU's economic agreements with African, Caribbean, and Pacific (ACP) states were in violation of free trade rules. The Lomé Convention, later replaced by the Cotonou Partnership Agreement, gave special market access to the ACP states, a configuration of states that was itself an EU creation, making the accords discriminatory and therefore non-compliant. In 2001, the WTO ruled that the EU had until January 1, 2008 to negotiate WTO-compliant accords with the ACP states. In 2002, the EU began negotiations for economic partnership agreements (EPAs). Ironically, the EPAs might be undermining the EU's image as a supporter of African regionalism.

The special trading relationship between the EU and Africa began in 1957, with the Treaty of Rome, which created European Development Funds (EDF) for technical and financial aid to African countries still colonized and with which some European Economic Community states had historical ties. The first EDF ran from 1958 to 1963. This economic relationship evolved into the Lomé accords, which were followed by the Cotonou Partnership Agreement and finally the EPAs.

Lomé I (1975), which coincided with the fourth EDF, initiated preferences for most exports to the Europeans from the ACP states, which consisted of Europe's former colonies. Lomé I also introduced the STABEX system under which ACP states are compensated for the shortfall in export earning due to fluctuations in the price or supply of commodities. Quotas and guaranteed prices for bananas and sugar mostly benefited Caribbean states, Mauritius, Guyana, Fiji, and Barbados, while southern African countries benefited from beef and veal protocols which permitted a 90 percent refund of tax normally paid on imports (European Commission 2013b). Lomé II (1979) introduced a system for mining similar to the STABEX, called the SYSMIN system. Lomé I and II also included funding on infrastructure, such as road building, bridges, hospitals, and schools, as well as supporting sustainable agriculture. Lomé III (1984) focused on self-sufficiency and food security, while Lomé IV (1989) emphasized promoting human rights, democracy and good governance, strengthening the position of women, protecting the environment, decentralizing cooperation, diversifying ACP economies, promoting the private sector, and increasing regional cooperation (European Commission 2013b). By 2000, the ACP grouped together a wide variety of states, 79 in total, including 48 from Africa, many of which likely did not see themselves as having much in common with the others.

As the millennium approached, the EU was determined to do something different to assist Africa. Despite considerable economic aid, trade protocols, and the STABEX and SYSMIN systems, Africa was falling further behind in terms of development but also in its trade relations with the EU. The ACP states' share of the EU market had declined from 7 percent in 1976 to 3 percent in 1998. Sixty percent of total exports were concentrated in only ten products. From 1960 to 1992, Africa's GPD per capita grew at an average annual rate of only 0.4 percent, compared with 2 percent for developing states overall. Adding to this negative picture, European citizens were increasingly frustrated with the lack of progress, viewing Africa as riddled with corruption and therefore a poor investment (European Commission 2013b). In response to these concerns, the EC and ACP states moved to a new model for development.

On June 23, 2000, in Cotonou, Benin, the countries signed the ACP–EC Partnership Agreement, commonly called the Cotonou Agreement. The agreement covers trade issues until February 2020. Cotonou continues many of the Lomé principles, such as special access to the European market for the former colonies, but adds a political dimension and makes eradicating poverty a central goal of the partnership. The parties have twice revised the accord, in June 2005 and March 2010. The agreement covers three "pillars": development cooperation, economic and trade cooperation, and politics.

Cotonou includes a specific focus on regionalism, which was emphasized even more strongly in the second revision. For example, it states there will be a "particular emphasis placed on regional integration, including at the continental level" (Article 2) and that EPAs should, "as development instruments, aim to foster smooth and gradual integration of the ACP States into the world economy, especially by making full use of the potential of regional integration and South–South trade" (Article 36) (*Second Revision of the Cotonou Agreement* 2010). The language referring to continental integration is clearly meant to highlight the role of the African Union (Africa and Europe in Partnership 2010).

The non-reciprocal trade preferences ran afoul of GATT/WTO rules that disallow discrimination among members, except when members are forming a preferential trade agreement or a customs union. The EU sought and won a waiver from the WTO to continue the preferences through December 2007, after which new agreements would replace Cotonou provisions or the states would have to revert to existing agreements, such as the Generalized System of Preferences, a less favorable set of tariffs. Since 2002, the parties have been negotiating EPAs but have continually missed deadlines (Bilal and Stevens 2009).

The EU asked ACP states to put themselves into one of several regional negotiating groups, which did not coincide with existing RTAs. The African groupings are West Africa, Central Africa, Eastern and Southern Africa, East African Community, and SADC (European Commission 2006). The EU's request put African states in the awkward position of having to choose which group to join. Some have labeled the EPA configurations "flawed from the start" (Erixon 2012) and have called "the lack of reflection on the potential lessons" of EPA negotiations "staggering" (Bilal 2012).

The EU has been aggressively working to sell the EPAs as an improvement over prior trade agreements. For example, the EU created a 46-page brochure, filled with photographs from the ACP states and quotes of people supporting the EPAs. This Zambian farmer's testimony is typical:

> With the support of the EU and its agencies, we have also seen lots of improvements in customs procedures: they are much quicker now and work more efficiently for business shipments . . . Overall, we are now almost twice as fast on all our routes – some even take only a third of what they used to. (European Commission 2011)

The brochure, as well as the EU Commission's *EPA News: Weekly Digest* and countless reports and articles covering and promoting EPAs, demonstrates how hard the EU is working to persuade Africans (and Europeans) of the value of the proposed trade agreements.

The EPAs, however inadvertently, may be undermining African regionalism. First, the way in which the African states have organized themselves is inconsistent with the regional accords. The SADC EPA group is not the SADC at all; rather it is the five SACU states plus Mozambique and Angola, for a total of seven of the 15 SADC members. As of May 2013, not even all of these states had signed the interim agreement; only Mozambique, Botswana, Lesotho, and Swaziland had signed (European Commission 2013a). Malawi, Mauritius, Madagascar, Zambia, and Zimbabwe, all members of SADC, are participating as part of the Eastern and Southern Africa (ESA) group. This splits both the SACU and the SADC members into separate agreements. For SACU, these separate agreements are inconsistent with the customs union, since by definition members of a customs union cannot have different trading policies. The EU's approach was seen by some analysts and African officials as heavy-handed, unjustified, and damaging to the customs union.[4]

Second, even within the EPA groups, states negotiated different terms. Table 12.3 shows the varying liberalization schedules for the SADC members. In only one region, the East African Community, does more than one country have the same commitments as the others. The terms of liberalization – how quickly the African state must finish reducing or eliminating tariffs, how soon it must start this process, and what percentage of its tariff schedule it can exclude from the EPA – appear to reflect the state's individual negotiating skills and the EU's own economic interests: states with a strong hand and interests consistent with the EU's were able to get a better deal than those without these features. In general, those with

Table 12.3   Liberalization schedules for SADC members

Duration	Under 15 years	15-20 years	20+ years
	Botswana	Zambia	Tanzania
	Lesotho	Zimbabwe	
	Madagascar		
	Mauritius		
	Mozambique		
	Namibia		
	Seychelles		
	Swaziland		
Liberalization starts	Under 2 years	2-5 years	6+ years
	Botswana	Madagascar	Tanzania
	Lesotho	Seychelles	Zambia
	Mauritius	Zimbabwe	
	Mozambique		
	Namibia		
	Swaziland		
Exclusions	Under 15 per cent	15-20 per cent	20+ per cent
	Botswana	Madagascar	Mozambique
	Lesotho	Namibia	Zambia
	Mauritius	Tanzania	Zimbabwe
	Seychelles		
	Swaziland		

Source: The Interim Economic Partnership Agreements between the EU and African States, European Centre for Development Policy Management, 29.

weaker skills and interests inconsistent with the EU have agreed to open up more of their markets to EU imports sooner than other states (Bilal and Stevens 2009). The extreme example of a state able to drive a hard bargain is South Africa, which has strong negotiating skills and a favorable status quo trading system.

As Bilal and Stevens (2009) note, "little consideration seems to have been given to the complexity and importance of existing regional integration efforts in the context of the EPA negotiations" (Bilal and Stevens 2009: 37). Whether the EU has made a major miscalculation that will further undermine regionalism or just a minor misstep that can be easily corrected, the data show that regionalism has not yielded the desired fruit.

NEW DIRECTION IN AFRICAN REGIONALISM: RESOURCE REGIONALISM

The lack of success with regional trade agreements raises questions about whether there might be other forms of cooperation more likely to yield the desired results. Although understudied by IPE scholars, I argue that *resource regionalism* may be one of the keys to improved economic development, through increased foreign direct investment, improved governance, and more reliable access to energy. In this section, I highlight two resource regionalism issues in Africa: regional electricity grids, or power pools as they are known in Africa, that rely on natural resources (coal, water, sun, and wind); and rivers that cut across state borders, creating ecological and often economic regions (Hancock 2013).

With encouragement and funding from the World Bank, the EU, USAID, and other international organizations and states, sub-Saharan African states created four regional "power pools," which are regional electricity grids that allow power sharing: Southern African Power Pool (SAPP), East African Power Pool, West African Power Pool, and Central African Power Pool. These power pools were created over a decade, starting with SAPP, which was created in 1995, one year after the end of apartheid, and ending with the East African pool, created in 2005. Tanzania may eventually link the different power pools, leading to a continent-wide grid. North Africa also has a power pool, started in 1989, called the Comité Maghrébin de l'Electricité. Table 12.4 shows the members of the various pools and their connections to existing economic integration agreements.

The regional power pools are designed to lower electricity prices and expand access, by encouraging trade and investment in electricity. The SAPP followed from analysis demonstrating that southern Africa would see significant economic and access advantages from regional electricity integration and increased electricity trade using market mechanisms to set prices (Robinson 1993; Lewis 1994; Rubbers 1994; Eberhard and Van Horen 1995). These calculations were based on optimistic assumptions, but they were persuasive enough to move the political leaders of the 12 SADC members to create and sign the legal framework for the SAPP. From 1997 to 2000, USAID's Equity and Growth through Economic Research (EAGER) program funded a partnership between Purdue University and SAPP to create models for electricity trade among the SAPP members (Bowen et al. 1999). International organizations and states are now funding training for those who regulate the electricity sector, with the incentive of creating more efficient regional electricity markets (Kapika and Eberhard 2013). While analysts have found that short-term market trading of electricity between states happens mostly at the margins

Table 12.4   African power pools

Regional group	Year founded	Linked economic agreement members	Status
Southern African Power Pool (SAPP)	1995	Southern African Development Community (SADC): Angola, Botswana, Democratic Republic of Congo (DRC), Lesotho, Malawi, Mozambique, Namibia, South Africa, Swaziland, Tanzania, Zambia, Zimbabwe	As of 2012, Angola, Malawi, and Tanzania were not connected to the grid; the Grand Inga dam project was estimated at $80 billion.
West African Power Pool (WAPP)	1999	Economic Community of Western African States (ECOWAS): Benin, Burkina Faso, Cabo Verde, Côte d'Ivoire, the Gambia, Ghana, Guinea, Guinea-Bissau, Liberia, Mali, Niger, Nigeria, Senegal, Sierra Leone, Togo	Key components include projects linking Benin, Côte d'Ivoire, Ghana, Nigeria, and Togo; developing a second-generation hydropower project and interconnecting Guinea, Guinea-Bissau, the Gambia, and Senegal; and connecting Burkina Faso, Côte d'Ivoire, and Mali.
Central African Power Pool (PEAC – Pool Energétique de l'Afrique Centrale)	2003	Economic Community of Central African States (ECCAS): Cameroon, Central African Republic, Chad, Republic of Congo, Equatorial Guinea, Gabon	Smallest, least integrated pool. Mini-power pool with eastern DRC, Rwanda, and Burundi
East African Power Pool (EAPP)	2005	Burundi, Djibouti, DRC, Egypt, Eritrea, Ethiopia, Kenya, Rwanda, Somalia, Sudan, Tanzania, and Uganda.	Electricity trade through Kenya–Uganda, Burundi–DRC–Rwanda. Overall, lack of infrastructure, institutions, and technical capacity.

and that longer-term purchasing agreements are bilateral rather than multilateral, the grid clearly enables these purchases, and the institutional structure of the SAPP allows for regular meetings to discuss issues that may affect more than one utility.[5]

The African regional power pools link directly to regional water issues. The SAPP enables South Africa, which relies on coal for 95 percent of its electricity, to buy hydroelectricity from the Democratic Republic of Congo (DRC), Zambia, and Mozambique (Wild 2013). Proponents expect the proposed $80 billion Grand Inga dam in the DRC to generate double the capacity of China's Three Gorges dam, providing even more energy for the SAPP. The Congo river, which widens to about three miles in some areas, empties into the Atlantic Ocean near the equator, creating a massive plume that accounts for 40–80 percent of total carbon productivity and making it one of the largest carbon sinks on the planet. This raises issues of how the dam will affect other states in the region. Critics have raised concerns about the DRC's massive debt and high levels of corruption (the DRC is ranked 160 out of 176 on the Corruption Index (Transparency International 2013)), and questioned whether the Congolese people will really get any of the electricity, as opposed to South Africa, mining companies, and even Europeans (International Rivers 2013).

The River Congo and its Inga dam are just one example of how water is a regional resource issue. Water often cuts across borders, linking ecological regions in two or more states. In Africa, 14 states have high dependencies (defined as more than 50 percent) on exogenous fresh water resources (Libiszewski 1999: 118). With high dependencies, states are sensitive to any changes in the quantity or quality of their water supply. In addition, those living upriver have a privileged position, since any of their economic activity that affects the water will be passed on to those downstream.

While water for drinking and agriculture has significant political and economic consequences, water also intersects with energy issues, because of hydropower and because other types of energy can be highly water intensive, straining supplies and creating regional conflicts. Hydroelectric plants require that water reservoir or river levels be maintained. Thermal plants, which include plants fueled by coal, natural gas, biomass, and nuclear energy, require water for steam, cooling, and other processes related to electricity generation. Water quality in terms of temperature, turbidity, and pollution can affect the performance of plants and even cause shutdowns (Sauer and Klop 2010).

Large-scale hydro is considered the most efficient and cost-effective source of renewable energy. Africa has significant potential in this area, with only about 7 percent currently tapped (World Energy Council 2013: 9). However, since Africa is almost entirely water scarce or water stressed, dams for hydropower will raise issues about water use, including whether states can afford new forms of electricity generation, the drain that some resource exploration (mining, for example) might put on countries, and the conflicts between using water for energy, agriculture, and drinking.

Damming rivers for hydroelectric plants does not remove much water from the river, but it does affect seasonal patterns of water discharge, which may be needed for downstream states for agricultural purposes. Water released in the winter is of no help to summer crops, and water released during wet seasons can lead to flooding. Damming rivers can lead to reduced salinity and some water loss due to evaporation. Construction may also affect the migration of fish (Libiszewski 1999: 123). These issues can lead to state conflicts, but they also create a resource-based region, which might lead to greater cooperation and governance and economic growth. According to Libiszewski, the critical factors that determine how well states handle these potential conflicts include the "degree of dependency on exogenous sources of water, the distribution of power between adjacent states, and the relationship of an antagonistic versus cooperative tradition in inter-state relations" (Libiszewski 1999: 123). States are most likely to resolve favorably issues when there is an existing institutional and legal framework (Libiszewski 1999: 128).

Water management reforms are occurring around the world. In a classic story of the power of epistemic communities, after more than 30 years of discussion and debate, water professionals came to agree on the Integrated Water Resources Management (IWRM) as the right format for governing water (Swatuk 2008: 26). The United Nations declared 2005–15 the International Decade for Action "Water for Life," stating that the IWRM is the "approach that has now been accepted internationally as the way forward for efficient, equitable and sustainable development and management of the world's limited water resources and for coping with conflicting demands" (United Nations 2013). The consensus on the IWRM approach coincided with the end of apartheid and South Africa joining SADC, making the region a prime focus for the approach. At the same time, the region suffered extreme weather events – severe drought followed by flooding – which brought attention to water management. Water thus became the focal point for enhanced regional cooperation (Swatuk 2002, 2005, 2008). Water governance in turn can lead to improvements in energy, agriculture, and other factors needed for increased trade.

These two cases – power pools and water governance – demonstrate the overlap between resources and regional integration and thus suggest new ways for IPE scholars to think about the relationship between trade and regionalism, and their end goals of improved development in Africa and other parts of the developing world. In addition, RTAs may be playing an additional role in African development. It might be that RTAs are weak in terms of increasing levels of intra-group trade, but they are helping create regions for other development-related purposes, such as through the power pools, which are needed not only for trade but for state development. The RTAs should be judged not just by their stated economic agenda, but also by the ways in which they are reinvigorating themselves through new, previously unplanned missions, such as serving as the building blocks for the electricity grids and for other development purposes, such as the ECOWAS program for increasing renewable energy (ECOWAS Center for Renewable Energy and Energy Efficiency 2013). The AU's current commission chair, Nokosazana Dlamini-Zuma, recently espoused the importance of regional infrastructure:

> For her, the founding vision of a borderless Africa with a single market, freedom of movement for labour and capital must underpin the continent's development strategy. The struggle has now moved on, she says, to organizing the ports, the continental highways and power plants that will change people's lives but require unprecedented cooperation. (Jobson and Kantai 2013)

These extensions of the original mission may well become critical in the ultimate goal of further developing Africa and reducing poverty.

CONCLUSION

While Africa has numerous formal economic regional agreements, including the oldest customs union in the world, these accords are not achieving their primary goals of greater economic development and lower poverty rates in Africa. A variety of political and economic factors are significant barriers to African states trading more within their sub-regions and to increasing overall trade levels. The EU's trade negotiations with Africa, forced by WTO rules, are further undermining Africa's regional trade accords. This lack of progress suggests that these formal accords may not be the right means to the end. In addition, rapidly rising Chinese investment into Africa may further undermine regional trade, as China does not show any interest in promoting regional agreements. I argue that a promising area for future research and funding for African development and poverty reduction is *resource regionalism*, in which natural resources used for energy and other purposes create and maintain regions. With the support of the US, the EU, the UN, the World Bank, the African Development Bank and others, Africa has already created regional electricity grids, linking states together for more efficient energy markets, and developed water governance instruments. These types of development efforts are more likely to yield the growth that Africa is seeking, and may in the end improve the performance of the formal regional trade accords that have currently failed to produce results.

NOTES

1. Earlier versions of this chapter were presented at the conference on "Europe from the Outside In," Berlin, December 15–17, 2011 and at the International Studies Association annual convention, San Francisco, CA, April 3–6, 2013. Grants from the Colorado European Union Center for Excellence and the Colorado School of Mines supported two field research trips in 2011 and 2013 to South Africa and Botswana.
2. I include the European Community only once, rather than adding it for each enlargement.
3. Interviews with members of European Union Directorate-General for Development and Relations with African, Caribbean and Pacific States, December 14, 2010, Brussels.
4. Author interviews with government officials and analysts in Brussels, Pretoria, and Gaborone (Botswana), in December 2010 and in February and August 2011, confirm that at least some SACU members see the EPA process as a threat to the SACU agreement, and even to SADC, given the way in which the states have configured themselves for negotiations. Those interviewed spoke on condition of anonymity.
5. Interviews with members of the Botswana Power Corporation, August 2013.

REFERENCES

Africa and Europe in Partnership (2010), *The Revised Cotonou Agreement and Its Implications*, available from: http://www.africa-eu-partnership.org/partnerships/revised-cotonou-agreement-and-its-implications (accessed June 20, 2013).
Afrika, Jean-Guy K. and Gerald Ajumbo (2012), *Informal Cross Border Trade in Africa: Implications and Policy Recommendation*, Abidjan: African Development Bank.
Antkiewicz, Agata and John Whalley (2005), "China's New Regional Trade Agreements," *World Economy*, **28** (10), 1539–57.
Bach, Daniel C. (2003), "New Regionalism as an Alias: Regionalization through Trans-State Networks," in J. Andrew Grant and Fredrik Söderbaum (eds.), *The New Regionalism in Africa*, Aldershot, UK: Ashgate.
Balassa, Bela A. (1961), *The Theory of Economic Integration*, Homewood, IL: R.D. Irwin.
Berg, Andrew and Anne O. Krueger (2003), *Trade, Growth, and Poverty: A Selective Survey*, IMF Working Paper No. 03/30, Washington, DC: IMF, pp. 1–51.
Bicchi, Federica (2006), "'Our Size Fits All': Normative Power Europe and the Mediterranean," *Journal of European Public Policy*, **13** (2), 286–303.
Bilal, Sanoussi (2012), "The New EU Trade, Growth and Development Agenda: A Step Too Short," in Dirk Willem te Velde (ed.), *The Next Decade of EU Trade Policy: Confronting Global Challenges?*, London: Overseas Development Institute, pp. 19–20.
Bilal, Sanoussi and Christopher Stevens (2009), *The Interim Economic Partnership Agreements between the EU and African States: Contents, Challenges, and Prospects*, ECDPM Policy Management Report 17, Maastricht: European Centre for Development Policy Management.
Bischoff, Paul-Henri (2012), "What's Been Built in Twenty Years? SADC and Southern Africa's Political and Regional Security Culture," *Strategic Review for Southern Africa*, **34** (2), 63–91.

Bøås, Morten and Karin Dokken (2002), *Internasjonal Politikk og Utenrikspolitikk i Afrika sør for Sahara*, Oslo: Universitetsforlaget.

Börzel, Tanja A. and Thomas Risse (2009), *Diffusing (Inter-)Regionalism: The EU as a Model of Regional Integration*, Working Paper Series No. 7, September, Berlin: Kolleg-Forschergruppe (KFG).

Bowen, Brian H., F.T. Sparrow and Zuwei Yu (1999), "Modeling Electricity Trade Policy for the Twelve Nations of the Southern African Power Pool (SAPP)," *Utilities Policy*, **8**, 183–97.

Bradford, Colin, Jr. and Naomi Chakwin (1993), *Alternative Explanations of the Trade–Output Correlation in East Asian Economies*, OECD Development Centre Technical Paper, Paris: OECD Development Centre.

Chandy, Laurence, Natasha Ledlie and Veronika Penciakova (2013), *The Final Countdown: Prospects for Ending Extreme Poverty by 2030*, Washington, DC: Brookings Institution.

Chipman, John S. (1965), "A Survey of the Theory of International Trade: Part 1, The Classical Theory," *Econometrica*, **33** (3), 477–519.

Christ, Nannette and Michael J. Ferrantino (2011), "Land Transport for Export: The Effects of Cost, Time, and Uncertainty in Sub-Saharan Africa," *World Development*, **39** (10), 1749–59.

Clemens, Michael A. and Jeffrey G. Williamson (2004), "Why Did the Tariff–Growth Correlation Change after 1950?," *Journal of Economic Growth*, **9** (1), 5–46.

Deardorff, Alan V. and Robert M. Stern (2009), "Alternatives to the Doha Round," *Journal of Policy Modeling*, **31** (4), 526–39.

Dollar, David and Aart Kraay (2002), "Growth Is Good for the Poor," *Journal of Economic Growth*, **7**, 195–225.

Draper, Peter (2012), "Breaking Free from Europe: Why Africa Needs Another Model of Regional Integration," *International Spectator*, **47** (1), 67–82.

Duina, Francesco (2006), *The Social Construction of Free Trade: The European Union, NAFTA, and Mercosur*, Princeton, NJ: Princeton University Press.

Eberhard, Anton and C. Van Horen (1995), *Poverty and Power: Energy and the South African State*, East Haven, CT: UCT Press and London: Pluto Press.

Economic Commission for Africa (2010), *The Development of Trade Transit Corridors in Africa's Landlocked Countries*, African Trade Policy Centre Briefing No. 10, Addis Ababa: UN Economic Commission for Africa.

Economic Commission for Africa, African Union and African Development Bank (2010), *Assessing Regional Integration in Africa, IV: Enhancing Intra-African Trade*, Addis Ababa: UN Economic Commission for Africa.

Economic Commission for Africa, African Union and African Development Bank (2012), *Assessing Regional Integration in Africa, V: Towards an African Continental Free Trade Area*, Addis Ababa: UN Economic Commission for Africa.

ECOWAS Center for Renewable Energy and Energy Efficiency (2013), available from: http://www.ecreee.org (accessed April 21, 2014).

Erixon, Fredrik (2012), "The EC Communication on Trade, Growth, and Development: Comment," in Dirk Willem te Velde (ed.), *The Next Decade of EU Trade Policy: Confronting Global Challenges?*, London: Overseas Development Institute, pp. 15–16.

European Commission (2006), *A New Approach in the Relations between European Union and Eastern and Southern Africa Countries*, Luxembourg: European Publications Office.

European Commission (2011), *Economic Partnership Agreements (EPAs): African, Caribbean, and Pacific Voices Speak Up for Trade and Development*, Luxembourg: European Publications Office.

European Commission (2013a), *EU meets Eastern and Southern African Partners to Discuss EPA Implementation*, available from: http://trade.ec.europa.eu/doclib/press/index.cfm?id=897 (accessed April 21, 2014).

European Commission (2013b), *The Lomé Convention*, available from: http://ec.europa.eu/europeaid/where/acp/overview/lome-convention/lomeitoiv_en.htm (accessed April 21, 2014).

Frankel, Jeffrey A. and David Romer (1999), "Does Trade Cause Growth?," *American Economic Review*, **89** (3), 379–99.

Gibb, Richard and Karen Treasure (2011), "SACU at Centenary: Theory and Practice of Democratising Regionalism," *South African Journal of International Affairs*, **18** (1), 1–21.

Greenaway, David, Wyn Morgan and Peter Wright (2002), "Trade Liberalisation and Growth in Developing Countries," *Journal of Development Economics*, **67** (1), February, 229–44.

Grugel, Jean B. 2004. "New Regionalism and Modes of Governance: Comparing US and EU Strategies in Latin America," *European Journal of International Relations*, **10** (4), 603–26.

Guvele, Cesar and Sue Lautze (2000), *Unofficial Cross-Border Exports from Southern Sudan to Kenya*, Medford, MA: Feinstein International Famine Center, Tufts University.

Haggard, Stephan (1997), "Regionalism in Asia and the Americas," in Edward D. Mansfield and Helen V. Milner (eds.), *The Political Economy of Regionalism*, New York: Columbia University Press, pp. 20–49.

Hancock, Kathleen J. (2009), *Regional Integration: Choosing Plutocracy*, New York: Palgrave.

Hancock, Kathleen J. (2011), "Regional Integration in a Global Context: Implications for Sub-Saharan Africa," *Connections: Paper Series on Transatlantic Trade and Development Policy Issues*, **5**, July 26.

Hancock, Kathleen J. (2013), "Comparative Regionalism and Natural Resources: A Focus on Africa," paper prepared for the International Studies Association annual convention, San Francisco, CA.

Helpman, Elhanan (1988), *Growth, Technological Progress, and Trade*, Cambridge, MA: National Bureau of Economic Research.

International Rivers (2013), available from: http://www.internationalrivers.org (accessed April 21, 2014).

Jobson, Elissa and Parselelo Kantai (2013), "Pan-Africanism is More Important than Ever – Dlamini-Zuma," *Africa Report*, May 20.

Kapika, Joseph and Anton Eberhard (2013), *Power-Sector Reform and Regulation in Africa: Lessons from Kenya, Tanzania, Uganda, Zambia, Namibia and Ghana*, Cape Town: Human Sciences Research Council.

Kraay, Aart (2004), *When Is Growth Pro-Poor? Evidence from a Panel of Countries*, World Bank Policy Research Paper No. 3225, Washington, DC: World Bank.

Lawrence, Mark and Hadija Mohiddin (2004), *Djibouti Livelihood Profiles*, Nairobi: Famine Early Warning System Network (FEWSNET) and United States Agency for International Development (USAID).

Leith, J. Clark and John Whalley (2004), "Competitive Liberalization and the US–SACU FTA," in Jeffrey J. Schott (ed.), *Free Trade Agreements: US. Strategies and Priorities*, Washington, DC: Institute of International Economics, pp. 331–58.

Lewis, W.P. (1994), "Issues and Options for Interconnection in Southern Africa," *Journal of Energy in Southern Africa*, **5** (3), 61–6.

Libiszewski, Stephan (1999), "International Conflicts over Freshwater Resources," in Mohamed Suliman (ed.), *Ecology, Politics, and Violent Conflict*, New York: Zed Books, pp. 115–38.

Mattli, Walter (1999), *The Logic of Regional Integration: Europe and Beyond*, Cambridge: Cambridge University Press.

Matusz, Steven J. and David Tarr (1999), *Adjusting to Trade Policy Reform*, Policy Research Working Paper No. 2142, Washington, DC: World Bank.

Mbekeani, Kennedy K. (2010), "Infrastructure, Trade Expansion and Regional Integration: Global Experience and Lessons for Africa," *Journal of African Economies*, **19** (Supp. 1), i88–i113.

McCarthy, Colin (2003), "The Southern African Customs Union in Transition," *African Affairs*, **102**, 605–30.

Muchomba, Evelyn and Buzz Sharp (2006), *Southern Sudan Livelihood Profiles: A Guide for Humanitarian and Development Planning*, Nairobi: Southern Sudan Centre Census, Statistics and Evaluation (SSCCSE) and Save the Children UK.

Nkrumah, Kwame (2013), "The People of Africa Are Crying for Unity," *New African*, available from: http://www.newafricanmagazine.com/special-reports/other-reports/10-years-of-the-au/kwame-nkrumah-the-people-of-africa-are-crying-for-unity (accessed June 20, 2013).

Portugal-Perez, Alberto and John S. Wilson (2008), *Why Trade Facilitation Matters to Africa?*, World Bank Policy Research Working Paper No. 4719, Washington, DC: World Bank.

Qureshi, Mahvash Saeed and Charalambos G. Tsangarides (2011), *Exchange Rate Regimes and Trade: Is Africa Different?*, Working Paper Series, Helsinki: World Institute for Development Economic Research (UNU-WIDER).

Raballand, Gael and Patricia Macchi (2008), "Transport Prices and Costs: The Need to Revisit Donors' Policies in Transport in Africa," paper read at the Fourteenth BREAD Conference on Development Economics, Chicago, IL.

Reiter, Joakim (2003), "The EU–Mexico Free Trade Agreement: Assessing the EU Approach to Regulatory Issues," in Gary P. Sampson and Stephen Woolcock (eds.), *Regionalism, Multilateralism and Economic Integration: The Recent Experience*, Tokyo: United Nations University Press, pp. 62–99.

Robinson, P.B. (1993), "Energy," in *Economic Integration in Southern Africa*, Abidjan: African Development Bank.

Rodríguez, Francisco and Dani Rodrik (1999), *Trade Policy and Economic Growth: A Skeptic's Guide to the Cross-National Evidence*, NBER Working Paper No. 7081, Cambridge, MA: National Bureau of Economic Research.

Rodrik, Dani (1995), "Getting Interventions Right: How South Korea and Taiwan Grew Rich," *Economic Policy*, **20**, 53–97.

Rubbers, P.J.E. (1994), "Advantages of Interconnections and the Creation of a Power Pool in Southern Africa," *Journal of Energy in Southern Africa*, **5** (3), 67–72.

Sachs, Jeffrey D. and Andrew Warner (1995), "Economic Reform and the Process of Global Integration," *Brookings Papers on Economic Activity*, **26** (1), 1–118.

Salvatore, Dominick (2004), *International Economics*, Hoboken, NJ: John Wiley & Sons.

Sauer, Amanda and Piet Klop (2010), *Over Heating: Financial Risks from Water Constraints on Power Generation in Asia: India, Malaysia, Philippines, Thailand, Vietnam*, London: World Resources Institute.

Schott, Jeffrey J. (2004), "Assessing US FTA Policy," in Jeffrey J. Schott (ed.), *Free Trade Agreements: US. Strategies and Priorities*, Washington, DC: Institute of International Economics, pp. 359–81.

Sebitosi, Adoniya Benaya and Richard Okou (2010), "Re-Thinking the Power Transmission Model for Sub-Saharan Africa," *Energy Policy*, **38**, 1448–54.

Second Revision of the Cotonou Agreement, Agreed Consolidated Text (2010), available from: http://ec.europa.eu/development/icenter/repository/second_revision_cotonou_agreement_20100311.pdf (accessed April 21, 2014).

Singh, Tarlok (2010), "Does International Trade Cause Economic Growth? A Survey," *World Development*, **33** (11), 1517–64.

Söderbaum, Fredrik (2004), *The Political Economy of Regionalism: The Case of Southern Africa*, Basingstoke: Palgrave Macmillan.

Söderbaum, Fredrik and Ian Taylor (2008), "Considering Micro-Regionalism in Africa in the Twenty-First Century," in Fredrik Söderbaum and Ian Taylor (eds.), *Afro-Regions: The Dynamics of Cross-Border Micro-Regionalism in Africa*, Uppsala, Sweden: Nordiska Afrikainstitutet, pp. 13–31.

Swatuk, Larry A. (2002), "The New Water Architecture in Southern Africa: Reflections on Current Trends in Light of Rio+10," *International Affairs*, **78**, 507–30.

Swatuk, Larry A. (2005) "Political Challenges to Implementing IWRM in Southern Africa," *Physics and Chemistry of the Earth*, **30**, 11–16.

Swatuk, Larry A. (2008), "A Political Economy of Water in Southern Africa," *Water Alternatives*, **1** (1), 24–47.

Taylor, Ian (2011), "South African 'Imperialism' in a Region Lacking Regionalism: A Critique," *Third World Quarterly*, **32** (7), 1233–53.

Teka, Tegegne and Alemayehu Azeze (2002), *Cross-Border Trade and Food Security in the Ethiopia–Djibouti and Ethiopia–Somalia Borderlands*, OSSREA Development Research Report Series 4, Addis Ababa: Organization for Social Science Research in Eastern and Southern Africa.

Thomas, Vinod, John Nash and Associates (1991), *Best Practices in Trade Policy Reform*, Oxford: Oxford University Press.

Transparency International (2013), available from: http://www.transparency.org/country #COD (accessed March 17, 2013).

Uganda Bureau of Statistics and Bank of Uganda (2012), *The Informal Cross Border Trade Survey Report, 2011*, Kampala: Uganda Bureau of Statistics and Bank of Uganda.

Umar, Abdi and Bob Baluch (2007), *Risk Taking for a Living: Trade and Marketing in the Somali Region*, Addis Ababa: UN-OCHA and Pastoral Communications Initiative Project.

United Nations (2013), *Water for Life Decade, Integrated Water Resources Management*, available from: http://www.un.org/waterforlifedecade/iwrm.shtml (accessed March 15, 2013).

Vamvakidis, Athanasios (2002), "How Robust Is the Growth–Openness Connection? Historical Evidence," *Journal of Economic Growth*, **7** (1), 57–80.

Viner, Jacob (1950), *The Customs Union Issue*, New York: Carnegie Endowment for International Peace.

Weber, Max ([1922] 1978), *Economy and Society: An Outline of Interpretive Sociology*, (eds.) Guenther Roth and Claus Wittich, Berkeley: University of California Press.

Weintraub, Sidney (2004), "Lessons from Chile and Singapore Free Trade Agreements," in Jeffrey J. Schott (ed.), *Free Trade Agreements: US. Strategies and Priorities*, Washington, DC: Institute of International Economics, pp. 79–94.

Wild, Franz (2013), "South Africa Secures Energy Promise from Congo's Inga Dam," *Bloomberg*, March 8, available from: http://www.bloomberg.com/news/2013-03-08/south-africa-secures-energy-promise-from-congo-s-inga-dam.html (accessed April 21, 2014).

World Bank (2013a), *Doing Business: Smarter Regulations for Small and Medium-Size Enterprises*, Washington, DC: World Bank.

World Bank (2013b), *GDP Ranking*, available from: http://data.worldbank.org/data-catalog/ GDP-ranking-table (accessed April 21, 2014).

World Bank (2013c), *Poverty*, available from: http://data.worldbank.org/topic/poverty (accessed June 20, 2013).

World Bank (2013d), *Regional Integration in Africa*, available from: http://go.worldbank. org/89J65V2HB0 (accessed April 21, 2014).

World Bank (2013e), *WDI Online: World Development Indicators*, available from: http:// devdata.worldbank.org/dataonline/ (accessed June 20, 2013).

World Energy Council (2013), *World Energy Issues Monitor*, London: World Energy Council.

World Trade Organization (2013a), *The Doha Round*, available from: http://www.wto.org/ english/tratop_e/dda_e/dda_e.htm (accessed April 21, 2014).

World Trade Organization (2013b), *Regional Trade Agreements Information System*, available from: http://rtais.wto.org/ui/PublicMaintainRTAHome.aspx (accessed June 20, 2013).

13. Multilateral institutions and African economic integration*[1]

Bernard Hoekman

INTRODUCTION

The average level of import protection around the world has dropped to the 5–10 percent range (Kee et al. 2009). In conjunction with technological changes that greatly reduced trade costs – telecommunications, the Internet, containerization and other improvements in logistics – the result was a sustained boom in world trade. The value of global trade in goods and services passed the US$20 trillion mark in 2011 (WTO 2012) or 59 percent of global GDP, up from 39 percent of GDP in 1990.[2] This increase in internationalization was due in no small part to ever greater "vertical specialization," with firms and plants in different countries specializing in different parts of the value chain for a product. The share of manufactures in total exports of developing countries increased from just 30 percent in 1980 to over 70 percent today, with a substantial proportion of this consisting of intra-industry trade – the exchange of similar, differentiated products. Since the 1990s intra-industry trade ratios for high-growth developing and transition economies have risen to 50 percent or higher. Much of this consists of intra-regional trade. For example, about half of all East Asian exports of manufactured goods go to other East Asian economies.

Of course, there is substantial variation across countries and regions. Sub-Saharan African countries in particular remain heavily dependent on natural resources and agricultural products. And, although there has been a sea change in trade policy everywhere, the poorest countries, many of which are in Africa, tend to have the highest barriers. Africa is also one of the least integrated continents in terms of "connectivity," reflecting weaknesses in infrastructure and limited regional integration. There has been progress in the last decade in pursuit of regional economic integration among subsets of African states, but to date the continent as a whole and the various sub-regions have not seen the shift towards intra-industry trade, vertical specialization and participation in international supply chains that has been a driver of growth in other parts of the world. This is particularly unfortunate because global value chains offer an opportunity for firms in Africa to engage in international production in a way that was much less feasible 20–30 years ago. Integration into a supply chain allows a firm to specialize in a narrow activity and add value to a product that can be sold anywhere in the world. But preconditions for this are that trade barriers are low, because being part of a supply chain means many of the inputs that are needed must be imported from foreign firms that are "upstream" in the chain, and that trade costs are low enough to make production profitable.

Many different institutions and groups play a role in supporting the economic integration of African economies, including states, business, intergovernmental organizations and NGOs. In this chapter I discuss what two types of international organizations (IOs) can do in this regard, and whether there are opportunities to do better. I will limit my focus to trade (the WTO) and multilateral development organizations (primarily the World Bank) and the relationship between these two types of IOs – an issue that is sometimes discussed under the heading of "coherence." Although the focus is mainly on the WTO and the World Bank, much of the discussion applies as well to other international trade institutions such as regional trade agreements and to other providers of development assistance.

It is important to note at the outset that the discussion will not do justice to what development organizations do, as they are active on many fronts that are directly or indirectly relevant to economic integration. Much of their activity aims at bolstering productivity performance, for example by strengthening the investment climate, increasing human capital and improving public health. All of these impact on economic opportunities and outcomes. A country's trade-related policies are determined by governments. Trade IOs can be used by governments to establish rules of the game for policies, and development IOs can advise on the design of institutional frameworks to support an open trade regime and provide financial and technical support to improve trade-related infrastructure, both hard (roads, ports, etc.) and soft (policies, standards upgrading, export promotion services, border management procedures, etc.). The extent to which IOs do this depends in part on whether trade competitiveness and economic integration are priorities for a government. The effectiveness of the support provided also depends importantly on governments, as this will be determined in part by the ability to coordinate across ministries and regulatory bodies as well as providers of technical and financial assistance. At the end of the day much of the burden of greater coherence rests on governments both individually and collectively, as all IOs are governed by their members.

What follows very briefly summarizes some of the main reasons identified in the literature as to why Africa has seen less diversification and specialization in processing activities and "intermediate" parts of international value chains for goods. This is followed by a discussion of the role IOs can play and have played in addressing these various factors, in particular the global trade organization, the GATT/WTO and the multilateral development organizations. The chapter goes on to assess what might be done to bolster the effectiveness of IOs in supporting African economic integration, both regionally and into the world economy, and suggests some implications for trade governance at both the national and the global level. The chapter then concludes.

FACTORS AFFECTING AFRICAN ECONOMIC INTEGRATION

African countries are active traders – the ratio of trade to GDP is often above 60 percent. What distinguishes African trade is the dominance of natural resources and agricultural exports and the very limited intraregional trade that takes place (less than 10 percent of the total, as measured by official trade statistics).[3] The prevailing pattern of trade reflects endowments and very high trade costs.[4] Many African countries are rich in natural resources, and most have large pools of relatively unskilled labor. High trade costs are the result of many factors, including trade policy. Tariffs or the rules of origin that apply among countries that have free trade agreements are examples, as are inefficient border management practices and nontariff barriers such as onerous compliance and conformity assessment processes, and restrictive regulations affecting the cross-border movement of trucks, traders, and products such as food.[5]

Transport costs are high for many African nations simply because of geography. Many countries are land-locked and thus far from sea ports located in other countries, making the efficiency of transport corridors and border crossings of paramount importance for firm-level competitiveness. Lowering trade costs is therefore not "simply" a matter of dealing with nontariff measures that apply at borders. Equally important in many countries are internal trade costs associated with frequent controls and stopping of trucks moving along corridors. To a significant extent the trade cost policy agenda also revolves around improving the performance of services sectors: reducing the costs of service inputs for firms and increasing the variety and quality of producer and backbone services such as transport are important determinants of the competitiveness of firms and farmers. Their ability to produce and sell their products on local, national and global markets and the rate of return they will obtain depends on the availability and cost of services (Francois and Hoekman 2010). Wages in much of Africa are among the lowest in the world, making the region potentially attractive for investment in relatively unskilled labor-intensive export production of the type that has tended to be a key feature of the development strategy undertaken by Asian countries, most recently and notably China. As real wages in China continue to increase, African countries become more attractive for manufacturing and processing investment, but the speed and extent to which this will happen will depend in part on reducing trade costs.

Achieving this is a complex, multi-dimensional challenge. Trade liberalization has an important role to play, but much of the agenda revolves around administrative practices and procedures. One example is border management – enhancing the efficiency of enforcing regulatory and fiscal policies (McLinden et al. 2010). Another example is making greater progress in achieving regional integration objectives, which can create larger markets and lower the costs of transit transport – a key factor for land-locked countries in particular (Arvis et al. 2010). The importance of reducing the costs of accessing and transiting neighboring markets and attaining scale and agglomeration economies through convergence of administrative procedures and trade-related regulatory regimes is a major motivation underpinning regional integration efforts in Africa.

While regional cooperation is important, much of the policy agenda involves autonomous, unilateral reforms. The potential benefits associated with a concerted effort to facilitate trade are large. A global dataset compiled by Arvis et al. (2013) suggests that improving logistics performance could reduce average bilateral trade costs ten times more than an equivalent percentage reduction in average tariffs. A report by the World Economic Forum (WEF), Bain and the World Bank (WEF et al. 2013) examines supply chain barriers to international trade and concludes that these are far more significant impediments than tariffs. It suggests that concerted action to reduce supply chain barriers to achieve a level that is equivalent to 50 percent of best practice observed in the world today could increase world GDP over six times more than removing all tariffs. The projected gains for African countries are among the highest, in the range of 10 percent of GDP or more, reflecting the high levels of barriers that prevail (Figure 13.1). This is an area where making progress requires cooperation and coordination across a range of institutions and stakeholders in a country, in part because there are investment costs associated with realizing these gains. This is a good example of the need for greater coherence, including in terms of what trade and development IOs do.

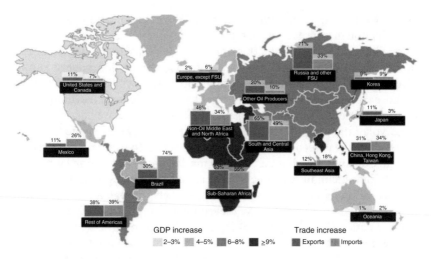

Note: Based on 2007 baseline.

Source: Ferrantino et al., The Benefits of Trade Facilitation – A Modelling Exercise, in WEF et al. (2013).

Figure 13.1   Projected impact of reducing supply chain barriers to 50 percent of best practice

AFRICAN TRADE POLICIES AND THE GATT/WTO

The global trade regime has provided a framework for countries to define trade policy disciplines commitments and a mechanism through which these can be enforced. The scope and coverage of policy disciplines has expanded steadily since the creation of the GATT in 1947, as has membership. Some 30 countries have acceded to the WTO since 1995, including many small developing and transition economies, as well as China and Russia. A noteworthy feature of the accession process is that it entailed much more far-reaching policy commitments and reforms than those African countries made when they became contracting parties to the GATT (Braga and Cattaneo 2009). Although accession takes too long and is too much subject to idiosyncratic demands by existing WTO members, the result of the process is generally that countries undertake numerous reforms, and, perhaps more importantly, for a period of time there is an explicit focus by government on the trade regime and trade policy institutions.

Engagement by African states in the trading system has been characterized by insistence on more favorable and differential treatment. This was associated with an import substitution industrialization strategy and non-participation in multilateral rounds of tariff reduction and trade liberalization. The basic rationale for this approach was that developing countries needed to foster industrial capacity to reduce import dependence and to diversify away from traditional commodities. Diversification was needed because commodities were held to be subject to long-term declining terms of trade reflecting low income elasticity of demand, as well as short-term price volatility, and offered little scope for employment creation. At the same time it was recognized that exports were important as a source of foreign exchange and that the national market might be too small for a protected domestic industry to be able to realize economies of scale. This led to calls for preferential access to export markets through a general system of preferences that would give developing countries better than most favored nation (MFN) treatment in industrialized countries (Hudec 1987).

The end result was limited preferential access to OECD markets, as "sensitive" items tended to be excluded, and significant anti-export bias as a result of high rates of protection that were exempt from trade negotiations. The strategy of "less than full reciprocity" in GATT/WTO trade negotiations helps explain the long-standing tariff peaks and escalation in OECD countries: as these were on items of interest to African and other developing countries the lack of engagement implied no incentive to lower them.

The strategy of not offering trade policy concessions has continued to be pursued in the WTO context. Least developed countries (LDCs), which are mostly located in Africa, were granted "the round for free" in the Doha Development Agenda (DDA) negotiations: it was agreed that they were not required to make any reductions in their tariff bindings. The focus of African countries has been on improving and defending preferential access to major export markets, not just OECD markets but also those of the rapidly growing emerging economies, and expanding or improving provisions for special and differential treatment.[6] Progress was made in the post-2001 period following the launch of the DDA in expanding duty-free, quota-free (DFQF) market access for LDCs. This is a significant achievement, but it also had a downside by pitting developing countries against each other (DFQF extends only to the LDCs and not to other countries that may be very similar in terms of per capita income and other development indicators) and focusing attention on the preference erosion losses that might occur if the DDA were to lead to a substantial reduction in the applied MFN tariffs of preference-granting countries. This dynamic is illustrated most notably in the resistance by the United States to extending DFQF treatment to Asian LDCs (Bangladesh, Cambodia, Laos), which is driven in part by concern that doing so would erode the value of the preferential market access provided under the African Growth and Opportunities Act (AGOA).

Particularly striking has been the limited degree to which attention has been given to subjects that matter greatly for competitiveness and that could therefore help improve trade conditions in African countries. Two areas stand out in this regard, services and trade facilitation. Both are of critical importance, as policy reforms affecting these areas can have a major impact on trade costs confronting firms and farmers.

On the positive side of the ledger, a major achievement was the launch of the "aid for trade" (AFT) initiative and the establishment of the Enhanced Integrated Framework for Trade-Related Technical Assistance. Although not formally tied to the DDA, these initiatives signified recognition by the WTO membership that market access and rules were not enough. The aid for trade initiative is a mechanism to engage development agencies more in the trade integration agenda and helps to raise the profile of trade issues in the process of determining priorities for investment and policy reform at the country level. The major challenge and opportunity looking forward is to do more to link AFT with the negotiation and implementation of specific commitments in policy areas such as services and trade facilitation, as it is there that the potential gains for African countries are the largest.

The WTO can help countries to deal with the "real trade costs" agenda through agreements on frameworks that embody good practices and establish focal points for regular dialogue and monitoring of progress in implementation of good practices. The trade facilitation negotiations in the Doha Round illustrate how the WTO could be used by developing countries to make a difference on the ground for traders and producers. A key feature of the trade facilitation talks was a decision by developing countries to introduce a formal link between implementation of any agreement and the provision of financial and technical assistance. Another feature of the negotiations was to engage the specialized agencies with expertise in the area in the process. Examples include the World Customs Organization, UNCTAD, the IMF and the World Bank. These agencies undertook assessments at country level of the trade facilitation situation, gaps and priorities, and can provide the assistance needed for implementation of reforms. The Doha Round process raised national awareness of the importance of trade facilitation and influenced the development community as well. A plethora of research on the net benefits of facilitating trade induced by the launch of the negotiations identified the high rate of return of investments in this area and the high opportunity cost of not dealing with the issue. As a result, the number of projects and level of resources allocated to this area increased significantly relative to the late 1990s and early 2000s.

Emulating this approach in other areas of trade-related regulation could help make the WTO a more effective mechanism to assist countries reduce trade costs and improve competitiveness. Perhaps the most obvious and important area is services. Hoekman and Mattoo (2013) argue that progress in this area would be enhanced by taking regulatory concerns and constraints seriously. Liberalization of services policies is constrained by the great diversity in regulation and regulatory capacity. Mechanisms that bring together sectoral regulators, trade officials and business to assess current policies and to identify beneficial reforms are needed. Strengthening the relevant implementing institutions will require the engagement of a variety of national, regional and international institutions.

This is an area where greater "coherence" is needed between trade organizations such as the WTO that establish rules of the trade game and the trade and development organizations that have the technical expertise, resources and country presence to support reform processes. Moving in this direction implies a shift away from the long-standing insistence on special and differential treatment (SDT) in the WTO, which is more about exceptions and exemptions as opposed to constructive engagement and mobilization of support to help governments put in place better policy frameworks and achieve national objectives. Traditional SDT has been a weak reed that has generated little in the way of direct benefits and arguably has resulted in significant opportunity costs in terms of benefits forgone (Hoekman 2005). It has meant less market access in areas of export interest (continued tariff escalation and peaks in major export markets during the 1970s and 1980s, for example) and less in the way of benefits from applying WTO trade policy disciplines, including very limited use of WTO dispute settlement procedures and the WTO's transparency mechanisms.[7]

Key elements of the SDT strategy pursued by many developing countries are arguably misconceived because they do little to address the key factors that matter for competitiveness and that could therefore help improve trade performance. Four areas stand out in this regard: tariffs; the cost and quality of service inputs; reducing the trade-impeding effects of nontariff measures (NTMs); and trade facilitation and border management. Policy reforms affecting these areas can have a major positive impact in terms of reducing the trade costs confronting firms and farmers. A large and expanding body of research has documented that the potential benefits for the world as a whole of action in these areas are substantial (Decreux and Fontagné 2011; Laborde et al. 2011; WEF et al. 2013). DFQF access for LDCs and AFT are both important post-2001 achievements, but much depends on how the latter is used to help firms benefit from the former.

Given that average MFN tariffs are declining steadily, the value of

DFQF treatment is inherently limited. It can only partially make up for the high trade costs that confront African enterprises. The key challenge and priority is improving the domestic "trade environment." AFT can help, but how it is allocated and how much it is used are very much a function of what governments want to use it for, and whether they make trade a priority area for investment and reform. AFT allocation and effectiveness are also a function of the "supply side." Demand may exceed supply, and there are invariably important coordination challenges to be overcome within government, as well as across and within development agencies.

INTERNATIONAL FINANCIAL AND DEVELOPMENT ORGANIZATIONS

The international financial institutions (IFIs) played a significant role in supporting trade reforms in developing countries in recent decades. They have a mandate to engage governments on the content of trade policy and to provide advice on, and analysis of, trade policies and trade-related reforms. They also have the ability to identify the need for complementary reforms and investments and engage in policy dialogue on areas critical for competitiveness (e.g., Reis and Farole 2012). Examples include the level of the (real) exchange rate, the exchange rate regime, and the monetary and fiscal policies that affect these variables. The IFIs could complement technical analysis and advice on the design of policies with financial resources to assist countries to implement reforms and improve supply capacity. Between 1987 and 2004, for example, the World Bank allocated some 8 percent of its total loans and credits to programs and projects aimed at trade policy reforms and strengthening trade-related institutions and infrastructure (e.g., product standards, customs) (World Bank 2006). The IMF supported economic adjustment programs in 34 Sub-Saharan African countries between 1993 and 2003. In 31 of these countries, programs were implemented that included trade policy reform conditions (Wei and Zhang 2006). The World Bank and IMF programs were generally informed by extensive analysis and research on trade issues, ranging from the design of reforms to assessments of the impacts and results of different types of trade policies. Several influential multi-country case studies of prevailing trade policy regimes and economic performance played a role in identifying priorities for reform in the mid- to late 1980s (e.g., Bhagwati 1978; Krueger 1978; Choksi et al. 1991; Thomas et al. 1991).

One focus of these programs was to reduce disincentives to engage in export production, boost export performance and improve resource allocation, thereby making economies more robust to changes in the world economy, whether these are technological in nature or short-term exogenous shocks. The objective was to increase incentives for investments in new activities and products so as to diversify the economy and generate new sources of foreign exchange. A key part of many programs was to enable firms to have access to the inputs they needed at world market prices, thereby allowing them to compete on a level playing field with foreign competitors, and confronting firms with competition from imports, thereby ensuring that resources went to sectors in which a country had a comparative advantage. Creating an incentive framework that would generate a more efficient allocation of domestic labor and capital was seen as a precondition for sustaining higher economic growth over time.

Trade reforms supported by the IFIs generally had common features: a removal of quantitative restrictions (QRs) on imports and exports; a reform of the structure of the tariff, generally moving towards a simpler and more transparent system of a limited number of tariff bands; the removal of tariff exemptions of various kinds; reducing net taxation of agriculture; and lowering the average level of the tariff. Frequently the tariff structure that was recommended involved higher tariffs on final products than on inputs – the idea being to afford industries a continued positive rate of effective protection against imports. The experience of many countries that implemented such trade reform packages, including in Africa (e.g., Benin, Côte d'Ivoire, Gambia, Malawi, Zambia), was that tariff revenue declines, a major concern for many low-income countries, were offset by the removal of tariff exemptions, the tariffication of quotas and the mobilization of other tax bases (Baunsgaard and Keen 2010; Keen and Mansour 2010). Over time, as economic activity increased and trade expanded, tariff revenues might even increase as a result of import growth.

Reforms generally went beyond narrow trade policy (tariffs, quotas). In many cases programs included an extensive focus on macroeconomic management driven by the need to move countries towards a more sustainable fiscal situation and control inflation. In many instances trade reforms included a devaluation of the real exchange rate. Depreciation created incentives to switch expenditures away from imports, thus helping to move the balance of payments towards surplus. Devaluation also played an important political economy role in helping to implement and sustain trade liberalization: by making imports more costly, some of the protection that was lost through lower trade barriers was offset. Conversely, devaluation made it easier for export-oriented firms to expand output and generate employment opportunities for workers in import substituting sectors that were negatively affected by liberalization. Complementary measures that were often pursued included the introduction of indirect tax systems (excises, value added taxation) and projects to bolster the supply side of the economy: efforts to restructure firms or industries with a view to improving efficiency, investments in infrastructure and education, and so on.

There have been many assessments of the trade reform programs and the assistance provided by the IFIs through the early 2000s (see for example World Bank, 1992, 2001, 2006; Dean et al. 1994; Sharer 1998; Wei and Zhang 2006). While reform programs did not always have the desired effects and many were not sustained, the reforms increased growth rates by generating additional investment into the tradable sectors.[8] Whatever the relative importance of the different drivers of reform, the result was a significant reduction in anti-export bias, greater neutrality in the incidence of policies across sectors, a reduction in the relative taxation of agriculture compared to other sectors (Anderson 2009), and increases in investment, output and trade. This also occurred in Africa, although to a lesser extent than in other regions. Africa is the only region that still taxes farmers (Anderson and Masters 2009). But similarly to other parts of the world the magnitude of the rate of relative taxation has fallen – and greater trade openness in Africa has led to higher rates of growth (Bruckner and Lederman 2012).

Since the early 2000s World Bank support activities have put more emphasis on the reduction of real trade costs. The World Bank Group is the largest provider of financial assistance for trade integration if one uses the OECD definition of aid for trade.[9] Africa is the largest recipient of World Bank AFT and has seen its share in the Bank's overall support for trade activities rise to over one-third.[10] The increasing emphasis on trade competitiveness and trade facilitation and logistics reflects demand for assistance in these areas from governments and a recognition that improving border management (the administrative procedures associated with the movement of goods across borders) and transport services policies can have a major impact on firm-level competitiveness and helps explain the lack of diversification in many African countries.[11] Without action to reduce transport costs from remote areas, increase connectivity and facilitate the movement of goods, services and people across borders, specialization opportunities cannot be fully exploited, if at all, and the potential gains from trade will not be maximized. Poor roads and ports, poorly performing customs, weaknesses in border management, inadequate regulatory capacity, limited access to finance and poor business services are all areas where development assistance can help to improve matters.

Trade policy was a central element of many IMF programs in the 1980s and 1990s. From 2000 on less attention was given to trade matters in IMF lending, although trade policy is a standard element of IMF surveillance activities. The average number of trade policy conditions in IMF programs fell from over 2 to under 0.5 between 1998 and 2007.

As of the late 2000s the traditional focus on trade liberalization was no longer visible in most country programs – insofar as trade was an element of lending programs, policy conditions mostly pertained to customs (IMF 2009). The decline in focus on trade policy was a reflection of different factors, including lower tariffs in most countries, the limited connection between specific trade policies and macroeconomic performance, learning from the East Asian crisis (where many were of the view that a number of the trade-related conditions that were imposed by the Fund could not be justified as having a macroeconomic rationale) and a sense that with the establishment of the WTO and the increasing prominence of PTAs the need to focus on national trade policies had become weaker. A corollary of the shift away from trade conditionality by the IMF was a drop in the extent of trade policy analysis by Fund staff. In the late 1990s, three-quarters of Fund staff reports included analysis of trade policy matters; as of 2006 the number had fallen to one-quarter (IMF 2005, 2009).[12]

CHALLENGES, GAPS AND OPPORTUNITIES

The foregoing discussion illustrates that the World Bank has been providing substantial assistance to African countries aimed at improving trade competitiveness and that this has been rising in the last decade. The same is true of other development IOs such as the African Development Bank (AfDB) and the United Nations Development Programme (UNDP), and bilateral donors such as the UK's Department for International Development (DFID) and the US Agency for International Development (USAID).

There are a number of areas in which more could be done. One is to provide more effective support for integration of African markets for goods, services and people. This is not to say that this is a subject that is ignored by policymakers and the international agencies. The New Partnership for Africa's Development (NEPAD) is a focal point for regional cooperation and integration. The AfDB supports regional cooperation and integration efforts by lending for multi-country projects and assisting African regional economic communities (RECs). The NEPAD initiative raised the profile of the regional integration agenda in AfDB activities, both policy based (e.g., banking and financial standards) and infrastructure development. The AfDB hosts the Africa Infrastructure Consortium Secretariat, and is tasked with facilitating cooperation on infrastructure development between itself, the AU, NEPAD, RECs and the members of the Consortium. Priority is being given by the AfDB to the promotion and development of regional infrastructure, in partnership with the AU and the UN Economic Commission for Africa.

While the regional lens has been used as a focal point for assistance by the World Bank and other development organizations, the types of projects that have been pursued are mostly country-specific, reflecting the country-centric operating model that characterizes the way the IOs are organized. Lending by the development banks (AfDB and World Bank) for policy reforms that would support regional trade arguably is too limited owing to the difficulties in securing agreement between countries and achieving agreement on guarantees for multi-country loans (Hoekman and Njinkeu 2012). Loans by the IOs can be made only to revenue earning, credit-worthy regional entities, unless repayment obligations are assumed by member governments. Many regional bodies are not revenue earning and are dependent on financial contributions from their member governments, which themselves often face serious fiscal constraints. More fundamentally, regional projects are less likely to find their way into national development plans as a result of coordination problems. A challenge then is to ensure that sufficient attention is given to determining the relative direct importance of regional projects and cooperation for countries, and the potential positive externalities that could be achieved, and finding solutions in cases where country-specific capacity constraints preclude the appropriate level of regional cooperation (supply of a regional public good).

Another, more specific challenge is to devote greater attention in the context of integration efforts to matters such as trade facilitation and expanding trade in services (integrating services markets). These are areas that increasingly are getting more attention from policymakers, creating opportunities to increase the coherence of what the IOs do in both areas and by doing so supporting greater progress on African economic integration (World Bank 2011a). At present full use is not being made of these opportunities. One illustration of this is the limited support that African countries have been giving to the trade facilitation talks in Geneva. Another is the lack of engagement in efforts to agree on liberalization of services trade and investment policies, and for dealing with nontariff measures more generally. By not leveraging the WTO process to make progress in facilitating trade and reducing trade costs, a significant opportunity cost is incurred. Particularly worrisome in this regard are some of the arguments that are offered as to why African countries should resist accepting new disciplines on trade facilitation (Ismail 2012) or avoid taking action to liberalize access to services markets. By not doing so – or, equivalently, by insisting on a mercantilist quid pro quo for agreeing to move forward on trade facilitation that they do not have the market power to achieve – firms and workers in Africa will continue to be confronted with higher trade and operating costs that preclude them from integrating into value chains (Draper and Lawrence 2013).

The greater focus by IOs like the World Bank on economic integration and increasing trade competitiveness in the decade following the launch of the DDA is a reflection of greater demand for assistance by governments in these areas. The increasing demand for – and engagement in – trade facilitation projects suggests a disconnect between the positions that are often taken in Geneva and what governments are doing at home. There is less of a disconnect when it comes to the manner in which use is made of the development IOs, but their support could be made more effective. Arguably IOs can do more to provide more effective assistance for putting in place the institutional mechanisms to launch and sustain the processes that are needed to make major inroads on trade costs. Trade facilitation, dealing with NTMs and integrating services markets are much more complex than traditional trade liberalization (Cadot and Malouche 2012; Hoekman and Mattoo 2013; WEF et al. 2013).

Tariffs can be reduced at the stroke of a pen by the minister of finance; regulatory reform cannot. Bringing the relevant players together, including the business community and the regulatory agencies, is a precondition for establishing a performance baseline and thus a common understanding of the impacts on traders and investors and the opportunity costs that are incurred (Cadot et al. 2012). Establishing trust is paramount if the various parties are to engage fully and openly. Greater coherence requires mechanisms that are used to build agreement on what the priorities are from an integration perspective, and to define what policy disciplines could usefully be embedded in trade agreements, as well as a means to agree with development IOs what support should be provided and who will provide it, and to mobilize business in monitoring implementation and outcomes. A major factor impeding progress in the WTO, as well as in PTAs, both North–South such as the economic partnership agreements with the EU (see Chapter 12 by Hancock) and among African nations, in dealing with NTBs, facilitating trade in goods and liberalizing services-related transactions is that there is often no concrete action plan, performance metrics and indicators, and "ownership" of such an agenda. This requires not just creating institutional mechanisms that allow participation by all the main stakeholders and that have solid governance and accountability features, but sustained engagement and support for the people and entities that are tasked with managing such mechanisms and processes.

What follows takes a "supply chain perspective" to illustrate several types of opportunities that exist for greater coherence and effectiveness. For reasons already noted, supply chains offer significant prospects for African firms to increase their participation in regional and global trade.

As shown in Figure 13.1, reducing supply chain trade barriers will have large positive effects on trade and incomes, because African trade costs are particularly high. Moreover, the redistributive impacts of taking action to lower trade costs are less stark than those associated with reducing import tariffs.[13] A supply chain lens is also helpful in identifying where IOs like the World Bank can be more effective in the provision of trade-related assistance from an economic integration perspective *and* in informing the design of rules of the game that would be beneficial to embed in trade agreements.

A company's ability to participate in supply chains depends greatly on government policy choices such as the extent of restrictions on market access at home and in export markets, and the efficiency of border management and transport and logistics services. Even if tariffs on exported goods are zero, firms that confront high and uncertain border costs, complex and restrictive rules of origin, and inefficient and unpredictable logistics services will not be able to compete with firms in countries that do not confront such costs. A major challenge in making progress to reduce trade costs is to determine what exactly needs to be done. Often it is not enough to fix just one thing or another. In practice a "bundle" of policy-induced constraints may need to be addressed for a supply chain to become feasible, or for firms to invest in the facilities that are needed to make a value chain work.

A report by the World Economic Forum, Bain & Co. and the World Bank (WEF et al. 2013) concludes that a necessary condition for a comprehensive approach to reducing supply chain barriers is for governments to engage with the business community. Firms that are involved in the management of value chains, that provide transport and logistics services or that are engaged in wholesale and retail distribution can all provide information on the factors that affect (reduce) supply chain efficiency. A first challenge is therefore to elicit this information from them. A central component of any such effort is the creation of mechanisms to collect data on factors affecting supply chain operations. These data can then be used to identify "clusters" of policies that jointly generate the major supply chain barriers for industries that are particularly important or that have the greatest potential (based on inputs from business and economic analysis). A second challenge is therefore to design and put in place mechanisms that can be used to identify these priority clusters of policies and agree on a specific implementation action plan to address the different policy-induced constraints that are identified. A third challenge is to ensure that this process includes feedback loops between government and firms to allow everyone to monitor progress, which again will have to include a mechanism through which data can be channeled on whether performance indicators are improving.[14]

This may seem a rather obvious prescription but such approaches are rarely pursued with an explicit focus on what matters from a supply chain perspective. Instead, governments (and thus IOs) tend to focus on specific policy areas such as customs, transport, standards and so on. A supply chain lens would ensure that a cross-cutting approach is taken towards identifying barriers, and that what matters most from an investment or operations viewpoint will be identified. A practical constraint that may impede initiatives along these lines is unwillingness by firms to provide data or to inform the government about some of the constraints that they face (e.g., related to corruption or other abuse of power).[15] This suggests a role for IOs – to be facilitators that help to design and put in place mechanisms that assure firms of confidentiality in the case of sensitive information and that assure governments that the information that is being tabled is accurate.

Another role could be to support mechanisms to identify proposed priority areas for action that will promote the general interest as opposed to benefiting only a few companies. In practice, many of the policies that impede economic integration are regulatory in nature; they are generated by a multiplicity of agencies that impose compliance requirements on firms and traders.[16] Very often there is little if any communication or coordination among such agencies. Making progress in removing or reducing the supply chain barriers that prevail requires coordination across many government agencies as well as engagement with industry. Involving economic agencies such as competition authorities that will take an economy-wide view and focus on the interests of consumers would help ensure that efforts are directed at reforms that will promote the general welfare. Steps in this direction can be made through the creation of a high-level body that has the mandate to bring the relevant regulatory bodies and enforcement agencies together, enhance the understanding of all concerned regarding the effects of the status quo on trade and identify approaches that can reduce negative trade impacts while not impinging on the achievement of regulatory objectives.

Such approaches can also be pursued with a view to furthering regional integration and more generally the negotiation of trade agreements. A "whole of the supply chain" approach will help ensure that in negotiating the removal of barriers a comprehensive approach is pursued as opposed to one that centers primarily on specific policy instruments. International trade agreements tend to take a silo approach, addressing policy areas in isolation. Lowering supply chain barriers requires a more flexible and cross-cutting approach that spans all policy measures that impact on trade logistics, including those affecting services such as transport and distribution, as well as those related to border protection and management, product health and safety, foreign investment, and the movement of business people and service providers. In this regard there is great scope for greater coherence between what is needed from an economic integration perspective and the approach that is taken in trade agreements.

Another approach that can enhance coherence and thus the effectiveness of assistance is to focus on NTMs and services. International cooperation can do more to help support economic integration through processes that aim to deal with the main constraints that impede progress in reducing the incidence of NTMs and opening services markets to greater competition. The negotiation literature stresses that negotiators need to learn about the preferences and interests of other parties, as well as their own, and this is a process that takes time. Negotiations invariably involve a complex process of interaction between domestic groups that results in an understanding of negotiating objectives and priorities. Learning is critical when it comes to the substance of policy rules – officials and stakeholders need to understand what the implications are of a given proposed rule and how it will impact on the economy. Hoekman and Mattoo (2013) argue that establishment of "knowledge platforms" – fora aimed at fostering a substantive, evidence- and analysis-based discussion of the impacts of sector-specific regulatory policies and NTMs – could help build a common understanding of where there are large potential gains from opening markets to greater competition, the preconditions for realizing such gains, and options to address possible negative distributional consequences of policy reforms. Generating information on the impact and experience with reform programs that were pursued in other countries could help governments both assess prevailing policies and institutions in their own nations and identify policy reform options.

Such fora could fulfill a number of roles:

1. They could be a mechanism through which information is generated on prevailing regulatory measures and their effects on prices and trade flows.
2. They could enhance knowledge of experiences and impacts in other countries, in the process identifying alternative options or good practices through collection and sharing of information. Such learning could help ensure that regulations and standards that are adopted reflect local conditions and capacities for effective implementation.
3. By bringing together representatives of a range of countries, including officials, regulators, and services suppliers, governments could discuss and learn about alternative approaches that have been pursued in practice to address the political economy constraints that may impede pro-competitive regulatory reform.

4. They could identify the need for external financial and technical assist-
    ance and thus help governments allocate aid for trade more effectively.

Any mechanism to identify good practices in regulation must be
broad-based and tap into knowledge across the globe for a specific sector
or issue. International sectoral organizations such as the International
Telecommunication Union (for information and telecommunications services), the Bank for International Settlements, the International Accounting
Standards Board and the Berne Union (for financial sector-related standards and regulation), the International Organization for Migration (for
migration and cross-border movement of people), and networks of sectoral
regulators and related institutions (such as the International Competition
Network) could be the focal points for specific activities. The same applies
to entities such as the Asia Pacific Economic Forum, the OECD, UN agencies and business associations. In practice knowledge platforms may best
be designed on a regional basis, linked to PTAs and regional institutions
(such as regional development banks). A few initiatives along these lines
have been launched in recent years, including one on professional services
in the context of the Common Market for Eastern and Southern Africa
(COMESA) (Dihel 2012).

CONCLUSION

Much progress arguably has been made in the last decade to increase the
degree of coherence in what development IOs do to respond to the priorities areas in which governments seek support. Progress has also been
made to make the global trading system a more effective instrument to
support economic integration, including the move by the EU through its
Everything But Arms DFQF initiative for LDCs, similar initiatives by a
number of other OECD countries, and the Aid for Trade initiative. But a
good case can be made that there is still much that can be done to improve
coherence of policies and impact of the support that is provided by IOs.
As far as participation in the WTO is concerned, the continued insistence
on traditional forms of special and differential treatment is arguably an
opportunity lost. The trade facilitation, services and NTM agendas that
are on the table in the WTO are all policy areas that are of great importance from a development perspective. Economic integration can be an
effective instrument to improve development outcomes. A new approach
that revolves around a positive agenda could have a much greater impact
in supporting economic integration. Pursuing such an agenda would help
to improve coherence by creating focal points in the WTO that can be used

by governments to pursue desirable reforms, and by development IOs not just to support implementation of what are agreed to be good practices but to help put in place complementary measures to increase the benefits of implementation of trade commitments.

Agreement on binding (enforceable) disciplines is an important role of the WTO and PTAs. But trade cooperation can and should go beyond the negotiation of binding rules of the game. Mechanisms of the type discussed in this chapter can be pursued not just at the national or regional level but at the global (WTO) level. Reducing the trade-impeding effects of regulation requires consultative processes and dialogue through which agents can increase their understanding of the issues and the options that may exist to reduce trade costs without doing harm to the objectives that underlie regulation. There is no reason why existing WTO committees and groups cannot do more to have such exchanges and to promote greater learning about country experiences, not just involving government officials but drawing on data and information provided by businesses and other IOs.

More fundamentally, there is arguably a need to go beyond business as usual in the approaches that are taken by governments to facilitate trade. Shifting from pursuit of cooperation on a policy instrument basis (tariffs, licensing, customs valuation, services, IPRs, etc.) to a supply chain-informed approach could do much to make trade agreements and trade assistance more relevant to business, resulting in greater trade expansion by creating greater incentives for investment and job creation. This will be difficult to do given that it implies much more coordination across government and regulatory agencies and structured engagement with the business community. It will also be challenging for development organizations, as the same challenge arises there: to cut through the many silos that have been created to provide support to specific "sectors," for example transport, or to deal with specific policy areas, for example customs reform. A supply chain focus would imply that all of the main bottlenecks, chokepoints and sources of uncertainty and variability would be on the table, not just those aspects that a government agency happens to request assistance on. It would also help improve coherence by encouraging greater cooperation and coordination across IOs and other development organizations by identifying a cluster of areas where action is needed.

NOTES

*   This chapter was written before the trade facilitation package was negotiated in Bali at the end of 2013.

1. An earlier draft of this chapter was presented at the conference "Trade Governance: Integrating Africa into the World Economy through International Economic Law," Mandela Institute, Witwatersrand University, Johannesburg, March 7–8, 2013. I am grateful to Dominique Njinkeu for helpful comments.
2. Trade openness ratios were calculated from the World DataBank (Global Economic Prospects).
3. See Chapter 12 by Hancock and World Bank (2012). Informal trade within Africa is significant, so the actual figure is higher. However, this mostly comprises low-value items and trade in foodstuffs. While important from a welfare perspective – this type of trade generates revenue for the small traders involved (who are often women) – it does not consist of the type of specialization that has supported growth in other parts of the world.
4. Policies in the rest of the world also affect Africa's export structure and trade volumes. Tariff peaks and tariff escalation in major export markets have had a negative effect on incentives to do more processing in Africa. The extensive support given to agricultural production in many OECD countries, combined with limited preferential market access programs for African producers of certain commodities, for example sugar, created incentives against diversification and upgrading and supported status quo bias because of the rents involved.
5. There is a large literature focusing on the factors affecting African trade perform-ance and measuring the relative performance and the incentive structure confronting firms and farmers in Africa. See the annual World Bank reports *Doing Business* and *Global Monitoring Report*; Anderson and Masters (2009) on agricultural trade policies; Borchert et al. (2012) on services trade policies; and Arvis et al. (2012) for measures of logistics performance.
6. See Apecu (2011) for a very comprehensive, in-depth analysis of the engagement by African countries on the various subject areas covered by the WTO and the DDA.
7. There is of course an active debate on whether WTO rules restrict the ability of gov-ernments to pursue development objectives. In my view arguments that the WTO has "kicked away the ladder" are largely incorrect – governments continue to have a very substantial degree of "policy space" to pursue measures that aim at offsetting market failures and creating an enabling business environment. Insofar as there are specific WTO disciplines that are deemed to be too constraining, there are numerous channels to relax these, ranging from requests for waivers to the (re-)negotiation process – as was done in the case of TRIPS and access to medicines and action by developing countries to safeguard the ability to use export subsidies (see Hoekman and Kostecki 2009).
8. See for example Wacziarg and Welch (2008) for a careful analysis of performance of a large number of countries before and after trade reform. See also Greenaway et al. (2002). Krueger (2003) discusses the importance of the interplay between politics and the nature of governments across countries and the effectiveness of economic policies and policy reform.
9. The OECD/WTO definition of AFT includes trade policy and regulation, economic infrastructure (ports, roads, airports, telecommunications and energy), capacity build-ing, and trade-related budget support. Because it is impossible to distinguish which part of an infrastructure project is for a nontradable sector, the OECD considers all loans for infrastructure as AFT.
10. See World Bank (2011b).
11. According to the World Bank's annual *Doing Business* report, on average it takes three times as many days, nearly twice as many documents and six times as many signatures to trade in many African countries than in high-income economies (see for example Djankov et al. 2010; Freund and Rocha 2010; and Hoekman and Nicita 2011).
12. The IMF participates in the Enhanced Integrated Framework for Trade-Related Technical Assistance to LDCs, which among other things aims to help ensure that LDCs include relevant trade-related priorities in their Poverty Reduction and Strategy Papers (PRSPs). In principle IMF surveillance can help inform this process, and the

IMF can provide technical assistance in specific areas (such as customs). The IMF created the Trade Integration Mechanism (TIM) in 2004, an instrument to help countries where multilateral trade liberalization might create balance of payments problems. The TIM is not a new facility, however, but aims to make IMF assistance more predictably available. To date, three member countries (Bangladesh, the Dominican Republic and the Republic of Madagascar) have obtained support under the TIM.

13. This is because supply chain barriers often do not generate much in the way of rents, but instead simply raise costs. In contrast, an import tariff, for example, generates revenues for the government and rents for import-competing industries that are paid for by consumers. Liberalization distributes income from producers to consumers, while removal of many supply chain barriers will increase real incomes by lowering the costs of goods.

14. The aim here is not simply to give the private sector – whether local or multinational – what they want and increase their profits. The focus is on what will enhance the general welfare by reducing trade costs that are redundant, thereby benefiting consumers and increasing real incomes.

15. Only one out of some 20 companies that were the source of detailed case studies of the types of supply chain barriers that prevail in their operations on specific trade lanes or in specific countries were willing to be named in the WEF et al. (2013) report.

16. Most NTBs are due to the enforcement of regulatory provisions that are either product-specific or industry- or activity-specific.

REFERENCES

Anderson, K. (ed.) (2009), *Distortions to Agricultural Incentives: A Global Perspective, 1955–2007*, Washington, DC: Palgrave Macmillan and World Bank.

Anderson. K. and W. Masters (eds.) (2009), *Distortions to Agricultural Incentives in Africa*, Washington, DC: World Bank.

Apecu, Joan (2011), "African Participation at the WTO: Legal and Institutional Aspects, 1995–2010," PhD dissertation, Graduate Institute, Geneva.

Arvis, J.F., G. Raballand and J.F. Marteau (2010), *The Cost of Being Landlocked: Logistics Costs and Supply Chain Reliability*, Washington, DC: World Bank.

Arvis, J.F., M. Mustra, L. Ojala, B. Shepherd and D. Saslavsky (2012), *Connecting to Compete 2012: The Logistics Performance Index and Its Indicators*, Washington, DC: World Bank.

Arvis, J.F., Y. Duval, B. Shepherd and C. Utoktham (2013), *Trade Costs in the Developing World: 1995–2010*, World Bank Policy Research Working Paper No. 6309, Washington, DC: World Bank.

Baunsgaard, T. and M. Keen (2010), "Tax revenue and (or?) trade liberalization," *Journal of Public Economics*, **94** (9–10), 563–77.

Bhagwati, J. (1978), *Anatomy and Consequences of Exchange Control Regimes*, Cambridge, MA: National Bureau of Economic Research.

Borchert, I., B. Gootiiz and A. Mattoo (2012), *Policy Barriers to International Trade in Services: Evidence from a New Database*, World Bank Policy Research Working Paper No. 6109, Washington, DC: World Bank.

Braga, C. and O. Cattaneo (2009), *Everything You Always Wanted to Know about WTO Accession (But Were Afraid to Ask)*, World Bank Policy Research Paper No. 5116, Washington, DC: World Bank.

Bruckner, M. and D. Lederman (2012), *Trade Causes Growth in Africa*, World Bank Policy Research Working Paper No. 6007, Washington, DC: World Bank.

Cadot, O. and M. Malouche (eds.) (2012), *Non-Tariff Measures: A Fresh Look at Trade Policy's New Frontier*, London: CEPR and World Bank.

Cadot, O., M. Malouche and S. Sáez (2012), *Streamlining Non-Tariff Measures: A Toolkit for Policy Makers*, Washington, DC: World Bank.

Choksi, A., M. Michaely and G. Papageorgiou (1991), *Liberalizing Foreign Trade*, Oxford: Basil Blackwell.
Dean, J., S. Desai and J. Riedel (1994), *Trade Policy Reform in Developing Countries since 1985: A Review of the Evidence*, World Bank Discussion Paper No. 267, Washington, DC: World Bank.
Decreux, Y. and L. Fontagné (2011), *Economic Impact of Potential Outcome of the DDA*, CEPII Working Paper No. 2011-23, Paris: CEPII.
Dihel, N. (2012), "Knowledge Platforms to Support Trade Integration in Africa: Progress with Services," presentation, December 17.
Djankov, S., C. Freund and C. Pham (2010), "Trading on Time," *Review of Economics and Statistics*, **92** (1), 166–73.
Draper, P. and R. Lawrence (2013), "How Should Sub-Saharan African Countries Think about Global Value Chains?," mimeo.
François, J. and B. Hoekman (2010), "Services Trade and Policy," *Journal of Economic Literature*, **48** (3), 642–92.
Freund, C. and N. Rocha (2010), *What Constrains Africa's Exports?*, World Bank Policy Research Working Paper No. 5184, Washington, DC: World Bank.
Greenaway, D., W. Morgan and P. Wright (2002), "Trade Liberalization and Growth in Developing Countries," *Journal of Development Economics*, **67** (1), 229–44.
Hoekman, B. (2005), "Operationalizing the Concept of Policy Space in the WTO: Beyond Special and Differential Treatment," *Journal of International Economic Law*, **8** (2), 405–24.
Hoekman, B. and M. Kostecki (2009), *The Political Economy of the World Trading System*, 3rd edn., Oxford: Oxford University Press.
Hoekman, B. and A. Mattoo (2013), "Liberalizing Trade in Services: Lessons from Regional and WTO Negotiations," *International Negotiation*, **18**, 131–51.
Hoekman, B. and A. Nicita (2011), "Trade Policy, Trade Costs and Developing Country Trade," *World Development*, **39** (12), 2069–79.
Hoekman, B. and D. Njinkeu (2012), "Aid for Trade and Export Competitiveness: New Opportunities for Africa," in D.O. Ajakaiye and T.A. Oyejide (eds.), *Trade Infrastructure and Economic Development*, Studies in Development Economics, London: Routledge.
Hudec, R. (1987), *Developing Countries in the GATT Legal System*, London: Trade Policy Research Centre.
IMF (International Monetary Fund) (2005), "Review of Fund Work on Trade," Policy Development Review Department, mimeo.
IMF (International Monetary Fund) (2009), *IMF Involvement in International Trade Policy Issues*, Independent Evaluation Office report, Washington, DC: IMF.
Ismail, F. (2012), "Towards an Alternative Narrative for the Multilateral Trading System," *SouthViews* (South Centre), **40** (7), November.
Kee, H.L., A. Nicita and M. Olarreaga (2009), "Estimating Trade Restrictiveness Indices," *Economic Journal*, **119** (534), 172–99.
Keen, M. and M. Mansour (2010), "Revenue Mobilisation in Sub-Saharan Africa: Challenges from Globalisation I – Trade Reform," *Development Policy Review*, **28** (5), 553–71.
Krueger, A. (1978), *Liberalization Attempts and Consequences*, Cambridge, MA: National Bureau of Economic Research.
Krueger, A. (2003), *Political Economy of Policy Reform in Developing Countries*, Cambridge, MA: MIT Press.
Laborde, D., W. Martin and D. van der Mensbrugghe (2011), *Measuring the Impacts of Global Trade Reform with Optimal Aggregators of Distortions*, World Bank Policy Research Working Paper No. 5665, Washington, DC: World Bank.
McLinden, G., E. Fanta, D. Widdowson and T. Doyle (eds.) (2010), *Border Management Modernization*, Washington, DC: World Bank.
Reis, J.G. and T. Farole (2012), *Trade Competitiveness Diagnostic Toolkit*, Washington, DC: World Bank.
Sharer, R. 1998. *Trade Liberalization in IMF-Supported Programs*, Washington, DC: IMF.

Thomas, V., J. Nash and Associates (1991), *Best Practices in Trade Policy Reform*, Oxford: Oxford University Press.

Wacziarg, R. and K. Welch (2008), "Trade Liberalization and Growth: New Evidence," *World Bank Economic Review*, **22** (2), 187–231.

Wei, Shang-Jin and Zhiwei Zhang (2006), *Do External Interventions Work? The Case of Trade Reform Conditions in IMF-Supported Programs*, NBER Working Paper No. 12667, Cambridge, MA: National Bureau of Economic Research.

World Bank (1992), *Trade Policy Reforms under Adjustment Programs*, Washington, DC: World Bank.

World Bank (2001), *Adjustment Lending Retrospective: Final Report*, Washington, DC: World Bank.

World Bank (2006), *Assessing World Bank Support for Trade, 1987–2004*, Washington, DC: World Bank.

World Bank (2011a), *Leveraging Trade for Development and Inclusive Growth: The World Bank Group Trade Strategy, 2011–2021*, available from: http://siteresources.worldbank.org/TRADE/Resources/WBGTradeStrategyJune10.pdf (accessed September 15, 2013).

World Bank (2011b), *What Is the World Bank Doing on Aid for Trade?*, available from: http://siteresources.worldbank.org/INTRANETTRADE/Resources/AfTbookletFINAL.pdf (accessed September 15, 2013).

World Bank (2012), *De-Fragmenting Africa: Deepening Regional Trade Integration in Goods and Services*, Washington, DC: World Bank.

WEF (World Economic Forum), Bain & Co. and World Bank (2013), *Enabling Trade: Valuing Growth Opportunities*, available from: http://www3.weforum.org/docs/WEF_SCT_EnablingTrade_Report_2013.pdf (accessed September 10, 2013).

WTO (World Trade Organization) (2012), *International Trade Statistics, 2012*, Geneva: WTO.

14. The EU, China and trade in 'green' technologies: cooperation and conflict
Maria Garcia

INTRODUCTION

Since the Chinese leadership handover in November 2012, little has changed in the overarching dynamics of Sino-European economic relations. Trade and investment relations, a mainstay of the relationship over the past decades, have continued to solidify despite the financial crisis in Europe. They have led to the increased importance of China as a market and a source of inward investment. Behind the headlines of quotas, anti-dumping measures and other trade conflicts, China and the EU are key to each other's economic survival, as the EU is China's top trade partner and China is the EU's second partner. Within the current environment, where policy-makers across the world propose exporting their way out of the crisis (particularly in high-value technological and knowledge-based products and services), their relative dependence on one another increases further. As both partners turn to the 'greening' of the economy as a response to the crisis, the opportunities for cooperation, as well as the risks of competition in the relationship, are heightened. The 2012–13 EU–China solar panel trade dispute and the 2011–12 dispute over rare earth mineral exports are significant examples of this new reality. Drawing on official policy documents and material from open-ended personal interviews with policy-makers and diplomats, this chapter presents an overview of these disputes within the context of the overarching Sino-European economic relationship. Focusing on the underlying interests and circumstances behind these disputes, the chapter explains the evolution of the dispute as a function of changes in the industry as well as in energy policies in the EU and China. The chapter shows that the divergent interests over time cause fractures within the EU that weaken its position vis-à-vis China, and how the intricacies of global production lines and international investment opportunities and choices complicate the realization of policy-makers' future development plans. Finally, it suggests that cooperation on 'green economy' developments has been a key feature of the Sino-European relationship in recent decades, which the current disputes, and more competitive environment, risk undermining.

THE CONTEXT OF EU–CHINA ECONOMIC RELATIONS

Trade Relationship

China's economic transformation into a market socialist economy and its consistent economic growth have been the focus of a wide body of literature and analysis (Bramall 2000; Naughton 2007; Breslin 2009; Blecher 2010). This unprecedented transformation initially focused on exports and the incorporation into global markets. Crucial to this was the accession of China into the WTO in late 2001, in spite of internal conflict regarding the desirability of opening up the Chinese economy to foreign competition (Blecher 2010). China's dramatic rise in share of global trade and magnified significance in global markets since its accession to the WTO have meant that its trade with the European Union has increased sharply, in terms both of imports and of exports, to the extent that in 2013 it was the world's second largest economic relation. The EU represented the second largest market for Chinese goods in 2012, accounting for 15.4 per cent of all Chinese exports, and was the first source of imports for China.[1] For the EU, China was its main supplier, accounting for 16.2 per cent of imports, and its second market, purchasing 8.5 per cent of all EU exports (behind the USA's 17.3 per cent) (DG Trade 2013).

Whilst the EU runs a small trade surplus in commercial services with China, this is dwarfed by the deficit in trade in goods. Despite an initial drop in the EU of Chinese imports of 13.6 per cent in 2009, and a significant rise in EU exports to China of 37.6 per cent in 2010 and 20.3 per cent in 2011, growth in EU exports to China slowed down again in 2012 to just a 5.5 per cent increase (DG Trade 2013). The financial and economic crisis that has so harshly affected Europe and the USA since 2008 has not, thus far, dramatically altered the economic relationship between the EU and China (see Figures 14.1 and 14.2).

China's export capacity has spurred complications with the EU and other partners given these trade deficits. Cases of anti-dumping measures, quota restrictions and others have been brought against it by its key trade partners, the USA and the EU (Moller and Kutkowski 2005; Hufbauer et al. 2006; Brown 2007; Comino 2007), as one measure to stem the deficits. What makes the particular case of the EU even more complicated is the fact that such actions must be undertaken by the EU as a whole, as the European Commission's Trade Commissioner acts on behalf of all member states. The amalgamation of individual member state preferences as well as interest group preferences is complex and at times opaque. A tendency towards consensual decision-making in the

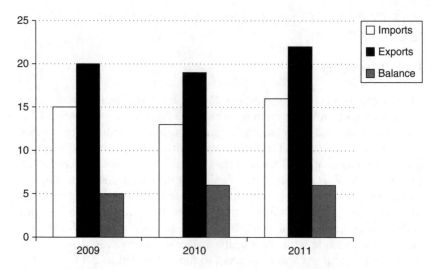

Note: In billion euros.

Source: Eurostat Comtext data in EU Trade website 2013.

Figure 14.1   EU27–China trade in commercial services

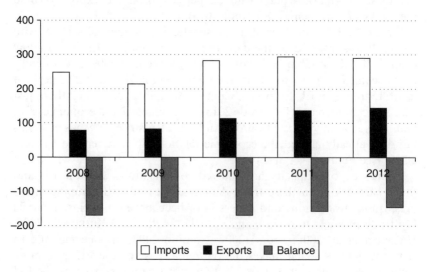

Note: In billion euros.

Source: Eurostat Comtext data in EU Trade website 2013.

Figure 14.2   EU27–China trade in goods

Council of the EU Trade Ministers' meetings dilutes the core objectives of individual member states in global trade relations.[2] EU–China economic relations display a large degree of heterogeneity amongst EU member states, which translates into divergent preferences that must be reconciled into one policy to be executed by the European Commission (DG Trade) on behalf of the Union.[3] Germany, France, Italy, the United Kingdom, the Netherlands, Belgium, Sweden and Spain account for more than 80 per cent of the transactions. All of them display deficits with China, although the largest deficits relate to the Netherlands, the United Kingdom and Italy, which represent over half of the entire deficit of the EU27 (Beneyto et al. 2011: 16). The disproportionate acceleration of imports and exports has taken the trade deficit to a cumulative growth rate of over 23 per cent from 1995 until the onset of the international crisis.

However, the overall trade deficit data disguises the complexity of the international trade relations that underpin the data. Chinese imports into the EU include intra-firm imports in cases where European firms have invested in production facilities in China. Increases in imports, which are implicitly understood as a negative development within the trade statistics, also reflect positive developments in other sectors. For instance, imports of Chinese commodities sustain certain parts of the European retail industry. In recent years, imports of competitively priced Chinese photovoltaic (PV) panels have reduced prices in Europe, encouraging a surge in their adoption by consumers (often further promoted through government subsidies) and in an industry specializing in their installation and maintenance. Similarly, Chinese exports of telecommunications equipment have benefited European service providers, which can reduce costs with these devices. Thus, Spain's telecommunications provider Telefónica has become the largest external private client of China's Huawei, which in mid-2012 overtook Sweden's Ericsson to become the world's largest telecoms equipment maker ('Who's Afraid?' 2012). Not only have Huawei's more affordable devices enabled Telefónica to further its growth and leadership position in South American markets, but both companies have signed services contracts as well, with Telefónica's UK section O2 signing Huawei for a five-year network service contract (Global Telecoms Business 2012). This reveals the complexity of the relations that underlie the official trade statistics, notwithstanding which the EU's trade deficits with China are a worrying sign of an unbalanced relationship, especially as almost half of all EU exports to China originate in one member state, Germany. Divergent interests of domestic constituencies, some of which specialize in exporting parts for final production lines in China and others of which have invested in production facilities in China, and retailers that depend on

Chinese imports have led to complex and fluctuating EU responses to the rise of China (Shu 2010).

Other issues marring the relationship include many of the technical, sanitary and phytosanitary measures that have become obstacles to exports from China, affecting more than 15 per cent of exporting firms, which highlights the need to adapt national legislation to the standards required by the vast majority of its trading partners (Beneyto et al. 2011: 24). However, China too has increasingly learnt from its WTO experience and has likewise increased its participation in the 'non-tariff barrier game', as one European diplomat described it, but in ways that are compatible with its WTO membership.[4]

Investment Relationship

Although trade accounts for the more visible and substantial part of Sino-European economic relations, increasing investment flows are also gaining significance. Despite the financial and economic crisis, EU investment flows to China have continued and, perhaps because of the opportunities afforded by the EU's need for liquidity, China's foreign direct investment (FDI) flows into the European Union have increased dramatically over the last few years. Chinese FDI in Europe increased by 337 per cent between 2007 and 2010, as evidenced in Figure 14.3.

Some high-profile cases have included investments in iconic brands like car manufacturer Volvo, French winery Chateau de Viaud, French resort Club Med, or foods like the UK's Weetabix. Acquisitions have also abounded in the eurocrisis-stricken countries, such as the lease of the operations of the Greek port Piraeus, showrooms in Ireland to exhibit Chinese exports, and a 21 per cent participation by the Three Gorges Project Corporation in Energias de Portugal and a 25 per cent stake in the Portuguese electricity network (see Hanemann and Rosen 2012), and recently NHA Group acquired 20 per cent of the Spanish NH hotel group. These investments are consistent with China's entering the second phase of its 'going out' strategy for investment abroad. If phase one focused on acquiring energy and raw materials (hence investments in extraction and infrastructure in Africa and Asia) to secure its own industrial growth, phase two targets entering into the developed markets and acquiring know-how, technologies and established brands.[5] Investments in Europe, including the eurozone periphery, follow this business strategy. However, the eurocrisis has created additional opportunities for investment in the EU, as the declining value of the euro has also cheapened the cost of these investments. Moreover with the currency losing value it seems sensible for Chinese companies to use some of the euros they have accumulated

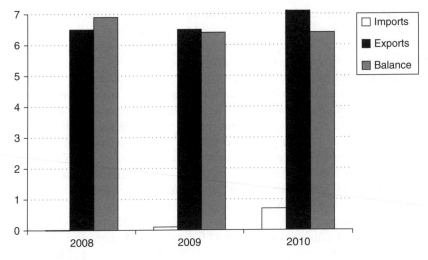

Note: In billion euros.

Source: Eurostat Comtext data in DG Trade website 2012.

Figure 14.3 *EU27–China FDI flows*

through their exports to the eurozone. Whilst the Chinese economic leadership might not wish for a collapse of the euro (which it holds as foreign exchange currency, although not to the extent of the US dollar),[6] and is clearly concerned about the decline in demand from its major market, its current attitude to Europe is marked by a clear sense of business acumen. Although China's leadership has shown its commitment to Europe and the euro, not least through purchases of bonds at the height of the eurocrisis (see Otero-Iglesias 2013), China and its state and private enterprises will not support Europe at any cost, but rather are shopping around for the best business opportunities.[7] More significantly, investments in Europe, thus far, also represent less than a fifth of Chinese FDI abroad, which has been destined mostly to securing resources in other resource-rich developing states.

From a European perspective, these FDI flows are relatively minor. Although important in absolute values (€3.1 billion in 2011), FDI inflows into the EU from China accounted for just 1.4 per cent of total FDI inflows, compared to 47 per cent originating in North America. More significant in value have been EU investments in China (€617 billion, representing 20 per cent of Chinese FDI inflows), yet, even then, total EU FDI outward stocks in Asia accounted for 15 per cent of total EU investments abroad compared to 58 per cent represented by North America (DG Trade 2013). In terms of FDI the relationship with North America remains crucial. This is, of course, motivated partly by tradition (the accumulation of FDI stocks over decades), but also by more open investment environments in North America and Europe and more consistent legal frameworks, which are likely to be further harmonized if the Transatlantic Trade and Investment Partnership (TTIP) negotiations succeed. By contrast, European (and other foreign) enterprises have experienced difficulties investing in China in the past,[8] accounting for lower levels of investment than elsewhere. To bolster investments in both directions, the European Commission's DG Trade is now prioritizing the negotiation of an investment agreement with China, using the competence over investment that it was granted in the Lisbon Treaty (DG Trade 2013).

Other European concerns in this economic relationship regard infringements of intellectual property rights (IP)[9] by an industry specializing in forgeries of consumer goods, as well as resulting from technology and know-how transfers via investments and joint ventures. Difficulties for competitive European service companies bidding for public procurement[10] contracts are another contentious issue, and the European Commission even suggested in 2012 that it too would close the European public procurement market to companies from states that have closed public procurement markets ('EU to Restrict Foreign Access' 2012). However, threats of retaliation from China and the USA,[11] and opposition from key EU member states (Germany, the UK and the Netherlands), meant that the Commission dropped the proposal. Frederik Erixon and Razeen Sally (2010: 13) have documented some of these actions as part of the creeping protectionism that states across the world (including the EU) have enacted as part of their stimulus package policy responses to the economic and financial crisis. The European Commission's Directorate-General for Trade (DG Trade) has been stressing all these aspects, as well as increased non-tariff barrier obstacles for exports, in its general trade policy papers, like *Global Europe: Competing in the World* (European Commission 2006a) and *Trade, Growth and World Affairs* (European Commission 2010a), with regard to all states, and also in its specific policy papers on China (European Commission 2006b) since before the start of the crisis. DG Trade's objectives are to internationalize and institutionalize what has been described as its 'deep trade' agenda (Lamy 2002; Young and Peterson 2006).[12] Deep trade refers to the incorporation of the so-called Singapore issues which were meant to be negotiated at the WTO.

These so-called Singapore issues (market access facilitation, public procurement, services liberalization and competition policy, as well as 'strengthen[ing] sustainable development through ... bilateral trade relations ... incorporating new co-operative provisions in areas relating to labour standards and environmental protection') are the core strategic aims that the EU pursues in its relations with Asia (European Commission 2006a: 12). These are addressed via dialogues with China, and the negotiations for a Partnership and Cooperation Agreement that started in 2007. Given the importance of the Chinese market and the challenges it presents, these issues are even more forcefully portrayed in the DG's policy papers specifically on economic relations with China, which insist on the need to 'get China right' and to establish 'fair trade' practices between the two partners to redress the current unbalanced relationship (European Commission 2006b). These challenges on the European side are particularly pressing, as these are precisely the economic areas in which European companies are most competitive and in which the EU has priorities in its trade policies.

Institutional Relationship

A complex institutional relationship has developed to address these as well as other issues, especially through the creation of a Strategic Partnership since 2003. The Partnership, which revolves around three pillars (a Strategic Dialogue pillar, a trade pillar and a people-to-people pillar), has been criticized for lacking a genuine strategic component (Smith and Xie 2010; Taneja 2010; Holslag 2011). In fact EU representatives have conceded that the Strategic Dialogue needs to be imbued with meaningful content.[13] According to Beneyto et al. (2011: 18) the Strategic Partnership was 'clearly directed, first toward a political dimension', including global issues like reduction of weapons of mass destruction, security of energy supply, and international terrorism, and, on the other hand, an economic dimension. A key element of the Partnership is the upgrading of the current legal basis of the relationship (the outdated 1985 Trade and Economic Cooperation Agreement) to a Partnership Cooperation Agreement (PCA), which whilst not as inclusive in scope as the free trade agreements and association agreements the EU has subscribed with other partners, would create a clear legal framework for cooperation and especially for increased trade and investment. Indeed, the economic pillar is the one in which diplomats agree a greater effort has been invested thus far. However, negotiations have been ongoing since 2007 and are still far from resolution. Within the PCA negotiations the European Union initially resorted to linkage of issues (as it does in other negotiations) to leverage its market power.[14] However, Chinese reluctance to negotiate anything other than economic matters led to an eventual separation of the economic and political negotiations, regardless of which both are currently more or less stalled.

The economic aspect of the Dialogue is the area in which both parties are most interested, and has been institutionalized since April 2008 through the High-Level Economic and Trade Dialogue Mechanism. This Dialogue remains difficult, especially in view of recent escalation of protectionist measures. Recent difficulties notwithstanding, through this Dialogue, and the more technical (and depoliticized ones) on customs procedures, non-tariff barriers, and so on, there has been an emphasis on the importance of collaboration between the EU and China on customs matters for the treatment of goods moving between the two blocks. Other contentious issues are also being addressed through the High-Level Economic Dialogue. For instance, the parties have expressed their desire to 'create a favourable environment to promote innovation and protection of IPR to ensure favourable and regulatory conditions' (EU–China High-Level Economic Dialogue 2010).

GROWTH STRATEGIES, THE CRISIS AND SOLAR PANELS

Europe 2020 and European Trade Policy

The European Commission's 2006 'Global Europe' trade strategy signalled a new era of a more outwardly aggressive EU trade policy, which left behind some of its prior rhetorical niceties regarding trade and development and instead overtly pursued a competitiveness-driven policy of market opening and liberalization to the benefit of EU industries (see Woolcock 2007; Garcia 2013). Concerned with lack of progress in opening markets at the WTO, and with growth in emerging competitor markets, DG Trade emphasized market access and creating a 'level playing field' for European exports of goods and, more importantly, services, which make up 70 per cent of EU GDP. Relations with India, Russia and of course China are prioritized in this and subsequent policy papers (European Commission 2006a, 2006b), as the aim is to foster European competitiveness in services and high-tech by opening other markets (and it is precisely these emerging economies that limit access to foreign enterprises).[15]

Trade Commissioner Karel De Gucht's 2010 'Trade, Growth and World Affairs' trade policy continued the competitiveness agenda put forward by his predecessor Peter Mandelson in 2006. However, in the midst of the economic and financial crisis that followed the collapse of Lehman Brothers, it placed a greater emphasis on the contribution of exports to potential growth and recovery in Europe. The policy paper claimed a direct link between more open trade and GDP growth in Europe, greater consumer choice and lower prices, and more employment in Europe (European Commission 2010a: 5), not only justifying the EU's liberal trade policy, but also articulating the external dimension of the EU's own internal strategy for growth and future development, Europe 2020.

Europe 2020 is an overarching EU strategy that covers all areas of economic development, from economic governance (including fiscal oversight and constraints) to macroeconomic policies and social and employment policies, as well as external economic relations.[16] This agenda refines and strengthens some of the economic and social objectives prioritized at the turn of the century by the EU through the Lisbon Strategy, which hoped to create the most competitive knowledge-based economy in the world, through the protection of intellectual property, the fostering of innovation, technical education, and specialization in the export of high-value-added high technology and services.[17] Deadlines were missed, and the onslaught of the crisis made the need for a broad strategy all the more pressing. Europe 2020 reiterates the aims of the Lisbon Strategy and further focuses on a transformation into a low-carbon economy based on sustainability and a clean and high-tech industry, in which training and technical and innovative training are key economic drivers. It aims to improve employment in Europe through the creation of jobs in these target sectors, not just for intra-EU consumption but also for exports. Key aims of Europe 2020 rely on exporting high-technology, a low-carbon economy and innovations abroad. The focus on a low-carbon economy is also consistent with the EU's climate change and environmental policy. In '20 20 by 2020', the EU committed itself to increasing its use of renewable energy, so as to reach 20 per cent of energy consumption by 2020, as well as ambitious carbon emission targets, in line with the EU's support of the UN Climate Change Framework and with the EU's desire to be a world leader in environmental matters (see Lightfoot and Burchell 2005). In this sense trade policy is a crucial factor in achieving the 2020 aims, and it is unsurprising that the EU's current trade policy is so focused on gaining opportunities for these targeted sectors abroad.

Europe 2020 and Green Technologies

Green technologies are, thus, a cornerstone of the Europe 2020 strategy. Until the onset of the crisis, the EU was the world leader in these technologies. Wind and solar power, in particular, had experienced significant successes. Denmark's Vestas was the world's top manufacturer of wind turbines. The domestic policies of various EU member states had encouraged the uptake of wind and solar power in Europe, motivated partly by a need to meet emission reduction targets agreed internationally, desires to reduce energy dependence on imports of fossil fuels and on volatile global prices, and even promotion of the domestic high-technology industry. Consequently, Germany has become the world leader in terms of installed capacity for solar power generation.

Two interlinked phenomena derived from globalization have challenged the EU's leadership position in this area, and with it some of its 2020 objectives. Firstly, successful European green technology firms, in a bid to increase profitability and market share and to supply foreign markets, commenced to move production capacity outside Europe. Vestas, for instance, set up production lines in China. Lower labour costs helped reduce prices and, more importantly, facilitated entry into the Chinese marketplace, where as the next section highlights the government has tended to favour wind and solar farms with higher domestically produced content. China's government promoted these types of investments so as to facilitate technology transfers. Moreover, cooperation in green economy developments has been a key facet of the EU–China relationship.

Secondly, as demand for green power supplies increased in Europe and elsewhere, foreign companies, too, have been keen to increase capacity so as to meet that demand. As a result, global prices for green power equipment have dropped dramatically in recent years. This has been particularly true in the PV panel sector. Lower prices have facilitated the adoption of the technology, particularly in Europe. It has led to increased service jobs involved with the installation and upkeep of domestic solar panels, as well as solar and wind farms. However, lower prices and increased competition from manufacturers abroad, particularly in China, have caused strife in the manufacturing sector within Europe.

The EU–China Solar Panel Dispute

Against this backdrop, in July 2012, some EU solar panel manufacturers grouped themselves within the association ProSun[18] and placed a formal complaint against Chinese producers of solar panels, claiming they were able to sell them below production costs in Europe (dumping) thanks to government subsidies, and that this threatened to put the European manufacturers out of business. Following EU legal procedures, once the request was received the European Commission opened an investigation on 6 September 2012 into possible Chinese dumping practices in this field (Bloomberg 2012; European Commission 2012), and a further investigation into subsidies of solar panels on 8 November 2012, which has engendered a more tense relationship with China in the past few years.[19] For its part, on 7 November 2012 China requested the opening of a panel at the WTO to investigate the legislation of EU member states (specifically

Greece and Italy) on feed-in tariffs that require certain domestic manufacture components for the equipment as a breach of GATT 1994 (WTO 2012). Simultaneously, China opened its own anti-dumping and anti-subsidy investigation into European exports of polysilicon (material used in solar panels) to China. The latter was resolved in March 2014, when the German polysilicon producer Wacker Chemie AG and the Chinese Ministry of Commerce (MOFCOM) agreed to settle the proceedings through a price undertaking (European Commission 2014a).

In the first months of 2013, as part of the investigation, the European Commission started listing all PV equipment coming into the EU at the border as a first step to possible anti-dumping duties.[20] When the European Commission commenced listing all PV equipment coming into the EU at the border, and requesting extra information from Chinese manufacturers, the latter complied. Meanwhile the Chinese government and Chinese Chamber of Commerce had made efforts to persuade EU member states to stop the imposition of sanctions, including various trips to Europe to offer alternatives to the European Commission (which were rejected). China's premier Li Keqiang, on his first trip abroad, visited several European capitals, amongst other things, to avert the imposition of tariffs on PV panels. Germany's government, which had been ambivalent on the matter, positioned itself against the tariffs after Li's visit. Notwithstanding this, and the fact that 15 member states oppose the tariffs and only six actually support them, the European Commission voted in favour of initiating temporary tariffs on Chinese PV imports on 6 June 2013, as its report had found that Chinese panels were entering the EU at an 88 per cent price reduction (European Commission 2013a), which allowed them to gain an 80 per cent share of the EU solar panel market (Reuters 2013a). Duties were not set at 88 per cent, but instead at 11.5 per cent for the first two months, during which time negotiations with China continued. If no amicable solution had been reached, the EU would have imposed tariffs of 47.6 per cent from August 2013 (European Commission 2013a).[21] However, after frenzied diplomacy by Beijing, including a visit by Li Keqiang to European capitals, the conflict was resolved by means of a voluntary price undertaking. This meant that Chinese exporters who participate in the undertaking agree to sell their products in the EU at a minimum price, as explained further in the next section. China's retaliation had included launching its own investigation into the dumping of European wine in China and European wine subsidies on 7 July 2013 (having threatened to do so a month earlier). These actions targeted in particular France and Italy, the main supporters of EU solar panel tariffs, and major European wine exporters.[22] China's wine imports increased by 8.9 per cent in 2012, with a third of all imports originating in the EU. Overall,

EU exports to China account for 1 per cent of total exports, and whilst tariffs could potentially be damaging to lesser-known wines from Spain, which in 2012 accounted for a sharp rise in EU wine exports to China, potential tariffs are less likely to harm French wine sales in China, where the expense and prestige factor account for the majority of sales (Reuters 2013b). More significantly, Chinese leaders also threatened to apply tariffs to EU high-end car exports and equipment, something that could be more damaging, particularly to Germany's exporting interests. The unequal effects of potential Chinese retaliation on EU member states increased the division that already exists amongst them, therefore increasing pressure to negotiate a solution with China.

European Divisions and the Solar Panel Dispute

Given the high stakes, both sides created incentives for the other party to actively seek a negotiated solution. On the European side, the 'conflicted trade power' nature of the EU (Meunier and Nicolaidis 2006) was made evident in the intense pressure DG Trade was placed under by various member states. Sweden, the UK, Ireland, the Netherlands and Denmark, in particular, opposed the European Commission's tough stance on the issue, with the Danish Trade Minister Pia Olsen Dyhr stating at a press conference that 'We're very much against using trade defense mechanisms unless we can really show there is evidence that they are using subsidies, and we cannot do that' (Reuters 2013a). Germany too, concerned with threats to its car exports, after Li Keqiang's visit expressed its opposition, to the annoyance of EU Trade Commissioner Karel De Gucht, who claimed that unless Europe stood together on the issue they would lose, in a case of what Peter Gumbel (2013) argues demonstrates the divisive effect of Chinese investment in Europe amongst member states' stances on China, especially in the context of the financial crisis.

One reason many EU states opposed the measures is the relatively small size of the solar panel industry in Europe. EurObserv'ER (2013: 128) estimates that the PV industry in the EU employs 311 930 people between direct and indirect jobs (e.g. installation and maintenance component parts) and generates a turnover of €45.9 billion. Around 110 000 of these jobs are in Germany. However, it was Italy (55 000), France (62 275) and Spain (12 000), alongside Lithuania, that were reported to have voted in favour of proceeding with anti-dumping measures on China, in a non-binding consultation vote in May 2013; four states abstained, and the others voted against ('Majority of EU States' 2013). The European Commission's (2013a) investigation estimated that 25 000 jobs could be lost in the EU as a result of Chinese PV dumping and export subsidies.

However, an independent report by Prognos estimated that 242 000 EU jobs would be lost if the duties were imposed on Chinese PV in parts of the solar power sector devoted to installation and maintenance, and among manufacturers that use Chinese PV as components (Ehrentraut et al. 2013). De Bièvre and Eckhardt (2011) have argued that, in terms of the EU's anti-dumping policy, well-organized protectionist industrial sectors tend to win the day in persuading the Commission, instead of consumers, importers and retailers. The solar panel case, which represented the largest case of its kind ever investigated by the Commission based on the value of PV imports (€21 000 million), followed this trend. A quarter of PV manufacturers in Europe joined to create ProSun, with the specific aim of giving the European Commission evidence of Chinese dumping and initiating an investigation and anti-dumping measures.

Given intense member state pressure, China's stance and the importance of the overarching economic relationship, China and the EU had clear incentives to reach an agreement. On 27 July 2013, EU Trade Commissioner De Gucht announced that both sides had reached an amicable agreement on the solar panel matter. Rather than impose duties on Chinese solar panels, Chinese manufacturers agreed to present a price undertaking (a minimum price for the products) that the Chinese government presented to EU negotiators, and which EU negotiators accepted, pending a formal favourable vote by EU member state governments at the Council meeting of 6 August 2013 (European Commission 2013b). The EU Trade Commissioner expressed his confidence 'that this price undertaking will stabilise the European solar panel market and will remove the injury that the dumping practices have caused to the European industry' (European Commission 2013b), although ProSun rejected the deal and have announced their plans to challenge it in the courts (ProSun 2013). The Commission's investigation on subsidies continues. Whilst it was hoped that the avoidance of tariffs would facilitate the resolution of China's threatened actions against European wines, Chinese investigations of the sector continued until, in March 2014, the European and Chinese wine industries, represented by the European Committee of Wine Companies (CEEV) and the Chinese Alcoholic Drinks Association (CADA) respectively, reached an agreement for technical cooperation and exchanges, which led to the Chinese wine producers withdrawing their claims to the Chinese Ministry of Commerce to investigate EU dumping and subsidies (European Commission 2014b).

De Gucht's strong stance on the matter may be as much motivated by his Directorate's findings in the investigation, and its overarching concern with establishing a 'fair' playing field (European Commission 2006b), with China more actively applying WTO rules, as with bolstering the

Directorate's own position within the EU system vis-à-vis other negotiations with China and potential investment negotiations, as well as ongoing negotiations with other states, in particular the USA. The PV dispute displayed in a very public way different preferences amongst EU member states, divergences with the Commission's more aggressive stance on the application of trade policy and rules, and the complex intricacies of the principal–agent relationship that underpins the EU's trade policy (Elsig 2007; Billiet 2009; Dür and Elsig 2011). In this particular case, DG Trade's policy of aggressive market opening, creating a level playing field for EU firms, was trumped by the immediate interests of member states in staving off retaliatory measures by China on more significant exporting sectors. Interestingly, the interests of consumers, and the EU's own commitments to enhance the use of 'green energies', have featured far less in the debate surrounding the dispute.[23]

In other cases, member states have allowed the European Commission to take a more forceful stance. China has been the target of around 42 per cent of the EU's anti-dumping investigations since 2007 (Davis 2009: 6), and the EU has brought various cases before the WTO appellate body against it.[24] Europe's more aggressive predisposition is reflected in the rare earth mineral case. China's restriction on the export of rare earth minerals, crucial for the production of alternative energy generators as well as most high-technology manufactures, upon which the 2020 strategy hinges, resulted in the EU asking the WTO to open two panels to investigate the matter. The first panel was presented by the EU, Japan and the USA in 2011 in a concerted effort to force China to continue supply of these minerals, as it accounts for 95 per cent of the world's production of some of the minerals. In 2012 the EU presented another panel for a different list of rare minerals, this time alone. Baroncini (2013) convincingly argues that the EU could have opted to conduct an investigation that would allow it to gain access to Chinese decision-makers in the field of rare earth mineral extraction and to continuously monitor procedures there, rather than merely gaining some compensation through the WTO appellate body's resolution. For the EU, which currently is the world leader in alternative energy technology, and has committed itself to increased usage (up to 20 per cent of energy from renewable sources) through the 20 20 by 2020 strategy, this presents a significant problem. As with the solar panel case, DG Trade is taking an active position to gain leverage with China and ensure that some high-technology production remains in Europe, but, as the subsequent section shows, China's own industrial and development policy pushes it towards greater domestic production, and even damaging overcapacity, as in the solar panel case, can be at odds with this strategy.

Explaining China's Reaction to the Dispute: China's Industrial Model and Renewable Energy Policy

China's export-led growth following on from Deng Xiaoping's reforms accelerated after it joined the WTO (see Bramall 2000; Blecher 2010). Its large state-owned enterprises (SOEs) and managed economy have enabled the world's speediest industrialization, which has also resulted in large surpluses with trading partners. As already noted, the economic and financial crisis that began in 2008, and has been particularly damaging to the USA and the EU, has begun to redress the EU's trade deficit with China slightly. An impact of this in China has been to generate greater awareness within Chinese policy-making elites of the need to promote internal consumption and lessen dependence on the European and American markets, a political and developmental aim that preceded the onset of the crisis, but has gathered strength since. The new leadership team under Xi Jinping has shown commitment to this goal and to further the internal development of China in order to tackle the social inequality that has arisen from rapid development and industrialization, as laid out in the 12th Five-Year Plan (2011–15). Key objectives in the plan include progressing up the value-added chain, manufacturing high technology domestically, improving innovation and also addressing the social and environmental consequences of industrialization. A preference for technology and cleaner development and the exploitation of low-carbon-economy opportunities mirror the EU's own aims in the 2020 strategy.

In order to achieve the priorities of saving energy, relying on Chinese energy sources, protecting nature and improving livelihoods as set out in the 12th Five-Year Plan (2011–15), the Chinese government's 2012 Energy Policy has encouraged efficiency (decreased by 16 per cent the energy consumption per point of GDP) and increased usage of renewable energy sources, including solar power (Information Office 2012). Although China's renewable energy policy dates back to the Energy and Renewable Energy Development of 1996, the greatest progress and industrial growth have been achieved in the 2000s, with greater emphasis on the environmental aspects, the substitution of fossil energy and the development of the renewable energy industry with independent design capacity (Shi 2010: 204). Because of the high initial costs, economic incentives for the development and use of renewable energy include tax reduction and exemptions on the import of equipment, half value-added tax on renewable energy companies, and discounted interest loans (mostly for wind power promotion, solar energy and large and medium-sized marsh gas projects) (Zhang et al. 2009). All states have in this respect subsidized the uptake of solar and other green power sources. Many have done so through support of end users, although increasingly European states are passing the costs on to users and removing the remaining subsidies (*Renewable Energy Magazine* 2013). In China, prices for renewable electricity are set by the government based on the principle of 'rate of return', that is, cost plus a reasonable return on capital, and there is a fiscal subsidy policy in place for renewable energy development, demonstration projects and bidding prices of renewable energy power, as well as direct investment funds from the Ministry of Finance. However, there are many obstacles that have prevented the uptake of renewable energy in China arising from high production costs, inadequate grid facilities that are unable to support the more irregular flow of solar and wind-generated electricity, rapid growth in installation but incomplete usage, and competition amongst SOEs and smaller private companies (Shi 2010: 212).

The Solar Power Industry in China

Solar power energy in China, in particular, presents a paradox. On the one hand, China has become one of the world's top manufacturers of PV panels and equipment, overtaking early leaders in PV production (the United States, Germany and Japan) (Algieri et al. 2011: 7277), and boasts a capacity that is one and a half times total global demand (European Commission 2013a). On the other hand, uptake of the technology has lagged far behind manufacturing capabilities. In recent years a comprehensive production chain has emerged, including polysilicon feedstock, silicon slices, silicon carbide, solar panels and modules, solar power systems and PV power stations (Hu 2012: 2). Chinese companies have now mastered some of the processes for which they previously relied on imports like polysilicon production. By 2011, China was responsible for 38 per cent of the world's production of the latter. In the same year, PV batteries production increased 100 per cent with respect to the previous year in China, with a manufacturing cost 30 per cent below international levels given the economies of scale, technology and cheaper labour (Hu 2012: 3). In this sense, PV production has been a success story in terms of the Chinese government's pursuit of domestic design capacity and production. To further this and other high-technology sectors, as well as to limit some of the environmental degradation caused by their exploitation, the Chinese government enacted export restrictions on rare earth minerals, spurring two WTO cases against it led by the advanced economies of the West. A side effect of this measure was the government's encouraging foreign high-technology and green technology firms to establish production lines in China, where they would have access to rare earths, in exchange for jobs and technology transfer.

Meanwhile, domestic PV power generation on a large scale began in 2009 with the launch of large-scale projects such as 'PV Building', the 'Golden Sun Demonstration Project' and the 'Dunhuang Desert PV Station Tendering'. In 2011, in order to stimulate the growth of the PV power generation market, the government initiated a PV feed-in tariff. That year, 2.2 million KW PV power generating capacity was installed, bringing the total up to 3 million KW (Hu 2012: 3), which alongside the promotion of wind power has turned China into the largest future market for renewable energy equipment.

Its market has encouraged Western market leaders to invest in manufacturing capacity in China and to transfer the required high-end technology and know-how, as Danish wind turbine manufacturer Vestas has done ('To Conquer' 2010). However, whilst Chinese demand is growing slowly, Chinese manufacturing capacity has increased dramatically since 2006. Chinese renewable equipment overcapacity has lowered global prices for these products, facilitating the assimilation of the technologies throughout the world, but has also placed great strain on Western manufacturers like the USA's Solyndra, which filed for bankruptcy, or various German PV firms (Hollersen 2013). Yet the same problem is affecting Chinese manufacturers. Lower prices mean that China's US$30 billion solar power industry, which is overbuilt and heavily in debt, despite continued government support to prevent job losses, is also under threat (Goossens 2012).

In 2012 Suntech Power Holdings, the world's largest solar panel maker, announced the reassignment of 1500 workers in its PV cell factory in Wuxi, and in March 2013 it was forced into Chinese bankruptcy procedures ('Suntech Pushed' 2013). Also in 2012, LDK Solar, China's second largest maker of solar wafers, was forced to sell a 20 per cent stake to a renewable energy investor part-owned by the city of Xinyu, where the company is located. In April 2013, *Energy and Capital* reported that LDK had defaulted on a bank loan and was also facing severe financial difficulties ('China's Next?' 2013). In 2012, Chinese solar power manufacturers posted losses of US$987 million, and, although the government intervened to support the largest manufacturers with loans and by encouraging state-owned banks to extend credit to the companies (Goossens 2012), the problems worsened in 2013. However, the government itself would prefer consolidation of companies and mergers, and in December 2012 announced it would stop additional support to the sector ('China's Next?' 2013). Regional governments, on their part, are loath to allow their local solar industry to fail. The ensuing social tensions have led to a rift in EU–China relations over the solar power industry, and the government's support for this sector accounts for the attention that this particular trade dispute, unlike others, has aroused. Of the anti-dumping measures put in place by the European Commission in 2011 and 2012, 48 per cent had China as their target. They included tariffs on tiles, bicycles and a host of other issues but have largely been contained within the normal relationship.

China's extreme reaction to the solar panel case, launching a WTO investigation into EU members state subsidies to install solar panels (WTO 2012), and initiating its own anti-dumping investigation against European wines, threatening luxury cars and chemicals, can be understood only in the context of the internal turmoil that the solar power industry is suffering within China, and its own retreating support to the industry. Moreover, the industry has already been facing US tariffs since May 2012,[25] and the prospect of tariffs from the EU market, which is four times larger than that of the USA, would have been damaging, as it would be difficult to shift sales elsewhere. Perhaps more significant is what is at stake. Beyond the solar panel industry, for over a year the European Commission has also been mulling over an investigation into Chinese subsidies in the telecommunication sector. From a Chinese perspective, it is the principle of foreign interference in its domestic industrial policy that is far more irritating and worrying, and hence why it elicits such a response.[26]

CONCLUDING REMARKS

In view of the EU's core Europe 2020 and trade policy paradigms, and China's own contrasting development policy, it seems likely that difficulties in the relationship will continue into the future. However, as one diplomat put it, within this relationship 'a lot of people have made and are still making a lot of money', and as long as those opportunities exist the relationship will expand. In the aftermath of the crisis, one interesting phenomenon has been the reshaping of EU member states' interest in China. These internal divisions (and the ones of the eurocrisis) have weakened the EU's leveraging position with respect to China, and China (and other partners) can also take advantage, as some EU member states will lobby the European Commission for a more open policy. The EU–China economic relationship will continue to be crucial to both partners, but will probably experience changes in the future.

The problem with current growth policies basing hopes for recovery on the green economy and technological exports is that it assumes steady demand for your exports abroad. As everyone tries to do this the demand side of the market will dry up. Furthermore, the exponential growth created by free trade, and even the existence of a genuinely free trade system, has been questioned.[27] Notwithstanding this, within the Strategic Partnership, cooperation on the environment and peacekeeping is increasing, and the institutionalization of dialogues is in itself a success. China and the EU do share a host of common interests globally (multipolarity, peacekeeping, a low-carbon economy, securing trade lanes, counterterrorism and development) and, whilst complicated, their maturing relationship increasingly bears a resemblance to the EU–USA partnership, where trade and political tensions are frequent despite extensive collaboration in other areas.

NOTES

1. Europe's share in total Chinese exports has been decreasing from around 20 per cent since 2008 (DG Trade 2013).
2. The complex interests at play in EU trade policy-making are highlighted in the concept of a 'conflicted trade power' as described in Meunier and Nicolaidis (2006). Meunier and Nicolaidis (1999) and Meunier (2000) also describe EU trade policy-making in detail, and Dür (2008) focuses on the incorporation of interests into the policy.
3. Literature describing the EU's trade policy mechanisms as a principal–agent relationship between the Council of the EU and the European Commission and the tensions within this relationship includes Damro (2007) and da Conceicao-Heldt (2011).
4. Interview with European diplomat, Beijing, August 2012.
5. Investment in Europe is facilitated by the absence of an EU-wide body exercising oversight over incoming investment like the USA's Committee on Foreign Investment (see Meunier 2012).
6. China has already started exchange swap agreements with key trade partners (Russia and Japan) to pay in their own currencies or even to bypass currencies completely by bartering oil and commodities (with Russia), showing a clear desire by these other crucial actors to limit their exposures to volatile US dollars and euros.
7. Interview with European official, Beijing, August 2012.
8. In 2012 China relaxed its rules on foreign direct investment and ownership. Previously foreign firms had to engage in joint ventures, and had more restricted rights.
9. Intellectual property rights include copyright of creative works, geographic indicators of wines, spirits and agricultural and traditional goods, and innovation patents.
10. Public procurement refers to the awarding of government contracts for infrastructure construction (roads, bridges and public works), operation of ports and airports, providing IT services to government-funded bodies or even contracts for security, catering and cleaning, amongst others.
11. China is negotiating its entry into the WTO's Global Procurement Agreement (GPA), which binds signatories to more transparent procurement procedures. The USA is a member, yet European companies complain about 'Buy American' campaigns. Final adoption of an upgraded version of the GPA is still pending. Its adoption may resolve some of the procurement confrontations in the future.
12. Young and Peterson (2006) explain the EU's deep trade agenda as a response to a new trade environment where behind-the-doors issues are more relevant, there are more actors (parliaments and NGOs), and EU and US dominance is challenged by the newly industrialised and developing states.
13. Interview with EU officials, Beijing, August 2012.
14. See Damro (2012) and Garcia (2012) *inter alia*.
15. EU negotiations of free trade agreements with Latin American (Central America, Peru and Colombia) and Asian countries (Singapore and South Korea, and ongoing negotiations with Malaysia, Vietnam, Japan and Thailand), as well as Eastern Europe, North Africa and recently the USA, are part of its strategy to negotiate market opening in services and public procurement and to secure advantageous regulations.

16. The different policy areas covered by the strategy and related documentation can be found at European Union (2013).
17. See European Commission (2010b).
18. ProSun represents a small group of PV manufacturers. Through fear of potential retaliation from China, member names are kept secret (ProSun 2013).
19. Interviews with European representatives, Beijing, August 2012.
20. Within the EU, the Alliance for Affordable Solar Energy has been campaigning to put a stop to any possible duties.
21. In its investigation the European Commission established that Chinese solar panels should be 88 per cent more expensive, but it will not be implementing tariffs of 88 per cent.
22. The official investigation was announced on 1 July 2013, with 20 July the final date for all exporting companies to register with the two companies carrying out the study on behalf of China's Ministry of Commerce, MOFCOM. On 30 July, European wine companies were selected for detailed investigations – with companies that willingly registered for the study standing to benefit from lower taxes than those that did not. The final decision was due on 1 July 2014, and it was anticipated that a preliminary tax might have been put in place in early 2014 while waiting for the final results ('China Solar' 2013). However, the investigation was concluded in April 2014, soon after the EU determined in its investigation into subsidies for solar panels in China that it need not adopt any measures, as the government had withdrawn its large-scale support for the industry and determined that no dumping was taking place; therefore no tariffs have been levied on EU wine exports to China.
23. In part this may be due to the fact that, since the start of the crisis, EU emissions have decreased (through less industrial activity), and, as world coal prices have dropped, in part as a result of the USA's excess export capacity driven by its shale gas production, EU states including Germany have actually increased their use of carbon in their energy mix in the last few years.
24. When China joined the WTO in 2001 it was not granted market economy status, which makes it easier for states to impose anti-dumping measures on China. In 2016 it will be granted market economy status within the WTO.
25. Some of the effects of these tariffs were reduced by using Taiwan as a point of departure for the exports.
26. Interviews with diplomats, Beijing, August 2012.
27. Dunkley (2006) offers a thorough and enlightening challenge to common assumptions regarding the merits of free trade.

REFERENCES

Algieri, B., A. Aquino and M. Sucurro (2011), 'Going "Green": Trade Specialisation Dynamics in the Solar Photovoltaic Sector', *Energy Policy*, **39**, 7275–83.
Baroncini, E. (2013), 'The WTO Disputes on Chinese Natural Resources and the EU Litigation Strategy in the Light of the Lisbon Treaty', paper presented at the EU and Emerging Powers Conference, European Parliament, Brussels, 29–30 May.
Beneyto, J.M., A. Soroza, I. Hurtado and J. Corti (2011), *Political Dialogue in EU–China Relations*, Documento de Trabajo Serie Unión Europea No. 50, Madrid: CEU Instituto Universitario de Estudios Europeos.
Billiet, S. (2009), 'Principal–Agent Analysis and the Study of the EU: What about the EC's External Relations?', *Comparative European Politics*, **7** (4), 435–54.
Blecher, M. (2010), *China against the Tides: Restructuring through Revolution, Radicalism and Reform*, London: Continuum.
Bloomberg (2012), 'EU Solar Panel Makers Demand China Tariffs with Second Complaint', 26 September, available from: http://www.bloomberg.com/news/2012-09-25/eu-solar-

companies-demand-china-tariffs-with-subsidy-complaint.html (accessed 27 September 2012).

Bramall, C. (2000), *Sources of Chinese Economic Growth 1978–1996*, Oxford: Oxford University Press.

Breslin, S. (2009), 'Understanding China's Regional Rise: Interpretations, Identities and Implications', *International Affairs*, **85** (4), 817–35.

Brown, C. (2007), *China's WTO Entry: Anti-Dumping, Safeguards and Dispute Settlement*, NBER Working Paper No. 13349, Cambridge, MA: NBER.

'China's Next Bankrupt Solar Stock?' (2013), *Energy and Capital*, 18 April, available from: http://www.energyandcapital.com/articles/chinas-next-bankrupt-solar-stock/3297 (accessed 25 April 2014).

'China Solar Panel Agreement Brings Hope for European Wine Producers' (2013), *Decanter*, 29 July, available from: http://www.decanter.com/news/wine-news/584204/china-solar-panel-agreement-brings-hope-for-eu-wine-resolution (accessed 29 July 2013).

Comino, A. (2007), 'A Dragon in Cheap Clothing: What Lessons Can Be Learned from the EU–China Textile Dispute', *European Law Journal*, **23** (6), 818–38.

Conceicao-Heldt, E. da (2011), 'Variation in EU Member States' Preferences and the Commission's Discretion in the Doha Round', *Journal of European Public Policy*, **18** (3), 403–19.

Damro, C. (2007), 'EU Delegation and Agency in International Trade Negotiations: A Cautionary Comparison', *Journal of Common Market Studies*, **45** (4), 883–903.

Damro, C. (2012), 'Market Power Europe', *Journal of European Public Policy*, **19** (5), 682–99.

Davis, L. (2009), *Ten Years of Anti-Dumping in the EU: Economic and Political Targeting*, ECIPE Working Paper No. 02/2009, Brussels: ECIPE.

De Bièvre, D. and J. Eckhardt (2011), 'Interest Groups and EU Anti-Dumping Policy', *Journal of European Public Policy*, **18** (3), 339–60.

DG Trade (2013), 'EU–China Trade Relations', available from: http://ec.europa.eu/trade/creating-opportunities/bilateral-relations/countries/china/ (accessed 20 July 2013).

Dunkley, G. (2006), *Free Trade: Myth, Reality and Alternatives*, London: Zed Books.

Dür, A. (2008), 'Bringing Economic Interests Back into the Study of EU Trade Policy-Making', *British Journal of Politics and International Relations*, **10** (1), 27–45.

Dür, A. and M. Elsig (2011), 'Principals, Agents, and the European Union's Foreign Economic Policies', *Journal of European Public Policy*, **18** (3), 323–38.

Ehrentraut, O., F. Peter, S. Schmutz and L. Krampe (2013), *The Impact of Anti-Dumping and/or Countervailing Measures on Imports of Solar Modules, Cells and Wafers from China on EU Employment and Value Added*, Berlin: Prognos, available from: http://afase.org/sites/default/files/docs/action/prognos_employment_and_value_added_effects_of_ad_cvd_solar_14_february_2013_management_summary.pdf (accessed 30 July 2013).

Elsig, M. (2007), 'The EU's Choice of Regulatory Venues for Trade Negotiations: A Tale of Agency Power?', *Journal of Common Market Studies*, **45** (4), 927–48.

Erixon, F. and R. Sally (2010), *Trade, Globalisation and Emerging Protectionism since the Crisis*, ECIPE Working Paper No. 2, Brussels: ECIPE.

EU–China High-Level Economic Dialogue (2010), '3rd Meeting Declaration', 21 December, MEMO/10/698.

EurObserv'ER (2013), *The State of Renewable Energies in Europe*, 12th EurObserv'ER Report, 2012 edn, Paris: EurObserv'ER, available from: http://www.energies-renouvelables.org (accessed 30 July 2013).

European Commission (2006a), *Global Europe: Competing in the World*, Brussels: European Commission.

European Commission (2006b), *Global Europe: EU–China Trade and Investment: Competition and Partnership*, Brussels: European Commission.

European Commission (2010a), *Trade, Growth and World Affairs: Trade Policy as a Core Component of the EU's 2020 Strategy*, COM(2010) 612, Brussels: European Commission.

European Commission (2010b), *Lisbon Strategy Evaluation Document*, SEC(2010) 114, 2

February, Brussels: European Commission, available from: http://ec.europa.eu/europe2020/pdf/lisbon_strategy_evaluation_en.pdf (accessed 25 May 2013).

European Commission (2012), 'EU Initiates Anti-Dumping Investigation on Solar Panels from China', Memorandum, 6 September, available from: http://trade.ec.europa.eu/doclib/press/index.cfm?id=829 (accessed 27 September 2012).

European Commission (2013a), 'EU Imposes Provisional Anti-Dumping Sanctions on Chinese Solar Panels', 4 June, Press Release IP/13/501, available from: http://europa.eu/rapid/press-release_IP-13-501_en.htm (accessed 5 June 2013).

European Commission (2013b), 'Commissioner De Gucht: We Found an Amicable Solution in the EU–China Solar Panels Case That Will Lead to a New Market Equilibrium at Sustainable Prices', Memorandum, 27 July, available from: http://trade.ec.europa.eu/doclib/press/index.cfm?id=955 (accessed 27 July 2013).

European Commission (2014a), 'Trade Defence Instruments: European Commission Welcomes EU Industry's Agreement with China in the Polysilicon Anti-Dumping and Anti-Subsidy Cases', Press Release, 18 March, available from: http://trade.ec.europa.eu/doclib/press/index.cfm?id=1044.

European Commission (2014b), 'European Commission Welcomes Agreement Reached between European and Chinese Wine Industries Which Will Put an End to China's Anti-Dumping and Anti-Subsidy Cases', Press Release, 21 March, available from: http://trade.ec.europa.eu/doclib/press/index.cfm?id=1048.

European Union (2013), 'Europe 2020', available from: http://ec.europa.eu/europe2020/europe-2020-in-a-nutshell/eu-tools-for-growth-and-jobs/index_en.htm (accessed 10 July 2013).

'EU to Restrict Foreign Access to Tenders' (2012), *EUObserver*, 21 March, available from: http://euobserver.com/news/115658 (accessed 20 September 2012).

'Failure to Win Contracts Is EU Companies' Fault' (2009), *EUObserver*, 19 September, available from: http://euobserver.com/china/28658 (accessed 20 September 2012).

Garcia, M. (2012), 'The European Union: "Transformative Power Europe" versus the Realities of Economic Interests', *Cambridge Review of International Affairs*, doi 10.1080/09557571.2011.647762 (read online first 29 May 2012).

Garcia, M. (2013), 'From Idealism to Realism? EU Preferential Trade Agreements', *Journal of Contemporary European Research*, **9** (3).

'Germany Will Stop Subsidising Solar in 2018' (2013), *Renewable Energy Magazine*, 10 July, available from: http://www.renewableenergymagazine.com/article/germany-will-stop-subsidising-solar-in-2018-20130710 (accessed 10 July 2013).

Global Telecoms Business (2012), 'Telefonica Picks Huawei for UK services', 24 May, available from: http://www.globaltelecomsbusiness.com/Article/3035255/Sectors/25198/Telefnica-O2-picks-Huawei-for-UK-services.html (accessed 6 June 2013).

Goossens, E. (2012), 'The Downside of China's Clean Energy Push', *Businessweek*, 21 November, available from: http://www.businessweek.com/articles/2012-11-21/the-down side-of-chinas-clean-energy-push (accessed 20 May 2013).

Gumbel, P. (2013), 'Guess Who's Bullish on Europe? China's New Investment Play', *Business Time*, 3 June, available at http://business.time.com/2013/06/03/europ-new-wave-chinese-acquisitions/#ixzz2WaQqmkFy (accessed 10 July 2013).

Hanemann, T. and D. Rosen (2012), 'China Invests in Europe: Patterns, Impacts and Policy Implications', Rhodium Group, available from: http://rhg.com/wp-content/uploads/2012/06/RHG_ChinaInvestsInEurope_June2012.pdf (accessed 25 July 2013).

Hollersen, W. (2013), 'Chasing the Sun: German and Chinese Solar Firms Battle for Survival', *Der Spiegel*, available from: http://www.spiegel.de/international/business/german-and-chinese-solar-firms-fight-for-survival-a-835367.html (accessed 20 July 2013).

Holslag, J. (2011), 'The Elusive Axis: Assessing the EU–China Strategic Partnership', *Journal of Common Market Studies*, **49** (2), 293–313.

Hu, R. (2012), 'A Bright Future for China's Solar Power Industry', *Clean Energy Perspectives*, **5**, 2–3.

Hufbauer, G., Y. Wong and K. Sheth (2006), *US–China Trade Disputes: Rising Tide, Rising Stakes*, Washington, DC: Institute for International Economics.

Information Office of the State Council (2012), *China's Energy Policy 2012*, reproduced in full in English at: http://www.chinadaily.com.cn/cndy/2012-10/25/content_15844539.htm (accessed 20 May 2013).

Lamy, P. (2002), 'Stepping Stones or Stumbling Blocks: The EU's Approach towards the Problem of Multilateralism versus Regionalism in Trade Policy', *World Economy*, **25** (10), 1399–1413.

Lightfoot, S. and J. Burchell (2005), 'The European Union at the World Summit on Sustainable Development: Normative Power Europe in Action', *Journal of Common Market Studies*, **43** (1), 75–95.

'Majority of EU States Oppose Chinese Solar Panels Duties' (2013), *Telegraph*, 27 May, available from: http://www.telegraph.co.uk/finance/china-business/10082940/Majority-of-EU-states-oppose-Chinese-solar-panel-duties.html (accessed 25 July 2013).

Meunier, S. (2000), 'What Single Voice? European Institutions and EU–US Trade Negotiations', *International Organization*, **54** (1), 103–35.

Meunier, S. (2012), 'Political Impact of Chinese Foreign Direct Investment in the European Union on Transatlantic Relations', European Parliament Briefing Paper, available from: http://www.scholar.princeton.edu/smeunier/files/meunier_final.pdf (accessed 20 May 2013).

Meunier, S. and K. Nicolaidis (1999), 'Who Speaks for Europe? The Delegation of Trade Authority in the European Union', *Journal of Common Market Studies*, **37** (3), 477–501.

Meunier, S. and K. Nicolaidis (2006), 'The European Union as a Conflicted Trade Power', *Journal of European Public Policy*, **13** (6), 906–25.

Moller, J. and A. Kutkowski (2005), 'The EU Anti-Dumping Policy towards Russia and China: Product Quality and the Choice of an Analogue Country', *World Economy*, **28** (1), 103–36.

Naughton, B. (2007), *The Chinese Economy: Transitions and Growth*, Cambridge, MA: MIT Press.

Otero-Iglesias, M. (2013), 'The Euro and Global Economic Governance', in *Brussels–Beijing: Changing the Game*, Report No. 14, Paris: EU Institute for Security Studies, pp. 29–36.

ProSun (2013), available from: http://www.prosun.org (accessed 30 July 2013).

Reuters (2013a), 'EU Free Trade States Urge Quick Resolution of Chinese Solar Panel Dispute', 14 June, available from: http://www.reuters.com/article/2013/06/14/us-eu-china-trade-idUSBRE95D0FX20130614 (accessed 10 July 2013).

Reuters (2013b), 'In China, Fake European Wine More Worrying than Tariffs', 9 June, available from: http://www.reuters.com/article/2013/06/09/us-china-wine-fakes-idUSBRE 95801Q20130609 (accessed 10 June 2013).

Shi, D. (2010), 'China's Renewable Energy Development Targets and Implementation Effect Analysis', in M. Parivizi Amineh and R. Yang (eds), *Globalization of Energy: China and the European Union*, Leiden: Brill Academic Publishers, pp. 201–26.

Shu, M. (2010), 'Dealing with an Emerging Economic Power: The EU's Trade Policy towards China', paper presented at PSA 60th Annual Conference, Edinburgh, 30 March.

Smith, M. and H. Xie (2010), 'The European Union and China: The Logics of Strategic Partnership', *Journal of Contemporary European Research*, **6** (4).

'Suntech Pushed to Chinese Bankruptcy Court' (2013), *Wall Street Journal*, 20 March, available from: http://online.wsj.com/article/SB100014241278873245578045783720827338278 60.html (accessed 6 June 2013).

Taneja, P. (2010), 'China–Europe Relations: The Limits of Strategic Partnership', *International Politics*, **47** (3), 371–87.

'To Conquer Wind Power, China Writes the Rules' (2010), *New York Times*, 14 December, available from: http://www.nytimes.com/2010/12/15/business/global/15chinawind.html?ref=windpower&_r=0 (accessed 25 April 2014).

'Who's Afraid of Huawei?' (2012), *Economist*, 4 August, available from: http://www.economist.com/node/21559922 (accessed 25 April 2014).

Woolcock, S. (2007), *European Union Policy towards FTAs*, ECIPE Working Paper No. 3/2007, Brussels: ECIPE.

WTO (World Trade Organization) (2012), 'China Files Dispute against EU and Certain Member States', 5 November, http://www.wto.org/english/news_e/news12_e/ds452rfc_05nov12_e.htm (accessed 20 April 2013).

Young, A.R. and J. Peterson (2006), 'The EU and the New Trade Politics', *Journal of European Public Policy*, **13** (6), 795–814.

Zhang, Y., W. Han, X. Jing, G. Pu and C. Wang (2009), 'Development Strategies for Wind Power Industry in Jiangsu Province, China: Based on the Evaluation of Resource Capacity', *Energy Policy*, **37**, 2079–86.

PART IV

THE GLOBAL GOVERNANCE OF TRADE: WHO IS ACCOUNTABLE AND WHO GOVERNS?

15. Trade policy review and dispute settlement at the WTO
Marc D. Froese

The Trade Policy Review Mechanism (TPRM) was established at the GATT in 1989, and was one of the first substantive institution-building outcomes of the Uruguay Round of multilateral trade negotiations (Ostry 1997: 201). It is also one of the most significant examples of a workable transparency-enhancing mechanism in the realm of international economic law (Marceau and Hurley 2012). The Trade Policy Review Body offers multilateral oversight and Secretariat research and support that constitute trade policy review (TPR) at the WTO (Barton et al. 2006: 18–19). By the end of 2011, the TPRM had undertaken 256 individual reviews of members' trade policies, and had developed a process by which the world's largest traders receive the most scrutiny, with the four largest traders (the US, the EU, Japan, China) being reviewed every two years, the following 16 largest economies reviewed every four years and the remainder 137 undergoing review every six years.[1]

In the years immediately following implementation, a number of scholars examined the implications of the new mechanism for policy transparency among members of the GATT, and later the WTO (Qureshi 1990; Curzon Price 1991). Given the fact that much of this interest in the TPRM occurred before the WTO's Dispute Settlement Mechanism (DSM) was created, very little attention has been devoted to the study of policy review as its functions relate to the DSM (Chaisse and Chakraborty 2007).

This chapter tackles the thorny issue of predictability in transnational litigation patterns and attempts to answer the following three questions (Slaughter 2003).[2] If an issue is raised in trade policy review, is it likely to be subsequently challenged in dispute settlement? If so, is the issue likely to be raised by a regional trading partner, and is the respondent likely to lose the case? The first question is the most important in analytical terms, and the other two follow logically from it. Research has shown that dispute settlement is associated with trade volumes in two ways. First, members tend to trade within regions and members with high trade volumes tend to use dispute settlement processes more (Francois et al. 2008). Second, trading partners with intensive exchange patterns have more opportunity for trade irritants to arise, and are likely to possess the legal capacity to address them (Bown 2005). Consequently these countries use dispute settlement more often than partners with low trade volumes and sparse exchange patterns. This latter dynamic is clearly presented in the dispute settlement patterns of the largest traders, particularly the United States and the European Union (Leitner and Lester 2011). Even so, only a small amount of research examines dispute settlement in terms of the potential predictability of litigation patterns. So it is relevant to ask if the North American trading partners, with their high trading volumes and dense trade ties, are more likely than other members to pursue issues raised in TPRs through litigation at the WTO.

The chapter first examines the place of trade policy review in the larger institutional frame of the WTO. It reviews key pieces of the literature and then situates the TPRM in relation to the Dispute Settlement Mechanism. Trade monitoring is not intended to be integrated into the dispute settlement process. The information gathered is not grounds for a dispute, nor can it be considered evidence in the adjudication process. Clearly this chapter does not seek to argue that trade policy review is used by the membership as a first step in the dispute settlement process. Rather, it wonders whether policy review may be considered an opening round in a series of diplomatic and legal exchanges that may culminate in the Dispute Settlement Body (DSB)'s panel process. As a mechanism that attempts to simultaneously perform a surveillance function, which implies enforcement and stresses the obligations of members, and a transparency function, which implies voluntary compliance and the enlightened self-interest of states, trade monitoring is functionally related to the adjudication process in that both are integral to the resolution of trading frictions. The chapter then undertakes an empirical study of trade policy review in Canada, the US and Mexico, and attempts to answer the three questions posed above. Finally, the chapter places this study into a larger context, and draws a number of policy implications for member governments.

Within the political economy of international economic law, the questions of how to ensure adequate transparency at the national and international levels as well as how to define the role that surveillance plays in the successful functioning of governance institutions are timely and relevant. Over the coming decades, furthering the cause of transparency at the WTO will require that scholars develop a more systematic study of transparency, relating it not only to the processes of commercial arbitration, but also to the larger questions of state–market interaction, and the place of the WTO in the ongoing adjustment processes that constitute global economic integration (Kindleberger 1951; Rogers 2006).

TRADE POLICY REVIEW AT THE WTO

When the World Trade Organization was created on January 1, 1995, the TPRM was integrated as Annex 3 of the Marrakesh Agreement. It was designed to "contribute to improved adherence by all Members to rules, disciplines and commitments . . . by achieving greater transparency in, and understanding of, the trade policies and practices of Members."[3] The two primary functions of the General Council, which is the main governing body of the WTO, consisting of representatives from each member country, are to meet as the Dispute Settlement Body and the Trade Policy Review Body, and in each of these aspects to oversee the smooth functioning of the WTO Agreement and the Secretariat.

The TPRM's objectives are to provide a window on members' domestic policies, to analyze the impact of those policies on the multilateral trading system, to improve members' understanding of WTO rules and processes and thereby to contribute to a more transparent system for the regulation of international trade (Trebilcock and Howse 2005: 584–5). Importantly, the TPRM is not designed to impose new obligations on members, nor is it intended to be a starting point for dispute settlement. Secretariat reports tend to focus on the larger contours of members' trade policies, emphasizing liberalization gains made over time, and discussing issue areas in general terms rather than delving into the statistical study of trade liberalization, as other reporting organs do.

Most literature on the TPRM is more than a decade old, with scholarly interest peaking in the late 1990s (Laird 1999). The Dispute Settlement Mechanism, with its binding decisions, appellate body and high-stakes drama of litigious confrontation (not to mention the clash between national priorities and multilateral commitments), displaced much study of trade policy review. Given the general satisfaction with the overall functioning of the trade policy reviews, it is likely that the mechanism would have continued to operate below the radar of most scholars, except that the financial crisis of 2008 raised the specter of rising global protectionism, making policy review a higher priority once more (Howse 2002; Lamy 2010).

The scholarly literature on the TPRM attempts to come to terms with the dichotomous functions of trade policy review, which are surveillance to ensure ongoing compliance with rules, and transparency that builds the political legitimacy necessary for the trade liberalization process. The literature on the TPRM can be divided into three broad thematic streams. The first interrogates the mechanics of institutional success and deals with the ability of the WTO to make progress towards a more liberal trading order. This stream contains the literature primarily concerned with the factors that make the TPRM more or less successful. It critiques the institutional shape of the TPRM insofar as the literature aims to reform aspects of trade policy review that may contribute to suboptimal outcomes.

For example, Zahrnt (2009) advocates a mechanism "resolutely aimed at shaping domestic politics," which analyzes "the economy-wide costs of protectionism and [identifies] winners and losers on a sectoral basis." This is a perspective that is resolutely sanguine about the possibilities inherent in the multilateral trade project. Keesing (1998) is similarly oriented towards the development of a muscular multilateralism, but understands better the limits of an institutionalized liberalization project. He argues for a more detailed approach to trade policy review and suggests that a more successful TPRM needs, first, to improve the "quality and scope of the TPRs themselves," second, to allocate more resources to the review process and, third, to disseminate TPRs more widely in order to realize their full prescriptive potential (Keesing 1998: 49).

Prescriptions for increasing the quality of TPRs range from taking a longer-term, historical perspective to the analysis of a member's trade policy trajectory, to paying more attention to what Keesing calls "the bottom line," the actual cost to business of state policies and practices (Keesing 1998: 50). This literature is policy oriented and ultimately argues that better international institutions lead to better domestic trade policies. Thus the main strength and weakness of this approach are its essentially liberal and institutional optimism about the possibility of better rules to achieve more effective outcomes.

The second theme focuses on the role of transparency in developing a politically legitimate trading order. Daly notes that structural reform and unilateral trade liberalization are "greatly facilitated by high degree of domestic transparency," and in his study of TPRs in the Asia-Pacific region he singles out Australia for its commitment to maintaining a transparent trade policy environment (Daly 2011). Similarly, Valdes emphasizes the reciprocal nature of transparency at the national and international levels, and suggests that successful economic management includes trade liberalization, because openness at both the national and the international level is a basic requirement of global economic integration (Valdes 2010).

In this theme, transparency is defined as the availability of knowledge about institutional processes and a general awareness of the costs and benefits of current policies and practices (Rogers 2006: 1303–09). Spriggs argues for an International Transparency Institution that provides more information on trade policy than does the TPRM and operates outside the messy multilateral process of ensuring adherence to multilateral rules (Spriggs 1991: 176). He suggests that an institution dedicated to providing as much information about trade policy as possible, while operating outside the ongoing processes of multilateralism, would be able to cover three conventional aspects of trade practice: practices specifically allowed by GATT, practices tacitly allowed by GATT, and practices that contravene GATT rules. This may be termed a muscular, if somewhat distant, form of transparency in which surveillance is the purview of a public body that exists outside the processes of multilateralism and therefore operates at a remove from the complex political realm in which the WTO operates. Such a system of expanded oversight is one possible future for the Trade Policy Review Mechanism, but it would require a system of international economic law that is further developed than are the current institutions of global economic governance (Koskenniemmi 2006).

Such an institution could provide a significant service to the international economy, but it remains unclear whether removal from the processes of liberalization would improve the political legitimacy of policy prescription. Perhaps, as Mah (1997) suggests, the overall improvement of the TPRM will occur over time, as the process becomes more stable, and also through a simultaneous attempt to improve the mechanism so that, rather than generating information "only to gain greater adherence to the existing GATT rules," it can also produce information that is useful in the larger project of developing the international rule of law (Mah 1997: 56). Transparency, in this regard, ought to be part of a larger project to create a robust and legitimate system of law.

The final theme examines institutional surveillance and the disciplinary features of trade multilateralism. Qureshi (1990) locates the TPRM within the dichotomy between transparency and enforcement, in which transparency is defined as "the highest level of clarity and candour on the part of the contracting party under review," and enforcement implies compulsion or, more broadly considered, "measures designed to induce adherence to norms" (Qureshi 1990: 147). He concludes that, while the WTO is not a mechanism of enforcement in the compulsive sense, it may have unforeseen consequences for developing countries. Twenty years on this concern has not proven to be entirely substantial, but Qureshi's point about the subtle differences between the voluntary act of policy transparency and the inducements required for greater adherence is certainly salient.

Curzon Price notes the important internal policing function carried out by the TPRM, arguing that it facilitates "mutual surveillance" of members' trading policies (Curzon Price 1991: 227). She also suggests that the TPRM is at the forefront of a larger process by which the trade regime is increasingly pushing into the "protected domain" of sovereign states. This understanding of the TPRM as having a role in probing the consistency of domestic policy is significant to our understanding of the place of trade policy review vis-à-vis dispute settlement. Chaisse and

Chakraborty (2007) produced the first such study of trade policy review in the context of dispute settlement and concluded that the TPRM may be considered an enforcement mechanism. Even so, they are careful to note that "it intervenes before the dispute resolution, as an attempt to avoid any litigation with a combination of consultation and negotiation" (Chaisse and Chakraborty 2007: 179). This literature review has suggested that the TPRM operates at a far enough remove from other features of the WTO to be only indirectly related to their functions, but Chaisse and Chakraborty are perhaps correct to wonder about a closer functional relationship than is frequently assumed.

Together, these three themes in the literature speak to the larger issue of how to consider the TPRM's role in the global trading system. The WTO is a knowledge-driven institution and, because of the central role that information plays in negotiation and dispute settlement, the TPRM has grown in importance (Ostry 1997: 194). Even so, as the literature above suggests, there is an ongoing, if somewhat diffuse, debate about how to think about the TPRM's place in the global trading system. Does it lack the teeth necessary for proper enforcement of rules, has it been captured by the processes of multilateralism or, to arrange the questions differently, is it perhaps too narrowly focused on maintaining institutional buy-in, when it should be focused on supporting the larger goals of international economic law? In this debate the scholarship discussed above has noted substantial complications involved in the process of developing a system designed for both surveillance and transparency.

We may integrate these many strands of thought through a basic functionalist perspective on trade policy review. Functionalism has deep roots in the study of the politics of international law (Morgenthau 1940). As a broadly articulated approach to understanding the place of law amongst political actors, it is perhaps the dominant method for organizing the comparative empirical observation of legal institutions and conceptualizing the evolution of legal relations over time (Michaels 2006). Functionalist theory in law and the social sciences is based upon the ontological assumption that social organization, whether a society, body of law or international institution, can be viewed as an explicable system, "a collection of interdependent parts, with a tendency towards equilibrium" (Pribetic 2008: 5). Legal institutions that organize political relations exist because they serve a function and maintain (or at least exist at the nexus of) a political consensus that is necessary for their continued existence (Rittich 2005).

An empirical study of institutional function such as this one benefits greatly from the rigor of functional approaches in the social sciences. However, legal functionalism in its modern iterations has been criticized from a number of corners (Ehrenberg 2009). The main criticism of functionalism is that, even when it works well as a method for comparing legal systems and institutions, it "does not draw any normative consequences from it, for example about what future law should look like" (Husa and Smits 2011: 557). Even so, the strength of the functional approach lies in its basic orientation towards a multidisciplinary and empirical set of social scientific methods. In the social world the identification of patterns and the raising of questions about the extension of these patterns into the future require that political or legal research simultaneously asks and answers the formal question of "Why does this institution do what it does?" while raising the stakes with the functionalist question of "Why does this institution continue to do what it does?" or, to put it into even more basic terms, "Why does this institution continue to exist?" Importantly, functionalism does not often address the larger qualitative questions that confront global governance such as "Why this institution in this time and place?," although, even here, a strong argument has recently been made for broadening and deepening a functional approach to studying global governance (Dunoff and Trachtman 2009).

Legal functionalism has made significant strides towards describing and theorizing the place of postwar legal institutions in the global political economy (De Coninck 2009). In the context of international institutions for economic integration, we may assert, without putting too fine a point on it, that the form of international economic law is determined by institutional constraints, historical institutional development trajectories and the larger world of ideas and perceptions (Whytock 2009). Meanwhile the functions of international economic law are shaped by social need, economic interest and political contingency.

The Trade Policy Review Mechanism appears to be something of a hybrid institutional organ designed to fill a role that reflects both the trade regime's historical institutional development trajectory and the political contingencies of twenty-first-century trade politics, not the least of which is the ongoing specification of international economic law itself (Charnovitz 2011). The TPRM has a surveillance function, with an enforcement implication, and this is a factor in the negotiation of treaty obligations. It also maintains an important transparency function, which implies that voluntary compliance is necessary in the resolution of trade friction through dispute settlement. Both of these functions, surveillance and transparency, are essential to the TPRM's role as primary transmission point for information collected for and by members on national trade policies. The surveillance function stresses the responsibility of the institution to organize and maintain a multilateral vigilance against free riding, while the transparency function stresses the responsibility of the membership to maintain and make available information about national trade policies in the spirit of enlightened self-interest. In simplest terms, we may think of surveillance as being linked to the enforcement of treaty obligations and of transparency as being associated with the inducement to compliance with DSB decisions.

In political scientific terms, a functionalist understanding of the Trade Policy Review Mechanism is an intervention into the ongoing political economic debate about the possible outcomes for both state and non-state actors of the institutionalization processes currently under way at the global level (Keohane and Milner 1996). Institutionally oriented social scientists have shown that international institutions such as the WTO and the IFIs follow a relatively path-dependent trajectory with a certain leeway for evolutionary change that responds to the changing global economic and political environment (Pierson and Skocpol 2002). In this way rules shape international interaction, and the ongoing evolutionary development of multilateral institutions is posited to be somewhat predictable, insofar as any social pattern can be reliably predicted in a system lacking an overarching authority.

Realists and nationalists, on the other hand, argue that institutionalization processes are never certain, because the dynamics of state power are sure to influence institutional outcomes, not to mention the overall trajectory of institutional development (Mearsheimer 2003; Drache 2004). The author of this chapter is agnostic in this particular regard about the relationship between power and the larger trajectory of international institutionalization, but particularly interested in the intersection of institutionalist and realist modes of thought, where a close examination of processes at the international level reveals the complexity of causation in the ongoing development of international economic law (Winham 1992; Oliver 2009). In short, the tension between transparency and surveillance can be best understood in terms of the TPRM's relationship to other WTO functions, and, while much has been written on trade policy review in the context of multilateral negotiation, little has been written about its relationship to dispute settlement.

How should scholars of global governance and trade think about the TPRM? Is it a part of the negotiation process, or a part of the dispute settlement process? Is it a part of both and, if so, does it carry out similar roles in each? The following empirical study suggests that the best argument for a functionalist perspective on trade policy review is that it highlights the subtle differences in the way scholars think about transparency and surveillance goals and outcomes. Examining dispute settlement alongside trade policy review suggests that the TPRM can and ought to be considered as a central feature of the knowledge-gathering process that underpins trade liberalization, but students of global trade must be

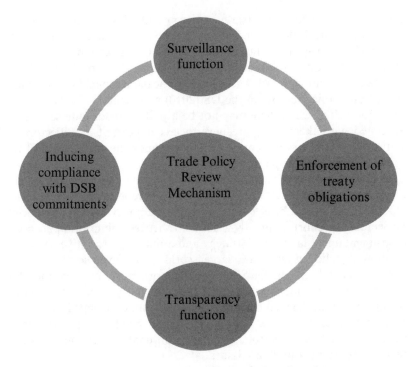

Figure 15.1   A basic functionalist conception of trade policy review

circumspect when linking the TPRM's processes to dispute settlement. Perhaps, in the final balance, conceptualizing the TPRM between transparency and surveillance requires that we locate its functional role outside both negotiation and dispute settlement (see Figure 15.1).

TRADE POLICY REVIEW AND DISPUTE SETTLEMENT

The Trade Policy Review Mechanism has been conceptualized as a body for enhancing multilateral transparency that encourages access to information and voluntary compliance with dispute settlement and as an institution for surveillance that attempts to induce compliance with treaty obligations. A functionalist analysis locates the TPRM's role in the larger trade regime between these functions, and over the past two decades it has evolved to become a central feature of the WTO system.

This section examines 16 reviews of the trade policies of Canada (six reviews), the United States (seven reviews) and Mexico (three reviews). Even though the TPRM came online in 1989, the dataset includes only trade policy reviews undertaken after the WTO Agreement entered into force in 1995 in order to obtain an accurate depiction of trade irritants as they stand in relation to WTO governance. The data also includes the most recent trade policy reviews in the US (2010) and Canada (2011) with the expectation that, while there may not be a pattern of dispute settlement associated with them, they are nevertheless important as reflectors of contemporary trade policy concerns and bear upon the implications of the study set out in the "Implications" section.

Trade policy reviews have been criticized for their generalist approach to policy review, and certainly the government reports tend to be less a self-study and more a brief overview of general policy directions. Indeed, the Secretariat report frequently walks a line between description of recent governmental legislation and strategy and a mildly prescriptive contextualization of policy in relation to larger world events. Even so, the package of governmental reports, the Secretariat's report, the minutes of the TPR meetings, and each member's written questions fairly accurately pinpoint the big issues that the membership is concerned about, from Mexican contingency measures and internal regulation, to Canadian supply management and investment controls, and American contingency measures and dispute settlement compliance issues.

The process of trade policy review became more streamlined as the 1990s progressed, but documentation also became more voluminous and complex. There is a general template for laying out information in the Secretariat report and minutes of the meeting, but overall clarity of issues raised by the membership varies by country, with some members preferring a point-by-point discussion of trade issues in their verbal comments, while others prefer to refer to their trading relationship to the member under review in more general terms. Likewise written questions range from the general to the specific, and from the laudatory to the critical. Even so, given the number of members participating, a fairly comprehensive list of trading issues emerges from the available documentation. The reader should note that this study identifies only trade issues that may be potentially litigated at the WTO, and does not consider barriers that are associated with continuing negotiation at the General Agreement on Trade in Services (GATS) such as the regulation of professions and the movement of natural persons.[4]

It is likely to be impossible to empirically measure the success of the TPRM in terms of its role in enforcing treaty obligations, or in terms of the overall inducement of compliance with dispute settlement obligations – at least at this point in time, given the current data. But it is possible to gain some empirical sense of the relationship of the TPRM to the WTO's juridical processes. In particular, this section will answer the following three questions. First, if a trade issue is raised in trade policy review at the WTO, is it likely to be subsequently challenged in dispute settlement? In order to answer this question, we will examine the number of trade issues raised in Secretariat reports and the minutes of meetings of trade policy reviews and then look at the number of complaints received by Canada, the US and Mexico following each policy review process. Second, are the issues discussed in trade policy review likely to be challenged by a regional trading partner? Finally, is the respondent likely to lose the case? Taken together, these three questions move forward our discussion of the role of the TPRM by giving a more complete picture of how the chronology of cyclical policy review interacts with the WTO's juridical mechanisms.

Question 1: If a Trade Issue Is Raised in Trade Policy Review at the WTO, Is It Likely to Be Subsequently Challenged in Dispute Settlement?

In order to answer this question we need to discover how many issues are raised at the TPRB, and look at how many complaints each country receives following each trade policy review. Finally, we need to divide the number of disputes by the average number of issues raised to get some sense of the correlation between disputes and trade issues.

1A: How many trade issues are raised in the Secretariat reports and minutes of the meetings of each TPR for Canada, the US and Mexico?
In analyzing the 16 TPRs for North American members, the main trade issues raised in the Secretariat reports and minutes of the meetings are isolated. Written questions and responses are not included, because there are dozens of small issues raised, a vast majority of which are simply requests for information about the specifics of legislation and policy. They may represent real barriers to trade, or they may represent other interests on the part of the questioning government. However, the substantive issues raised by the Secretariat and the issues raised by members orally represent issues that are widely considered to be of interest both to regional trading partners and to the larger membership of the WTO system.

Figure 15.2 shows how many issues were raised across the three national jurisdictions in TPRs generated between 1996 and 2011. Only TPRs undertaken since the WTO came into being and policy review was made public online are included. An average of 22.5 trade issues are identified over all TPRs, with Mexico accounting for a higher average of 31.6, and Canada and the US accounting for an average of 20.8 and 20 issues respectively. Overall, Mexico's first two TPRs covered more issues than have the

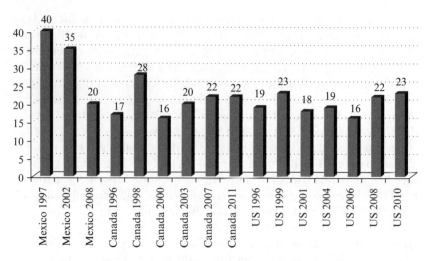

Source: WTO trade policy reviews: Mexico, Canada and the USA.

Figure 15.2   Number of issues raised in North American trade policy reviews

reviews of Canada and the US, which stands to reason given Mexico's recent history of market liberalization and the movement towards multi-party democracy (for a full breakdown of issues raised in policy review see the Appendix to this chapter).

1B: How many complaints does each country receive within the periods following each TPR grouped by category?

The Trade Policy Review Mechanism has a rough template it uses for the format of TPRs, but the issues raised, the terminology used and the order in which specific issues are discussed vary across TPRs. In order to better categorize trade issues for study, I have divided the issues discussed in trade policy reviews into six categories, and then grouped dispute settlement according to those categories. The standardized categories are as follows:

1.   tariffs and border measures – including customs procedures, customs valuation, numerous duties and quantitative restrictions;
2.   contingency measures – including antidumping duties, countervailing measures and safeguards;
3.   standards and technical regulations – including sanitary measures, technical barriers to trade, rules of origin, labeling requirements and environmental regulations;
4.   internal regulation – including business taxation, corporate govern-

ance, trade legislation such as the American Trade Act of 1974 and its Section 301 provisions, and national security measures affecting trade;
5. subsidies, competition and government procurement – including export and production subsidies, various forms of financial assistance to business, export promotion, local content requirements, state trading and monopolies, certain forms of export prohibition, measures relating to agri-food exports, export insurance and guarantees, and the regulation of government procurement;
6. measures relating to investment, trade in services and intellectual property rights enforcement – including the regulation of foreign investment, investment limits, the regulation of service provision, and the regulation and enforcement of intellectual property rights.

Table 15.1 shows the number of complaints received by each member in the period following trade policy review. Because not all complaints result in a panel, both the number of complaints and the number of resulting panels in each period are flagged. For example, the five-year period following Mexico's 1997 TPR saw six complaints notified to the DSM, of which just one resulted in a full panel process. The others were eventually suspended. Likewise, in the period after its 1996 TPR, the US received 30 complaints, covering the entire spectrum of trade issues, and 11 of those went all the way to panel.

An astute observer will note that the number of complaints declined over time, and that certain types of cases feature more prominently for each country (see Figure 15.3). One feature of its regulatory framework that Mexico shares with the US and Canada is a reliance upon contingency measures to protect domestic producers, and predictably they draw a significant plurality of all complaints. Mexico also drew complaints about its tariffs and border measures and its internal regulation, in particular certain tax measures. Canada received the most complaints about its subsidy regimes, competition policies and government procurement. This reflects the basic regulatory differences that exist side by side in the closely integrated markets of Canada and the US, and also reflects well-publicized trade wars involving agricultural goods and softwood lumber. The vast majority of complaints against US trade policy and practice involved antidumping measures. In fact a full 70 complaints in this period were directed against an array of American contingency measures.

1C: How many complaints come to the DSM and how many result in panels, compared to the number of issues raised in trade policy review?
The number of issues shown in Question 1A are taken and divided by the number of complaints and the number of panels to get a number

Table 15.1   Complaints sorted by trade policy review

TPR	Trade Policy Review Mechanism	Dispute Settlement Mechanism
	Trade issue	Case(s)
Mexico		
1997	Tariffs and border measures	1 complaint.
	Contingency measures	4 complaints – resulted in 1 panel.
	Standards and technical regulations	1 complaint.
2002	Tariffs and border measures	1 complaint.
	Contingency measures	4 complaints – resulted in 3 panels.
	Standards and technical regulations	1 complaint.
	Internal regulation	1 complaint – resulted in 1 panel.
2008	No complaints, no panels.	
Canada		
1996	Internal regulation	1 complaint – resulted in 1 panel.
	Subsidies, competition and government procurement	6 complaints – resulted in 3 panels.
	Measures relating to investment, services and intellectual property rights enforcement	2 complaints – resulted in 1 panel.
1998	Measures relating to investment, services and intellectual property rights enforcement	1 complaint – resulted in 1 panel.
2000	Subsidies, competition and government procurement	2 complaints – resulted in 2 panels.
2003	Contingency measures	1 complaint.
	Standards and technical regulations	1 complaint – resulted in 1 panel.
	Subsidies, competition and government procurement	1 complaint.
2007	Measures relating to investment, services and intellectual property rights enforcement	1 complaint – active case.
2011	Tariffs and border measures	1 complaint – active case.
US		
1996	Tariffs and border measures	6 complaints – resulted in 3 panels.
	Contingency measures	11 complaints – resulted in 3 panels.
	Standards and technical regulations	6 complaints – resulted in 2 panels.

Table 15.1 (continued)

TPR	Trade Policy Review Mechanism	Dispute Settlement Mechanism
	Trade issue	Case(s)
	Internal regulation	3 complaints – resulted in 1 panel.
	Subsidies, competition and government procurement	3 complaints – resulted in 1 panel.
	Measures relating to investment, services and intellectual property rights enforcement	1 complaint – resulted in 1 panel.
1999	Contingency measures	17 complaints – resulted in 11 panels.
	Internal regulation	2 complaints – resulted in 1 panel.
	Subsidies, competition and government procurement	1 complaint.
	Measures relating to investment, services and intellectual property rights enforcement	3 complaints – resulted in 1 panel.
2001	Contingency measures	20 complaints – resulted in 9 panels.
	Standards and technical regulations	1 complaint – resulted in 1 panel.
	Internal regulation	1 complaint.
	Subsidies, competition and government procurement	1 complaint – resulted in 1 panel.
2004	Contingency measures	10 complaints – resulted in 5 panels.
	Standards and technical regulations	1 complaint – resulted in 1 panel.
	Subsidies, competition and government procurement	1 complaint.
2006	Contingency measures	3 complaints – resulted in 1 panel.
	Subsidies, competition and government procurement	3 complaints – resulted in 1 panel.
2008	Contingency measures	6 complaints – resulted in 6 panels.
	Standards and technical regulations	5 complaints – resulted in 4 panels.
2010	Contingency measures	3 complaints – active cases.

Source: WTO Dispute Settlement Database.

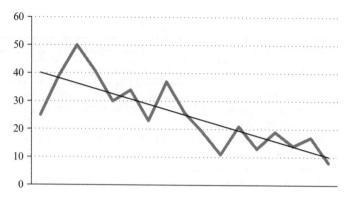

Source: Worldtradelaw.net statistical database.

Figure 15.3   The decline of complaints at the WTO, 1995–2011

that gives some sense of the relationship between trade policy review and dispute settlement (see Table 15.2). There are three facts to note. First, the number of complaints notified to the DSB per issue raised in trade policy review is very low. Second, relatively few complaints reach the panel stage. This fact holds true for all three countries, although the US saw more complaints reach the panel process by far. In 1996, a high-water mark for complaints directed against the US, there were about 1.6 complaints for every issue raised by the TPR. This does not represent complaints made in all issue areas, across the board, but rather suggests that certain significant issue areas, most notably contingency measures, attracted a great number of complaints, as shown in Table 15.1. Third, the number of complaints expressed as a proportion of trade issues raised and number of panels expressed as a proportion of trade issues tended to decline over time. In fact, the decline is very significant and reflects the overall decline in number of complaints brought to the DSM.

In summary, answering the first question–If a trade issue is raised in trade policy review at the WTO, is it likely to be subsequently challenged in dispute settlement?–required three sets of facts: the number of trade issues identified in TPRs, the number of complaints received by each member in the period following each TPR, and the number of complaints received per issue area. I also noted the general downward trend in complaints. Most issues raised in policy review are not subsequently brought to dispute settlement. Even so, it appears that the rather general concerns highlighted by trade policy review, as we discussed above, are fairly good predictors of the sorts of disputes brought to the Dispute Settlement Body. For example, many of the concerns discussed in American TPRs involved

Table 15.2   *Complaints and panels divided by number of issues raised in*
             TPRs

TPR	Issues raised	Complaints	Complaints / issues	Panels	Panels / issues
Mexico					
1997	40	6	0.15	1	0.025
2002	35	7	0.2	4	0.11
2008	20	0	0	0	0
Canada					
1996	17	9	0.53	5	0.29
1998	28	1	0.04	1	0.04
2000	16	2	0.13	2	0.13
2003	20	3	0.15	1	0.05
2007	22	1	0.05	active	n/a
2011	22	1	0.05	active	n/a
US					
1996	19	30	1.58	11	0.58
1999	23	23	1	13	0.57
2001	18	23	1.28	11	0.61
2004	19	12	0.63	6	0.32
2006	16	6	0.38	2	0.13
2008	22	11	0.5	10	0.45
2010	23	3	0.13	active	n/a

contingency measures, and predictably these are the complaints that most frequently came to the panel process. And now we move to issues raised by regional trading partners and the probability of losing a challenge brought to the Dispute Settlement Body.

Question 2:   Is the Issue Likely to Be Raised by a Regional Trading Partner?

The regional partners in the NAFTA context account for somewhere between 20 and 40 percent of complaints. It is particularly telling that, in the case of the junior partners, all regional complaints came from the United States. In the case of the US, the other large trading bloc, the European Union, accounted for 32 complaints, or 28 percent of the total, reaffirming research that points to a relationship between trading volumes and the use of dispute settlement, particularly in the case of the world's largest traders. Nevertheless, usage of the DSM does not track precisely with trading volumes; it is more of a loose association. The

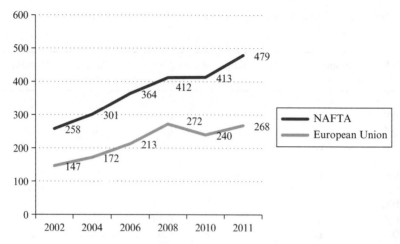

Note: Exports in billions of US dollars.

Source: US Census Bureau; USA Trade Data Online Database; NAICS Commodities.

Figure 15.4   US exports to the NAFTA partners and to the EU

NAFTA partners have, for quite some time, accounted for a larger value of American exports than does Europe, as Figure 15.4 shows.

Mexico has received 13 complaints, six of which came from a regional trading partner. In this case, all regional complaints, which account for 46 percent of the total, came from the United States. Canada has received 17 complaints in total, with five, or 29 percent, coming from a regional partner. In this case again all came from the US. The United States has received 113 complaints, and 24, or 21 percent, have come from a regional trading partner. Of those 24 complaints, 15 originated in Canada, and nine came from Mexico (see Figure 15.5). Overall, regional partners account for approximately 25 percent of complaints.

Question 3:   Is the Respondent Likely to Lose at Panel?

The final issue, of whether the respondent is likely to lose the case, deals with a concept that is difficult to quantify in the context of the WTO because cases are complex and frequently require multiple findings that may simultaneously validate and invalidate certain state practices. Therefore a typology of dispute settlement success is necessary in the context of North American states defending existing practice in the shadow of recent policy review:

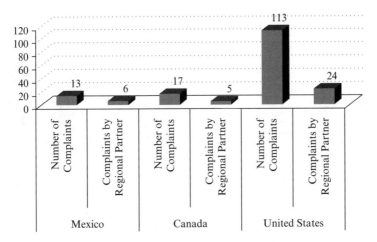

Source: Worldtradelaw.net Statistical Database.

Figure 15.5   Complaints, global and regional

1. Win: The panel and/or appellate body upholds all or almost entirely all of the measures challenged by the complainant.
2. Partial win: The panel and/or appellate body upholds a majority of the respondent's trade measures in question, but also uncovers inconsistencies between state practice and the relevant agreement(s).
3. Partial loss: The panel and/or appellate body disallows a majority of the policy or legislative measures in question, but also confirms certain aspects of the respondent's policies and/or legal reasoning.
4. Loss: The panel and/or appellate body strikes down all or almost entirely all of the respondent's policy measure and/or practice in question.

3A: What percentage of complaints that go to panel are loss/partial loss and win/partial win?

A vast majority of complaints that make it to the panel process result in a win for the complainant, or at least what passes for a win in dispute settlement, in that the panel disallows a majority of the policy measures or practices at issue. The panel process does not use the language of national court systems in which a case can be won or lost per se, but rather speaks in terms of particular policies and laws that are challenged in the context of a member's treaty obligations (Steger 2004: 121–52). Of Mexico's five panels, all may be considered a loss for the Mexican state. Seven of Canada's nine panels are coded as a loss/partial loss. In relative terms,

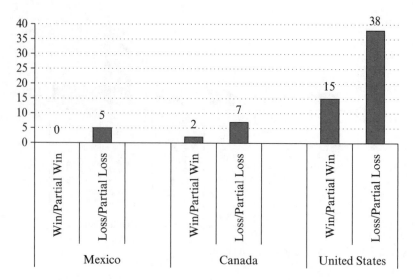

Source: Worldtradelaw.net Dispute Settlement Commentaries.

Figure 15.6   North American win/loss rate at panel

the US won more panels than Canada or Mexico, but still lost at panel a majority of the time, chalking up 38 loss/partial losses, to 15 partial win/ wins (see Figure 15.6). Overall, complainants won/partial-won against North American respondents approximately 75 percent of the time.

3B: What percentage of cases brought by regional partners are loss/ partial loss and win/partial win?

This last question goes to the heart of the issue of WTO dispute settlement among regional partners. All five of the challenges brought against Mexican trade policies came from the US, and Mexico lost all of them. Turning to Canada, of the nine cases that went to panel during the period, four of them were brought by a North American trading partner (the US), and three were losses and one was a win. Canada arguably won DS 276 – Measures Relating to Exports of Wheat and Treatment of Imported Grain, because the panel upheld the main issue, Canada's use of the Canadian Wheat Board to market and sell the wheat of Western Canadian farmers. The US had argued that using a state trading enterprise (STE) to sell wheat abroad was a form of subsidy, because an STE does not operate on the basis of commercial considerations alone. The panel disagreed, suggesting that, as long as a state and its STEs obeyed the prime directive of non-discrimination, there was a place for state trading in the world trading system. However, the panel found Canada's treatment of imported American grain traveling by Canadian rail to be discriminatory, and disallowed portions of Canadian legislation in that regard (Froese 2010).

Finally turning to the United States, of the 53 panels, 11 were brought by a North American trading partner. Three cases were brought by Mexico, two cases (DS 217/234 and DS 384/386) were jointly brought by Canada and Mexico, and six were brought by Canada. Table 15.3 shows the American win/loss record as it pertains to North American dispute settlement. Of the four cases that the US won, two came from Canada, and two from Mexico. Three of these cases deal with American contingency measures (DS 194, DS 221 and DS 282), and one deals with American dolphin-safe labeling regulations for tuna. In the loss column, six of the seven cases brought by a regional trading partner challenge American contingency measures, and a vast majority of those (including DS 217/234 – the so-called Byrd Amendment challenge) are directly connected to the long-running softwood lumber trade war between the US and Canada.

In summary, issues raised by the TPRM are not very good predictors of future trade challenges, at least not in the sense that members raise individual issues that correlate closely with future complaints at the DSB. However, the TPRM is a good predictor of member sentiment, in the sense that issues that dominate TPRs tend also to be challenged at the DSM. The best examples are Canada's agri-food protections and American contingency measures. Of course, there are other issues that never get raised and become significant panels. The best examples are the two GATS cases, DS 204, Mexico – Measures Affecting Telecommunications Services, and DS 285, United States – Measures Affecting Cross-Border Supply of Gambling and Betting Services. The issues raised in these panels were never mentioned in their respective prior TPRs.

That leaves the issue of regionalism and trade policy review. Regional partners tend to challenge the big issues that pique member sentiment, from American challenges of Mexican contingency measures to American challenges of Canadian subsidy programs and Canadian/Mexican challenges of American antidumping processes. The data suggests that, at least in the context of North America, trading volumes may be as close a predictor of DSM usage as is the level of regional economic integration. The next section moves from these discussions of the place of the TPRM in the WTO system and its relationship to dispute settlement in order to examine the implications for the future of trade relations in the context of international economic law.

Table 15.3 *North American dispute settlement with the United States as the respondent*

Win/partial win		Loss/partial loss	
Case	Complainant	Case	Complainant
DS 194 US – Measures Treating Export Restraints as Subsidies	Canada	DS 217/234 US – Continued Dumping and Subsidy Offset Act of 2000	Canada and Mexico
DS 221 US – Section 129(c)(1) of the Uruguay Round Agreements Act	Canada	DS 236 US – Preliminary Determinations with Respect to Certain Softwood Lumber from Canada	Canada
DS 282 US – Antidumping Measures on Oil Country Tubular Goods from Mexico	Mexico	DS 257 US – Final Countervailing Duty Determination with Respect to Certain Softwood Lumber from Canada	Canada
DS 381 US – Measures Concerning the Importation, Marketing and Sale of Tuna and Tuna Products	Mexico	DS 264 US – Final Dumping Determination on Softwood Lumber from Canada	Canada
		DS 277 US – Investigation of the International Trade Commission in Softwood Lumber from Canada	Canada
		DS 344 US – Final Antidumping Measures on Stainless Steel from Mexico	Mexico
		DS 384/386 US – Certain Country of Origin Labeling (COOL) Requirements	Canada and Mexico

Source: Worldtradelaw.Net Dispute Settlement Database.

IMPLICATIONS

The preceding study offers theoretically informed and somewhat coun-terintuitive findings about the relationship between trade policy review and dispute settlement. Below are the three most significant implications for future policy analysis and scholarly study of the Trade Policy Review Mechanism as it relates to dispute settlement:

1. Partners with dense trade ties (particularly large trading nations) are usually active users of the DSM, but policy review is not necessarily a reliable predictor of dispute settlement trends.

    This chapter began with the hypothesis that issues raised in TPRs are subsequently challenged in dispute settlement by partners with dense trade ties. If this were the case, the data would have shown issues raised in TPRs challenged more often between Canada, the US and Mexico than those challenges brought by states outside the North American partnership. Instead the data shows that dispute settlement happens between partners with dense trade ties, which includes the trading partners in North America, but the TPRM does not neces-sarily predict dispute settlement. In fact the best relationship between issues raised in trade policy review and those challenged in dispute settlement involves those issues that may be termed headline issues – large irritants raised by multiple members and dominating the pro-ceedings. It is important to note that dispute settlement involving the measures at issue may already be under way at the time of the policy review. It may be more accurate to suggest that, in at least some of these instances, issues raised at the Trade Policy Review Body follow rather than lead dispute settlement.

2. Although there is not a dichotomous, tit-for-tat, pattern in which dispute settlement follows policy review, there are still substantive relational linkages that deserve study.

    Ultimately, the study above shows that the relationship between trade policy review and dispute settlement should not be read with the positive goal of prediction, despite the rather provocative hypothesis posed at the beginning of this chapter. Rather, the goal ought to be a more complete understanding of the functional connection between trade policy review and dispute settlement. The TPRM ought not to be considered as related only to the liberalization negotiation process and therefore somewhat remote from dispute settlement, nor ought it to be considered in the somewhat simple terms of a disciplinary func-tion, and therefore of lesser importance than dispute settlement itself, with its binding decisions and well-developed judicial processes.

In order to move beyond this dichotomy, the empirical study above takes a functionalist view of the Trade Policy Review Mechanism in which a multilateral transparency mechanism operates in the liminal space between transparency and surveillance, in which it simultaneously offers members greater access to information and an opportunity to meet treaty obligations. This functionalist view, in turn, elucidates Bagwell and Staiger's (2002) argument about the place of trade policy review and dispute settlement in the multilateral trading system. Following Maggi (1999), they suggest that the role of dispute settlement is to achieve the gains from "an aggregation of enforcement power" (Maggi 1999: 109). A key benefit of a multilateral trading system over a network of bilateral trade agreements, for example, is that it facilitates greater cooperation because enforcement becomes a multilateral affair. Similarly the TPRM plays a complementary role by gathering and disseminating information and monitoring compliance with the goal of greater multilateral cooperation.

3. Ultimately, scholars and policy makers ought to keep one eye on the evolving issue of transparency because, although the WTO has made strides forward, the future legitimacy of dispute settlement will likely hinge upon a greater willingness to open up more of the adjudication process to public scrutiny.

In terms of policy making, a wider focus shifts perspective away from the WTO's negotiation processes, thereby aligning our view of dispute settlement issues with an understanding of the TPRM's role in the larger goal of transparency in the trading system. Furthermore, it suggests that trade policy reviews ought to be studied with an eye to future dispute settlement issues, if only because the larger concerns raised at review are likely to end up in front of a panel, if they have not already at the time of review. Finally, it suggests that policy makers ought to consider transparency and surveillance as two sides of the same coin. Any transparency mechanism is worth only as much as states are willing to invest in complying with their treaty obligations.

The very fact that the study did not find a tit-for-tat relationship between policy review and dispute settlement likely means that the TPRM is functioning as it should, as an information-gathering transparency mechanism first, and as a reflector of trading irritants second. It is somewhat paradoxical that, when considered in the context of dispute settlement, the job of the Trade Policy Review Body becomes simultaneously more prominent and less amenable to easy characterization. Even so, its relative success is undisputed, and in December 2006 the General Council of the WTO adopted a second provisional transparency mechanism in order to clarify and strengthen notification obligations for regional trade agreements (Crawford 2007). If the TPRM were a disciplinary body, firmly oriented towards surveillance and therefore being more strongly associated with treaty enforcement, its reports and meetings would likely be more predictive of issues that arise in dispute settlement. However, as a consultative and information-transmitting mechanism it is oriented entirely towards neither surveillance nor transparency. To further complicate matters, it exists within a political matrix, in the complex terrain of trade multilateralism, and its role is to straddle, or exist between, two functions, and so its reviews are a somewhat poor predictor of trade issues bound for dispute settlement.

CONCLUSION

This chapter has suggested that trade policy review may be studied in the context of dispute settlement not because of unintended institutional consequences or because it is linked by bonds of law and politics to a disciplinary agenda per se, but because the Secretariat's report, the meeting of the TPRB and the written questions attempt to describe and discuss national policies that have been flagged by other members as problematic in the context of trade. Similarly, dispute settlement has been a concerted attempt to take trade irritants out of an anarchic international system where state power in its many forms determines outcomes, and place it in a transparent legal process that emphasizes the rule of law over the rule of wealth and power. The TPRB and the DSB are part of the same broad institutional process of trade liberalization in which irritants are identified, categorized, rendered visible through multilateral mechanisms and hopefully resolved through the application of international legal remedies agreed upon by all parties. As a result, trade policy review, however one reconciles its benefits and drawbacks, remains functionally essential to both the success of future negotiations and the ongoing effectiveness of the WTO's judicial processes.

NOTES

1. For a comprehensive overview of the institutional parameters of trade policy review, go to the WTO's dedicated site for trade monitoring at http://www.wto.org/english/tratop_e/tpr_e/tpr_e.htm.
2. In particular see Slaughter (2003: 191–3), where Slaughter notes that the term "transnational litigation" used to be used to describe litigation in national courts that dealt with

legal issues in more than one national jurisdiction. However, the term has evolved with what she terms the rise of a global community of courts, so that it now also denotes litigation by states and sometimes investors at supranational courts, such as the Dispute Settlement Body at the WTO.
3. WTO Agreement, Annex 3, para. A(i).
4. See the schedules of commitments and lists of exemptions to sectoral negotiations at the GATS at http://www.wto.org/english/tratop_e/serv_e/serv_commitments_e.htm.

REFERENCES

Bagwell, K. and R.W. Staiger (2002), *The Economics of the World Trading System*, Cambridge, MA: MIT Press.
Barton, J., J. Goldstein, T. Josling and R. Steinberg (2006), *The Evolution of the Trade Regime: Politics, Law, and the Economics of the GATT and the WTO*, Princeton, NJ: Princeton University Press.
Bown, C.P. (2005), "Participation in WTO Dispute Settlement: Complainants, Interested Parties and Free Riders," *World Bank Economic Review*, **19** (2), 287–310.
Chaisse, J. and D. Chakraborty (2007), "Implementing WTO Rules through Negotiations and Sanctions: The Role of Trade Policy Review Mechanism and Dispute Settlement System," *University of Pennsylvania Journal of International Economic Law*, **28** (1), 153–85.
Charnovitz, S. (2011), "What Is International Economic Law?," *Journal of International Economic Law*, **14** (1), 3–22.
Crawford, J.-A. (2007), "A New Transparency Mechanism for Regional Trade Agreements," *Singapore Yearbook of International Law*, **11**, 133–40.
Curzon Price, V. (1991), "GATT's New Trade Policy Review Mechanism," *World Economy*, **14** (2), 227–38.
Daly, M. (2011), *Evolution of Asia's Outward Looking Economic Policies: Some Lessons from Trade Policy Reviews*, World Trade Organization Economic Research and Statistics Division, Geneva: World Trade Organization.
De Coninck, J. (2009), "Overcoming the Mere Heuristic Aspirations of (Functional) Comparative Legal Research? An Exploration into the Possibilities and Limits of Behavioral Economics," *Global Jurist*, **9** (4).
Drache, D. (2004), *Borders Matter: Homeland Security and the Search for North America*, Black Point, NS: Fernwood Publishing.
Dunoff, J.L. and J.P. Trachtman (2009), "A Functional Approach to Global Constitutionalism," *Harvard Public Law Working Papers*, available from: http://ssrn.com/abstract=1311983 (accessed August 8, 2012).
Ehrenberg, K.M. (2009), "Defending the Possibility of a Neutral Functional Theory of Law," *Oxford Journal of Legal Studies*, **29** (1), 91–113.
Francois, J.F., H. Horn and N. Kaunitz (2008), *Trading Profiles and Developing Country Participation in the WTO Dispute Settlement System*, ICTSD Dispute Settlement and Legal Aspects of Trade, available from: http://ictsd.org/downloads/2009/02/trading_profiles.pdf (accessed April 16, 2014).
Froese, M.D. (2010), "Trade Friction, Dispute Settlement and Structural Adjustment, or Why Canada-Wheat Doesn't Matter in North American Trade Relations," *Estey Centre Journal of International Law and Trade Policy*, **11** (1), 46–66.
Howse, R. (2002), "From Politics to Technocracy – and Back Again: The Fate of the Multilateral Trading Regime," *American Journal of International Law*, **96** (1), 94–117.
Husa, J. and J. Smits (2011), "A Dialogue on Comparative Functionalism," *Maastricht Journal of European and Comparative Law*, **18**, 554–8.
Keesing, D.B. (1998), *Improving Trade Policy Reviews in the World Trade Organization*, Washington, DC: Institute for International Economics.

Keohane, R.O. and H.V. Milner (1996), *Internationalization and Domestic Politics*, New York: Cambridge University Press.

Kindleberger, C.P. (1951), "Group Behavior and International Trade," *Journal of Political Economy*, **59** (1), 30–46.

Koskenniemmi, M. (2006), *Fragmentation of International Law: Difficulties Arising from the Diversification and Expansion of International Law*, Report of the Study Group of the International Law Commission, Geneva: United Nations International Law Commission.

Laird, S. (1999), "The WTO's Trade Policy Review Mechanism – From Through the Looking Glass," *World Economy*, **22** (6), 741–64.

Lamy, P. (2010), *Report to the TPRB from the Director-General on Trade-Related Developments*, Geneva: World Trade Organization.

Leitner, K. and S. Lester (2011), "WTO Dispute Settlement 1995–2010: A Statistical Analysis," *Journal of International Economic Law*, **14** (1), 191–201.

Maggi, G. (1999), "The Role of Multilateral Institutions in International Trade Cooperation," *American Economic Review*, **89**, 190–214.

Mah, J.S. (1997), "Reflections on the Trade Policy Review Mechanism in the World Trade Organization," *Journal of World Trade*, **31** (5), 49–56.

Marceau, G. and M. Hurley (2012), "Transparency and Public Participation in the WTO: A Report Card on WTO Transparency Mechanisms," *Trade, Law and Development*, **4** (1), 19–44.

Mearsheimer, J.J. (2003), *The Tragedy of Great Power Politics*, New York: W.W. Norton & Company.

Michaels, R. (2006), "The Functional Method of Comparative Law," in M. Reimann and R. Zimmermann (eds.), *The Oxford Handbook of Comparative Law*, Oxford: Oxford University Press.

Morgenthau, H.J. (1940), "Positivism, Functionalism and International Law," *American Journal of International Law*, **34** (2), 260–84.

Oliver, M.J. (2009), "Economic History and International Political Economy," in M. Blyth (ed.), *Routledge Handbook of International Political Economy (IPE): IPE as a Global Conversation*, New York: Routledge.

Ostry, S. (1997), *The Post-Cold War Trading System: Who's on First?*, Chicago: University of Chicago Press.

Pierson, P. and T. Skocpol (2002), "Historical Institutionalism in Contemporary Political Science," in I. Katznelson and H.V. Milner (eds.), *Political Science: The State of the Discipline*, New York: W.W. Norton and Company, pp. 693–721.

Pribetic, A.I. (2008), "A Strategic Functional Approach to International Commercial Arbitration," *ICFAI Journal of Alternative Dispute Resolution*, **7** (2), 37–58.

Qureshi, A.H. (1990), "The New GATT Trade Policy Review Mechanism: An Exercise in Transparency or 'Enforcement'?," *Journal of World Trade*, **24** (3), 147–60.

Rittich, K. (2005), "Functionalism and Formalism: Their Latest Incarnations in Contemporary Development and Governance Debates," *University of Toronto Law Journal*, **55** (3), 853–68.

Rogers, C.A. (2006), "Transparency in International Commercial Arbitration," *University of Kansas Law Review*, **54** (5), 1301–38.

Slaughter, A.-M. (2003), "A Global Community of Courts," *Harvard International Law Journal*, **44** (1), 191–219.

Spriggs, J. (1991), "Towards an International Transparency Institution: Australian Style," *World Economy*, **14** (2), 165–80.

Steger, D.P. (2004), *Peace through Trade: Building the World Trade Organization*, London: Cameron May.

Trebilcock, M.J. and R. Howse (2005), *The Regulation of International Trade*, 3rd edn., London: Routledge.

Valdes, R. (2010), *Lessons from the First Two Decades of Trade Policy Reviews in the Americas*, Geneva: World Trade Organization Economic and Statistics Division.

Whytock, C.A. (2009), "Legal Origins, Functionalism and the Future of Comparative Law," *Brigham Young University Law Review*, **6**, 1879–1906.

Winham, Gilbert R. (1992), *The Evolution of International Trade Agreements*, Toronto: University of Toronto Press.

Zahrnt, V. (2009), *The WTO's Trade Policy Review Mechanism: How to Create Political Will for Liberalization?*, ECIPE Working Papers, Brussels: European Centre for International Political Economy.

APPENDIX

Table 15A.1 Trade policy review and dispute settlement in North America

TPR	Trade Policy Review Mechanism	Dispute Settlement Mechanism		
	Trade issue	Case(s)	Complainant	Win/loss for respondent
Mexico				
199V7	Tariffs and border measures	DS 53 Mexico – Customs Valuation of Imports	European Communities	Case suspended.
	Contingency measures	DS 101, 132 Mexico – Antidumping Investigation of High-Fructose Corn Syrup (HFCS) from the United States; DS 203 Mexico – Measures Affecting Trade in Live Swine; DS 216 Mexico – Provisional Antidumping Measure on Electric Transformers	DS 101, 132 – US; DS 203 – US; DS 216 – Brazil	DS 101, 132 – loss; DS 203 – case suspended; DS 216 – case suspended.
	Standards and technical regulations	DS 232 Mexico – Measures Affecting the Import of Matches	Chile	Case suspended.
	Internal regulation			
	Subsidies, competition and government procurement			
	Measures relating to investment, services and intellectual property rights enforcement			

377

Table 15A.1 (continued)

TPR	Trade Policy Review Mechanism	Dispute Settlement Mechanism		
	Trade issue	Case(s)	Complainant	Win/loss for respondent
2002	Tariffs and border measures	DS 298 Mexico – Certain Pricing Measures for Customs Valuation and Other Purposes	Guatemala	Case suspended.
	Contingency measures	DS 295 Mexico – Definitive Antidumping Measures on Beef and Rice; DS 314 Mexico – Provisional Countervailing Measures on Olive Oil from the European Communities; DS 331 Mexico – Antidumping Duties on Steel Pipes and Tubes from Guatemala; DS 341 Mexico – Definitive Countervailing Measures on Olive Oil from the European Communities	DS 295 – US; DS 314 – EC; DS 331 – Guatemala: DS 341 – EC	DS 295 – loss; DS 314 – case suspended; DS 331 – loss; DS 341 – loss.
		DS 284 Mexico – Certain Measures Preventing the Importation of Black Beans from Nicaragua	Nicaragua	Case suspended.
	Internal regulation	DS 308 Mexico – Taxes on Soft Drinks and Other Beverages	United States	Loss.
	Subsidies, competition and government procurement			

			United States	Loss.
		Measures relating to investment, services and intellectual property rights enforcement		
2008		Tariffs and border measures		
		Contingency measures		
		Standards and technical regulations		
		Internal regulation		
		Subsidies, competition and government procurement		
		Measures relating to investment, services and intellectual property rights enforcement		
Canada 1996		Tariffs and border measures		
		Contingency measures		
		Standards and technical regulations		
		Internal regulation	DS 31 Canada – Certain Measures Concerning Periodicals	United States	Loss.
		Subsidies, competition and government procurement	DS 70, 71 Canada – Measures Affecting the Export of Civilian Aircraft; DS 103, 113 Canada – Measures Affecting the Importation of Milk and the Exportation of Dairy Products; DS 139, 142 Canada – Certain Measures Affecting the Automotive Industry	DS 70, 71 – Brazil; DS 103, 113 – US, New Zealand; DS 139, 142 – Japan, EC	DS 70, 71 – loss; DS 103, 113 – loss; DS 139, 142 – loss.

TPR	Trade Policy Review Mechanism	Dispute Settlement Mechanism		
	Trade issue	Case(s)	Complainant	Win/loss for respondent
	Measures relating to investment, services and intellectual property rights enforcement	DS 114 Canada – Patent Protection of Pharmaceutical Products; DS 117 Canada – Measures Affecting Film Distribution Services	DS 114 – EC; DS 117 – EC	DS 114 – partial loss; DS 117 – case suspended.
1998	Tariffs and border measures			
	Contingency measures			
	Standards and technical regulations			
	Internal regulation			
	Subsidies, competition and government procurement			
	Measures relating to investment, services and intellectual property rights enforcement	DS 170 Canada – Term of Patent Protection	United States	Loss.
2000	Tariffs and border measures			
	Contingency measures			
	Standards and technical regulations			

Year	Subject matter	Case	Party	Outcome
	Internal regulation Subsidies, competition and government procurement	DS 222 Canada – Export Credits and Loan Guarantees for Regional Aircraft; DS 276 Canada – Measures Relating to Exports of Wheat and Treatment of Imported Grain	DS 222 – Brazil; DS 276 – US	DS 222 – loss; DS 276 – partial win.
	Measures relating to investment, services and intellectual property rights enforcement			
	Tariffs and border measures			
2003	Contingency measures	DS 338 Canada – Provisional Antidumping and Countervailing Duties on Grain Corn from the United States	United States	Case suspended.
	Standards and technical regulations	DS 321 Canada – Continued Suspension of Obligations in the EC – Hormones Dispute	European Communities	Partial win.
	Internal regulation Subsidies, competition and government procurement	DS 354 Canada – Tax Exemptions and Reductions for Wine and Beer	European Communities	Case suspended.
	Measures relating to investment, services and intellectual property rights enforcement			

Table 15A.1 (continued)

TPR	Trade Policy Review Mechanism	Dispute Settlement Mechanism		
	Trade issue	Case(s)	Complainant	Win/loss for respondent
2007	Tariffs and border measures			
	Contingency measures			
	Standards and technical regulations			
	Internal regulation			
	Subsidies, competition and government procurement			
	Measures relating to investment, services and intellectual property rights enforcement	DS 412 Canada – Certain Measures Affecting the Renewable Energy Generation Sector	Japan	Active case.
2011	Tariffs and border measures	DS 426 Canada – Measures Relating to the Feed-In Tariff Program	European Communities	Active case.
	Contingency measures			
	Standards and technical regulations			
	Internal regulation			
	Subsidies, competition and government procurement			

Measures relating to investment, services and intellectual property rights enforcement

US
1996

Tariffs and border measures	DS 24 United States – Restrictions on Imports of Cotton and Man-Made Fiber Underwear; DS 33 United States – Measures Affecting Imports of Woven Wool Shirts and Blouses; DS 39 United States – Tariff Increases on Products from the European Communities; DS 111 United States – Tariff Rate Quota for Imports of Groundnuts; DS 165 United States – Import Measures on Certain Products from the European Communities; DS 118 United States – Harbor Maintenance Tax	DS 24 – Costa Rica; DS 33 – India; DS 39 – EC; DS 111 – Argentina; DS 165 – EC; DS 118 – EC	DS 24 – loss; DS 33 – loss; DS 39 – case suspended; DS 111 – case suspended; DS 165 – loss; DS 118 – case suspended.
Contingency measures	DS 49 United States – Antidumping Investigation Regarding Imports of Fresh or Chilled Tomatoes from Mexico; DS 63 United States – Antidumping Measures on Imports of Solid Urea from the Former German Democratic Republic; DS 78 United States	DS 49 – Mexico; DS 63 – EC; DS 78 – Colombia; DS 89 – Korea; DS 97 – Chile; DS 99 – Korea; DS 136, 162 – EC; DS 138 – EC; DS 166 – EC; DS 167 – Canada	DS 49, 63, 78, 89, 97 – cases suspended; DS 99 – mutually agreed solution; DS 136, 162 – loss; DS 138 – partial loss; DS 166 – partial loss; DS 167 – case suspended.

Table 15A.1 (continued)

TPR	Trade Policy Review Mechanism	Dispute Settlement Mechanism		
	Trade issue	Case(s)	Complainant	Win/loss for respondent
		– Safeguard Measures against Imports of Broom Corn Brooms; DS 89 United States – Imposition of Antidumping Duties on Imports of Color Television Receivers from Korea; DS 97 United States – Countervailing Duty Investigation of Imports of Salmon from Chile; DS 99 United States – Antidumping Duty on Dynamic Random Access Memory Semiconductors of One Megabit or Above from Korea; DS 136, 162 United States – Antidumping Act of 1916; DS 138 United States – Imposition of Countervailing Duties on Certain Hot-Rolled Lead and Bismuth Carbon Steel Products Originating in the United Kingdom; DS 166 United States – Definitive Safeguard Measures on Imports of		

Standards and technical regulations	Wheat Gluten from the European Communities; DS 167 United States – Countervailing Duty Investigation with Respect to Live Cattle from Canada DS 85, 151 United States – Measures Affecting Textiles and Apparel Products; DS 2 United States – Standards for Reformulated and Conventional Gasoline; DS 100 United States – Measures Affecting Imports of Poultry Products; DS 144 United States – Certain Measures Affecting the Import of Cattle, Swine and Grain from Canada; DS 58 United States – Import Prohibition of Certain Shrimp and Shrimp Products	DS 85, 151 – EC; DS 2 – Venezuela; DS 100 – EC; DS 144 – Canada; DS 58 – India, Malaysia, Pakistan, Thailand	DS 85, 151 – cases suspended; DS 2 – loss; DS 100 – case suspended; DS 144 – case suspended; DS 58 – loss.
Internal regulation	DS 6 United States – Imposition of Import Duties on Automobiles from Japan under Sections 301 and 304 of the Trade Act of 1974; DS 38 United States – The Cuban Liberty and Democratic Solidarity Act; DS 152 United States – Sections 301–310 of the Trade Act of 1974	DS 6 – Japan; DS 38 – EC; DS 152 – EC	DS 6 – case suspended; DS 38 – case suspended; DS 152 – win.
Subsidies, competition and government procurement	DS 88, 95 United States – Measures Affecting Government Procurement; DS 108 United States	DS 88, 95 – EC, Japan; DS 108 – EC	DS 88, 95 – case suspended; DS 108 – loss.

Table 15A.1 (continued)

TPR	Trade Policy Review Mechanism	Dispute Settlement Mechanism		
	Trade issue	Case(s)	Complainant	Win/loss for respondent
	Measures relating to investment, services and intellectual property rights enforcement	– Tax Treatment for "Foreign Sales Corporations" DS 160 United States – Section 110(5) of the US Copyright Act	European Communities	Partial loss.
1999	Tariffs and border measures			
	Contingency measures	DS 177, 178 United States – Safeguard Measures on Imports of Fresh, Chilled or Frozen Lamb Meat from New Zealand and Australia; DS 179 United States – Antidumping Measures on Stainless Steel Plate in Coils and Stainless Steel Sheet and Strip from Korea; DS 184 United States – Antidumping Measures on Certain Hot-Rolled Steel Products from Japan; DS 192 United States	DS 177, 178 – New Zealand, Australia; DS 179 – Korea; DS 184 – Japan; DS 192 – Pakistan; DS 202 – Korea; DS 206 – India; DS 212 – EC; DS 213 – EC; DS 214 – EC; DS 217/234 – Australia, Brazil, Chile, EC, India, Indonesia, Japan, Korea, Thailand, Canada, Mexico; DS 218 – Brazil; DS 221 – Canada; DS 225 –	DS 177, 178 – loss; DS 179 – loss; DS 184 – loss; DS 192 – partial win; DS 202 – partial loss; DS 206 – partial win; DS 212 – partial loss; DS 213 – partial loss; DS 214 – case suspended; DS 217, 234 – loss; DS 218 – case suspended; DS 221 – win; DS

386

| Contingency measures | – Transitional Safeguard Measure on Combed Cotton Yarn from Pakistan; DS 202 United States – Definitive Safeguard Measures on Imports of Circular Welded Carbon Quality Line Pipe from Korea; DS 206 United States – Antidumping and Countervailing Measures on Steel Plate from India; DS 212 United States – Countervailing Measures Concerning Certain Products from the European Communities; DS 213 United States – Countervailing Duties on Certain Corrosion-Resistant Carbon Steel Flat Products from Germany; DS 214 United States – Definitive Safeguard Measures on Imports of Steel Wire Rod and Circular Welded Quality Line Pipe; DS 217/234 United States – Continued Dumping and Subsidy Offset Act of 2000; DS 218 United States – Countervailing Duties on Certain Carbon Steel Products from Brazil; DS 221 United States – Section 129(c)(1) of the Uruguay Round Agreements Act; DS 225 United | EC; DS 236 – Canada; DS 239 – Brazil | 225 – case suspended; DS 236 – loss; DS 239 – case suspended. |

Table 15A.1 (continued)

TPR	Trade Policy Review Mechanism	Dispute Settlement Mechanism		
	Trade issue	Case(s)	Complainant	Win/loss for respondent
	Contingency measures	States – Antidumping Duties on Seamless Pipe from Italy; DS 236 United States – Preliminary Determinations with Respect to Certain Softwood Lumber from Canada; DS 239 United States – Antidumping Duties on Silicon Metal from Brazil		
	Standards and technical regulations			
	Internal regulation	DS 194 United States – Measures Treating Export Restraints as Subsidies; DS 200 United States – Section 306 of the Trade Act of 1974 and Amendments Thereto	DS 194 – Canada; DS 200 – EC	DS 194 – win; DS 200 – case suspended.

Subsidies, competition and government procurement	DS 180 United States – Reclassification of Certain Sugar Syrups	Canada	Case suspended.
Measures relating to investment, services and intellectual property rights enforcement	DS 176 United States – Section 211 of the Omnibus Appropriations Act of 1998; DS 186 United States – Section 337 of the Tariff Act of 1930 and Amendments Thereto; DS 224 United States – US Patents Code	DS 176 – EC; DS 186 – EC; DS 224 – Brazil	DS 176 – partial win; DS 186 – case suspended; DS 224 – case suspended.
2001 Tariffs and border measures Contingency measures	DS 244 United States – Sunset Review of Antidumping Duties on Corrosion-Resistant Carbon Steel Flat Products from Japan; DS 247 United States – Provisional Antidumping Measure on Imports of Certain Softwood Lumber from Canada; DS 248, 249, 251, 252, 253, 254, 258, 259 United States – Definitive Safeguard Measures on Imports of Certain Steel Products; DS 257 United States – Final Countervailing Duty Determination with Respect to Certain Softwood Lumber from Canada; DS 264 United States – Final Dumping	DS 244 – Japan; DS 247 – Canada; DS 248 et al. – Brazil, China, EC, Japan, Korea, New Zealand, Norway, Switzerland; DS 257 – Canada; DS 264 – Canada; DS 268 – Argentina; DS 274 – Chinese Taipei; DS 277 – Canada; DS 280 – Mexico; DS 281 – Mexico; DS 282 – Mexico; DS 294 – EC; DS 296 – Korea	DS 244 – win; DS 247 – case suspended; DS 248 et al. – partial loss; DS 257 – partial loss; DS 264 – partial loss; DS 268 – loss; DS 274 – case suspended; DS 277 – loss; DS 280 – case suspended; DS 281 – case suspended; DS 282 – win; DS 294 – loss; DS 296 – win.

Table 15A.1 (continued)

TPR	Trade Policy Review Mechanism	Dispute Settlement Mechanism		
		Case(s)	Complainant	Win/loss for respondent
	Trade issue	Determination on Softwood Lumber from Canada; DS 268 United States – Sunset Reviews of Antidumping Measures on Oil Country Tubular Goods from Argentina; DS 274 United States – Definitive Safeguard Measures on Import of Certain Steel Products; DS 277 United States – Investigation of the International Trade Commission in Softwood Lumber from Canada; DS 280 United States – Countervailing Duties on Steel Plate from Mexico; DS 281 United States – Antidumping Measures on Cement from Mexico; DS 282 United States – Antidumping Measures on Oil Country Tubular Goods from Mexico; DS 294 United States – Laws, Regulations		

Year	Category	Case	Country	Result
		and Methodology for Calculating Dumping Margins ("Zeroing"); DS 296 United States – Countervailing Duty Investigation on Dynamic Random Access Memory Semiconductors (DRAMS) from Korea		
	Standards and technical regulations	DS 243 United States – Rules of Origin for Textiles and Apparel Products	India	Win.
	Internal regulation	DS 250 United States – Equalizing Excise Tax Imposed by Florida on Processed Orange and Grapefruit Products	Brazil	Case suspended.
	Subsidies, competition and government procurement	DS 267 United States – Subsidies on Upland Cotton	Brazil	Partial loss.
	Measures relating to investment, services and intellectual property rights enforcement			
	Tariffs and border measures			
2004	Contingency measures	DS 310 United States – Determination of the International Trade Commission in Hard Red Spring Wheat from Canada; DS 311 United States – Reviews of Countervailing Duty on Softwood	DS 310 – Canada; DS 311 – Canada; DS 319 – European Communities; DS 322 – Japan; DS 324 – Thailand; DS 325 – Mexico; DS 335 – Ecuador; DS	DS 310 – case suspended; DS 311 – case suspended; DS 319 – case suspended; DS 322 – loss; DS 324 – case suspended;

Table 15A.1 (continued)

TPR	Trade Policy Review Mechanism	Dispute Settlement Mechanism		
	Trade issue	Case(s)	Complainant	Win/loss for respondent
2004	Tariffs and border measures			
	Contingency measures	Lumber from Canada; DS 319 United States – Section 776 of the Tariff Act of 1930; DS 322 United States – Measures Relating to Zeroing and Sunset Reviews; DS 324 United States – Provisional Antidumping Measures on Shrimp from Thailand; DS 325 United States – Antidumping Determinations Regarding Stainless Steel from Mexico; DS 335 United States – Antidumping Measure on Shrimp from Ecuador; DS 343 United States – Measures Relating to Shrimp from Thailand; DS 344 United States – Final Antidumping Measures on Stainless Steel from Mexico; DS 345 United States – Customs Bond Directive	343 – Thailand; DS 344 – Mexico; DS 345 – India	DS 325 – case suspended; DS 335 – loss; DS 343 – loss; DS 344 – loss; DS 345 – loss.

Standards and technical regulations	for Merchandise Subject to Antidumping/Countervailing Duties DS 320 Canada/United States – Continued Suspension of Obligations in the EC – Hormones Dispute	European Communities	Partial win.
Internal regulation	DS 317 United States – Measures Affecting Trade in Large Civil Aircraft	European Communities	Case suspended.
Subsidies, competition and government procurement			
Measures relating to investment, services and intellectual property rights enforcement			
Tariffs and border measures			
2006 Contingency measures	DS 346 United States – Antidumping Administrative Review on Oil Country Tubular Goods from Argentina; DS 350 United States – Continued Existence and Application of Zeroing Methodology; DS 368 United States – Preliminary Antidumping and Countervailing Duty Determinations on Coated Free Sheet Paper from China	DS 346 – Argentina; DS 350 – European Communities; DS 368 – China	DS 346 – case suspended; DS 350 – loss; DS 368 – case suspended.

Table 15A.1 (continued)

TPR	Trade Policy Review Mechanism	Dispute Settlement Mechanism		
	Trade issue	Case(s)	Complainant	Win/loss for respondent
	Standards and technical regulations			
	Internal regulation			
	Subsidies, competition and government procurement	DS 353 United States – Measures Affecting Trade in Large Civil Aircraft (Second Complaint); DS 357 United States – Subsidies and Other Domestic Support for Corn and Other Agricultural Products; DS 365 United States – Domestic Support and Export Credit Guarantees for Agricultural Products	DS 353 – European Communities; DS 357 – Canada; DS 365 – Brazil	DS 353 – loss (awaiting appeal); DS 357 – case suspended; DS 365 – case suspended.
	Measures relating to investment, services and intellectual property rights enforcement			
	Tariffs and border measures			
2008	Contingency measures	DS 379 United States – Definitive Antidumping and Countervailing	DS 379 – China; DS 382 – Brazil; DS 383 – Thailand;	DS 379 – partial win; DS 382 – loss; DS

394

	Duties on Certain Products from China; DS 382 United States – Antidumping Administrative Reviews and Other Measures Related to Imports of Certain Orange Juice from Brazil; DS 383 United States – Antidumping Measures on Polyethylene Retail Carrier Bags from Thailand; DS 399 United States – Measures Affecting Imports of Certain Passenger Vehicle and Light Truck Tires from China; DS 402 United States – Use of zeroing in Antidumping Measures Involving Products from Korea; DS 404 United States – Antidumping Measures on Certain Shrimp from Vietnam	DS 399 – China; DS 402 – Korea; DS 404 – Vietnam	383 – loss; DS 399 – win; DS 402 – loss; DS 404 – loss.
Standards and technical regulations	DS 381 United States – Measures Concerning the Importation, Marketing and Sale of Tuna and Tuna Products; DS 384/386 United States – Certain Country of Origin Labeling (COOL) Requirements; DS 392 United States – Certain Measures Affecting Imports of Poultry from China; DS 406 United States – Measures Affecting the Production and Sale of Clove Cigarettes	DS 381 – Mexico; DS 384/386 – Canada, Mexico; DS 392 – China; DS 406 – Indonesia	DS 381 – win (awaiting appeal); DS 384, 386 – loss; DS 392 – loss; DS 406 – win (awaiting appeal).

Table 15.4.1 (continued)

TPR	Trade Policy Review Mechanism — Trade issue	Dispute Settlement Mechanism — Case(s)	Complainant	Win/loss for respondent
	Internal regulation			
	Subsidies, competition and government procurement			
	Measures relating to investment, services and intellectual property rights enforcement			
2010	Tariffs and border measures			
	Contingency measures	DS 420 United States – Antidumping Measures on Corrosion Resistant Carbon Steel Flat Products from Korea; DS 422 United States – Antidumping Measures on Certain Shrimp and Diamond Saw Blades from China; DS 424 United States –	DS 420 - Korea; DS 422 – China; DS 424 – EU	DS 420 – active; DS 422 – active; DS 424 – active.

Standards and technical
regulations
Internal regulation
Subsidies, competition
and government
procurement
Measures relating to
investment, services and
intellectual property
rights enforcement

Antidumping Measures on Imports
of Stainless Steel Sheet and Strip in
Coils from Italy

Source: WTO Dispute Settlement Database; Worldtradelaw.net Dispute Settlement Commentaries.

16. Looking back, looking forward: multilateral and regional trade governance
Wei Liang

INTRODUCTION

The World Trade Organization (WTO) is seen as one of the pillar institutions in global economic governance and aims to promote free trade globally. As it operates on a one-country-one-vote consensus basis, and has an effective dispute settlement mechanism, it has been viewed by many as the most legitimate and enforceable multilateral institution in global governance. However, today it has to deal with one big institutional challenge: its 160 member states are unable to reconcile their divergent interests in order to break the deadlock and conclude the 13-year-long Doha Development Round (DDR) negotiation. The stalled negotiation can be attributed to many factors, including the lack of political will of the key members, a decline of US leadership in multilateralism, the imbalanced agenda setting, the unexpected global financial crisis in 2008 and the following global recession. In addition, developing countries are frustrated by the apparent disengagement of the developed countries and in multilateralism their retreat to regional trade agreements (RTAs).

In the past decade, RTAs that deeply liberalize trade between two or more countries have proliferated. Almost all the members of the WTO are now members of at least one RTA. Mongolia, the only exception, is also proactively negotiating bilateral free trade agreements (FTAs) with Japan and China. The average African country belongs to four different agreements, and the average Latin America country belongs to seven agreements.[1] More negotiations are under way.

While research on the WTO and RTAs is not short on theoretical argument, there are still important gaps in understanding the domestic and international factors that have contributed to the policy preferences of the states toward the WTO and RTAs. What are the benefits and limitations of both multilateralism and regionalism? What are the changes in global commerce that have renewed the interest of developed and developing countries in RTAs? Is the relationship between the two more complementary or conflicting? What are the implications of RTA proliferation for the credibility and future development of global trade governance? What are the challenges of negotiating RTAs for the developing countries? This chapter aims to address these questions.

THE EVOLUTION OF THE MULTILATERAL TRADE REGIME: THE GATT YEARS

The post-World War II era witnessed the remarkable development of multilateralism, exemplified by the growth in the international trade system. Out of the ashes of a world economy torn by war and depression, the Great Depression, a world trading regime, the General Agreement on Tariffs and Trade (GATT), was created to promote world peace through trade liberalization and international cooperation. US secretary of State Cordell Hull reaffirmed his belief that international economic discord and competition rendered political cooperation improbable: "to me it seemed virtually impossible to develop friendly relations with other nations in the political sphere so long as we provoked their animosity in the economic sphere."[2] With the failed effort in creating the International Trade Organization (ITO), the GATT was the result of policy compromise of the key Western countries, primarily between the United States and the United Kingdom.[3] It created a few straightforward but important rules that have governed world trade ever since, including the most-favored-nation principle, reciprocity, non-discrimination, national treatment, special and differential treatment and single undertaking in multilateral negotiation.

During the GATT years, the trade regime was developed and evolved through eight rounds of multilateral trade liberalization negotiations. The GATT was established to promote trade negotiation in 1947, and following that the GATT sponsored multilateral negotiations in 1949 (Annecy), 1951 (Torquay), 1956 (Geneva), 1960–61 (the Dillon Round), 1963–67 (the Kennedy Round), 1973–79 (the Tokyo Round) and 1988–93 (the Uruguay Round). When the Western European countries had a slow recovery from war, their governments chose to maintain protectionist policies, inconvertible currency and capital control to insulate them from international competition. Hence, in the early years of the GATT, the US made many unilateral market access concessions. From the 1960s (the Kennedy Round), the focus of the multilateral negotiation turned to tariff reductions on industrial goods. It led to a bold cut of 35 percent in tariffs among all the participating countries. In the 1970s, in response to the chaos in the international monetary system and the export surge from West Germany, Japan and other Asian tigers, many members of the GATT began to increase the use of non-tariff barriers (NTBs). Hence addressing NTBs became the top priority of the Tokyo Round negotiation. The far-reaching agreement reached in the Tokyo Round included the six legal codes covering a range of NTBs, including customs valuation procedures, import licensing, technical standards for products, subsidies and countervailing duty measures, government procurement and anti-dumping duty procedures.

The most comprehensive negotiation during the GATT years was the Uruguay Round, which redefined the scope of the trade issues covered by the trade regime and further established new major trade rules to make the GATT compatible with the changing world economy. As a result, new issues such as services, investment and intellectual property were added to the negotiation agenda for the first time. Developing countries preferred to negotiate only old trade issues like tariff reduction, as they insisted that they were not sufficiently developed to make any concession on the new issues without causing devastating effects on their future development.[4] To compromise, developed countries agreed to make concessions on the issues that they had long tried to avoid, evidenced by the gradual elimination of the multi-fiber agreement for textiles and a substantial cut in agricultural tariffs and subsidies. For most of the GATT's history, developing countries played only a marginal role, with few concessions made and few gains received. The domination of the US and its Western allies in the GATT multilateral trade negotiation was challenged for the first time in the Uruguay Round.[5] Led by India and Brazil, developing countries were able to participate proactively in the negotiation and successfully gain in the areas of traditional trade that are crucial to their development, namely textiles and agriculture.

THE WTO IN ACTION: IS THE DOHA ROUND DEAD?

As part of the result of the successful conclusion of the Uruguay Round on December 15, 1993, the World Trade Organization was established to formally replace the less institutionalized GATT and less legalized GATT dispute settlement mechanism. It is well accepted that the more enforceable WTO dispute settlement mechanism has added teeth to this international organization that most others lack. The WTO not only expanded trade rules to cover many new trade-related issues, but also strengthened the scope, procedure and enforcement of dispute settlement in the WTO.

What accounted for the long-drawn-out negotiation of the Doha Round? First, it had a defect at the stage of agenda setting. One of the major tasks of the WTO is to continue the trade liberalization negotiation. The WTO moved quickly to carry out its mandate to sponsor a new round of negotiation. But the developing countries were generally hostile to the idea of including an ambitious list of trade-related issues beyond traditional border measures in the new round of negotiation. By appealing to the norm of sovereignty and development, developing countries rejected the proposal made by the developed countries to include the so-called Singapore issues[6], including investment policy, competition policy, labor standards and government procurement, at the Singapore ministerial meeting in 1996. Moreover, some developing countries faced serious domestic challenges and resistance in complying with the 1994 Uruguay Round agreements, particularly in the areas of intellectual property rights protection (TRIPS), trade-related investment measures (TRIMs) and food safety (SPS).[7]

The main purpose of the ministerial meeting in Seattle in 1999 was to launch a new multilateral round, the Millennium Round, in order to continue the effort of liberalizing trade and elaborating international rules. But the critics of the WTO in the US and around the world organized protests to oppose globalization and trade liberalization, including labor unions, environmentalists, students and consumer advocates. They gathered in downtown Seattle chanting "No new round, turn around."[8] They believed that the creation of the new trade regime had reinforced the trend of concentration of corporate control and had had a vast impact on many social institutions and programs, including public health, environmental protection, education, cultural issues and poverty alleviation. The Doha Round was thus launched nearly two years later in the city of Doha, Qatar in November 2001, as a display of global solidarity following September 11 attacks.[9]

However, the finalized negotiation agenda was considerably less favorable to the developed country advocates of the Doha Round, mostly the EU, the US and Japan, than the original proposal.[10] With the exclusion of some important Singapore issues from the negotiation agenda and with the expectation that, in negotiations on agriculture, the EU and Japan would be asked mostly to make difficult concessions, they became more suspicious and passive in the Doha Round negotiation. Indeed, one important calculation of agenda setting for multilateral negotiation is that a comprehensive package would permit exchanges of concessions across sectors, hence generating a win–win agreement with balanced terms for all members. Although the Doha Round negotiation was labeled the "Doha Development Round" (DDA), developed countries have not embraced this mandate whole-heartedly. The process of the negotiation was still dominated by self-interested calculation of national interest and domestic concerns.[11]

Second, the Doha Round of WTO negotiation has been notable for the more active participation and far greater use of coalitions by its developing country members than in earlier GATT rounds. During earlier rounds, the European Community and the US typically talked bilaterally first. When the G4 (the US, the EU, Canada and Japan) were able to reach a provisional settlement, they widened the process to encompass other parties.[12] Developing countries tended to assume a passive role in the negotiation by availing themselves of GATT's balance-of-payments and development exceptions.[13] Only a handful of large developing countries were active in the Uruguay Round, such as Brazil, India, Argentina, Colombia, Uruguay and Egypt. Since the collapse of the Soviet camp and the end of the Cold War, a large number of transition economies and developing countries joined the GATT/WTO. With the establishment of the WTO in 1995, 31 countries joined the organization through a formal accession process. Currently another 24 countries are negotiating entry into the organization.[14] The majority of WTO's new members are developing countries and transitional economies. For example, China acceded to the WTO in 2001, when the Doha talks were launched. Moreover, many developing countries that had long been GATT parties opened their markets in the 1990s. Their embrace of globalization made those developing countries more engaged in market access negotiations in the Doha Round talks. The near-universal membership of the WTO has also made policy preference convergence and negotiation position coordination a true challenge. Thanks to strategic coalitions such as the G20, G33, African Groups and Recently Acceded Members (RAMs), developing countries have been able to exercise greater influence in the Doha talks than in the previous multilateral rounds. Undeniably such coalitions have empowered developing countries in multilateral negotiations through collective effort, but they may also serve as a double-edged sword in global economic governance. Most of these developing countries' coalitions are focused on highlighting the established "North–South" or "developing–developed" divisions, which has contributed to the widening of the gap between developed and developing countries' positions and thus made the conclusion of the Doha talks more difficult.

Third, the WTO is a rule-based institution, and it has some fundamental negotiation principles, which have increasingly been questioned by some WTO members as barriers to reaching a Doha agreement. The WTO is consensus based, so the negotiated commitments and disciplines need to be accepted and implemented by all parties. As WTO members have to accept this type of all-or-nothing agreement, a single undertaking is critical. The principle of single undertaking, "nothing is agreed until everything is agreed," was enunciated in the Punta del Este Declaration of 1986. This principle was introduced to protect the interests of less powerful members in the WTO in order to ensure that they would reach a win–win agreement by gaining ground on the issues they care about when they make concessions to more powerful states. Though the WTO is not as efficient or democratic as desired, the principles of consensus and single undertaking help to protect the interests of the developing member states.[15] But some other analysts and practitioners believe that this critical aspect of global governance has undermined the efficiency of the multilateral trade negotiation and partially contributed to the failure of reaching the Doha agreement despite the fact that WTO members have reached consensus on over 80 percent of the issues under negotiation.[16] The round covers 20 topics, from agriculture, industrial goods market access, services and environmental goods and services to food aid, fishery subsidies and trade facilitations. For instance, although WTO members have already reached consensus on trade facilitation, and a potential agreement on that will benefit all, especially the developing states, member countries could not agree upon this "stand-alone" item.

The ninth WTO ministerial meeting, held in Bali, Indonesia on December 3–6, 2013, made an important breakthrough in this long-lasting principle of single undertaking. The 160 trade ministers, after five days of intense negotiations, finally agreed to sign off an unprecedented "early harvest" trade deal. The Bali package adopted decisions on the ten texts regarding the three pillars of the Bali package: trade facilitation, some agricultural issues, and select development-focused provisions.[17] This small step is seen as an effort made by all parties to revive the Doha talks.

Fourth, the rise of emerging economies, in particular Brazil, India, China and South Africa (BICS), and their coalitions in trade negotiations have altered the power balance in the WTO. This new trend of multipolarity thwarted the enthusiasm of some developed countries toward multilateralism. BICS countries gained this new importance in global trade governance not because of the fact that they account for 42 percent of the world population and 18 percent of world GDP, but because they have the potential to develop faster than the relatively stagnant developed countries. This has become even more prominent since the 2008 financial crisis, when most developed countries suffered from severe economic recession. BICS countries suffered far less than any other major economies and gradually became the engine of global economic recovery. According to the IMF, China alone contributed to 37.4 percent of world GDP growth in 2012, while the US's share was 10.2 percent.[18] With the rapid economic growth of these emerging economies, they have gained a new competitiveness in global commerce. China now accounts for almost half of America's total trade deficit, up from less than one-third in 2008.[19] Moreover, rising income in these countries also made them the fastest-growing markets for the developed countries, which explains why the developed countries care more about their market access to these emerging economies than in the earlier rounds. The former chief negotiator of the US, Susan Schwab, explicitly pointed out that the big problem of Doha was that developed countries made clear concessions, but their market access gains from the BICS countries were unclear.[20] Some analysts argued that it was the fear of competition from a dominant China that inhibited progress of the Doha negotiation.[21] Hence, developed and BICS countries disagree on the balance of rights and responsibilities that emerging economies should carry in the Doha negotiation. For the US and other developed countries, WTO rules should be made stricter and emerging economies should not receive any special treatment.[22] The emerging economies argue that their average GDP per capita is still low and their development should be supported by the developed members in the WTO.[23] From the perspective of global governance, the greater participation and influence of the BICS countries will make the institution more democratic and transparent. However, it has also brought efficiency issues. At the current stage, Brazil, China and India are influential enough to be invited to the "green room negotiation," which is composed of a core group of WTO members to coordinate their policy positions before substantial progress can be made among the larger group of members. In a consensus-based institution such as the WTO, they can become the de facto "blocker" of any agreement. But they have not had the economic power and political influence to effectively persuade the developed countries to accept the proposals they suggested.

RISING REGIONALISM AND RTAS

There has been a surge of RTAs since the 1990s, and many have been concluded recently. As of July 30, 2013, some 575 notifications of RTAs, counting goods, services and accessions separately, had been received by the GATT/WTO. Of these, 379 were in force. Of these RTAs, free trade agreements (FTAs) and partial scope agreements account for 90 percent, while customs unions account for 10 percent.[24] During this wave of regionalism, it is no longer mainly the EU and the US negotiating with neighboring countries, as every country is negotiating RTAs, including many developing countries. In Asia, the number of completed FTAs increased from 3 to 76 between 2000 and April 2013, and more are under negotiation.[25]

What are the drivers for RTAs? First, it is relatively easier to reach RTA agreement than multilateral agreement, as only two or a few like-minded states are involved. When a country is getting impatient with the slow progress of multilateral negotiation, it will turn to regional agreements to obtain reciprocal trade liberalization commitments. This is best illustrated by the fact that interest in regionalism increased in the 1980s and early 1990s,[26] as the prospect for a successful conclusion of the Uruguay Round seemed unpromising. Over the last decade, even more RTAs came into effect, while the Uruguay Round and the Doha Round made very slow progress. Second, a domino effect has driven non-member countries to join the existing RTAs or create their own. When a country's major trading partners form trade blocs, it creates pressure on others to follow owing to the cost of exclusion.[27] For example, in order to restore the competitiveness of its business abroad, which had deteriorated as a result of the trade and investment diversion caused by the NAFTA and the Mexico–EU Free Trade Agreement, Japan chose to negotiate its own FTA with Mexico.[28] In this way, Japanese firms can enjoy comparable market access conditions in Mexico to their main competitors, such as American and European firms. Third, RTAs can easily be adopted as a foreign policy tool to promote trade and investment between a country and its strategic partners. The political and security imperatives are pushing states to cooperate more economically and to form closer economic partnerships, illustrated by the recently concluded China–Taiwan FTA and US–South Korea FTA and the ongoing FTA negotiations such as the Trans-Pacific Partnership (TPP) and the US–EU Transatlantic Trade and Investment Partnership (TTIP) negotiation.

Compared with multilateralism, RTAs often can achieve deeper trade liberalization and economic integration among the member states. GATT Article XXIV.8 provides that the duties and other restrictive regulations of commerce are eliminated on "substantially all the trade" between the members of regional trade agreements. In general, the liberalization ratio[29] of FTAs between two developed countries (North–North) or between a developed and a developing country (North–South) is much higher than that of FTAs between two developing countries (South–South). Developed countries have established comprehensive templates for the FTAs they negotiate, with the inclusion of many WTO-plus provisions, and many Singapore issues beyond the existing WTO rules, such as competition policy, environmental and labor standards, IPR and investment policy.

As neither the GATT nor the WTO has been able to agree on what is meant by "substantially all the trade," many countries may still seek exceptions and flexibilities in order to protect their domestic sensitive products. The EU set a precedent for excluding sensitive agricultural sectors from its FTAs with Mexico and South Africa. These precedents were seized upon by Japan in its current economic partnership agreement (EPA) negotiations.[30] It made no liberalization commitments on many agricultural products such as rice, wheat and starch in all of its EPAs. As a result, the liberalization ratio of Japan's EPAs is relatively lower, with

84.4 percent (Japan–Singapore EPA) to 88.4 percent (Japan–Philippines EPA), than those of US FTAs, which are higher than 95 percent.[31] Compared with developed countries, developing countries have had the tendency to sign "shallow" FTA agreements. They continue to evade the above-mentioned WTO-plus rules on substantial trade liberalization by relying on their developing country status and the special and differential treatment granted to developing countries. Hence, many of the South–South FTAs deal only with tariff reduction. In terms of the nature of the agreement, some FTAs signed by Japan and China are called cooperation and partnership agreements, which have evolved as formalized management agreements to facilitate bilateral economic interaction.[32] The variation of the forms chosen, the different scope and terms of the agreement negotiated and the different policy objectives achieved have further complicated the significance and effect of RTAs in the trade system.

The fundamental limitation of the RTAs have made them the second-best choice for many developing countries. RTAs are clear violations of non-discrimination in the application of trade policy, a fundamental principle of the GATT/WTO, even though both the GATT and the WTO make explicit allowance for preferential trade agreement among their members. FTAs are discriminatory against non-parties and tend to divert trade to their inclusive parties. We still don't have sound empirical evidence to support the belief of proponents of "regionalism that total trade creation will outweigh trade diversion."[33] Considering Mexico's trade volume with the US before and after it joined the NAFTA, it seems that the new market share gained by Mexico in the US market as a member of NAFTA is at the price of shrinking some market share of some other developing countries.

The other caveat of the RTAs is the increased transaction cost in dealing with the problem of "trade deflection." Complex rules of origin (ROOs) have to be specified. The bureaucratic complexity of ROOs makes them more costly and less attractive to business. There are now more than 50 FTAs in effect in East Asia. Still the "noodle bowl" produces overlapping ROOs requirements, which are impediments for business, especially the small and medium enterprises. The Asian Development Bank (ADB) conducted firm-level surveys in six countries, Japan, China, Korea, Singapore, Thailand and the Philippines, which show that only about 28 percent of firms in the sample use FTA preferences for exporting their goods.[34] Companies have to navigate different rules and regulations associated with varying agreements. The various ROO requirements are particularly business-unfriendly today, as economic globalization has brought highly globalized production networks. A simple manufacturing product may easily require the imports and exports of raw materials and intermediate parts from various markets, best illustrated by the example of the travels of a T-shirt.[35]

The revived regionalism has put many developing countries in a difficult position. Economically, developing countries tend to benefit more from multilaterally liberalizing for all WTO members rather than preferentially liberalizing trade to a few countries. In multilateral negotiations, the economic interest of the developing countries is better protected by global rules and norms such as the "special and differentiated treatment" and the "development mandate" granted to the developing countries in the WTO. They can gain further bargaining chips in the negotiation through coalition building. But, when a developing country negotiates FTAs with a developed country, it often has little leverage in the negotiation owing to its dependence on the developed market. The EU opened free trade negotiations with 78 African, Caribbean and Pacific (ACP) countries in 2002. But, 11 years later, the negotiations are still ongoing. African countries such as Ivory Coast and Ghana have no intention of implementing their part of the interim EPA concluded with the EU, as they feel that this trade deal could not ultimately deliver on its development promises. But recently the EU threatened to withdraw its special trade preferences by 2014 to countries not showing commitment to proceed with their interim agreement.[36]

Moreover, it seems that both developed and developing countries have reservations about this type of North–South FTA. From the perspective of developed countries, it is hard to convince the domestic audiences that FTAs with developing countries would not threaten the labor-intensive jobs at home. On the other hand, developing countries are concerned about the inclusion of WTO-plus issues such as a more legalized dispute settlement mechanism, more stringent IPR protection and more liberal investment policy. Developing countries are also concerned about the inclusion of strict regulations regarding labor and the environment when they negotiate FTAs with developed countries. To developing countries, these can be disguised protectionism and will allow the developed countries to employ sanctions to restrict the flow of goods from developing countries into their market. The US Congress refused to ratify the US–Colombia FTA until more sophisticated articles on labor and environmental standards were renegotiated. In recent years, the proliferation of South–South FTAs has provided the opportunity to diversify trade, yet free trade agreements between developing countries tend to be shallow and less complementary, as they may share similar comparative advantage and trade profiles. Moreover, the developing countries, with limited purchasing power, tend to offer smaller market opportunities to each other. Consequently, the mutual gains from such South–South FTAs are limited.

WHERE ARE THE RTAS HEADED?

This new wave of RTAs has spread quickly around the world as compared to the regionalism of the 1990s. The changing political economy of the international trade system has also transformed the form and content of RTAs today. While the focus of multilateralism is still on trade in goods and services, a number of US- and EU-dominated FTAs began to shift the focus from eliminating cross-border barriers to reducing behind-border barriers.

The most salient example is the TPP negotiation, a proposed regional FTA negotiated by 12 APEC members, including the US, Australia, New Zealand, Brunei, Singapore, Chile, Peru, Malaysia, Canada, Mexico, Vietnam and Japan. South Korea and Thailand may join later. The US negotiator has labeled it a "twenty-first-century, high-standard negotiation." A total of 29 chapters of the agreement, covering 21 trade areas, are under discussion. They are well beyond the traditional trade issues. Investment policy, competition policy, IPR protection and disciplines on state-owned enterprises (SOEs) are the major issues in the ongoing TPP negotiation. Among them, one most difficult issue area is IPR enforcement. Though the TPP negotiation is held in secret, based on the information revealed the US is trying to negotiate IPR protection provision that is the same as or even beyond that of US domestic law. For example, on the patent protection of new pharmaceutical products, the US currently adopts its protection for five years in principle (also five years in Australia and New Zealand), but insists the protection period should be extended to ten years under the TPP agreement. Japan proposes eight years of protection.[37]

While negotiations have yet to begin, the US–EU TTIP is moving closer to reality. By December 2013, Brussels and Washington, DC had finished two rounds of negotiation. As the average tariffs for both countries are just 3–4 percent, addressing non-tariff barriers and trade rules such as food safety[38] will be the primary objective of this trade deal. Up to 80 percent of the overall gains from this agreement are expected to come from cutting costs imposed by bureaucracy and regulations, as well as from liberalizing trade in services and public procurement.[39]

Assuming that trade regionalism is outcompeting the WTO to reflect new developments in global trade, what are the main features of twenty-first-century trade? Richard Baldwin summarizes it as the trade–investment–services nexus. The underlying logic of the GATT/WTO is the exchange of market access; thus reciprocity is critical for domestic ratification. But today the main goal of RTAs is to establish disciplines that foster the trade–investment–services nexus, and a commitment for domestic reform is more important than market access per se.[40] Similarly, the global supply chain business model emphasizes the role played by investment in changing trade patterns.[41] Another ongoing RTA negotiation, the Regional Comprehensive Economic Partnership (RCEP), can best illustrate this point. RCEP was launched at the East Asia Summit in November 2012 in Phnom Penh, Cambodia to consolidate and upgrade the existing six ASEAN+1 agreements between ASEAN and China, Japan, South Korea, India, Australia and New Zealand respectively. It is different from TPP and TTIP in that the main driver of the RCEP negotiation is not to make new trade rules, but to support the spread of sophisticated global production networks underlying the rise of factory Asia and to reduce the risk of an Asian "noodle bowl" of multiple trade rules in overlapping Asian trade agreements.[42]

The above-mentioned TPP, TTIP and RCEP are all mega-regionalism that has involved a wide range of states. The proposed deals attract much public attention, as, if concluded successfully, they will have the potential to restructure the global trade system. Together, the US–EU TTIP trade bloc encompasses nearly 50 percent of global GDP, 30 percent of global trade in goods and 40 percent of global trade in services. This could speed up a retreat of the two most influential economies from multilateral leadership and spur another wave of FTA proliferation. The economic importance of the RCEP is also striking. The grouping covers 49 percent of the world's population and accounts for 30 percent of world GDP. It also makes up 29.3 percent of world trade, 26.4 percent of world FDI inflows and 22.4 percent of world FDI outflows.[43] With the size of total GDP, market and population included, the rules created by this mega-regionalism will have a direct spillover effect on multilateralism.

The growing number of FTAs achieved and implemented by the WTO members raises the question as to whether the WTO is still the major force for future trade liberalization. Will the TPP and TTIP serve as the building blocks for a more viable future multilateral trade system by signaling the new agenda and responding to the twenty-first-century trade challenges? Or will the US and EU efforts on regional pacts divert their resources and attention from their essential commitment on multilateralism?

CONCLUSION: WHAT NEXT? CAN WE LIVE WITHOUT DOHA?

This chapter links the multilateral process with the development of RTAs. The collective effort made by many developing countries to withdraw the four Singapore issues from the DDA agenda is viewed by many as a positive trend to make the WTO more democratic and development-friendly. However, the attempt to prevent certain industrialized countries from establishing working groups and bringing the Singapore issues under the auspices of the WTO has motivated them to shift attention to the RTAs. The activism of the emerging BICS powers in the Doha Round negotiation also frustrated the developed countries, not only because the BICS powers have become more influential in the negotiation but also because of the perception that if emerging economies do not make concessions commensurate with their new economic importance then "there is not enough on the table" to support the covered agenda.

The renewed interest of countries in FTAs, particularly US- and EU-dominated FTAs, may suggest that the current Doha agenda is increasingly irrelevant to the developed countries and no longer reflects the changing business interests in those countries. During the Uruguay Round negotiation, pharmaceutical companies and the software and entertainment industries all lobbied for the conclusion and ratification of an agreement, as they expected the benefit would be substantial from the TRIPS and TRIMs agreements. Today, the business communities in developed countries do not lobby strongly for the conclusion of Doha agreement, as the key issues of their concerns are not included in the Doha agenda.

By 2013, it was widely accepted that the Doha Round negotiation had reached an impasse. Since the July 2008 breakdown, there has been little progress to break the deadlock. Impasses are not new in the history of multilateral trade negotiation, but this time there is a strong sense of pessimism that the round will be delayed indefinitely. It is still too early to predict whether the signing off of the Bali package will bring the momentum back to the Doha negotiation. The real concern shared by many is that the gap between the economic reality of today and the trade rules governing them is widening, as the existing multilateral trade rules were made almost two decades ago.

The spread in FTAs, and especially the intensification of FTA activity in Europe, Asia and the Americas, is likely to continue as multilateralism is outpaced by new development in the global marketplace and the changing power balance in the WTO. Moreover, the negotiation of mega-regionalism such as the TPP and US–EU TTIP will reshape the global trading system by implementing new trade rules across the regions and eventually further weaken the centrality of the WTO, as long as the WTO continues to focus only on the traditional trade issues.

NOTES

1. L. Baccini, A. Dur, M. Elsig and K Milewicz (2011), "Preferential Trade Agreements: A New Dataset in the Making," WTO Staff Working Paper ERSD-2011-10, available from: http://www.wto.org/english/res_e/reser_e/ersd201110_e.pdf (accessed May 27, 2013).
2. Cordell Hull (1948), *The Memoirs of Cordell Hull*, London: Hodder & Stoughton, p. 353.
3. John H. Barton, Judith L. Goldstein, Timothy E. Josling and Richard H. Steinberg (2008), *The Evolution of the Trade Regime: Politics, Law, and Economics of the GATT and the WTO*, Princeton, NJ: Princeton University Press.
4. Gilbert Winham (1998), "Explanations of Developing Country Behavior in the GATT Uruguay Round Negotiation," *World Competition Law and Economics Review*, **21**, 109–34.
5. Amrita Narlikar (2003), *International Trade and Developing Countries: Coalitions in GATT and WTO*, London: Routledge.
6. Ministers from WTO member countries decided at the 1996 Singapore ministerial conference to set up new working groups: on trade and investment, on competition policy, on transparency in government procurement and on trade facilitation. These four issues are called the "Singapore issues."
7. John Odell (2002), "The Seattle Impasse and Its Implications for the World Trade Organization," in Daniel L.M. Kennedy and James D. Southwick (eds.), *The Political Economy of International Trade Law*, Cambridge: Cambridge University Press.
8. International Trade Reporter (BNA) at 1980 (December 1, 1999). Quoted in Odell, "The Seattle Impasse and Its Implications for the World Trade Organization."
9. Alan Beattie (2011), "Counting the Cost of Al-Qaeda's Chief," *Financial Times*, May 9, available from: http://www.ftchinese.com/story/001038454.
10. Interview with EU official, Geneva, June 2012.
11. Fizel Ismail (2012), *Is the Doha Round Dead? What Is the Way Forward?*, Brooks World Poverty Institute (BWPI) Policy Paper 167, May, Manchester: BWPI.
12. David A. Deese (2008), *World Trade Politics: Power, Principles and Leadership*, London: Routledge.
13. Syed Javed Maswood and Larry Crump (eds.) (2007), *Developing Countries and Global Trade Negotiations*, London: Routledge.
14. WTO Accession Gateway, http://www.wto.org/english/thewto_e/acc_e/acc_e.htm.
15. Robert Wolfe (2008), "Can the Trading System Be Governed? Institutional Implications of the WTO's Suspended Animation," ch. 9 in Alan Alexandroff (ed.), *Can the World Be Governed? Possibilities for Effective Multilateralism*, Waterloo, ON: Center for International Governance Innovation and Wilfrid Laurier University Press.
16. Biswajit Dhar (2013), "The Future of the World Trade Organization," ch. 14 in Richard Baldwin, Masahiro Kawai and Ganeshan Wignaraja (eds.), *Future of the World Trading System: Asian Perspectives*, London: Centre for Economic Policy Research, p. 124.
17. ICTSD, "Historic Bali Deal to Spring WTO, Global Economy Ahead," Bridges Daily Update #5, December 7, available from: http://ictsd.org/i/wto/wto-mc9-bali-2013/bridges-daily-updates-bali-2013/180991/ (accessed November 11, 2013).
18. *Economist* (2012), "Absent Friends: World Economic Growth Is Originating Almost Exclusively from the Emerging World," January 24.
19. *Economist* (2010), "Fear of the Dragon," January 7.
20. Susan Schwab (2011), "After Doha: Why the Negotiations Are Doomed and What We Should Do about It," *Foreign Affairs*, May/June.
21. Aaditya Mattoo, Francis Ng and Arvind Subramanian (2011), *The Elephant in the "Green Room": China and the Doha Round*, Policy Brief 11-3, Washington, DC: Peterson Institute for International Economics.
22. Fred Bergsten (2011), "US Trade Policy and the Doha Round: An Alternative View," *VoxEU.org*, May 18.

23. Xiaozhun Yi, speech delivered at the LDCs Round Table on WTO Accessions, Beijing, May 30, 2012. Pradeep S. Mehta (2010), "India's Role in Doha Negotiations," *The News*, Pakistan, November 28.
24. WTO Regional Trade Agreements Gateway, http://www.wto.org/english/tratop_e/region_e/region_e.htm.
25. Masahiro Kawai and Ganeshan Wignaraja (2013), "Policy Challenges Posed by Asian FTAs," ch. 10 in Richard Baldwin, Masahiro Kawai and Ganeshan Wignaraja (eds.), *Future of the World Trading System: Asian Perspectives*, London: Centre for Economic Policy Research, p. 85.
26. That is, Canada, Mexico and the United States signed the NAFTA in 1992, and Mercosur was signed in 1991 by Argentina, Brazil, Uruguay and Paraguay.
27. R.E. Baldwin (1995), "A Domino Theory of Regionalism," in R.E. Baldwin, P. Haaparanta and J. Kiander (eds.), *Expanding Membership in the European Union*, Cambridge: Cambridge University Press.
28. The loss of Japan's exports to Mexico caused by the NAFTA was estimated to be 395.1 billion yen, or $3.2 billion, which would result in a loss of employment for 31 824 people. See Japan–Mexico Joint Study Group on the Strengthening of Bilateral Economic Relations (2002), *Final Report*, p. 14 note 1, available from: http://www.mofa.go.jp/region/latin/mexico/relation0207/part2.pdf (accessed October 15, 2013).
29. A liberalization ratio is the ratio of items whose tariffs will be abolished within ten years.
30. John Ravenhill (2003), "The New Bilateralism in the Asia Pacific," *Third World Quarterly*, **24** (2), 308.
31. Japan's Cabinet Office (2010), "The Comparison of the Liberalization Ratios of Japan's EPAs and FTAs by the US, EU, Etc.," in Japan's Cabinet Office, *Hōkatsuteki keizai renkei ni kansuru kentō jōkyō* [Analysis on a comprehensive economic partnership], October, 19 (in Japanese), available from: http://www.mofa.go.jp/mofaj/gaiko/fta/pdfs/siryou20101106.pdf (accessed March 2, 2013).
32. John Whalley (2008), "Recent Regional Agreements: Why So Many, Why So Much Variance in Forms, Why Coming So Fast, and Where Are They Headed?," *World Economy*, pp. 517–33.
33. Claude E. Barfield (1996), "Regionalism and U.S. Trade Policy," in Jagdish Bhagwati and Arvind Panagariya (eds.), *The Economics of Preferential Trade Agreements*, Washington, DC: AEI Press, p. vii.
34. Masahiro Kawai and Ganeshan Wignaraja (eds.) (2011), *Asia's Free Trade Agreements: How Is Business Responding?*, Cheltenham, UK and Northampton, MA, USA: Edward Elgar Publishing.
35. Pietra Rivioli (2009), *The Travels of a T-Shirt in the Global Economy: An Economist Examines the Markets, Power, and Politics of World Trade*, Hoboken, NJ: John Wiley & Sons.
36. Sanoussi Bilal (2012), "Trade Talks between Europe and Africa: Time to Bring the Curtain Down?," *Guardian*, July 12, available from: http://www.theguardian.com/global-development/poverty-matters/2012/jul/12/trade-talks-europe-africa (accessed May 5, 2013).
37. Interview with a trade official from TPP negotiating countries, November 2013.
38. Heidi Moore (2013), "The US–EU Trade Deal Could Take Monsanto's GM Crops off the Table," *Guardian*, May 15.
39. European Commission Press Release (2013), "US and Brussels Concluded Second Round of TTIP Negotiation," November 15, available from: http://trade.ec.europa.eu/doclib/press/index.cfm?id=988 (accessed October 12, 2013).
40. Richard Baldwin (2011), *21st Century Regionalism: Filling the Gap between 21st Century Trade and 20th Century Trade Rules*, WTO Staff Working Paper ERSD-2011-08, May, Geneva: WTO.
41. Roderick Abbott (2012), "The Future of the Multilateral Trading System and the WTO," ch. 2 in Ricardo Melendez-Ortiz, Christophe Bellmann and Miguel Rodriguez

Mendoza (eds.), *The Future and the WTO: Confronting the Challenges*, July, Geneva: ICTSD.

42. M. Kawai and G. Wignaraja (2013), *Patterns of FTAs in Asia: A Review of Recent Evidence*, Policy Studies 65, Honolulu, HI: East West Center.
43. Ganeshan Wignaraja (2013), "Evaluating Asia's Mega-Regional RTA: The Regional Comprehensive Economic Partnership," *VOX*, April 6, available from: http://www.voxeu.org/article/mega-regionalism-asia (accessed October 11, 2013).

17. Rotating checks and balances in international economic law[1]

Ari Afilalo

The international trade system of the post-World War II twentieth century mirrors the general hallmarks that have animated the collectivity of States during that period. Sovereign States joined international organizations seeking to provide predictability and order, but without infringing on the individual State's right to its territorial and regulatory inviolability, the essence of "sovereignty" in that age. The legitimacy of international law depended, in most areas of international law, not only on its substantive desirability but on its respect for the State as the virtually exclusive authority to legislate, police and otherwise act within its borders free of outside interference. True, international law would formally assert its preemptive and self-imposing nature, but no international organization would have the power to impose its norms on a recalcitrant jurisdiction.

In the trade realm (and probably generally for international law and institutions) this structural design created what can be conceptualized as a "vertical system of checks and balances."[2] Each sphere, international and domestic, sought to advance goals that, while not necessary unfriendly to the other sphere's *telos*, tempered it with conflicting considerations. For example, the GATT sought to open up barriers to trade, and domestic environmental regulation slowed down the movement of goods across disparate regulatory areas. The GATT itself did not include an environmental code addressing the circumstances in which environmental concerns would warrant derogating from free movement principles. Instead, it checked itself by limiting its reach and applicability within the domestic realm, and providing as a formal matter that individual States might choose their level of regulation as long as they did not discriminate against foreign products.

The transformation of the international economic landscape that we have experienced since the last decade of the twentieth century is eroding the structure of international relations that made this system of checks and balances so central to international economic law. Economic assets are no longer closely associated with a nation and national boundaries, and the concept of trade among nations based on comparative advantage no longer has the logical sense backed by basic facts on the ground that it had. Important regulatory areas have escaped domestic control and come within the realm of international systems, often controlled by "networks" of government officials or international tribunals, or even associations of private parties or multi-national corporations with sufficient power over the relevant subject matter area.[3]

This is a direct result of the evolution of Statecraft from the welfare nation-state of the twentieth century into what has been called the "post-modern State"[4] or the "market-state."[5] As has always been the case in the international economic legal field, norms and institutions reshape themselves in response to the evolution of the domestic constitutional structure of the State. As was bound to happen, the liberalization of trade in goods and services not only resulted in more commerce, but also caused the horizontal integration of economies that were previously associated with the nation. This makes a trade system based on comparative advantage for economics and sovereignty sheltering for politics less of a perfect fit for the domestic configuration of the age. And no system will be timeless, even comparative advantage. Protectionism accorded with Industrial Age economies seeking to consolidate and, once consolidated, those economies acquired national industries and sectors for which trading on the basis of comparative advantage made sense. Once the discrete "black boxes" that constitute the nation-state map evolve into the intertwined, cross-owned, globalized markets that we now experience, the system must again evolve and move beyond comparative advantage.[6]

I start with a description of the notions of Statecraft that are relevant to this exposition, and move on to apply them to selected issues in the international trade and investment fields. My goal is to show that the international–national checks and balances of the twentieth century, based on an equilibrium between the two realms, must be replaced by a substantive, norms-based system that must make choices at each level instead of merely delegating the sovereign power to choose.

THE STATE AND STATECRAFT

The "State" is not an immutable entity. It evolves through foundational structures that differ sharply from one era to the next. Each era is characterized by foundational hallmarks of Statecraft as then in effect. The "state-nation" corresponds, in Professor Bobbitt's historical analysis, to the consolidation of the State and its markets. The State drew on the nation and outside resources to strengthen itself. Mercantilism, protectionism, laissez-faire policies that tolerated bust-and-boom cycles, and even colonialism were compatible with the state-nation ethos, but would become obsolete and even dangerous policies in the next era. They all contributed to the strengthening and consolidation of an economy and a nation that would ultimately be closely associated with each other, but, when consolidation was achieved and the time arrived to trade more liberally so as to free up global resources for local redistribution, those policies were bound to create existentially dangerous frictions among the commercial powers. Entering into a treaty like the GATT, which as a formal matter allowed the States to draw on a larger pool of resources without compromising their redistributive choices, accorded with the legitimacy hallmarks of the day, whereas the "state-nation" had no use for a collaborative system that would interfere with its resource-accumulation enterprise.

Different constitutional architectures result in different internal legal systems and ways of relating to other States in the collective system. The nation-state legitimizes itself by ensuring "regulatory welfare" and "entitlements welfare." Regulatory welfare refers to the regulation of the economic and social aspects of the State, and the concomitant rise of an administrative State apparatus to enforce the applicable norms. The administrative State as we came to know it in the twentieth century regulated health, labor, the environment, resource conservation, worker safety, consumption, investor protection and many other areas where State intervention was deemed necessary to correct market outcomes. Entitlements welfare includes the support work of the nation-state to ensure that the nation, by and large, lives within a minimally adequate set of standards. The French shorthand "RMI," standing for minimal revenue of insertion, captures the notion. Its goal is to give everyone, without questions or conditions, a handout designed to guarantee basic survival. This aspect of welfare encompasses the various regimes adopted by Western States to ensure minimum standards of living for their subjects. These include unemployment benefits, retirement pensions, health insurance, minimum income guarantees, housing aid, aid to families with children, education, and other welfare tools adopted by European States to ensure that their nations would not fall below a minimal safety net level.[7]

The international trade order follows the foundational hallmarks of domestic "Statecraft," in the sense of the basic set of norms that animates the domestic system. Each successive epochal definition of the State is reflected, in time, by a complementary trade ideology.[8] The state-nation draws on its inner resources to solidify its metropolis and in the process creates a nation. Mercantilism, "gunboat diplomacy" and a general lack of collaborative international institutions of the type we came to know in the twentieth century made sense for those systems. Comparative advantage, and the political and legal structures that implemented it into the GATT treaty, accords with the nation-state because in theory it does not threaten the regulatory choices of the nation-state. In other words, Fukuyama declaring the "end of history" only saw the end of a particular historical era, and our entrance into the next one.[9] Through each era, the State will change, interact with the global order, change it, and change again through the reverberation of the global change.

In the next section, I will show how the GATT and the WTO systems implemented a vertical system of checks and balances to shelter the regulatory space that the nation-state needed, and argue that the sovereignty-sheltering system is not as indispensable an element of the international trade order now that we seem to be graduating away from the age of the nation-state. Relying on the past order, when its foundational assumptions have changed, is a danger that the international trade system has faced before. It is important to notice and identify the nature of the signs of transformation because, much like applying protectionism when States should be trading based on comparative advantage, an old institutional and normative architecture is likely to harm the relations among the trading nations and fail to enable fully the potential of the age.

THE WTO AS THE INTERNATIONAL FACE OF THE NATION-STATE EPOCH

Trade is the domain of the World Trade Organization and regional trade organizations such as the North America Free Trade Agreement (NAFTA). These organizations established institutions and norms that are characteristic of the nation-state. Their membership was decidedly State-to-State. Disputes were handled without involving private parties. The negative integration norms of the treaty did not threaten the domestic right to regulate. The international economic rules would not have a direct effect.[10] Government officials carefully selected the disputes that implicate weighty enough national interests to bring them before an international court. In doing so, they weighed limited resources and the possibility of retaliation for their own violation before initiating legal proceedings. As "rational choice" theory teaches, States will bargain in the marketplace of violations to determine which claims should be withdrawn in exchange for the other side's agreement to give up a grievance of its own and which disputes should be prosecuted to their bitter end.[11] Likewise, "networks" of government officials forge bonds across borders to create a loose but effective network of law makers and enforcers.[12]

The limited liability of the State enshrined in trade law is consistent with the origins and theoretical foundations of the General Agreement on Tariffs and Trade (GATT) and the WTO as a child of the nation era. The original GATT carefully maintained a structure that sheltered State sovereignty. As Keynes famously expressed, the lawyers as "poets of Bretton Woods" married after World War II a good economic idea with a politically palatable treaty system.[13] The three "pillars" of trade, tariffs reduction operating in conjunction with most-favored nation, national treatment, and ban on quotas and like measures, aimed to open borders without dictating national policy. The architecture of the GATT insulated national taxation and regulation from potential infringement by international norms. It identified in Article XX of the GATT Agreement regulatory areas of concern carrying special potential to encroach on the free movement of goods, such as the environment, resource conservation and public order, and carved out exceptions for legitimate measures in those areas. Generally speaking the GATT left redistributive justice to the jurisdiction of the national political actors. The UK could follow a cradle-to-grave welfare model, Japan an indicative planning structure, and the United States a tax-and-spend (or not) set of policies in pursuit of their version of the good life. The GATT merely required them not to charge foreign products duties in excess of their bindings, not to treat them less favorably than competitive domestic products, and not to impose quotas. In doing so, however, the GATT did not mandate any specific national legislation.[14]

John Ruggie captured this bargain with his "embedded liberalism" shorthand.[15] This captured the ability of the State to legislate at the level of its choosing free of constraints from conflicting norms of international law.[16] The GATT system's adoption of the core pillars that liberalized trade without infringing on domestic policy made it palatable for modern liberal democracies to accept the treaty.

Of course, this is only the law "in the books," and every student of trade knows that the law "in action" leaves significant areas of pressure against national law. Domestic regulation of economic and social activities, especially in subject matter areas where different jurisdictions tend to have disparate levels of regulation, will often burden trade. The job of trade courts is to sort out the regulatory space in which international law should not intrude. When the United States tells Indonesia that it will not allow its clove cigarettes onto the American market, is it favoring the menthol cigarette industry or pursuing a health goal? Can Argentina, faced with the possibility of yet another financial crisis, require trading partners to shoulder some of the costs of shoring up local currency reserves? When the European Union bans beef with hormones or asbestos, is it pursuing a valid domestic policy or again sheltering competitive domestic products? The great questions of trade have often hinged on the judgment call of a tribunal in favor of the domestic regulatory space or, alternatively, on the side of the free movement of goods.

Nonetheless, despite these tensions, and in fact as the great controversies that accompany each significant tension demonstrate, the twentieth-century international trade framework provides States with a prophylactic protection against international intrusion that embodies the vertical checks and balances that its founders had in mind. These checks and balances are found in several safety nets: the sensitive issues arising in the area of tension between sovereignty and international legal norms are left to a State-to-State system that limits exposure. Even when consultations are initiated, the matter may be resolved or dropped well before the case reaches active litigation. Even if the case reaches active litigation, the tribunal will be limited by substantive treaty norms that, although aiming to eliminate barriers to trade and foster the free movement of goods, enshrine a strong boundary designed to prevent intrusion into the State's regulatory system. As described above, the tribunal is in theory not permitted to evaluate the State's domestic choice as to the level of regulation within a permitted subject matter area.[17] And, even if the State loses the case altogether, it will be given a comfortable period of time to bring its system into compliance. The trade system is creating obstacles to sovereignty challenges precisely because, when trade encroaches on the sovereign right to regulate, it should act within self-contained confines.[18]

This system of checks and balances is based on the premise that States participating in the system have the type of control over their national economies that was characteristic of the nation-state era. Each system, domestic and international, is driven principally by the substantive norms that further their respective basic purposes. The international system favors free movement of goods and more *laissez-faire* economic policies. The domestic system provides a countervailing measure of regulations intended to further health, labor, consumer protection, the environment, investor choices and other interests. The balance is struck by the boundary placed around the domestic system, and the insistence that it leave ample regulatory space to the domestic redistributive choices. This is all the more important because the WTO has gradually supplemented the core GATT pillars with agreements that go beyond the negative injunctions and discriminatory rationale of the treaty and require that States comply with affirmative requirements, such as the Sanitary and Phytosanitary (SPS) Agreement, the Technical Barriers to Trade (TBT) Agreement or TRIPS. Going beyond an anti-discrimination rationale for invalidating a national measure creates a potentially higher level of pressure on State sovereignty.

The next section of this chapter will explore investment treaties, and show how they reflect a new, post-nation-state form of international regulation. I will argue that it is essential to understand the current evolution of the international system and Statecraft to properly evaluate and structure this new kind of international economic law. My conclusion is that the system of checks and balances is "rotating" from a vertical to horizontal position, in line with the intertwined and diffuse nature of the factors of production in the globalized marketplace.

INVESTMENT

Investment treaties embody in principle a different rationale than trade law. At their core, they aim to give private investors a direct cause of action against the central government of the host State. They are the product of a very different history. The very same modern liberal democracies, led by the United States, for which sheltering sovereignty in the trade context had been so important insisted that their investors should have the right to bring a claim against the States wherever they do business. They rejected domestic courts as the venue for investor claims as unreliably biased and demanded instead an international neutral arbitral forum. They sought to hold the central governments of the host States responsible for violations committed by any branch of government, whether executive, legislative or judicial, and whether central, regional or local. These tribunals, the West insisted, should have the power to award damages to make whole aggrieved investors and compensate them for treaty violations, and the awards should be enforceable in domestic courts under normal principles of arbitration law.

This stance arose from long-standing historical disputes following decolonization. The "North" insisted that independence came with the responsibility to comply with established international law doctrines, such as the requirement that expropriation be made only upon payment of fair market value, national treatment principles mirroring those set forth in the GATT, minimal standards of protection protecting foreign businesses against administrative unfairness, violations of due process (as understood in the West), and other measures thought to be arbitrary, as well as international neutral venues. The South, for its part, viewed these arguments as aggressive attempts to keep economic control over their territories and resources even after relinquishing political control. Paying compensation for property that was misappropriated by a foreign enterprise in the first place violated essential norms of fairness. Applying neutral standards to foreign businesses would allow them to exploit labor and resources without conferring any lasting benefits to the domestic economy. And the "Calvo Doctrine" categorically rejected the grant of jurisdiction to international tribunals applying norms outside of the domestic law of the land.[19] Domestic courts would apply as they saw fit domestic standards adopted independently of the colonizer and its yoke. This too was an indispensable element of the self-determination package.

After the fall of the Berlin Wall and the gradual rise of what we describe in shorthand as globalization, the Northern view came to prevail in the form not of a multilateral investment treaty imposed on the South but, instead, of an extensive network of investment treaties. The countries that previously were the standard-bearers of the South (e.g. Mexico) now accepted the Western view in international agreements like the Investment Chapter of the NAFTA, which essentially codifies the United States' long-held views.

The former South, a group now including some of the world's fastest-growing economies, the manufacturing centers of the consumer societies, and the holders of Western currencies and debt that keep the former North afloat, accepted and started to use, as its own weapons, legal systems that contemplate private party access, the award of damages, and virtually unreviewable decisions by specialized bodies. The International Centre for Settlement of Investment Disputes (ICSID) and the United Nations Commission on International Trade Law (UNCITRAL) became the forum for arbitration, under the aegis of the United States and the World Bank respectively, of the investment disputes. Investment law came to encompass virtually all situations where a traditional trade cause of action would lie. If Indonesia files a complaint against the United States alleging that the ban on clove cigarettes violates the national treatment provisions of the GATT, its cigarette distributors may file a parallel complaint under the national treatment of the applicable treaty. If Argentina revokes the permit of financial services companies from Panama because it needs to retain capital in the country and the Panamanian government files a complaint under Article XI of the GATT, the private interests from Panama may seek to recover damages under the takings or minimum standards of protection clauses of the investment treaty. The rationale for the overlap is simple. Trade is carried on by investors and their companies. There is no way to draw a distinction between the activity and the person conducting it. And, therefore, the GATT regulates trade, and the investment treaties regulate the traders' investments (i.e. their companies, the money they lend or contribute, the assets that their activities produce), but both systems speak to the same commercial reality.

The consequences of the overlap do not sit well with the twentieth-century legal mind and its habit of operating under a system of vertical checks and balance. The upshot of collapsing investment into trade could be an explosion of high-stakes litigation, overshadowing and taking over the delicately balanced system of trade integration of the WTO. Indeed, I have reviewed all of the WTO cases arising under the main pillars of trade (national treatment, non-tariff barriers, tariffs, SPS and TBT), and found that applying investment law to a trade cause of action yields a near perfect correlation of outcomes.[20] A company that sues under any of these treaty provisions will most likely win in investment if it wins in trade. If it faces an uncertain outcome in trade, it will face the same uncertainty, for the same reasons, in investment. And, if it loses in trade, it will most likely also lose in investment.

Again, this near perfect correlation is a function of the overlap between trade and the private parties carrying on the trade. It is not surprising, yet it unsettles the customary balance of the international legal system as we have come to know it, and its establishing checks and balances, by containing individual remedies and drawing a hard boundary sheltering States. And this is true not only in trade but in all of the areas of international law where the international system is careful to speak to States only, and to speak to them with respect. How would UN members react if they were subject to binding, effective and recurring lawsuits from individuals for violations of treaties adopted under the aegis of that organization? Individuals aggrieved by a violation of treaties covering such disparate subject matter as social and economic rights, the law of the sea, air pollution, or civil liability for the transport of civil arms simply do not have access to courts or directly effective law. And yet we can see the nascent signs of a world where the horizontal relations among individuals gradually pierce the previously sacrosanct "sovereignty veil": international criminal courts, the rise of human rights as a potential new basis to overcome the presumption of territorial inviolability, the evolution of Europe into a polity where the States' veto rights enshrined in such basic foundations as the Luxembourg Accords no longer have any meaningful relevance, human rights courts, and so on.

The classical exposition of international law and its relation to individual States posits that States accept becoming part of an international system that touches on virtually every area of commercial and social life, without insisting on the right to participate more meaningfully in law making, because States are accustomed to "exit selectively" the strictures of the system when its norms do not accord with domestic policies that it finds overriding.[21] The more integrated systems, with the European Union at one extreme, will expect and tolerate more individual participation. More classical international systems, including the vast majority of treaty frameworks, will tolerate little if any individual participation and leave the conversation about enforcement and interpretation to the States, guided and limited by their limited and prudential concerns.

And yet the new age challenges our habits of thinking and pressures the checks and balances system to shift away, in more and more instances and in more and more subject matter areas, from a vertical architecture. The economic world gives us one of the clearest views of this evolving order. The evolved international economic landscape and the transformation of Statecraft warrant a review of the classical assumptions related to sovereignty. The opening up of borders to trade has resulted in the integration of economic actors that were normally associated with national borders, into an intertwined, cross-owned globalized market. Interventionist policies and regulatory welfare no longer have an easily identifiable body of target subjects. Cross-border undertakings cannot be associated easily with one State or the next, and Keynesian expenditures are often as likely to assist economic interests in other countries. This is exacerbated by the relationships of inter-dependence among some States, which may hold massive debt or currency of others, or depend on export of their goods to their markets. Further, tools of intervention on the market such as monetary policies have lost much of their effectiveness because of the commodification of currencies and other instruments over which the States used to hold much more control. The explosion of methods of communication that cause information to travel at real-time speed has further contributed to the loss of control and transformation of States from the traditional "black boxes" to market actors in a diffuse world where the power they have been used to wielding has been eroded.

In this new marketplace, it is not surprising that the rising forces of the private sector are asking for access to legal systems that used to be the exclusive province of the States. And the overlap between trade and capital, and the import of classical norms of international economic law into investor-to-State litigation, should not be quickly condemned as an abuse of checks and balances as we know them, but evaluated in light of what can be conceptualized as the "horizontalization" of the international landscape. Like every legal system, the new system that will be subject to abuse as well as legitimate use. Australia's plain packaging laws, for example, were challenged before the WTO by an impressive array of States, including the European Union, Brazil, Egypt, Ukraine, Honduras, the Dominican Republic and New Zealand.[22] The WTO complainants argued that the plain packaging laws violated the TBT Agreement, the TRIPS Agreement, and Article III of the GATT. Philip Morris (PM) Asia, for its part, brought a direct challenge seeking damages under investment law. The investment filings by PM Asia follow a similar structure and, in addition, raise investment-specific causes of action, such as expropriation and denial of minimum standards of treatment under customary international law. By rejecting and failing to abide by those obligations, PM Asia claims, Australia deprived it of basic assumptions upon which its investment in that country relied. PM Asia's arguments essentially replicate those made before the WTO with respect to potential GATT violations. Australia responded by advancing a vehement argument that essentially tells the tribunal that the legislation amounts to a legitimate exercise of its police power, which is part of a comprehensive government strategy to reduce smoking rates in Australia. Australia, speaking the language of the nation-state era, advances an argument that would be a "home run" back then:

> It is not the function of a dispute settlement provision such as that contained in Article 10 of the BIT to establish a roving jurisdiction that would enable a BIT tribunal to make a broad series of determinations that would potentially conflict with the determinations of the agreed dispute settlement bodies under the nominated multilateral treaties. This is all the more so in circumstances where such bodies enjoy exclusive jurisdiction.[23]

At the same time as it is advancing traditional nation-state arguments, Australia is also meeting PM's claims on its investment terms. Thus, Australia claims that PM Asia acquired its shares in PM Australia in February 2011, with full knowledge that the decision had been announced by the Australian government to introduce plain packaging, and also in circumstances where various other members of the Philip Morris group had repeatedly made clear their objections to the plain packaging legislation, which objections had not been accepted by the Australian government. In other words, Australia argues that an investor cannot make a claim for breach of the fair and equitable treatment standard or of expropriation in circumstances where 1) a host State has announced that it is going to take certain regulatory measures in protection of public health, 2) the prospective investor, fully advised of the relevant facts, then acquires some form of an interest in the object of the regulatory measures, and 3) the host State acts in the way it has said it is going to act. In addition, the WHO and the Secretariat of the Framework Convention on Tobacco Control have each made submissions to the Australian government strongly supporting the legislation.

This is the right language, that of investment, expectations, and balancing the rights of investors with the police power of the State. Of course sovereignty and the international nature of the matters are relevant to the analysis. But the investment treaty jurisprudence should shift away from analyzing claims that overlap with the WTO framework through the exclusive lens of traditional checks and balances vertically applied. Otherwise, the tribunals will not provide a venue for the horizontal claims that the globalized marketplace needs. We stand at an evolutionary stage similar to that which the twentieth-century institutions experienced when asked to reject protectionism and embrace comparative advantage. We often think of those actors as oblivious to the "truth of comparative advantage," whereas they were simply unfamiliar with the emerging truth of the nation-state. Today's institutions are unfamiliar with the new truth, and the wheels of history are rolling without them. The debate has shifted, and we do not know precisely where it will lead us, but we do know that we have to adjust our foundational assumptions and start steering with Statecraft rather than against it.

NOTES

1. I build in this piece on thoughts and ideas developed with Professor Dennis Patterson, my co-author for the book, *The New Global Trading Order: The Evolving State and the Future of Trade*, Cambridge: Cambridge University Press, 2008, and colleague for regular intellectual exchanges. My thanks to him for a long-lasting partnership of the sort any academic seeks and cherishes. My thanks also to Yuval Nir, a brilliant young attorney I am privileged to work with and learn from on a daily basis, and to Liran Kandinov, the most recent legal talent I discovered, who contributed outstanding research.
2. I use this term to refer to a self-contained international legal system which checks itself by refraining from asserting any power over the domestic sovereign regulatory space. For example, as I explain below, international economic law has until recently limited itself in theory to removing barriers to trade and enabling the freer movement of goods and services. On a basic theoretical level, the international trade system as originally adopted did not assert any right to legislate on any substantive issue of domestic law that might affect international commerce, such as health or safety regulations. As long as a State did not impose a prohibited barrier to trade, it was free to act as it pleased. The upshot was that the system did not impose from above the optimal levels of taxation, regulation or redistributive justice generally. Of course, in practice, the free movement of goods put pressure on domestic regulation and created tensions that became the bread and butter of students of trade, but this framework lay at the theoretical core of the treaty. The mixture of self-containment in international law with its articulation of standards that States were bound to respect (e.g. the removal of the right to act in a protectionist manner, the international balancing) is what I mean by vertical checks and balances. See, for an excellent discussion, Thomas Cottier, *The Impact of Justiciability and Separation of Powers in EC Law*, available from: http://www.peacepalacelibrary.nl/ebooks/files/326919783.pdf.
3. Anne-Marie Slaughter frequently discussed the efficiencies provided by government networks, particularly regulatory networks. She described governance through a complex global web of "government networks" whereby government officials (legislators, police investigators, judges, financial regulators, etc.) exchange information and coordinate activity across national borders to solve problems resulting from the daily grind of international interactions. See for example A.-M. Slaughter (2000), "Government Networks: The Heart of the Liberal Democratic Order" and G. Fox and G. Nolte (2000), "Intolerant Democracies," both in G. Fox and B. Roth (eds.), *Democratic Governance and International Law*, Cambridge: Cambridge University Press, pp. 214, 217, 223–4. See also for example Ari Afilalo and Dennis Patterson (2008), *The New Global Trading Order: The Evolving State and the Future of Trade*, Cambridge: Cambridge University Press, chs. 5, 6, pp. 81–146.
4. Robert Cooper (2003), *The Breaking of Nations*, New York: Atlantic Books, p. 76. Cooper writes: "The kind of world we have depends on the kind of states that compose it: for the pre-modern world, success is empire and failure is chaos. For the modern, success entails managing the balance of power and failure means falling back into

war or empire. For the postmodern state, success means openness and transnational cooperation."

5. Philip Bobbitt (2002), *The Shield of Achilles: War, Peace and the Course of History*, New York: Knopf, pp. 24–33.
6. See Patrick M. McFadden (1995), "Provincialism in United States Courts," *Cornell Law Review*, **81** (4), at 44–5. McFadden explains that: "[Black-box] theory conceives international law as imposing its obligations only on each state as a whole, and not on any of its constituent organs. It is a matter for each state to determine which of its organs shall execute the nation's international responsibilities, and each of these organs, consequently, must await an internal signal to operate." See also Ward Ferdinandusse (2003-4), *Out of the Black-Box? The International Obligation of State Organs*, Brooklyn Journal of International Law, 29, 48 and a review of Andrew T. Guzman (2009), *How International Law Works: A Rational Choice Theory*, New York: Oxford University Press by Anthony Carty (2009) *Melbourne Journal of International Law*, **10**, 691.
7. See for a general discussion, for example, Afilalo and Patterson, *New Global Trading Order*, chs. 1–3, and other sources cited therein.
8. Cooper, *Breaking of Nations*, p. 76.
9. According to Fukuyama, the liberal democratic model soundly beat fascism and communism because, simply put, it was a better idea. The liberal democratic model had no problem besting the fascist ideology of expansionism and racial superiority. In time, it defeated the Marxist ideology – in part because of the growth of a strong and expansive middle class, resulting from (among other factors) the welfare policies of the nation-state – as it had radically changed the social reality in which Marx wrote. In the end, Fukuyama argued, all good government would be organized along the lines of the liberal democratic model, which would be applied to govern an ethnic or otherwise discrete nation and would protect the rights of minorities. See Francis Fukuyama (1989), "The End of History?," *National Interest*, Summer.
10. The NAFTA, in addition to its Investment Chapter, gives in some instances access to its dispute resolution systems. The Side Agreement on Labor, for instance, includes a procedure according to which, if the parties fail to resolve the dispute between themselves, the council may convene an arbitration panel, which prepares a report. If it is found that a party "persistently failed" to enforce its laws, the disputing parties will prepare an action plan and, if the parties do not agree or if the plan is not fully implemented, the panel can be reconvened. If the panel finds that the plan was not implemented, the offending party can be fined. If the fine is not paid, NAFTA trade benefits can be suspended to pay the fine.
11. Jack L. Goldsmith and Eric Posner (2005), *The Limits of International Law*, New York: Oxford University Press. See also the discussion in Robert Z. Lawrence (2007), *The United States and WTO Dispute Settlement System*, CSR No. 25, New York: Council on Foreign Relations; and in E.U. Petersmann (2007), "Why Rational Choice Theory Requires a Multilevel Constitutional Approach to International Economic Law: The Case for Reforming the WTO's Enforcement Mechanism," Law and Economics Research Paper Series Working Paper No. 2007-19, July, University of St. Gallen Law School.
12. See for example Slaughter, "Government Networks," pp. 214, 217, 223–4.
13. Robert Howse (2002), "From Politics to Technocracy and Back Again: The Fate of the Multilateral Trading Regime," *American Journal of International Law*, **96**, at 95–6.
14. See also for example Afilalo and Patterson, *New Global Trading Order*, ch. 4.
15. See John Gerard Ruggie (1982), "International Regimes, Transactions, and Change: Embedded Liberalism in the Post War Economic Order," *International Organization*, **36** (2), International Regimes, 385–8. According to Professor Ruggie, the GATT "embedded liberalism" in that each State participant enjoys, at least in theory, the sovereign right to establish and operate a domestic system of its choice, and at the same time removed barriers to trade and created a more efficient trading system. Each nation can maintain its identity and specific domestic programs, ranging from universal education to the supply of subsidized metro tickets to large families, all the while participating in a liberalized system of trade that generates more global resources to share.

16. See for example WT/DS135/ R, Measures Affecting Asbestos and Asbestos Containing Products, Panel report (adopted September 18, 2000), Section 3.19, p. 9.
17. Much has been written about the extent to which WTO law actually meddles with regulatory levels and redistributive justice choices, and at least one WTO tribunal has explicitly stated that it was doing so. As a general legal architectural matter, however, it is clear that the WTO and international economic law generally perceive that their legitimacy depends on the deployment of meaningful restraints.
18. This system resembled the classical international organizations of the time such as the United Nations or the European Union, whose basic laws were premised on the inviolability of the participating States' right to be free from interference by others. See for example Ari Afilalo and Dennis Patterson (2012), "Statecraft and the Foundations of European Union Law," ch. 11 in Julie Dickson and Pavlos Eleftheriadis (eds.), *Philosophical Foundations of European Union Law*, Oxford: Oxford University Press, describing how European treaties, for example, although more ambitious than any international treaty in force at the time, still provided a substantial level of protection of the member States' ability to legislate. Each member State could, to a certain extent, remain a "black box," in which it enjoyed freedom to determine how best to support the welfare of its nations, free from interference by European law.
19. Bernardo M. Cremades (2004), "Disputes Arising out of Foreign Direct Investment in Latin America: A New Look at the Calvo Doctrine and Other Jurisdictional Issues," *Dispute Resolution Journal*, **59**, 78, 80. See also Alexia Brunet and Juan Agustin Lentini (2007), "Arbitration of International Oil, Gas, and Energy Disputes in Latin America," *Northwestern Journal of International Law and Business*, **27**, 591.
20. Ari Afilalo, *Failed Boundaries: The Near-Perfect Correlation between State-to-State WTO Claims and Private Party Investment Rights*, Jean Monnet Working Paper 01/13; available from: http://centers.law.nyu.edu/jeanmonnet/papers/13/documents/JMWP01 Afilalo.pdf.
21. Joseph H.H. Weiler (1991), "The Transformation of Europe," *Yale Law Journal*, **100**, 2403–83.
22. See for example WT/DS434/1 (March 13, 2012), WT/DS435/1 (April 4, 2012) and WT/DS441/R (July 18, 2012), Australia – Tobacco Products and Packaging, Request for Consultations.
23. WT/DS434/1, WT/DS435/1 and WT/DS441/R, Australia – Tobacco Products and Packaging, Australia's Response, para. 35.

PART V

TRADE AS GLOBALIZATION

18. "Using ideas strategically": non-state actors and the politics of trade
Silke Trommer

INTRODUCTION

A new witticism about the relationship between the World Trade Organization (WTO) and so-called "civil society" has emerged in trade circles in recent years. Accordingly, some trade insiders half-humorously, half-nostalgically declare that they miss the protesters of the early 2000s at WTO headquarters in Geneva. Some jokingly reminisce about pushing through hordes of demonstrators in order to attend WTO Ministerial Conferences. The more seriously expressed view that civil society actors have found a new liking for the WTO, because nothing happens at the WTO anymore, has equally gained traction among trade experts. The assessments build on the assumption that corporate and non-corporate non-state groups constitute two distinct and essentially different sets of trade political actors and that the latter's relationship with trade institutions is necessarily confrontational. The protests around the WTO Ministerial Conference in Seattle in 1999 have become a powerful piece of collective memory that helps to cement this view.

The 1999 events sparked a debate on the merits and challenges for a more inclusive trade politics under the post-sovereign conditions resulting from growing governance complexity in the globalization process. Commentators on one side of the spectrum of opinions identified lacking knowledge about international institutions and/or lacking appreciation of the benefits of corporate-driven globalization as the root causes of what they saw as non-corporate non-state actors' misguided criticism of global trade. Commentators on the other side of the spectrum pointed to a liberal ideological bias in favor of corporate non-state actors as one prime culprit for the conflictual state of affairs. Overall, the debate has reified the idea, if only by leaving it unquestioned, that the sharp distinction between corporate and non-corporate actors in trade political analysis and commentary is warranted, seemingly because both pursue fundamentally different political goals through fundamentally different methods of advocacy. This feature separates the international political economy (IPE) literature on trade from broader conceptualizations in the social sciences that see "civil

431

society" as encompassing not only voluntary associations, social movements and the family, but also corporate interest groups.

While we have become accustomed to taking the distinction for granted in the IPE literature, sharp criticism has been raised against this methodological and analytical choice elsewhere. Burstein charged over 20 years ago that "there is no theoretical justification for distinguishing between social movement organizations and interest groups. There exist simple organizations – 'interest organization' – trying to influence public policy" (Burstein 1999: 19). Examining the campaigns of corporate and non-corporate actors on the Agreement on Trade-Related Aspects of Intellectual Property Rights (TRIPS), Sell and Prakash (2004) argued that the analytical distinction between corporate and non-corporate groups makes too many assumptions about the motivations for actions and the strategies of either set of actors, for which the authors could find no empirical confirmation. They claimed that, rather than capturing a state of affairs in the real world, the distinction "is rooted in the analytical bifurcation of 'ideas' and 'interests'" which "mirrors the rationalist/materialist versus constructivist/normative 'divide' in IPE scholarship" (Sell and Prakash 2004: 148).

Civil society is heterogeneous, both as a social phenomenon and as a theoretical notion. Scholte has pointed out that civil society means different things to different people. He finds four main contemporary usages in the global governance literature alone (Scholte 2011).[1] The usages arguably come with varying assumptions about how the state does or should interact with the different spheres or iterations of civil society. To grapple with this problem, trade scholars have attempted to produce more detailed categorizations. Bellmann and Gerster (1996), for example, have identified professional associations, research institutions and non-governmental organizations (NGOs) in trade politics. While professional associations are directly concerned with production and exchange through the global economy and incorporate trade unions and commercial groups, research institutions and NGOs are expected to be less immediately affected by changes in trade policy measures.

Other scholars have suggested that attitudes equally play an important role in the way in which state and non-state actors interact in trade politics. Scholte has differentiated non-state actors according to three basic attitudes, which constitute broad orientations that can and do overlap in practice. Conformers, such as corporate business associations, commercial farmers' unions and economic research institutes, "follow mainstream discourses of trade theory and broadly endorse the existing aims and activities of the WTO." Reformers, such as trade unions, human rights advocates, development NGOs, environmental groups, consumer protection activists and gender equality organizations, "aim to change the thinking, rules and procedures of the WTO . . . to redress alleged undesirable effects of the existing trading order." They typically argue for a democratization of trade politics by increasing the breadth and depth of public participation. Rejectionists "regard the existing global trade regime as incorrigible" and advocate its contraction or complete abolition according to the slogan "shrink or sink" (Scholte 2004: 150).

Building on the assumption that the first category aims to conform to existing norms, rules and institutional arrangements, while the latter two categories aim to transform them, although in different ways, I have proposed an attitudinal approach to trade political actors based on a distinction between conformist and transformative claims (Trommer 2014). Trade institutions appear to cooperate more readily with conformist groups (Williams 2011). The research of Gerlach (2006) and Hannah (2011) has further shown that trade institutions resist pressure from corporate actors that oppose a given trade political reform, suggesting that attitudinal factors play a role in the overall explanatory framework for trade political outcomes.

In this chapter, I scrutinize the various debates that non-corporate and transformative advocacy on trade issues has sparked in the IPE literature since the advent of the WTO. Breaking with the tradition in trade scholarship of sharply differentiating "the private sector" and "civil society," I use the term "non-state actor" to refer to any group that makes trade political claims and that is not representative of a state or public institution. Although I focus on non-corporate non-state actors in this chapter, the categorical adjustment is analytically meaningful, because it avoids common assumptions and/or prescriptions about the nature of relations in the conceptual state–private sector–civil society triangle, if only by putting corporate and non-corporate actors on the same footing as non-state groups that aim to influence trade policy outcomes.

As an immediate consequence of this perspective, we are bound to notice that the common accusation that civil society organizations are not only "self-appointed," but also "fungible . . . and divisible, frequently combining and dividing according to circumstances or objectives" (Robertson 2000: 1123) applies to corporate actors in the same way. This brings us full circle to Sell and Prakash's argument that "the similarities between business and NGO 'campaigns' far outweigh their differences" and that therefore policy formation in the field "can be usefully viewed as a contest between two interest groups, without normatively privileging one group over another" (Sell and Prakash 2004: 144).

I start out with a discussion of standard IPE approaches to trade policy formation that typically either marginalize or entirely sideline non-corporate interests in their analytical frameworks. The approaches build on a reductionist portrayal of society assumed to consist solely of government officials and economic agents. I then show that shifts in the mechanisms and regulatory reach of trade policy since the last decades of the General Agreement on Tariffs and Trade (GATT) have brought non-corporate actors to the fore, which in turn has sparked the above-mentioned debates about the legitimacy of conceptually separate "civil society" actors in trade politics vis-à-vis the assumed more "natural" involvement of the state and the corporate sector.

In the following section, I argue that, because trade policy is today increasingly about domestic regulatory adjustments, rather than removing trade barriers at the border, our analytical convention that trade politics equals contestation between "free trade" and "protectionist" interests breaks down. As a result of the increasing politicization of global trade rules that affect an ever broader spectrum of domestic rules, and in accordance with Sell and Prakash's finding, contemporary trade politics is a field in which both state and non-state actors use a number of material and ideational strategies to shape trade policy-making in accordance with their own normative preferences that cannot be appropriately subsumed under "free trade" or "protectionist" policy goals. I conclude that the IPE of trade literature is in need of new analytical concepts to grasp the contemporary politics of trade policy formation effectively, which go beyond the state–private sector–civil society triangle and beyond what Draper and Lawrence have called "tired old debates about free trade versus protection" (Draper and Lawrence 2013).

THE ABSENCE OF SOCIETY IN THE IPE OF TRADE

According to Williams, trade institutions are "founded on liberal economic principles" which contain an inherent bias that "support[s] certain discursive practices and marginalize[s] particular values and orientations" in trade policy-making. As a result, "the dominant position of liberal economic thought in academia and policy-making circles serves to normalize this orientation and renders this bias invisible" (Williams 2004: 197). I have argued that the dominant position relies on a methodological choice made in political economy in the late nineteenth century, which conflates society with its industries and assumes that the welfare of the latter is the adequate proxy for the welfare of the former (Trommer 2014).

Much trade political controversy arises from the fact that the methodological choice misrepresents how trade policy impacts on society by denying its societal and environmental effects. In this section, I first outline the standard IPE approach to trade policy formation and expose the absence of broader society from its analytical lens.[2] In a second step, I show how society "came back" into trade politics during the 1980s and 1990s to spark a controversial debate, not only about trade policy, but also about the role of broader societal interests in trade policy formation.[3]

Writing in the year of the Seattle WTO Ministerial Conference, Milner summed up the chief explanatory factor in the IPE literature of trade with the following statement: "groups seek protection or liberalization because such policies increase their income" (Milner 1999: 95). For standard IPE approaches, trade politics is a function of corporate non-state actors' interests, states' political and economic ambitions and the institutional setting in which trade political controversy is placed domestically and glo-bally. The distinct trade policy preferences of specific domestic economic sectors, or "special interests," are expressed in terms of "free trade," that is to say removing trade barriers, and "protectionism," that is to say mount-ing or maintaining trade barriers. The role of the state is to negotiate trade concessions with partner countries in pursuit of increasing its economic welfare and geopolitical might. At the domestic level, those domestic eco-nomic sectors that lose out in the overall trade bargain can be "bribed," to use Stolper and Samuelson's expression, into accepting a given trade policy line (Stolper and Samuelson 1941: 73).

Non-corporate societal interests are either completely absent or sidelined in this strand of the trade literature. The "rest of society" is typically con-ceptualized as a relatively gray mass of consumers who experience diffuse economic benefits and costs from trade rules (Woolcock 2005; Young and Peterson 2006). Because concentrated gains and losses resulting from trade policy adjustments mainly affect import-competing and export-competing interests, corporate agents are expected to hold a monopoly of influence in trade politics (Frieden and Rogowski 1996). Because NGOs do not dispose of the information about constituency preferences or market conditions that affect decision-makers' chances for re-election or re-appointment, their opportunities to impact on trade policy processes are seen as very limited (Dür and De Bièvre 2007).

Building on the assumption that trade policy affects economic factors of life only, scholars in the special interest tradition deduct policy preferences of corporate actors from the structures of the global economy (e.g. Hiscox 2002) or consider a given country's endowments in economic factors, such as labor, capital or land, in order to explain trade policy outcomes (e.g. Rogowksi 1990). To varying degrees, alleged non-economic considerations and ambitions (e.g. Ruggie 1982; Lake 1988) or the specificities of a given political or institutional setting (e.g. Elsig 2002) are considered to be part of the explanatory puzzle. How these goals become formulated, however, and what role the non-corporate spheres of society might play in this process are left obscure.

As a result, a number of trade political puzzles cannot be solved on the basis of the traditional approach. Why non-corporate actors launch trade campaigns in the first place is, for example, a research question that cannot fully be answered under this lens. The scholarship in particular laments that the interaction of ideas and interests is poorly understood in the IPE of trade literature (Milner 1999) and recommends an entire overhaul of the standard theoretical approach, "although it is the culmination of half a century of research" (Ethier 2007: 622).

The perspective underlying standard IPE approaches to trade policy formation reflects the political setting of the GATT years, when trade reform consisted mainly of lowering or dismantling tariffs and tariffication of quotas in a number of predominantly industrial and manufacturing sectors. However, with the gradual expansion of the trade agenda since the 1980s, trade rules have moved beyond borders. The Uruguay Round from 1986 to 1994 extended the scope of trade in goods regulations to previously excluded fields and codified the conditions under which member countries to the multilateral system could make use of policy exceptions. Multilateral agreements such as the General Agreement on Trade in Services (GATS), the TRIPS and the Agreement on Sanitary and Phytosanitary Measures (SPS) as well as the growing number of preferential trade agreements included provisions that had repercussions for governments' policy space in domains such as public health, education, environmental protection, labor standards and so forth (Ostry 2009). Procedural changes to the dispute settlement mechanism in the institutional transformation from GATT to WTO made the arbitration process of the multilateral organization more effective (Jackson 1997). This new legalism produced enforceable restrictions of domestic policy space through reform at the international level.

The role of corporate non-state actors in pushing for the institutional transformation from GATT to WTO is well documented (Ostry 2002; Chimni 2006). Through the new legalism, corporate actors regained influence in global trade policy-making. Aside from negotiations, they regularly participated in the filing of trade disputes and contributed to states' legal submissions (Matthews 2002). Corporate activism at the international level created momentum for its critics to engage with trade. As Wilkinson has pointed out, in trade policy "business groups are over-represented at the national and international levels; it is in recognition of this that civil society organizations have sought to engage and redress something of the balance" (Wilkinson 2002: 208).

During the Uruguay Round, critical observers started raising concerns over trade institutions' so-called "democratic deficit." They started using the term "GATTastrophe" to denounce undemocratic trade policy-making (Croome 1995; Rikkilä and Sehm Patomäki 2001). In doing so, they responded to rising insecurities about the effects of globalization (Williams 2004). Esty noted that "the WTO appears simultaneously to be at the leading edge of the economic integration process and yet curiously old-fashioned and out of step with some modern norms, particularly those involving good public decision-making" (Esty 2002: 8). The most far-reaching academic calls for inclusion of non-corporate and transformative groups have come from legal trade scholarship since the mid-1990s (Charnovitz 1996; Shell 1996; Lacarte 2004). The democratic deficit constituted one element of the so-called "legitimacy gap" in the multilateral trading system, which contributed to negotiating failures within the WTO and triggered strong and at times violent reactions against the organization on the outside (Ricupero 2001).

In political practice, Hocking has subsequently identified a move away from the traditional "club model" of trade policy-making since the 1999 WTO Ministerial Conference in Seattle towards what he has termed a "multistakeholder model" of trade governance (Hocking 2004). "What appears to be happening," he noted, "is that rules of engagement between the key sets of actors – government, business and NGOs – are gradually being shaped, based on shared interests in trading resources – knowledge, legitimacy and access – which each possess in differing degrees" (Hocking 2004: 26). This suggests that we witness an ongoing shift in the legitimization of trade policy outcomes that hinges on the consultation of hitherto disengaged interests. It is compatible with the observation in broader economic governance that non-state actors play increasingly important roles as globalization progresses and global governance complexity is on the rise (O'Brien et al. 2000).

The accountability literature has tried to address the concerns that a gradual move towards a multi-stakeholder model and broader debates about the democratic deficit and the legitimacy gap has produced. As Williams has pointed out, "there are conflicting views on the actors to whom the WTO should be accountable" (Williams 2011: 110). He argued that changes in the trade regime and notably the expansion of the global trade agenda "bring the WTO into direct engagement with groups (such as consumers, farmers or workers) that may not be adequately represented by national governments" and concluded on these grounds that "civil society actors could have a legitimate role to play in WTO governance" (Williams 2011: 112). Differences of assessment of the WTO's nature, as a predominantly intergovernmental or predominantly supranational organization, have come with differences of opinion on where the appropriate level for oversight should lie, as predominantly in domestic politics or predominantly in global governance institutions.

Overall, the debate has reinforced the assumption that non-corporate advocacy in trade policy-making requires justification, while the relevance of corporate groups appears to be self-evident. A number of scholars have charged that non-corporate actors have less legitimacy in participating in trade policy formation because they expect these actors to be less affected by trade policy choices (Dunoff 1998; Robertson 2000). Others have doubted that international economic policy-making is the appropriate governance level for non-corporate non-state actors' engagement (Capling 2003).

Considering the challenges that multilayered global governance and fragmented state authority pose, Scholte has asked: "How can post-sovereign conditions be fashioned to yield adequate popular participation, open debate, consultation and representation as well as transparency and democratic accountability?" (Scholte 2004: 147). He has argued that broad involvement can improve the situation but maintained that benefits do not automatically result from opening up the policy process to non-corporate groups. Rather, he invited trade officials and "civil society" groups to clarify their objectives in trade policy, to institutionalize their relations, to improve staff capacity, to coordinate their activities and to "consciously nurture attitudinal change that promotes more constructive dialogue" (Scholte 2004: 158). Wilkinson has criticized the fact that non-corporate organizations, and particularly those from the global South, have been factually marginalized in global trade talks. He has identified a risk that this development could "reinforce the Western bias already existent in the WTO particularly, and global governance more generally" (Wilkinson 2002: 207).

Conceiving of non-state actors as a meaningful analytical group, Charnovitz has explained that the main concern about their rising role in world politics comes as their level of influence increases or, put simply, stems from their "role as a political actor" (Charnovitz 2005: 33). In similar fashion, my previous research has indicated that controversies about the representativity and/or legitimacy of a given non-state actor in trade political processes are tied into controversies over trade political substance (Trommer 2014). A West African trade official most clearly expressed this to me in a personal interview when pointing out: "We [trade officials] only ask them [civil society] 'Who do you represent?' when we disagree with what they're saying."[4] My previous research on the evolution and application of participatory trade politics in West African regional integration organizations has examined a case where Scholte and Wilkinson's concerns have been addressed and mediated through trade political practice that institutionalized political conflict between state and various non-state actors within trade institutions, rather than suppressing conflicts by excluding transformative voices from the decision-making process (Trommer 2014).

On the whole, few scholars have addressed questions of non-state actor participation in trade policy formation at the domestic level, but focused on the WTO instead. This is somewhat surprising since, according to the WTO, members' governments present the appropriate policy level for civil society input into trade policy formation, and not the WTO (WTO 1996). Sapra has further highlighted a need for the reform of domestic trade policy-making processes to enhance transparency and non-state actor involvement. She has warned that the academic discussion needs to move away from NGO participation in Geneva to "include the broader category of non-state actors and their role in the WTO system of multi-level governance at both the international and domestic levels" (Sapra 2009: 71).

In view of the recent transformations of the global trading system, the focus on the WTO seems ever less warranted. Today, the rule-making function of the multilateral organization is disputed. While its policy debate and adjudication function are still prominently used, several big trading economies pursue their agendas through preferential trade agreements under Article XXIV GATT and Article V GATS. In addition, plurilateral agreements under Annex 4 of the WTO Agreement are experiencing a revival in the multilateral realm. As the channels of global trade governance continue to multiply and the member-driven character of the WTO becomes more apparent again, the domestic level is likely to be the prime focus for trade advocacy. In addition, the above-mentioned expansion of the trade agenda brings trade politics into more direct confrontation with other societal interests and contributes to the increasingly political nature of global trade.

THE INCREASINGLY POLITICAL NATURE OF GLOBAL TRADE

Williams has explained that "the extension of trade rules into new areas has reinvigorated the historical conflict between domestic interest groups supportive of trade liberalization and those groups intent on protecting national and sectional interests from further economic liberalization" (Williams 2004: 194). In this section, I argue that the conflict has also changed in nature, because it has become more complex, involving a greater number of interests, and at the same time shifted terrain, expanding substantially beyond questions of income gains and losses for economic agents as trade barriers stand or fall. I first outline the concrete impacts of the adjustments in the global trade agenda for the politics of trade and for the "free trade" versus "protectionism" controversy. I then present Sell and Prakash's finding on the similar behavior of business and NGO networks in TRIPS politics and highlight further successful transformative advocacy from the global trade system. In doing so, I provide an account of the increasingly political nature of global trade and its implications for studies of non-state actors in trade politics.

The trade literature tends to make a sharp distinction between civil society, the private sector and labor, and sees civil society as less immediately affected by trade policy choices than the other sectors. Skeptical scholars have deduced conclusions about civil society trade activism's misguided nature from this trade political ontology. Robertson, for example, held that civil society organizations "seek access to WTO meetings to redress 'labor conditions, development problems, environmental damage, consumer protection and gender irregularities' – none of which is WTO's business" (Robertson 2000: 1122). The assessment is in direct contradiction with other observations in the literature that the expansion of the global trade agenda that has taken place since the Uruguay Round implied that trade affects policy areas that global economic governance had not traditionally regulated (Young and Peterson 2006).

This conflict in the literature replicates one of the key conflicts in contemporary trade politics. Practically, the expansion of the agenda created resistance to new trade rules from the affected interests (Klug 2008). Theoretically, the traditional sectoral bargain approach based on a reduction of society to its special interests henceforth fails to capture the politics of trade adequately. Today, trade politics of course continues to be a matter of which type of economic operator, such as capital, labor or the state, gains income and which loses income in the overall trade bargain. This is however not only implemented through classical market opening techniques such as the removal of tariff barriers. It also includes regulatory intervention in domestic regimes, which forges market conditions that favor certain economic operators' interests over those of others.

The content of what constitutes the appropriate "free trade" policy has become more contested in the context of a steadily rising number of WTO members and an expansion of topical issues. As one result of this process, the standard political economy terms "free trade" and "protectionism" have lost analytical usefulness and explanatory power. This is not a new phenomenon in political economy, but rather an iteration of the broader insight that even economic concepts do not have fixed meanings. Thus, "how groups understand economic concepts may be complex, ambiguous, indeed contradictory compared to high theory" (Trentmann 1998: 238).

When the trade economist Jacob Viner complained in the magazine

Foreign Affairs during GATT negotiations in 1947 that "there are few free-traders in the present day world, no one pays any attention to their views and no person in authority anywhere advocates free trade," he was referring to the fact that a club of 23 mainly industrialized countries could not envisage more ambitious reforms than taking down select, very high, post-war tariffs in a limited number of economic sectors, namely industrial and manufacturing goods (Viner 1947: 613). Depending on the WTO delegation one talks to, free trade can loosely include providing market access opportunities in services and government procurement sectors, dismantling export subsidization schemes for agricultural products, expanding and deepening the reach of intellectual property protection, and so forth.

The shift blurs the traditional conceptual categories of the IPE of trade, as the trade diverting impacts of so-called "trade liberalization" become more obvious.[5] Intellectual property protection and certain forms of service concessions are for example regulatory reforms that have little to do with "free trade" on an allegedly level playing field according to a given comparative advantage. Instead, these reforms establish new forms of monopoly or opportunities for monopolization through regulatory interference with local, national, regional and global markets. As under protectionism, the type of intervention chosen to create a "free" market determines which economic operators gain over others.

Variations in the meanings of the terms "free trade" and "protectionism" and the perceptions attached to them constitute ideas that fulfill discursive and rhetorical functions in international trade policy-making. Ford has pointed out that global South countries are commonly perceived in trade negotiations as pursuing protectionist trade policy lines, while global North countries are often thought of as free traders. She has argued that these perceptions are part of what she has called the global "trading culture" and, while factually misleading, impact on the dynamics of trade negotiations (Ford 2003).

At the same time, the fact that trade rules not only affect economic activity, but also interact with the way society functions more broadly, became more apparent as a result of the institutional shift from GATT to WTO elaborated in the previous section. It is more obvious today, and partly a result of the expansion of the trade agenda, that trade policy choices have concrete impacts on long term socio-economic and environmental processes, including, but not limited to, climate change, energy, global social justice, public health, food security and human rights, as the trade agenda continues to expand. This alters the nature of the political conflict underlying trade controversies.

Reflecting on the lessons from the events in and around the Seattle 1999 Ministerial Conference, Dymond and Hart noted that rule-making under the WTO "intrudes deeply into domestic policy and raises critical issues of governance in terms of the power of democratic governments to control economic development and influence the distribution of its benefits across society" (Dymond and Hart 2000: 34). In this context, von Bülow has asserted that:

> the traditional distinction between two antagonistic sets of actors, protectionist and free traders, does not reflect the reality accurately, simply because it over-simplifies and distorts the debate in this new context of trade negotiations . . . The increased politicization of trade debates makes theories in the political economy literature that try to explain the formation of domestic coalitions based on factor endowments incomplete, at best. (von Bülow 2010: 47)

It is today more obvious than ever that trade policy affects society at large, not only through affecting the economic situation of a given country's industries and thus creating effects in people's income levels, but also through forging the environmental and social conditions and standards by which the vast majority of people on the planet live their lives. This is not a matter of sectoral bargains only, which continue to experience changes in income partly as a result of variations in trade rules, among many other factors, but constitutes a broader political struggle over the adequate modes for shaping societies' ongoing material, social and political transformations in the globalization process. Put differently, in view of the WTO Director-General's assertion that trade and climate need a joint agenda (WTO 2009), for example, the position that sectoral interests should determine this agenda to the exclusion of other societal interests looks less self-evident, but requires justification.

The relevance of Sell and Prakash's contribution to the literature has to be seen in the broader context of increasing analytical problems connected to the use of the terms "free trade" and "protection." In their paper "Using Ideas Strategically," the authors challenged "the notion that NGOs are different from businesses" in trade politics "because they pursue principled beliefs while businesses pursue material interests" (Sell and Prakash 2004: 143). They argued that this idea is an oversimplification of reality that sidelines the fact that NGO and business networks are both driven by ideals and material concerns at the same time, and that the similarities in their strategies to pursue their competing normative frameworks outweigh the differences.

Their paper analyzed two campaigns in the field of trade-related intellectual property rights. In a first step, they examined "why and how a transnational network of multinational corporations succeeded in grafting its agenda onto the 1994 Agreement on Trade-Related Intellectual Property Rights (TRIPS) negotiations of the Uruguay Round of the

GATT" (Sell and Prakash 2004: 144). They then considered the fact that the same network was unable to convince US policy-makers in the subsequent controversy over HIV/AIDS medication to pursue perceived TRIPS violations of developing countries. The authors found that, in the case of the HIV/AIDS campaign, "another transnational network, this time led by NGOs, has succeeded in grafting its agenda onto U.S. policy" (Sell and Prakash 2004: 144).

Sell and Prakash used the same explanatory framework to account for both policy outcomes. They borrowed the key insight from the political opportunity structure and public policy literatures that "both structure and agency matter in influencing policy outcomes" (Sell and Prakash 2004: 145). Arguing that "behind every idea there is an interest . . . and interests are guided by normative ideas," they "identify key competing ideas in a debate, whose interests they serve, how they are promoted, and how effectively they are deployed" (Sell and Prakash 2004: 148). For this purpose they did not differentiate between different types of non-state actors, because they found both NGOs and businesses to have instrumental interests and normative concerns.

The authors showed how the business network initially "successfully promoted the frame that 'patents = free trade + investment = economic growth,' which became the normative building block of the TRIPS agreement" (Sell and Prakash 2004: 145). The NGO network was later successful in framing the HIV/AIDS problem as one of overly restrictive intellectual property rules making medication inaccessible, sidelining the business communities' frame that saw poverty and poor governance as the root causes. In their paper, Sell and Prakash traced how:

> competing transnational networks: (a) identified a policy crisis; (b) explicated their normative positions and policy goals; (c) mobilized a transnational network of actors with congruent goals; (d) set the policy agenda by constructing the problem, disseminating favorable information to key players, and providing a normative frame to interpret this information; and (e) brought about substantive and normative changes in the policy regime. (Sell and Prakash 2004: 152)

In sum, they argued that "each campaign grafted new normative frames onto existing ones; the business campaign grafted IPR protection onto free trade, while the NGO campaign grafted IPR onto public health. Both succeeded in producing normative and substantive changes in policy outcomes" (Sell and Prakash 2004: 144). They concluded that "adhering to rigidly defined categories often distorts the analysis and imports hidden assumptions that are more normative than analytic. Our position is that both business and NGO networks have their share of principled beliefs and instrumental goals. Hence, their actions and strategies should be viewed through a common framework" (Sell and Prakash 2004: 152).

Successful non-corporate advocacy has been reported since the early days of the multilateral trading system. Research has, for example, indicated the involvement of non-corporate non-state actors in several high-profile trade issues from early on in the days of the multilateral trading system. In the Shrimp–Turtle case, the WTO's Appellate Body made the controversial decision that it, as well as the panels of first instance, might, on a discretionary basis, accept and consider amicus curiae briefs from, *inter alia*, non-governmental organizations and private individuals (Howse 2003). Legal trade scholarship has categorized non-corporate non-state actors as a relevant set of social actors in the area of international trade, because these actors engage the debates that structure and produce the law (Lang 2007).

Based on case studies in the areas of labor standards, intellectual property and investment rules, Murphy has found that NGO activities serve an agenda-setting function at the WTO. NGOs publicize neglected trade-related issues, persuade others to support their positions, enhance the resources of less developed member states and highlight normative rationales for policy change (Murphy 2010). In addition, non-corporate non-state actors have helped to initiate a number of WTO disputes and have helped to bring certain issues onto the negotiating agenda, for example the Cotton Initiative. This campaign was based on the notion that developed country WTO members needed to free-trade in agriculture for developing country exports (Heinisch 2006). The example supports the view that "free trade" is an idea that any trade political actor can strategically refer to in order to provoke a certain policy outcome, where the context of the situation suggests this discursive tool would help to produce the desired result.

The fact that all of these examples are taken from policy areas that were not covered under the GATT system supports my broader argument that the institutional shift to the WTO has made our standard analytical categories for trade policy formation defunct. An outdated ontology of the basic trade political conflict as evolving around the question of on-the-border barriers for trade in goods continues to underlie our habitual conceptualization of trade politics. It encourages skewed analytical concepts, namely essentially different private sector and civil society actors using distinctly different strategies to achieve one of two possible outcomes: "protection" or "free trade." As a result, trade policy formation theory struggles to address what the politics of trade are currently about, namely competing normative preferences for the purposes and the functions of the trading activity in bringing about competing normative scenarios for global futures. As further evidenced in debates about the various financial and debt crises since 2008, the way in which interests and ideas interact and shape each other in political economy processes are key elements for policy outcomes in and around the (world) economy.

CONCLUSION

Global trade flows are embedded in and constitutive of broader social and economic organization. As trade governance stays in motion, so should our analytical tools. In 1947 the GATT became the first international institution in history dedicated to administering the rules of global trade. Forty years later, the Uruguay Round purported a shift in the topical reach of trade issues and in the level of institutionalization and legalization. Today, 20 years after the conclusion of the Uruguay Round, the rapid expansion of Jagdish Bhagwati's famous "spaghetti bowls of obligations" (Bhagwati and Panagariya 1996) continues fueling the system's fragmentation and raises questions as to whether it will continue to be predominantly multilateral in character in the future.

At the same time, new discourses arise in policy circles and pose challenges to the traditional understanding of the nature of the trading activity itself. The global value chain perspective sees the high level of import intensity in export production as the foundation of an unprecedented level of inter-dependency among countries across the world economy. "Supply chains are mostly about making things internationally," Baldwin has recently explained, "while today's WTO . . . rules are primarily aimed at governing the international selling of things" (Baldwin 2013). The WTO Secretariat has engaged in a statistical re-writing exercise under its "Made in the World" initiative. The initiative attempts to account for individual countries' trade by tracing the value that each adds along a production chain, rather than by final value of a product. A number of WTO members have attacked the perspective as an attempt to revive the Washington Consensus and see it as hiding an aggressive liberalization agenda that downplays the necessity to address the imbalances of the system (Ismail 2012). The controversy is one of the latest examples that show how ideas about the world enable the pursuit of certain interests over others and how interests can influence the shaping of ideas about how the world functions in return.

Overall, the topical expansion of the trade agenda and the legalization that were introduced during the GATT's Uruguay Round have repoliticized trade as a policy field. With regard to non-state actor participation in trade political processes, the core debate revolves around the question of legitimacy. Its contours are currently delineated by a taken-for-granted view on how trading interacts with socio-economic and political organization more broadly, which is anachronistically based on a GATT-style trade politics and infuses analytical tools with distinct normative preferences. In other words, the view prioritizes the impacts of trade flows on corporate actors over the impacts of global trade flows on other socio-economic processes within the compartmentalized field of trade governance. These underlying assumptions confirm the expectation that non-corporate non-state actors are fundamentally different from corporate non-state actors in trade policy-making, and ultimately encourage the view that the former are irrelevant, a nuisance or less entitled to engage with trade policy-making than the latter.

As the work of Burstein (1999) and Sell and Prakash (2004) has shown, there is neither a theoretical justification nor an analytical need for this sharp distinction. At the same time, the debate has, intentionally or unintentionally, reified the expectation that differences between state, corporate and non-corporate actors in trade politics cannot be overcome. Whether this is an empirically valid assumption is one research question that the scholarship could turn some attention to as we aim to make positive contributions to long-standing political deadlocks in global trade politics. An overhaul of our analytical categories for trade policy formation as suggested in this chapter is one step in the direction of building new theoretical approaches that can adequately capture the contemporary politics of trade.

NOTES

1. The four contemporary usages are "a general quality of a given human collectivity," "an arena where citizens congregate to deliberate on the actual and prospective circumstances of their collective life," "the sum total of associational life within a given human collectivity" and "the aggregate of so-called non-governmental organizations" (Scholte 2011: 33–4).
2. For a detailed review of the trade policy formation literature see Milner (1999) or more recently Capling and Low (2010).
3. For idea of a "double movement" see Polanyi ([1944] 2001).
4. Personal interview with ECOWAS official, July 21, 2009, Dakar.
5. For the first conceptualization of trade diversion and trade creation as macro-economic phenomena see Jacob Viner (1950). Under trade diversion, trade flows increase owing to a beneficial regulatory setting in the importing country (in Viner's example low tariffs), rather than owing to the existence of a comparative advantage on the side of the exporter.

REFERENCES

Baldwin, Richard (2013), "The WTO and Global Supply Chains," February 23, available from: http://www.eastasiaforum.org/2013/02/24/the-wto-and-global-supply-chains (accessed April 16, 2014).

Bellmann, Richard and Christophe Gerster (1996), "Accountability in the World Trade Organization," *Journal of World Trade*, **30** (6), 31–74. Bhagwati, Jagdish N. and Arvind Panagariya (1996), *The Economics of Preferential Trade Agreements*, Cambridge, MA: MIT Press.

Bülow, Marisa von (2010), *Building Transnational Networks: Civil Society and the Politics of Trade in the Americas*, Cambridge: Cambridge University Press.

Burstein, Paul (1999), "Social Movements and Public Policy," in Marco Giugni, Doug McAdam and Charles Tilly (eds.), *How Social Movements Matter*, Minneapolis: University of Minnesota Press, pp. 3–21.

Capling, Ann (2003), "Democratic Deficit, the Global Trade System and 11 September," *Australian Journal of Politics and History*, **49** (3), 372–9.

Capling, Ann and Patrick Low (2010), *Governments, Non-State Actors and Trade Policy-Making: Negotiating Preferentially or Multilaterally?*, Cambridge and Geneva: Cambridge University Press and World Trade Organization.

Charnovitz, Steve (1996), "Participation of Nongovernmental Organizations in the World Trade Organization," *University of Pennsylvania Journal of International Economic Law*, **17** (1), 331–58.

Charnovitz, Steve (2005), "Accountability of Nongovernmental Organizations (NGOs) in Global Governance," paper prepared for the Conference on Global Administrative Law, New York University Law School, April 22–23.

Chimni, B.S. (2006), "The World Trade Organization, Democracy and Development: A View from the South," *Journal of World Trade*, **40** (1), 5–36.

Croome, John (1995), *Reshaping the World Trading System: A History of the Uruguay Round*, Geneva: World Trade Organization.

Draper, Peter and Robert Lawrence (2013), "How Should Sub-Saharan African Countries Think about Global Value Chains?," *Bridges Africa Review*, **2** (1), available from: http://ictsd.org/i/competitiveness/158175/ (accessed April 16, 2014).

Dunoff, Jeffrey (1998), "The Misguided Debate over NGO Participation at the WTO," *Journal of International Economic Law*, **1** (3), 433–56.

Dür, Andreas and Dirk De Bièvre (2007), "Inclusion without Influence? NGOs in European Trade Policy," *Journal of Public Policy*, **27** (1), 79–101.

Dymond, William and Michael Hart (2000), "Post-Modern Trade Diplomacy: Reflections on the Challenges to Multilateral Trade Negotiations after Seattle," *Journal of World Trade*, **34** (3), 21–38.

Elsig, Manfred (2002), *The EU's Common Commercial Policy: Institutions, Interests and Ideas*, Aldershot, UK: Ashgate.

Esty, Daniel (2002), "The World Trade Organization's Legitimacy Crisis," *World Trade Review*, **1** (1), 7–22.

Ethier, William (2007), "The Theory of Trade Policy and Trade Agreements: A Critique," *European Journal of Political Economy*, **23** (3), 605–23.

Ford, Jane (2003), *A Social Theory of the WTO: Trading Cultures*, Basingstoke, UK: Palgrave Macmillan.

Frieden, Jeffrey and Ronald Rogowski (1996), "The Impact of the International Economy on National Policies: An Analytical Overview," in Robert Keohane and Helen Milner (eds.), *Internationalization and Domestic Politics*, Cambridge: Cambridge University Press, pp. 25–47.

Gerlach, Carina (2006), "Does Business Really Run EU Trade Policy? Observations about EU Trade Policy Lobbying," *Politics*, **26** (3), 176–83.

Hannah, Erin (2011), "NGOs and the European Union: Examining the Power of Epistemes in the EC's TRIPS and Access to Medicines Negotiations," *Journal of Civil Society*, **7** (2), 179–206.

Heinisch, Elinor (2006), "West Africa versus the United States on Cotton Subsidies: How, Why and What Next?," *Journal of Modern African Studies*, **44** (2), 251–74.

Hiscox, Michael (2002), *International Trade and Political Conflict: Commerce, Coalitions and Mobility*, Princeton, NJ: Princeton University Press.

Hocking, Brian (2004), "Changing the Terms of Trade Policymaking: From the 'Club' to the 'Multistakeholder' Model," *World Trade Review*, **3** (1), 3–26.

Howse, Robert (2003), "Membership and Its Privileges: the WTO, Civil Society, and the Amicus Brief Controversy," *European Law Journal*, **9** (4), 496–510.

Ismail, Faizel (2012), "Towards an Alternative Narrative for the Multilateral Trading System," presentation to UNCTAD TDB panel discussion, Geneva, September 18.

Jackson, John H. (1997), *The World Trading System: Law and Policy of International Economic Relations*, Cambridge, MA: MIT Press.

Klug, Heinz (2008), "Law, Politics, and Access to Essential Medicines in Developing Countries," *Politics and Society*, **36** (2), 207–46.

Lacarte, Julio (2004), "Transparency, Public Debate and Participation by NGOs in the WTO: A WTO Perspective," *Journal of International Economic Law*, **7** (3), 683–6.

Lake, David (1988), *Power, Protection and Free Trade: International Sources of U.S. Commercial Strategy, 1887–1939*, Ithaca, NY: Cornell University Press.

Lang, Andrew (2007), "Reflecting on 'Linkage': Cognitive and Institutional Change in the International Trading System," *Modern Law Review*, **70** (4), 523–49.

Matthews, Duncan (2002), *Globalizing Intellectual Property Rights: The TRIPs Agreement*, London: Routledge.

Milner, Helen (1999), "The Political Economy of International Trade," *Annual Review of Political Science*, **2**, 91–114.

Murphy, Hannah (2010), *The Making of International Trade Policy: NGOs, Agenda-Setting and the WTO*, Cheltenham, UK and Northampton, MA, USA: Edward Elgar Publishing.

O'Brien, Robert, Anne Marie Goetz, Jan Aart Scholte and Marc Williams (2000), *Contesting Global Governance: Multilateral Economic Institutions and Global Social Movements*, Cambridge: Cambridge University Press.

Ostry, Sylvia (2002), "The Uruguay Round North–South Grand Bargain: Implications for Future Negotiations," in Daniel Kennedy and James Southwick (eds.), *The Political Economy of International Trade: Essays in Honor of Robert E. Hudec*, Cambridge: Cambridge University Press, pp. 285–300.

Ostry, Sylvia (2009), "The World Trade Organization: System under Stress," in Steven Bernstein and W. Coleman (eds.), *Unsettled Legitimacy: Political Community, Power and Authority in a Global Era*, Vancouver: University of British Columbia, pp. 259–79.

Polanyi, Karl ([1944] 2001), *The Great Transformation: The Political and Economic Origins of Our Time*, Boston, MA: Beacon Press.

Ricupero, Rubens (2001), "Rebuilding Confidence in the Multilateral Trading System," in Gary Sampson (ed.), *The Role of the World Trade Organization in Global Governance*, Tokyo: United Nations University Press, pp. 37–58.

Rikkilä, Lena and Katarina Sehm Patomäki (2001), *Democracy and Globalisation: Promoting North–South Dialogue*, Helsinki: Hakapaino.

Robertson, David (2000), "Civil Society and the WTO," *World Economy*, **23** (9), 1119–34.

Rogowski, Ronald (1990), *Commerce and Coalitions: How Trade Affects Domestic Political Alignments*, Princeton, NJ: Princeton University Press.

Ruggie, John (1982), "International Regimes, Transactions, and Change: Embedded Liberalism in the Postwar Economic Order," *International Organization*, **36** (2), 379–415.

Sapra, Seema (2009), "The WTO System of Trade Governance: The Stale NGO Debate and the Appropriate Role for Non-State Actors," *Oregon Review of International Law*, **11** (1), 71–108.

Scholte, Jan Aart (2004), "The WTO and Civil Society," in Brian Hocking and Steven McGuire (eds.), *Trade Politics*, London: Routledge, pp. 146–61.

Scholte, Jan Aart (2011), "Global Governance, Accountability and Civil Society," in Jan Aart Scholte (ed.), *Building Global Democracy? Civil Society and Accountable Global Governance*, Cambridge: Cambridge University Press, pp. 8–41.

Sell, Susan and Aseem Prakash (2004), "Using Ideas Strategically: The Contest between Business and NGO Networks in Intellectual Property Rights," *International Studies Quarterly*, **48** (1), 143–75.

Shell, G. Richard (1996), "Trade Stakeholders Model and Participation by Nonstate Parties in the World Trade Organization," *University of Pennsylvania Journal of International Economic Law*, **17** (1), 358–82.

Stolper, Wolfgang and Paul Samuelson (1941), "Protection and Real Wages," *Review of Economic Studies*, **9** (1), 58–73.

Trentmann, Frank (1998), "Political Culture and Political Economy: Interests, Ideology and Free Trade," *Review of International Political Economy*, **5** (2), 217–51.

Trommer, Silke (2014), *Transformations in Trade Politics: Participatory Trade Politics in West Africa*, London: Routledge.

Viner, Jacob (1947), "Conflicts of Principle in Drafting a Trade Charter," *Foreign Affairs*, **25** (4), 612–28.

Viner, Jacob (1950), *The Customs Union Issue*, Washington, DC: Carnegie Endowment for International Peace.

Wilkinson, Rorden (2002), "The Contours of Courtship: The WTO and Civil Society," in Rorden Wilkinson and Steven Hughes (eds.), *Global Governance: Critical Perspectives*, London: Routledge, pp. 193–211.

Williams, Marc (2004), "Contesting Global Trade Rules: Social Movements and the World Trade Organization," in Lourdes Benería and Savitri Bisnath (eds.), *Global Tensions: Challenges and Opportunities in the World Economy*, London: Routledge, pp. 193–206.

Williams, Marc (2011), "Civil Society and the WTO: Contesting Accountability," in Jan Aart Scholte (ed.), *Building Global Democracy? Civil Society and Accountable Global Governance*, Cambridge: Cambridge University Press, pp. 105–27.

Woolcock, Stephen (2005), "Trade Policy: From Uruguay to Doha and Beyond," in Helen Wallace, William Wallace and Mark A. Pollack (eds.), *Policy-Making in the European Union*, Oxford: Oxford University Press, pp. 377–99.

WTO (World Trade Organization) (1996), *Guidelines for Arrangements on Relations with Non-Governmental Organizations*, Decision adopted by the General Council, July 18, WT/L/162.

WTO (World Trade Organization) (2009), "Lamy Underscores the Urgency of Responding to Climate Crisis," November 2, available from: http://www.wto.org/english/news_e/sppl_e/sppl140_e.htm (accessed April 16, 2014).

Young, Alasdair and John Peterson (2006), "The EU and the New Trade Politics," *Journal of European Public Policy*, **13** (6), 795–814.

19. Capitalism in large emerging economies and the new global trade order[1]
Christian May and Andreas Nölke

INTRODUCTION

Large emerging economies have increased their share of the global economy quite substantially over the last few decades. While discussions about the international political economy previously centered on the US, the EU and Japan, such a focus is difficult to uphold today. In particular China, India and Brazil have surpassed the established economies in terms of GDP growth, trade growth and industry value added growth during the last 30 years (Figure 19.1).

Although these figures fluctuate quite substantially every year, there are no sound reasons to assume that this long-term tendency is likely to reverse any time soon. Correspondingly, countries such as Brazil, China and India

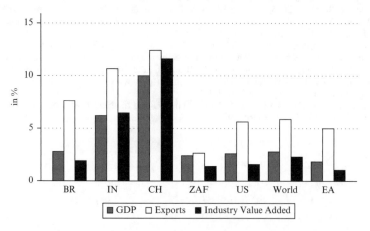

Notes:
Average growth of GDP, exports and industry value added, average annual percentage growth, 1980–2010.
ZAF=South Africa; EA=Euro Area.

Source: World Bank.

Figure 19.1 Economic dynamics of large emerging economies

have to be increasingly counted as heavyweights that shape the future of the global economy. Moreover, they have recently begun to organize themselves in order to coordinate their positions vis-à-vis the global economic order. Examples of this coordination include the institutionalized cooperation between India, Brazil and South Africa (IBSA), the BASIC alliance (also including China) and the BRICS grouping (additionally including Russia). In the long term, we may thus assume that we are witnessing not only a shift in economic importance in favor of large emerging economies, but also a conscious effort by the latter to influence global economic rules.

The likely consequences of the rise of the large emerging economies for the global economic order have been discussed widely in recent years (for example Hurrell 2006; Cooper et al. 2007; Subacchi 2008). However, they have so far focused only on getting a seat at the table (such as larger voting rights in the Bretton Woods institutions and participation in the Basel Committee) and have only just begun to outline their demands for specific policies. Thus, on the substance of this new global economic order, many of the existing accounts are either heavily speculative or, in contrast, purely descriptive and thus unable to make any substantial statement regarding the likely future course of events.

Our approach is based on the assumption that we need to develop clear analytical perspectives on the behavior of large emerging economies with regard to the global economic order if we want to go beyond description and/or speculation. In this chapter we develop a "second image" perspective, in the terminology of Waltz (2001), by highlighting the importance of domestic economic structures for the explanation of global economic policies (Singer 1961). In contrast to liberal theories of international relations (Moravcsik 1997; Schirm 2013), however, we do not focus on the interactions between domestic societal interest groups and governments, but rather study the broad capitalist structures that have evolved in large emerging markets. The reason is twofold: on the one hand, we are interested in the long-term evolution of emerging markets' stance towards the global economic order. Such a research interest does not lend itself well to the demarcation of issue-specific preferences of particular interest groups in individual countries, which is the usual approach of these liberal theories. On the other hand, we are deeply skeptical about the application of conventional liberal-pluralist models of democratic policy making to countries such as China, but also Brazil and India. Instead, we assume – in a more historical-institutionalist perspective – that the type of capitalism dominating in the large emerging economies will also determine their long-term preferences regarding the global economic order; that is, they will want to make sure that global economic rules do not inhibit the functioning of their domestic economic order (Fioretos 2011). More specifically, we are situating our analysis in the critical institutionalist approach within comparative capitalism (May and Nölke 2013), which means that we are comparing national capitalist institutions from a perspective that highlights the historical evolution of specific forms of capitalism based on their mode of integration into the global political economy and on domestic class struggles. From this perspective, we argue that there are important commonalities between the national varieties of capitalism that have developed in the large emerging markets, and that this new type of capitalism is an important determinant of the future global economic order.

Correspondingly, the next section of this chapter sketches some important aspects of this new type of capitalism. We highlight that capitalism in large emerging markets is dominated by national development strategies, which are being coordinated by alliances of domestic capitalists and fractions of the state, held together by reciprocal exchanges. The chapter then discusses the implications that the emergence of this form of capitalism entails for global trade regulation. Crucial findings include a clear preference for reciprocal bilateral instead of universalist multilateral agreements, and an aversion to central issues of the World Trade Organization (WTO) Singapore agenda, in particular regarding the freedom of investment rule that might challenge the dominance of national capital. Finally, we step back from the particular issues of global trade regulation and move towards more general implications of our findings for the global economic order. Here we find inspiration in the sociological work on coordination by Karl Polanyi (1977, [1944] 2001) and apply this approach to the broad lines of global economic regulation. Seen from this perspective, a global order dominated by the large emerging markets can be considered as a non-liberal order based on reciprocal exchanges, in contrast to market coordination in the liberal postwar economic order, and to (proposed) coordination by redistribution in the New International Economic Order of the late 1960s and early 1970s.

The emphasis of our empirical discussion is on trade. Arguably, it is easier to come to a thorough assessment of recent changes as well as the development of clear perspectives for further development of the global economy if we focus our discussions on one particular issue area (and then compare findings with those on other issue areas).[2] In contrast to issue areas such as production or finance, trade is a particularly important issue for the study of the global political economy, especially given the existence of a powerful global trade institution (the WTO). The empirical focus of our discussion is on the very large emerging economies (in particular China, India, Brazil and South Africa), not only because these economies are at the centre of the various emerging economies' associations, but also because we assume that the type of capitalism in (rather autonomous) large emerging economies differs quite clearly from the type of smaller "dependent market economies" (Nölke and Vliegenthart 2009). We exclude Russia from our analysis, since Russia mainly qualifies as a natural resources exporter, more similar to Saudi Arabia than to rapidly industrializing countries such as Brazil, India and China.

LARGE EMERGING ECONOMIES AS A DISTINCT TYPE OF CAPITALISM

From a second image-perspective, "the internal structure of states determines not only the form and use of military force but external behavior generally" (Waltz 2001: 125). This means that we have to look inside large emerging economies to learn about their international behavior. Since the economic structures in these countries are relatively similar, we argue for a common and particular model of capitalism that heavily influences their external preferences.

The point of departure of our stylized account of capitalism in large emerging economies is the observation that this type of capitalism can best be depicted as a "state-permeated market economy" (Nölke 2012; Nölke et al. 2013).[3] State-permeated market economies are dominated by domestic capitalists who are working fairly closely in various alliances with government agencies and ministries, mostly based on informal personal relations. In contrast to the situation in dependent market economies, such as the Czech Republic or Slovakia, national control over the economy is maintained by avoiding a sell-out to (Western) multinational companies. In contrast to the model of the East Asian developmental state, state-permeated market economies are not hierarchically and formally coordinated by a central body, and do not rely on exports as the backbone of their economic model. Below we will illustrate some core traits of this ideal type with a focus on the institutional spheres highlighted by comparative capitalism scholarship, such as corporate governance, sources of investment finance, industrial relations and education and training (Jackson and Deeg 2006), enlarged by our own concern with the particular mode of integration into the global economy. Next, we will focus in greater detail on corporate governance and on global economic integration, given that these areas are most crucial for an understanding of the stance of these countries towards the global trade order.

State-Permeated Capitalism: In a Nutshell

Corporations from emerging economies are typically not dominated by dispersed shareholders and the organized forces of global capital markets (mutual funds, pension funds, investment banks, hedge funds, etc.), but are family owned or state controlled. Family and state ownership might even be counted among the "distinguishing features" of non-triad multinationals (Goldstein 2007: 148). Foreign direct investments (FDI) and selected privatizations are welcome as long as they do not challenge the predominance of national capital. The latter depends on such modernization in order to provide for the conditions of its own expansion; therefore it supports the selective opening of the producing sector for foreign investments. Usually, however, investments are financed by retained earnings of firms and bank credit by state-controlled banks. Raising funds for investments on global stock markets, in turn, does not play a significant role. Industries in emerging economies profit from very low average wages, which are accompanied by low social spending (with the recent exception of Brazil). Emerging economies spend relatively little on R&D and innovation, mostly because new technologies are imported through FDI and practices of reverse engineering and imitation but also because industrial development in emerging economies requires high labor input, which again makes investment in human resources a minor priority. In order to support (large) national firms, product markets are heavily protected and FDI is discouraged. As a consequence, large firms in emerging economies are able to develop in sheltered domestic markets and enter the global market only in a late stage. Central banks in emerging economies actively seek to stabilize external financial relations by accumulating currency reserves in order to prevent volatility in the exchange rate from compromising the competitiveness of domestic firms. Overall, the model of capitalism in emerging economies is characterized by strong but differentiated activity of the state and a high level of protection of domestic firms, albeit in a very selective way. This is because much coordination in emerging economies is based on reciprocal personal relations between state officials at various levels and managers of large domestic firms. In the following, we discuss these two key features in greater detail.

Control by Domestic Owners

In contrast to capitalism in the European Union and the United States, companies in the large emerging markets are dominated by domestic owners. This feature can be illustrated with the relationship between inward FDI and the size of the economy (Figure 19.2). The Chinese and Indian economies, especially, are still overwhelmingly dominated by domestic capitalists: either by the state or by highly concentrated private ownership.

While capitalism in emerging economies is neither one-sidedly state con-

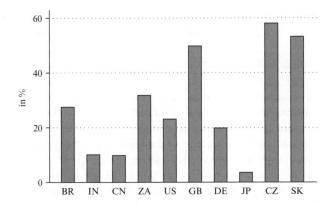

Note: ZA=South Africa; DE=Germany.

Source: UNCTAD.

Figure 19.2   FDI inward stock as percentage of GDP

trolled nor market led, the presence of domestic business communities is crucial. These communities are a result of two characteristic features: high concentration of private ownership and control along with a state that is able to allocate crucial resources. Most Indian companies are dominated by the founding family (Allen et al. 2006: 21). It is no exaggeration to assert that the Indian economy is governed by business houses, with the heads of them being eminent persons of Indian social life (Piramal 1996; Dutta 1997). Family-owned businesses are also "the typical business arrangement of the Brazilian bourgeoisie" (Abu-El-Haj 2007: 106). Obviously, owning families have more long-term stakes in their businesses than anonymous shareholders. As a consequence, much coordination is based on personal relations and reciprocal trust. Historically, the state acted (and still acts) as a gatekeeper to important resources, such as licenses for production in India or low-interest credit in Brazil. Wherever the state has something crucial to distribute, actors depending on such resources tend to seek exclusive access and, over time, personal relations between business and state managers are established. Although Chinese business relations are more fragmented than in Brazil or India, personal connections are key as well. Under pressure to fulfill growth benchmarks set by the central state, provincial bureaucrats and businesses cooperate very closely. As an effect, decisions over activities of enterprises are taken within public–private growth communities (Wank 2001; ten Brink 2010). These business communities become stronger owing to the competition they face from rival communities in other provinces. Here, too, reciprocity between economic actors provides for reliable and long-term coordination.

Selective Protection from External Competitors

The model of capitalism in large emerging economies is not universally protectionist, but its institutional set-up includes a number of genuinely non-liberal traits. More specifically, emerging economies do not follow an export-led growth path. In contrast to the East Asian "tiger states," in which a strong developmental state fueled a strict export orientation, growth in emerging economies is increasingly driven by domestic consumption (for China, see for example Brandt and Thun 2010: 1558). Moreover, investment strategies of firms are heavily shaped by the macroeconomic preferences of state agencies. For this reason, the state channels large amounts of credit through ministries and, in particular, state-controlled development banks (Musacchio and Lazzarini 2012). Such preferential support for local companies by way of advantageous credit conditions often allows domestic firms to be more competitive than foreign companies. Furthermore, the state acts as a giant consumer of goods and services. Especially with regard to infrastructure and public procurement, foreign firms are structurally excluded from these markets. Such protection from external competitors allows local firms to follow long-term maturing strategies without being subject to short-term interests by shareholders from global capital markets and price pressures by powerful foreign multinationals.

Protection of domestic firms from external competition, even at the cost of conflicting with international norms, is a common policy of all catch-up strategies. Historically, this has been a crucial element of developmentalist policies. First, "infant" firms copy or reinvent products for the domestic market that is shielded by high tariffs and later, as products become competitive in the world market, states follow an aggressive export orientation. However, today's emerging economies keep on walling off the domestic market even though many companies are by no means infant anymore. They use a differential system of product market regulations that favor national firms to take advantage of their large domestic markets (Figure 19.3).

The privileged position of large national companies, which are often long-established local market players, is thus strengthened by restrictive trade policies. Although these policies are meant to be developmentalist, emerging countries tacitly accept their protectionist side effects. Preferential support for large national companies comes in a mixture of direct (for example the provision of state credit) and indirect (by the provision of a favorable macroeconomic framework) means. A crucial element is the provision of macroeconomic stability. As most emerging

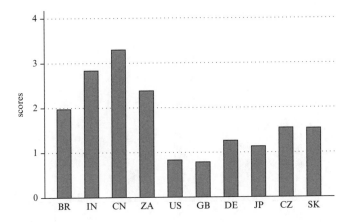

Notes:
Index scale of 0–6 from least to most restrictive.
ZA = South Africa; DE = Germany.

Source: OECD (www.oecd.org/economy/pmr).

Figure 19.3   Product market regulation in emerging and OECD countries, 2008

economies experience economic instability, including debt crises, inflation and the deterioration of world market prices, states actively seek to stabilize the value of their currency. This is done mainly by accumulating foreign reserves. The main objective is to prevent abrupt devaluation of the national currencies as a reaction to external shocks and crises. It became a priority across central banks after the Asian Crisis, where East Asian central banks were forced to devaluate against the dollar owing to speculative attacks. The lack of sufficient foreign currency to pay for imports often forced developing countries into short-term borrowing and unwanted trade liberalization (see Richter 2013). Contemporary emerging economies aim to avoid both, as it hinders long-term development strategies and correspondingly results in these countries amassing foreign currency. By now, most of them are able to cover a year of import payments from their currency stocks, whereas they could do so only for five to eight months during the mid-1990s (Figure 19.4).

The main goal behind the accumulation of foreign reserves is not an artificial undervaluation of the national currency to stimulate export-led growth. On the contrary, sudden devaluation should be avoided. What lies behind the large reserves is the establishment of a stable macroeconomic framework that makes it reasonable for domestic firms to invest in capital goods in order to create a competitive industrial base, instead of sticking

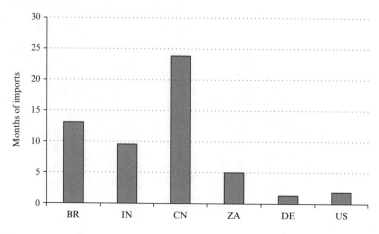

Notes:
In months of imports.
ZA=South Africa; DE=Germany.

Source: World Bank database.

Figure 19.4   Foreign currency reserves of emerging economies

to simple assembling and the export of primary goods. Thus, emerging economies of the twenty-first century, such as Brazil, China and India, follow a developmentalist agenda but differ strongly from the East Asian new industrializing countries such as Korea and Taiwan in at least two ways. Firstly, the state engages in various ways with the economy, but without commanding or planning it from overarching "growth ministries" (Woo-Cumings 1999). Secondly, the interplay of the various institutions of "BRIC capitalism" enables high growth rates, albeit not based on excessive exports.

TRADE-RELATED IMPLICATIONS OF THE INCREASING IMPORTANCE OF EMERGING ECONOMIES

If we apply the second image-view to the international political economy of trade, we expect the external behavior of Brazil, India and China to follow the underlying preferences of their internal economic structures. Consequently, we observe a strongly inward-looking, non-liberal and reciprocal stance towards global trade.

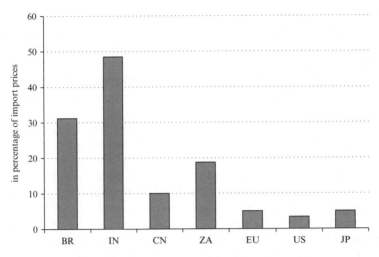

Notes:
Average bound *ad valorem* tariff.
ZA=South Africa.

Source: WTO (2012a, 2012b).

Figure 19.5 *Average tariff rate, compared to other largest traders (excluding Russia)*

Continuing Protection of National Product Markets

Although they are slowly reducing, average tariffs in emerging economies are still high compared to other major trading countries (Figure 19.5).

With tariffs being at least four times higher than in the EU and the US, emerging economies are far from submitting to a global free trade agenda. Moreover, the relatively low tariff rate for China is, in our view, not a sign of China's free trade commitments. On the contrary, we find it highly unlikely that Chinese capitalists will leave the market of the rising middle classes over the next decades to foreign competitors that are exporting to rather than investing in China.

Enduring Opposition to Deep Liberalization (of Ownership) via WTO Singapore Issues

As the large emerging economies are not heavily dependent on exports, their integration into the global trade system is selective and fragmentary. During the last ten years, they have succeeded in emancipating themselves from foreign assistance and associated conditionalities. As a consequence, they were able to protect their economic systems from pressures to remove capital barriers and ownership restrictions. The same applies to the attempt of Western countries to open emerging (and developing) economies via trade-related deep integration (Claar and Nölke 2012). Measures of deep integration, also called "Singapore issues" or "WTO plus," were proposed by the EU and the US more than a decade ago, but were turned down consistently by a coalition of emerging and developing economies. From the perspective developed in this chapter, this will most likely be an enduring state of affairs.

Investment rules are linked with trade relations because their regulation crucially touches upon the possibility of Western firms being active in emerging economies. Facing high tariff and non-tariff barriers, foreign firms might endeavor to enter large emerging economies by setting up branches in these countries. The establishment of emerging economies has been accompanied since the 1980s by a reorientation of foreign investors in the (semi-)periphery, who switched their focus away from the exploitation of labor and raw materials in developing countries (let alone the political priorities of the Cold War) towards their growing domestic markets. Such ambitions however are hampered by strong restrictions on FDI in the large emerging economies. Often, emerging economies allow FDI only conditionally, for example by forcing foreign investors to engage in joint ventures with local companies or by inhibiting transnational mergers and acquisitions. As a consequence, trade negotiations in the GATT and WTO increasingly expanded into these realms, such as the GATT Agreement on Trade-Related Investment Measures (TRIMs) and the inclusion of competitions policy and public procurement into the Singapore issues. However, the issue of public procurement transparency has been dealt with only marginally in the WTO. It is excluded from the General Agreement on Trade in Services (GATS), and negotiations on this were halted after the Cancún ministerial meeting in 2003 (WTO 2004). The deadlock in Cancún was due not only to conflicting views on agriculture but also to fundamental rifts over the Singapore issues (Narlikar and Tussie 2004). This has not fundamentally changed during the last ten years, in spite of repeated initiatives by the EU and the US (Nölke and Claar 2012). The selective regulation of public procurement, investment and competition is a crucial pillar of state-permeated capitalism, and any compromise on these issues would potentially undermine the competitive strength of emerging economies.

A Shift from WTO Universal Trade Agreements to Bilateral Reciprocal Trade Agreements

The practice of controlling the inflow of imports by high levels of product market regulation and tariffs is reflected in the increased importance of bilateral and other reciprocal trade agreements (Figure 19.6).

While recent trade agreements by the EU and the US with Morocco, Papua New Guinea and Fiji are of minor global importance, agreements of emerging economies span huge trading blocs, such as the Mercosur, the Mercosur–India and the ASEAN–China agreements. Most reciprocal trade agreements by emerging economies are with other countries of the Southern hemisphere, which tend to form overlapping Southern trade groupings. By now, this is an explicit aim of the BRICS group, which announced in their Joint Delhi Declaration of 2012 their aim to "build upon our synergies and to work together to intensify trade and investment flows among our countries to advance our respective industrial development and employment objectives" (BRICS 2012). This would not be particularly challenging for the developed world if it involved only trade. What matters more is that the BRICS are planning to enable payments for inter-BRICS trade in local currency, which means in renminbi, not US dollars (McNally 2012). As the combined share of Brazil, India, China and South

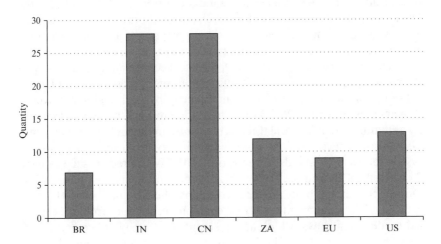

Note: ZA=South Africa.

Source: WTO RTA Database.

Figure 19.6   Reciprocal trade agreements, 2003–11 (goods only)

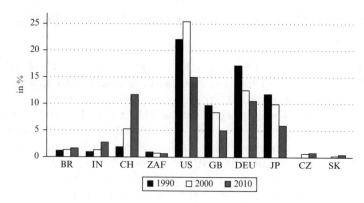

Notes:
Trade as sum of exports and imports of goods and services.
ZAF=South Africa; DEU=Germany.

Source: World Bank.

Figure 19.7   Shifting shares in global trade

Africa already amounts to nearly 20 per cent of world trade (Figure 19.7), or more than the US share, this poses a potential challenge to the dollar-based trade regime. The challenge behind the currency conflict between the USA and China is therefore not so much about a short-term advantage by an undervalued renminbi, but about the perspective of an alternative trade and monetary system. But, in order to function as alternative trade currencies, renminbis, rupees and reais will have to become stable and trustworthy means of exchange for which sufficient foreign reserves are available.

South–South trade therefore is increasingly bypassing global universal principles as codified in WTO rules. Instead, it follows the rule of reciprocity as manifested in bilateral trade agreements, and it could well evolve into a BRICs-managed payment system. In this way, from the late 1990s this system increasingly stands in opposition to the WTO trade regime. Almost 75 per cent of all complaints by Brazil, India and China before the WTO Dispute Settlement Body are targeted against the EU and the US (Horn et al. 2011). The fundamental shift by emerging economies from an export-led model to an inward-looking development strategy at the end of the 1990s has thrown into doubt the current global free trade regime (Blustein 2009: 238). The "Southern turn" represents a suitable exit strategy for those countries that have developed a specific type of capitalism. As these countries are ever more important to the global economy, this particular configuration of Southern capitalism has dramatic consequences for the world economic order.

MARKET, REDISTRIBUTION AND RECIPROCITY: LONG-TERM IMPLICATIONS FOR THE GLOBAL ECONOMIC ORDER

But why do large emerging economies display reciprocal and non-liberal modes of economic regulation, and what are its long-term consequences? In order to make sense of the recent changes in trade policies and to extrapolate the contours of a global economic order dominated by the large emerging markets, we now turn to categories developed by Karl Polanyi.

Market, Redistribution and Reciprocity in Polanyi

In *The Great Transformation* Polanyi distinguished between three principles of economic order or "forms of integration" beyond the market: reciprocity, redistribution and household production (Polanyi [1944] 2001: 49–56). For good reason he later included household production in the category of redistributive economic organization (Polanyi 1977: 41). Generally, he stresses the socializing aspect of economic relations. Indeed, he argues that such forms of economic integration represent different modes of societalization (*Vergesellschaftung*). Reciprocity, redistribution and the market represent three principles of economic organization.

- Reciprocity aims to achieve symmetry among parties. The classic case of reciprocity is the gift–countergift chain, through which economic relations are established. Polanyi refers to the system of trade between the Trobriand Islands as a highly sophisticated institution of economic exchange (Polanyi [1944] 2001: 52–3). He also points out that gifts do not need to be of equal but of "appropriate" value, a discerning criterion for the valuation of goods, as opposed to prices, which requires abilities for interpretation and empathy.
- Redistributive economies collect goods and other values centrally and distribute them according to pre-formulated criteria among members of a society. This does apply for instance to household economies, although all large-scale economies require some form of redistribution (Polanyi [1944] 2001: 53). Political economies vary according to the extent to which they are organized on the basis of redistribution. Modern states establish systems of taxation, and some even provide for extensive welfare arrangements, while socialist economies are, in principle, entirely redistributive.
- To speak about market economies means that the political economy is dominated by the price mechanism. However, this mechanism

can be effective only if the economy is organized not symmetrically or centrally, but diffusely. A major feature of markets is their anonymity: they not only enable instant transactions between strangers but also guarantee equal prices for any market participant. In this way, economic relations are intended to achieve distance, or "arm's length," instead of closer proximity between members. Anonymity implies that the economic order must be exclusively based upon market relations, that is, that no other social relations, such as kinship, friendship, loyalty or enmity, should interfere as "intervening" norms of coordination. Consequently, such interventions are known as "market distortions" in market societies.

Polanyi's analysis of the rise of the liberal market society as a corollary to the rise of capitalism, and how this differs from many non-capitalist societies, both sheds light on different national economic systems and helps to explain the emergence of, and change in, the current global political economy. As we shall see, the postwar economic order was dominated by liberalism before it was challenged by the redistributive principles of the new international economic order (NIEO). A global economic order dominated by the large emerging markets, however, will probably be dominated by principles of reciprocity.

Market Coordination: The Liberal Postwar International Economic Order

The Pax Americana established an order in which key liberal institutions became more and more institutionalized on the global level. At its heart was the principle of freedom, or the freedom of individual actors to engage in economic actions as they so choose (see Sørensen 2006). Market coordination epitomizes economic freedom because actors act neither upon command, as in a hierarchical coordination, nor upon loyalty, as in reciprocal coordination. Only in markets are economic agents able to pursue their goals without regard to fellow actors. Markets therefore must be de-contextualized and anonymous. Equal treatment should ensure that strangers can enjoy the same benefits as locals. This principle is exhibited for instance in the most-favored-nation treatment provisions within the GATT and the WTO.

Since the internalization of the economy was central to the postwar global economic order, liberal political principles have been important for its justification (van der Pijl 1984). But internationalization did not proceed without tensions. Globally, the system experienced the same constellation that Polanyi identified for the emerging bourgeois, or capitalist, society: while one class strives to maximize wealth, another class tries to protect itself from dislocation. He accurately predicted the perspective of the emerging bourgeois class: "The poor man shall be satisfied in his end: Habitation; and the gentleman not hindered in his desire: Improvement" (Polanyi [1944] 2001: 36).

By the 1960s, most countries were not part of the liberal club; that is, they were not characterized by the liberal principles of governance laid out above. They danced, and still dance, to different beats. Liberal universalism was not in their interest. It certainly did not correspond with their actual life experience, because in many countries capitalism existed only in "islands": the big cities, industrial districts, special processing zones and so forth. It was often absent in the rural hinterland, where people generally produced for their own needs instead of the market. Their integration into the world economy was conditional upon their need to maintain "habitation" – the ability to protect their economic existence. This became the backbone of the movement for a new international economic order in the 1970s.

Coordination by Redistribution: The New International Economic Order

The dominant mode of international economic regulation in the postwar period has been the market, both politically and economically. Since this has been neither a natural order, nor one that is complementary to non-market forms of regulation, it required the elimination of all other forms of governance. But, with the same action, it made inevitable, in Polanyi's words, a "counter-movement" ([1944] 2001: 136–57). Ruggie's depiction of the postwar international economic order as an "embedded liberalism" compromise, in which the rigidities of the international market are limited by domestic political intervention (Ruggie 1982), slightly distorts the picture for two reasons: Firstly, this compromise, as negotiated by a leading group of capitalist states, excluded most of the world from the basic understanding about protecting the integrity of national economies (Ruggie 1982). Secondly, it is now understood to be a static configuration which lasted only until the early 1970s, when the US abandoned the dollar convertibility and financial markets were, in turn, liberalized. However, during this period the formerly excluded colonies and third world countries emerged as significant actors, and Western liberalization pressures on these economies intensified, not least because of the activity of multinational corporations. When the G-77 organized around the NIEO issue, their main objective was protection: first to maintain an economic order that "fitted" with their domestic social structures and later to overcome the vicious circle of dependent underdevelopment (Frank 1969). As Craig Murphy pointed out, the ideas behind the NIEO were of both an economic and a political nature (Murphy 2005: 107–13). Yet the "core of the NIEO ideology" (Murphy 2005: 107) consisted of an alternative project for the design of the postwar international system. Political leaders of the South in the 1940s envisaged an international order based on inter-state solidarity within the UN where:

> each state had the duty to aid the economic development of every other state, that this aid should be given no matter what political and economic disagreements a country might have with another country's economic ideology or economic policies. It was, for example, the duty of a capitalist state to aid the economic development of socialist states. (Murphy 2005: 109)

It can be argued that political and economic exclusion fostered the radicalization of Southern positions. As we know, the postwar system was characterized by several key principles, but certainly not solidarity. This had the effect of marginalizing Southern demands. The implicit ideas of fairness and equality were further frustrated by economic arguments about deteriorating terms of trade, which became more radical in their evolution from Raul Prebisch in the 1950s to Andre Gunder Frank in the 1960s. By then, the NIEO project adopted not only the principle but also the "duty" of redistribution: from this perspective the wealth of the North is a direct result of the South's poverty. For this reason, the NIEO aimed for a redistribution of global wealth.

Even if perhaps the imagination of inter-state solidarity by the early NIEO movement was idealistic, any chance for its realization became illusory in the wake of bloc rivalry and US interventionism. Any economic system based on redistribution must establish a centralist institutional structure, and a common sense of community, such as that of a "nation," is often indispensable. Both were missing from the postwar global system, which is why the NIEO movement was stuck in an antagonistic position vis-à-vis the developed countries. Most importantly, the NIEO could not become a counter-hegemonic force, because it never corresponded to the internal structures of most G-77 countries, which were, in fact, usually not based on solidarity. In contrast, even the postwar embedded liberalism dissolved after the 1970s, giving way to neoliberalism, an economic order where market principles dominated not only international institutions but also increasingly all economic and social sub-systems.

Coordination by Reciprocity: A State-Permeated Economic Order

The rise of the emerging economies may be considered to provide an opportunity for changing the global order. Will this order turn away from the market principle and towards redistribution as demanded by those countries four decades ago? From our perspective, however, any new world economic order that is led by the large emerging economies would be based much less on liberal or redistributive principles, and much more on reciprocity. This is not because the emerging economies adhere to a particular ideology of reciprocity, although notions of "fairness" and "balance" often come to the fore in their statements at international negotiations, but because their domestic economies developed institutions that were able to convert a reciprocal form of coordination into a comparative advantage. Our basic assumption is therefore that from the emerging economies' point of view there is no point in regulating their external relations in a fundamentally different way than their domestic ones.

Where personal relations between national capitalists and state agencies effectively coordinate the economy, there is no need for formal contracts, since interpersonal trust ensures the execution of reciprocal obligations. These reciprocal relationships are preserved over many decades, as for example in India, and they are often strongly connected to society-wide norms. It is difficult to make sense of Chinese capitalism without considering *guanxi* as a fundamental reciprocal principle of daily life (Michailova and Worm 2003; Ledeneva 2008). Similar to *blat* in Russia, it delineates patterns of loyalty and mutual obligations that, despite all differences, effectively create communities because members enjoy privileges not available to outsiders. In Brazil, in contrast, loyalty plays out in widespread patronage (Boeckh 2003). While the sources and characteristics of this mode of coordination are different, common to all is their reciprocal character and the fact that political and economic regulation becomes "privatized."

In sum, "selectivity" is one characteristic feature of capitalism in emerging economies. Loyalty networks establish state–business communities through their active (re-)production of reciprocal relations. As true communities, they constitute in-groups that provide exclusive "club goods" of which only members can take advantage. While this poses strong objections from a Western point of view concerning universalism, there are good reasons to consider these modes of regulation to be thoroughly embedded in general social values and principles. Selective regulation is not only legitimate within their respective social settings but also effective. It apparently brings about results for enterprises that are just as efficient and productive as those under Anglo-Saxon market-led governance. We can therefore speak of a successful institutional complementarity that enables steady growth. For Western observers, this is perceived as clientelism, protectionism and patronage, but, in the absence of liberal universalistic principles, such patterns are well-established modes of social order.

As highlighted above, there are strong indications that the trade policies of the large emerging economies are informed by these domestic structures. Emerging markets try to protect the close linkages between domestic capital and the state. At the same time, they extend the reciprocity principle governing these relationships to the global economic order by, for example, pursuing bilateral trade agreements over global ones. From the perspective developed in this chapter, any global economic order which reflects the power shift towards the large emerging markets will be non-liberal. It will reject universalist principles of order valid for the domestic and the international level. In particular, it will not be centered around market-compatible equality of access for all participants, but selective policy making and implementation as well as preferential treatment of specific economic actors. Thus one cannot expect a further consolidation of global liberal institutions with their emphasis on free access for all. To the extent that the external behavior of the large emerging economies is based on the dominant economic structures in these countries, we may expect the evolution of what has been a liberal, market-based, global economic order into one dominated by the principle of reciprocity.

NOTES

1. This chapter is based on findings of a research project on the nature of capitalism in Brazil, India, China and South Africa, started in June 2012 at Goethe University Frankfurt, Germany (www.bics.uni-frankfurt.de). We gratefully acknowledge support by the German Research Council (Deutsche Forschungsgemeinschaft/DFG, No. 855/3-1) and research assistance by Hauke Feil, Sabine Englert and Sahil Mathur. We are indebted to Patrick Bond, Sacha Dierckx, Kevin Gray and Jim Mittelman for valuable comments and suggestions.
2. For broader, more superficial studies see Nölke and Taylor (2010) and Nölke (2011).
3. The following depiction refers to a theoretical ideal type. Specific countries are more or less identical with this ideal type, and may move towards the type or away from it over time. Currently, China is most close to this ideal type, followed by India; South Africa and Brazil are more distant, with the latter recently moving towards the ideal type.

REFERENCES

Abu-El-Haj, Jawdat (2007), "From Interdependence to Neo-Mercantilism: Brazilian Capitalism in the Age of Globalization," *Latin American Perspectives*, **34** (5), 92–114.
Allen, Franklin, R. Chakrabarti, S. De, J. Qian and M. Qian (2006), "Financing Firms in India," Working Paper 06-08, University of Pennsylvania, Wharton Financial Institutions Center.
Blustein, Paul (2009), *Misadventures of the Most Favored Nations: Clashing Egos, Inflated Ambitions, and the Great Shambles of the World Trade System*, New York: Public Affairs.
Boeckh, Andreas (2003), "Der gefesselte Gigant: Politik und Reform(un-)fähigkeit in Brasilien," in Gerd Kohlhepp (ed.), *Brasilien: Entwicklungsland oder tropische Grossmacht des 21. Jahrhunderts?*, Tübingen: Attempto, pp. 57–80.

Brandt, Loren and Eric Thun (2010), "The Fight for the Middle: Upgrading, Competition, and Industrial Development in China," *World Development*, **38** (11), 1555–74.
BRICS (2012), "BRICS Delhi Declaration," available from: http://www.brics.utoronto.ca/docs/120329-delhi-declaration.html (accessed April 16, 2013).
Brink, Tobias ten (2010), *Strukturmerkmale des chinesischen Kapitalismus*, MPIfG Working Paper 10-1, Cologne: Max Planck Institute for the Study of Societies.
Claar, Simone and Andreas Nölke (2012), "Tiefe Integration: Konzeptuelle Grundlagen," *Journal für Entwicklungspolitik*, **28** (2), 8–27.
Cooper, Andrew F., Agata Antkiewicz and Timothy M. Shaw (2007), "Lessons from/for BRICSAM about South–North Relations at the Start of the 21st Century: Economic Size Trumps All Else?," *International Studies Review*, **9** (4), 673–89.
Dutta, Sudipt (1997), *Family Business in India*, New Delhi: Response/Sage.
Fioretos, Orfeo (2011), *Creative Reconstructions: Multilateralism and European Varieties of Capitalism*, Ithaca, NY: Cornell University Press.
Frank, Andre Gunder (1969), *Capitalism and Underdevelopment in Latin America*, New York: Monthly Review.
Goldstein, Andrea (2007), *Multinational Companies from Emerging Economies*, New York: Palgrave Macmillan.
Horn, Henrik, Louise Johannesson and Petros C. Mavroidis (2011), *The WTO Dispute Settlement System 1995–2010: Some Descriptive Statistics*, IFN Working Paper No. 891, Stockholm: Research Institute for Industrial Economics.
Hurrell, Andrew (2006), "Hegemony, Liberalism and Global Order: What Space for Would-Be Great Powers?," *International Affairs*, **82** (1), 1–20.
Jackson, Gregory and Richard Deeg (2006), *How Many Varieties of Capitalism? Comparing the Comparative Institutional Analyses of Capitalist Diversity*, MPIfG Discussion Paper 06-2, Cologne: Max Planck Institute for the Study of Societies.
Ledeneva, Alena (2008), "Blat and Guanxi: Informal Practices in Russia and China," *Comparative Studies in Society and History*, **50** (1), 118–44.
May, Christian and Andreas Nölke (2013), "Kritischer Institutionalismus in der Vergleichenden Kapitalismusforschung: Konzeptionelle Überlegungen und Forschungsprogramm," in Ian Bruff, Matthias Ebenau, Christian May and Andreas Nölke (eds.), *Vergleichende Kapitalismusforschung: Stand, Perspektiven, Kritik*, Münster: Westfälisches Dampfboot, pp. 103–18.
McNally, Christopher A. (2012), "Sino-Capitalism: China's Reemergence and the International Political Economy," *World Politics*, **64** (4), 741–76.
Michailova, Snejina and Verner Worm (2003), "Personal Networking in Russia and China: Blat and Guanxi," *European Management Journal*, **21** (4), 509–19.
Moravcsik, Andrew (1997), "Taking Preferences Seriously: A Liberal Theory of International Politics," *International Organization*, **51** (4), 513–53.
Murphy, Craig N. (2005), *Global Institutions, Marginalization, and Development*, London: Routledge.
Musacchio, Aldo and Sergio Lazzarini (2012), "Leviathan in Business: Varieties of State Capitalism and Their Implications for Economic Performance," available from: http://papers.ssrn.com/sol3/papers.cfm?abstract_id=2070942 (accessed January 22, 2013).
Narlikar, Amrita and Diana Tussie (2004), "The G20 at the Cancun Ministerial: Developing Countries and Their Evolving Coalitions in the WTO," *World Economy*, **27** (7), 947–66.
Nölke, Andreas (2011), "Non-Triad Multinational Enterprises and Global Economic Institutions," in Dag Harald Claes and Carl Hendrik Knutsen (eds.), *Governing the Global Economy: Politics, Institutions, and Economic Development*, London: Routledge, pp. 277–91.
Nölke, Andreas (2012), "The Rise of the 'B(R)IC-Variety of Capitalism': Toward a New Phase of Organized Capitalism," in Henk Overbeek and Bastiaan van Apeldoorn (eds.), *Neoliberalism in Crisis*, Basingstoke: Palgrave Macmillan, pp. 117–37.
Nölke, Andreas and Simone Claar (2012), "Tiefe Integration in der Praxis der Nord-Süd-Beziehungen: Vergleichende Perspektiven," *Journal für Entwicklungspolitik*, **28** (2), 80–98.

Nölke, Andreas and Heather Taylor (2010), "Non-Triad Multinationals and Global Governance: Still a North–South Conflict?," in Morten Ougaard and Anna Leander (eds.), *Business and Global Governance*, London: Routledge, pp. 156–77.

Nölke, Andreas and Arjan Vliegenthart (2009), "Enlarging the Varieties of Capitalism: The Emergence of Dependent Market Economies in East Central Europe," *World Politics*, **61** (4), 670–702.

Nölke, Andreas, Tobias ten Brink, Simone Claar and Christian May (2013), "The Rise of Emerging Economies: Expanding 'Varieties of Capitalism' into 'Global Political Economy,'" paper presented at the International Studies Association Annual Convention, San Francisco, April 5.

Pijl, Kees van der (1984), *The Making of an Atlantic Ruling Class*, London: Verso.

Piramal, Gita (1996), *Business Maharajas*, New Delhi: Viking.

Polanyi, Karl (1977), *The Livelihood of Man*, New York: Academic Press.

Polanyi, Karl ([1944] 2001), *The Great Transformation: The Political and Economic Origins of Our Time*, Boston, MA: Beacon Press.

Richter, Thomas (2013), "When Do Autocracies Start to Liberalize Foreign Trade? Evidence from Four Cases in the Middle East and North Africa," *Review of International Political Economy*, **20** (4), 760–87.

Ruggie, John G. (1982), "International Regimes, Transactions and Change: Embedded Liberalism in the Postwar Economic Order," *International Organization*, **36** (2), 379–415.

Schirm, Stefan (2013), "Global Politics Are Domestic Politics: A Societal Approach towards Divergence in the G20," *Review of International Studies*, **39** (3), 685–706.

Singer, J. David (1961), "The Level-of-Analysis Problem in International Relations," *World Politics*, **14** (1), 77–92.

Sørensen, Georg (2006), "Liberalism of Restraint and Liberalism of Imposition: Liberal Values and World Order in the New Millennium," *International Relations*, **20** (3), 251–72.

Subacchi, Paola (2008), "New Power Centres and New Power Brokers: Are They Shaping a New Economic Order?," *International Affairs*, **84** (3), 485–98.

Waltz, Kenneth N. (2001), *Man, the State, and War: A Theoretical Analysis*, New York: Columbia University Press.

Wank, David L. (2001), *Commodifying Communism: Business, Trust, and Politics in a Chinese City*, Cambridge: Cambridge University Press.

Woo-Cumings, Meredith (1999), *The Developmental State*, Ithaca, NY: Cornell University Press.

WTO (World Trade Organization) (2004), *Decision Adopted by the General Council on 1 August 2004*, Document WT/L/579.

WTO (World Trade Organization) (2012a), *International Trade Statistics 2012*, Geneva: WTO.

WTO (World Trade Organization) (2012b), *World Tariff Profiles 2012*, Geneva: WTO.

20. Food is different: globalization, trade regimes and local food movements
Elizabeth Smythe[1]

INTRODUCTION

> Food is different. It is not a typical commodity because it affects so many people – and the environment – in such intimate ways. Food has the power to move us to action. Food is both personal (it affects our bodies) and political (it affects the world). (Rosset 2006: 79)

Food (the word is derived from an old English term of Germanic origin referring to fodder) is normally thought of as a nutritious substance that we eat or drink, which is necessary, at some minimal level, to the maintenance of life. In contrast, agriculture refers to the cultivation of crops in fields or the rearing of animals. The crops produced may or may not include edible substances we would call food. My use of the term 'food' in this chapter is intended to shift the focus in the discussion of the WTO to capture what Peter Rosset notes, that is, that food is not a typical traded commodity; it is different. Eating food is the most intimate act of consumption, necessary to our survival and well-being, tied up in culture and community. But a global food system has emerged as a result of liberalized markets, new technologies and financialization which has increased the distance between producers and eaters of food. The system has destroyed livelihoods of some and created both crises of hunger alongside abundance, and malnutrition alongside rising obesity levels. The uneven impacts of this global food system have raised issues about the quality, safety and provenance of food, and the justness of the food system. This is evident in the wide array of civil society actors in both the global South and the North and broader publics who are increasingly attentive to food issues. I examine the World Trade Organization (WTO) within this broader context, going beyond the Agreement on Agriculture (AoA), the failed agricultural negotiations in the Doha Round, or a particular trade dispute. In this way, I look at the struggles which have emerged over the global food system that have been shaped by WTO rules and, in turn, how these struggles challenge the future of the WTO and the legitimacy of those rules. I begin with a brief discussion of the development of the global food system.

THE GLOBAL FOOD SYSTEM

The global food regime, according to McMichael, can be characterized as a:

> 'corporate food regime', organized around a politically constructed division of agricultural labour between Northern staple grains traded for Southern high-value products (meats, fruits and vegetables).The free trade rhetoric associated with the global rule (through states) of the World Trade Organisation suggests that this ordering represents the blossoming of a free trade regime, and yet the implicit rules (regarding agro-exporting) preserve farm subsidies for the Northern powers alone, while Southern states have been forced to reduce agricultural protections and import staple, and export high-value, foods. (McMichael 2009: 148)

As Figure 20.1 indicates, agricultural trade, while lagging behind other products, has expanded steadily since the 1950s. About 80 per cent of this trade is in food products (WTO 2012).

Within this system are powerful players, both state and non-state actors, including what Oxfam calls the 'food superpowers', those countries dominating food exports. Led by the United States, whose food exports rose from US$135 billion in 1961 to almost US$12 trillion in 2006 (FAO 2009: table c.1), other countries, including Brazil, China, Canada and Australia, along with the European Union, are major exporters. At the same time they are food importers, the EU and the US being the largest. The EU, the US and (for some products) Japan provide high levels of subsidies to large domestic producers, which ultimately benefit food processors and facilitate the spread of cheap junk food, leading to dumping and trade distortions.

Export expansion occurred within the context of the extraordinary growth in the market power of agrifood corporations such as ADM, Cargill, Bunge and Dreyfus, which as of 2012 controlled 90 per cent of the global grain trade (Murphy et al. 2012), and the dominance of corporations like Monsanto in seeds. Corporate concentration also led to a handful of giant firms dominating both processing and retailing. For example, in the case of beef in the United States four firms control 83.5 per cent of the supply (Holt-Giménez and Shattuck 2011: 111). Within global supply chains, supermarkets have come to play a dominant role as chief beneficiaries of value added along the chain and enforcers of private standards. As Busch notes, 'the top five are well-known global retailers: Wal-Mart (USA), Carrefour (France), Tesco (UK), Metro (Germany), and Ahold (The Netherlands)' (Busch 2010). Trade expansion, especially in pre-packaged goods, and rising production do not mean that all is well. Many concerns have developed around the nature of this system, and

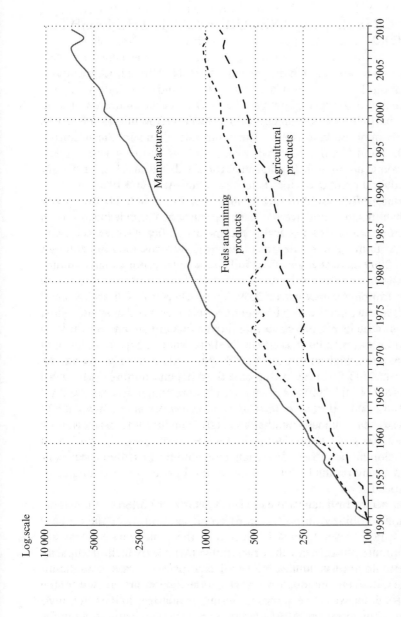

Log scale

Note: Volume indices, 1950=100.

Source: WTO (2011b).

Figure 20.1 World merchandise trade volume by major product group, 1950–2010

recent food crises have brought them into focus, raising questions about governance of the food system.

FOOD CRISES, FOOD SECURITY AND THE RIGHT TO FOOD

Food crises have appeared in the past, and the UN's Food and Agricultural Organization (FAO), established in 1945, had a mandate to address hunger. As McKeon (2010) argues, however, the FAO was able, as a result of food crises in the 1970s and the process of World Food Summits, to develop a mandate around issues of food security and development. According to the FAO, 'Food security exists when all people at all times have physical and economic access to safe and nutritious food that meets their dietary needs and food preferences for an active healthy life' (FAO 1996).

The concept focuses on the availability of food, the stability or security of supply, utilization and access. The corporate food regime has not been able to ensure food security, and it became a significant issue once again in 2007. After more than a decade of downward trends, food prices began to rise in 2003 and, as Figure 20.2 indicates, began a very sharp upward trend in 2007.

While dropping somewhat in 2009, prices were still well above previous levels and within a year had begun sharply increasing again. Of most concern was the increase in price volatility and its impact on more vulnerable food importing countries especially those where incomes are low and food costs are a high proportion (50–70 per cent) of family income. As of 2012 the FAO listed 66 low-income food deficit countries (LIFDCs). Explanations for the 2007–08 price increase were numerous, and the FAO listed them in its report *The State of Food Insecurity in the World* (FAO 2011: 11). They included: weather shocks (droughts), the promotion of biofuels (subsidized), depreciation of the US dollar, economic growth in large developing countries, diet changes including increased meat consumption, rising production costs (linked to oil price increases) and commodity speculation.

Two immediate impacts of the price increases are of interest. Vulnerable populations mobilized in protest in 61 countries, and 21 of the protests were violent. A second impact occurred at the policy level, as governments' options to deal with the crisis ranged widely. A lack of capacity led some to do nothing, while others looked to price controls, subsidies to consumers, drawing down reserve stocks, reducing import taxes or, in the case of food commodity exports, imposing export restrictions. An FAO survey of 77 countries in 2008 found that about one-quarter of countries

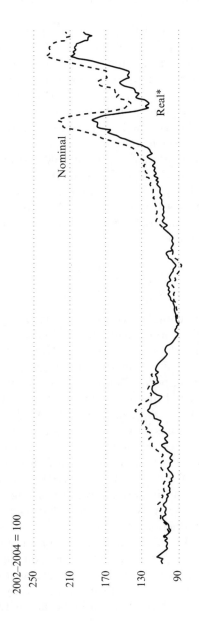

2002–2004 = 100

Nominal

Real*

* The real price index is the nominal price index deflated by the world Bank Manufactures Unit Value index (MUV) groups' indices weighted with the average export share of each of the groups.

Note: The FAO Food Price Index tracks changes in the prices of a basket of food commodities and consists of the average of five commodity groups' indices weighted with the average export share of each of the groups.

Source: FAO (2012).

Figure 20.2   FAO Food Price Index

475

imposed some kind of export restrictions, exacerbating price increases (Sharma 2011). As I indicate below, this issue emerged on the WTO policy agenda.

The food crisis also drew attention to institutions and agreements relating to food, including international human rights law. The UN Universal Declaration of Human Rights (of 1948) and the Covenant on Economic, Social and Cultural Rights, in effect since 1976, have recognized a right to food for decades. However, the appointment by the UN Human Rights Commission of the first Special Rapporteur on the Right to Food in 2000 raised the profile of this issue, though low food prices, declining levels of investment in agriculture, and eroding agricultural aid reflected international priorities of the time. The food price spike of 2007–08 and the appointment of a the new Rapporteur Olivier De Schutter gave the issue currency. The right to food and the need for states to work toward realizing it were recognized during the 2009 World Summit on Food Security in Rome. As a result, the role of trade and trade rules in advancing or impeding this right began to receive attention.

FOOD MOVEMENTS

A third element of the changing context has been the rise, along with the corporate food regime, of food movements in reaction to it. Such movements are active in both the global South and the North as local, regional and global manifestations of resistance to this regime and the rules and policies that are seen to support it. One of the most significant, La Via Campesina (LVC), developed out of a network of peasant and farmer-based organizations from South, Central and North America, as well as Europe (Borras 2008). It has grown to 148 peasant and small farmer organizations in 69 countries, including the National Farmers Union (NFU) and the Quebec-based Union Paysanne in Canada, along with the National Coalition for Family Farming in the US. Since its creation in 1993, LVC has played an important role in challenging the food regime and international trade rules and in articulating an alternative vision of agricultural production (Martinez-Torres and Rosset 2010: 149). This vision focuses on what and how food is produced, and the scale of production. Its fierce opposition to organizations like the WTO and regional trade agreements is well known. LVC articulated the key principles of food sovereignty in 1996 and subsequently elaborated them further through a number of international meetings and networks to include:

The right of peoples to healthy and culturally appropriate food produced through ecologically sound and sustainable methods, and their right to define their own food and agriculture systems. It puts those who produce, distribute and consume food at the heart of food systems and policies rather than the demands of markets and corporations ... Food sovereignty prioritises local and national economies and markets. (Desmarais 2007: 134)

The increased resonance of the food sovereignty frame at the global and the local level is clear in even a cursory examination of the language and rhetoric of these very diverse movements and coalitions (Andrée et al. 2014). LVC has also played a role within a broader international coalition, the International Planning Committee on Food Sovereignty (IPCFS) (www.foodsovereignty.org; Borras 2008), which in 2002 identified 'the need to give primacy to food security and food sovereignty principles when considering trade measures'.

A second group of organizations addressing the global food system and trade rules is what has been called the Food Justice Advocates (Clapp 2012). Based in the North but driven by an altruistic solidarity with those in the South (Reitan 2007), they have played an important role in articulating concerns about the international financial and trading system and provided strong moral critiques of it. While more reformist in their views of trade rules, these organizations have had the capacity to provide analysis and advocacy functions that other networks and coalitions can draw on. Since the global food crisis of 2007–08 they too have turned their attention to the global food system, and in particular to the plight of small producers in the global South. Oxfam's Grow Campaign is a good example. While differing from Via Campesina and wanting to avoid the 'romanticisation' of the peasant (Oxfam 2011: 52), the report focuses on small producers as part of the solution to the food crisis, and links the issue directly to climate change. Its approach to trade rules is less radical than LVC calling for an end to trade distorting agricultural subsidies. Oxfam argues that, 'far from reducing the importance of OECD agricultural liberalization, soaring food prices make it more important than ever' (Oxfam 2011: 47). It is critical, however, of the way trade rules limit countries' policy space and argues that 'poor countries need the freedom to determine the extent and pace of their own agricultural market opening' (Oxfam 2011: 47).

In addition to the NGO advocacy and small producer movements that form part of the LVC and IPCFS, a vast array of non-producer food movements have emerged in Europe, North America and elsewhere, including within the food superpower countries. Pollan (2010) aptly describes the movements as a 'big lumpy tent', ranging from environmentalists to consumer groups, public health and anti-poverty activists, organic gardeners and others who are critical of the prevailing food system. The growing distance from food producers, rising food imports and new technologies have generated a growing unease among eaters (Blay-Palmer 2008) about their food. Well-publicized food scares have added to concerns about the provenance of their food. As Morgan et al. note, provenance encompasses much more than just place, but also includes:

> a spatial dimension (its place of origin), a social dimension (its methods of production and distribution), and a cultural dimension (its perceived qualities and reputation). The social dimension is particularly important because it helps consumers to deal with the ethical issues in globally dispersed food supply chains. (Morgan et al. 2006: 3)

This concern is reflected in the growth of local food movements, the organic food market and fair trade labels. Underlying these developments are a range of concerns about GM crops, the sustainability of the industrial food system, animal welfare and the safety and quality of the food being eaten.

THE WTO AND FOOD

It is within this changing food context that we look at the WTO and how it has addressed trade rules and the issues around the production and provenance of food. We begin with the Agreement on Agriculture.[2]

Agreement on Agriculture

The GATT Agreement on Agriculture, finalized at the end of the Uruguay Round of trade negotiations in 1994, ended the exemption of agriculture from GATT principles. The difficult negotiations reflected the sensitivity of the sector and demonstrated that 'members of the WTO are not yet ready to treat agriculture in the same way as other products' (McMahon and Desta 2012). The agreement did however initiate reform processes focusing on three 'pillars' of commitments: increased market access, elimination of export subsidies and ending trade distorting domestic subsidies, along with an agreement to further negotiations. The 2001 Doha Ministerial meeting incorporated these into the Doha Development Round (DDR) as part of a single undertaking. The implementation of the AoA, however, was uneven both in advancing the agenda of liberalization and in fairly distributing its benefits. While limits to export subsidies saw some progress and the transparency of non-tariff trade barriers was increased, the progress on reducing domestic subsidies was slower. The agreement allowed support for domestic agriculture through categorization of measures into amber (trade distorting), blue and green (trade neutral) boxes and some ambiguity and flexibility in what measures went in which box. Opening developing country markets in the context of little movement of the large Northern countries on market access or subsidies led to dumping and low-cost imports destroying local producers in the South. In some cases this generated high levels of dependence on food imports. It also led to stronger developing country coalitions within the WTO challenging the traditional dominance of the US and EU. The G20 coalition, led by Brazil and India, demanded greater reductions in subsidies and, to better protect themselves from import surges, safeguard mechanisms (SSMs) and exemptions from significant tariff reductions for special products. US and EU concessions on subsidies and safeguards were part of the trade-off for increased access for non-agricultural products (NAMA) in developing countries.

Agriculture was a significant part of DDR negotiations and reached a critical point in the 2006–07 period. The Bush administration, pressured by the major agribusiness players such as Archer Daniels Midland, rejected the proposals on SSMs (Schoenbaum 2011). Despite intensive periodic efforts to end it, the impasse was formally recognized in December 2011. In the meantime the global food crisis had emerged.

WTO AND THE FOOD CRISIS

On the one hand the proponents of agricultural trade liberalization embraced the food and financial crises as opportunities to pressure negotiators to conclude the DDR. WTO Director-General Lamy told the WTO's General Council and Trade Negotiating Committee (TNC): 'We have all witnessed the financial turbulence we are in and the hikes in energy and food prices that are affecting severely many of your countries. At a time when the world economy is in rough waters, concluding the Doha Round can provide a strong anchor' (WTO 2008). His assertions were supported by other proponents of trade liberalization, such as President of the World Bank and former US Trade Representative Robert Zoellick, who argued that a key solution to the food crisis 'is to break the Doha Development Agenda impasse' (OWINFS 2008). In contrast, 243 organizations critical of the WTO, including smaller agricultural producer movements in the global South, saw it differently:

> We believe the Doha Round as is currently envisioned will intensify the crisis by making food prices more volatile, increasing developing countries' dependence on imports, and strengthening the power of multinational agribusiness in food and agricultural markets. Developing countries are likely to lose further policy space in their agriculture sector, which would in turn limit their ability to deal

with the current crisis and to strengthen the livelihoods of small producers. The inability to manage the current food crisis is an illustration of the failure of three decades of market deregulation in agriculture. (OWINFS 2008)

These were not the only critics of the WTO. Beginning in 2009, the UN's Rapporteur on the Right to Food Olivier De Schutter turned his attention to the contribution of WTO rules to advancing the right to food. This included a debate with Secretary-General Lamy in 2009, and a May 2011 draft report critical of the WTO. In a speech to WTO delegates in December 2011, De Schutter (2011) accused the WTO and Lamy of 'defending an outdated vision of food security' which relied on 'food systems where the most efficient producers with the biggest economies of scale are relied upon to feed food-deficit regions, and where the divide only gets bigger'. He argued that, with such a

> trade-centric approach, we miss the simplest of win–wins. If we were to support developing world small-holders, who are often the poorest groups, we could enable them to move out of poverty, and enable local food production to meet local needs. In this context, trade would complement local production, not justify its abandonment. (Green 2011)

What was needed, he claimed, was more national policy space to limit price volatility, a policy space that WTO rules were reducing. Lamy's response in the form of a letter and notations by the WTO Secretariat appeared on the WTO website. Lamy argued that the AoA allows for flexibility in relation to food security and that trade could play an important role in achieving food security, and he criticized domestic measures to address food security as costly and trade distorting (WTO 2011a).

Two priority issues, food aid and export restrictions, are also addressed in WTO rules. Concerns regarding the situation of the 77 WTO members that are net food importing developing countries (NFIDCs) led Egypt, a country highly dependent on food imports, to put forward proposals exempting NFIDCs from export restrictions on foodstuffs by both developing and industrialized countries. NFIDCs, however, would still be allowed to use such restrictions for their own food security. The proposal called for a ban on export restrictions on food destined for humanitarian assistance delivered by the World Food Programme (WFP). Food security proposals were dropped from the agenda shortly before the WTO Ministerial meeting in December 2011, however, owing to a lack of consensus on specific measures. The chair's summary of discussions indicated that ministers called for exporters not to impose export restrictions on food aid purchased by the World Food Programme – an issue the G8 and G20 group of countries had addressed earlier as well. The chair also noted members' support for a work programme on trade and food price volatility, and its impact on LDCs and net food importing developing countries ('WTO Members Drop' 2011). The impasse on the DDR, the meagre outcomes on food security, and increased questioning of the once unassailable premise that liberalized trade in agriculture was the answer suggest that food was something the WTO, despite having swallowed the AoA, was having a hard time digesting. Food, however, is also implicated in many of the ongoing functions of the WTO, including disciplining, through processes of dispute resolution, national use of non-tariff measures which might pose barriers to trade.

WTO TRADE DISPUTES, FOOD STANDARDS AND THE SPS AND TBT AGREEMENTS

While the AoA dealt with market access in terms of barriers such as tariffs and quotas, the GATT/WTO system has long recognized that domestic measures can pose import barriers but at the same time accepts that states have obligations to ensure the safety of food products and limit the spread of diseases and pests. As a consequence the WTO has two agreements which address regulatory measures that could pose trade barriers. The first, the Agreement on Sanitary and Phytosanitary (SPS) Measures, deals with food safety, and the second, the Technical Barriers to Trade (TBT) Agreement, addresses regulatory measures adopted to deal with consumer safety, health or environmental protection, including product labelling.

The Agreement on SPS Measures allows, along with Article 20 of the GATT, a state to regulate beyond safety and human health 'to protect human, animal or plant life or health', but measures must be 'based on scientific principles and not maintained without sufficient scientific evidence'. In the interests of harmonization, states 'shall base measures on international standards, guidelines or recommendations, where they exist'. States may go beyond international standards, but only if the justification is scientifically based risk assessment. The SPS Agreement does not reference any broader societal or environmental concerns, or recognize any justification not rooted in scientifically based risk assessment.

The TBT Agreement covers non-safety aspects of food, including labelling, and seeks to harmonize national requirements so as not to create 'unnecessary obstacles to international trade'. But it also affirms the right of countries to take 'measures necessary to ensure the quality of their exports, for the protection of human, animal or plant life or health, of the environment, or for the prevention of deceptive practices' (WTO Agreement on Technical Barriers to Trade 2011). While protection of the environment is referenced, in contrast to the SPS, measures 'shall not be more trade-restrictive than necessary to fulfil a legitimate objective'. What constitutes a legitimate objective appears to be limited to national security requirements, the prevention of deceptive practices, and protection of human health or safety, animal or plant life or health, or the environment, and does not necessarily encompass providing consumers with full information about the provenance of their food. All such regulations should be transparent, notified to the WTO and affected states in a timely and transparent way, be based on international standards, be the least trade restrictive possible, and follow most favoured nation (MFN) and non-discrimination provisions of the WTO.

As Figures 20.3 and 20.4 indicate, notifications to each committee have increased significantly, a fourfold increase over the past 20 years for the TBT. The SPS Committee total since 1995 is in excess of 13000, and annual notifications peaked in 2010. An analysis of the SPS notifications notes that a large proportion of these involved regulations related to food safety, in particular 22 per cent, the largest proportion, related to meat and edible offal. The largest number of notifications came from the United States (WTO 2011c). A certain amount of the increase is due to education and outreach to inform WTO members about the need to notify, what and how to notify, and the development of a simpler online notification system.

While it is difficult to say what the underlying rationale for each measure was, the overall trend suggests that the increase in agricultural trade, in particular food exports, in the past two decades has been accompanied by an increase in domestic measures related to food. A number of these measures resulted in trade disputes which have proven to be long, acrimonious and difficult to resolve. Trade liberalization proponents argue that many measures are disguised protectionism designed to protect domestic producers and deserve to be challenged under WTO rules. I argue, however, that many reflect public concerns about the provenance of food and that efforts to agree on standards and harmonize national regulations based on them have proven difficult because, as indicated at the outset, food is indeed different. The challenge is agreeing on uniform standards regarding food, especially where the science is limited or uncertain, or where important social values and priorities differ.

THE BATTLE OVER FOOD STANDARDS: REGULATIONS AND TRADE DISPUTES

Three international standard setting bodies are referenced in the SPS and TBT agreements. These bodies, such as the World Organisation for Animal

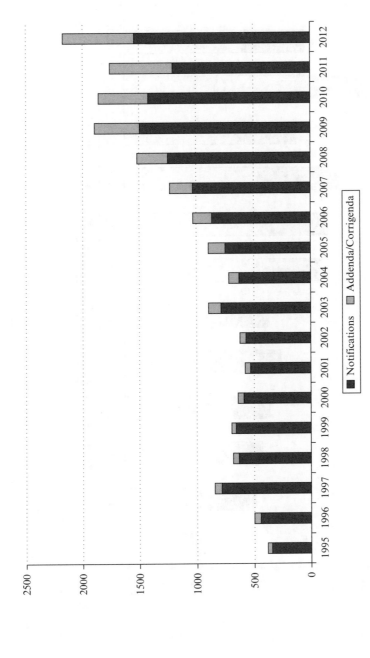

Source: WTO Committee on Technical Barriers to Trade (2013).

Figure 20.3   Number of TBT notifications since 1995

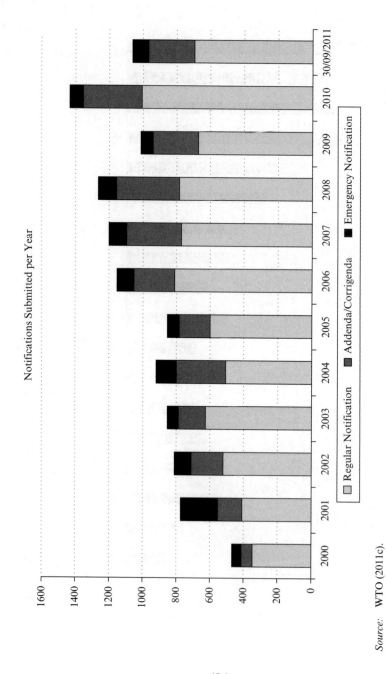

Notifications Submitted per Year

Regular Notification   Addenda/Corrigenda   Emergency Notification

Source: WTO (2011c).

Figure 20.4   SPS notifications since 2000

Health (OIE) and the Codex Alimentarius, engage in processes of defining best practices and standards that affect the production and handling of animals and food products. The Codex Alimentarius has played the major role in defining and developing food standards.

A joint body of the FAO and the World Health Organization (WHO), Codex was founded in 1962 with a mandate to develop food standards 'protecting the health of consumers' and to harmonize them to ensure 'fair practices in the food trade'.[3] The Codex Commission meets annually in Rome (FAO) or Geneva (WHO). Committees carry out much of the work dealing with functional issues (such as general principles, labelling, and limits on pesticide or veterinary drug residues in food) and commodity areas (such as milk products or meat) as well as geographic regions. National chairs of Codex committees host the committee's work, that is, chair and fund the Secretariat and annual committee meeting costs. Canada has hosted the food labelling committee's work for many years, while the US hosts the committee dealing with veterinary drug residues in food. The development of new food standards follows an eight-step process of proposals, discussion papers and decisions by the relevant committee that a standard should be developed. Once developed, the draft standard is circulated to members for comment and may be revised and ultimately adopted.

Codex standards serve as a benchmark and justification to the WTO as to whether national food regulations constitute unjustifiable barriers to trade. As a result the Codex Commission, along with the WTO, became a site of struggle over states' rights to regulate food and food eaters' rights to know the provenance of food. National rules that deviate from (i.e. exceed) Codex standards in response to consumer or other civil society demands could become the subject of trade disputes and targets for WTO-authorized trade retaliation. On the other hand, if a state's regulatory practice becomes the Codex standard it is thus insulated from challenges to that regulation as an unjustified trade barrier (Buckingham 2000). Codex standards can reduce or expand the national policy space for food regulation and, as a result, standard setting processes have become more politicized, reflected in its growing state membership (181) and the increased involvement of trade officials, and non-state actors, both corporations and non-governmental organizations (NGOs) (Veggeland and Borgen 2005). In contrast to the situation at the WTO, non-state actors can be formal observers at Codex meetings, speak during deliberations and lobby national delegations (Smythe 2009). Given the increasing demand for, and complexity of, food production standards and the small size of the Codex Secretariat, developing a standard can take years, be highly acrimonious, and have important consequences for food exports and trade disputes. One such example is GM food labelling.

GM Food

Genetically modified (GM) commercial crop production is concentrated in soybeans, maize, canola and cotton. Major producers are the United States, Canada, Argentina, Brazil and China. As early adopters of biotechnology, the US and Canada became heavily invested in GM crops, with close links between the biotechnology industry, universities and governments. With the influence of the biotechnology industry came limited regulation based on the concept of 'substantial equivalence', which assumed that, if the GM product in its components was the same as those products already deemed safe, the product would in its entirety be considered safe. Thus labelling of products containing genetically modified organisms (GMOs) in North America was voluntary, and the presence of GM crops was pervasive. It is estimated that there are GMOs in over 70 per cent of food on the shelves of US supermarkets. Yet even in North America a range of public concerns about their safety, environmental impacts, crop contamination and accidental releases remain. Strong intellectual property rules and market concentration have afforded biotechnology corporations even more power over access to seeds, another concern for critics (Prakash and Kollman 2007; Smythe 2009).

The European Union was much slower to adopt these crops, hesitated to approve them and has gone in a different regulatory direction. In 1998, as a result of food scares, public distrust of regulators, division among EU members, and strong consumer and food retailer opposition, a moratorium was placed on further GM crops approvals until EU-wide mandatory labelling and traceability rules were put into place. On 2 July 2003 the European Parliament approved two laws requiring the labelling of food containing GM products based on the consumers' right to know. Given the impact of the EU's GM moratorium on North American food exports, the US (June 2003) and then Canada (August 2003) launched a trade dispute claiming that the moratorium had restricted imports of food products and violated WTO obligations under the SPS and TBT agreements. The final Report of the Dispute Panel, released in September 2006, did find that the EC:

> acted inconsistently with its obligations under Articles 5.1 and 2.2 of the SPS Agreement with regard to all of the safeguard measures at issue, because these measures were not based on risk assessments satisfying the definition of the SPS Agreement and hence could be presumed to be maintained without sufficient scientific evidence. (WTO 2006: 6)

Even though it could be said that the US and Canada 'won' a victory at the WTO, it did not mean that North American GM crops and food would be able to easily access the EU market. While the United States and Canada had opted for voluntary labelling of foods derived from GM crops, the EU had gone for mandatory labelling above a very low threshold. In North America, 'voluntary' meant no labelling of GM food, as the powerful food processing and retailing sectors decided such labels would deter consumers. In contrast, in the EU, mandatory labelling of all products led food processors and retailers to reject GM food products, fearing consumers' strong aversion to them, which limited North American exports.

Not surprisingly, the issue of mandatory labelling for GM foods arose within the Codex. Preliminary work began in its Committee on Food Labelling in 1991. A full debate in October 1994 centred around whether labelling should be required only when there were health and safety concerns and whether it should be required if the food products in question did not differ substantively from traditional equivalents. The battle over GM food labelling or what the Codex calls 'Foods and Food Ingredients Obtained through Certain Techniques of Genetic Modification/Genetic Engineering' went on for the next 20 years (see Smythe 2009). The United States, Canada and a number of other food exporters (many in South America), along with the biotechnology industry and food processors, argued that mandatory labelling was unnecessary, since such foods were substantially equivalent to existing foods. They also argued that labels would be perceived as a warning to consumers regarding the food's safety, but, based on scientific assessments, such food had been deemed safe. In contrast the European Union, Norway, Japan and a number of countries in Africa and Asia argued in favour of mandatory labels. The EU, Norway and consumer organizations made the case for labels based on the consumers' right to know what is in their food. Over time the anti-mandatory labelling side lost ground and, when it appeared that standards supportive of mandatory labelling might be approved, it tried to stop work on GM labelling entirely. Repeated attempts at compromises finally resulted in a compilation of existing labelling standards relevant to GM foods and a preamble to that section of the standards acknowledging the variety of approaches (i.e. mandatory and voluntary) that states had adopted to GM foods in their national standards. The US made one final effort to further weaken the wording, but after being deserted by allies gave up the fight in July 2011 at the Codex Commission. While weak, the Codex text appears to be permissive of these differing approaches, putting any trade challenge based on its standard in doubt.

Despite pressure from the biotechnology and agricultural sectors and some members of Congress to launch another trade complaint against EU regulations, uncertainty about its likely success based on the TBT obligations and the need for European cooperation to rescue the sinking Doha negotiations in 2007–08 led to US restraint (Schramm 2007: 96).

Country of Origin Labelling

While knowing what is in food and how it is produced is an important aspect of the provenance of food, most eaters want to know where it was produced. The close connection of food to a land or *terroir* is a long-standing one, and where a food was produced was often historically linked to its qualities. Designations of regions and control over those designations, called in WTO parlance 'geographic indications', have been a subject of debate and division in the WTO that cannot be dealt with here. Rather I look at the growing demand to know where food comes from that is part of a reaction against the global food system.

Food eaters want to know a food's origin for a variety of reasons, such as wanting to consume local food so as to reduce the distance food is transported. Some lack confidence in standards in other food producing jurisdictions, whether it relates to health, safety or animal welfare, or want to privilege local producers, however defined, in their food purchases. Standards and rules regarding labelling the origin of food have, however, been the source of trade disputes.

Both the WTO and the Codex have guidelines on food labelling in terms of origins. The WTO does permit the labelling of a product's origin under Article 9, referring to marks of origin. But labelling requirements are subject to WTO principles outlined above under the TBT Agreement. In the Codex, standards of labelling for origin are covered in the *General Standard for the Labelling of Prepackaged Foods*, section 4.5, which states:

> 4.5.1   The country of origin shall be declared if its omission would mislead or deceive the consumer.
>
> 4.5.2   When food undergoes processing in a second country which changes its nature, the country in which the processing is performed shall be considered to be the country of origin for its purposes of labelling. (Codex 2010)

The standard thus does not require labelling for origin. An attempt to initiate work on mandatory country of origin labelling in 2000 was limited by a lack of consensus in the Codex Committee on Food Labelling, which became apparent in 2002 and again in 2004. While the UK, a number of European countries, consumer groups and some public health NGOs favoured mandatory labelling, major food exporters, especially the United States, supported by Canada, opposed it (Smythe 2014). Those favouring mandatory labelling pointed to the strong consumer desire indicated in surveys to know the origins of their food, the confusion among consumers about where their food came from and the rather misleading use retailers made of voluntary labels. None of these arguments persuaded enough delegates to proceed, and the Codex Commission stopped work on the issue. In the meantime, however, a number of countries feeling increasing pressure moved to mandatory labelling. Ironically one of them was the United States.

US regulations on labelling the origin of goods go back to the Tariff Act of 1930, but the current issue dates from the Consumer Right to Know Act of 2001, introduced by a North Dakota senator, which called for the labelling of beef, lamb, pork and fresh fruit and vegetables at final point of sale according to their country of origin. Similar bills introduced in the Senate and various amendments and horse trading related to the Farm Bill eventually resulted in a list of products, including meat, that required country of origin labelling (COOL). The ensuing six-year battle over the measure initially pitted a group of smaller-scale livestock producers, small farmers, and environmental and consumer organizations against all the largest livestock producers, processors and food retailers, the Bush Administration and the US Department of Agriculture (USDA). Tactics to stop COOL included heavy lobbying by the industrial food system, delaying appropriations and funding to the USDA to implement the programme, and a presidential veto of the Farm Bill that was overridden. This period also saw a presidential election campaign in 2008 and the development of food movements which broadened the pro-COOL coalition. When it was clear the measure would be implemented, US officials made an initial notification to the WTO on 26 June 2007 calling for comments.

The 2008 election brought in a President who had promised COOL. His Agriculture Secretary quickly requested that processors tighten up labelling further to clarify where animals were born, raised and slaughtered. This led eventually to a trade dispute with Canada and later Mexico. After negotiations failed to resolve the dispute, the formal WTO process began in the spring of 2010. The May 2011 preliminary and the November final ruling went against the United States. The panel report and a brief summary of the arguments help us see how such cases challenge not only those who desire national regulations allowing consumers to know the origins of food, but the WTO itself. Canada and Mexico (along with a number of third-party submissions) claimed the COOL measures violated sections of the TBT Agreement, disadvantaged their producers, and thus led to de facto discrimination. The US argued on its side that the measure was not discriminatory and was based on the need to inform consumers who wish to know the origins of their meat and who have not been served well by confusing voluntary labelling schemes.

The panel's final ruling acknowledged the legitimacy of the US goal of informing consumers but found that the measure as implemented was discriminatory and unduly trade restricting. The difficulty for both the US regulators and meat eaters is the high level of integration of the North American meat market and the industrial style of livestock and meat production, which sees large-scale movements of live animals across borders for fattening, slaughtering, processing and packaging. The need to clearly identify where animals are born, reared and slaughtered would, in the view of the Canadian government and large-scale livestock producers, lead to a need to separate and identify Canadian product. With a highly concentrated meat processing industry, the additional costs could lead processors to pay lower prices to Canadian producers. Given that US consumers were not served well by voluntary schemes it has been difficult to determine an alternative that would be acceptable. The Office of the US Trade Representative (USTR) found that it could not reconcile the pro- and anti-COOL sides in an effort to revise the label rules in February 2012 ('USTR Abandons' 2012) to conform with the WTO's ruling. To satisfy demands to know the origin of meat it had few options other than appealing against the WTO ruling, which the US announced it would do on 23 March 2012. The US lost its appeal, but subsequent modifications of the US regulations have failed to satisfy Canada, which in May 2013 announced it would be reviewing potential areas for trade retaliation under WTO rules given the continued de facto discrimination against Canadian beef in the US market. The issue of meat, what goes into it and how it is produced, in addition to knowing where it comes from, is especially sensitive. One of the longest, most acrimonious trade disputes under the SPS related to meat. Another case on that issue may well be looming for the WTO.

INDUSTRIAL LIVESTOCK, RESIDUES, HORMONES AND MEAT

The WTO SPS Committee annual report for 2011 (WTO Secretariat 2011) had two lengthy paragraphs discussing what the US, supported by Canada, Brazil and a number of South American delegates, claimed were significant barriers to meat exports to China and Chinese Taipei (i.e. Taiwan). The measures banned the import of meats which contained residue of the drug ractopamine – an additive to pork and cattle feed widely used in North American meat production. After strong US trade pressure a bilateral agreement between Taiwan and the United States in March 2012 to open that market to US beef resulted in protests and piles of US meat being burnt in front of Taiwan's legislature. This dispute reflects the challenges of trying to harmonize food regulations based on 'sound science' and the sensitivity of various publics to what is in, and not in, their meat. The long and painful effort at the Codex to agree on international standards for maximum residue levels (MRL) of various veterinary drugs such as ractopamine shows the extent to which the standards, or the absence of standards, drive trade disputes. Comparisons with the first trade dispute under the SPS Agreement at the WTO, the beef hormones case of 1997 and its equally complicated 14-year history, show how regulatory differences persist and 'winning' a trade case does not necessarily lead to improved market access, as Canadian and US beef exporters discovered.

Ractopamine[4] is a drug given to pigs and cattle to promote weight gain and is normally given right up to the point of slaughter. The drug had been approved in the US since 1999 for pigs and since 2002 for cattle and is widely used in meat production involving intensive livestock feeding operations. Low-fat meat increases the value of the animal to the producer. Many countries (160), however, ban its use and do not allow meat with residue to be sold or imported.

Standards are dealt with by the Codex Committee on Residues of Veterinary Drugs in Food (CCRVDF), which is hosted and chaired by the United States. Draft standards are debated and discussed and, once consensus is reached, go on to formal approval at the full Codex Commission meeting. Given its mandate, however, the committee is heavily reliant on expert advice provided by the Joint Expert Committee on Food Additives (JECFA), an FAO/WHO-constituted body of experts which Codex relies on for scientific opinions. It had provided the committee with assessments in 2004 and 2006 on ractopamine and recommended maximum levels of residue in muscle, fat, liver and kidneys. These were incorporated into draft standards. However, the EU indicated in the 17th session of the committee that such drugs under EU directives in 1997 and 2002 were not approved for non-therapeutic use in animals. In light of the work of the Codex, the European Union's Food Safety Authority (EFSA 2009) re-visited the issue in 2009, consulting experts, who questioned JECFA's methodology and testing. The drug had also been banned for use in China, and Chinese regulators raised concerns in 2010 about JECFA's failure to assess residues in organs such as lungs which are regularly consumed in China. This case provides a very powerful example of regulatory differences in the context of a disagreement on what the science says, which is difficult to dismiss as simply a measure designed to protect domestic meat producers.

In July 2011 the draft standards from the CCRVDF came before the full Commission after being stuck at the second last stage for six years. Opponents of any standard (i.e. no level of residue is acceptable) include the EU, China, Norway, Switzerland and many other countries, along with consumer health and other NGOs. Supporters included the United States, Canada, Brazil, Australia, New Zealand and other meat producers in South America, along with processing and meat industry associations. Efforts to find common ground in 2010–11 failed, while the Codex Commission chair, seeing no consensus, suggested holding the standard in abeyance. However, the US and its allies pushed to force a vote on the standard at both the 2011 and the 2012 meeting. The Codex normally operates on consensus and views votes as a sign of failure of the process. After procedural wrangling and votes on voting, the 2011 Commission failed to adopt the standard (Codex Alimentarius Commission 2011). By 2012 the US and its allies, after pressing for a vote and lobbying members vigorously, were able to 'win' approval of the standard by two votes in a late evening session. The EU delegate declared that the EU would not change its law and along with China argued that approval of the standard when countries representing over 70 per cent of the world's pork eaters opposed it would raise serious questions about the legitimacy of the Codex process (Codex Alimentarius Commission 2012). With agreement on the standard, some observers expected that countries like Brazil and the US would launch trade challenges against the EU and China. Instead, the opposite has occurred. The beef hormones case provides some interesting parallels to the ractopamine case and indicates the difficulty of assuming that the adoption of global standards will lead to regulatory harmonization and better market access. Indeed, it provides a cautionary tale for the WTO.

Lessons from the Beef Hormone Case

The US brought the first trade dispute based on the SPS Agreement against the EU in 1997 after negotiations failed to resolve the issue. The WTO panel ruled against the EU on the grounds that the ban on US beef treated with hormones violated the SPS Agreement because the EU had not conducted a science-based risk assessment. This did not afford US hormone-treated beef market access, but rather led to an EU study of the risks to human health from hormone-treated meat and further EU regulations in 2003. US trade retaliation and more negotiations followed. Another WTO ruling in 2008 did not so clearly favour the US because, while it allowed the US to continue trade retaliation, it also upheld the EU ban. This stalemate led to further negotiations to solve the impasse bilaterally. A deal with the Obama administration was reached in May 2009, which opened the EU market gradually to US high-quality beef produced without growth-promoting hormones and certified by the US Department of Agriculture Non-Hormonal Cattle Treated Program (Johnson and Hanrahan 2010). Canada negotiated a similar agreement.

Almost 100 per cent of cattle in US commercial feedlots used hormones, because it produces leaner, lower-fat meat. Producers in Canada, Australia, New Zealand, South Africa, Mexico and Chile also used these hormones. What this case indicates, however, is that within the EU, aside from concerns around the safety and science, there is a powerful combination of producer and consumer interests that make any change in EU regulations highly unlikely no matter what a WTO panel might decide. Consumer meat scares and concerns about human impacts of hormones in meat in the 1970s in France and Italy and the trauma of BSE meat in the 1990s have rendered EU regulators highly cautious and European consumers concerned about what is in their meat (Eurobarometer 2010). The only way the US has been afforded access is to forgo the use of such hormones. A similar situation is emerging regarding ractopamine.

The response of Russian and Chinese regulators to the Codex standard was to ban imported meat produced using ractopamine. China, the world's largest pork consumer and 'the third largest market for U.S. pork with sales of over $800 million last year, demanded pork from the United States to be verified ractopamine free by a third party by March 1 2013' (Bottemiller 2012). The response, however, was not necessarily one of heading to Geneva, although both the United States Trade Representative Ron Kirk and the Canadian Minister threatened to do that. In the case of Brazil, where ractopamine had been approved and used, the response was to ban its use in Brazil to ensure continued export market access. Similarly to what happened in the hormones in beef case, both the United States and Canada began processes for bilateral agreements and certification of ractopamine-free meat and meat processing facilities for access to the Russian market. A major US processor of pork, Smithfield, began a similar development of dual-track meat production to meet the demands of the Chinese market ('CEO' 2013), despite having claimed a few months earlier that ractopamine was a 'safe and effective FDA feed supplement that has been widely used in the hog-farming industry for years' (Smithfield 2013).

These cases show the extent to which disputes involving food, despite the SPS and TBT agreements, have proven difficult to resolve at the WTO. The reliance on standards of bodies like the Codex has not proven to be an effective solution in creating standards and harmonizing food regulations to facilitate trade. Rather, the Codex has itself become a site of political struggle over standards regarding the production and labelling of food. While the food superpowers and the corporate food regime still play very influential roles at the Codex, regulatory differences are providing spaces where a range of other voices, including those of consumers and food activists, are heard. Demands at the national level to know the provenance of food are generating pressure even on major food producers to regulate.

CONCLUSION

Food is indeed different. While a global food system has emerged facilitated by trade liberalization, its impact has been uneven, as it destroys small-scale peasant agriculture in some regions of the world and increases some countries' dependence on food imports. It has increased the distance between sites of food production and eaters and rendered the latter wary of what is in their food and how it is produced. The emergence of the global food crisis in 2007–08 raised further issues around food security. Reactions to the global corporate food regime have emerged in the form of the food movements described in this chapter. These developments provide the context within which I have examined some aspects of the WTO in relation to food, including two important aspects, the first the Agreement on Agriculture and negotiations in the Doha Round and the second relating to non-tariff measures and trade disputes.

The implementation of the AoA and further negotiations have proven a challenge for the WTO as questions remain about the ability to eliminate subsidies while providing sufficient protection and policy space for vulnerable countries. Unable to complete negotiations, the WTO has also come under pressure and criticism in terms of food security and the extent to which WTO trade rules have furthered or limited it. Even where the WTO might acted on export restrictions, the results have been meagre.

Those who focus on the WTO as an organization implementing and enforcing trade rules often point to its dispute resolution processes as an area of success in disciplining the use of non-tariff measures considered to be protectionist. The SPS and TBT agreements are supposed to provide a means by which legitimate regulations can be justified and protectionist measures subjected to trade challenges. Legitimate justification includes reference to international standards. Harmonized or mutually recognized standards then would provide the basis to resolve such disputes. The experience of food standards at the Codex and its relationship to the WTO suggest that this process has proven to be complex and many disputes intractable. A growing public interest in the provenance of food has been reflected in regulations and measures that even when challenged and found to be in violation of trade rules remain in place, particularly among countries with the capacity to resist trade retaliation and engage in lengthy trade litigation. Trends in notification of SPS and TBT measures suggest that such cases will proliferate rather than diminish. Cases which appear either to limit consumers' right to know how and where their food was produced or to reduce the policy space for regulators to have control over these questions risk eroding the legitimacy of the WTO even further.

The growing concern and unease among many eaters about the provenance of their food, the justness of the existing food system and looming threats to food security that derive from many sources, including the inter-linked challenges of climate change and financialization, mean that concerns about food are likely to augment, not diminish. Food is indeed different and will prove to be a challenge to the future and legitimacy of the WTO.

NOTES

1. The support of the Canadian Social Science and Humanities Research Council for this research is gratefully acknowledged.
2. The WTO Agreement on Agriculture defines in its Annex 1 'agricultural products by reference to the harmonised system of product classification – the definition covers not only basic agricultural products such as wheat, milk and live animals, but the products derived from them such as bread, butter and meat, as well as all processed agricultural products such as chocolate and sausages. The coverage also includes wines, spirits and tobacco products, fibres such as cotton, wool and silk, and raw animal skins destined for leather production. Fish and fish products are not included, nor are forestry products' (WTO 2012).
3. See the Codex website at http://www.codexalimentarius.org/.
4. Ractopamine hydrochloride, which is a beta agonist, speeds up the heart rate of the animal to produce heavier, leaner, more muscled animals. Produced by Elanco Animal, a division of the Eli Lilly drug company, it is mixed into feed under the brand name Paylean. To be effective it must be fed to animals right up until shortly before slaughter. The result is that a small amount of drug residue remains in the meat.

REFERENCES

Andrée, Peter Jeffrey Ayres, Michael Bosia and Marie Josée Massicotte (eds) (2014), *Globalization and Food Sovereignty: Global and Local Change in the New Politics of Food*, Toronto: University of Toronto Press.
Blay-Palmer, Allison (2008), *Food Fears*, Aldershot, UK: Ashgate Press.
Borras, Saturnino M., Jr (2008), 'La Via Campesina and Its Global Campaign for Agrarian Reform', *Journal of Agrarian Change*, **8** (2–3), 258–89.
Bottemiller, Helena (2012), 'Dispute over Drug in Feed Limiting US Meat Exports', *Food and Environment Reporting Network*, 25 January, available from: http://thefern.org/2012/01/dispute-over-drug-in-feed-limiting-u-s-meat-exports (accessed 7 July 2012).
Buckingham, Don (2000), 'The Labeling of GM Foods: The Link between the Codex and the WTO', *Agbioforum*, **3** (4), 209–12.
Busch, Lawrence (2010), 'Fairy Tales Do Come True? The Surprising Story of Neoliberalism and World Agriculture', *Sociologia Ruralis*, **50** (4), 331–51.
'CEO: Half of Smithfield's U.S. Pork Will Soon Be Off Ractopamine' (2013), *Chicago Tribune*, 14 May.
Clapp, Jennifer (2012), *Food*, Cambridge: Polity Press.
Codex (2010), *General Standard for the Labelling of Prepackaged Foods*, available from: www.codexalimentarius.net/download/standards/32/CXS_001e.pdf (accessed 25 March 2012).
Codex Alimentarius Commission (2011), Report, 34th Session, Geneva, 4–9 July, available from: www.codexalimentarius.net/download/report/765/REP11_FLe.pdf (accessed 21 March 2012).
Codex Alimentarius Commission (2012), Report, 35th Session, Rome, July.

De Schutter, Olivier (2011), *The World Trade Organization and the Post-Global Food Crisis Agenda: Putting Food Security First in the International Trade System*, Activity Report of the United Nations Special Rapporteur on the Right to Food, November.

Desmarais, Annette (2007), *La Via Campesina: Globalization and the Power of Peasants*, Black Point, NS: Fernwood.

EFSA (European Food Safety Authority) (2009), 'Scientific Opinion Safety Evaluation of Ractopamine', *EFSA Journal*, **1041**, 1–52.

Eurobarometer (2010), *Food-Related Risks*, Eurobarometer 354, prepared for the European Food Safety Authority, November.

FAO (Food and Agricultural Organization) (1996), Rome Declaration on World Food Security and World Food Summit Plan of Action, World Food Summit, 13–17 November, Rome.

FAO (Food and Agricultural Organization) (2009), *FAO Statistical Yearbook*, Rome: UN.

FAO (Food and Agricultural Organization) (2011), *The State of Food Insecurity in the World*, available from: http://www.fao.org/docrep/014/i2330e/i2330e.pdf (accessed 14 March 2011).

FAO (Food and Agriculture Organization) (2012), *Food Price Index*, available from: http://www.fao.org/worldfoodsituation/wfs-home/foodpricesindex/en/ (accessed 18 March 2012).

Green, Duncan (2011), 'Food Fight at the WTO', blogpost, 20 December, available from: http://www.oxfamblogs.org/fp2p/?p=8058 (accessed 20 March 2012).

Holt-Giménez, Eric and Amy Shattuck (2011), 'Food Crises, Food Regimes and Food Movements: Rumblings of Reform or Tides of Transformation', *Journal of Peasant Studies*, **38** (1), 109–44.

Johnson, Renée and Charles Hanrahan (2010), *The U.S.–EU Beef Hormone Dispute*, Washington, DC: Congressional Research Service 7-5700, Report R40449, available from: www.crs.gov (accessed 21 March 2012).

Martinez-Torres, Maria Elena and Peter M. Rosset (2010), La Via Campesina: The Birth and Evolution of a Transnational Social Movement', *Journal of Peasant Studies*, **37** (1), 149–75.

McKeon, Nora (2010), *The United Nations and Civil Society: Legitimating Global Governance – Whose Voice?*, New York: Zed Books.

McMahon, Joseph A. and Melaku Desta (2012), 'The Agreement on Agriculture: Setting the Scene', in Joseph A. McMahon and Melaku Desta (eds), *Research Handbook on the WTO Agriculture Agreement*, Cheltenham, UK and Northampton, MA, USA: Edward Elgar Publishing.

McMichael, Philip (2009), 'A Food Regime Genealogy', *Journal of Peasant Studies*, **36** (1), 129–69.

Morgan, Kevin, Terry Marsden and Jonathan Murdoch (2006), *Worlds of Food: Place, Power and Provenance in the Food Chain*, New York: Oxford University Press.

Murphy, Sophia, David Burch and Jennifer Clapp (2012), *Cereal Secrets: The World's Largest Commodity Traders and Global Trends in Agriculture*, Oxfam Research Report, August, Oxford: Oxfam.

OWINFS (Our World Is Not for Sale) (2008), 'The WTO's Doha Round Will Not Stop the Food Crisis: Time for Real Solutions', letter from 243 organizations from more than 50 countries on the food crisis, June.

Oxfam (2011), *Growing a Better Future: Food Justice in a Resource Constrained World*, available from: www.oxfam.org (accessed 10 March 2011).

Pollan, Michael (2010), 'The Food Movement Rising', *New York Review of Books*, 10 June.

Prakash, Aseem and Kelly Kollman (2007), 'Biopolitics in the US: An Assessment', in Robert Falkner (ed.), *The International Politics of Genetically Modified Food: Diplomacy, Trade and Law*, Basingstoke, UK: Palgrave, pp. 103–17.

Reitan, Ruth (2007), *Global Activism*, New York: Routledge.

Rosset, P. (2006), *Food Is Different: Why We Must Get the WTO Out of Agriculture*, New York: Zed Books.

Schoenbaum, Thomas J. (2011), 'Fashioning a New Regime for Agricultural Trade: New Issues and the Global Food Crisis', *Journal of International Economic Law*, **14** (3), 593–611.

Schramm, Daniel (2007), 'The Race to Geneva: Resisting the Gravitational Pull of the WTO in the GMO Labeling Controversy', *Vermont Journal of Environmental Law*, **9** (3), 94–129.

Sharma, Ramesh (2011), *Food Export Restrictions: Review of the 2007–2010 Experience and Considerations for Disciplining Restrictive Measures*, FAO Commodity and Trade Policy Research Working Paper No. 32, available from: http://www.fao.org/fileadmin/templates/est/PUBLICATIONS/Comm_Working_Papers/EST-WP32.pdf (accessed 14 March 2011).

Smithfield (2013), 'Smithfield Well Positioned to Meet Rising Demand for Ractopamine-Free Pork', 21 February.

Smythe, Elizabeth (2009), 'In Whose Interests? Transparency and Accountability in the Global Governance of Food', in J. Clapp and Doris Fuchs (eds), *Corporate Power in Global Agrifood Governance*, Cambridge, MA: MIT Press, pp. 93–124.

Smythe, Elizabeth (2014), 'Food Sovereignty, Trade Rules and the Struggle to Know the Origins of Food', in Peter Jeffrey Ayres Andrée, Michael Bosia and Marie Josée Massicotte (eds), *Globalization and Food Sovereignty: Global and Local Change in the New Politics of Food*, Toronto: University of Toronto Press.

'USTR Abandons Regulatory COOL "Fix" in Face of Stakeholder Division' (2012), *Inside US Trade*, 2 March.

Veggeland, Frode and Svein Ole Borgen (2005), 'Negotiating International Food Standards: The World Trade Organization's Impact on the Codex Alimentarius Commission', *Governance*, **18** (4), 675–708.

WTO (World Trade Organization) (2006), *European Communities: Measures Affecting the Approval and Marketing of Biotech Products: Reports of the Panel*, WT/DS291/R, 292/R, 293/R, 29 September, Geneva: WTO.

WTO (World Trade Organization) (2008), 'Lamy Signals Start of "Horizontal Process" in Negotiations', News items, Trade Negotiations Committee, 17 April, available from: http://www.wto.org/english/news_e/news08_e/tnc_17apr08_e.htm (accessed 14 March 2011).

WTO (World Trade Organization) (2011a), 'Lamy Rebuts UN Food Rapporteur's Claim that WTO Talks Hold Food Rights "Hostage,"' 14 December, available from: http://www.wto.org/english/news_e/news11_e/agcom_14dec11_e.htm (accessed 20 March 2012).

WTO (World Trade Organization) (2011b), *International Trade Statistics*, available from: http://www.wto.org/english/res_e/statis_e/its2011_e/its11_charts_e.htm.

WTO (World Trade Organization) (2011c), *Overview Regarding the Level of Implementation of the Transparency Provisions of the SPS Agreement*, Note by the Secretariat, G/SPS/GEN/804/Rev.4, 13 October, Geneva: WTO.

WTO (World Trade Organization) (2012), *Trade Topics: Agriculture*, available from: http://www.wto.org/english/tratop_e/agric_e/ag_intro01_intro_e.htm (accessed 20 March 2012).

WTO Committee on Technical Barriers to Trade (2011), *Sixteenth Annual Review of the Implementation and Operation of the TBT Agreement*, Note by the Secretariat, G/TBT/29, 8 March, Geneva: WTO.

WTO Committee on Technical Barriers to Trade (2013), Eighteenth Annual Review of the Implementation and Operation of the TBT Agreement, G/TBT/33, 27 February, Geneva: WTO.

'WTO Members Drop Food Security Proposals for Ministerial' (2011), *Bridges*, **15** (42), 7 December.

WTO Secretariat (2011), *Report on the Activities of the WTO SPS Committee and Other Relevant WTO Activities from January 2010 through March 2011*, CAC/34 INF/3, presented to Codex Commission, 4–9 July, Geneva: WTO.

21. The political economy of international migration law[1]

Joel P. Trachtman

This chapter develops a political economy analysis of international migration, and suggests the implications of this analysis for international legal rules relating to migration. As Grossman and Helpman put it, at the conclusion of their leading work on the political economy of protectionism in trade:

> A next step might be to assess the relative desirability of alternative international "rules of the game." Such rules limit the policy choices open to national governments and change the nature of the strategic interactions between elected officials and their constituents. Our framework could be used to generate predictions about what domestic policies will emerge from the political process in different [international] institutional settings, and therefore to evaluate which rules give rise to preferred policy outcomes.[2]

Given existing wide disparities in wage rates across borders, global welfare would be greatly increased by permitting greater mobility of labor. However, the international political economy academy and the international law academy have devoted much less attention to migration than to international trade or finance, both theoretically and empirically.[3] The welfare factors themselves are complex and variegated, and welfare analysis would require individual country evaluation, and customized solutions, with the possibility for change over time. Thus, there is no single political economy model that can apply to all states, and no monolithic set of international legal rules that can be advanced as the key to unlocking these great welfare increases. Rather, a framework agreement that allows states, through analysis and negotiations, to discover and implement their own reciprocal welfare-enhancing regimes is the only feasible path.

In this chapter, I examine how welfare economics concerns, and others, are mediated through national political processes, and how the resulting national political equilibria may result in an international political equilibrium. I then take up the Grossman and Helpman challenge to assess the relative desirability of international legal rules to change the nature of the strategic equilibrium, both between governments and within domestic coalition politics. Once we evaluate the domestic politics of states arising from the distributive consequences of migration, we must also recognize that other factors, including recession, income inequality, history, ignorance, demagogic scapegoating, chauvinism, and even racism may be added to the forces that determine policy, and that the alchemy of domestic coalitions is complex. In this brief treatment, I cannot do more than mention these important factors.

Within each state, some groups of individuals will be harmed by liberalization, while some will be helped. In order to assess domestic political dynamics, we must analyze and synthesize the domestic coalition politics of migration. Those domestic workers who compete with immigrants may experience reduced wages and, unless adjustment assistance is provided, reduced welfare. This result is not certain, nor is the magnitude necessarily very great. Nor does it appear that immigrant workers generally consume public services excessively. However, in certain cases it may be that some segments of native workers are hurt significantly or that immigrants consume greater amounts of public services than they contribute. Alternatively, perhaps workers and voters may succumb to prejudice or demagogic appeals, and therefore oppose immigration.[4]

It is worthwhile to compare the political economy of migration with the political economy of trade. The standard political economy account of protectionism in trade in goods is as follows. Domestic manufacturers for domestic consumption, perhaps supported by domestic labor, are interested in protection against imports in order to increase their profitability. Domestic manufacturers for domestic consumption are more concentrated, and therefore better organized and more powerful politically, than domestic consumers interested in cheap imports. Being better organized than consumers, domestic manufacturers for domestic consumption succeed in determining policy.[5]

In contrast, one would assume generally that domestic manufacturers that compete with imports, domestic manufacturers seeking to export, domestic workers in complementary industries, and domestic consumers would all welcome immigrants, who are presumed to bring reduced labor costs. However, for some multinational corporations that already have the advantage of being able to access foreign labor markets at low prices, it may be more advantageous to locate labor intensive activities in cheap labor markets, which may not benefit from higher prevailing wages, minimum wages, collective bargaining, or costly safety standards. At the same time, these multinational corporations may wish to deprive their domestic competitors of cheap labor by promoting immigration restrictions. This presents the possibility of bootlegger–Baptist coalitions between multinational corporations, on the one hand, and wealthy country unskilled labor, on the other hand, in support of restrictions on immigration.

Some domestic employers may prefer illegal immigration to legal immigration, because of the bargaining power they may hold in relation to illegal immigrants. These employers may lobby against policies that would liberalize legal migration, while possibly opposing enforcement of restrictions on illegal immigration. Along with nativists, these employers may form another type of bootlegger–Baptist coalition.

We might expect better-organized producer interests, combined with diffuse consumer interests, to be able to overcome less well-organized labor interests. As suggested above, much would depend on the extent to which producer interests benefit from use of illegal immigrants, or derive a competitive advantage from differential access to cheap labor markets abroad. In addition, much would depend on the extent of labor organization. If labor interests were less well organized, or otherwise weaker, under the standard political economy simplification that government decision-makers are rational political support-maximizers, we would expect government policy to be favorable to immigration. Indeed, Freeman argued in 1995 that "there is in general an expansionary bias in the politics of immigration in liberal democracies such that official policies tend to be more liberal than public opinion and annual intakes larger than is politically optimal."[6]

As suggested above, politics is driven by more than just welfare, and it is certainly driven by the intra-national distributive aspects of welfare. That is, the politics of migration policy involves complex historical, social, patriotic, chauvinistic, and other factors, and experience has shown that it is too much to expect politicians consistently to play to the best interests or to the greater virtues of their constituents. Second, politics involves the examination not just of aggregate effects, but of effects on particular interest groups. Furthermore, political analysis requires examination of the relative intensity of the preferences and influence of these particular interest groups: their concern and clout.

Therefore, this chapter begins at the local level, and then moves to the global, or in this case international, level. Once we are able to establish a set of parameters that determine national policies with respect to migration, we are able to turn to the international politics of migration. Once we understand the national politics and the international politics, we can examine the potential role of international law.

Political economy analysis thus has three important dimensions.

- First, at the domestic level, how and to what extent are the distributive outcomes indicated by welfare economics transformed into political pressure in domestic politics? This is a question both of economic effects and of the mediation of economic effects through political and social mechanisms. What additional parameters are important to political decision-making regarding migration?

- Second, at the international level, how do states fail to achieve welfare-enhancing agreements or transactions owing to strategic problems or other market failures?
- Third, the prior two dimensions interact to present a cooperation problem in connection with international migration. In order for welfare-enhancing international agreements to be entered into, they must engage the domestic politics of member states. They require the assembly of domestic coalitions that have the political power to approve international agreements that will be acceptable to foreign counterparties. In order to convince foreign counterparties to engage in reciprocal concessions, they require the assembly or contingent assembly of domestic coalitions that have the political power to induce continued compliance with the relevant agreement. Compliance coalitions may be supported, in part or in whole, by international legal commitments that include the threat of specific or diffuse, formal or informal, retaliation, or of other types of consequences. How is this cooperation problem different from that experienced in other areas, such as international trade in goods and services? What are the implications of these differences for legal structures?

This chapter is an exercise in normative political economy, insofar as it examines the extent to which existing national and international political equilibria are consistent with the maximization of global, national, and individual welfare. Alternative legal rules and institutions may allow achievement of welfare-enhancing domestic and international political equilibria.

ENDOGENOUS POLICY MODELS OF TRADE AND IMMIGRATION

Grossman and Helpman develop a paradigmatic model of trade politics in which owners of particular factors organize a lobbying group in order to influence the government by political contributions. Grossman and Helpman focus on the campaign contributions channel of influence on government.[7] In this model, the motivation of lobbyists to contribute to political campaigns is not necessarily to affect the outcome of elections, but to "buy influence."

In the Grossman–Helpman model, each interest group has a "contribution schedule" linked to various alternative policy vectors. In response, government chooses a policy vector in order to maximize a weighted sum of 1) contributions and 2) national social welfare. National social welfare is part of the calculus because it is assumed to affect votes. The Grossman–Helpman model relates an industry's equilibrium protection to its political organization, its ratio of domestic output to net trade, and the elasticity of import demand or export supply. The equilibrium is that set of contribution schedules such that each lobby's schedule maximizes the aggregate utility of the lobby's members, taking as a given the schedules of other lobby groups.

Grossman and Helpman assume a small competitive economy, for which free trade is optimal. Under that assumption, government interventions in the form of tariffs or subsidies may be assumed to be motivated by political considerations, rather than national welfare. The standard trade model of protectionism explains protection in national public welfare terms by reference to terms of trade[8] externalities, and holds that protectionism can be welfare-improving only for a large country (with market power), which can use trade barriers to improve its welfare as compared with free trade.[9]

One commonly accepted extension of the Grossman–Helpman approach to the domestic political economy of trade recognizes the possibility of linking the interests of domestic producers for export to the interests of domestic consumers through *reciprocal* free trade agreements. By virtue of these agreements, the political power of domestic producers *for export* is added to the political power of domestic consumers, overcoming the political power of domestic producers that compete with imports for domestic consumption. The possibility of reciprocal international trade agreements induces an anti-protection coalition to form, in support of liberalization pursuant to these agreements. Thus, the domestic political economy of trade is critically linked, by reciprocal trade agreements, to the international political economy of trade.

Is this approach to international trade relations adaptable to migration?[10] Migration does not display the same pattern of domestic interests as trade. In the migration context, destination state manufacturers, both for domestic consumption and for export, would generally be expected to be in favor of liberalized immigration. Facchini et al.[11] suggest that migration politics is strongly affected by political contributions by manufacturers, as well as by labor union activity. However, destination state manufacturers may experience difficulties in organizing, as the breadth of interest in immigration could result in collective action problems unless immigration policy is selective by sector. Facchini et al. assume selectivity in their model of protection against immigration:

> We show that in equilibrium, in a given sector, the amount of protection afforded to labor, i.e. the restrictiveness of the migration policy adopted by the

government, depends on both the lobbying expenditures made by organized labor, as well as on the expenditures made by capital (which is its complement). In particular, if labor in a sector spends larger amounts, ceteris paribus it will obtain higher levels of protection from foreign inflows of workers to that sector and, hence, it will lower the equilibrium number of immigrants. At the same time, if organized business owners spend higher amounts, this will ceteris paribus make migration policy in that sector less restrictive and, therefore, increase the number of immigrants.[12]

In the Facchini et al. model, a lobby for labor and a lobby for capital engage in a non-cooperative game where each chooses an amount to pay in order to maximize its own net welfare.[13] It is uncertain, however, to what extent the sectoral divisions assumed by Facchini et al. actually exist. In the U.S., for example, there are few formal distinctions between different occupations at the legislative level, where lobbying is expected to operate.

If destination states had no market power, as Grossman and Helpman assume with respect to importing states, then the Facchini et al. model would seem to provide a plausible tool by which to analyze immigration policy. However, popular destination states seem to wield important market power, allowing them to improve their welfare at the expense of migrants and home states. The ability to import labor at a price lower than the price that would otherwise apply, by using policy measures to extract some of the income from the imported worker, or to extract welfare from the home state, seems analogous to the use of tariffs to increase domestic welfare at the expense of foreign welfare. Market power of this type might be a more important factor in connection with less skilled labor than in connection with highly skilled labor. Even wealthy states may find that they must compete in order to attract highly skilled labor.

Some destinations, such as the U.S., the E.U., Canada, Australia, and other wealthy states, undoubtedly are attractive to immigrants. Part of this attraction arises from the wages that can be earned in these destinations, presumably owing to high levels of productivity. This strong attraction may give rise to market power, in the sense that supply of immigration opportunities is limited, demand for immigration opportunities is high, and the governments of the destination countries have control of entry. Of course, market power also requires that a state be sufficiently large as a fraction of the global economy to affect the world price of labor through its policies. Do these leading destination states use market power to extract welfare gains from immigration? Consider the following possibilities:

- First, states with market power in this context may exert that power by accepting immigrants and denying the home state of the immigrants the ability to tax those migrants – declining to implement

Handbook of the international political economy of trade

a Bhagwati tax.[14] By doing so, the destination state may impose a negative externality on the home state.[15]

- A second, related, way by which states with market power may exert their power is to accept only highly skilled immigrants – those who will make a positive contribution in terms of an immigration dividend and in terms of a fiscal contribution. Thus, we can interpret brain drain as a negative externality imposed by the destination state on the home state.

- Third, it is also possible that destination states could use their market power to impose discriminatory taxes or other burdens on immigrants, or to deny immigrants public benefits that are available to natives, causing immigrants to give up some of the surplus from migration that they might otherwise capture.[16] Considering the U.S. relationship with Mexican or other illegal immigrants, it may be that denial of public services or public transfer payment benefits could be understood as discriminatory provision of public benefits, with the same motivation and effect. Of course, illegal immigrants are more likely to suffer from this type of "discrimination." Under U.S. law, illegal immigrants are denied certain public benefits. So, could it be that a preference for illegal immigration can be explained in terms of negative externalities?[17]

These types of measures are likely to provide disincentives for migration, in a way that may reduce global welfare insofar as migration would otherwise be efficient.[18] Indeed, it may be that a sufficient rationale for states to cooperate in this area is simply to agree to suppress these types of measures in order to increase volumes of migration, and thereby enhance global welfare. According to this rationale, states could agree to increase international migration, and thereby increase global welfare, provided that they are able to agree on the distribution of the gains.

Note, however, that the home state is not necessarily directly harmed by the destination state exercise of market power, or does not feel the full welfare loss caused by the destination state policy, and so may not be sufficiently motivated to negotiate to protect its emigrants. On the other hand, if home states sought more actively to tax their emigrants, they might understand refusal by destination states to enforce these taxes as harmful, and discrimination might reduce amounts available for remittances or to be used for investment upon return. Temporary migration arrangements may provide greater incentives for home states to protect their emigrants: under these arrangements, the goal of the home state is to have migrants send remittances and then return with capital, skills, and contacts.

To the extent that these types of policy externalities are recognized by the home state, it may have incentives to negotiate with the destination state over their reduction. Robert Staiger explains this motivation in the trade context as follows:

> Beginning from the inefficient trade policy choices made in the presence of this international cost-shifting, the purpose of international trade negotiations is then clear: to provide an avenue by which foreign exporters can have their interests represented in the trade protection choices of the national governments to whose markets these exporters seek access, and thereby to face those governments with internationally appropriate incentives that lead them to choose internationally efficient levels of trade protection.[19]

Note that this is a political representation argument. The goal in migration is also to induce destination states to choose internationally efficient levels of restriction on immigration. To paraphrase Staiger, the goal is to provide an avenue by which emigrants and those left behind in home states can have their interests represented in immigration policies of destination state governments. To the extent that destination state governments take these interests into account, they will be more likely to choose internationally efficient levels of immigration protection.

In the trade context, the terms of trade approach, focusing on the exercise of market power, seems only to provide a rationale for negotiations among states with market power. As noted above, economists expect that welfare-maximizing states without market power would unilaterally make policy choices that are internationally efficient, since they cannot gain welfare by raising barriers.[20] Furthermore, they therefore expect that states with market power would see little benefit from negotiating agreements with states that lack market power.[21] There is no clear understanding regarding the extent of poor or small states' market power, except an understanding that it is generally less than that of wealthy and rich states.

In the migration context, it appears that states without market power frequently do not impose restrictions on immigration. One reason, no doubt, is that the demand to immigrate to those states is, by definition, not very great: their productivity rates generally do not result in increased wages for immigrants. But the important point here is that states without market power in migration would have little to bargain with in a transaction limited to reciprocal liberalization of migration. On the other hand, we must remember that, in this context, market power is relative. Thus, a middle-income developing country may have market power as a destination state vis-à-vis a lower-income developing country: it may be attractive for residents of the latter to migrate to the former, in order to realize wage gains.

In the trade model addressing terms of trade externalities, the role of

506 Handbook of the international political economy of trade

international law is to allow states credibly to commit to exercise reciprocal restraint. Even in a model that does not include terms of trade externalities, in which states are failing to achieve optimal volumes of trade, and therefore are failing to achieve maximum global welfare, international law could play a similar role in allowing states credibly to commit to exercise restraint, or to make compensation, as appropriate.

This type of cooperation problem has often been modeled, assuming a certain structure of payoffs, using the prisoner's dilemma game. The assumption is that the states could be better off if neither of them defected, but that each is individually better off if it defects while the other cooperates, and is worst off if it cooperates while the other defects. The dominant solution – the expected behavior – is defection by all states. However, by using international legal rules to make negative the payoffs from defection, states are able to achieve the collectively optimal outcome of mutual cooperation.

Table 21.1a is a diagram of the prisoner's dilemma, as applied to trade. In this set of assumed payoffs, if international legal rules can impose a cost on defectors (states that fail to liberalize or impose terms of trade externalities) greater than 1 (in Table 21.1b, for illustration, I use 1.5), then they will decide to liberalize instead. In Table 21.1b, the dominant solution for each player is to liberalize: no matter what State B does, the best payoff for State A is to liberalize.

If, in the migration context, home states saw themselves as harmed by the kinds of negative externalities described above imposed by destination states in connection with migration, and if the positions were symmetrical, a similar set of payoffs might arise. Alternatively, if states saw themselves as harmed by global failure to achieve optimal volumes of migration, a similar strategic setting, based on a public goods problem, might arise. On the basis of the example of trade, we might too quickly assume that international migration agreements could play a similar role. However, as I have suggested, the explanations developed in connection with the political economy of trade do not neatly map into the migration context: while the

Table 21.1a   A trade prisoner's dilemma game without international legal rules

| | | State B | |
		Liberalize	Defect
State A	Liberalize	2,2	0,3
	Defect	3,0	1,1

*Table 21.1b   A trade prisoner's dilemma game plus international legal
            rules imposing penalties for defection (no longer a prisoner's
            dilemma)*

		State B	
		Liberalize	Defect
State A	Liberalize	2,2	0,1.5
	Defect	1.5,0	−0.5,−0.5

welfare economics analysis bears some limited similarities, and the international setting may be comparable, the domestic political economy parameters are different. There are important reasons why we do not observe international agreements for liberalization of migration.

Greenaway and Nelson state that there is little empirical research on immigration policy with a direct link to endogenous policy modeling, in part owing to 1) weak evidence of economic impact, and 2) strong evidence of noneconomic forces in determining preferences.[22] They find that "endogenous policy models of migration policy seem to provide very little analytical leverage."[23] One reason is that "there is no equivalent, long-lived, group-based politics surrounding immigration."[24] Greenaway and Nelson conclude that "trade is seen as national and essentially economic; while immigration is local and essentially social."[25] However, this conclusion may be seen as more an observation of a result than an identification of a cause. A casual observer of U.S. immigration politics might conclude that immigration is becoming more like trade: group-based, national if not international, and essentially economic. Indeed, Willmann,[26] commenting on Greenaway and Nelson, finds counterevidence in the work of Borjas[27] and Mayda. Willmann cites examples of political positions that seem consistent with economic expectations.[28]

MAPPING THE DESTINATION STATE POLITICAL ECONOMY OF MIGRATION

In order to develop some simple schematics of the possible coalition dynamics in the political economy of the destination state[29] regarding migration, comparable to the model of the political economy of the importing state regarding trade described above, it is necessary to make a number of simplifying assumptions and to exclude much detail. These assumptions are supported by the discussion above.

For simplicity's sake, I largely exclude from these schematics factors other than economic welfare and political representation in connection with economic welfare. Hatton and Williamson find that, in the long run, "the New World countries tried to protect the economic position of their scarce factor, the unskilled worker."[30] They find "no compelling evidence that xenophobia or racism was driving immigration policy in the New World economies," once you ignore Asian exclusions and absent Africans. This does not mean that these factors are unimportant, but the purpose of these schematics is not to determine how states will necessarily behave, or what kind of international legal commitments they will necessarily establish. Rather, it is to develop an idea of the way that the welfare economics considerations may be translated into political pressures, the strategic constraints that domestic interests face, and the strategic constraints that states face, in order to be able to suggest how international legal commitments may facilitate the achievement of these goals. By doing so, I hope to develop an idea of the broad parameters of possible international legal commitments in this area.

This strategy is predicated on a simplifying assumption that welfare considerations will be strong and may, over time and in appropriate contexts, overcome some of the contextual, social, historical, and political factors. Furthermore, these factors do not necessarily always militate against liberalization. So, these schematics are simplifications. However, an international negotiation toward an agreement would necessarily involve states determining their positions based on all of the relevant factors, not only welfare.

I assume that citizens seek to influence their own governments through two main channels: 1) political contributions, and 2) voting. Governments act in response to utility functions based on an attempt to maximize a weighted sum of these two components: they maximize political support.[31]

As noted above, there is a domestic coalition-building game, and a linked international cooperation game: thus, migration policy is a two-level game in the Putnam sense.[32] The question raised by this chapter is whether governments may find it useful to enter into international agreements in order to induce the formation of domestic political coalitions in support of liberalization. I describe the domestic coalition-building problem textually, and show how it may drive an international coordination or cooperation game with game theory matrices. I show that, at least under certain hypothesized circumstances where, without international agreements, pro-liberalization forces would not be successful in inducing formal liberalization, international agreements may increase the possibility of formation of pro-liberalization coalitions.

In the following four subsections, I develop four simple schematics of possible structures of political support for liberalization of immigration.

The first two schematics use the assumption, based on Heckscher–Ohlin theory, that unskilled labor would migrate to where it is scarce, and skilled labor would migrate to where it is scarce. Opposition also follows Heckscher–Ohlin theory: the scarce factor in the destination state has the most to lose in connection with immigration. The third schematic adds the possibility of capital mobility or offshoring, or illegal immigration. The fourth schematic assumes that wealthy country labor has no interest in migrating to poor countries. Under this schematic, potential reciprocity within migration policy would play no role, as wealthy country labor would not seek access to poor country markets.

1. Symmetric labor markets. First, I develop a schematic in which two states are symmetric, with equal endowments of labor, including equal proportions of skilled and unskilled labor. This schematic could describe migration between poor or middle-income states, or migration between wealthy states. An example might be the migration relationship between the U.S. and the E.U. Here, engineers, doctors, or professors might migrate in search of a particular type of position or better pay. Although I assume symmetry in terms of general endowments, it would be likely that some states might have an advantage in producing a particular type of worker. France would be expected to produce better chefs than the U.S., while the U.S. might be expected to produce better basketball players than France. (While this schematic is based on the Heckscher–Ohlin model, since there is no differential between the two states in relative abundance and scarcity, migration cannot be said to be motivated by Heckscher–Ohlin factors.)
2. Asymmetric labor markets with two-way migration. Second, I develop a schematic that assumes asymmetry, where one state has abundant skilled labor while the other has abundant unskilled labor. Here, the relationship between Spain and Morocco, or between the U.S. and Mexico, is an example. Generally, developing countries are likely to have greater abundance of unskilled labor, while developed countries have greater abundance of skilled labor.
3. Asymmetric labor markets with offshoring or illegal immigration. Third, I add to the asymmetric context the possibility of offshoring or illegal immigration as an alternative to liberalization of migration.
4. Asymmetric labor markets with one-way migration. Fourth, I develop a schematic that assumes asymmetry, but, contrary to Heckscher–Ohlin theory, assumes that poor country labor flows only toward the wealthy country: wealthy country natives do not wish to migrate to the poor country.

These schematics are structured in bilateral terms. Obviously, multilateral arrangements will be more complex. Indeed, multilateral arrangements with most-favored-nation non-discrimination may be very difficult to achieve where they include relationships of both symmetry and asymmetry, and both "two-way street" migration relationships and "one-way street" relationships.

1 Symmetric Labor Markets: A Coordination (Stag Hunt) Game

Assume two symmetric states: domestic labor and foreign labor are symmetric overall in quantity and skill level. Assume that, in each economy, skilled labor is abundant and unskilled labor is scarce. (This schematic would also apply to the opposite: symmetric economies where unskilled labor is abundant and skilled labor is scarce.) Levels of productivity and wages are closely aligned. In this context, there may be little reason for migration, and little by way of welfare gains to be captured by liberalizing migration. Conversely, there may be little reason to *oppose* immigration, because it brings no pressure on wages in the destination country. On the other hand, within certain sectors, such as cooking, language training, software engineering, or baseball, some countries might produce more highly skilled workers than others. This would constitute a basis for migration, within the particular sector. It might also constitute a basis for protectionism by the competing domestic workers.

Nielson suggests that, generally, agreements among countries that are geographically proximate and at similar levels of development entail greater liberalization of labor mobility.[33] Ghosh suggests that migration liberalization agreements among countries of similar levels of income are most likely to emerge and survive.[34]

In Table 21.2, I set forth a stylized conjecture as to the likely positions of different broad groups under this condition of labor market symmetry. I first describe each state's unilateral policy, and then examine how a regime of reciprocity would affect the groups' positions. I then explain my reasons for characterizing each group's position as I do. The main difference between the non-reciprocal case and the reciprocal case is that the abundant labor factor, seeing opportunities abroad that could be opened up by reciprocity, favors reciprocal liberalization. In some cases, this will be sufficient to change the balance of lobbying power, resulting in a new, pro-reciprocal liberalization equilibrium. Indeed, this may be especially true in particular vocational sectors and not true in other vocational sectors. So it may be that an international agreement that differentiates by vocational sector, in which states make schedules of liberalization commitments by vocational sector, would allow states to make the most precise choices in

Table 21.2   Symmetric labor markets with equal productivity

	Scarce labor	Abundant labor	Capital	Consumers
No reciprocity	Opposed to liberalization	Weakly in favor of liberalization	Weakly in favor of liberalization (symmetry reduces returns)	Weakly in favor of liberalization (dispersed)
Reciprocity	Opposed to liberalization	More strongly in favor	Weakly in favor	Weakly in favor (dispersed)

this field. This would allow a kind of cross-vocational reciprocity, in which, for example, the U.S. opens its market to French chefs in return for France opening its market to U.S. basketball players.

Scarce labor factor opposes liberalization
Assume, consistent with Heckscher–Ohlin, that unskilled workers believe that they are hurt by immigration.[35] Unskilled workers therefore oppose liberalization of immigration. However, under conditions of equal productivity and symmetry, with little wage differential between the symmetric states, and little expected migration, this opposition may not be strong. As noted above, certain sectors may demonstrate greater concern than others.

Capital weakly supports liberalization
Domestic capital supports liberalization of immigration.[36] Benefits to capital may include greater labor market flexibility. As wage differentials are assumed not to be significant, the benefits to capital are not great, and therefore the support is not strong.

Furthermore, capital may have a more difficult time organizing in connection with immigration than in connection with trade liberalization, because of accentuated collective action problems, unless the state permits sector-selective immigration policy. In connection with trade, tariffs are industry- or product-specific, as are many subsidies, giving rise to concentrated incentives for lobbying. Immigration policy may not be product- or industry-specific, at least at the legislative level, and so there may be temptations to free ride. This will vary by state. While many states require labor market certification, it is unclear to what extent this type of certification is susceptible to lobbying influence. Some states have point systems or other devices for preferring individuals with certain vocations over others. On the other hand, the WTO General Agreement on Trade in Services (GATS) allows states to make vocation-specific commitments.

Consumers weakly support liberalization

Except to the extent that they compete with immigrants for consumption opportunities, consumers would benefit in welfare terms from immigration. However, as the wage differentials are not significant, the likely savings to consumers would not be great. Moreover, as in trade, consumers are often not sufficiently organized to articulate this preference in destination country politics.

Abundant labor factor weakly supports liberalization

Abundant types of workers benefit from liberalization to the extent that there are complementarities by virtue of which increased immigration of unskilled workers may increase the returns to skilled workers. These are not powerful incentives for skilled workers to advocate liberalization, and the actual position of the abundant type of workers would depend on many factors.[37] As noted above, one important caveat is that, within certain sectors, skilled workers may benefit from liberalization.

Abundant labor factor seeks mobility – reciprocation

Assume that domestic abundant labor believes that it would benefit from its own international mobility, allowing its workers to emigrate to where they are scarce, in search of higher prices. This benefit is presumed to accrue to the segment of labor that is plentiful. But note that, under the assumption of symmetry, mobility is not as valuable as it would be under an assumption of asymmetry. This benefit gives plentiful labor a modest added incentive to seek foreign liberalization.[38] Again, within certain sectors, we might see greater interest in mobility.

Mobility of labor allows workers to "countervail" multinational corporation mobility, allowing labor to seek the highest wages. Furthermore, foreign labor mobility would increase foreign labor bargaining power and price, and therefore reduce the possibility that domestic multinational corporations might offshore to foreign labor. However, for the same reason that the scarce labor factor's opposition is weak in this symmetric context, mobility in this context does not provide great incentives for support by the abundant factor. As noted above, however, one important caveat is that, within certain vocations, workers may benefit more from liberalization, and so, to the extent that liberalization can be differentiated by vocation, there may be stronger support for liberalization in some vocations than in others.

Thus, it is possible that the added factor of reciprocal foreign liberalization, perhaps with the possibility for differentiation by vocation, could induce the formation of a coalition between capital and abundant labor, along with consumers, to overcome scarce labor's opposition to liberalization of immigration. However, note that, while capital supports liberalization of immigration at home, it is unlikely to support increased emigration by virtue of liberalization of immigration abroad. Thus, reciprocal liberalization may actually reduce capital's support. The actual position of capital would depend on the extent to which capital is a complement for emigrant labor, and the degree of mobility of capital. Mobile capital might actually benefit from a more efficient allocation of labor between countries.

On the other hand, it may be that, if the true costs and benefits are quite different depending on the sector involved, we would observe sectorally differentiated positions among workers.

Adjustment and voters
Under this symmetric context, the gains from liberalization are not likely to be very great. Therefore, the surplus generated may not be sufficient to cover the costs of adjustment assistance plus its administration. It may be that unskilled labor simply absorbs any loss that accrues to it – this loss is not likely to be great. If the gains from liberalization accrue largely to capital, it might be appropriate to tax capital in order to acquire funds to provide adjustment assistance. If the gains accrue largely to migrants, which is likely, it may be useful to impose some type of charge or tax on migrants in order to capture a sufficient portion of the surplus to be able to provide adjustment assistance. The U.S. charges such a fee in connection with its H1-B visa program. If these domestic institutional arrangements could be made, a wider range of reciprocal commitments to liberalize would become feasible. All other things being equal, if we can assume that liberalization improves global welfare, and if this redounds to the general benefit of voters, we might expect a slight impulse toward liberalization. This impulse would be vulnerable to being countervailed by concern for those who lose their jobs, and by a variety of noneconomic factors.

Coordination game
Given all these factors, it may be that the best outcome for both states is reciprocal liberalization. Under these circumstances, this game could be understood as a coordination game, like a stag hunt, in which each state government does better in this political support game if it seeks liberalization, but only if other states reciprocally liberalize. The critical question, then, is whether states may provide assurance to one another regarding their liberalization. This assurance need not be great, as there are not strong incentives to defect. This may explain why liberalization of migration among wealthy states generally appears to require no international legal commitments to provide additional incentives for compliance. Note that the inducement to domestic skilled labor to support liberalization is

foreign market access. If foreign market access can be achieved without liberalizing at home – without reciprocation – domestic skilled labor will still be satisfied. But liberalizing at home does not harm domestic skilled labor, and so the only reason to defect would be the concerns of unskilled labor.

Under the stag hunt, which is a type of "assurance" game, each state may obtain smaller payoffs – in our case, a lower level of gains from liberalization – by seeking protection for its own workers, without providing liberalization for foreign workers, while the other state liberalizes. But, if states are able to coordinate to forgo settling for lower payoffs from their own protection in favor of greater payoffs from global mobility, they will all be better off. Part of these increased payoffs will come from increased global output. Cooperation may break down if players are uncertain about the preferences and strategy of others.

The stag hunt game is derived from a Rousseauvian fable of cooperation among hunters.[39] Unless all hunters are committed to catching the stag, it will escape. Each individual hunter may be tempted by a passing rabbit. Each hunter prefers a share of stag to an individual portion of rabbit, but is uncertain about whether other hunters are sufficiently committed to capturing stag. The analogy to international migration policy is as follows: each state prefers its share of global liberalization of migration (stag), but may be distracted by the opportunity to obtain local protection (rabbit), especially if it is unsure of the commitment of other states. (See Table 21.3.)

In international legal or organizational terms, a stag hunt context may require a lesser level of international legal inducements to compliance, compared to a prisoner's dilemma context, because each player's best strategy is to cooperate in global liberalization. Sufficient clarity regarding the definition of the cooperative behavior, monitoring to ensure compliance, and modest penalties should be sufficient. Note that we are assuming symmetry of preferences: no player actually prefers protection. However, Sandler shows that, as the number of players increases, depending on

Table 21.3   A stag hunt game

		State B	
		Hunt stag/ global liberalization	Chase rabbit/ local protection
State A	Hunt stag/global liberalization	4,4	1,3
	Chase rabbit/local protection	3,1	3,3

whether gains are dependent on uniform compliance, coordination can become quite difficult.[40]

Externalities

I have assumed no labor market externalities in this model – no benefits that accrue more broadly than to the specific groups named. However, if skilled labor is scarce (even where unskilled labor is also scarce), and brings positive fiscal, growth, or other externalities, while unskilled labor brings negative externalities, this game could be transformed into a prisoner's dilemma (illustrated in Table 21.1) between governments seeking to attract and retain skilled labor, depending on the magnitude of the effects and how the political constituencies influence government decisions. Given positive externalities of this type, states would compete to attract skilled labor. There is evidence that increasing numbers of wealthy states see themselves in such competition for skilled labor. International agreements might be used to resolve the prisoner's dilemma (to change the payoff structure so that it is a different game), assuming that the aggregate payoffs from cooperation exceed the aggregate payoffs from defection.

2 Asymmetric Labor Markets with Equal Productivity: A "Prisoner's Dilemma" or "Bully" Game

Now, assume that domestic labor and foreign labor are asymmetric in skill level: labor in State A is largely high-skilled, while labor in State B is largely low-skilled. (See Table 21.4.)

Under this assumed asymmetry, as contrasted with schematic 1, there are significant gains from trade: aggregate welfare in each of State A and State B can be increased by reciprocal liberalization. This is an important

Table 21.4   Asymmetric labor markets with equal productivity

	Scarce labor	Abundant labor	Capital	Consumers
No reciprocity	Strongly opposed to liberalization	Weakly in favor of liberalization	Strongly in favor of liberalization	Weakly in favor (dispersed)
Reciprocity	Strongly opposed to liberalization	Strongly in favor	Still strongly in favor, but reciprocity may reduce returns owing to emigration	Weakly in favor (dispersed)

part of each government's utility function, and may help to induce the government to enter into international legal commitments to unlock this welfare increase.

Scarce labor factor opposes liberalization

Given that these states have asymmetric labor markets, under Heckscher–Ohlin, mobility (if made available without selectivity between classes of labor) is likely to benefit skilled labor in State A and unskilled labor in State B, and conversely is likely to harm unskilled labor in State A and skilled labor in State B.[41] Actual positions, here and in connection with other factors, would depend on cross-elasticities of substitution among the various factors of production. Therefore, we would expect unskilled labor in State A to oppose liberalization, while skilled labor in State B opposes liberalization.

Capital strongly supports liberalization

Besides the migrants themselves, capital is the main beneficiary of liberalization of immigration. Here, under asymmetry, there are greater cross-country price differences, strengthening capital's support for liberalization.

Consumers weakly support liberalization

Except to the extent that they compete with immigrants for consumption opportunities, consumers would be likely to benefit in welfare terms from immigration. Here, under asymmetry, there are greater cross-country price differences, strengthening consumer support for liberalization. However, as in trade, consumers are not well organized to articulate this preference in destination country politics.

Abundant labor factor weakly supports liberalization

Abundant labor may benefit from liberalization by virtue of increased immigration of complementary types of workers. These complementary workers may increase the returns to the abundant types of workers. These are not powerful incentives to advocate liberalization.

Abundant labor factor seeks mobility – reciprocation

As in the symmetric case, however, the abundant factor believes that it would benefit from its own international mobility, allowing its workers to emigrate to where they are scarce, in search of higher prices. This benefit gives plentiful labor an added incentive to seek foreign liberalization, as discussed above.

Thus, the added possibility of reciprocal foreign liberalization induces the formation of a coalition among capital, the abundant labor factor, and consumers to overcome the scarce labor factor's opposition to liberalization of immigration.

However, note that, while capital supports liberalization of immigration at home, it is less likely to support increased emigration by virtue of liberalization of immigration abroad, at least with respect to scarce labor factors. So, we would expect to see some diversity of position within capital: some employers would benefit from increased immigration, while others would be harmed by increased emigration. Thus, *unselective* reciprocal liberalization may actually reduce capital's support. *Selective* reciprocal liberalization – by which the partner state liberalizes its immigration policy only with respect to factors abundant in the first state – would help to overcome this problem.

Cooperation game
Under these circumstances, each state would generally have strong interests in liberalization by the other state, but would prefer – in terms of political contributions and votes from scarce labor – to avoid its own liberalization. This strategic setting may give rise to a prisoner's dilemma-type situation, in which each state is best off protecting while the other state liberalizes, but both states are better off if both liberalize than if both protect. See Table 21.1a.

In this asymmetric schematic, international legal rules could play a role in migration similar to that described above with respect to international legal rules in trade (see Table 21.1b): international legal rules could be entered into by states in order to resolve the prisoner's dilemma, allowing states to achieve greater welfare.

Note the difference between the role of international legal rules in schematic 1 and the role described here in the context of schematic 2. Schematic 1 involved principally a coordination game, in which international legal rules are useful in order to provide a focal point, but each player has incentives to cooperate. Schematic 2, on the other hand, involves a prisoner's dilemma in which each party has an incentive to play a strategy that would confer harm on the other party. However, sufficiently strong international legal rules, changing the payoffs so that states comply, may restrain this behavior.

A reciprocal agreement to liberalize would create increased surplus, possibly allowing government to utilize this surplus to redistribute to those harmed (the scarce factor). Arrangements within each state in order to compensate previously scarce labor for the loss of its market power may be necessary to induce agreement. If the gains accrue largely to capital, it may be appropriate to tax capital in order to acquire funds to provide adjustment assistance. If the gains accrue largely to migrants, which is likely, it may be useful to impose some type of charge or tax on migrants in order to capture a sufficient portion of the surplus to be able to provide adjustment assistance.[42] If these domestic institutional arrangements could be made, a wider range of reciprocal commitments to liberalize would become feasible.

Externalities
Alternatively, if skilled labor brings sufficient positive fiscal, growth, or other externalities while unskilled labor brings sufficient negative externalities, this game could be transformed into a "bully" game between governments, depending on the magnitude of the effects and how the political constituencies influence government decisions. In this bully game, the state that has abundant high-skilled labor may have little incentive to liberalize reciprocally, in order to encourage outflows of high-skilled labor in exchange for inflows of low-skilled labor, particularly if it will have to compensate its low-skilled labor for its losses. (See Table 21.5.)

Note that protection by State A with liberalization by State B is not only State A's dominant strategy, but also the efficient outcome of this game: it maximizes the joint payoffs. State A's payoffs from protection are derived from its ability to avoid harm to its unskilled labor, and its ability to avoid loss of skilled labor where State B also protects. State B does not have a dominant strategy, but, if State B understands State A's dominant strategy to protect, it can increase its payoff from 0 to 1 by playing "liberalize" while State A protects. Assuming that State A understands State B's dilemma, it will simply protect. This strategic setting may describe the typical relationship between developed countries and developing countries. It is not attractive to developing countries from a distributive standpoint.

3 Asymmetric Labor Markets with Mobile Capital/Offshoring or Illegal Immigration

In the prior schematics, capital has not played a decisive role, in part because it is not allied with labor, as it often is in the trade context. Yet 1) offshoring or 2) illegal immigration may give capital a further source

Table 21.5   A "bully" game with asymmetric payoffs

		State B (chicken player)	
		Liberalize	Protect
State A (deadlock player)	Liberalize	1,2	0,3
	Protect	3,1	2,0

Table 21.6   *Asymmetric labor markets, with mobile capital/offshoring or illegal immigration (position of country of immigration)*

	Scarce labor	Abundant labor	Capital	Consumers
No reciprocity	Weaker opposition	Weakly in favor of liberalization	Less strongly in favor of liberalization	Weakly in favor
Reciprocity	Weaker opposition	Strongly in favor of liberalization	Reciprocity may reduce returns owing to emigration, reducing support	Weakly in favor

of power that is not necessarily dependent on affirmative government action.[43] The ability to offshore, or to hire illegal immigrants, reduces the benefits of protection to scarce labor, thereby reducing its opposition to legal immigration. Indeed, as suggested above, simple liberalization of trade in goods or services plays a similar role. However, greater capital mobility, and greater access to illegal immigrants, will reduce the returns to capital from liberalization of immigration, reducing its support for formal liberalization. (See Table 21.6.)

"That immigration and trade are substitute ways to obtain the same output suggests that changes in the number of immigrants will have less effect on native incomes in the presence of relatively free trade than they otherwise would."[44] This is a critical point, as it suggests that resistance to immigration may be reduced as trade in goods and services is liberalized. While this proposition depends on whether migration and trade are complements or substitutes, the threat value of offshoring might persist even where they are complements. Perhaps this point helps to account for the ability of the European Union to engage in extensive liberalization of labor movement, and suggests that multilateral liberalization of markets for goods, services, and investment will facilitate, and yet render less valuable, liberalization of labor movement. Interestingly, globalization in one factor supports globalization in other factors, by reducing the returns to protection. Thus, workers, and their unions, must recognize the alternatives available to them and their opponents as they decide what policy to support. Technological or institutional change that makes it possible to offshore jobs to developing countries with lower wages is analytically similar, assuming free trade in the products of this work, to a policy change relaxing restrictions on immigration.[45] For example, U.S. farmers are increasingly shifting production to Mexico in order to overcome barriers to immigration in the U.S.[46]

This type of change would ordinarily benefit owners of firms and owners of complementary inputs, including complementary workers, while hurting those whose work it replaces. With declining trade protection, increasing liberalization of foreign investment, and technological advances, offshoring must be understood as a growing strategic alternative available to firms. It may be that, in some contexts, support for relaxation of formal immigration controls is a superior alternative from the standpoint of unions, compared to the default alternative of allowing offshoring.

Furthermore, if illiberal formal migration policies will result in greater informal migration, with unorganized and vulnerable[47] illegal immigrants competing with organized labor in the destination state, then organized labor might find some attraction in managed formal migration.[48] Watts suggests that labor unions may form a coalition with employers in favor of legal immigration.

In an asymmetric context, offshoring or illegal immigration may reduce the value to domestic scarce labor of blocking formal liberalization of immigration. Under these circumstances, domestic labor may determine to support increased formal migration, as legal immigrants might join unions and would be subject to destination country cost structures, resulting in less competitive pressure than under the alternatives. Thus, offshoring and illegal immigration would tend to promote greater permission from labor for formal migration to the wealthy state. On the other hand, these same factors of capital mobility or offshoring, or illegal immigration, might reduce the returns to capital from liberalization of migration.

4 Asymmetric One-Way Flow with Compensation

Despite Heckscher–Ohlin theory, there is some reason to believe that, for citizens of popular destination states, there may not be great interest in migration to the typical sending states. As suggested above,[49] under some circumstances, both skilled and unskilled workers may flow toward the high-skilled country – the wealthy country.[50] "This is, of course, what happens in the real world, suggesting that richer countries do indeed enjoy superior technology to poor countries, and that endowments alone cannot explain differences in income, or for that matter trade patterns and factor flows."[51] (See Table 21.7.)

Abundant skilled labor in State A does not support reciprocity
I assume here that the skilled labor in the skilled labor abundant country is not interested in migrating to the unskilled labor abundant country,

Table 21.7   Asymmetric one-way flow: unequal productivity (position of country of immigration)

	Scarce labor	Abundant labor	Capital	Consumers
No reciprocity	Strongly opposed to liberalization	Weakly in favor of liberalization	Strongly in favor of liberalization	Weakly in favor (dispersed)
Reciprocity	Strongly opposed to liberalization	No change— no interest in emigration	Still in favor, with enhanced benefits for investment	Weakly in favor (dispersed)
Reciprocity with side payment	Less opposed if side payment is used for adjustment or increase in export opportunities	More favorable if side payment is used for increase in export opportunities	Increased support if side payment provides increased investment or trade opportunities	May increase support if side payment is used to reduce taxes

because the wages are substantially lower. Therefore, it is not valuable to State A's abundant skilled labor to secure liberalization by State B, so State A labor does not support liberalization by State A, and reciprocity within the migration field is not appealing.

Capital supports liberalization
Under circumstances of asymmetry, capital is strongly in favor of liberalization. However, as in the prior schematics, I assume that State A capital is not sufficiently powerful by itself to procure a policy of liberalization.

Bully game
State A's dominant strategy will likely be to protect, and it will protect unless some other arrangements are made to induce a different move by State A. The payoffs may be similar to the bully game scenario described in connection with the externalities variation of schematic 2. Thus, the question is whether State A constituencies could be given increased incentives to support liberalization, in order to unlock an expected global welfare increase from liberalized migration.

Side payments or linkage

Although a side payment might result in an efficient solution, it might also be unappealing for State B to make financial compensation to State A. However, it is possible that if, for example, State B were willing to liberalize in relevant high-value-added services sectors, under the GATS, 1) State A capital might find this opportunity valuable, and 2) State A skilled labor might benefit from opportunities to be employed or otherwise to provide services to State B. A similar type of side payment or linkage could arise from investment liberalization in State B, providing opportunities for State A capital and State A skilled labor.

This provides an argument for cross-sectoral linkage, by which two efficient policy changes that do not have the political support to be effected alone may be viable together under linkage. This is similar to what is believed to have happened *within* the trade field, where mercantilism balances mercantilism. In fact, now that wealthy states have few tariff barriers, while developing states still have substantial tariff barriers, the outlines of a "grand bargain" toward a virtuous cycle of efficiency may be identified: wealthy states allow greater immigration of skilled and unskilled workers, perhaps also agreeing to enforce a Bhagwati tax, while poor states reduce tariffs and barriers to investment and high-value-added services.

Migration fee or Bhagwati tax

Another alternative or additional type of "side payment" is to allow State A to achieve compensation by imposing a special fee or tax on immigrants.[52]

> [B]ecause most of the gains from immigration accrue to the immigrants rather than to the residents of destination countries . . . there is little incentive for destination countries to ease immigration restrictions. The only way I can think of to increase the receptivity of destination countries to accept more immigrants would be to redistribute the benefits of immigration so that a greater share of the benefits flow to natives and a lower share of the benefits to immigrants. The "radically economic" policy here would be to use the price system to equilibrate the market for immigrants rather than to ration entry. An immigrant receiving country could charge admission fees or auction immigration visas or place special taxes on immigrants, and use those funds to redistribute the gains from immigration to existing citizens.[53]

Thus, the institutional capacity of home and destination states to jointly charge a migration fee might allow them to enjoy a greater portion of the surplus from migration. This capacity might transform the payoff structure of the migration schematic into more of a collective action problem between states, with greater incentives for cooperation. Of course, the problem with a migration fee alone is that it would not necessarily provide incentives for any particular political group to lobby for liberalization of immigration. So, the migration fee might be used to fund adjustment assistance in the destination state, and perhaps development assistance in the home state.

Any proposal of a special fee or tax on immigrants would have to separate itself from the stigma associated with the early-twentieth-century "head taxes" imposed by the U.S. and Canada in order to deter Chinese immigration.

TOWARD A RATIONALE FOR INTERNATIONAL LAW OF MIGRATION

The above analysis suggests that different states will have different strategic positions, that different economic sectors within these states will have different strategic positions, and even that different occupational groups will have different strategic positions. Thus, it is clearly impossible to specify a single arrangement for international cooperation, or even to predict whether international cooperation will occur.

However, we know that, in the aggregate, liberalization is expected to provide increased surplus, and, assuming 1) that there are mechanisms that can be devised to overcome the strategic problems that may exist between different domestic constituencies, and between different states, and 2) that the increased surplus exceeds the cost of its capture, we would expect states to move to do so. This chapter is an exercise in institutional imagination intended first to evaluate whether the surplus may exceed the cost of its capture, and how states may move to capture it. That they have not made these moves generally thus far does not mean that such moves are not available: it would be difficult to argue that the international legal system as we see it is already efficient. Some may argue that capital markets, with their clear pricing, narrow profit motives, and numerous transactions, are already efficient, and that therefore new transactions cannot result in profits. However, the international legal system is far less efficient, so we may expect that new transactions of the nature described above could make the parties better off.

In order to move forward, it will be necessary to analyze different states, different sectors within states, and different occupations within those sectors, in order to understand the strategic position of each. Then, once we know what game is being played, we can evaluate which international legal rules, if any, are useful in order to allow for the maximum net payoffs.

A framework agreement that allows for states to agree on the structure of reciprocity, to allow sending states to share in the benefits of liberalization through a Bhagwati tax or other mechanism, to make side payments through linkage to other areas of liberalization, and to make side payments through immigration fees, would establish an appropriate institutional framework, and would minimize the transaction costs, for states to negotiate optimal arrangements. While such a framework agreement might best be legally binding, it is possible that it might alternatively be best kept informal. In international law, the distinction may have only subtle behavioral implications.

Assuming that liberalization of migration is potential Pareto efficient, it may be that states are unable to achieve the efficient liberalization unless a move is made toward actual Pareto efficiency: toward compensation of states and individuals that are otherwise made worse off.

The national political economy of international migration is complex, and mediates imperfectly the welfare considerations, which are themselves complex. However, even an imprecise assessment of the interplay of interest and power yields insights into the possibility that international legal rules may play a role in committing other states to act, in order to support domestic coalitions that will support liberalization. The game theoretic abstractions developed here are merely conjectures as to the possible interplay of interest and power, but the research discussed in this chapter makes these conjectures plausible.

NOTES

1. This chapter is based on portions of my 2009 book *The International Law of Economic Migration: Toward the Fourth Freedom*, Kalamazoo, MI: Upjohn Institute.
2. Gene Grossman and Elhanan Helpman (1994), "Protection for Sale," *American Economic Review*, **84** (4), 833–50, at 849.
3. Giovanni Facchini, Anna Maria Mayda and Prachi Mishra (2007), *Do Interest Groups Affect Immigration?*, IZA Discussion Paper No. 3183, Bonn: Institute for the Study of Labour.
4. Riccardo Faini, Jaime de Melo and Klaus Zimmermann (1999), *Migration: The Controversies and the Evidence*, Cambridge: Cambridge University Press, pp. 6–7.
5. Mancur Olson (1965), *The Logic of Collective Action: Public Goods and the Theory of Groups*, New York: Schocken Books; and World Trade Organization (2007), *World Trade Report*, Geneva: World Trade Organization.
6. In a liberal democracy, it is possible to define optimal immigration policy as "that preferred by the median voter where voters are utility-maximizers with complete information." Gary P. Freeman (1995), "Modes of Immigration Politics in the Liberal Democratic States," *International Migration Review*, **29** (4), 881–902, at 883.
7. Grossman and Helpman, "Protection for Sale," p. 849.
8. "Terms of trade" refers to the relative prices of a state's imports and exports. States may improve their terms of trade, and their welfare, by reducing the price of their imports relative to exports or increasing the price of their exports relative to imports.
9. Under this model, international trade agreements are understood to be beneficial in order to avoid a "beggar thy neighbor" trade war in which states, in a strategic prisoner's dilemma, obtain suboptimal outcomes by imposing terms of trade externalities on one

another. Kyle Bagwell and Robert W. Staiger (1999), "An Economic Theory of GATT," *American Economic Review*, **89** (1), 215–48; Kyle Bagwell and Robert W. Staiger (2001), "Reciprocity, Non-Discrimination and Preferential Agreements in the Multilateral Trading System," *European Journal of Political Economy*, **17** (2), 281; and Kyle Bagwell and Robert W. Staiger (2002), "The Economics of the World Trading System," *European Journal of Political Economy*, **17** (2), 281–325.

10. Harry R. Clarke (1994), "Entry Charges on Immigrants," *International Migration Review*, **28** (2), 338.

11. Facchini et al., *Do Interest Groups Affect Immigration?*

12. Facchini et al. thus assume that migration policy can be disaggregated into sectoral components. This assumption raises significant questions regarding the extent to which *migration policy* is disaggregated into specific sectoral components. Facchini et al., *Do Interest Groups Affect Immigration?*, p. 4.

13. Their model, following Grossman and Helpman, does not include the ability of lobbies to influence voting, except to the extent that this is captured in the amount of the lobby's expenditures. Grossman and Helpman, "Protection for Sale."

14. A "Bhagwati tax" is a tax levied by the home state on the income of a migrant. It was proposed by Jagdish Bhagwati as a response to brain drain.

15. The fact that the home state does not protest, and perhaps does not see this state of affairs as the imposition of a negative externality, is not necessarily determinative. Many externalities seem "natural" until they are identified and sought to be internalized.

16. Sam Bucovetsky (2003), "Efficient Migration and Income Tax Competition," *Journal of Public Finance Theory*, **5** (2), 249.

17. An empirical test might examine the scope of "differential fiscal treatment" in different destination states, and compare it to the proportion of legal versus illegal immigration in those states. The hypothesis is that the greater the differential fiscal treatment, the greater the immigration.

18. Below, I suggest that discriminatory taxation of immigrants may, under limited circumstances, be useful to promote liberalization or to reduce transfer program-motivated migration.

19. Robert W. Staiger (2006), "What Can Developing Countries Achieve in the WTO?," *Journal of Economic Literature*, **44** (2), 428–42.

20. Staiger, "What Can Developing Countries Achieve?"

21. WTO, World Trade Report.

22. David Greenaway and Douglas Nelson (2006), "The Distinct Political Economies of Trade and Migration Policy: Through the Window of Endogenous Policy Models, with a Focus on North America," in Federico Foders and Rolf J. Langhammer (eds.), *Labor Mobility and the World Economy*, Berlin: Springer-Verlag, p. 305.

23. Greenaway and Nelson, "Distinct Political Economies," p. 312.

24. Greenaway and Nelson, "Distinct Political Economies," p. 314.

25. Greenaway and Nelson, "Distinct Political Economies," p. 315.

26. Greenaway and Nelson, "Distinct Political Economies," p. 315.

27. George J. Borjas (2003), "The Labor Demand Curve Is Downward Sloping: Reexamining the Impact of Immigration on the Labor Market," *Quarterly Journal of Economics*, **118** (4), 1335–74.

28. Greenaway and Nelson, "Distinct Political Economies," p. 329.

29. I do not try to model the political economy of the home state, but this would be an important exercise in connection with attempts to evaluate the possibility that home states would enter into international migration agreements.

30. Timothy J. Hatton and Jeffrey G. Williamson (2005), *Global Migration and the World Economy: Two Centuries of Policy and Performance*, Cambridge, MA: MIT Press, p. 179.

31. Grossman and Helpman substitute aggregate social welfare for voting. They do so partly, it appears, because aggregate social welfare is a proxy for voting, and partly because they have a hybrid model of government official behavior that may partially reflect fidelity to public welfare. Grossman and Helpman, "Protection for Sale." In the

politics of immigration policy, domestic employers would largely deploy political contributions, while labor unions could deploy both political contributions and voting.

32.   Robert D. Putnam (1988), "Diplomacy and Domestic Politics: The Logic of Two-Level Games," *International Organization*, **42** (3), 427–60.

33.   Julia Nielson (2003), "Labour Mobility in Regional Trade Agreements," in Antonia Carzaniga and Aaditya Matto (eds.), *Moving People to Deliver Services*, Washington, DC: World Bank and Oxford University Press, pp. 93–4.

34.   Bimal Ghosh (2007), "Managing Migration: Towards the Missing Regime," in Antoin Pécoud and Paul de Guchteneire (eds.), *Migration without Borders: Essays on the Free Movement of People*, Paris and New York: UNESCO and Berghahn, p. 102.

35.   This set of assumptions seems slightly more pessimistic than the economic reality, but it seems to comport with popular opinion regarding the effects of immigration.

36.   Facchini et al., *Do Interest Groups Affect Immigration?* on the contributions of labor and capital to policy.

37.   Illegal immigration, as opposed to legal immigration, accentuates negative effects on labor. Labor prefers legal to illegal immigration, because legal immigration maximizes the bargaining power of immigrants, allows unionization of immigrants, and allows gradualism or regulation of immigration. Therefore, where the alternative to increased legal immigration is increased illegal immigration, labor may support increased legal immigration.

38.   In the two-country, symmetrical, model I have been assuming, the abundant labor factor may not seek mobility, because the other country has a symmetrical labor market.

39.   Kenneth Abbott (1989), "Modern International Relations Theory: A Prospectus for International Lawyers," *Yale Journal of International Law*, **14**, 335.

40.   Todd Sandler (2008), "Treaties: Strategic Considerations," *University of Illinois Law Review*, **1**, 155.

41.   Hiscox suggests that highly skilled workers may already have greater mobility across sectors, and therefore may be less concerned about migration. M.J. Hiscox (2002), *International Trade and Political Conflict: Commerce, Coalitions, and Mobility*, Princeton, NJ: Princeton University Press.

42.   Hatton and Williamson, *Global Migration and the World Economy*, p. 382.

43.   It may be dependent upon government inaction; that is, offshoring could be prohibited or otherwise deterred. In the 2004 presidential elections in the U.S., John Kerry, the Democratic nominee, referred to companies that offshored as "Benedict Arnold" companies. Saritha Rai (2004), "An Industry in India Cheers Bush's Victory," *New York Times*, November 4, available from: http://www.nytimes.com/2004/11/04/business/worldbusiness/04outsource.html (accessed February 3, 2008).

44.   James P. Smith and Barry Edmonston (1997), *The New Americans: Economic, Demographic and Fiscal Effects of Immigration*, Washington, DC: National Academy Press, p. 147.

45.   Sanjay Jain, Devesh Kapur and Sharun Mukand (2006), "Outsourcing and International Labor Mobility: A Political Economy Analysis," in Federico Foders and Rolf J. Langhammer (eds.), *Labor Mobility and the World Economy*, Berlin: Springer, pp. 187–204.

46.   Of course, Mexico benefits from free trade in goods under NAFTA, and transport costs are relatively low. Julia Preston (2007), "Short on Labor, Farmers in U.S. Shift to Mexico," *New York Times*, September 5.

47.   Undocumented workers benefit from fewer labor rights protections than authorized workers or citizens. American Federation of Labor–Congress of Industrial Organizations, "Testimony of Jonathan P. Hiatt, General Counsel, AFL-CIO, Before the U.S. House of Representatives Committee on the Judiciary, Subcommittee on Immigration, Citizenship, Refugees, Border Security and International Law, dated May 24, 2007," available from: http://www.aflcio.org/issues/civilrights/immigration/upload/Hiatt_Test.pdf (accessed February 3, 2008).

48.   J. Watts (2002), *Immigration Policy and the Challenge of Globalization: Unions and Employers in an Unlikely Alliance*, Ithaca, NY: Cornell University Press.

49. Daniel Trefler (1993), "International Factor Price Differences: Leontief was Right!," *Journal of Political Economy*, **101**, 961–87; and D. Trefler (1998), "Immigrants and Natives in General Equilibrium Trade Models," in J.P. Smith and B. Edmonston (eds.), *The Immigration Debate: Studies on the Economic, Demographic, and Fiscal Effects of Immigration Policy Options*, Washington, DC: National Academy Press, 206–38.
50. Gordon Hanson (2007), *The Economic Logic of Illegal Immigration*, Council Special Report No. 26, Washington, DC: Council on Foreign Relations, p. 14.
51. James R. Markusen (1983), "Factor Movements and Commodity Trade as Complements," *Journal of International Economics*, **14** (3–4), 341–56.
52. Richard B. Freeman (2006), *People Flows in Globalization*, NBER Working Paper No. 12315, Cambridge, MA: National Bureau of Economic Research, available from: http://www.nber.org/papers/w12315 (accessed November 3, 2007); Clarke, "Entry Charges on Immigrants."
53. Freeman, *People Flows in Globalization*, p. 33.

PART VI

THE FUTURE OF TRADE

22. The design of social standards in EU and US preferential trade agreements
Evgeny Postnikov

INTRODUCTION

Preferential trade agreements (PTAs) have become ubiquitous in the global trade order. Their quick proliferation has been the direct result of the failure of multilateral trade negotiations in the late 1990s and early 2000s. Trade liberalization is easier to achieve at the bilateral or regional level, and many countries have opted for signing bilateral PTAs with their trading partners.

Modern trade agreements can serve various purposes, in addition to trade liberalization, and can differ in terms of the scope of issue coverage, the degree of legal binding, and enforcement mechanisms. Recent PTAs signed by various states not only remove tariff and non-tariff barriers to trade but also try to tackle various regulatory aspects extending beyond just trade liberalization. Trade-related issues, such as investment, competition policy, intellectual property rights, labor rights and environmental standards, have become an integral part of PTAs, especially those signed by the developed states. These issues are termed the deep-trade agenda or WTO-extra, as they require a level of commitment going beyond the WTO requirements and cover areas not included in the multilateral trade regime (Horn et al. 2010). Sometimes they are also referred to as behind-the-border provisions, since they target domestic laws of agreement signatories, requiring the harmonization or mutual recognition of standards. Many studies in international political economy have examined the causes and consequences of the rise of bilateralism in the world trade system, citing various international and domestic factors, such as fear of trade diversion, bargaining leverage in the WTO, regime type, and veto players (e.g. Baldwin 1993; Mansfield and Reinhardt 2003; Ravenhill 2008; Baccini 2010; Mansfield and Milner 2010; Hicks and Kim 2012). Yet the literature has remained noticeably silent about the diverse features of today's trade agreements, including various behind-the-border provisions, which has been noticed by some scholars (e.g. Baccini et al. 2011).

The European Union (EU) and the United States have become the champions of bilateral trade liberalization and have concluded PTAs with various trading partners across the globe in the race for gaining access to new markets.[1] Both have also spearheaded the inclusion of behind-the-border provisions in their PTAs, which they often use as the vehicles for exporting their domestic regulations. Importantly, both the EU and the United States increasingly include social provisions, such as labor and environmental standards, in their bilateral agreements, aiming at mitigating the adverse effects of trade liberalization on society. Given the difficulty of including this type of regulation at the multilateral level owing to the intransigent positions of developing countries, the United States and the EU incorporate these issues in their PTAs, where they have more bargaining leverage. The agreement partners are compelled to accept these regulations if they want to get access to attractive EU and US markets.

However, despite the similarity in terms of the inclusion of such provisions, their design varies widely between US and EU agreements. The United States tries to export some of its domestic standards, while the EU emphasizes international rules, such as the ILO core labor standards and multilateral environmental agreements. Furthermore, the former relies on a more coercive approach towards the enforcement of social issues, while the latter prefers a much softer approach. This is quite puzzling if one considers the importance the EU traditionally attaches to social issues within its own Single Market and the purported role of a normative power in international affairs and defender of the social dimension of globalization (see Manners 2002; Orbie et al. 2011).

Thus, the aim of this chapter is two-fold. First, it will delineate the EU and US approaches towards the inclusion of social standards in their PTAs, tracing their evolution throughout the 2000s. Second, it will try to explain why there is a difference between the two approaches and why it persists over time, despite the general convergence between the EU and US regarding bilateral trade liberalization. In doing so, it will argue for the need to incorporate domestic political factors into our knowledge about PTAs in order to allow for the understanding of their diverse features, while highlighting the importance of one such factor – the degree of trade policy executives' autonomy from interest groups and legislators.

Before comparing EU and US approaches, it is important to note that, arguably, social standards in PTAs represent a distinct type of trade policy, as they are not concerned with market expansion and competition but rather with mitigating negative aspects of trade liberalization. Young (2007) provides a useful typology of current trade policy issues, which fall into three main categories: 1) at-the-border issues, dealing with trade liberalization, such as tariffs and quotas; and behind-the-border issues, divided into 2) commercial policy, dealing with differences in domestic regulatory regimes on services, investment and government procurement (the so-called Singapore issues), and 3) social trade policy, dealing with market failures, such as sanitary and phytosanitary rules, technical barriers to trade, core labor rights and the environment. This chapter aims to elucidate the political dynamic behind the latter type.

EU AND US APPROACHES TOWARDS SOCIAL STANDARDS IN PTAS

Scholars have noted the significantly different design of social standards in EU, as opposed to US, PTAs, with regard to both their content and their degree of enforcement (Grynberg and Qalo 2006; Heydon and Woolcock 2009; Horn et al. 2010). In particular, a seminal study by Horn et al. (2010) explores a wide range of WTO-plus and WTO-extra[2] provisions in EU and US PTAs and finds that the former are generally characterized by greater "legal inflation" than the latter, with the exception of social standards, which are, curiously, more legally binding and enforceable in US agreements. In the same vein, Grynberg and Qalo (2006) find that the United States pursues a more punitive approach towards the enforcement of its labor standards, resorting to the use of sanctions to ensure compliance, while the EU relies on softer measures, emphasizing non-coercive means of enforcement, such as dialogue and consultations with governments and civil society in its trading partners. These distinct approaches have been rather consistent throughout agreements with various partners.

NAFTA was the first US PTA to provide comprehensive coverage of labor and the environment in its side chapters, known as the North American Agreement on Labor Cooperation (NAALC) and the North American Agreement on Environmental Cooperation (NAAEC). All later agreements treat labor and environmental standards in the main part of the agreement together with other trade-related issues. The US–Jordan agreement concluded in 2000 includes social standards in the main body of the agreement, giving them the same treatment as trade issues, and uses the sanctions-based approach towards their enforcement. It serves as the basic model for all later PTAs negotiated by the United States (Grynberg and Qalo 2006).[3] The agreement also contains the requirements to maintain a minimum wage and health and safety regulations which are not part of the ILO 1998 Declaration. US trading partners can lose trade privileges or be made to pay fines for failing to enforce their domestic labor and environmental laws. The most recent US PTAs negotiated after 2007 also envision sanctions for failure to comply with ILO rules and multilateral environmental agreements (MEAs) the parties have signed.

The first EU PTA to include separate non-binding chapters on labor and the environment was the EU–Chile Association Agreement (AA) signed in 2002. The EU's approach towards bilateralism evolved significantly throughout the 2000s, culminating in a pro-active stance outlined in the European Commission's (2006) communication *Global Europe: Competing in the World*. The first "new generation" PTA is the EU–Korea FTA (2010), which includes the legally binding sustainable development chapter, covering both labor and the environment. This chapter is used as a model in later EU agreements. Yet the strong emphasis on dialogue and cooperation as a means of enforcing social standards remains unchanged between the "old" and "new" generation of agreements, and non-compliance with the rulings of the dispute settlement body cannot lead to sanctions. Civil society dialogue and intergovernmental consultations are supposed to ensure effective implementation of social standards, and expert panels can rule on cases of non-compliance but can issue only recommendatory opinions.

As far as the content of social standards is concerned, the EU has traditionally eschewed exporting its own comprehensive set of rules pertaining to labor and the environment, opting instead for the ILO core labor standards and MEAs. This approach remained constant between the so-called "old" and "new" generation of EU PTAs.

EXPLAINING THE DIFFERENCES BETWEEN THE EU AND US APPROACHES

What can explain these differences between the EU and US approaches towards the inclusion of social standards in PTAs and especially their enforcement? Even if the rapid signing of bilateral PTAs is largely driven by international systemic factors, such as geo-economic competition between the EU and the United States (see Sbragia 2010), these factors can hardly account for variation in the design of social provisions in PTAs. Kim (2012) argues that the general public in the United States favors "fair trade," which compels policy makers to include labor standards in trade agreements. His argument can be extended to the case of the EU, where citizens are also pro-fair trade either for ethical reasons or because of disguised protectionism. Furthermore, labor unions and environmental NGOs on both sides of the Atlantic actively lobby their governments to include social provisions in trade agreements. Why then, given such similarity of views on the social trade agenda in the EU and the United States, do we observe a different design of social standards in PTAs in terms of their scope and enforcement? This chapter argues that in order to understand the differences between social provisions in EU and US PTAs we need to examine the causal links between domestic political factors and their effects on various PTA features.

PTA Design and Trade Policy Making

Scholars have long acknowledged that trade policy is the outcome of the domestic political process. When taking stock of the international trade literature, Milner (1999) notes that international trade policy outcomes can be viewed as a function of certain societal preferences channeled through a combination of domestic political institutions. The literature on trade policy making is vast and allows for a relatively solid understanding of domestic factors responsible for the shape of traditional, at-the-border, trade policy issues. Despite some disagreements about whether the benefits of trade liberalization accrue mainly to societal interests divided along class or industry lines and the role of the mobility of factors of production (Rogowski 1987; Hiscox 2001), there is a broad agreement that trade policy produces domestic winners and losers. It is hypothesized that the winners from trade liberalization, mostly export-oriented industries, will typically lobby their governments for more trade openness, while the losers, mostly domestically oriented, import-competing industries, will do the opposite. Thus, many studies emphasize the importance of trade policy coalitions in setting the trade policy agenda (Alt et al. 1996). Their success will depend on their ability to mobilize and use the institutional channels provided by the domestic political system. These channels can help actors overcome their collective action problem and gain access to the main decision makers, such as legislators, on whose vote trade policy depends, as the well-known example of the farming lobby shows.

Both formal and socio-economic institutions matter for channeling the preferences of various domestic groups into policy outcomes, as they determine different patterns of interest aggregation (Garrett and Lange 1995; Milner 1999). This happens by influencing both the distributional policy demands of the private sector and the macroeconomic constraints on governments. Institutions also determine whose preferences are heard and the overall responsiveness of the government to societal actors. In addition to the material interests, scholars also highlight the importance of non-material factors, such as policy makers' ideas, in explaining trade policy outcomes (e.g. Goldstein 1993).

At the same time, very little is known about trade policy making in non-traditional issue areas, such as behind-the-border provisions. Young (2007) argues that policy making on traditional and social trade issues is characterized by different patterns of domestic politics. While extant political economy models are well suited to explaining the outcomes of traditional trade policy by attributing causal power to the interests of winners and losers of trade liberalization, they do poorly in trying to explain the outcomes of social trade policy, because the distribution of costs and benefits in this case is less clear, and significant uncertainty exists with regard to the goals of such policy.

First, unlike traditional trade issues, social issues in trade are characterized by less severe distributional conflicts for domestic groups, because material gains and losses are diffuse and cut across multiple constituencies. This, in turn, can affect the intensity of actors' preferences. For example, the advocates of environmental provisions in trade agreements can belong to various factors of production or economic sectors and be united only by holding similar values. When stakes are more value-driven, the intensity of societal preferences and the degree of lobbying pressures might decrease. As beneficiaries of social provisions in trade agreements can come from various factors of production and industrial sectors, they might be less organized than traditional winners and losers of trade liberalization. In addition to firms interested in cheap labor and labor unions fearing social dumping, social issues in trade mobilize other actors, such as human rights activists and environmental NGOs. They can often be perceived as poorly organized value communities connected by their normative vision of the appropriateness of regulating certain aspects of international trade rather its material consequences. The collective action problem they face when trying to influence the agreement agenda is potentially greater than the one faced by the winners and losers from different industrial sectors. For example, NGOs trying to advocate the enforcement of core labor rights in PTAs will have fewer resources at their disposal to lobby negotiators than well-organized business interests.

Second, as in traditional trade policy, domestic institutions also mediate societal preferences on non-trade issues. They can lessen the collective action problem faced by domestic groups trying to influence the agreement agenda, for example, by providing more channels for labor activists to make their concerns heard by politicians, or make it more severe when such channels are not easily accessible. For instance, the multi-level structure of the EU might have an effect on the actors' lobbying strategies in terms of multiplying the channels available to them, both national and supranational, but might also make their efforts less targeted by increasing the number of policy makers that they need to reach, as noted by the scholars of EU lobbying (e.g. Coen 2009).

In sum, actors' interests and ideas channeled through domestic institutions are responsible for the shape of social provisions in PTAs, just as in traditional trade policy. Yet what preferences are at play and whose preferences are translated through institutions differ in this case. Thus, variation in the design of social provisions in EU and US PTAs is a function of different patterns of domestic politics in the EU and the United States respectively, particularly the constellation of societal preferences and institutions through which these preferences are channeled. Yet what these preferences are and how they translate into the trade policy agenda need to be investigated. The next section explains the difference between the EU and US approaches towards the inclusion of social standards in their PTAs by utilizing the framework outlined here.

SOCIETAL ACTORS' PREFERENCES IN THE EU AND THE UNITED STATES

There are multiple societal actors, such as labor groups, environmental NGOs and organized businesses, that lobby trade policy makers in order to realize their preferences with regard to social standards in trade agreements. According to the theory of international trade, labor in the developed world is a factor of production which would be negatively affected by trade liberalization, as capital would find it easier to escape to other jurisdictions, according to the Stolper–Samuelson theorem and the logic of the race to the bottom. Trade liberalization can also negatively impact the environment, as producers from the developed world will be incentivized to move production to jurisdictions with less stringent environmental regulations where the cost of production might be lower, which in turn will put the environment under more strain. Thus, when it comes to trade liberalization, the high stakes for both labor and environmental groups stem from their fear of competition with cheaper and less regulated labor and laxer environmental regulation in the PTA partners. It is widely believed that bilateral trade liberalization can create a race-to-the-bottom dynamic, whereas producers will be able to reap greater benefits at the expense of workers' interests or the environmental concerns. This is also known as social dumping in EU parlance.

Both labor and environmental groups in the EU have advocated strongly for making social provisions more comprehensive in terms of the scope and more enforceable. For example, the European Trade Union Confederation (ETUC) has consistently criticized the lack of enforcement of social standards in EU PTAs. It wants to see the EU not only rely on the international norms and standards but also export parts of its own domestic regulation, stating that "Europe should seek to project its standards outside the Union through all its policies," which would include additional social rights such as the right to employment and protection of maternity and health and safety (ETUC 2006). The European Parliament is one of the main platforms for EU-level lobbyists, including labor and environmental interests. Its Committee on International Trade also published a report advocating the establishment of a comprehensive social development chapter and complained about the lack of enforcement of labor standards in the new generation of EU PTAs, referring to social standards in US PTAs and their enforcement as the model to follow (European Parliament 2010).[4] European environmental NGOs also advocated for stronger environmental clauses in PTAs and insisted on moving away from viewing trade liberalization as the sole objective of EU trade policy, seeking more synergy between trade and sustainable development, which would include full-fledged environmental protocols as part of EU trade agreements (WWF 2001). Ultimately, labor and environmental groups in the EU were unsuccessful, as the EU PTAs do not include enforceable social provisions and require the parties to follow only the minimal standards defined by the ILO or MEAs in addition to their domestic rules already on the books.

On the other hand, labor and environmental groups in the United States were able to realize their preferences with regard to the inclusion of social standards in US trade agreements more successfully. After the failure to safeguard labor rights through the WTO by the 1990s, US labor unions became strong advocates of enforceable labor provisions in all US trade deals. Beginning with NAFTA, all US agreements contain enforceable social standards. Furthermore, labor unions and environmentalists were largely dissatisfied with NAFTA's side chapters and insisted on including social standards in the main text of PTAs, which would make them be treated on a par with trade issues. Environmental groups also insisted on using US trade agreements as a way to promote sustainable development.[5] As it appears, the US approach towards social standards in PTAs has been largely dictated by the concerns of labor and environmental groups, as it shifted away from side chapters on labor and the environment towards the inclusion of comprehensive and enforceable social standards in the main text of trade agreements. As argued above, to understand these different trajectories followed by the EU and the United States attention needs to be paid to the institutional factors.

EU Trade Policy Institutions and Social Standards in PTAs

EU trade policy has a supranational set-up, as authority with regard to trade policy making is delegated by member states to the European Commission, which conducts all negotiations. The Commission, a powerful unelected supranational executive presiding over the multi-level decision-making system of the EU, is more insulated from societal interests than executives in national political systems. However, throughout the

1990s, as trade-related issues were increasingly put on the agenda, member states tried to take back control. Thus, they ensured that the EU's Council of Ministers, an intergovernmental body representing member states' interests, takes part in the process of making trade agreements involving trade-related issues or any association agreement between the EU and another country that includes political issues. This resulted in the so-called "mixed" agreements, where member states' governments retain veto power on certain trade-related issues, such as intellectual property rights, trade in services and social provisions (Meunier and Nicolaïdis 1999). Thus, in order to fully understand the outcomes of the trade policy-making process on social standards in trade agreements, it is important also to look at the preferences of not only EU-level interest groups but also EU legislators in the Council of Ministers.

When it comes to EU social trade policy, there is a lack of consensus among the member states' governments about the specifics of behind-the-border provisions in trade agreements, in particular core labor standards. As the question of social standards within the WTO was deliberated in the EU during the 1990s, different member states held diverging views. For example, conservative governments in Germany and the UK at the time were opposed to the inclusion of such standards, whereas Belgium and France were in favor of it (Waer, quoted in Orbie et al. 2011). Furthermore, there were sharp ideological disagreements among social-democratic and liberal parties within the member states as to the extent to which social issues should be a part of the trade agenda, as many believed they might jeopardize the overarching goal of trade liberalization. Elsig (2007) notes that EU enlargement only increased the degree of heterogeneity among the governments. Orbie and Babarinde (2008) highlight the lack of both vertical and horizontal coherence in the EU's promotion of the social trade agenda, which is a function of disagreements among member states over the desirability of certain development goals and different foreign policy priorities. Bossuyt (2009) also finds that many member states had only vague ideas about social issues in trade. In sum, there appears to be a lack of unity among the member states' governments as to the extent to which social standards need to be addressed in trade agreements. Overall, governments want to include social provisions in bilateral PTAs, but there is no well-formulated position on their scope, enforceability or extent of legal obligation, which means that the mandate given to Commission officials is rather ambiguous.

These disagreements among the member states' governments and the vague institutional mandate create a permissive situation for the executives in the Commission in terms of pursuing their own agenda for social provisions in trade agreements. Commission officials in the Directorate-General

(DG) Trade have an incentive to act strategically, foreseeing differences among governments and balancing carefully among various ideological platforms and possible scenarios for the design of social standards. An attempt to export the EU's own social policy through PTAs and make social provisions more enforceable by employing sanctions could certainly invite a harsh response from more liberal member states, whereas not paying enough attention to social concerns would most likely displease the social-democratic governments. Thus, in the institutional environment characterized by uncertainty over the preferences of legislators, the reliance on international rules set by the ILO and multilateral environmental treaties has become the way for the European Commission to deal with the heterogeneity of member states' preferences. These international rules help to frame the agreement agenda with regard to social standards so as to avoid potential conflicts that could delay the negotiation process.

As far as the influence of societal actors in the EU is concerned, both labor and environmental groups have several lobbying channels at their disposal. Owing to the shared competencies between the Commission and national governments, interest groups are prompted to lobby at several different levels, including the Commission, the Council of Ministers and national executives. Various scholars have noted that Brussels has become the prime location for interest groups' venue shopping in terms of securing the best access to policy makers and influencing policy outcomes (Long and Lörinszi 2009). However, lobbying in the EU differs from that in national systems, as it has been traditionally top-down, with the Commission playing a central role in terms of selecting interest groups whose input it wants to have in the policy-making process (Woll 2009). This has been especially relevant for EU external trade policy, as the Commission can use the top-down lobbying to increase its legitimacy as the agenda-setter in this policy area (Coen 2009).

Thus, in 1998 the Commission created a novel institutional mechanism for the stakeholders in EU trade policy known as the Civil Society Dialogue. It includes various civil society actors, such as public and private actors' associations, NGOs and businesses, whose representatives regularly meet with Commission officials and receive updates from them about the course of negotiations. Interest groups are also encouraged to use this mechanism to provide their input in the negotiation process. However, the Civil Society Dialogue plays only a consultative role wherein societal actors are not allowed to influence the course of negotiations directly or to have access to the negotiation texts. By using the Civil Society Dialogue the Commission can give preferential access to various groups and enhance its role of agenda-setter for EU trade policy.

The Civil Society Dialogue is not the only mechanism which interest groups can use to influence Brussels officials working on trade. Other EU institutions representing societal interests can provide additional channels for societal actors lobbying in the EU. The European Parliament and the European Economic and Social Committee (EESC) are both supposed to act as representatives of civil society in Brussels. However, the role of the European Parliament in trade policy was inconsequential until after the ratification of the Treaty of Lisbon in 2009, which excluded a crucial influence channel for societal actors. Similarly, the EESC performs only a consultative function in EU policy making, and does not participate in trade negotiations. Overall, the multi-level nature of the EU decision-making system makes lobbying efforts more diffuse and less effective, as interest groups need to target different levels of government simultaneously, especially when there is a lack of coherence among those levels and interest groups themselves lack crucial material resources.

Thus, European Commission officials are insulated from interest groups' pressure and member states' control. As a result of this institutional configuration, trade policy executives in the EU are able to exercise a large degree of autonomy when it comes to designing social provisions in PTAs. It is not surprising then that interest groups in the EU lobbying for stricter social standards in trade agreements are not able to achieve what they want. The European Commission acts as a policy entrepreneur, capturing the agenda on PTAs' social standards and exercising influence over the design of PTAs' social provisions. It acts strategically to account for potentially conflicting preferences among the member states' governments and designs social provisions accordingly, while at the same time advancing its own views on the role of labor and environmental standards in EU trade agreements. In doing so, it resorts to the international rules, the ILO's core labor standards and multilateral environmental agreements. These international standards are defined very broadly and represent the least controversial, minimal set of rules which reflect the interests of all involved parties. Importantly, they also reflect EU trade policy executives' own normative ideas about social standards.

These ideas are outlined in two main documents. The "social dimension of globalization" approach promoted by Pascal Lamy emphasizes the importance of ILO core labor standards and social cooperation in a non-binding, non-coercive fashion (European Commission 2001). The "global Europe" approach advanced by Peter Mandelson in 2006 with the publication of *Global Europe: Competing in the World* (European Commission 2006) prioritized trade liberalization, but also aimed at linking trade with sustainable development, putting labor and the environment under the same heading. Both documents indicate that trade policy executives in the European Commission had a strong preference for relying on international rules and avoiding coercive measures when dealing with both labor and environmental standards in the EU's bilateral agreements, thereby demonstrating the EU's strong commitment to the multilateral approach in world affairs. Peter Mandelson (2006) has aptly summarized the EU's approach towards social standards trade agreements:

> The EU has always rejected a sanctions-based approach to labour standards – and that will continue. But equally, we can do more to encourage countries to enforce basic labour rights, such as the ILO core conventions, along with environmental standards – not simply in principle, but in practice. Cooperation and social dialogue are certainly important. Transparency, through an independent mechanism, will also help us highlight areas where governments should take action against violations of basic rights. We are also considering an incentives approach.

US Trade Policy Institutions and Social Standards in PTAs

Whereas the supranational structure of the EU trade policy making enables executive preferences to trump societal ones, the case of social standards in US PTAs reveals a very different domestic political dynamic. According to the institutional arrangement of US trade policy, Congress delegates the negotiating authority to the US President acting through the United States Trade Representative (USTR). This can be done in the form of the Trade Promotion Authority (TPA), which allows for the accelerated ratification of trade agreements, also known as the fast-track procedure. It gives a mandate to the executive to conclude agreements in an accelerated manner and without holding it hostage to the Congressional voting. However, legislators make sure that Congress retains control through not only the *ex post* control mechanism of ratification but also the *ex ante* control mechanism by specifying the mandate for the executive authority. Thus, the fast-track procedure is subject to Congressional oversight in the form of the regular TPA renewal by Congress. As the latter is the major institution representing societal interests, it is receptive to the preferences of both labor and environmental groups.

The last TPA was renewed by the 2002 Trade Act and stipulated that all US trade agreements must contain labor and environmental safeguards. The inclusion of these standards in US trade deals was required as a condition of renewing the TPA, which means that the President appeals to labor and environmental interests when negotiating agreements falling under the fast-track procedure. Various observers attribute this to the stalemate over the TPA owing to the importance of labor and environmental issues for the Congress in the 1990s when a number of bilateral agreements were negotiated (Brainard and Shapiro 2001). When the renewal of the TPA was discussed in the 1990s and early 2000s, labor unions in particular pressed for putting labor standards on the agenda, as they thought that weaker labor regulations in developing countries would create a competitive disadvantage for US producers (Carbaugh 2010: 203). They also argued that making environmental and labor rules part of secondary agreements, as in the case of the supplementary chapters of NAFTA, would result in weaker enforcement of labor and environmental standards by US trading partners. Many Congressional Democrats in the House of Representatives also opposed PTAs as such in the 1990s, as organized labor and environmental groups are their constituency. This, in turn, put pressure on the Bush administration to incorporate labor and environmental standards into trade agreements as a side payment to these constituents in order to maintain support for renewing the TPA (Hudson Teslik 2007). The pressure on the executive to include labor and environmental standards was very strong, as labor and environmental interests were crucial for winning a majority in the House to approve PTAs.

Thus, it is not surprising that all US PTAs negotiated under the TPA have enforceable labor and environmental provisions. US trading partners must enforce their domestic laws, and a failure to do this will result in either fines or the suspension of trade privileges. Furthermore, the reference to not only existing domestic standards but also the requirement to include the minimum wage is a direct reflection of the unions' concern about unequal competition with cheap labor in the developing world (Grynberg and Qalo 2006).

The TPA expired in 2007 and so did its provisions for safeguarding labor and environmental interests. Yet the Democrats had control of both the House and the Senate in 2006, and it was widely believed that social provisions in trade had to be strengthened. Thus, even after the expiry of the TPA, any future agreement would have to include enforceable labor and environmental standards if it were to be ratified by Congress. In fact, the latter made clear that there would be no movement towards any new trade deals until the issue was resolved. This became institutionalized in the Bipartisan Trade Deal in 2007, also known as the May 10th agreement, which not only ensures the inclusion of labor and environmental principles in PTAs but also strengthens the level of safeguards. Now, all US trade agreements are expected to have sanctions for not only the failure to comply with domestic labor and environmental laws, as was the case with previous PTAs, but also the failure to enforce ILO labor standards and multilateral environmental agreements they have joined. These new measures largely reflect the dissatisfaction of unions and environmentalists with the previous agreements that did not have such clauses.[6]

The fact that the US administration had to bow to Congress and include labor and environmental standards in US PTAs is a direct result of societal actors and legislators' control over the autonomy of trade policy executives. The oversight mechanisms in the form of the strict negotiating mandate and the ratification process have ensured that labor and environmental interests are reflected in all US agreements. These mechanisms decrease the executive's insulation from societal interests and the incentive to pursue its own agenda, irrespective of those interests, contrary to the case of the EU. Unlike their European counterparts, US labor and environmental interests have a powerful and well-institutionalized channel for lobbying – Congress – in addition to trying to influence the USTR directly through the Labor or Trade and Environment Policy Advisory Committees, where they do not have a final say. Thus, the USTR simply has no choice but to respond to the pressures from Congress if it wants agreements to be ratified. For this reason, it is not surprising that the coercive approach towards social standards, characteristic of all US PTAs, as well as the expansion of the scope of coverage and enforcement of labor and environmental provisions, directly reflects the unions' and environmentalists' concerns over the race to the bottom and the success of their lobbying efforts. Furthermore, despite the fact that labor and environmental actors represent somewhat different constituencies, Congressional politics facilitates an alliance between the two groups, as it allows them to lobby legislators more effectively and enables legislators to appeal to a wider range of societal interests.

Unlike European Commission officials, USTR officials find their hands tied by the Congressional mandate, which makes it impossible for them to pursue their own preferences with regard to the agreement agenda. USTR officials' own views do not play a role in the agreement agenda-setting process. Thus, the existing institutional structure of US trade policy making is not conducive to the realization of the executive preferences, unlike the case in the EU. This difference between EU and US institutional structures mediating the degree of executive autonomy and success of societal lobbying explains why US PTAs contain surprisingly stricter social standards than those signed by the EU. Domestic political institutions are the key to understanding the design of social standards in trade agreements.

An objection might be raised that social standards in EU and US PTAs are an outcome of the bargaining process between the EU, the US and their trading partners. Yet there is no evidence of third countries' influence over the EU and US approaches. In general, countries want to get access to the lucrative European and American markets and are induced to act as policy takers at the negotiation table. The decision to include WTO-extra provisions in PTAs is precisely the result of bargaining power asymmetries between the developed and developing countries at the bilateral level. As far as US agreements are concerned, the stipulation to include the enforceable social standards is constitutionally protected through the TPA and the Bipartisan Trade Deal, which severely restricts the room for maneuver of American negotiators. US trading partners have to accept social standards as a fait accompli to avoid ratification failure, which would jeopardize the much wanted access to the American market. US PTA partners might be able to influence the scope of social standards only marginally, for example when it comes to the size and conditions of the fine that has to be paid for the failure to enforce social standards, but not the coercive approach per se (Bierman and Campbell 2004). EU trading partners are compelled to accept social standards precisely because of the language of international standards and the absence of sanctions, which makes them look less coercive and protectionist.

CONCLUSION

Today's trade policy happens increasingly behind the border, and social standards are a crucial part of it. Labor and environmental provisions have become an important element of all EU and US PTAs. Furthermore, as the preference for "fair trade" grows stronger among both policy makers and their constituents in the developed world, social standards will feature even more prominently on the trade policy agenda. Yet significant differences exist between the EU and US approaches towards the content and enforcement of these standards. This chapter has demonstrated that the nature of these differences lies in the distinct patterns of trade policy making in the EU and the United States. It argued that, in order to understand these differences, as well as the design of PTAs more generally, it would be expedient to move beyond the analysis of international systemic factors and look more closely at the role of domestic factors, such as the constellation of political actors and their ideas, interests and policy-making institutions. The difference between the EU and US approaches towards social standards in PTAs exists as a result of the differing levels of executive authority insulation from the pressure of societal actors and control of legislators that characterize trade policy making in the EU and the United States. The analysis of other behind-the-border provisions in PTAs would also have to incorporate domestic political and institutional factors for the sake of a comprehensive explanation of PTA design, which has been long overdue (see Baccini et al. 2011).

The attempt to redirect the analytical focus to the analysis of various institutional features of PTAs made here can prove beneficial for several reasons. First, social provisions have become an omnipresent feature of many PTAs. Importantly, even some of the latest South–South agreements include labor and environmental chapters, notably those initiated by Chile and South Korea. Understanding the roots of this trend can shed light on the processes of trade policy making in various political and institutional contexts, enhancing our understanding of contemporary trade policy. Second, PTAs that differ in terms of institutional design are likely to yield different outcomes in the partner countries, as the literature on institutional design of international agreements has long argued (e.g. Rosendorff and Milner 2001). Showing the effects of social provisions in EU and US agreements is beyond the scope of this chapter but should be seen as a fruitful direction for future research. Do sanctions used by the United States work? Or is the dialogical approach promoted by the European Union more efficient in terms of improving labor rights and environmental laws in partner countries? Through what mechanisms do these approaches affect domestic outcomes in EU and US trading partners? These are some questions that could be examined by future studies. Third, as the EU and the US start to negotiate PTAs with the developed countries, whose domestic social standards can be even higher, what will be the negotiation dynamic? Will they be able to dictate their standards to third parties in exchange for market access as they have done thus far with the developing countries, which do not possess equal bargaining power? Labor and environmental standards in the trading system can be viewed as particularly valued commodities by some states, as they touch upon deeply entrenched societal norms. Ironically, social standards in PTAs could become the stumbling blocks in the negotiation process, undermining the whole function of bilateral agreements as an alternative to the complexities of the WTO system. The prolonged negotiation of the EU–Canada Free Trade Agreement, and the disagreements between the parties over the shape of social provisions, is a case in point. Finally, as the European Union and the United States themselves begin to negotiate the Transatlantic Trade and Investment Partnership (TTIP), the question of labor and environmental standards will come to the fore even more strongly, testing our knowledge of international trade negotiations and providing an impetus to the richer analysis of new trade issues.

NOTES

1. The EU has a supranational authority in trade policy, including the negotiation and signing of trade agreements.
2. Social standards fall under WTO-extra provisions, as they are not currently covered by the multilateral rules of trade, whereas measures to liberalize trade beyond the WTO requirements are part of WTO-plus provisions.

3. However, there are variations within this approach, depending on concrete PTAs, but the presence of coercion, in the form of either a fine or sanctions, as the means of enforcement is a constant feature of all US agreements (see Bolle 2013).
4. The following quote is revealing: "The US Administration and Congress having agreed that 'all of our FTA environmental obligations will be enforced on the same basis as the commercial provisions of our agreements – same remedies, procedures, and sanctions,' it is hard to see why Europe should settle for less" (European Parliament 2010: 9).
5. It should be noted that often labor and environmental constituencies include groups that oppose free trade altogether. However, the official position of AFL-CIO as well as major environmental NGOs on US trade agreements is less negative as long as they include enforceable social standards.
6. The agreements that include these new provisions are US–Colombia, US–Panama and US–Korea.

REFERENCES

Alt, James E., Jeffrey Frieden, Michael J. Gilligan, Dani Rodrik and Ronald Rogowski (1996), "The Political Economy of International Trade: Enduring Puzzles and an Agenda for Inquiry," *Comparative Political Studies*, **29** (6), 689–717.
Baccini, Leonardo (2010), "Explaining Formation and Design of EU Trade Agreements: The Role of Transparency and Flexibility," *European Union Politics*, **11** (2), 195–217.
Baccini, Leonardo, Andreas Dür, Manfred Elsig and Karolina Milewicz (2011), *The Design of Preferential Trade Agreements: A New Dataset in the Making*, Staff Working Paper ERSD-2011-10, Geneva: World Trade Organization.
Baldwin, Richard (1993), *A Domino Theory of Regionalism*, NBER Working Paper No. 4465, Cambridge, MA: National Bureau of Economic Research.
Bierman, Leonard and Jason Campbell (2004), "Negotiating a Template for Labor Standards: The U.S.–Chile Free Trade Agreement," Harvard Law School.
Bolle, Mary Jane (2013), *Overview of Labor Enforcement Issues in Free Trade Agreements*, CRS Report for Congress RS 22823, Washington, DC: Congressional Research Service.
Bossuyt, Fabienne (2009), "The Social Dimension of the New Generation of EU FTAs with Asia and Latin America: Ambitious Continuation for the Sake of Policy Coherence," *European Foreign Affairs Review*, **14** (5), 703–42.
Brainard, Lael and Hal Shapiro (2001), *Fast Track Trade Promotion Authority*, Policy Brief 91, Washington, DC: Brookings Institution.
Carbaugh, Robert J. (2010), *International Economics*, Mason, OH: South-Western.
Coen, David (2009), "Business Lobbying in the European Union," in David Coen and Jeremy Richardson (eds.), *Lobbying the European Union: Institutions, Actors, and Issues*, Oxford: Oxford University Press, pp. 145–68.
Elsig, Manfred (2007), "The EU's Choice of Regulatory Venues for Trade Negotiations: A Tale of Agency Power?," *Journal of Common Market Studies*, **45** (4), 927–48.
ETUC (European Trade Union Confederation) (2006), "ETUC Demands a Refocusing of EU Trade Strategy in Line with Europe's Social and Development Objectives," available from: http://www.etuc.org/a/2899 (accessed August 7, 2013).
European Commission (2001), *Promoting Core Labour Standards and Improving Social Governance in the Context of Globalisation*, COM(2001) 416, July 18, Brussels: European Commission.
European Commission (2006), *Global Europe: Competing in the World*, COM(2006) 567, October 4, Brussels: European Commission.
European Parliament (2010), *Human Rights, Social and Environmental Standards in International Trade Agreements*, 2009/2219 (INI), November 25, Brussels and Strasbourg: European Parliament.

Garrett, Geoffrey and Peter Lange (1995), "Internationalization, Institutions, and Political Change," *International Organization*, **49** (4), 627–55.

Goldstein, Judith (1993), *Ideas, Interests, and American Trade Policy*, Ithaca, NY: Cornell University Press.

Grynberg, Roman and Veniana Qalo (2006), "Labour Standards in US and EU Preferential Trading Agreements," *Journal of World Trade*, **40** (4), 619–53.

Heydon, Kenneth and Stephen Woolcock (2009), *The Rise of Bilateralism: Comparing American, European and Asian Approaches to Preferential Trade Agreements*, Tokyo: United Nations University Press.

Hicks, Raymond and Soo Yeon Kim (2012), "Reciprocal Trade Agreements in Asia: Credible Commitment to Trade Liberalization or Paper Tigers?," *Journal of East Asian Studies*, **12** (1), 1–29.

Hiscox, Michael J. (2001), "Class versus Industry Cleavages: Inter-Industry Factor Mobility and the Politics of Trade," *International Organization*, **55** (1), 1–46.

Horn, Henrik, Petros C. Mavroidis and André Sapir (2010), "Beyond the WTO? An Anatomy of EU and US Preferential Trade Agreements," *World Economy*, **33** (11), 1565–88.

Hudson Teslik, Lee (2007), *Fast-Track Trade Promotion Authority and Its Impact on U.S. Trade Policy*, Council on Foreign Relations, available from: http://www.cfr.org/trade/fast-track-trade-promotion-authority-its-impact-us-trade-policy/p13663 (accessed August 7, 2013).

Kim, Moonhawk (2012), "Ex Ante Due Diligence: Formation of PTAs and Protection of Labor Rights," *International Studies Quarterly*, **56** (4), 704–19.

Long, Tony and Larisa Lörinszi (2009), "NGOs as Gatekeepers: A Green Vision," in David Coen and Jeremy Richardson (eds.), *Lobbying the European Union: Institutions, Actors, and Issues*, Oxford: Oxford University Press, pp. 162–79.

Mandelson, Peter (2006), "Trade Policy and Decent Work," speech at the EU Decent Work Conference on Globalization, available from: http://europa.eu/rapid/press-release_SPEECH-06-779_en.htm?locale=en (accessed August 7, 2013).

Manners, Ian (2002), "Normative Power Europe: A Contradiction in Terms?," *Journal of Common Market Studies*, **40** (2), 235–58.

Mansfield, Edward D. and Helen V. Milner (2010), "Regime Type, Veto Players, and Preferential Trade Arrangements," *Stanford Journal of International Law*, **46** (2), 219–42.

Mansfield, Edward D. and Eric Reinhardt (2003), "Multilateral Determinants of Regionalism: The Effects of GATT/WTO on the Formation of Preferential Trading Arrangements," *International Organization*, **57** (4), 829–62.

Meunier, Sophie and Kalypso Nicolaïdis (1999), "Who Speaks for Europe? The Delegation of Trade Authority in the EU," *Journal of Common Market Studies*, **37** (3), 477–501.

Milner, Helen V. (1999), "The Political Economy of International Trade," *Annual Review of Political Science*, **2**, 91–114.

Orbie, Jan and Olufemi Babarinde (2008), "The Social Dimension of Globalization and EU Development Policy: Promoting Core Labor Standards and Corporate Social Responsibility," *Journal of European Integration*, **30** (3), 459–77.

Orbie, Jan, Myriam Gistelinck and Bart Kerremans (2011), "The Social Dimension of EU Trade Policies," in Jan Orbie and Lisa Tortell (eds.), *The European Union and the Social Dimension of Globalization: How the EU Influences the World*, London: Routledge, pp. 148–55.

Ravenhill, John (2008), "Regionalism," in John Ravenhill (ed.), *Global Political Economy*, Oxford: Oxford University Press, pp. 172–210.

Rogowski, Ronald (1987), "Political Cleavages and Changing Exposure to Trade," *American Political Science Review*, **81** (4), 1121–37.

Rosendorff, B. Peter and Helen V. Milner (2001), "The Optimal Design of International Trade Institutions: Uncertainty and Escape," *International Organization*, **55** (4), 829–57.

Sbragia, Alberta (2010), "The EU, the US, and Trade Policy: Competitive Interdependence in the Management of Globalization," *Journal of European Public Policy*, **17** (3), 368–82.

Woll, Cornelia (2009), "Trade Policy Lobbying in the European Union: Who Captures

Whom?," in David Coen and Jeremy Richardson (eds.), *Lobbying the European Union: Institutions, Actors, and Issues*, Oxford: Oxford University Press, pp. 277–97.

WWF (2001), "Environment and Trade in the European Union's Inter-Regional Agreements," WWF European Policy Office, May, available from: assets.panda.org/downloads/WWFPartIII_trade.pdf (accessed August 7, 2013).

Young, Alasdair R. (2007), "Trade Politics Ain't What It Used to Be: The European Union in the Doha Round," *Journal of Common Market Studies*, **45** (4), 789–811.

23. Trade and the Internet: policies in the US, the EU and Canada[1]

Susan Ariel Aaronson and Rob Maxim

Edward Snowden, the computer whiz who leaked details of the National Security Agency (NSA's) controversial PRISM program, probably didn't aim to undermine US–EU free trade talks in July 2013. However, Snowden's revelations that America was collecting phone calls and Internet communications of foreign citizens, as well as using the Internet to spy on allied governments, drove a wedge between the two trade giants. Within days the EU Parliament announced an investigation, the German Prosecutor General began looking into espionage charges[2] and German Chancellor Angela Merkel expressed her support for tougher rules governing the privacy of EU citizens' data.[3] French President François Hollande flirted with the idea of calling off negotiations for the Transatlantic Trade and Investment Partnership (TTIP),[4] while President Hendrik Ilves of Estonia argued that the right response to PRISM should be to create a secure "European cloud" with high data protection standards.[5]

The PRISM program became a trade issue because, like goods and services, information online is traded across borders. That information is stored in servers controlled by big Internet companies, which are almost all US-based. These American companies have to comply with NSA directives, but at the same time these companies may be violating European data protection (also known as privacy) standards. As a result, EU policymakers are determined to achieve stronger privacy protection for European citizens and greater control over cloud services. EU officials see free trade negotiations with the US as an appropriate venue to achieve these goals. However, the revelations about PRISM may jeopardize more than just trade talks between the US and the EU.

Concerns about the relationship between privacy, national security and digital trade are not new, and may stem from the contradictory nature of the Internet. On one hand, the global Internet is creating a virtuous circle of expanding growth, opportunity and information. On the other hand, some policymakers and market actors are taking steps that undermine access to information, reduce freedom of expression and splinter the Internet. Almost every country has adopted policies to enforce intellectual property rights, protect national security or thwart cyber-theft, hacking and spam. Nevertheless, other nations may be taking steps to limit access to information and/or violating the rights and privacy of netizens. Repressive states such as Iran, Russia and China openly censor many sites for political reasons. However, even countries like the US which have committed to a free and open Internet tread a fine line between freedom and security. Today, policymakers must find a balance between these policy objectives online.

Internet freedom can be defined as the promotion, protection and enjoyment of human rights on the Internet. Internet openness is the collection of policies and procedures that allow netizens to make their own choices about applications and services to use and which lawful content they want to access, create, or share with others. As technology, politics and culture change over time, citizens and policymakers are rethinking how to advance both freedom and openness on the web.

Not surprisingly, netizens and policymakers have not figured out how to balance Internet openness and stability. On one hand, advocates of Internet openness want policymakers to play a minimal role regulating the actions of networks, companies and individuals online. They want to build on the longstanding ethos of the Internet, which defines the web as a platform separate from government and governed by net neutrality, open standards and multi-stakeholder participation. On the other hand, policymakers must find a delicate balance between intervention and non-intervention to preserve the open Internet. To preserve Internet freedom and openness, they must respect freedom of information, expression, due process, and the right to privacy. To respect these human rights accruing to individuals, sometimes governments must act to maintain Internet openness; at other times, policymakers must refrain from acting. However, to promote Internet resilience and stability, policymakers must act in the interest of multiple stakeholders (or empower others to act) to restrict the free flow of information across borders, enforce copyright or thwart cyber-crime, hacking and spam.

This chapter examines how three trade behemoths and Internet powers (the US, Canada and the EU) use trade policies to govern the Internet at home and across borders. All three use trade agreements to encourage e-commerce, reduce online barriers to trade, and develop shared policies in a world where technology is rapidly changing and where governments compete to disseminate their regulatory approaches. Moreover, the three want the same goals: to encourage the free flow of information; to encourage Internet freedom; and to reduce cyber-instability. However, they do not always agree on what goals should be digital trade priorities (the what) or how to achieve these goals. As an example, in the EU and Canada, privacy is a basic human right as well as a consumer right. These governments are unwilling to reduce privacy protections in the interest of negotiating language in trade agreements to encourage the free flow of information, a priority in the US. Moreover, the 28 nations of the EU, along with the US and Canada, do not always agree on the best methods for protecting privacy, when to restrict (or censor) information, or how to do so without altering the basic character of the Internet. These disagreements are manifested in how and when each Internet power uses trade policy to promote Internet freedom. But these are not the only differences among the three big trading nations. The US and the EU, but not Canada, use export controls, trade bans or targeted sanctions to protect Internet users in other countries or to prevent officials of other countries from using Internet-related technologies in ways that undermine the rights of individuals abroad. Of the three, the US is the first to monitor other governments' Internet policies as potential trade barriers.[6]

Many people may not recognize how trade policies affect the Internet. Herein, we discuss how trade policies, agreements, bans and strategies could affect Internet openness, Internet governance and Internet freedom, but we do not discuss telecommunications or e-commerce issues. We note that, despite the shared goal of promoting Internet openness and stability, the three trade behemoths do not consistently cooperate. Without such cooperation, we may see a more fragmented web, more digital protectionism and fewer e-opportunities.

ATTITUDES TOWARDS INTERNET GOVERNANCE – HOW HAS TRADE POLICY BECOME A TOOL TO REGULATE THE INTERNET?

The US, the EU and Canada share the same Internet, support the current ad hoc multi-stakeholder system, and oppose greater UN or governmental control of the web. Yet the US, the EU and Canada have fundamentally different approaches to Internet governance at the national level and in trade agreements.[7] Moreover, the three trade giants have not developed a flexible set of shared principles that do three things: encourage global information flows; ensure that regulators do not discriminate between foreign and domestic firms facilitating, creating or receiving those information flows;[8] and effectively balance national and international norms for Internet openness and Internet stability.

Although the US argues that the system governing the Internet is global and diverse, US actors and norms play an outsized role on the information superhighway. US companies such as Facebook, Google, Yahoo and Twitter dominate much of the web. Moreover, Internet gov-

BOX 23.1   WHAT DO WE MEAN BY INTERNET FREEDOM?

What is the state of Internet freedom?

- In July 2012, the United Nations Human Rights Council approved a resolution to support the "promotion, protection, and enjoyment of human rights on the Internet." The resolution A/HRC/20/L.13 affirms that people have the same rights online as they do offline, and these rights are "applicable regardless of frontiers." The resolution says states should promote and facilitate access to the Internet.
- The UN Special Rapporteur on the promotion and protection of the right to freedom of opinion and expression, Frank La Rue, has said governments should not block access to the Internet. He stressed that all states are obligated "to promote or to facilitate the enjoyment of the right to freedom of expression and the means necessary to exercise this right, including the Internet. Hence, States should consult with all segments of society to make the Internet widely available, accessible and affordable to all." His warning applies to how trade policies are made: they must be developed in a transparent and accountable manner.*
- However, activists and human rights officials have not achieved a clear and widely accepted definition of Internet freedom. Until recently, activists and human rights officials focused on the specific human rights that are instrumental to creating, protecting and sharing information on the web such as the right to privacy, freedom of expression, and access to information. However, governments must provide an appropriate regulatory framework for the Internet to function in an open, efficient and responsible manner. An appropriate regulatory framework includes government respect for due process, political participation, freedom of expression, and rule of law.
- Access to the Internet is a fundamental human right in France, Finland and Costa Rica. Estonia and Greece stipulate that the state has legal obligations to provide access. Member states of the Council of Europe agreed that they have an obligation to provide or allow access to the Internet.

> (The Council of Europe promotes common and democratic principles based on the European Convention on Human Rights within 47 European countries.)
>
> - In countries such as Brazil and India, governments provide a wide range of public services on the web, including healthcare and education, and hence must exert some control. These states argue that governments must actively intervene online to ensure Internet freedom.
> - Many democracies, including India, Brazil and the United States, actively censor the web and at times abuse the privacy rights of their citizens.
> - Meanwhile, officials in Iran and China (among other nations) have walled off the Internet and are essentially creating national intranets.
>
> * See UN Human Rights Council, "Report of the Special Rapporteur on the Promotion and Protection of the Right to Freedom of Opinion and Expression, Frank La Rue, A/HRC/17/27.

ernance reflects the influential role of US early web actors who wanted an ad hoc, multi-stakeholder, bottom-up and self-regulatory approach to Internet governance. However, because US (and to a lesser extent Canadian and European) companies have such huge market presence on the web, policymakers in other governments may distrust US motives. Policymakers and citizens in other countries may perceive US policymakers as acting in the interest of US companies and not in the general public interest.

Meanwhile, many other major trading nations with global clout and strong Internet presence have put forward different ideas about the role of the state online. The Chinese[9] and Russian[10] governments argue that governments must safeguard and control the Internet. For example, the Russian government now plans to use deep packet inspection to monitor the Russian Internet, which could breach citizens' privacy and free speech rights.[11] The Chinese and Russian governments have become increasingly vocal about rethinking Internet governance and have proposed greater international control over the Internet.[12] At the same time, many developing countries are just beginning to set the ground rules for the Internet in their countries.[13] Policymakers in some developing countries such as India or middle-income nations such as Brazil believe that governments should do more to control the Internet.[14] Officials in these countries make the case that greater governmental control will help them provide public goods

---

BOX 23.2   WHAT INTERNATIONAL LAWS APPLY TO THE INTERNET?

The Internet is a decentralized network of networks, operated by several multi-stakeholder organizations such as the Internet Society, the Internet Engineering Task Force, the World Wide Web Consortium, the regional internet registries and the Internet Corporation for Assigned Names and Numbers. It is affected by international telecommunications regulations, which are made by a UN subagency, the International Telecommunication Union. Trade rules also regulate the Internet, by regulating trade in goods, information and services.

International law applies to cyberspace. Cyber-activities may in certain circumstances constitute uses of force if they create physical damage. Countries have rights to self-defense online, but responses must correspond to principles of necessity and pro-portionality. International human rights law applies online, where everyone has the right to opinion and expression, and the right of access to information.

---

online, such as education and healthcare, and foster innovation and economic growth throughout the country.[15]

In recent years officials have developed several sets of principles to guide government action on the Internet. The Organisation for Economic Co-operation and Development (OECD), a forum for industrialized nations and think tank on global issues, has spearheaded many of these efforts and called for a holistic approach to Internet governance at the national and international level.[16] The US, the EU and Canada have worked internationally to develop principles to ensure an open and stable Internet. Some 34 nations have also agreed to principles to encourage free expression online.[17] However, these principles are neither universal nor binding. Hence, government officials have sought other venues to address cross-border Internet issues.

Trade agreements and policies have become an important source of rules governing cross-border information flows. First, policymakers recognize that, when we travel the information superhighway, we are often trading. And Internet usage can dramatically expand trade.[18] Secondly, officials from the three trade giants understand that the Internet is not only a tool of empowerment for the world's people, but a major source of wealth for US, European and Canadian business. Some 65–70 percent of the world's population is not yet online, so it is not surprising that these govern-ments see a huge potential for growth in e-commerce.[19] US, European and Canadian policymakers want both to protect their firms' competitiveness and to increase market share. Finally, these officials understand that, while some domestic laws can have worldwide reach, domestic laws on copyright, piracy and Internet security do not have international legitimacy and force. Hence, they recognize they must find common ground on globally accepted rules governing cross-border data flows.[20] They can achieve these internationally accepted rules within bilateral, regional or broader multi-lateral trade agreements.[21]

Trade agreements regulate how entities may trade and how nations may use protectionist tools. These agreements initially covered only border measures such as tariffs and quotas. Since the 1970s, however, policy-makers have gradually expanded trade agreements to include domestic regulations such as health and safety regulations, competition policies and procurement rules. So, when countries block services or censor informa-tion on the Internet, policymakers from other countries may argue that these states are erecting barriers to Internet-related trade. (A trade barrier is a law, regulation, policy or practice that impedes trade.) One hundred and fifty nine countries rely on an international organization, the World Trade Organization (WTO), to establish the rule of law on international trade.

The WTO is a set of rules defining how firms can trade and how poli-cymakers can protect producers and consumers from injurious imports. But it is much more; it also serves as a forum for trade negotiations and settles trade disputes through a binding system. In the Internet arena, the WTO acts to promote market access, to preserve open telecommunication networks and to harmonize policies that can affect international trade.[22] Although the WTO does not explicitly regulate Internet services per se, it regulates trade in the goods and services that constitute e-commerce.[23] There are 74 members of the WTO that have agreed to implement the Information Technology Agreement. The signatories have eliminated tariffs on many of the products that make the Internet possible, such as semiconductors, set-top boxes, digital printers and computers.[24] Since 1998, the members of the WTO have agreed not to place tariffs on data flows. But members have also disagreed on how the WTO should affect national Internet policies. The WTO's dispute settlement body has already settled two trade disputes related to Internet issues (Internet gambling and China's state trading rights on audiovisual products and services).[25] Alas, the member states have not found common ground on how to reduce new trade barriers to information flows.[26] In 2011, several nations rejected a US and EU proposal in which members would have agreed not to block

Internet service providers (ISPs) or impede the free flow of information online.[27] Moreover, the members of the WTO have made little progress on adding new regulatory issues such as privacy and cyber-security that challenge Internet policymakers.[28]

Although trade policymakers can see the benefits of trade rules as a tool to govern the Internet and encourage information flows, some individuals question whether the WTO should even address Internet openness issues. First, the WTO regulates the behavior of states, not individuals or firms.[29] As a result, individuals and firms involved in online transactions have no way to directly represent their interests at the WTO. Second, information is a global public good; access to information is a basic human right under international human rights law. Hence, governments have a responsibility to ensure that their citizens have access to information through transparency mechanisms.[30] The WTO does have clear rules on transparency (access to information), due process, and political participation related to trade rulemaking. Some scholars have asserted that these rules may, without intent, encourage some democratic rights in member states.[31] But the WTO does not address specific human rights and has no authority to prod member states to provide an enabling regulatory context for the protection of these rights and other human rights fundamental to Internet freedom such as the right to privacy[32] or the right to free expression.[33] Third, the WTO moves slowly (as decisions are made by consensus), and thus cannot keep up with the development of new technologies. Fourth, many new online activities will require cooperative global regulation on issues that transcend market access – the traditional turf of the WTO. These issues will require policymakers to think less about ensuring that their model of regulation is adopted globally and more about achieving interoperability among different governance approaches.[34]

Because members have made little progress in trade talks at the WTO, the US, the EU and other countries have begun to use bilateral and regional free trade agreements (FTAs) to address e-commerce and other Internet issues. (These bilateral or regional agreements have many of the same problems mentioned above.) The US, the EU and Canada also use their FTAs to prod other governments to adopt a similar approach to regulation and enforcement. Thus, some observers see these agreements as governance agreements.[35] Table 23.1 summarizes how the US, the EU and Canada address Internet issues in their trade agreements.

We divide this chapter into the major issues surrounding trade policy and the Internet, and then compare the three trade giants' respective approaches to these issues.

Table 23.1   Case study free trade agreements: provisions that can enhance or reduce Internet openness

	EU	USA	Canada
Intellectual property rights provisions	Strong enforcement: +/− (actionable provisions)	Strong enforcement: +/− (actionable provisions)	Encourage cooperation: +/− (no binding language)
Privacy	Human/consumer right: +/− (no binding language)	Consumer right: +/− (no binding language)	Human/consumer right: +/− (no binding language)
Free flow		Free flow: + (proposed binding language)	Cross-border data flows: + (no binding language)
Server location		No restrictions: + (proposed binding language)	

Note: + enhance; − reduce.

Source: All tables and charts are from Susan Ariel Aaronson with Miles D. Townes (2012), "Can Trade Policy Set Information Free? Trade Agreements, Internet Governance, and Internet Freedom," policy brief, available from: http://www.gwu.edu/~iiep/governance/taig/CanTradePolicySetInformationFreeFINAL.pdf.

FREE FLOW OF INFORMATION AND SERVER LOCATION – SHOULD TRADE AGREEMENTS DELINEATE CLEAR EXCEPTIONS TO THE FREE FLOW OF INFORMATION?

Free Flow and Server Location Provisions: The US

The US is home to the world's largest and most influential Internet industries, and not surprisingly these companies have organized to influence trade policies and agreements. Google was the first company to argue that government restrictions on data flows and server location requirements might be a barrier to trade.[36] But Google was not the only company concerned with this issue: manufacturers and retailers also use data to cut costs, raise quality of services and optimize energy use. In 2011, the National Foreign Trade Council (NFTC), an export-oriented lobbying group with a diverse membership of multinational manufacturers, banks and tech companies, called for provisions to facilitate the free flow of information and to challenge restrictions on the flow of information as trade barriers.[37]

Soon thereafter, the US Trade Representative (USTR), who negotiates trade agreements for the US, began to develop language to encourage the free flow of information as well as policies to thwart "data protectionism."

US policymakers had many reasons to be responsive to these firms. When governments restrict information flows, companies have fewer viewers and customers for their sites, content and apps. Moreover, the US has been one of the leading advocates for Internet freedom and recognized that policies designed to facilitate the free flow of information could have spillovers for individuals.

If US policymakers included these provisions in trade agreements with developing countries, policymakers from other countries might gradually learn to value the open Internet. Yet US policymakers do not argue that facilitating the free flow of information will enhance Internet freedom and openness. Instead, policymakers make economic arguments; they stress that countries open to the free flow of information will grow faster, be more productive and receive more investment.[38] This strategy makes sense, as developing countries are more likely to be responsive to economic rather than human rights arguments. However, because policymakers have not linked free flow provisions to efforts to maintain Internet openness and freedom, US Internet trade policy seems incoherent and disconnected from US Internet foreign policy.

Although US trade agreements have long included language related to e-commerce,[39] the US and the Republic of Korea were the first states to include principles related to Internet openness and Internet stability in the electronic commerce chapter of the US–Korea FTA.[40] The language in this FTA was extensive. First, the two nations agreed to accept electronic signatures and included provisions designed to protect consumers online.[41] Second, the two nations agreed to encourage the free flow of information. Article 15.8 of the agreement says: "the Parties shall endeavor to refrain from imposing or maintaining unnecessary barriers to electronic information flows across borders."[42] However, this provision does not forbid the use of such barriers, nor does it define necessary or unnecessary barriers. Hence the reader does not know if legitimate online exceptions to free flow such as cyber-security measures or privacy regulations are necessary or not. It is unclear if one party could use this language to challenge another party's use of such barriers. Moreover, a party could always justify using such barriers under WTO exceptions to protect national security (the Chinese argument) or to protect public morals (the Russian argument).

In 2011 the US proposed actionable language in the Trans-Pacific Partnership (TPP), a regional Asia-Pacific trade agreement being negotiated by 12 countries, which could enhance Internet openness. In 2012 at George Washington University, Deputy Assistant USTR for Telecommunications

Policy Jonathan McHale noted that the USTR suggested rules that would allow data, as a default, to flow freely across borders.[43] The US wants to include language obligating TPP countries not to block the cross-border transfer of inbound and outbound data over the Internet. Additionally, the US has pushed rules prohibiting countries from requiring that data servers be located in their country as a business condition, as well as provisions allowing businesses to operate in countries via e-commerce platforms without establishing a commercial presence in the country.[44]

Officials from some of the TPP parties have not responded enthusiastically to these provisions. Some countries in the negotiation, such as Vietnam, have extensive restrictions on the Internet. Moreover, some TPP countries and individuals fear that this requirement that e-commerce platforms not be located at home is a national security issue.[45] Australia and New Zealand are concerned that foreign server locations could undermine their citizens' privacy rights. According to *Inside U.S. Trade*, in September 2012, Australia tabled alternative language to ensure that the data-flow proposal would be consistent with its privacy laws. Australia wants TPP countries to put in place restrictions on the free flow of data, as long as the country can justify that they are not disguised barriers to trade. As of October 2012, seven of the nine countries negotiating supposedly preferred this approach.[46] The US responded to Australian demands by proposing a more ad hoc strategy, which adheres to the Asia-Pacific Economic Cooperation Privacy Framework: firms could develop their own strategies to guard sensitive data, but each government would make this commitment enforceable through domestic institutions, such as the Federal Trade Commission (FTC) in the US.[47] As of this writing, TPP negotiators have not yet found language that all the countries can accept.[48]

The US may be encountering significant opposition to free flow provisions because the US and some of its TPP negotiating partners have different positions on the role of privacy, approaches to regulating privacy, and attitudes regarding the free flow of information. As noted above, the US wants to ensure data can flow freely across borders with only narrow exceptions. However, Australia, New Zealand and Canada have made protection of privacy rather than the free flow of information a top priority for international rules governing cross-border information flows. Meanwhile, countries such as Malaysia and Vietnam have not yet developed regulations to balance privacy and free flow; the US hopes that the TPP will influence these regulations and enhance the free flow of information.[49]

Members of Congress and activist groups are also concerned about these provisions and the TPP in general. In June 2012, some 131 members of Congress criticized the USTR's strategy on the negotiations and asked for additional consultations.[50] While generally supportive of the objective of free flow, these legislators are concerned about how the US negotiates in the age of the Internet; they want a more transparent and open process. Six months later, Senator Ron Wyden laid out a "freedom to compete" agenda that centered on promoting free flow domestically through legislation, and globally through trade.[51] First, he called for barring ISPs from slowing users' connections in order to discriminate against content providers. Next he called for limits on the ability of ISPs to cap user data. Third, he promoted legislation that would penalize false representations, but strengthen fair use, enhance due process and provide due process for seizures of property. Finally, he stated that Congress should provide the Obama administration with statutory negotiating instructions to seek open Internet disciplines in all trade discussions. Meanwhile, some activists argue that these free flow provisions are outweighed by the copyright provisions in the TPP, which they believe unfairly punish netizens for sharing copyrighted information on the web.[52] Activists in Australia, New Zealand, Canada and Mexico are also organizing to express their concerns about the Internet provisions proposed for the TPP.[53]

Free Flow Provisions: Canada and the EU

Although Canada's recent FTAs contain some language designed to encourage cross-border data flows, the language is not binding. Canada has included provisions on a permanent moratorium on customs duties applied to digital products delivered electronically, as well as on transparency, protection of consumers and personal information, and cooperation in the electronic commerce chapters of its previous agreements.[54] In the 2011 Canada–Colombia FTA, Canada notes the importance of:

> (a) clarity, transparency and predictability in their domestic regulatory frameworks in facilitating . . . electronic commerce; (b) encouraging self-regulation by the private sector to promote trust and confidence in electronic commerce . . . (d) ensuring that . . . electronic commerce policy takes into account the interest of all stakeholders . . . and (f) protecting personal information in the on-line environment.

Canada's recent FTAs also state that "each Party shall endeavor to guard against measures that unduly hinder trade conducted by electronic means." Finally, the parties agree to cooperate to maintain cross-border flows of information.[55] The EU has not included free flow of information language in its recent trade agreements.

Trade officials from both Canada and the EU say that, despite their support for Internet freedom, their countries would not include actionable provisions regarding the free flow of information and/or server location language in trade agreements. In July 2013 the Canadian Chamber of Commerce, in partnership with the US Chamber of Commerce, began to push for new data standards in future free trade deals, beginning with the Trans-Pacific Partnership. The effort was designed to stamp out policies that the organizations labeled "digital protectionism," such as Internet censorship and domestic data storage laws. Meanwhile, Canadian Privacy Commissioner Jennifer Stoddart expressed her support for a major overhaul of the federal Personal Information Protection and Electronic Documents Act (PIPEDA), in order to develop more adequate policies related to cloud computing, data mining software, government surveillance and cyber-threats.[56]

Under current EU policy, data may not enter or leave Europe unless the destination has privacy standards on a par with those of the EU. The EU has classified America's privacy standards as below those of the EU, so as a result a "Safe Harbor Agreement" is in place allowing data to flow only to companies that show privacy standards equivalent to those of Europe. However, Edward Snowden revealed that many of the companies within the Safe Harbor Agreement were providing personal data to the United States government. As a result, some policymakers in the European Union have expressed deep skepticism of America's insistence on free flow provisions.[57] In the EU, personal information and privacy go hand in hand. While the US plans to push for strong free flow provisions in TTIP,[58] US policymakers may struggle to convince European trade officials that free flow, data protection and surveillance can all be accommodated without undermining basic rights.

In recent years the US, the EU and Canada have also relied on voluntary principles, or soft law, to guide their work on the free flow of information and server location issues. In April 2012, the US and the European Union signed a set of non-binding trade-related principles for information and communication technology (ICT) services. The principles address commercial issues such as transparency, open networks, cross-border information flows and the digital divide, but say nothing per se about Internet freedom or the broader regulatory context to facilitate Internet openness.[59] Meanwhile the EU and Canada have been negotiating a free trade agreement since October 2009. The negotiators will address intellectual property and cross-border trade in services, but are unlikely to discuss free flow language or Internet freedom.[60] Finally, as part of the Security and Prosperity Partnership of North America, the US, Canada and Mexico signed "A Framework of Common Principles for Electronic Commerce" in June 2005, in which they agreed to "identify, monitor and address impediments to the free flow of information that unnecessarily impede cross-border trade or impose an unreasonable burden on the business community."[61]

However, here too they made no mention of Internet freedom or the broader regulatory context that supports Internet openness.

US efforts to advance the free flow of information with language in trade agreements have long met opposition from some trade partners, which fear that this strategy could make it harder for their governments to protect other important goals, such as privacy. These difficulties have been compounded by the June 2013 revelations of NSA snooping. Although the free flow of information could have positive spillovers for market actors online, efforts to promote it have remained ensnared. One of the biggest roadblocks to an agreement on the free flow of information comes from concerns about privacy.

DATA PROTECTION LAWS, PRIVACY AND TRADE – SHOULD TRADE AGREEMENTS REGULATE PRIVATE INFORMATION CROSSING BORDERS?

In 2010, Facebook CEO Mark Zuckerberg said that "privacy is dead" because of the Internet.[62] Zuckerberg may be wrong; netizens increasingly demand that governments protect their data online. As consumers and citizens, they are both winners and losers when information is collected, processed and analyzed across borders.[63] They benefit from cheaper and greater access to information; but their information may not be secure. As Canada's Privacy Commissioner stressed:

> Individuals throughout the world rely on common information and communication technologies; they share information, videos and photos using a few highly popular social networking platforms; they play online games using the same platforms and they conduct searches using the same search engines. As a result, when one of these global companies . . . experiences a privacy breach (as we witnessed with Sony's PlayStation Network in 2011), millions of people worldwide can be affected.[64]

Nonetheless, netizens are learning to monitor their privacy and demanding that governments protect their rights online. A 2010 survey of 5400 adult users from 13 countries found some 84 percent of those polled are concerned about issues related to online security. Some 58 percent are concerned about being misled by inaccurate information or lies.[65] Under international human rights law, individuals have a right to privacy and to shield their information from use or misuse by others. Privacy is both a human and a consumer right. Individuals who have experienced identity fraud may find themselves with lower credit scores, stigma, stress and discrimination. Organizations that lose personal data may experience negative publicity, distrust and lawsuits.[66] However, barriers to trust are also barriers to access. As privacy is an issue of trust among online market actors, policymakers in the three case study countries have tried to balance protecting privacy with rules governing cross-border data flows.

The US, the EU and Canada have different definitions of privacy and distinct strategies to protect it. The US sees privacy as a consumer right. The EU and Canada see privacy as both a human and a consumer right.[67] The EU uses an extensive system of regulation that has broad effects on other nations' approaches to privacy. The United States uses a sectoral approach that relies on a mix of legislation, regulation and business self-regulation; recent US laws, including Sarbanes–Oxley, contain minimal guarantees of an individual's right not to have personal or confidential information exposed online.[68]

US, EU and Canadian policymakers recognize that trade is being distorted by the many different approaches to privacy. Some 100 countries have adopted regulations addressing cross-border data flows, although many major trading nations such as the US, China, India and Brazil do not have such laws. The US Department of Commerce did a study in 2009 of business concerns around data privacy and found six challenges: 1) restrictions on transferring data between jurisdictions; 2) the lack of a recognized US privacy authority to represent the interests of US industry and citizens internationally; 3) difficulty providing a clear articulation of the US approach; 4) obstacles to implementing global information management systems given conflicting foreign requirements; 5) jurisdictional ambiguity and security concerns over data held in the cloud; and 6) significant costs to track and comply with data protection laws in each country. Respondents also noted gaps in protection for consumers whose data are transferred across borders, since it is not always clear who has jurisdiction over data and what protections exist for foreign consumers.[69] Given this confusion, the OECD has tried to find common ground and interoperability among these various approaches to privacy and regulation of cross-border data flows.[70] In 1980, the members of the OECD issued the first guidelines for privacy regulations which delineated rights and responsibilities for governments, consumers, citizens, and companies transferring and processing data across borders.[71] Although the three trade giants are members of the OECD, they have favored their own approach to privacy when making trade policies. We begin with the EU system, which has become increasingly influential around the world.

Privacy: The EU

The European Union was an early leader in global efforts to advance privacy online. All 28 EU member states are also members of the Council of Europe, a group of 47 European countries, and as such they are required to secure the protection of personal data under human rights law.[72] Every EU citizen has the right to personal data protection, and firms can collect that data only under specific conditions.[73] The EU also requires member states to investigate privacy violations.[74]

The European Commission (EC)'s Directive on Data Protection went into effect in October 1998, and it prohibits the transfer of personal data to non-European Union countries that do not meet the EU "adequacy" standard for privacy protection. The EU requires other countries to create independent government data protection agencies and register databases with those agencies, and in some instances the EC must grant prior approval before personal data processing may begin. To bridge these differences in regulatory strategy, the US Department of Commerce in consultation with the European Commission developed a "Safe Harbor" Framework.[75]

The EU directive has had an effect on trade. Because of the importance of cross-border data flows to and from the 27 EU members, some nations such as India and China are weighing how to make their laws interoperable with EU privacy provisions.[76] Meanwhile, other countries such as the Philippines have adopted EU data protection policies.[77]

Some observers of the EU approach assert that the EU focuses on process rather than outcomes, or on promoting "effective good data protection practices."[78] The EC has decided to update its data protection rules to meet changes in technology and increased public concern about privacy.[79] After obtaining extensive public comment, the European Commission released its proposed regulation in January 2012. This regulation, as originally proposed by European Commission staff, includes: language granting a right to be forgotten, meaning companies must delete data at the request of consumers; individuals must directly give their consent for data processing; individuals will have easier access to their own data; and companies and organizations will have to notify individuals of serious data breaches without undue delay. The EU argued these changes are necessary to "make sure that people's personal information is protected, no matter where it is sent, processed or stored, even outside the EU, as may often be the case on the Internet."[80] The EU also noted that they will help business by replacing the patchwork of national rules, lowering costs, cutting red tape and providing "assurances of strong data protection whilst operating in a single regulatory environment."[81]

BOX 23.3   THE INTERNATIONAL SPILLOVERS OF DATA PROTECTION LAWS

International privacy and data protection laws have not been made interoperable. Transborder data flows involve many computers communicating on a decentralized network via a wide range of platforms including social networks, search engines and cloud computing. Personal data may be at risk when it travels across borders.

Over 60 countries have adopted data protection or privacy laws that regulate the flow of information on the Internet (and other ICT platforms). Data protection regulations and laws have:

- Different objectives: Some are designed to be legally binding human rights instruments; others such as the APEC Privacy Framework are designed to facilitate electronic commerce.
- Different rationales: To prevent circumvention of national data protection and privacy laws; to guard against data processing risks in other countries; to address difficulties in asserting data protection and privacy rights abroad; and to enhance online consumer confidence.
- Different legal reach: Some geographically based, others extraterritorial. If data is stored in the cloud in other countries, it may be hard for individuals to exercise their rights.
- Different 'default position': Some give regulators limited power to block data flows; others proceed from the assumption that personal data may not flow outside the jurisdiction unless a legal basis is present.
- Different approaches to dealing with ISPs and diverse legal liability.

The result is that there is little regulatory efficiency or consistency. The OECD suggests creating a default rule for transborder data flows, but it must incorporate human rights, trade, consumer protection and so on.

Source: Christopher Kuner (2011), *Regulation of Transborder Data Flows under Data Protection and Privacy Law: Past, Present and Future*, Digital Economy Paper No. 187, Paris: OECD, pp. 1–18, 22, 24, 30.

Since its release, the directive has received over 3000 proposed amendments, significantly delaying its passage through the Civil Liberties, Justice and Home Affairs Committee. The committee was originally scheduled to vote on the regulation in April 2013, but as of this writing had been forced to delay its vote three times, most recently at its June 19, 2013 meeting.[82] In addition to struggling under the weight of thousands of amendments, the NSA PRISM leaks contributed significantly to the decision to further delay the future vote. At the committee's June 19, 2013 meeting, European Commission Vice-President Viviane Reding stated that access by US authorities to the personal data of EU citizens under the PRISM program could be illegal under international law.[83] The revelations also spurred discussion that a clause on "disclosures not authorized by Union law" should be inserted back into the draft data protection regulation. The article would forbid companies from handing over the personal data of EU citizens to non-EU governments, unless the disclosure was done in accordance with a mutual legal assistance treaty or equivalent agreement.[84] As of this writing, the committee's delay has led to concern that the regulation would not be able to be adopted before European Parliament elections in May 2014. Failure to finalize the directive before European Parliament elections could force the entire process to restart.[85]

Despite its strong support for privacy as both a human and a consumer right, the EC has included only aspirational language on privacy in its free trade agreements. In its economic partnership agreements (EPAs) with developing countries, Articles 196 and 197 say in part: the parties recognize their "common interest in protecting fundamental rights and freedoms of natural persons, and in particular, their right to privacy, with respect to the processing of personal data."[86] In its recent free trade agreements such as EU–Korea, Chapter 6 of the agreement refers to trade in data, and Article 7.43 of the chapter on services says that each party should reaffirm its commitment to protect fundamental rights and freedom of individuals, and adopt adequate safeguards to the protection of privacy.[87]

Privacy: The US

One of the most important factors distinguishing the US from Canada and the EU is that the United States views privacy as a consumer right, whereas Canada and the EU consider privacy to be a fundamental human right. As a result, Canadian and EU citizens have stronger legal protections against violations of their privacy whether by governments or by corporations. Additionally, in contrast with the EU and Canada, the US does not have one broad privacy law related to data protection. Congress has passed several laws, such as the Electronic Communications Privacy Act of

1986 and the Children's Online Privacy Protection Act of 1998, and regulators have issued guidance, including the FTC Code of Fair Information Practices Online Report. (The FTC investigates and enforces many of these privacy policies.) However, these laws have major gaps; they do not require companies to get informed consent to use personal data, nor do they establish a baseline commercial data privacy framework. Congress has not been able to find common ground on new legislation. In February 2012, the White House announced a set of data privacy guidelines titled the "Consumer Privacy Bill of Rights," and the Department of Commerce convened companies, privacy advocates and other stakeholders to develop and implement enforceable privacy policies based on this proposed bill of rights.[88] However, no legislation has passed through Congress and become law. The US has publicly expressed its intent to make its approach to privacy interoperable with the privacy frameworks of its international partners.[89]

Since Congress has not written legislation on privacy in cross-border data flows, US officials have worked to accommodate the strategies of key US trade partners such as the EU. The Department of Commerce developed the US–EU Safe Harbor Framework, which permits transborder data flows to the United States for commercial purposes, with FTC enforcement as a backstop. Companies (except financial institutions and telecommunications common carriers) may apply to qualify for a Safe Harbor. Companies that accept the relevant voluntary, enforceable code are safeguarded, so long as their practices do not deviate from the code's approved provisions, with a certification. However, those firms that fail to comply with the code's provisions could be subject to an enforcement action by the FTC or a state Attorney General, just as a company's failure to follow the terms of its privacy policy or other information practice commitments might lead to investigation and enforcement under current US policy.[90] The US also has a Safe Harbor provision with Switzerland and is a supporter of the APEC Privacy Framework, which requires business to self-regulate.[91] Since the June 2013 NSA leaks, however, the EU has called into question whether Safe Harbor provisions go far enough toward protecting EU citizens. In July 2013 the European Parliament passed a resolution calling on the European Commission to conduct a full review of the US–EU Safe Harbor Agreement, in order to determine whether data passed on to the NSA by private US companies was in violation of the standards.[92]

While the US has included language related to consumer protection in past FTAs, it has not historically included specific privacy language. E-commerce chapters like those for the US–Panama agreement include general statements that the parties recognize the importance of protecting consumers online, and will cooperate on privacy;[93] however, these chapters do not contain specific mechanisms or policies for enforcing privacy standards. Nonetheless, that strategy may change owing to US–EU TTIP negotiations. The US and the EU are discussing areas for regulatory coherence in TTIP negotiations, and issues of privacy and data flows are among them. The United States wants to include rules that will ease the flow of data between the two parties.[94] However, the EU has stated that, while it is willing to discuss the issue, it will under no circumstances lower its own standards for data privacy.[95] How the two sides ultimately reconcile their positions will have a large effect on business, security and private citizens.

Privacy: Canada

Canada has developed strong national and provincial privacy protections. Canada's national privacy legislation, the Personal Information Protection and Electronic Documents Act, went into effect in 2001. The legislation established a new Privacy Commissioner, who reports to the Parliament and works to protect Canadians' privacy rights.[96] Each Canadian province also has privacy commissioners who have specific oversight responsibilities, including investigating, providing guidance, promoting proactive disclosure and educating the public.[97]

Privacy Canada has issued guidelines related to PIPEDA, noting that the legislation does not prohibit organizations in Canada from transferring personal information to an organization in another jurisdiction for processing. Under the law, "a transfer for processing is a 'use' of the information; it is not a disclosure." Canadian firms are supposed to advise customers that their personal information may be sent to another jurisdiction for processing and that while the information is in another jurisdiction it may be accessed by the courts, law enforcement and national security authorities.[98] Canadians seem increasingly reassured by these policies. According to the Privacy Commissioner's report to Parliament in 2011, in public opinion surveys commissioned by the Office of the Privacy Commissioner "the proportion of Canadians saying they feel they have less protection of their personal privacy in daily life than a decade previously has declined, from 71 percent in 2006 to 61 percent in 2011."[99]

Canada, like the EU, has not developed actionable language regarding privacy in its trade agreements. The signatories simply agree to cooperate on data privacy and consumer confidence. Article 1506: Protection of Personal Information says: "1. Each Party should adopt or maintain laws, regulations or administrative measures for the protection of personal information of users engaged in electronic commerce and 2. The Parties should exchange information and experiences regarding their domestic regimes for the protection of personal information."[100]

Although policymakers are beginning to address the privacy impact of data flows in trade agreements, the three trade giants have not found common ground on the trade spillovers of privacy rules. For example, some Canadian agencies have refused to send information to the US through email or data flows; they are concerned that such outsourcing could undermine Canada's security.[101] Many Canadians also believe their data can be put at risk by the US government because of Patriot Act data requirements. Hence, in 2004, the province of British Columbia passed legislation to restrict the disclosure of personal information outside Canada and expand the scope of personal liability and sanctions for contraventions of the British Columbia legislation. The law required public bodies to ensure that personal information "in its custody or under its control is stored only in Canada and accessed only in Canada."[102] In 2006, Nova Scotia established similar requirements. Quebec and Alberta also established provincial laws attempting to delineate when and how personal information controlled by public bodies could be shared.[103] More recently, Canada's provincial privacy commissioners expressed concerns that a new Canada–US perimeter security action plan could undermine Canada's privacy protections.[104]

Like the EC, Canada has made privacy a priority, but in contrast with the EU it has not attempted to export its approach. However, the Privacy Commission recognizes that Canadian officials will need to find ways to ensure that Canada's approach to privacy is workable beyond Canada's borders.[105]

Taken together, these different approaches to privacy may or may not distort trade, but they are creating regulatory incoherence. Policymakers are trying to make these approaches interoperable. As a result, privacy rules designed to promote trust among market actors online may both distort trade and, without intent, undermine Internet openness.

INTELLECTUAL PROPERTY RIGHTS ENFORCEMENT – CAN TRADE AGREEMENTS PROTECT ONLINE PROPERTY RIGHTS AND PRESERVE INTERNET OPENNESS?

The Internet has provided new platforms to exchange ideas, songs, news, pictures and other information. And, as the rise of Facebook, Pinterest, Weibo and Twitter reveal, people love to share online. However, when netizens share copyrighted information online, they may violate the rights of content creators.[106]

Under US, EU and Canadian intellectual property law, individuals can obtain limited exclusive rights to whatever economic reward the market may provide for their creations. These intellectual property rights (IPRs) provide a foundation with which intangible ideas generate tangible benefits to firms and workers. These rights are enforceable through government action and the courts. They are also enforceable through the WTO in an agreement called the Agreement on Trade Related Aspects of Intellectual Property Rights (TRIPS).[107] This agreement helped reduce non-tariff trade barriers stemming from different IPR regimes, and it also established transparency standards that require all members to publish laws, regulations and decisions on intellectual property. However, policymakers did not design copyright laws with an understanding of how people would share information online.[108] The US and EU approach to protecting IPR online is causing conflicts among high-tech firms, between netizens and their governments, as shown by the ACTA debate, between firms and their customers, and in trade relations, as with the US and Canada.

IPR Provisions: The US

Policymakers designed US copyright laws to protect rights holders, to encourage the creation of new knowledge and to protect intermediaries. First, individuals can use a copyrighted work for purposes such as criticism, comment, news reporting, parody and satire, teaching, scholarship or research according to the "fair use" doctrine created by the US Copyright Act of 1976.[109] Software developers, educational institutions, Internet search portals and others depend on "fair use" to provide or adapt information for consumers, students and users.[110] Several analysts have shown that these "fair use" provisions contribute to economic growth because individuals and firms learn from and build on the work of others.[111] Some other countries have "fair use," including Singapore, the Philippines, Korea, Malaysia and Israel, while the UK, Canada and Australia use the concepts of "fair dealing, which are not as broad or as flexible as the exceptions under fair use."[112] Secondly, the US recognizes that intermediaries should generally not be held liable for copyrighted material that is posted online. Hence, the US has laws that allow rights holders to petition intermediaries to take down infringing materials. Intermediaries are supposed to comply with these takedown requests in a transparent manner that follows US norms of due process.[113]

Because Congress has made the protection of IPR online a priority for domestic law and trade negotiations, the US includes extensive language related to IPR in its trade agreements.[114] However, the IPR chapters do not always include all the attributes of US copyright laws. Moreover, other countries have different approaches to protecting IPR and judging infringement.

The US Trade Representative has developed increasingly stringent enforcement language in its trade agreements. For example, in the US–Chile FTA (which went into force in 2004), each country is supposed to develop its own procedures for notice and takedown through an open and transparent process set forth in domestic law, for effective notifications of claimed infringement, and for effective counter-notifications by those whose material is removed or disabled through mistake or misidentification. The US also prevents FTA partners from using copyright limitations and exceptions in order to allow for the retransmission of television signals over the Internet without the authorization of both the rights holder of the content and the rights holder of the signal.[115]

In recent FTAs such as Korea, the US requires its FTA partners to provide copyright terms of 70 years (20 beyond the WTO requirement), and to make it illegal for companies or individuals to circumvent protection of copyrighted work. For example, the IPR chapter in the US–Korea Free Trade Agreement contains 35 pages of obligations which delineate "fair use" for research and non-infringing good faith activities related to online copyright. These provisions also delineate how content holders can inform service providers of materials that are supposedly infringing, as well as a due process strategy for those who claim they were mistakenly accused of infringement. The agreement includes several side letters addressing ISP obligations, copyright infringement on university campuses, enforcement against online piracy, and patent linkage. Korea also agreed to issue a policy directive establishing clear jurisdiction for effective enforcement against online piracy.[116] In the US proposal for the TPP, the provision requires an ISP to notify a user if it has posted infringing content and to take action against that subscriber's use of its service if the user does not take down the site.[117]

US policymakers recognize that language protecting online copyright in FTAs will not be sufficient to prevent online privacy. The US has only 19 FTAs in force and some not only contain less extensive IPR commitments, but were signed before the development of new file sharing technologies. Hence, the US has implemented a wide range of other enforcement strategies.[118] First, a senior US official now serves as the Intellectual Property Enforcement Coordinator in the White House.[119] The Intellectual Property Enforcement Coordinator's office reports on threats to US intellectual property from criminal violation.[120] Secondly, the US also conducts an annual review of its trade partners' IPR policies and practices. It creates a list of countries that don't offer "adequate and effective" protection of IPR, or "fair and equitable" market access to United States persons who rely upon intellectual property rights.[121] Thirdly, the US also lists countries and web sites as "notorious markets" in which pirated or counterfeit goods are reportedly available.[122] However, the US Congressional Research Service reports that this approach is not deterring online piracy.[123] The US government and US firms have sued users and file sharing sites.[124] The US has also taken steps to move the reach of US law beyond its borders, targeting intermediaries who set up web sites that share links to free access to copyright material across borders, such as Megaupload, and charging these individuals or companies with violating the Digital Millennium Copyright Act.[125] However, legal scholars and the courts are debating whether the law has extraterritorial application.[126]

Finally, the US was a major force behind a new treaty designed to bolster enforcement of IPR online. The Anti-Counterfeiting Trade Agreement (ACTA) was signed by the United States, Australia, Canada, Korea, Japan, New Zealand, Morocco and Singapore on October 1, 2011. The negotiating countries agreed that counterfeiting has huge economic costs and can lead to consumers purchasing substandard goods. However, some activists and Internet industry representatives in the US and around the world have argued that ACTA takes too punitive an approach towards enforcement, and by so doing could undermine the open Internet.[127]

Although the executives of both the EU and the US accepted ACTA, the EU Parliament and the 27 EU member states have not agreed to this treaty. After street and online protests, several EU governments announced that they no longer support ACTA.[128] In late February 2012, the European Commission announced that it was suspending consideration of the agreement and referred it to the European Court of Justice.[129] In July 2012, the European Parliament voted against ACTA. The European Economic and Social Committee (EESC), an arm of the EU, summarized European concerns:

> ACTA's approach is aimed at further strengthening the position of rights holders vis-à-vis the "public" . . . whose fundamental rights (privacy, freedom of information, secrecy of correspondence, presumption of innocence) are becoming increasingly undermined by laws that are heavily biased in favour of content distributors . . . Copyright pirates are perfectly capable of eluding any form of control on the flow of data on the Internet.[130]

Meanwhile, although the US Trade Representative insists Congress does not have to approve ACTA, some members of Congress disagree.[131]

In 2011, several members of Congress proposed legislation – the Stop Online Piracy Act (SOPA) and the Protect IP Act (PIPA) – to further protect copyrights on the Internet. Although the two bills were slightly different, they both required ISPs to shut down foreign web sites where copyrights were violated.[132] Although neither bill became law, they raised concerns in the US and abroad about extraterritoriality and due process. In conjunction with the debate over ACTA, the bills encouraged a broad public questioning about the effect of strong online copyright enforcement on the open Internet.

Meanwhile, in late 2011, Senator Ron Wyden and Representative Darrell Issa proposed a new approach, where content owners would ask the International Trade Commission to investigate whether a foreign web site profited from privacy. The foreign web site could rebut the claim to the Commission.

If the Commission ruled for the copyright holder, it could direct payment firms to stop doing business with the web site; it could not shut down the site only to determine infringement. The legislators who developed this strategy also created a web site where they answer public questions on the bill and encourage citizens to mark up and improve the legislation.[133] The bill's proponents argue:

> By approaching online infringement as an international trade issue, we are forced to consider not just ways to stop online infringement, but how the policies we enact impact things like cyber-security, efforts to promote digital exports and international diplomacy. Moreover because norms established in the US are likely to be advanced and replicated around the world, it is important that the US carefully consider how the policies it adopts are translated and received by other countries.[134]

Although the Wyden–Issa bill did not receive a vote in either the House or the Senate, it marked the first time that US policymakers weighed the broader regulatory context of Internet policies and how such policies might affect Internet openness.

America's current approach to protecting online copyright has many problems. First, the US demands that its trade partners focus funds and energy on enforcement, but this strategy does little to build public understanding and support for protecting copyright online. Secondly, the US strategy relies heavily on intermediaries to police the Internet for copyright violations. Although intermediaries such as Google, Twitter and Facebook have a mission of facilitating Internet openness and information exchange, under this strategy these intermediaries must monitor their customers. Companies are struggling to achieve this balance. Google provides a prominent example: every month it issues a takedown report, noting that it complies with over 90 percent of requests.[135] In May 2012, Google said it had received 1.24 million requests from 1296 copyright owners for removal, targeting 24 129 domains.[136] However, by July 2013 that number had risen to 14 million takedown requests per month from 3256 copyright owners, targeting 36 864 domains.[137] Although the company is extremely transparent, Google does not explain how and why it complied in one case and refused to comply in another.

Thirdly, the US approach does not consistently provide due process for individuals or firms accused of violating US copyright. Some countries use administrative or judicial procedures to decide what should be taken down and when. France and Spain have government agencies decide these issues, whereas in Chile the courts decide. The US Trade Representative has not favored this approach, because it can be time-consuming and may yield different results for copyright holders. For example, in the 2012 Special 301 report, the USTR urged Chile to "to amend its Internet service provider liability regime to permit effective action against piracy over the Internet."[138]

The US is increasingly encountering pushback abroad towards its online copyright policies. Some critics argue that the strategy lacks transparency, accountability and an independent appeals mechanism. They are seeking legal recourse. In both Canada and France, the courts have upheld the right to download and copy music and films, but did not clarify how many people can share these copies or downloads.[139] In Colombia, a US FTA partner, two senators recently filed lawsuits against copyright revisions to Colombian law, which were adopted to bring Colombia's laws into compliance with the US–Colombia FTA. The lawsuits make the case that the Colombian law restricts the rights of Internet users to access and disclose information as well as their rights to privacy under Colombian law.[140]

IPR Provisions: The EU

Like the United States, the European Union has strong and influential industries that have demanded a robust approach to protecting copyright online. But the 27 nations of the EU do not have a uniform approach to addressing this issue. Each European country makes its own decisions about when to remove content for violations of IPR.

Citizens in many European countries have become concerned about the focus on IPR enforcement and the implications of this strategy for an open Internet. In 2006, the Swedish government arrested the operators of the Pirate Bay, a file sharing site. In response, European citizens organized both civil society groups and a political party, the Pirate Party, to rethink IPR. Pirate parties exist today in multiple EU countries. They argue that the copyright system needs major reform, which cannot be done without addressing access, data retention, privacy and other related issues holistically.[141] In 2009 Sweden elected two Pirate Party members to the European Parliament.[142] In addition, Pirate Party candidates have been elected to the national legislature in Iceland[143] and the Czech Republic,[144] and hold several seats in state parliaments in Germany.[145]

Given widening criticism of its approach to online IPR, the European Commission, the executive branch of the EU, hopes to develop an updated EU-wide approach. On June 6, 2012, the European Commission kicked off an EU-wide public consultation.[146] Officials asked individuals and firms to comment on the failings of the current regime, such as notification procedures, the legal uncertainties of 27 different domestic legal regimes, and the potential for abuse where legal content is the subject of a takedown request.[147] However, the UK, Denmark, Slovenia, Belgium, Hungary and Sweden are opposed to EU-wide regulation and prefer to have a directive which would allow common rules and maintain individual state flexibility in administering online IPR.[148]

Although member states decide their own policies for when and how to protect IPR online, the EC makes trade policy for the member states and it develops the language in trade agreements. In 2005, the EC decided that it needed a new strategy to protect IPR online. The EC aimed to reduce IPR violations in third countries, and make the enforcement clauses in future bilateral or bi-regional agreements more operational, to clearly define what the EU regards as the highest international standards in this area, and what kind of efforts it expects from its trading partners. Trade officials acknowledged that, because it is difficult to detect the origin of the IPR violation and to effectively protect copyright, "EU policies should strive to improve the effectiveness and coordination of the police, the courts, the customs and the administration in general. It is also essential to ensure that the legal framework provides for deterrent sanctions."[149] Like the US, the EC is focused on enforcement, but policymakers also recognize that they must support government capacity to detect and enforce copyright violations online.

The EU began to make these changes in its EPAs, such as EU–Cariforum, as well as its recent free trade agreements. The EU included rules on the liability of ISPs in its draft FTA between the EU and ASEAN and in the EU–Korea Free Trade Agreement.[150] To meet its obligations to the EU, Korea changed its laws regarding fair use by online service providers to include acting as a conduit, caching, hosting, and information search. Korea also clarified exceptions to the prohibition against circumvention of technical protection measures online.[151]

As noted above, the EU and Canada are also negotiating an FTA known as the Comprehensive Economic and Trade Agreement (CETA). In July 2012 Michael Geist, Professor of Internet and E-Commerce Law at the University of Ottawa, leaked a copy of CETA's intellectual property chapter. The document, a draft chapter from February 2012, contained many provisions that directly copied language from ACTA.[152] Since ACTA had been defeated in the European Parliament just one week before the leak, the document caused controversy throughout the European Union. Opponents claimed it would become "ACTA through the backdoor" and that it undermined the will of the European people and their democratically elected representatives.[153] Two particularly contentious provisions involved verbatim copies of Articles 27.3 and 27.4 of ACTA.[154] The first, Article 27.3, promoted "cooperative efforts within the business community to effectively address trademark and copyright or related rights infringement." The second, Article 27.4, gave countries the authority to force ISPs to disclose the identities of copyright-infringing customers.[155] Opponents believed that both sections had a high potential to be abused, and that they could lead to violations of privacy.[156] Just two days after the leak, John Clancy, an EU spokesperson, confirmed via Twitter that the leaked text was real, but that the two articles were no longer part of the chapter.[157] However, concerns remained among CETA's opponents owing to the lack of transparency in the negotiating process. As a result, in February 2013 the European Commission released a factsheet dismissing the idea that CETA could become a backdoor ACTA, and reassuring EU citizens that CETA was not aiming to raise the level of protection or enforcement of IPR beyond the rules that were already applied in the EU.[158]

IPR Provisions: Canada

Canada recently updated its copyright laws to meet the demands of new technologies.[159] Parliamentarians began this process by examining demands for takedowns and found that the vast majority of copyright infringement notices were sent by either US studios, representing movies, music and television content, or software publishers, or by agents operating on their behalf. Policymakers learned that less than 2 percent of notices could be attributed to Canadian copyright holders.[160] Canada ultimately changed its policy to require ISPs to warn the potential infringer that posted the material rather than requiring the ISP to take down materials (notice and notice).

Canada also has a different approach to fair use, which it calls "fair dealing." It allows broad exemptions for non-commercial purposes such as education and parody. The Canadian courts have broadly interpreted fair dealing online.[161] The Canadian Supreme Court views teachers as well as ISPs as conduits of information.[162]

In general, Canada does not include IPR language in its free trade agreements, but rather encourages cooperation on IPR issues, as it did in the Canada–Colombia FTA.[163]

The Future Direction of Strategies to Enforce Online IPR

The public in the US and abroad have not generally been supportive of the US focus on enforcement. Although most web users recognize that, when they breach copyright they are stealing, many web users believe that it is ethical to download music and other copyrighted or trademarked items. A recent American Assembly poll found American Internet users oppose copyright enforcement when it intrudes on personal rights and freedoms. Some 57 percent oppose blocking or filtering if those measures block legal content, although 61 percent of those polled want sites such as Facebook to reject pirated copies of music and videos.[164]

Some individuals are concerned not only about the effectiveness of trade policies focused on enforcement, but about which entities do the enforcing and how that affects human rights. First, when individuals share infringing information online, they may also be sharing substantial amounts of non-infringing content. Moreover, people who download anonymously may also upload and vice versa. ISPs do not find it easy to figure out who posted what and who downloaded what (e.g. who is responsible). When corporate officials try to detect copyright violations in these circumstances they may, without intent, violate user rights to privacy and freedom of expression.[165] Policymakers are increasingly responsive to these concerns. For example, the UK and New Zealand are rethinking their approach to copyright online and offline.[166]

Thus, the current EU and US strategy for enforcing copyright online may without deliberate intent reduce Internet openness.

CHALLENGING INTERNET REGULATIONS AS BARRIERS TO TRADE – CAN TRADE RULES BE USED TO PROMOTE OPENNESS?

Barriers to Trade: The US

As noted above, the US is not only pushing for language in trade agreements to encourage the free flow of information, but also taking steps to challenge other countries' Internet policies as barriers to trade. Thus far, the US has used naming and shaming, rather than initiate trade disputes. However, in late 2011, the US sent a letter to the Chinese government asking it to explain its Internet policies. Under paragraph 4 of Article II of the General Agreement on Trade in Services (GATS), the US asked China to explain why some foreign sites were inaccessible in China, who decides when and if a foreign web site should be blocked, and if China had an appeal procedure for such blockage. Although China is required to respond under GATS, the US supposedly did not receive a formal reply. The US Trade Representative has also studied whether it could challenge Chinese Internet restrictions as a violation of WTO rules.[167] However, the US is unlikely to take this route, as policymakers would not want to create precedents that could limit the US or its allies' ability to restrict access to the Internet for national security reasons.[168]

The US has also identified privacy rules as a barrier to the free flow of information. For example, in its 2013 report on foreign trade barriers, the USTR argued that British Columbia and Nova Scotia's privacy laws discriminate against US suppliers, because they require that personal information be stored and accessed only in Canada.[169] The USTR claims these laws prevent public bodies from using US services when personal information could be accessed from or stored in the United States.[170] In its 2012 report, the US also cited Australia's approach to privacy, noting Australia's unwillingness to use US companies for hosting owing to concerns about privacy violations.[171] In 2013 the USTR noted that negative messaging about US privacy was on the decline, but that it had not disappeared. In July 2012 a new Australian law prohibiting the overseas storage of digital health records went into effect.[172] The US also complained about Japan's uneven approach to privacy and Vietnam's unclear approach.[173] Ironically, the US also argued that China's failure to enforce its privacy laws stifles e-commerce.[174]

In December 2012 the United States extended normal trade relations to Russia and Moldova.[175] The law contains a provision added by the House of Representatives that would expand the scope of the Special 301 report issued by the Office of the US Trade Representative each year. This provision mandates that the report include a description of laws, policies or practices by the Russian Federation that deny "fair and equitable treatment" to US digital trade.[176]

The US is also concerned that some governments have restricted information flows to the US because of the Patriot Act. The USTR notes that:

> US companies have faced obstacles to winning contracts with EU governments and private sector customers because of public fears in the EU that any personal data held by these companies may be collected by US law enforcement agencies. The United States is seeking to correct misconceptions about US law and practice and to engage with EU stakeholders on how personal data is protected in the United States.[177]

This effort has become more difficult in the face of the NSA privacy leaks.

Interestingly, Antigua challenged a US barrier to information flows at the WTO. The US allows domestic online gambling, but claimed that foreign sites could not effectively prevent fraud and money laundering. Although this objection seems reasonable, the dispute settlement body found that the US was discriminating among foreign and domestic purveyors of Internet gambling.[178]

Barriers to Trade: The EU and Canada

In 2010, European Commission Vice-President Neelie Kroes told Chinese officials that China's Internet censorship was a trade barrier that should be challenged at the WTO. However, the EC never launched a formal trade dispute.[179] The EU does not target other countries' privacy policies as trade barriers, although it does view national security policies as potential barriers to trade. In addition, the EU has expressed concerns about security policies for telecom equipment in both China and India. The Indian government asked firms to provide source codes and other sensitive information in case of security breaches, which led EU officials to express privacy concerns.[180] Canadian officials have not challenged other countries' privacy policies as barriers to trade.

The US, the EU and Canada have not found common ground on when privacy, national security and other considerations can be used to restrict the free flow of information and the location of data servers. Given these differences, policymakers need greater understanding of what domestic regulations may distort information flows and data on how these regulations affect trade, for example the dollar amounts of trade distortions.

PROMOTING INTERNET FREEDOM ABROAD THROUGH TRADE – SHOULD POLICYMAKERS USE TRADE AND OTHER STRATEGIES TO KEEP THE INTERNET OPEN?

Export Bans: The US and the EU

Canada, the EU and the US have often used trade policies, sanctions as well as incentives, to prevent repressive states from violating the rights of their citizens. However, the 2009 election protests in Iran and the 2011 protests in Egypt, Tunisia and other Middle Eastern states illuminated how social networking, cross-border information flows, and platforms such as Twitter could empower activists.[181] We also learned that repressive as well as democratic governments could use these platforms and web infrastructure to suppress dissent and block the free flow of information.[182]

The three case studies have considerable leverage to keep the web open. Many of these platforms, web sites and social networks, as well as the hardware that makes the web possible, are provided or produced by European, US and Canadian companies. Many of the US companies are publicly listed, and some European governments including France and Sweden are major investors in companies that export surveillance and communications equipment.[183] To prevent the abuse of these systems, US and EU officials have sanctioned bad actors and limited access to goods or services that government officials can use to spy on or monitor their citizens' activities online. For example, the US strictly controls which nations can buy Internet filtering tools or information suppression technologies. In July 2012, the US Department of Commerce added Internet filtering tools and information suppression technologies to items under strict export controls.[184]

Unfortunately sanctions can have unanticipated consequences for the citizens whom policymakers hope to assist. In 2012, *The Washington Post* reported that, although these sanctions are supposed to make it harder for Syrian officials to spy on dissidents, they also make it harder for activists in Syria to communicate online.[185]

So far, the US and other nations have not devised a clear approach to using trade incentives or disincentives. The US government also said that, although it has a wide range of sanctions in place for Cuba, Iran and Syria, it will grant licenses to companies that export instant messaging and other personal Internet services to those countries.[186] The US also eliminated export restrictions on "mass-market electronic products with encryption functions such as laptops and cell phones."[187]

Interestingly, the US strategy towards Internet openness and trade is being played out as the civil war rages in Syria. The Syrian government closed off the Internet for many of its citizens on November 29, 2012,[188] yet many government sites were in fact accessible because they were hosted by US companies. The government did so again in a 19-hour nationwide blackout on May 7–8, 2013.[189] The US government views such web hosting as a violation of the President's executive order on Syria, mentioned above. Ironically, the US is restricting the Internet at home in the interest of punishing the Syrian government for restricting the Internet abroad. The Department of State claimed this would promote the ability of Syrians to exercise their freedom of expression, although it is unclear how.[190] Canada and European countries also hosted some of these sites. They too must wrestle with how to protect the web abroad.

Neither the US, the EU nor Canada have developed clear guidance for firms as to when they can sell general-use technologies to repressive states. Some technologies, such as TOR or Blackberry Instant Messenger, can be deployed for good intent, for example to evade governments that abuse human rights. But the same technologies can be deployed for illegal purposes, such as terrorism, rioting or drug trafficking. Nor have the three collaborated to develop clear standards regarding whether these technologies can be sold abroad, when such sales should be monitored, and under what circumstances they should not be exported.

Promoting Internet Freedom: The US and the EU

The US, the EU and individual EU member states are trying to develop effective strategies to help activists in repressive states access the Internet and freely express their opinions online. However, the US and the EU have not developed principles regarding when and how they should act on behalf of netizens outside of the US and the EU.

Policymakers acknowledge that all governments block the flow of some information for moral, ethical, privacy, cyber-security or national security reasons. So officials understandably do not want to criticize the decisions of their democratically elected counterparts. Moreover, although the Internet is an obvious example of the global commons, where countries must collaborate in the broad public interest, policymakers from country A are reluctant to interfere in the affairs of country B or C. These policymakers recognize that they too would not like such interference. Thirdly, policymakers want to ensure that covert strategies to enhance Internet freedom abroad do not attract extensive attention and in so doing undermine, rather than increase, the ability of activists abroad to communicate and collaborate online.

Despite these difficulties, states are devising policies and funding innovative projects to promote Internet freedom. Sweden, the Netherlands, the EU and the US are among the most active proponents of Internet freedom.[191] The US brings human rights activists to Geneva, Washington and Silicon Valley to meet with fellow activists, as well as US and international government leaders, and members of civil society and the private sector working on technology and human rights issues.[192] The US government also helped establish the Global Network Initiative (GNI), a multisectoral partnership among business, human rights groups, academics and other interested parties. The Initiative has developed principles to guide the information technology industry on how to respect, protect and advance freedom of expression and privacy when faced with government demands for censorship and disclosure of users' personal information.[193] Yahoo,

Google, Evoca, Folksam and Microsoft, along with NGOs, churches and academics, participate in the GNI.

The EU Parliament established a €125 million fund to train and empower bloggers, online journalists and human rights defenders to circumvent censorship and evade cyber-attacks.[194] The EU also set up a program, "No Disconnect," to provide citizens in non-democratic countries with tools to fight "arbitrary censorship restrictions and protect against illegitimate surveillance."[195] With EU funding, EC officials are building a "European Capability for Situational Awareness," to aggregate and visualize up-to-date intelligence about the state of the Internet across the world.[196] Meanwhile, the US has given $70 million in grants to help citizens of repressive regimes use the Internet. These grants fund technology that helps these individuals communicate securely and freely.[197] However, some individuals have expressed concern that these technologies are not effective because they can be easily hacked, and they can be used by criminals as well as activists.[198]

Although Canada has issued several statements in support of Internet freedom, it has not made this a foreign policy priority. Despite the importance of the Internet as a platform for trade and for other sectors, none of the three trade giants uses trade capacity building to promote improved domestic Internet governance.

In sum, the US and the EU have adopted trade and foreign aid policies to support both Internet freedom and Internet openness. But these policies have not focused on the broader regulatory context of Internet governance at the national and international level, nor have they built a global consensus on when it is appropriate for governments to interfere in order to protect netizens abroad.

CONCLUSION

SOPA, PIPA and ACTA created an international dialogue about how to balance intellectual property rights and freedom of expression. Similarly, the 2013 NSA leaks brought about a new debate on issues of privacy and the free flow of information. Although the global community has been grappling with these issues, policymakers still have trouble weighing the implications of their choices on Internet freedom and openness. As a result, US and EU policies to promote cross-border information flows seem disconnected from policies to sustain the open web.

Although the Internet is facilitating trade, trade policies can serve both to enhance and to undermine Internet openness. Policymakers have not achieved consensus or interoperable policies among nations, which have

Table 23.2   The struggle to balance Internet stability and Internet freedom leads to policy incoherence

Country	Policy objective	Strategy	Implication for freedom and openness
US, EU, Canada	Advance Internet freedom.	Provide funds and technologies to ensure freedom of expression and access to the Internet.	Internet freedom may be advanced. Sometimes criminals may obtain evasive technologies.
US, EU, Canada	Protect privacy as a human and consumer right.	None of the countries has pressed for a global standard, but all three are pursuing interoperability.	Have not clarified when privacy rules act as a barrier to trade. Have not developed common ground on privacy as a human or consumer right.
US, EU, Canada	Protect national security and cyber-security.	Monitor and occasionally restrict access.	Have not clarified when policymakers can block access to information to support national security.
US	Challenge privacy regulations as a barrier to trade.	List in trade barrier report.	Send message protecting privacy should be subordinated to encouraging information flows.
US	Challenge concerns about server location and cloud computing as a barrier to trade.	List in trade barrier report.	Have not clarified if server requirements distort trade. Have not found national or international balance between privacy, server location and national security.
US, EU	Establish regulatory model and protect online IPR.	Insist that FTA partners adopt copyright protection model and focus on enforcement. Rely on intermediaries to enforce.	Put intermediaries in difficult position of reducing access to information, only some of which may violate copyright.
US	Use trade agreements to	Does not include provisions in	Unable to effectively promote Internet

Table 23.2   (continued)

Country	Policy objective	Strategy	Implication for freedom and openness
	facilitate the free flow of information among nations.	FTAs that address whole of regulatory governance to support an open Internet. Requires nations to include these provisions before achieving domestic consensus on Internet governance.	openness. Do not focus on broad vision of regulatory environment necessary to support an open Internet. Have not found shared approach to fostering free flow, server location, privacy, etc.
US, EU, Canada	Establish precedent and treaty to protect online copyright (ATCA).	Get major markets to sign on.	Send message that free expression and access to information are less important than protecting IPR. Focus on enforcement, but little effort to promote netizen understanding that online piracy is theft.

different priorities for privacy, security and the free flow of information. Moreover, policymakers have not figured out how to negotiate trade policies in a transparent, accountable and coherent manner supportive of the open Internet.

The US and the EU have made Internet freedom a priority. Yet neither the US nor the EU has clearly defined Internet freedom or developed a compelling and consistent argument as to why Internet freedom and openness are important to both economic growth and political stability.[199] While the US and the EU have both adopted a wide range of strategies to advance Internet freedom, they have not figured out how to help governments devise an appropriate domestic regulatory context to support Internet freedom and openness. Moreover, although the American, Canadian and EU governments generally share a vision of Internet freedom, they have not collaborated to define the role of governments in supporting an open Internet, or to determine when it is appropriate to interfere in the affairs of other countries to protect netizens.

Policymakers do not make Internet-related trade policies by weighing the implications of their choices for Internet openness. As a result, US, Canadian and EU policies to promote cross-border information flows seem disconnected from policies to sustain the open web.

NOTES

1. The MacArthur and Ford Foundations provided funds for this research.
2. "Growing Alarm: German Prosecutors to Review Allegations of US Spying" (2013), *Der Spiegel International*, June 30, available from: http://www.spiegel.de/international/germany/german-prosecutors-to-review-nsa-spying-allegations-a-908636.html (accessed August 5, 2013).
3. Ian Traynor (2013), "NSA Spying Row: Bugging Friends Is Unacceptable, Warn Germans," *Guardian*, July 1, available from: http://www.theguardian.com/world/2013/jul/01/nsa-spying-allegations-germany-us-france (accessed August 5, 2013); and Alan Travis (2013), "European Commission Backs Merkel's Call for Tougher Data Protection Laws," *Guardian*, July 15, available from: http://www.theguardian.com/world/2013/jul/15/european-commission-angela-merkel-data-protection (accessed August 5, 2013).
4. Matthew Price (2013), "Turn Back the Limousines: EU–US Trade Pact Faces Rocky Road," *BBC News*, July 1, available from: http://www.bbc.co.uk/news/world-europe-23126238 (accessed August 5, 2013).
5. Charlemagne (2013), "Reaching for the Clouds," *Economist*, July 24; and Monika Ermert (2013), "Nations Begin to Take Action against United States for NSA Spying," *Intellectual Property Watch*, July 12.
6. Under the Trade Act of 1974, revised to grant most favored nation (MFN) status to Russia, Congress agreed, "For calendar year and each succeeding calendar year, the Trade Representative shall include in the analyses and estimates under paragraph (1) an identification and analysis of any laws, policies, or practices of the Russian Federation that deny fair and equitable market access to United States digital trade." 112th Congress Public Law 208, available from: http://www.gpo.gov/fdsys/pkg/PLAW-112publ208/html/PLAW-112publ208.htm (accessed August 5, 2013).
7. The US approach to governance differs from that in the EU and Canada. European states generally have a history of corporatism, where business, government and labor work cooperatively, which is evident in the EC's approach to rethinking privacy and IPR provisions. Canada is somewhere in between the US and the EU model. Canadians see government as more of an enabler and partner, and Canadian policy-makers tend to govern from the center. On Europe, see Remarks of Marietje Schaake, November 2, 2012, at Congressional Internet Caucus Advisory Committee. Schaake is a member of the Committee on Foreign Affairs, EU Parliament. On Canada, see Crossing Boundaries, Canada 2020 Working Group (2012), *Progressive Governance for Canadians: What You Need to Know*, p. 23, available from: http://www.canada2020.ca/files/Canada_2020_CB_Book.pdf (accessed August 5, 2013).
8. Rohan Samarajiva and Hosuk Lee-Makiyama (2012), *Whither Global Rules for the Internet? The Implications of the World Conference on International Telecommunication (WCIT) for International Trade*, ECIPE Policy Brief No. 12, p. 3, available from: http://www.ecipe.org/publications/wcit/ (accessed August 5, 2013).
9. Information Office of the State Council of the People's Republic of China (2010), "White Paper on the Internet," June 8, available from: http://www.china.org.cn/government/whitepaper/node_7093508.htm (accessed August 5, 2013).
10. Beginning on November 1, 2012, the Russian agency Roskomnadzor (the Agency for the Supervision of Information Technology, Communications and Mass Media) has compiled lists of web sites to be blocked and instructs Internet service providers (ISPs) to block access. Host providers must also ensure they are not in breach of current law

by checking their content against the database of outlawed sites and URLs published in a special password-protected online version of the register open only to web hosters and ISPs. Federal Law of the Russian Federation No. 139-FZ of July 28, 2012, available from: http://en.wikipedia.org/wiki/Federal_law_of_Russian_Federation_no._139-FZ_of_2012-07-28 (accessed August 5, 2013).

11. Andrei Soldatov and Irina Borogan (2012), "The Kremlin's New Internet Surveillance Plan Goes Live Today," *Wired*, November 1, available from: http://www.wired.com/dangerroom/2012/11/russia-surveillance/all/ (accessed August 5, 2013).

12. On Russian and Chinese Views, Information Security Doctrine of the Russian Federation, approved by V. Putin September 9, 2000, available from: http://www.mid.ru/bdomp/ns-osndoc.nsf/1e5f0de28fe77fdcc32575d900298676/2deaa9ee15ddd24bc3257 5d9002c442b!OpenDocument, last searched 4/26/2014 (accessed August 5, 2013); Timothy L. Thomas (2001), "Information Security Thinking: A Comparison of US, Russian and Chinese concepts," July, available from: http://fmso.leavenworth.army. mil/ts/in-fosecu.htm (accessed August 5, 2013). On the proposals to rethink Internet governance at the ITU, see Grant Gross (2012), "US Tech Leaders Fear Proposed Internet Regulations, Taxes at ITU Meeting," *CNET*, May 12, available from: http:// www.pcworld.com/article/256596/us_tech_leaders_fear_proposed_Internet_regulatio ns_taxes_at_itu_meting.html (accessed August 5, 2013); and Eric Pfanner (2012), "Debunking Rumors of an Internet Takeover," *New York Times*, June 11, available from: http://www.nytimes.com/2012/06/11/technology/debunking-rumors-of-an-Internet-takeover.html?pagewanted=all (accessed August 5, 2013).

13. Scott J. Wallsten (2005), "Regulation and Internet Use in Developing Countries," *Economic Development and Cultural Change*, **53** (2), 501–23.

14. As example, India proposed a new UN Committee on Internet Related Policy (CIRP) at the 66th General Assembly on October 26, 2011. Recently under pressure, India has backed away from proposals advocating greater government control of the Internet. Sandeep Bamzai (2012), "Muzzlers of the Free Internet: India Is Lobbying for Bureaucrats to Run the Worldwide Web," *Daily Mail*, October 20, available from: http:// www.dailymail.co.uk/indiahome/indianews/article-2220692/How-India-helped-bunch-bureau-crats-custodians-Internet.html (accessed August 5, 2013).

15. Scott Wallsten (2002), *Regulation and Internet Use in Developing Countries*, World Bank Policy Research Working Paper No. 2979, December, p. 7, available from: http://papers.ssrn.com/sol3/papers.cfm?abstract_id=366100 (accessed August 5, 2013); Ministry of Foreign Affairs of the Netherlands (2011), "Background Paper: The Role of Governments in Protecting and Furthering Internet Freedom," available from: http://www.minbuza.nl/binaries/content/assets/minbuza/en/the_ministry/the-role-of-governments-in-protecting-Internet-freedom---freedom-online.pdf (accessed August 5, 2013); UN General Assembly Conference Secretariat (2001), "The Digital Economy: Integrating the LDCs into the Digital Economy," A/Conf.19/L.15, May 19; and Internet Governance Forum, TS Workshop 182 (2011), *Global Internet Related Public Policies: Is There an Institutional Gap?*, September, available from: http://www.intgovforum.org/cms/component/content/article/71-transcripts-/919-ts-workshop-182-global-Internet-related-public-policies-is-there-an-institutional-gap (accessed August 5, 2013).

16. OECD (2011), "The Role of Internet Intermediaries in Advancing Public Policy Objectives: Forging Partnerships for Advancing Policy Objectives for the Internet Economy," Part II, DSTI/ICCP/(2010)11/Final, June 22, pp. 32–3, available from: http://search.oecd.org/officialdocuments/displaydocumentpdf/?cote=DSTI/ICCP%282010%2911/FINAL&docLanguage=En (accessed August 5, 2013).

17. In June 2011, the 38 members of the OECD and Egypt agreed to the OECD Principles for Internet Policy Making. They agreed to promote and protect free flow of information, to limit Internet intermediary liability and to strengthen individual empowerment online, among other goals. Available from: http://www.oecd.org/Internet/innovation/48289796.pdf (accessed August 5, 2013). The Dutch government organized a meeting in 2011 for governments to stand up for free expression on the Internet. Some

17 governments have now agreed to join the Freedom Online Coalition. They include many members of the EU (but not the European Commission), Canada and the US, as well as developing countries Ghana, Kenya, the Maldives and Mongolia. The signatories agreed to share information about censorship, to collaborate to support free expression, to promote business responsibility in respect of the Internet and human rights and to promote Internet freedom. See http://www.government.nl/news/2011/12/14/coalition-of-countries-for-free-Internet.html (accessed August 5, 2013); and http://www.freedomonlinekenya.org/home (accessed August 5, 2013).

18. In a study of 27 developed and six developing countries Clarke and Wallsten found that a 1 percentage point increase in the number of Internet users correlates with a boost in exports of 4.3 percentage points. George R. Clarke and Scott J. Wallsten (2006), "Has the Internet Increased Trade? Developed and Developing Country Evidence," *Economic Inquiry*, **44** (3), 456–84.

19. OECD (2008), "The Future of the Internet Economy," Policy Brief, June, pp. 1, 2, available from: http://www.oecd.org/dataoecd/20/41/40789235.pdf (accessed August 5, 2013); Internet World Stats, available from: http://www.internetworldstats.com/stats.htm (accessed November 27, 2012).

20. Several scholars recognized that Internet restrictions could be trade barriers and that the world would need to develop shared rules for information flows. See Tim Wu (2006), "The World Trade Law of Censorship and Internet Filtering," available from: http://papers.ssrn.com/sol3/papers.cfm?abstract_id=882459 (accessed August 5, 2013); and Brian Hindley and Hosuk Lee-Makiyama (2009), "Protectionism Online: Internet Censorship and International Trade Law," December, available from: http://www.ecipe.org/media/publication_pdfs/protectionism-online-Internet-censorship-and-international-trade-law.pdf (accessed August 5, 2013).

21. Karen Coppock and Colin Maclay (2002), "Regional Electronic Commerce Initiatives: Findings from Three Case Studies on the Development of Regional Electronic Commerce Initiatives," Information Technologies Group, Harvard University, July, available from: http://cyber.law.harvard.edu/itg/libpubs/andes%20pubs/Regional_Ecommerce.pdf (accessed August 5, 2013).

22. The WTO was built on an international trade agreement, the General Agreement on Tariffs and Trade (GATT), which had governed trade since 1948. Since 1998, members have agreed not to put duties on e-commerce. See the Geneva Ministerial Declaration on Global Electronic Commerce (1998), WT/MIN (98/DEC/2), May 25. Also see Doha Ministerial Declaration (2001), November 14, para. 34, available from: http://www.wto.org/english/thewto_e/minist_e/min01_e/mindecl_e.htm#electronic (accessed August 5, 2013) and http://www.wto.org/english/thewto_e/whatis_e/tif_e/bey4_e.htm (accessed August 5, 2013). The WTO had an Internet tax moratorium from 1999 to approximately 2001, see http://www.tax-news.com/news/WTO_Ministers_Extend_Internet_Tax_Ban_For_2_Years____183.html (accessed August 5, 2013).

23. Sacha Wunsch-Vincent (2005), "WTO, E-Commerce and Information Technologies: From the Uruguay Round through the Doha Development Agenda: A Report for the UN IDT Task Force," Markle Foundation, available from: http://www.iie.com/publications/papers/wunsch1104.pdf (accessed August 5, 2013).

24. These zero tariffs are extended to all WTO members on a most favored nation basis. "Norway, Thailand Join Small-Group Discussions to Expand ITA" (2012), *Inside U.S. Trade*, July 20, available from: http://insidetrade.com/Inside-US-Trade/Inside-US-Trade-07/20/2012/norway-thailand-join-small-group-discussions-to-expand-ita/menu-id-172.html (accessed August 5, 2013). See the Geneva Ministerial Declaration on Global Electronic Commerce (1998), WT/MIN (98/DEC/2), May 25. Also see Doha Ministerial Declaration (2001), November 14, para. 34, available from: http://www.wto.org/english/thewto_e/minist_e/min01_e/mindecl_e.htm#electronic (accessed August 5, 2013).

25. "United States – Measures Affecting the Cross-Border Supply of Gambling and Betting Services," available from: http://www.wto.org/english/tratop_e/dispu_e/cases_e/ds285_e.

htm (accessed August 5, 2013); and "China – Measures Affecting Trading Rights and Distribution Services for Certain Publications and Audiovisual Entertainment Products," available from: http://www.wto.org/english/tratop_e/dispu_e/cases_e/ds363_e.htm (accessed August 5, 2013).

26. WTO (2012), "15 Years of the Information Technology Agreement: Trade, Innovation and Global Production Networks," p. 35, available from: http://www.wto.org/english/res_e/publications_e/ita15years_2012full_e.pdf (accessed April 26, 2014); and WTO (2012), "News on Information Technology Agreement," November 1, available from: http://www.wto.org/english/news_e/news12_e/ita_01nov12_e.htm (accessed August 5, 2013). However, discussions on free flow may be revived as part of a plurilateral agreement on the liberalization of services. See "WTO Members Seek Services Accord as Doha Stalls, US Says" (2012), *Bloomberg News*, March 2; and "US Steps Up Push for WTO Services Trade Talks" (2012), *Reuters*, March 2, available from: http://www.ecipe.org/media/media_hit_pdfs/ecipe-esf-seminar-in-brussels.pdf (accessed August 5, 2013).

27. The WTO's General Agreement on Trade in Services (GATS) sets limits as to when governments could block services (such as Internet services), but it is vague: Members can only invoke this exception to the rule "where a genuine and sufficiently serious threat is posed to one of the fundamental interests of society." General Agreement on Trade in Services (1994), 33 ILM, 1167, Article XIV, n. 5. On the US and EU proposal forbidding blocking, see "US Tables Second Part of TPP Data Proposal, But Talks Still Preliminary" (2011), *Inside U.S. Trade*, November 10.

28. Data protection regulations are exempted from scrutiny under the GATS as long as these regulations are not a disguised restriction on trade.

29. However, some of the WTO's disciplines directly affect commercial conduct, for example delineating a telephone company's obligation to treat customers in a non-discriminatory manner. I am grateful to USTR staff for that insight.

30. In fact, in the first session of the UN General Assembly, member states agreed: "Freedom of information is a fundamental human right and . . . the touchstone of all the freedoms to which the United Nations is consecrated." Inge Kaul, Isabelle Grunberg and Marc A. Stern (eds.) (1999), *Global Public Goods: International Cooperation in the 21st Century*, New York: Oxford University Press, available from: http://web.undp.org/globalpublicgoods/Executive_Summary/executive_summary.html#introduction (accessed August 5, 2013); Keith E. Maskus and Jerome H. Reichman (eds.) (2005), *International Public Goods and Transfer of Technology under a Globalized Intellectual Property Regime*, Cambridge: Cambridge University Press; and Toby Mendel (n.d.), "Freedom of Information as an Internationally Protected Human Right," available from: http://www.article19.org/data/files/pdfs/publications/foi-as-an-international-right.pdf (accessed August 5, 2013).

31. See Susan Ariel Aaronson and M. Rodwan Abouharb (2011), "Unexpected Bedfellows: The GATT, the WTO and Some Democratic Rights," *International Studies Quarterly*, **55** (2), June, 379–408.

32. GATS addresses protection of privacy as an exception, GATS XIV (c) (ii), available from: http://www.wto.org/english/docs_e/legal_e/26-gats_01_e.htm (accessed August 5, 2013); the WTO telecom agreement (5 (d)) also says: "a Member may take such measures as are necessary to ensure the security and confidentiality of messages, subject to the requirement that such measures are not applied in a manner which would constitute a means of arbitrary or unjustifiable discrimination or a disguised restriction on trade in services." See Telecom Annex, available from: http://www.wto.org/english/tratop_e/serv_e/12-tel_e.htm (accessed August 5, 2013).

33. On the WTO and human rights, see Susan Ariel Aaronson and Jamie Zimmerman (2007), *Trade Imbalance: The Struggle to Weigh Human Rights Concerns in Trade Policymaking*, Cambridge: Cambridge University Press, pp. 3–4, 18–19; and for a literature review see Monash Law School (2005), "WTO and Human Rights Literature Review," September, available from: http://www.law.monash.edu.au/castan-centre/projects/wto/wto-lit-review-05.pdf (accessed August 5, 2013).

34. For an excellent overview, see Mira Burri and Thomas Cottier (eds.) (2012), *Trade Governance in the Digital Age* (for the World Trade Forum), New York: Cambridge University Press.
35. Simon Evenett and Michael Meier (2008), "An Interim Assessment of the US Trade Policy of Competitive Liberalization," *World Economy*, **31** (1), 31–66; and Jean-Pierre Chauffour and Jean-Christophe Maur (2011), *Preferential Trade Agreement Policies for Development: A Handbook*, Washington, DC: World Bank, pp. 17–35.
36. Google (2010), "Enabling Trade in the Era of Information Technologies: Breaking Down Barriers to the Free Flow of Information," November 15; and Google letter to Don Eiss, Trade Policy Staff Committee, re Request for Public Comments to Compile the National Trade Estimate Report on Foreign Trade Barriers, Docket No. USTR-2011-0008.
37. NFTC (2011), "Promoting Cross-Border Data Flows: Priorities for the Business Community," available from: http://www.nftc.org/default/Innovation/PromotingCross BorderDataFlowsNFTC.pdf (accessed August 5, 2013).
38. Gary Locke, Secretary of Commerce (2011), "Remarks at U.S. Chamber of Commerce on Global Flow of Information on the Internet," June 16, available from: http://www.ntia.doc.gov/speech-testimony/2011/remarks-us-chamber-commerce-global-flow-information-internet (accessed August 5, 2013).
39. For a good overview of the earlier language see Brian Bieron and Usman Ahmed (2012), "Regulating E-Commerce through International Policy: Understanding the Trade Law Issues of E-Commerce," *Journal of World Trade*, **46** (3), 548–55. Bieron and Ahmed argue that earlier FTAs included binding language related to MFN for digital products, no customs duties on digital goods, cooperation, transparency in governance, and aspirational language for consumer protection.
40. As with earlier US FTAs, the parties agreed not to impose duties, fees or other charges related to e-commerce, to provide national treatment and MFN to e-commerce, and so on. The agreement went into force in 2012.
41. US International Trade Commission (2007), "Potential Economy Wide and Selected Sectoral Effects of the US–Korea Free Trade Agreement," Investigation No. TA-2104-24, Publication 3949, September, pp. 4–5 fn. 98, available from: http://www.usitc.gov/publications/pub3949.pdf (accessed August 5, 2013).
42. US–Korea FTA, Chapter 15, Article 15.8, "Electronic Commerce," available from: http://www.ustr.gov/trade-agreements/free-trade-agreements/korus-fta/final-text (accessed August 5, 2013).
43. "USTR Official: U.S. Still Faces Big Challenges on TPP Data Flow Proposal" (2012), *Inside U.S. Trade*, September 27, available from: insidetrade.com/Inside-US-Trade/Inside-U.S.-Trade-09/28/2012/ustr-official-us-still-faces-big-challenges-on-tpp-data-flow-proposal/menu-id-710.html (accessed August 5, 2013).
44. "TPP Countries to Discuss Australian Alternative to Data-Flow Proposal" (2012), *Inside U.S. Trade*, July 5, available from: http://insidetrade.com/Inside-US-Trade/Inside-U.S.-Trade-07/06/2012/tpp-countries-to-discuss-australian-alternative-to-data-flow-proposal/menu-id-710.html (accessed August 5, 2013).
45. Remarks of Rob Atkinson (2010), "Cloud Computing for Business and Society," Brookings Institution, Washington, DC, January 20, available from: http://www.brookings.edu/~/media/events/2010/1/20%20cloud%20computing/20100120_cloud_computing.pdf (accessed August 5, 2013). Also see Paul Taylor (2011), "Privacy Concerns Slow Cloud Adoption," *Financial Times*, August 2, available from: http://www.ft.com/intl/cms/s/0/c970e6ee-bc7e-11e0-adac-00144feabdc0.html (accessed August 5, 2013); and Jennifer Baker (2011), "EU Upset by Microsoft Warning on US Access to EU Cloud," *Computerworld*, July 5, available from: http://www.computerworld.com/s/article/9218167/EU_upset_by_Microsoft_warning_on_US_access_to_EU_cloud/ (accessed August 5, 2013).
46. "US, Australia Make Little Headway toward Resolving Differences on Data Flows" (2012), *Inside U.S. Trade*, September 12, available from: http://insidetrade.com/201209122409796/

WTO-Daily-News/Daily-News/us-australia-make-little-headway-toward-resolving-differences-on-data-flows/menu-id-948.html (accessed August 5, 2013).

47. "US, Australia Make Little Headway toward Resolving Differences on Data Flows" (2012), *Inside U.S. Trade*, September 12, available from: http://insidetrade.com/201209122409796/WTO-Daily-News/Daily-News/us-australia-make-little-headway-toward-resolving-differences-on-data-flows/menu-id-948.html (accessed August 5, 2013).

48. "TPP Negotiators in Malaysia Spending Most Time on Toughest Areas of Talks" (2013), *Inside U.S. Trade*, July 18, available from: http://insidetrade.com/Inside-US-Trade/Inside-U.S.-Trade-07/19/2013/tpp-negotiators-in-malaysia-spending-most-time-on-toughest-areas-of-talks/menu-id-172.html (accessed August 5, 2013).

49. "USTR Official: US Still Faces Big Challenges on TPP Data Flow Proposal" (2012), *Inside U.S. Trade*, September 24, available from: http://insidetrade.com/201209242411012/WTO-Daily-News/Daily-News/ustr-official-us-still-faces-big-challenges-on-tpp-data-flow-proposal/menu-id-948.html (accessed August 5, 2013).

50. "131 House Dems Criticize Direction of TPP; Demand Greater Transparency" (2012), *Inside U.S. Trade*, June 29; and author observations at event sponsored by this project, "Can Trade Agreements Facilitate the Free Flow of Information? The Trans-Pacific Partnership as a Case Study" (2012), Elliott School of International Affairs, Washington, DC, September 21, available from: http://www.gwu.edu/~iiep/events/tradeandinformation_tpp.cfm (accessed August 5, 2013).

51. "Senator Wyden Speech at 2013 CES" (2013), Office of Senator Ron Wyden, January 9, available from: http://www.wyden.senate.gov/news/blog/post/senator-wyden-speech-at-2013-ces (accessed August 5, 2013).

52. "Academics Describe US Clarifications in TPP Copyright Proposal" (2012), *Inside U.S. Trade*, September 14; and author observations at event sponsored by this project, "Can Trade Agreements Facilitate the Free Flow of Information? The Trans-Pacific Partnership as a Case Study" (2012), Elliott School of International Affairs, Washington, DC, September 21, available from: http://www.gwu.edu/~iiep/events/tradeandinformation_tpp.cfm (accessed August 5, 2013).

53. "After 30 Months of Negotiations, TPP Talks Still Have a Long Way to Go" (2012), *Inside U.S. Trade*, September 4; "Wyden, Issa Join Forces in Latest Effort for More Transparency in TPP" (2012), *Inside U.S. Trade*, September 6; "Academics Describe US Clarifications of Key Provisions in TPP Copyright Proposal" (2012), *Inside U.S. Trade*, September 12.

54. Government of Canada (2012), "Report of the Joint Study on the Possibility of a Canada–Japan Economic Partnership Agreement," March 7, available from: http://www.international.gc.ca/trade-agreements-accords-commerciaux/agr-acc/japan-japon/study-report_rapport-etude.aspx?lang=eng&view=d#19 (accessed August 5, 2013); and Canada–Jordan FTA, "E-Commerce Provisions," available from: http://www.international.gc.ca/trade-agreements-accords-commerciaux/agr-acc/jordan-jordanie/chapter3-chapitre3.aspx?lang=eng&view=d (accessed August 5, 2013).

55. Canada–Colombia Free Trade Agreement, Chapter Fifteen, "Electronic Commerce," available from: http://www.international.gc.ca/trade-agreements-accords-commerciaux/agr-acc/colombia-colombie/chapter15-chapitre15.aspx?view=d (accessed August 5, 2013).

56. Barrie McKenna (2013), "Businesses Push for Freedom to Share Personal Data across Borders," *Globe and Mail*, July 7, available from: http://www.theglobeandmail.com/report-on-business/economy/businesses-push-for-freedom-to-share-personal-data-across-borders/article13054771/ (accessed August 5, 2013).

57. "Data Mining Revelations Could Impact U.S. Business as EU Rewrites Rules," *Inside U.S. Trade*, June 13, available from: http://insidetrade.com/Inside-US-Trade/Inside-U.S.-Trade-06/14/2013/data-mining-revelations-could-impact-us-business-as-eu-rewrites-rules/menu-id-710.html (accessed August 5, 2013).

58. "U.S. Will Push for Rules Governing Data Flows in Trans-Atlantic Deal" (2013), *Inside*

U.S. Trade, July 12, available from: insidetrade.com/201307122440617/WTO-Daily-News/Daily-News/us-will-push-for-rules-governing-data-flows-in-trans-atlantic-deal/menu-id-948.html (accessed August 5, 2013).

59. European Union–United States Trade Principles for Information and Communication Technology Services (2012), April, available from: http://www.ustr.gov/webfm_send/2780 (accessed August 5, 2013).

60. European Commission, "International Affairs: Free Trade Agreements," available from: http://ec.europa.eu/enterprise/policies/international/facilitating-trade/free-trade/index_en.htm#h2-2 (accessed August 5, 2013); and Canada DFAIT, "Consultations towards a Canada–European Union Comprehensive Economic Agreement," available from: http://www.international.gc.ca/trade-agreements-accords-commerciaux/agr-acc/eu-ue/cepa-consult-apeg.aspx?lang=eng&view=d (accessed August 5, 2013).

61. Statement on the Free Flow of Information and Trade in North America (2005), June, available from: http://www.ic.gc.ca/eic/site/ecic-ceac.nsf/eng/gv00515.html (accessed August 5, 2013).

62. Emma Barnett (2010), "Facebook's Mark Zuckerberg Says Privacy Is No Longer a 'Social Norm,'" *Telegraph*, January 11, available from: http://www.telegraph.co.uk/technology/facebook/6966628/Facebooks-Mark-Zuckerberg-says-privacy-is-no-longer-a-social-norm.html (accessed August 5, 2013).

63. For an interesting analysis of this issue, see Michael Geist and Milana Homsi (2005), "Outsourcing Our Privacy? Privacy and Security in a Borderless Commercial World," *University of New Brunswick Law Journal*, **54**, 272–307.

64. Privacy Canada, *Privacy for Everyone: Annual Report to Parliament 2011: Report on the Personal Information Protection and Electronic Documents Act*, available from: http://www.priv.gc.ca/information/ar/201112/2011_pipeda_e.asp#toc3.5 (accessed August 5, 2013).

65. Soumitra Dutta, William H. Dutton and Ginette Law (2011), "The New Internet World: A Global Perspective on Freedom of Expression, Privacy, Trust and Security Online," INSEAD Working Paper No. 2011/89/TOM, April, pp. 9–11. The researchers analyzed public opinion on privacy in Australia and New Zealand, Brazil, Canada, China, France, Germany, Italy, India, Mexico, South Africa, Spain, the UK and the US.

66. Ian Brown (2011), "Privacy Attitudes, Incentives and Behaviors," available from: http://papers.ssrn.com/sol3/papers.cfm?abstract_id=1866299& (accessed August 5, 2013).

67. Sweden was the first government to establish privacy legislation, and today there are some 80 countries or entities with such laws. Steven Bellman, Eric J. Johnson, Stephen J. Kobrin and Gerald Lohse (2004), "International Differences in Information Privacy Concerns: A Global Survey of Consumers," *Information Society*, **20**, 313–24, available from: http://papers.ssrn.com/sol3/papers.cfm?abstract_id=1324721& (accessed August 5, 2013).

68. On US court cases see Martin Samson, Internet Library of Law and Court Decisions, available from: http://www.Internetlibrary.com/topics/right_privacy.cfm (accessed August 5, 2013); on Sarbanes–Oxley, see Public Law 107–204 – Sarbanes–Oxley Act of 2002, available from: http://www.gpo.gov/fdsys/pkg/PLAW-107publ204/content-detail.html (accessed August 5, 2013).

69. Department of Commerce Internet Policy Task Force, "Commercial Data Privacy and Innovation in the Internet Economy," pp. 44, 54, available from: http://www.commerce.gov/sites/default/files/documents/2010/december/iptf-privacy-green-paper.pdf (accessed August 5, 2013).

70. "Conference on Current Developments in Privacy Frameworks: Towards Global Interoperability" (2011), hosted by Ministry of Economy of Mexico, November 1, available from: http://www.oecd.org/document/23/0,3746,en_2649_34223_48443927_1_1_1_1,00.html#Agenda (accessed August 5, 2013).

71. OECD Guidelines on the Protection of Privacy and Transborder Flows of Personal Data (1980).

72. The Council of Europe promotes common and democratic principles based on the

European Convention on Human Rights and other reference texts on the protection of individuals. It is also home to the European Court of Human Rights, which clarifies European law related to human rights. Doc. 12695, July 29, 2011, "The Protection of Privacy and Personal Data on the Internet and Online Media," Report, Committee on Culture, Science and Education Rapporteur: Andreja Rihter, Slovenia, Socialist Group, available from: http://www.assembly.coe.int/ASP/Doc/XrefViewPDF. asp?FileID=13151&Language=EN (accessed August 5, 2013).

73. The Convention for the Protection of Individuals with Regard to Automatic Processing of Personal Data ("Convention No. 108") requires that personal data be processed fairly and securely for specified purposes on a legitimate basis only, and establishes that everyone has the right to know, access and rectify their personal data processed by third parties or to erase personal data which have been processed without authorization. The EU has not however devised an action plan for implementing Convention 108.

74. Future of Privacy Forum, available from: www.futureofprivacy.org/global; and Convention for the Protection of Individuals with Regard to Automatic Processing of Personal Data, available from: http://conventions.coe.int/Treaty/EN/Treaties/Html/108. htm (accessed August 5, 2013).

75. US Department of Commerce, "Safe Harbor," available from: http://export.gov/safe harbor/eu/eg_main_018476.asp (accessed August 5, 2013).

76. Interview with Rosa Barcelo, Privacy Coordinator, Policy Coordinator, European Commission, DG CONNECT, 7/24/2012. Also see Gregory Shaffer (2000), "Globalization and Social Protection: The Impact of EU and International Rules in the Ratcheting Up of US Data Privacy Standards," *Yale Journal of International Law*, **25**, Winter, available from: http://papers.ssrn.com/sol3/papers.cfm?abstract_id=531682 (accessed August 5, 2013).

77. Regarding Philippine adoption of legislation, based on the EU Data Protection Directive 95/46/EC and accords with APEC policies, "Senate Ratifies Bicam Report on Data Privacy Act" (2012), *Zambo Times*, June 6, available from: http://www.zam botimes.com/archives/48155-Senate-ratifies-bicam-report-on-Data-Privacy-Act.html (accessed August 5, 2013).

78. Neil Robinson, Hans Graux, Maarten Botterman and Lorenzo Valeri (2009), *Review of the European Data Protection Directive*, Cambridge: Rand Europe, p. 39.

79. European Principles and Guidelines for Internet Resilience and Stability (2011), March, available from: http://ec.europa.eu/information_society/policy/nis/docs/principles_ciip/ guidelines_Internet_fin.pdf (accessed August 5, 2013).

80. European Commission (2012), "Data Protection Reform: Frequently Asked Questions," MEMO/12/41, January 25, p. 2, available from: europa.eu/rapid/press-release_MEMO- 12-41_en.doc (accessed April 26 2014).

81. European Commission (2012), "Data Protection Reform: Frequently Asked Questions," MEMO/12/41, January 25, p. 3, available from: europa.eu/rapid/press-release_MEMO- 12-41_en.doc (accessed April 26 2014).

82. "EU Panel Data Protection Regulation Vote Delayed until Fall by Amendments, PRISM" (2013), *Bloomberg BNA*, July 1, available from: http://www.bna.com/eu-panel- data-n17179874844/ (accessed August 5, 2013).

83. "EU Panel Data Protection Regulation Vote Delayed until Fall by Amendments, PRISM" (2013), *Bloomberg BNA*, July 1, available from: http://www.bna.com/eu-panel- data-n17179874844/ (accessed August 5, 2013).

84. "EU Panel Data Protection Regulation Vote Delayed until Fall by Amendments, PRISM" (2013), *Bloomberg BNA*, July 1, available from: http://www.bna.com/eu-panel- data-n17179874844/ (accessed August 5, 2013).

85. "EU Panel Data Protection Regulation Vote Delayed until Fall by Amendments, PRISM" (2013), *Bloomberg BNA*, July 1, available from: http://www.bna.com/eu-panel- data-n17179874844/ (accessed August 5, 2013).

86. Available from: http://trade.ec.europa.eu/doclib/docs/2008/february/tradoc_137971.pdf (accessed August 5, 2013). Canada has similar provisions.

87. Chapter 6 of its model free trade agreements refers to trade in data, see http://
     trade.ec.europa.eu/doclib/docs/2008/february/tradoc_137971.pdf (accessed August 5,
     2013). Article 7.43, available from: http://trade.ec.europa.eu/doclib/docs/2009/october/
     tradoc_145166.pdf (accessed August 5, 2013).
88. See http://www.whitehouse.gov/the-press-office/2012/02/23/we-can-t-wait-obama-adm
     inistration-unveils-blueprint-privacy-bill-rights (accessed August 5, 2013). The bill of
     rights includes: a right to transparency – consumers have a right to easily understand-
     able information about privacy and security practices; respect for context – consumers
     have a right to expect that organizations will collect, use and disclose personal data in
     ways that are consistent with the context in which consumers provide the data; security –
     consumers have a right to secure and responsible handling of personal data; access and
     accuracy – consumers have a right to access and correct personal data in usable formats,
     in a manner that is appropriate to the sensitivity of the data and the risk of adverse con-
     sequences to consumers if the data are inaccurate; focused collection – consumers have
     a right to reasonable limits on the personal data that companies collect and retain; and
     accountability – consumers have a right to have personal data handled by companies
     with appropriate measures in place to assure that they adhere to the Consumer Privacy
     Bill of Rights.
89. Cameron S. Kerry (2011), "Second Annual European Data Protection and Privacy
     Conference, CFK Keynote Address, Trans-Atlantic Solutions for Data Privacy,"
     December 6, available from: http://www.ntia.doc.gov/speechtestimony/2011/cameron-
     f-kerry-keynote-address-european-data-protection-and-privacy-conference (accessed
     August 5, 2013). Kerry, the Commerce Department's General Counsel, noted that some
     3000 companies participate in Safe Harbor with the EU; he also stressed that the US
     adopted the Asia-Pacific Economic Cooperation's Cross Border Privacy Rules.
90. Department of Commerce Internet Policy Task Force, "Commercial Data Privacy
     and Innovation in the Internet Economy," pp. 44, 54, available from: http://www.com
     merce.gov/sites/default/files/documents/2010/december/iptf-privacy-green-paper.pdf
     (accessed August 5, 2013); and Department of Commerce, export.gov, Introduction to
     the US–EU and US Swiss Safe Harbor Frameworks, available from: www.export.gov/
     safeharbor (accessed August 5, 2013).
91. US Department of Commerce, "2009 Electronic Commerce Industry Assessment,"
     available from: http://web.ita.doc.gov/ITI/itiHome.nsf/0657865ce57c168185256cdb00
     7a1f3a/3771d41ba49c5cba852577440056dcd4/$FILE/Electronic Commerce Industry
     Assessment Public June 16.pdf (accessed August 5, 2013).
92. "European Parliament Calls for 'Full Review' of Data Transfer Agreement" (2013),
     Inside U.S. Trade, July 11, available from: insidetrade.com/Inside-US-Trade/Inside-
     U.S.-Trade-07/12/2013/european-parliament-calls-for-full-review-of-data-transfer-
     agreement/menu-id-172.html (accessed August 5, 2013).
93. Article 15.5 of US–Panama FTA, available from: http://www.ustr.gov/sites/default/files/
     uploads/agreements/fta/peru/asset_upload_file876_9540.pdf (accessed August 5, 2013).
94. "U.S. Will Push for Rules Governing Data Flows in Trans-Atlantic Deal" (2013), *Inside
     U.S. Trade*, July 12, available from: insidetrade.com/201307122440617/WTO-Daily-
     News/Daily-News/us-will-push-for-rules-governing-data-flows-in-trans-atlantic-deal/
     menu-id-948.html (accessed August 5, 2013).
95. "U.S. Will Push for Rules Governing Data Flows in Trans-Atlantic Deal" (2013), *Inside
     U.S. Trade*, July 12, available from: insidetrade.com/201307122440617/WTO-Daily-
     News/Daily-News/us-will-push-for-rules-governing-data-flows-in-trans-atlantic-deal/
     menu-id-948.html (accessed August 5, 2013).
96. Message from the Privacy Commissioner of Canada, available from: http://www.priv.
     gc.ca/aboutUs/message_e.cfm#contenttop (accessed August 5, 2013).
97. Office of the Information and Privacy Commissioner for British Columbia, *2011–12
     Annual Report*, Victoria, BC: Office of the Information and Privacy Commissioner for
     British Columbia, pp. 6–7.
98. Office of the Privacy Commissioner of Canada (2009), *Guidelines for Processing*

Personal Data across Borders, January, available from: http://www.priv.gc.ca/informa tion/guide/2009/gl_dab_090127_e.asp (accessed August 5, 2013).

99. Privacy Commissioner of Canada, "Privacy for All," available from: http://www.priv. gc.ca/information/ar/201112/2011_pipeda_e.asp#toc1 (accessed August 5, 2013).

100. Canada–Colombia Free Trade Agreement, Chapter Fifteen, "Electronic Commerce," available from: http://www.international.gc.ca/trade-agreements-accords-commerciaux/ agr-acc/colombia-colombie/chapter15-chapitre15.aspx?view=d (accessed August 5, 2013).

101. Information Technology Association of Canada, "Shared Services Canada Takes National Security Exception," available from: http://itac.ca/news/shared_services_ canada_takes_national_security_exception (accessed August 5, 2013).

102. Jason Young (2004), "BC Attempts to Regulate Outsourcing of Personal Information," November 4, available from: http://www.dww.com/?page_ id=1052 (accessed August 5, 2013); and Fred H. Cate (2008), *Provincial Canadian Geographic Restrictions on Personal Data in the Public Sector*, submitted to the Trilateral Committee on Transborder Data Flows, Centre for Information Policy Leadership, Hunton & Williams, pp. 1–2, available from: http://www.hunton.com/files/Publication/2a6f5831- 07b6-4300-af8d-ae30386993c1/Presentation/PublicationAttachment/0480e5b9-9309-40 49-9f25-4742cc9f6dce/cate_patriotact_white_paper.pdf (accessed August 5, 2013).

103. Fred H. Cate (2008), *Provincial Canadian Geographic Restrictions on Personal Data in the Public Sector*, submitted to the Trilateral Committee on Transborder Data Flows, Centre for Information Policy Leadership, Hunton & Williams, available from: http:// www.hunton.com/files/Publication/2a6f5831-07b6-4300-af8d-ae30386993c1/Presenta tion/PublicationAttachment/0480e5b9-9309-4049-9f25-4742cc9f6dce/cate_patriotact_ white_paper.pdf (accessed August 5, 2013).

104. Office of the Information and Privacy Commissioner for British Columbia, *2011–12 Annual Report*, Victoria, BC: Office of the Information and Privacy Commissioner for British Columbia, pp. 6–7.

105. Privacy Commissioner of Canada, "Privacy for All," available from: http://www.priv. gc.ca/information/ar/201112/2011_pipeda_e.asp#toc1 (accessed August 5, 2013).

106. Executive Office of the President (2012), *2011 US Intellectual Property Enforcement Coordinator Annual Report on Intellectual Property Enforcement*, March, Washington, DC: Executive Office of the President, pp. 10–11.

107. The TRIPS agreement covers: how nations should give adequate protection to intel- lectual property rights; how countries should enforce those rights; how to settle dis- putes on intellectual property between members of the WTO; and special transitional arrangements during the period when the new system is being introduced. The TRIPS agreement took effect on January 1, 1995; developed countries were given one year to ensure that their laws and practices conformed with the TRIPS agreement. Developing countries and (under certain conditions) transition economies were given five years, until 2000. Least-developed countries had 11 years, until 2006 – now extended to 2016 for pharmaceutical patents. Proponents of the TRIPS agreement argued that it would create a framework which encouraged domestic innovation, and, by protecting foreign IPR holders, gave them incentives to invest in production and research in the developing world. See http://www.wto.org/english/thewto_e/whatis_e/tif_e/agrm7_e.htm (accessed August 5, 2013).

108. Google (UK) (2011), "Submission to the Independent Review of Intellectual Property and Growth," March, p. 3, para. 3.5, available from: http://www.ipo.gov.uk/ipreview- c4e-sub-google.pdf (accessed April 26, 2014).

109. The US Copyright Act is 17 USC § 107. Much of the Internet industry grew in the US under the intellectual policy protecting fair use.

110. Thomas Rogers and Andrew Szamosszegi (2010), "Fair Use in the US Economy: Economic Contribution of Industries Relying on Fair Use," CCIA, pp. 11–12, available from: http://www.ccianet.org/CCIA/files/ccLibraryFiles/Filename/000000000354/fair- use-study-final.pdf (accessed August 5, 2013).

111. Thomas Rogers and Andrew Szamosszegi (2010), "Fair Use in the US Economy: Economic Contribution of Industries Relying on Fair Use," CCIA, pp. 11–12, available from: http://www.ccianet.org/CCIA/files/ccLibraryFiles/Filename/000000000354/fair-use-study-final.pdf (accessed August 5, 2013); and Jared Huber and Brian T. Yeh (2006), *Copyright Licensing in Music Distribution, Reproduction, and Public Performance*, CRS Report No. RL33631, August 20, Washington, DC: Congressional Research Service.
112. Brian Bieron and Usman Ahmed (2012), "Regulating E-Commerce through International Policy: Understanding the Trade Law Issues of E-Commerce," *Journal of World Trade*, **46** (3), p. 563.
113. The Digital Millennium Copyright Act is P.L. 105-304.
114. The Congress called on the executive to work to extend IPR protection to new and emerging technologies and to new methods of transmission and dissemination. Congress also wanted to bring other governments' IPR in line with US law (or to put it differently to extend US regulation to other markets). 2002 Bipartisan Trade Promotion Authority Act, P.L. 107-210, Sec. 2102(b)(4).
115. US–Chile FTA, Article 17.11, pp. 17-27–17-30), available from: http://www.ustr.gov/sites/default/files/uploads/agreements/fta/chile/asset_upload_file912_4011.pdf (accessed August 5, 2013).
116. Letters from Hyun Chong Kim and Susan C. Schwab (2007), June 20, available from: http://www.ustr.gov/sites/default/files/uploads/agreements/fta/korus/asset_upload_file948_12737.pdf (accessed August 5, 2013) and http://www.ustr.gov/sites/default/files/uploads/agreements/fta/korus/asset_upload_file948_12737.pdf (accessed August 5, 2013); US–Korea FTA, Articles 18.5, 18.7, available from: http://www.ustr.gov/sites/default/files/uploads/agreements/fta/korus/asset_upload_file273_12717.pdf (accessed August 5, 2013).
117. "In Shadow of ACTA, EU Drops Criminal IPR Provisions in CETA Talks" (2012), *Inside U.S. Trade*, November 2, available from: http://insidetrade.com/Inside-US-Trade/Inside-U.S.-Trade-11/02/2012/in-shadow-of-acta-eu-drops-criminal-ipr-provisions-in-ceta-talks/menu-id-172.html (accessed August 5, 2013).
118. US industries such as software, music, films and computer games rely on IPR protection. They lose billions of dollars in revenue through piracy and counterfeiting.
119. The US also has a portal on its IPR policies and enforcement, www.iprcenter.gov.
120. National Intellectual Property Rights Coordination Center, "Intellectual Property Rights Violations: A Report on Threats to United States Interests at Home and Abroad," available from: http://www.iprcenter.gov/reports/ipr-center-reports/IPR%20Center%20Threat%20Report%20and%20Survey.pdf/view (accessed August 5, 2013).
121. The Omnibus Trade and Competitiveness Act, P.L. 100-418 included the Special 301 provisions.
122. USTR (2011), "Out of Cycle Review of Notorious Markets," February 28, available from: http://www.ustr.gov/webfm_send/2595 (accessed August 5, 2013).
123. Shayerah Ilias and Ian F. Fergusson (2011), "Intellectual Property Rights and International Trade," CRS Report No. RL34292, February 17, p. 12, also see pp. 31–2, available from: http://www.ieeeusa.org/policy/eyeonwashington/2011/documents/ipr-tradeagreements.pdf (accessed August 5, 2013).
124. Torrent Freak (2012), "First Software Maker Joins Bit-Torrent Lawsuit Bonanza," November 16, available from: http://torrentfreak.com/first-software-maker-joins-bittorrent-lawsuit-bonanza-121116/ (accessed August 5, 2013).
125. Somini Sengupta (2012), "US Pursuing a Middleman in Web Piracy," *New York Times*, July 12, available from: http://www.nytimes.com/2012/07/13/technology/us-pursues-richard-odwyer-as-intermediary-in-online-piracy.html (accessed August 5, 2013). The sites associated with Megaupload were shut down by the United States Department of Justice on January 19, 2012. "Megaupload Extradition Case Delayed until March 2013" (2012), *BBC News*, July 10, available from: http://www.bbc.co.uk/news/technology-18779866 (accessed August 5, 2013).
126. Benjamin A. Neil and Richard W. Winelander (2010), "An Examination of Jurisdictional

Defenses Available to Foreign Defendants to Copyright Claims Brought in U.S. Courts," *Journal of International Business and Cultural Studies*, 3, available from: http://www.aabri.com/manuscripts/09334.pdf (accessed August 5, 2013); and Adam D. Fuller (2003), "Extraterritorial Implications of the Digital Millennium Copyright Act," *Case Western Reserve Journal of International Law*, **35** (1), p. 89.

127. On IPR as a customs problem see "Intellectual Property: Formal Council Meeting: Council Debates How and Where to Handle Counterfeit Trademarked Goods" (2012), *WTO News*, June 5, available from: http://www.wto.org/english/news_e/news12_e/trip_05jun12_e.htm (accessed August 5, 2013); and on concerns about ATCA see http://www.ifla.org/en/news/ifla-raises-concerns-about-acta (accessed August 5, 2013); http://www.publicknowledge.org/issues/acta (accessed August 5, 2013); and http://www.euroispa.org/news/63-Internet-industry-concerns-on-the-anti-counterfeiting-trade-agreement (accessed August 5, 2013).

128. Monika Ermert (2012), "Most EU Members Sign ACTA; SOPA-Style Protests Building," Intellectual Property Watch, January 27, available from: http://www.ip-watch.org/2012/01/27/most-eu-members-sign-acta-sopa-style-protests-building/?utm_source=weekly&utm_medium=email&utm_campaign=alerts (accessed August 5, 2013). Over 1.75 million people have signed a petition on avaaz.org urging EU members not to ratify ACTA. Infojustice.org (2012), "Resistance to ACTA in Europe Grows," February 8, available from: http://infojustice.org/archives/7886 (accessed August 5, 2013).

129. "EU Suspends Consideration of ACTA, Refers Treaty to Court" (2012), *RT News*, February 21, available from: http://rt.com/news/eu-suspends-acta-ratification-955/ (accessed August 5, 2013); and EC, "ACTA: The Anti-Counterfeiting Trade Agreement," available from: http://ec.europa.eu/trade/creating-opportunities/trade-topics/intellectual-property/anti-counterfeiting/ (accessed August 5, 2013).

130. "Opinion of the European Economic and Social Committee on the Communication from the Commission to the European Parliament, the Council, the European Economic and Social Committee and the Committee of the Regions – A Single Market for Intellectual Property Rights – Boosting Creativity and Innovation to Provide Economic Growth, High Quality Jobs and First Class Products and Services in Europe" (2012), COM(2011) 287 final, EESC, Brussels, January 18, p. 8, para. 3.1.3., p. 10, para. 4.5.5, available from: http://www.eesc.europa.eu/?i=portal.en.int-opinions.19154 (accessed August 5, 2013).

131. See http://www.mofa.go.jp/policy/economy/i_property/acta1201.html (accessed August 5, 2013).

132. See http://thomas.loc.gov/cgi-bin/bdquery/z?d112:h.r.3261 (accessed August 5, 2013); for a list of those concerned about the legislation see https://www.cdt.org/report/list-organizations-and-individuals-opposing-sopa (accessed August 5, 2013).

133. See http://keepthewebopen.com (accessed August 5, 2013); and http://keepthewebopen.com/assets/pdfs/faqs.pdf (accessed August 5, 2013).

134. See http://keepthewebopen.com/assets/pdfs/faqs.pdf (accessed August 5, 2013).

135. Many companies struggle to ensure free expression while not jeopardizing political stability. Google removed the anti-Islam video that set off riots in Egypt, Libya and other countries, during the week of September 11, 2012. However, Google did not block the film everywhere. Google was also asked by the US government to take down the video. Brian Womack (2012), "Google's YouTube Expands Anti-Islam Film Restriction in Asia," *Bloomberg News*, September 14, available from: http://www.bloomberg.com/news/2012-09-14/google-expands-anti-islam-video-restriction-to-india-indonesia.html (accessed August 5, 2013).

136. See http://www.google.com/transparencyreport/removals/government/countries/ (accessed August 5, 2013); David Kravets (2012), "Google Says It Removes 1 Million Infringing Links Monthly," *Wired*, May 24/, available from: http://www.wired.com/threatlevel/2012/05/google-infringing-link-removal/?utm_source=Contextly&utm_medium=RelatedLinks&utm_campaign=MoreRecently (accessed August 5, 2013).

137. See http://www.google.com/transparencyreport/removals/copyright/ (accessed August 5, 2013).
138. "US, Colombia Discuss Implementation of IP Provisions Due Next Year" (2012), *Inside U.S. Trade*, July 7, available from: http://insidetrade.com/Inside-US-Trade/Inside-U.S.-Trade-06/08/2012/us-colombia-discuss-implementation-of-ip-provisions-due-next-year/menu-id-710.html (accessed August 5, 2013).
139. Charlotte Waelde and Lilian Edwards (2005), "Online Intermediaries and Copyright Liability," WIPO Workshop Keynote Paper, Geneva, April, pp. 35, 51–2, available from: http://ssrn.com/abstract=1159640 (accessed August 5, 2013).
140. "Colombian Senators File Lawsuits against Copyright Bill Passed to Comply with Trade Agreement" (2011), June 8, available from: http://infojustice.org/archives/26337 (accessed August 5, 2013).
141. Jesse Brown (2011), "Pirate Politics Aren't Just for Hackers," *Maclean's*, September 21, available from: http://www2.macleans.ca/2011/09/21/pirate-politics-arent-just-for-hackers/ (accessed August 5, 2013).
142. "Christian Engström," European Parliament, available from: http://www.europarl.europa.eu/meps/en/96676/CHRISTIAN_ENGSTROM_home.html (accessed August 5, 2013); and "Amelia Andersdotter," European Parliament, available from: http://www.europarl.europa.eu/meps/en/108570/AMELIA_ANDERSDOTTER_home.html (accessed August 5, 2013).
143. "Iceland Vote: Centre-Right Opposition Wins Election" (2013), *BBC*, April 28, available from: http://www.bbc.co.uk/news/world-europe-22320282 (accessed August 5, 2013).
144. "Mgr. Libor Michálek, MPA," Senate of the Czech Republic, available from: http://www.senat.cz/senatori/index.php?lng=en&par_3=269 (accessed August 5, 2013); and "Czech Greens Are Back" (2012), European Green Party, October 22, available from: http://europeangreens.eu/news/czech-greens-are-back (accessed August 5, 2013).
145. See http://www.pp-international.net/about (accessed August 5, 2013); Pirate Codex, available from: http://www.pirates-without-borders.org/pirates-codex/ (accessed August 5, 2013); and Josh Kron (2012), "Open Source Politics: The Radical Promise of Germany's Pirate Party," *TheAtlantic.com*, September 21, available from: http://www.theatlantic.com/international/archive/2012/09/open-source-politics-the-radical-promise-of-germanys-pirate-party/262646/?single_page=true (accessed August 5, 2013).
146. See http://ec.europa.eu/yourvoice/ipm/forms/dispatch?form=noticeandaction (accessed August 5, 2013).
147. European Commission, "A Clean and Open Internet: Public Consultation on Procedures for Notifying and Acting on Illegal Content Hosted by Online Intermediaries," available from: http://ec.europa.eu/internal_market/consultations/2012/clean-and-open-Internet_en.htm (accessed August 5, 2013).
148. "UK Continues to Oppose New Single EU Data Protection Law Regime" (2012), *Out-Law.com*, November 13, available from: http://www.out-law.com/en/articles/2012/november/uk-continues-to-oppose-new-single-eu-data-protection-law-regime/ (accessed August 5, 2013).
149. EU (2005), "Strategy for the Enforcement of Intellectual Property Rights in Third Countries," 2005/C 129/03, p. 14, available from: http://trade.ec.europa.eu/doclib/docs/2010/december/tradoc_147070.pdf (accessed August 5, 2013).
150. EU–Korea Free Trade Agreement, available from: http://eur-lex.europa.eu/JOHtml.do?uri=OJ:L:2011:127:SOM:EN:HTML (accessed August 5, 2013). The EU–ASEAN negotiations are being paused because of rampant piracy and other factors. "EU Gives ASEAN 4.5 Million Euros for Intellectual Property" (2009), *Deutsche Presse Agentur*, October 21, available from: http://www.bilaterals.org/spip.php?article16126 (accessed August 5, 2013).
151. Jason J. Lee (2012), "Enactment of Korea–EU Free Trade Agreement Triggers Amendments to IP Laws," January 12, available from: http://www.bilaterals.org/spip.php?article20890 (accessed August 5, 2013).

152. "Intellectual Property Rights CETA: Draft IPR Chapter," available from: http://www.michaelgeist.ca/component/option,com_docman/task,doc_download/gid,114/ (accessed August 5, 2013).
153. Michael Geist (2012), "ACTA Lives: How the EU and Canada Are Using CETA as Backdoor Mechanism to Revive ACTA," July 9, available from: http://www.michaelgeist.ca/content/view/6580/135/ (accessed August 5, 2013); https://www.eff.org/deeplinks/2012/10/ceta-replicates-acta (accessed August 5, 2013); and "ACTA, CETA, Etc. Stop Denying Democracy!" (2012), *La Quadrature du Net*, October 24, available from: http://www.laquadrature.net/en/acta-ceta-etc-stop-denying-democracy (accessed August 5, 2013).
154. Michael Geist (2012), "ACTA Lives: How the EU and Canada Are Using CETA as Backdoor Mechanism to Revive ACTA," July 9, available from: http://www.michaelgeist.ca/content/view/6580/135/ (accessed August 5, 2013); Liat Clark (2012), "Acta's Worst Clauses Resurface in Canada–EU Trade Treaty, Verbatim," *Wired UK*, July 10, available from: http://www.wired.co.uk/news/archive/2012-07/10/acta-resurfaces-in-ceta (accessed August 5, 2013); and Melody Zhang (2012), "Leaked CETA Draft Provokes ACTA Comparisons, Transparency Worries," *OpenNet Initiative*, July 24, available from: https://opennet.net/blog/2012/07/leaked-ceta-draft-provokes-acta-comparisons-transparency-worries (accessed August 5, 2013).
155. Michael Geist (2012), "ACTA Lives: How the EU and Canada Are Using CETA as Backdoor Mechanism to Revive ACTA," July 9, available from: http://www.michaelgeist.ca/content/view/6580/135/ (accessed August 5, 2013).
156. Carolina Rossini (2012), "Canada–EU Trade Agreement Replicates ACTA's Notorious Copyright Provisions," *Electronic Frontier Foundation*, October 13, available from: https://www.eff.org/deeplinks/2012/10/ceta-replicates-acta (accessed August 5, 2013); and "Confirmed ACTA-like Outrageous Criminal Sanctions in CETA!" (2012), *La Quadrature du Net*, October 12, available from: http://www.laquadrature.net/en/confirmed-acta-like-outrageous-criminal-sanctions-in-ceta (accessed August 5, 2013).
157. David Meyer (2012), "Canada Trade Deal No Longer Borrows from ACTA: EU," *ZDNet*, July 11, available from: http://www.zdnet.com/canada-trade-deal-no-longer-borrows-from-acta-eu-7000000700/ (accessed August 5, 2013).
158. European Commission (2013), "The EU's Free Trade Agreement with Canada," February 1, available from: http://trade.ec.europa.eu/doclib/docs/2012/august/tradoc_149866.pdf (accessed August 5, 2013).
159. For information on the digital economy in Canada, see http://www.digitaleconomy.gc.ca/eic/site/028.nsf/eng/home (accessed August 5, 2013).
160. Paul Chwelos (2009), "Internet Service Providers Report, Executive Summary," available from: http://www.ic.gc.ca/eic/site/ippd-dppi.nsf/eng/ip01431.html (accessed August 5, 2013).
161. "Letting the Baby Dance" (2012), *Economist*, September 1, available from: http://www.economist.com/node/21561885 (accessed August 5, 2013).
162. Web site, Professor Michael Geist, Canada Research Chair in Internet and E-Commerce Law, University of Toronto, available from: http://www.michaelgeist.ca/content/view/6588/125/ (accessed August 5, 2013); and Nancy Situ (2012), "Considering Canada's Supreme Court Decisions in This Week's WIPO Proceedings," July 18, available from: http://www.ip-watch.org/2012/07/18/considering-canadas-supreme-court-decisions-in-this-weeks-wipo-proceedings/ (accessed August 5, 2013).
163. Canada–Colombia FTA, "E-Commerce Chapters," available from: http://www.international.gc.ca/trade-agreements-accords-commerciaux/agr-acc/colombia-colombie/chapter15-chapitre15.aspx?view=d (accessed August 5, 2013).
164. American Assembly (2011), "Copyright Infringement and Enforcement in the US, A Research Note," November, p.9, available from: http://piracy.americanassembly.org/wp-content/uploads/2011/11/AA-Research-Note-Infringement-and-Enforcement-November-2011.pdf (accessed August 5, 2013).
165. Waelde and Edwards found that ISPs are too receptive to takedown. They also need

to maintain extensive staff to ensure they are not breaching privacy or copyright. Charlotte Waelde and Lilian Edwards (2005), "Online Intermediaries and Copyright Liability," WIPO Workshop Keynote Paper, Geneva, April, pp. 30–31, available from: http://ssrn.com/abstract=1159640 (accessed August 5, 2013).

166. "Letting the Baby Dance" (2012), *Economist*, September 1, available from: http://www.economist.com/node/21561885 (accessed August 5, 2013).

167. "Obama Acts on FAC Petition against China's 'Great Firewall'" (2011), *FAC*, October 19, available from: http://www.firstamendmentcoalition.org/2011/10/obama-acts-on-fac-petition-against-chinas-Internet-censors/ (accessed August 5, 2013).

168. Brendan Greeley and Mark Drajem (2011), "China's Facebook Copycats Focus US on Trade as Well as Rights," *Bloomberg/Business Week*, March 10; and Letter from Ambassador Michael Puncke, US Ambassador to the WTO to Ambassador Yi Xiaozhun, China's Ambassador to the WTO, and Attachment (2011), October 17, available from: http://insidetrade.com/iwpfile.html?file=oct2011%2Fwto2011_2996a.pdf (accessed August 5, 2013).

169. US Trade Representative (2013), 2013 National Trade Estimate Report on Foreign Trade Barriers," March, pp. 60–61, available from: http://www.ustr.gov/sites/default/files/2013%20NTE.pdf (accessed August 5, 2013).

170. "USTR Flags Procurement, Data Flow Issues as New Barriers in Canada" (2012), *Inside U.S. Trade*, April 27, available from: http://insidetrade.com/Inside-US-Trade/Inside-U.S.-Trade-04/27/2012/ustr-flags-procurement-data-flow-issues-as-new-barriers-in-canada/menu-id-710.html (accessed August 5, 2013).

171. USTR (2012), "National Trade Estimate Report," available from: http://www.ustr.gov/sites/default/files/NTE Final Printed_0.pdf (accessed August 5, 2013). "A number of US companies have voiced concerns that various Australian government departments, such as the Department of Defense, the National Archives of Australia, the Department of Finance and Deregulation's Australian Government Information Management Office, and the State of Victoria Privacy Commissioner, are sending negative messages about cloud computing services to potential Australian customers in both the public and private sectors, implying that hosting data overseas, including in the United States, by definition entails greater risk and unduly exposes consumers to their data being scrutinized by foreign governments. In the case of the United States, many such concerns appear based on misinterpretation of applicable US law, including the US Patriot Act and regulatory requirements. In November 2011, new draft legislation was introduced into Parliament that would prohibit the overseas storage of any Australian electronic health records. This would pose a significant trade barrier for US information technology companies with data centers located in the United States or anywhere else outside of Australia. The bill has been referred to a Senate committee for inquiry."

172. USTR (2013), "2013 National Trade Estimate Report on Foreign Trade Barriers," March, p. 31, available from: http://www.ustr.gov/sites/default/files/2013%20NTE.pdf (accessed August 5, 2013).

173. USTR (2012), "National Trade Estimate Report," p. 216, available from: http://www.ustr.gov/sites/default/files/NTE%20Final%20Printed_0.pdf (accessed August 5, 2013).

174. USTR (2012), "National Trade Estimate Report," p. 96, available from: http://www.ustr.gov/sites/default/files/NTE%20Final%20Printed_0.pdf (accessed August 5, 2013).

175. Russia and Moldova Jackson–Vanik Repeal and Sergei Magnitsky Rule of Law Accountability Act of 2012, P.L. 112-208, available from: http://www.gpo.gov/fdsys/pkg/PLAW-112publ208/html/PLAW-112publ208.htm (accessed August 5, 2013); and "Presidential Proclamation – To Extend Nondiscriminatory Treatment (Normal Trade Relations Treatment) to the Products of the Russian Federation and the Republic of Moldova" (2012), White House, December 20, available from: http://www.whitehouse.gov/the-press-office/2012/12/20/presidential-proclamation-extend-nondiscriminatory-treatment-normal-trad (accessed August 5, 2013).

176. Sec. 203 – Reports on Laws, Policies, and Practices of the Russian Federation that Discriminate against United States Digital Trade, Russia and Moldova Jackson–Vanik

Repeal and Sergei Magnitsky Rule of Law Accountability Act of 2012, P.L. 112-208, available from: http://www.gpo.gov/fdsys/pkg/PLAW-112publ208/html/PLAW-112publ208.htm (accessed August 5, 2013).

177. USTR (2012), "National Trade Estimate Report," p. 166, available from: http://www.ustr.gov/sites/default/files/NTE%20Final%20Printed_0.pdf (accessed August 5, 2013).

178. Although the US argued it had to discriminate between domestic and foreign gambling web sites to avoid fraud, money laundering and organized crime, the US lost a trade dispute on this issue at the WTO. "United States – Measures Affecting the Cross-Border Supply of Gambling and Betting Services," available from: http://www.wto.org/english/tratop_e/dispu_e/cases_e/ds285_e.htm (accessed August 5, 2013); and Albena P. Petrova (2006), "The WTO Internet Gambling Dispute as a Case of First Impression: How to Interpret Exceptions under GATS Article XIV (a) . . .," *Richmond Journal of Global Law and Business*, **6** (1), 45–76, available from: http://rjglb.richmond.edu/archives/6.1/art2.pdf (accessed August 5, 2013).

179. Jian Junbo (2010), "Internet Claims Too Testy for China," *Asia Times*, May 27, available from: http://www.atimes.com/atimes/China/LE27Ad01.html (accessed August 5, 2013).

180. Commission Staff Paper Accompanying the Trade and Investment Report, available from: http://trade.ec.europa.eu/doclib/docs/2012/february/tradoc_149144.pdf (accessed August 5, 2013); and Report from the Commission to the European Council (2012), "Trade and Investment Barriers Report 2012," SWD(2012) 19 final, pp. 9, 15–16, available from: http://trade.ec.europa.eu/doclib/docs/2012/february/tradoc_149143.pdf (accessed August 5, 2013).

181. "Iran's Twitter Revolution" (2009), *Washington Times*, June 16, available from: http://www.washingtontimes.com/news/2009/jun/16/irans-twitter-revolution/ (accessed August 5, 2013); and Zoe Fox (2012), "How the Arab World Uses Facebook and Twitter," *Mashable*, June 8, available from: http://mashable.com/2012/06/08/arab-world-facebook-twitter/ (accessed August 5, 2013).

182. For the example of riots in the UK, see Josh Halliday (2011), "London Riots: How BlackBerry Messenger Played a Key Role," *Guardian*, August 8, available from: http://www.theguardian.com/media/2011/aug/08/london-riots-facebook-twitter-blackberry (accessed April 26, 2014); and "Technology and Disorder: The Blackberry Riots" (2011), *Economist*, August 13, available from: http://www.economist.com/node/21525976 (accessed April 26 2014). Also see https://www.nytimes.com/2011/08/12/world/europe/12iht-social12.html?_r=1dUSTRE7784EE20110809 (accessed August 5, 2013); http://www.aljazeera.com/indepth/opinion/2012/04/201241373429356249.html (accessed August 5, 2013); Anthony Faiola (2011), "London Riots: Britain Weighs Personal Freedoms against Need to Keep Order," August 11, available from: http://www.washingtonpost.com/world/europe/britain-weighs-personal-freedoms-against-need-to-keep-order/2011/08/11/gIQAMTO-S8I_print.html (accessed August 5, 2013). For the example of India, see Gardiner Harris and Malavika Vyawahare (2012), "Indian Government Defends Social Media Crackdown," available from: http://india.blogs.nytimes.com/2012/08/24/indian-government-defends-social-media-crackdown/ (accessed August 5, 2013).

183. See https://twitter.com/JeanBirnbaum/status/226348204160065537 (accessed August 5, 2013).

184. "BIS Offers Enhanced Enforcement Plan for Items Subject to Reform Effort" (2012), *Inside U.S. Trade*, July 19, available from: http://insidetrade.com/201207192404975/WTO-Daily-News/Daily-News/bis-offers-enhanced-enforcement-plan-for-items-subject-to-reform-effort/menu-id-948.html (accessed August 5, 2013).

185. James Ball (2012), "Sanctions Aimed at Syria and Iran Are Hindering Opposition, Activists Say," *Washington Post*, August 14, available from: http://www.washingtonpost.com/world/national-security/sanctions-aimed-at-syria-and-iran-are-hindering-opposition-activists-say/2012/08/14/c4c88998-e569-11e1-936a-b801f1abab19_story.html (accessed August 5, 2013).

186. "The US Boosts Exports of Internet Services to Closed Societies" (2010), *VOA*, March 10, available from: https://www.youtube.com/watch?v=qLDIQzpd5kcpress06252010. htm (accessed August 5, 2013).
187. Department of Commerce Bureau of Industry and Security (2010), "BIS Updates Encryption Export Rule; Revised Rule Streamlines Review Process, Enhances National Security," June 25, available from: http://www.bis.doc.gov/news/2010/bis_press06252010. htm (accessed August 5, 2013).
188. Martin Chulov (2012), "Syria Shuts Off Internet Access across the Country," *Guardian*, November 29, available from: http://www.theguardian.com/world/2012/nov/29/ syria-blocks-internet (accessed August 5, 2013); and "Syria: Internet and Mobile Communication 'Cut Off'" (2012), *BBC News*, November 29, available from: http:// www.bbc.co.uk/news/technology-20546302 (accessed August 5, 2013).
189. Ben Quinn (2013), "Syria's Internet in Apparent Blackout," *Guardian*, May 7, available from: http://www.theguardian.com/world/2013/may/07/syria-internet-blackout (accessed August 5, 2013); and "Syrian Internet Back after 19-Hour Blackout" (2013), *BBC News*, May 8, available from: http://www.bbc.co.uk/news/world-middle-east-22447247 (accessed August 5, 2013).
190. Amy Chozick (2012), "Official Syrian Web Sites Hosted in the United States," *New York Times*, November 30, available from: http://www.nytimes.com/2012/11/30/world/ middleeast/official-syrian-web-sites-hosted-in-us.html (accessed August 5, 2013); and Ron Deibert et al. (2012), "The Canadian Connection: One Year Later," available from: https://citizenlab.org/2012/11/the-canadian-connection-one-year-later/444 (accessed August 5, 2013).
191. See http://www.state.gov/secretary/rm/2011/12/178511.htm (accessed August 5, 2013); and http://www.state.gov/j/drl/rls/rm/2012/180958.htm (accessed August 5, 2013).
192. See http://geneva.usmission.gov/us-hrc/Internet-freedom-fellows-2012/ (accessed August 5, 2013).
193. See http://globalnetworkinitiative.org/ (accessed August 5, 2013).
194. See http://Internetfreedomfund.tumblr.com/ (accessed August 5, 2013).
195. See http://cordis.europa.eu/fp7/ict/fire/events/20120507-fire-nds-ws/ppts/01-no-discon nect-strategy-20120507-ag1.pdf (accessed August 5, 2013).
196. Ryan Gallagher (2012), "EU Plans Groundbreaking Project to Monitor Internet Censorship around the World," *Slate*, November 6, available from: http://www.slate. com/blogs/future_tense/2012/11/06/european_capability_for_situation_awareness_pro gram_to_monitor_internet.html (accessed August 5, 2013).
197. Deputy Assistant Secretary Dan Baer, "Live at State: Internet Freedom and US Foreign Policy," available from: http://www.state.gov/r/pa/ime/178707.htm (accessed August 5, 2013); and, as an example of a technology project the US funds, see the TOR project, designed to help individuals use the Internet anonymously, available from: http:// en.wikipedia.org/wiki/The_Tor_Project (accessed August 5, 2013). Also see Jay Newton-Small (2012), "Hillary's Little Startup: How the US Is Using Technology to Aid Syria's Rebels," *Time World*, June 13, available from: http://world.time.com/2012/06/13/hillarys-little-startup-how-the-u-s-is-using-technology-to-aid-syrias-rebels/ (accessed August 5, 2013).
198. See https://crypto.cat/ (accessed August 5, 2013); and debate at http://www.wired. com/threatlevel/2012/07/crypto-cat-encryption-for-all/all (accessed August 5, 2013); and http://www.wired.com/threatlevel/2012/08/wired_opinion_patrick_ball/all// (accessed August 5, 2013).
199. Richard Fontaine and Will Rogers (2011), *Internet Freedom: A Foreign Policy Imperative in the Digital Age*, June, Washington, DC: Center for a New American Security, pp. 12, 13.

Index

behind-the-border provisions 531–2, 539, 545
Belarus 206
Belgium 118, 539
Bellmann, R. 432
Beneyto, J. 329
Bernard, A. 123
beta convergence 74, 79, 80, 81, 83, 87, 89, 91, 97, 99, 101–3, 105
Bhagwati, Jagdish 228, 230, 445
'Bhagwati tax' 504, 522, 523–4
Bhala, Raj 194
BIA (best information available) 156–7
BICS (Brazil, India, China and South Africa) economies 403–4, 410
Bilal, S. 288
binding mechanisms 180–81
Bipartisan Trade Deal (2007) 543, 544
BITs (bilateral investment treaties) 138, 139–40, 146
blat 467
Bliss, C. 61
Blomstrom, M. 73
Bobbitt, Philip 415
Boix, C. 199
Bond, S. 214
'bootlegger–Baptist' coalitions 499–500
Borjas, G. 507
Börzel, T. 280
Bossuyt, F. 539
Bown, C. 166
Brazil
  and concerns over regionalism 231
  and current regionalism negotiations 239
  and declining relevance of WTO 403–4
  and domestic business ownership 455
  and FDI 137, 140
  and G-5 consensus group (proposed) 5–6
  and global food systems 472, 479
  and income inequality 50
  and industrial livestock 490
  and Internet freedom 554
  and reciprocal relationships 467
  and rise of large emerging economies 450–51, 452, 461–2
Breiger, R. 76

Bretton Woods system 228–9, 418, 451
BRIC (Brazil, Russia, India, China) economies 67, 404, 410, 451, 458, 461–2
Brunei 252, 253, 256, 260
BSE (bovine spongiform encephalopathy) 493
'bully game' 515, 518–19, 521
Bülow, M. von 442
Burstein, Paul 432, 446
Busch, L. 472
Bush, George W. 239, 240, 543
Byrd Amendment (2000) 161, 167–8, 170, 369
Byrd, Robert 161

CADA (Chinese Alcoholic Drinks Association) 335
'Calvo Doctrine' 420
Cambodia 252, 259
Canada
  and 'competitive liberalization' 242
  and data protection 563, 564, 569–70
  and FDI 142
  and free flow of information 22, 551, 561–3
  and global food systems 472
  and GM crops 486–7
  and IIT 121, 123, 127
  and industrial livestock 490–91, 492–3
  and Internet freedom 22, 551–2, 555–6, 557–8, 561–3, 569–70, 571, 577–8, 580–85
  and IPR provision 571, 577–8
  and mandatory food labelling 489–90
  and migration policy 503, 523
  and multilateralism 237
  and privacy standards 22, 551–2, 562, 563, 564, 569–70
  trade policy review example cases 357–8, 359–62, 364–70, 379–83
Canada–Colombia Free Trade Agreement (2011) 561
Canada–U.S. Free Trade Agreement (1987) 237
CAP (Common Agricultural Policy) 188, 194